Dictionary of Literary Biography • Volume Eighteen

Victorian Novelists
After 1885

Dictionary of Literary Biography

1: *The American Renaissance in New England*, edited by Joel Myerson (1978)

2: *American Novelists Since World War II*, edited by Jeffrey Helterman and Richard Layman (1978)

3: *Antebellum Writers in New York and the South*, edited by Joel Myerson (1979)

4: *American Writers in Paris, 1920-1939*, edited by Karen Lane Rood (1980)

5: *American Poets Since World War II*, 2 volumes, edited by Donald J. Greiner (1980)

6: *American Novelists Since World War II*, Second Series, edited by James E. Kibler, Jr. (1980)

7: *Twentieth-Century American Dramatists*, 2 volumes, edited by John MacNicholas (1981)

8: *Twentieth-Century American Science-Fiction Writers*, 2 volumes, edited by David Cowart and Thomas L. Wymer (1981)

9: *American Novelists, 1910-1945*, 3 volumes, edited by James J. Martine (1981)

10: *Modern British Dramatists, 1900-1945*, 2 volumes, edited by Stanley Weintraub (1982)

11: *American Humorists, 1800-1950*, 2 volumes, edited by Stanley Trachtenberg (1982)

12: *American Realists and Naturalists*, edited by Donald Pizer and Earl N. Harbert (1982)

13: *British Dramatists Since World War II*, 2 volumes, edited by Stanley Weintraub (1982)

14: *British Novelists Since 1960*, 2 volumes, edited by Jay L. Halio (1983)

15: *British Novelists, 1930-1959*, 2 volumes, edited by Bernard Oldsey (1983)

16: *The Beats: Literary Bohemians in Postwar America*, 2 volumes, edited by Ann Charters (1983)

17: *Twentieth-Century American Historians*, edited by Clyde N. Wilson (1983)

18 *Victorian Novelists After 1885*, edited by Ira B. Nadel and William E. Fredeman (1983)

Yearbook: 1980, edited by Karen L. Rood, Jean W. Ross, and Richard Ziegfeld (1981)

Yearbook: 1981, edited by Karen L. Rood, Jean W. Ross, and Richard Ziegfeld (1982)

Yearbook: 1982, edited by Richard Ziegfeld; associate editors: Jean W. Ross and Lynne C. Zeigler (1983)

Documentary Series, volume 1, edited by Margaret A. Van Antwerp (1982)

Documentary Series, volume 2, edited by Margaret A. Van Antwerp (1982)

Documentary Series, volume 3, edited by Mary Bruccoli (1983)

Dictionary of Literary Biography • Volume Eighteen

Victorian Novelists
After 1885

Edited by
Ira B. Nadel
University of British Columbia
and
William E. Fredeman
University of British Columbia

A Bruccoli Clark Book
Gale Research Company • Book Tower • Detroit, Michigan 48226
1983

Manufactured by Edwards Brothers, Inc.
Ann Arbor, Michigan
Printed in the United States of America

Copyright © 1983
GALE RESEARCH COMPANY

Library of Congress Cataloging in Publication Data
Main entry under title:

Victorian novelists after 1885.

 (Dictionary of literary biography; v. 18)
 "A Bruccoli Clark book."
 Includes index.
  1. English fiction—19th century—Bio-bibliography.
2. English fiction—19th century—History and criticism.
3. Novelists, English—19th century—Biography—Dictionaries. I. Fredeman, William E. (William Evan), 1928-
II. Nadel, Ira Bruce. III. Series: Dictionary of literary
biography; 18.
PR871.V54   1983   823'.8'09 [B]   82-24200
ISBN 0-8103-1143-7

Contents

Foreword...vii

Acknowledgments...ix

R. D. Blackmore (1825-1900).........................3
   Max Keith Sutton

Mary Elizabeth Braddon (1835-1915) 6
   Winifred Hughes

Rhoda Broughton (1840-1920)..........................15
   R. C. Terry

Robert Buchanan (1841-1901).........................18
   Christopher D. Murray

Samuel Butler (1835-1902) 23
   Lee E. Holt

Lewis Carroll (1832-1898).............................43
   Kathleen Blake

Wilkie Collins (1824-1889) 61
   Ira B. Nadel

Charles Lutwidge Dodgson
   (see Lewis Carroll)

Sir Arthur Conan Doyle (1859-1930).................77
   George Grella and Philip B. Dematteis

James Anthony Froude (1818-1894) 95
   Craig Turner

George Gissing (1857-1903)...........................103
   Jacob Korg

Thomas Hardy (1840-1928)............................119
   Norman Page

G. A. Henty (1832-1902)................................142
   Patrick A. Dunae

Thomas Hughes (1822-1896)...........................148
   George J. Worth

Eliza Lynn Linton (1822-1898) 153
   Dorothea M. Thompson

George MacDonald (1824-1905)......................158
   Marjory Lang

W. H. Mallock (1849-1923)............................164
   Barry V. Qualls

Henry Mayhew (1812-1887)............................167
   Anne Humpherys

George Meredith (1828-1909).........................172
   Michael Collie

George Moore (1852-1933).............................191
   Susan Dick

William Morris (1834-1896) 204
   Joseph R. Dunlap

John Henry Newman (1801-1890) 226
   Lionel Adey

Laurence Oliphant (1829-1888).......................231
   Tom Winnifrith

Margaret Oliphant (1828-1897).......................234
   Tom Winnifrith

Ouida (1839-1908)......................................239
   Roy B. Stokes

James Payn (1830-1898) 246
   R. C. Terry

Marie Louise de la Ramée
   (see Ouida)

Anne Thackeray Ritchie (1837-1919)...............251
   Barbara J. Dunlap

Mark Rutherford (1831-1913) 258
   Catherine Harland

Olive Schreiner (1855-1920) 270
   Joyce Avrech Berkman

Joseph Henry Shorthouse (1834-1903)............278
   Frederick J. Wagner

Robert Louis Stevenson (1850-1894)................281
   Robert Kiely

Mrs. Humphry Ward (1851-1920)....................297
   Esther M. G. Smith

William Hale White
   (see Mark Rutherford)

Mrs. Henry Wood (1814-1887)........................303
   Lionel Adey

Charlotte Mary Yonge (1823-1901)..................308
    Barbara J. Dunlap

Appendix

Literature at Nurse, or Circulating Morals
   329
    George Moore

From "The Decay of Lying" 338
    Oscar Wilde

Candour in English Fiction 342
    Thomas Hardy

The Present State of the English Novel, 1892
   346
    George Saintsbury

The Place of Realism in Fiction
   357
    George Gissing

The Future of the Novel....................................358
    Henry James

Contributors...365

Cumulative Index 369

Foreword

This volume of the *Dictionary of Literary Biography*, a companion to *Victorian Novelists Before 1885*, contains thirty-three entries that record the later development of Victorian fiction. In the work of Thomas Hardy, George Meredith, and George Moore, as well as in that of Miss Broughton, William Morris, and Mrs. Humphry Ward, a variety of new themes and situations begin to dominate the novel. These include the confrontation with spiritual crisis, as in Mrs. Ward's *Robert Elsmere* (1888); the problems of the independent woman, as in Meredith's *Diana of the Crossways* (1885); and the conflict between sexual frankness and the values of a new age, as in Hardy's *Jude the Obscure* (1895). In addition there appears a stronger recognition of the dualities of the self, as in Stevenson's *Strange Case of Dr. Jekyll and Mr. Hyde* (1886), and a vitriolic critique of the Victorian family, as in Samuel Butler's *The Way of All Flesh* (1903). But no single event or sudden development marks what various critics have called the emergence of the "problem novel."

Nonetheless, there is one significant transformation in the history of English fiction associated with the year 1885 that was to alter dramatically the character of the Victorian novel: the decline of the three-volume form of publication known as the triple-decker which, beginning with *Kenilworth* by Sir Walter Scott in 1821 and lasting for nearly seventy-five years, dominated nineteenth-century fiction.

Though three-volume publication remained common until 1894 and continued at least as late as 1897—the date of Algernon Gissing's *The Scholar of Bygate* (Hutchinson), the latest of the triple-deckers in the famous and massive collection of Robert Lee Wolff at Harvard—the affordable, one-volume novel quickly found new readers and achieved unprecedented sales.

This change ended the circulating libraries' control over public taste and publishing practices, which had begun in the early 1840s. By encouraging publishers to produce "library editions" of fiction, three-volume novels with an average of 325 pages per volume and with a total cost of thirty-one shillings and sixpence (approximately $40 today), the circulating libraries had maintained an iron grip on a form of publishing much criticized for the limited access it provided readers. Since the libraries charged only a guinea a year per volume (about $1.25 today), it made economic sense for readers to maintain subscriptions to them rather

However, the lending libraries exercised more than merely a business control over authors and publishers of fiction. In 1883, the largest and most formidable of these institutions, Mudie's Select Library, refused to stock George Moore's *A Modern Lover*, claiming that its title was offensive and its subject scandalous. Incensed, Moore retaliated by arranging to publish his next novel, *A Mummer's Wife* (1885), as a single volume; and in 1885 he brought out a one-volume revised edition of *A Modern Lover*. Priced at six shillings, both novels sold briskly, but Mudie's continued to refuse to stock Moore's work, notwithstanding the strong financial appeal of the one-volume novel, which had already begun to gain in popularity.

It was thus over the issue of censorship rather than that of format that Moore launched his famous attack on the circulating libraries, which signaled the death of the triple-decker—roughly within a decade. In the 1885 pamphlet *Literature at Nurse, or Circulating Morals* (reprinted in the appendix to this volume), Moore exposed the lending library's hypocrisy by printing a collection of carefully chosen passages from works freely circulated by Mudie's, many of which were more offensive than those sections in his own novels on which the library's rejection had been based. Each selection in Moore's pamphlet is followed by the reiterated refrain *"tell me, Mr. Mudie, if there be not in this doll just a little too much bosom showing, if there be not too much ankle appearing from under this skirt?"* Moore concludes by arguing that the circulating libraries, by virtue of the enormous power they exert over novelists and publishers, have inhibited both the talent of English writers and the development of British morals.

The move to publishing novels in an inexpensive, one-volume format led to manifest changes in writing, printing, and distribution. No longer was the cost of novels prohibitive; no longer was a membership in a circulating library necessary for one who wanted to read fiction, though libraries attempted to accommodate themselves to the new trend. In 1894, Arthur Mudie, son of the founder of Mudie's, explained to Richard Bentley, the best-known publisher of triple-deckers, that "with the one volume novel I can satisfy my subscribers much better, can keep within my margin, & can give them also which I am most anxious to do a far better supply of literature of *all* sorts." But the popularity of the lending library was already on the decline before Moore's attack, due to the phenomenal growth of reprints and novels in cheap series, which had started in the 1840s with the appearance of railway fiction generally called "yellow backs." As prices fell and new methods for the manufacturing of books appeared in the 1880s and later, more and more inexpensive editions began to be found in bookstalls. In 1896, George Newnes began the Penny Library of Famous Books, unabridged versions of favorite novels by Mayne Reid, Frederick Marrayat, and Dickens. During this same period, J. M. Dent began to publish the Temple Shakespeare, inexpensive editions of the Cambridge text of the playwright, and by 1906 Dent had founded the still-flourishing Everyman series. At the end of the Victorian era, the common reader had readier access to a greater supply of fiction than at any other time in the century.

The advent of single-volume fiction had important aesthetic consequences as well. Novelists were no longer required to pad their works with excessive dialogue, intricate plots, or wooden descriptions in order to meet the demands of publishers or printers. The art of "spreading out" a story so that it might fill three volumes gradually disappeared. Readers no longer had reason to complain with the writer Israel Zangwill that

> One idea makes one paragraph
> Two paragraphs make one page
> Twenty pages make one chapter
> Twelve chapters make one volume
> Three volumes make one tired.

In general novelists appear to have welcomed this shift in the mode of publication, which allowed them to write more concentrated stories focusing on better character development and scenes with significant detail, symbol, and limited dialogue. In 1885, the year of Moore's pamphlet attacking Mudie's, George Meredith, then reader of manuscripts for Chapman and Hall, advised George Gissing to revise *Isabel Clarendon* into two volumes. Gissing responded: "It is fine to see how the old three-vol. tradition is being broken through. Chapman tells me he much prefers two vols. & one vol. is becoming commonest of all. It is the new school, due to continental influence. Thackeray and Dickens wrote . . . with profusion and detail . . . to tell everything, & leave nothing to be divined. Far more artistic, I think, is the later method, of merely suggesting; of dealing with episodes, instead of writing biographies . . .—hinting, surmising, telling in detail what *can* so be told, & no more. In fact, it

approximates to the dramatic mode of presentment." Illustrating this alteration to a more condensed form of storytelling are such novels as Stevenson's *Treasure Island* (1883), H. Rider Haggard's *King Solomon's Mines* (1885), Moore's *Esther Waters* (1894), and Hardy's *Jude the Obscure* (1895), all published in inexpensive one-volume editions.

Of course, publication practices alone did not reshape the late-Victorian novel. The year 1885, while marking a revolutionary change in publishing history, was also notable for a series of events which altered permanently the artistic quality of Victorian and later fiction. Naturalism, soon to affect English novelists, solidified its place in France with the publication of *Germinal* by Émile Zola, and aestheticism was effectively launched in the English novel with the publication of Walter Pater's *Marius the Epicurean*. The year also saw the deaths of Victor Hugo and General Gordon; the births of D. H. Lawrence and Ezra Pound; the start of the publication of Ruskin's autobiography, *Praeterita*; and the publication of the first volume of the monumental *Dictionary of National Biography*. Gilbert and Sullivan premiered the *Mikado* and Richard Burton produced the first volume of his *Arabian Nights*, while British imperialism was put to a crucial test at Khartoum.

Epitomizing these changes, two years before the Diamond Jubilee of Queen Victoria, is James McNeill Whistler's 1885 lecture, "The Ten O'Clock." In this witty plea to sever art from its commitment to social reform, Whistler indicts the age for its timidity and conventionality. Radically, he declares that art is "selfishly occupied with her own perfection only—having no desire to teach—seeking and finding the beautiful in all conditions. . . ." Those Victorian novelists who lived beyond 1885 had to face the challenge of this new direction in art. In an 1886 article, Oscar Wilde admonished critics for prescribing to the public what to read: "to tell people what to read is as a rule either useless or harmful, for the true appreciation of literature is a question of temperament not of teaching." Such a precept was as upsetting as it was refreshing for the late-Victorian novelist, who, in his quest for readers, had to readjust his themes while he struggled with his form.

To our contributors, from several countries and three continents, and to the editorial staff of the *Dictionary of Literary Biography*, all of whom have cooperated to make this volume a truly Victorian enterprise, the editors wish to express their sincere thanks.

—Ira B. Nadel and W. E. Fredeman

Acknowledgments

This book was produced by BC Research. Karen L. Rood is senior editor for the *Dictionary of Literary Biography* series. Philip B. Dematteis was the in-house editor.

The production staff included Mary Betts, Joseph Caldwell, Patricia Coate, Angela Dixon, Anne Dixon, Lynn Felder, Joyce Fowler, Nancy L. Houghton, Sharon K. Kirkland, Cynthia D. Lybrand, Alice A. Parsons, Jean W. Ross, Walter W. Ross, Joycelyn R. Smith, Debra D. Straw, Robin A. Sumner, Meredith Walker, and Lynne C. Zeigler. Charles L. Wentworth is photography editor.

Valuable assistance was given by the staff at the Thomas Cooper Library of the University of South Carolina: Michael Freeman, Gary Geer, Alexander M. Gilchrist, W. Michael Havener, David Lincove, Roger Mortimer, Donna Nance, Harriet B. Oglesbee, Elizabeth Pugh, Jean Rhyne, Paula Swope, Jane Thesing, Ellen Tillett, and Beth S. Woodard.

Lola L. Szladits of the Henry W. and Albert A. Berg Collection of English and American Literature, New York Public Library, Astor, Lennox, and Tilden Foundation, was especially helpful in providing illustrations for this volume.

Dictionary of Literary Biography • Volume Eighteen

Victorian Novelists
After 1885

Dictionary of Literary Biography

R. D. Blackmore

(7 June 1825-20 January 1900)

Max Keith Sutton
University of Kansas

SELECTED BOOKS: *Poems by Melanter* (London: Hardwicke, 1854);

Epullia, as Melanter (London: Hope, 1854);

The Bugle of the Black Sea; or, The British in the East, as Melanter (London: Hardwicke, 1855);

The Fate of Franklin (London: Hardwicke, 1860);

Clara Vaughan: A Novel (3 volumes, London: Macmillan, 1864; 1 volume, New York: Harper, 1866);

Cradock Nowell: A Tale of the New Forest (3 volumes, London: Chapman & Hall, 1866; 1 volume, New York: Harper, 1866);

Lorna Doone: A Romance of Exmoor (3 volumes, London: Low & Marston, 1869; 1 volume, Philadelphia: Jacobs, 1869);

The Maid of Sker (3 volumes, Edinburgh & London: Blackwood, 1872; 1 volume, New York: Harper, 1872);

Alice Lorraine: A Tale of the South Downs (3 volumes, London: Low, Marston, Low & Searle, 1875; 1 volume, New York: Harper, 1875);

Cripps, the Carrier: A Woodland Tale (3 volumes, London: Low, Marston, Searle & Rivington, 1876; 1 volume, New York: Harper, 1876);

Erēma; or, My Father's Sin (3 volumes, London: Smith, Elder, 1877; 1 volume, New York: Harper, 1877);

Mary Anerley: A Yorkshire Tale (3 volumes, London: Low, Marston, Searle & Rivington, 1880; 1 volume, New York: Harper, 1880);

Christowell: A Dartmoor Tale (1 volume, New York: Harper, 1881; 3 volumes, London: Low,

Marston, Searle & Rivington, 1882);

The Remarkable History of Sir Thomas Upmore Bart MP, Formerly Known as "Tommy Upmore" (2 volumes, London: Low, Marston, Searle & Rivington, 1884; 1 volume, New York: Harper, 1884);

Springhaven: A Tale of the Great War (3 volumes,

R. D. Blackmore, 1882

London: Low, Marston, Searle & Rivington, 1887; 1 volume, New York: Harper, 1887);

Kit and Kitty: A Story of West Middlesex (New York: Harper, 1889; 3 volumes, London: Low, Marston, Searle & Rivington, 1890);

Perlycross: A Tale of the Western Hills (3 volumes, London: Low, Marston, Searle & Rivington, 1894; 1 volume, New York: Harper, 1894);

Fringilla: Some Tales in Verse (London: Elkin Mathews, 1895; Cleveland: Burrows, 1895);

Slain by the Doones (New York: Dodd, Mead, 1895); republished as *Tales from the Telling House* (London: Low, Marston, 1896);

Dariel: A Romance of Surrey (London & Edinburgh: Blackwood, 1897; New York: Dodd, Mead, 1897).

Blackmore's one famous story gave a name to a brand of cookies, to several British pubs, and to hundreds of baby girls born throughout the English-speaking world near the turn of the century. *Lorna Doone* (1869) even caused a legendary place—the "Doone Valley"—to appear on the official maps of Exmoor in southwestern England. A window in Exeter Cathedral pictures the heroine, the rustic hero, and the outlaw-villain in miniature;

tourists still come by the busload each year to visit the little church at Oare where Lorna was supposedly shot down at the altar. The story has appeared as a movie, a BBC television serial, and a classic comic. Yet the author of this "Romance of Exmoor" remains obscure, with most of his other books out of print and unread, even though they once gave him a claim to be considered with George Eliot and Thomas Hardy as an important novelist of the English countryside.

Blackmore was born in 1825 in the Berkshire village of Longworth, the second surviving son of a country curate, John Blackmore, whose father was a clergyman in North Devon. Richard's mother, Anne Bassett Knight, was the daughter of the Vicar of Tewkesbury. Christened Richard Doddridge in memory of his only notable literary ancestor, the hymn-writer Philip Doddridge, the boy lost his mother when he was three months old and was cared for by her sister, first at the Knights' family home at Newton Nottage on the south coast of Wales and later at Elsfield, outside of Oxford. He attended school at Bruton in Somerset and at South Molton in Devon before entering Blundell's School at Tiverton in Devon. There, under rough treatment from his schoolmates, he began to suffer from

Sker House on the Glamorganshire Coast near the ancestral home of Blackmore's mother's family. Sker House provided the setting for The Maid of Sker.

monthly installments of *Vanity Fair* (1847-1848), trying her hand precociously at fairy tales, domestic stories, and historical novels. In an unpublished memoir written during the last months of her life, she recalled "the quiet and safety of that shabby London where the muffin bell tinkled in the dusk at tea time, and where Punch could be heard two streets off." Her father, Henry Braddon, was a less-than-flourishing solicitor, the black sheep of a prosperous and well-established family from Cornwall; her adored mother, Fanny White Braddon, was the daughter of a ne'er-do-well Irishman. In the first days of their marriage, her parents were authors themselves after a fashion, collaborating on articles for Pitman's *Sporting Magazine* under the pseudonyms "Rough Robin" and "Gilbert Forester." Her brother, Edward, later a colonial civil servant and prime minister of Tasmania, and her sister, Margaret, were so much older that Mary Elizabeth spent her earliest years at home virtually as an only child.

The dark cloud of her childhood was associated with the misadventures of her charmingly irresponsible father. After he had finally deserted her mother, Mary Elizabeth, then in her early twenties, sought economic independence by taking to the stage under an assumed name like one of her own sensational heroines, in bold defiance of the usual Victorian restrictions on young women of respectable middle-class background. This theatrical interlude culminated in the production of her comedietta, *The Loves of Arcadia*, which opened at the Strand in March 1860. During that same spring she embarked on two other literary enterprises, a lengthy narrative poem on Garibaldi's Sicilian campaign, commissioned by an eccentric Yorkshire squire named John Gilby, and *Three Times Dead*, a cheerfully lurid potboiler originally brought out by an obscure provincial publisher and quickly republished as *The Trail of the Serpent* (1861) to capitalize on her sudden celebrity.

Before the end of the year, she was on her own in London, serving her apprenticeship as a writer of fiction while churning out highly spiced thrillers for the barely literate audience of the *Halfpenny Journal* and *Reynolds's Miscellany*. It was at this time that she met John Maxwell, a rising magazine publisher, who, like Jane Eyre's Mr. Rochester, was already possessed of a legal wife in a mental institution. For the next fourteen years, the period of her greatest fame, Miss Braddon's nonfictional secret was her domestic life with Maxwell, which eventually included their five illegitimate children. Scandal was

with difficulty kept at bay; when Maxwell quietly inserted a line in the newspapers to the effect that they had recently been married, a brother-in-law of the legal Mrs. Maxwell published clamorous denials.

Through all the social and personal strain of this early period, through the numerous pregnancies and the much-lamented loss of an infant son, Braddon continued to write furiously, averaging two triple-deckers a year for the mainstream market as well as founding the monthly *Belgravia* and keeping up her anonymous connection with the penny dreadfuls. Most of the time she worked under intense pressure, as she confided to her literary mentor, Sir Edward Bulwer-Lytton, with whom she maintained a regular correspondence: "I know that my writing teems with errors, absurdities, contradictions, and inconsistencies; but I have never written a line that has not been written against time—sometimes with the printer waiting outside the door." In a futile attempt to salvage one of

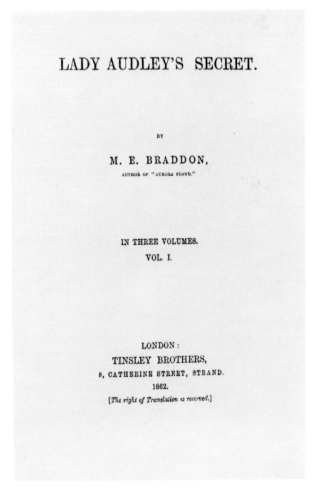

Title page for the novel that established Braddon's reputation

Maxwell's publishing ventures, she produced the first installment of *Lady Audley's Secret* overnight, later completing part of the second and the entire third volume "in less than a fortnight." From the outset of her career, Braddon proved to be a thoroughgoing professional and a shrewd businesswoman, writing unabashedly for profit, well aware of both the extent and limitations of her talent.

Lady Audley's Secret, an immediate *succès de scandale* that went on to become one of the top best-sellers of the century, was a prototype of the so-called sensation novel, a popular genre of the 1860s which insinuated crime, mystery, and illicit passion into the lives of ordinary middle-class characters as aspects of their familiar experiences. Braddon's notorious heroine, the fragile, fair-haired child-wife of an elderly baronet, perfectly fulfills the role of the Victorian domestic goddess until the fateful day that Sir Michael's nephew, Robert Audley, happens to visit with an old friend by the name of George Talboys. When George unaccountably disappears, Robert plays the part of amateur detective, finding to his astonishment that all the clues point directly to his beautiful young aunt, who had previously married his friend, borne a child and then faked her own death while George toiled in the gold diggings of Australia. Not only has Lady Audley committed bigamy and disposed of her superfluous husband by pushing him down an abandoned well, but she continues her career by dabbling in arson, setting fire at midnight to a nearby inn which houses both Robert Audley and a lower-class blackmailer. When she is finally unmasked, it turns out that she suffers from a hereditary condition of intermittent insanity. Although George Talboys reappears, having climbed out of the abandoned well and shipped for America, the unrepentant Lady Audley is forced to end her days in a Belgian madhouse. The outrageously sensational materials of Braddon's plot are qualified throughout by her amusingly ironic tone.

Braddon promptly followed up on her unexpected triumph with such sensational works as *Aurora Floyd* (1863), *John Marchmont's Legacy* (1863), *Birds of Prey* (1867), and *Charlotte's Inheritance* (1868). Although her popularity was staggering, her critical reception was decidedly hostile, par-

Braddon's application for entry of Lady Audley's Secret *in the Stationers' Register Book*
(Anderson Galleries, #4283, 9 December 1936)

ticularly in the higher-brow journals. She was accused of "animalism" and "sensuality"; she was mercilessly parodied; she was admonished for introducing what was known as "kitchen literature" into the respectable domain of the three-volume novel. *Lady Audley's Secret* was denounced on all sides as "one of the most noxious books of modern times." Because of her equivocal domestic position, Braddon was especially vulnerable to a double-edged attack from the reviewers, who rarely scrupled to sneer at her personal life under cover of criticizing her all-too-recognizably similar "bigamy novels."

Not even *The Doctor's Wife* (1864), an impressive adaptation of Flaubert's *Madame Bovary* (1856) and Braddon's first attempt at a novel of character rather than plot, managed entirely to escape the critical onslaught. In Braddon's version, Isabel Gilbert, the romantic young wife of an awkward country surgeon, becomes hopelessly infatuated with the dashing local squire, Roland Lansdell. Although Isabel is described as an "intellectual opium-eater" who prefers disembodied fantasy to actual involvement, and Roland is portrayed as an accomplished seducer who crudely demands a sexual return from her, Braddon allows their illicit passion to develop into a serious attachment, a love "too pure to have survived the stain of treachery and guilt." Unlike Madame Bovary, Isabel never commits adultery. Instead, Roland is brutally murdered by her father, a convicted criminal. The novel ends with Isabel, now widowed, devoting herself to philanthropy. Braddon admitted to being both fascinated and dismayed by her encounter with Flaubert's text; *The Doctor's Wife* represents a conscious anglicizing and feminizing of his major themes.

Despite her tremendous courage and unfailing good humor in all her difficulties, Braddon suffered a severe nervous breakdown following the death of her mother in November 1868. For the

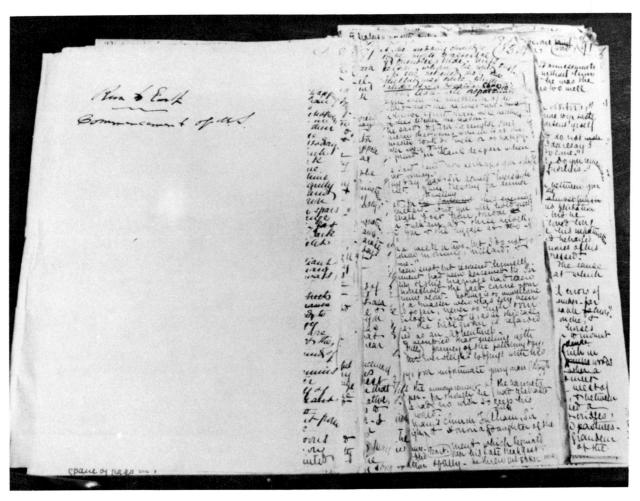

Manuscript for Run to Earth *(Collection of Robert Lee Wolff)*

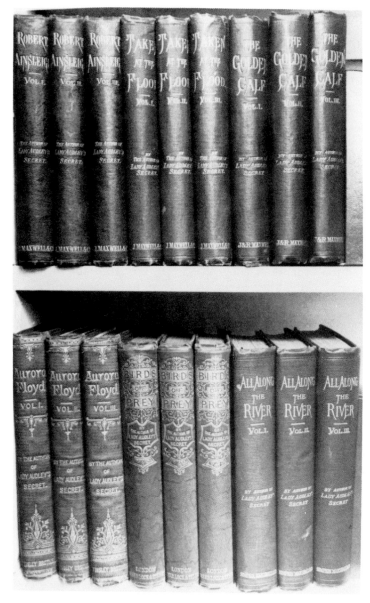

First editions, in three-volume format, of selected novels by Braddon (Collection of Robert Lee Wolff)

only time in her fifty-five-year career, she was unable to write; it was not until the spring of 1870 that her loyal public could again look forward to a new serial by M. E. Braddon. After a rather shaky start with a couple of routine sensational tales, she turned to the social novel in *The Lovels of Arden* (1871), a successful incursion into an area she had already exploited for *The Lady's Mile* (1866), her first novel without a murder.

Her steady output of fiction for the rest of her life gave evidence of her extraordinary versatility; once the fad for sensationalism had passed, she proved herself equally adept at biting social satire in novels like *Vixen* (1879), provincial domestic tragedy in *Joshua Haggard's Daughter* (1876), and historical romance in *Ishmael* (1884). The high quality of her work during this middle period reflects her increasing, if hard-won, security, both domestic and financial. At the death of Maxwell's first wife in 1874, her union with him was finally regularized, and they continued to live happily together until his death in 1895.

As a writer, Braddon never wearied or grew complacent; even in her sixties and seventies she remained a vital force in popular literature, experimenting with different genres and approaches, ultimately taking advantage of the new permissiveness around the turn of the century. When the old-fashioned triple-decker in which she had scored so many triumphs lingeringly expired during the 1890s, the durable Miss Braddon was ready with several complete one-volume manuscripts prudently tucked away in her desk. Among her twentieth-century novels are *The Infidel* (1900), another historical romance of which she wrote, "I like the book myself—I don't often like my books"; *The Rose of Life* (1905), which includes a sharp portrayal of her old friend Oscar Wilde; and *Dead Love Has Chains* (1907), a tragedy which shows her undiminished power even in old age. Describing herself as "an ancient story-spinner," she had no thoughts of quitting; she died in her eightieth year while still engaged in the revisions of *Mary*, a partially autobiographical work that appeared posthumously in 1916. Her last years had been characteristically busy, socially as well as professionally. Perhaps her greatest pleasure came from following and encouraging the career of her favorite son, the novelist W. B. Maxwell, with whom she regularly shared publication dates after his debut in 1892.

In spite of her slapdash methods of composition, in spite of the critical controversy that surrounded her early years and the total obscurity that descended after her death, M. E. Braddon was a popular novelist of genuine talent, a natural storyteller whose books, with their dry wit and flavor of worldliness, remain surprisingly fresh and readable. Not even her astonishing record of productivity over a period of more than half a century could exhaust her ready invention or her enthusiasm for her chosen craft. By sheer longevity and persistence, she not only outlasted her critics but went on to become an institution, no longer savaged in the periodicals but paid affectionate tribute as "part of England; she has woven herself into it; without her it would be different. . . . She is in the encyclopaedias; she ought to be in the dictionaries." Through times of cultural upheaval and

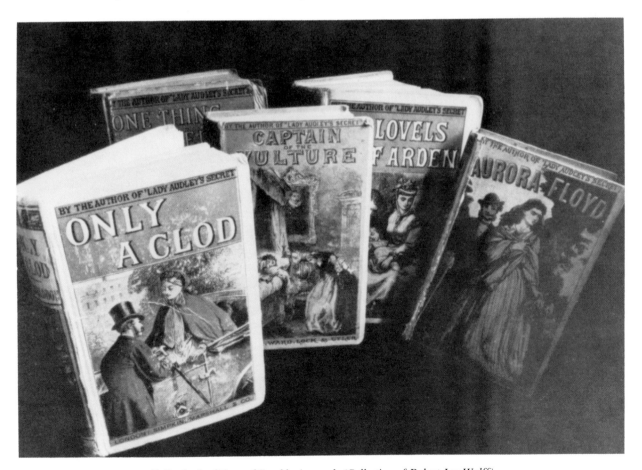

Yellowback editions of Braddon's novels (Collection of Robert Lee Wolff)

shifting fashion, she held on to the loyalty of her audience, which ranged from the humblest purchaser of a penny installment to the literary masters of three generations, mid-Victorian to Edwardian. Dickens, Thackeray, and Tennyson had all been gratefully ensnared by her serial mysteries; she was taken seriously by George Moore and Arnold Bennett; Thomas Hardy was sufficiently moved by his reading of *The Doctor's Wife* to recast its major themes in *The Return of the Native* (1878). As Robert Louis Stevenson wrote to her from Samoa, "It is something to be out and away greater than Scott, Shakespeare, Homer, in the South Seas, and to that you have attained." Only very recently has she been rediscovered by the academic critics, who have cited her career as an early example of female professionalism while re-evaluating her fiction as subversive of the official Victorian domestic mythology.

Braddon herself would have been the last to overestimate her contribution to English letters. In the heady days of her first success, she commented wryly on her own brand of sensationalism: "There's only one objection to the style—it's apt to give an author a tendency towards bodies.... And once you've had recourse to the stimulant of bodies, you're like a man who's accustomed to strong liquors, and to whose vitiated palate simple drinks seem flat and wishy-washy." As a seasoned professional, she offered much the same opinion in *The Rose of Life*: "Provided the showman clashes his cymbals loud enough, the unlettered millions are satisfied." The clasher of cymbals who wrote those words merits an honored place in the first rank of popular literature.

Other:

The Summer Tourist: A Book for Long and Short Journeys, edited by Braddon (London: Ward, Lock & Tyler, 1871).

Letters:

Robert Lee Wolff, ed., "Devoted Disciple: The Letters of Mary Elizabeth Braddon to Sir Edward Bulwer-Lytton 1862-1873," *Harvard Library Bulletin*, 22 (January & April 1974).

References:

Norman Donaldson, Introduction to M. E. Braddon, *Lady Audley's Secret* (New York: Dover, 1974);

Winifred Hughes, *The Maniac in the Cellar: Sensation Novels of the 1860s* (Princeton, N.J.: Princeton University Press, 1980);

W. B. Maxwell, *Time Gathered* (New York & London: Appleton-Century, 1938);

Michael Sadleir, *Things Past* (London: Constable, 1944);

Elaine Showalter, *A Literature of Their Own* (Princeton, N.J.: Princeton University Press, 1977);

Robert Lee Wolff, *Sensational Victorian: The Life and Fiction of Mary Elizabeth Braddon* (New York: Garland, 1979).

Rhoda Broughton

(29 November 1840-5 June 1920)

R. C. Terry
University of Victoria

BOOKS: *Not Wisely but Too Well* (3 volumes, London: Tinsley, 1867; 1 volume, New York: Appleton, 1868);

Cometh Up as a Flower: An Autobiography (2 volumes, London: Bentley, 1867; 1 volume, New York: Appleton, 1867);

Red as a Rose is She: A Novel (3 volumes, London: Bentley, 1870; 1 volume, New York: Appleton, 1870);

Good-bye, Sweetheart!: A Tale (3 volumes, London: Bentley, 1872; 1 volume, New York: Appleton, 1872);

Nancy: A Novel (3 volumes, London: Bentley, 1873; 1 volume, New York: Appleton, 1874);

Tales for Christmas Eve (London: Bentley, 1873); republished as *Twilight Stories* (New York: Transatlantic, 1948);

Joan: A Tale (3 volumes, London: Bentley, 1876; 1 volume, New York: Appleton, 1876);

Second Thoughts (2 volumes, London: Bentley, 1880; 1 volume, New York: Appleton, 1880);

Belinda: A Novel (3 volumes, London: Bentley, 1883; 1 volume, New York: Appleton, 1883);

Betty's Visions and Mrs. Smith of Longmains (London: Routledge, 1886; New York: Lovell, 1886);

Doctor Cupid: A Novel (3 volumes, London: Bentley, 1886; New York: Munro, 1886);

Alas!: A Novel (3 volumes, London: Bentley, 1890; 1 volume, New York: United States Book Company, 1890);

A Widower Indeed, by Broughton and Elizabeth Bisland (London: Osgood, 1891; New York: Appleton, 1891);

Mrs. Bligh: A Novel (London: Bentley, 1892; New York: Appleton, 1892);

A Beginner (London: Bentley, 1894; New York: Appleton, 1894);

Scylla or Charybdis?: A Novel (London: Bentley, 1895; New York: Appleton, 1895);

Dear Faustina (London: Bentley, 1897; New York: Appleton, 1897);

The Game and the Candle (London: Macmillan, 1899; New York: Appleton, 1899);

Foes in Law (London: Macmillan, 1900);

Lavinia (London: Macmillan, 1902);

Rhoda Broughton

A Waif's Progress (London: Macmillan, 1905);

Mamma (London: Macmillan, 1908);

The Devil and the Deep Sea (London: Macmillan, 1910);

Between Two Stools (London: Stanley Paul, 1912);

Concerning a Vow (London: Stanley Paul, 1914);

A Thorn in the Flesh (London: Stanley, Paul, 1917);

A Fool in Her Folly (London: Odhams, 1920).

In her novel *Good-bye, Sweetheart!* (1872), Rhoda Broughton categorizes two kinds of fiction: novels proper and novels improper, "novels that are milk for babes and novels that are almost too strong meat for men." The public considered hers to be of the latter kind, and lapped them up. Yet Rhoda Broughton may justly be rated considerably higher than as a writer of torrid love stories, chiefly for her insights into female psychology and for her contribution to the history of English manners.

The youngest of three daughters, Miss Broughton was born on 29 November 1840 at Segryd Hall, near Denbigh, Wales. Her grandfather was Sir Henry Delves Broughton; her father, a clergyman, held the living of Broughton, Staffordshire, where Rhoda grew up at the rectory. She was educated at home by her father, whose learning inspired her love of literature. With the aid of her uncle, Sheridan Le Fanu, she published anonymously her first two novels, *Not Wisely but Too Well* and *Cometh Up as a Flower*, in 1867. After that, living with her sister, first in Richmond and then in Oxford, where her conversational gifts made her a celebrity, she systematically turned out a novel almost every two years until her death on 5 June 1920. In all, she produced twenty-five novels and two

collections of stories, most of them serialized in *Temple Bar* before book publication by her devoted and patient publisher, George Bentley. She ended her career living in London, adored by a wide circle of artistic and aristocratic friends—among them Henry James, who knew her for almost a quarter of a century.

Charges that her writing was fast and frivolous surrounded her early work. Critics castigated her for her frankness about female sexuality and her want of propriety; her heroines, it seemed to Mrs. Oliphant, did not seem too particular in drawing the line between being made love to and making it. Certainly it seemed that Miss Broughton went out of her way to draw the critics' fire; and while she recoiled from the virulence of some of the criticism, she enjoyed shocking the straitlaced with a succession of tales about precocious young girls surrendering to disastrous love affairs or caught up in loveless marriages. Such is the pattern of *Not Wisely but Too Well* and *Cometh Up as a Flower*, which were

First editions of two novels by Broughton, both bound in chintz cloth. Second Thoughts *is reputed to be the first book so bound.*
(Collection of Robert Lee Wolff)

the first of her numerous successes, to be followed by such flamboyant works as *Red as a Rose is She* (1870), *Good-bye, Sweetheart!*, and several with the heroine's name, *Nancy* (1873), *Joan* (1876), and *Belinda* (1883).

Despising the mode of storytellers like Mrs. Craik or Charlotte Yonge, whose male characters she likened to "old governesses in trousers," Miss Broughton drew her men and women large. Her men are ruddy-cheeked philistines with gnarled throats and much in common with G. A. Lawrence's Guy Livingstone, though Miss Broughton did not welcome the comparison. Her fleshy heroines have healthy appetites and act with great spirit and brashness. In *Good-bye, Sweetheart!*, for example, Lenore Herrick dons peasant costume to check out the male talent in a Breton town and virtually picks up Paul le Mesurier. Despite misgivings he lets her persuade him to take her out in a boat by moonlight. The narrative is charged with images of water-lily cups as white chalices, and as Lenore stretches out her half-recumbent form, a moonbeam catches her white arm reaching for a bud which she offers to Paul: "Keep it as a memento of the fast girl who *would* go out boating with you, against your will, at ten o'clock at night—of the girl who *may be very good fun, if one goes in for that sort of thing, but is not your style.*" Impulsively she throws the bud into the river. He grabs for it and upsets the boat. Ashore she takes a nip of brandy, lets him wring out her petticoats, and returns to the hotel minus a shoe. All this is very typical Broughton. As Alfred Austin put it: "Life, verve, elasticity, pervade her pages."

Such elements are the saving grace of Broughton's conventional plotting and melodramatic endings. Again, *Good-bye, Sweetheart!* is typical: pride parts the two lovers and eventually Lenore dies of consumption. The heroines in Broughton's novels who appear so vigorously to kick over the traces, suggesting some valid concern in the authoress for quirks of behavior or feminine needs, have in the end to fit conventions of the popular novel and pay for their independence. For Rhoda Broughton was at bottom thoroughly moral and conventional herself. Thus the fizz and crackle of early parts of the novels tend to die out, and in the resolution of interesting human dilemmas the author is always bound by the prejudices of her age, one reason why Oscar Wilde could say of her she had that one touch of vulgarity that makes the whole world kin.

However, it is unwise to focus on the love scenes and their outcome, for Rhoda Broughton's merits lie elsewhere: in the way she expressed female passion with psychological acuity and painful awareness; in her lively plots, sinewy dialogue, and vividly realized English settings. She had a keen eye for the social milieu and class-determining marks, and like many Victorian novelists was fascinated by people on their way up or down. Such observation makes *Joan* and *Belinda* still readable (the latter contains also a portrait of Mark Pattison). Her work from about the time of *Nancy* abounds in more thoughtful studies of intricate domestic situations, with *Second Thoughts* (1880), *Doctor Cupid* (1886), *Mrs. Bligh* (1892), and *Foes in Law* (1900) being among the best. In addition she wrote a fine pair of stories of the supernatural, *Betty's Visions and Mrs. Smith of Longmains* (1886). Michael Sadleir decided that Rhoda Broughton's best works were the single-volume novels beginning with *Mrs. Bligh*. *A Beginner* (1894) and her last novel, *A Fool in Her Folly* (1920), both about young writers involved in love affairs, he argued, were probably fictionalized accounts of an unhappy romance in Broughton's own early life. There is no evidence on this point. The later novels show more sobriety and control, but the vitality and daring of her earlier work is diminished.

It is important to separate Miss Broughton's true contribution from her notoriety. She stands apart from sensationalists like Miss Braddon or the "wicked" romancers Ouida and Marie Corelli as a sound analyst of the female mind and a shrewd commentator on the domestic scene. At a time when women novelists humbugged a good deal, Rhoda Broughton's novels still have a refreshing pungency and candor.

References:

Ethel M. Arnold, "Rhoda Broughton as I Knew Her," *Fortnightly Review*, 114 (2 August 1920): 262-278;

Ernest Baker, *The History of the English Novel*, volume 10 (London: Witherby, 1939), pp. 211-213;

Helen Black, *Notable Women Authors of the Day* (Glasgow: David Bryce, 1893), pp. 37-44;

Michael Sadleir, *Things Past* (London: Constable, 1944), pp. 84-116;

R. C. Terry, *Victorian Popular Fiction* (London: Macmillan, forthcoming).

Papers:

Some manuscript material exists at the Humanities Research Center, University of Texas at Austin, and the Delves Broughton Collection, Cheshire Record Office.

Robert Buchanan

(18 August 1841-10 June 1901)

Christopher D. Murray
University of Regina

BOOKS: *Storm-Beaten: or, Christmas Eve at the "Old Anchor" Inn*, by Buchanan and Charles Gibbon (London: Ward & Lock, 1862);

Undertones (London: Chatto & Windus, 1863);

Idyls and Legends of Inverburn (London: Strahan, 1865);

London Poems (London: Strahan, 1866);

Ballad Stories of the Affections: From the Scandinavian (London: Routledge, 1866; New York: Scribners, Welford, 1869);

North Coast and Other Poems (London: Routledge, 1868);

David Gray and other Essays, Chiefly on Poetry (London: Low & Marston, 1868);

The Book of Orm: A Prelude to the Epic (London: Chatto & Windus, 1870);

Napoleon Fallen: A Lyrical Drama (London: Strahan, 1870);

The Drama of Kings (London: Strahan, 1871);

The Land of Lorne (2 volumes, London: Chapman & Hall, 1871; 1 volume, New York: Felt, 1871);

The Fleshly School of Poetry and other Phenomena of the Day (London: Strahan, 1872; New York: Boni & Liveright, 1926);

Saint Abe and His Seven Wives: A Tale of Salt Lake City (London: Strahan, 1872; New York: Routledge, 1872);

White Rose and Red: A Love Story (London: Strahan, 1873; Boston: Osgood, 1873);

Master-spirits (London: King, 1873);

The Shadow of the Sword (3 volumes, London: Bentley, 1876; 1 volume, New York: Appleton, 1877);

Balder the Beautiful: A Song of Divine Death (London: Mullan, 1877);

A Child of Nature: A Romance (3 volumes, London: Bentley, 1881; 1 volume, New York: Harper, 1881);

God and the Man (3 volumes, London: Chatto & Windus, 1881; 1 volume, New York: Munro, 1881);

Foxglove Manor: A Novel (3 volumes, London: Chatto & Windus, 1881);

The Martyrdom of Madeline: A Novel (3 volumes, London: Chatto & Windus, 1882; 1 volume, New York: Munro, 1882);

Ballads of Life, Love and Humour (London: Chatto & Windus, 1882);

Love Me Forever: A Romance (New York: Munro, 1882; London: Chatto & Windus, 1883);

Annan Water: A Romance (3 volumes, London: Chatto & Windus, 1883; 1 volume, New York: Munro, 1884);

A Poet's Sketch-Book: Selections from the Prose Writings of Robert Buchanan (London: Chatto & Windus, 1883);

The New Abelard: A Romance (New York: Lovell, 1883; 3 volumes, London: Chatto & Windus, 1884);

18

The Master of the Mine: A Novel (2 volumes, London: Bentley, 1885; 1 volume, New York: Munro, 1885);

Matt: A Story of a Caravan (London: Chatto & Windus, 1885); republished as *Matt: A Tale of a Caravan* (New York: Appleton, 1885);

Stormy Waters: A Story of To-day (3 volumes, London: Maxwell, 1885; 1 volume, New York: Munro, 1888);

The Earthquake; or, Six Days and a Sabbath (London: Chatto & Windus, 1885);

That Winter Night; or, Love's Victory (Bristol: Arrowsmith, 1886; New York: Harper, 1886);

A Look Round Literature (London: Ward & Downey, 1887);

The City of Dream: An Epic Poem (London: Chatto & Windus, 1888);

The Heir of Linne: A Novel (2 volumes, London: Chatto & Windus, 1888; 1 volume, New York: Munro, 1888);

On Descending into Hell: A Letter Addressed to the Right Hon. Henry Matthews, Q.C., Home Secretary, Concerning the Proposed Suppression of Literature (London: Redway, 1889);

The Moment After: A Tale of the Unseen (London: Heinemann, 1890; New York: Lovell, 1891);

Come, Live with Me and Be My Love: A Novel (2 volumes, New York: Lovell, 1891; 1 volume, London: Heinemann, 1892);

The Coming Terror and Other Essays and Letters (London: Heinemann, 1891; New York: United States Book Company, 1891);

The Wedding Ring: A Tale of To-Day (New York: Cassell, 1891);

The Outcast: A Rhyme for the Time (London: Chatto & Windus, 1891);

The Piper of Hamelin: A Fantastic Opera in Two Acts (London: Heinemann, 1893);

The Wandering Jew: A Christmas Carol (London: Chatto & Windus, 1893);

Woman and the Man: A Story (2 volumes, London: Chatto & Windus, 1893);

Red and White Heather: North Country Tales and Ballads (London: Chatto & Windus, 1894);

Rachel Dene: A Tale of the Deepdale Mills (2 volumes, London: Chatto & Windus, 1894; 1 volume, New York: Neely, 1894);

Lady Kilpatrick: A Novel (London: Chatto & Windus, 1895; New York: Rand, McNally, 1897);

The Charlatan, by Buchanan and Henry Murray (London: Chatto & Windus, 1895; New York: Neely, 1895);

Diana's Hunting: A Novel (London: Unwin, 1895; New York: Stokes, 1895);

A Marriage by Capture: A Romance of To-day (London: Unwin, 1896; Philadelphia: Lippincott, 1896);

Effie Hetherington: A Novel (London: Unwin, 1896; Boston: Roberts, 1896);

Is Barabbas a Necessity? (London: Buchanan, 1896);

The Devil's Case: A Bank Holiday Interlude (London: Buchanan, 1896);

The Ballad of Mary the Mother: A Christmas Carol (London: Buchanan, 1897);

Father Anthony: A Romance of To-day (London: Long, 1898; New York: Dillingham, 1900);

The Rev. Annabel Lee (London: Pearson, 1898);

The New Rome: Poems and Ballads of Our Empire (London: Scott, 1898);

Andromeda: An Idyll of the Great River (London: Chatto & Windus, 1900; Philadelphia: Lippincott, 1901);

The Voice of "The Hooligan": A Discussion of Kiplingism, by Buchanan and Sir Walter Besant (New York: Tucker, 1900);

Sweet Nancy: A Comedy in Three Acts (London: French, 1914).

A prolific writer with twenty-seven novels attributed to him, Robert Buchanan enjoyed remarkable success when he turned to fiction in the 1870s in an attempt to earn the living his verse had failed to provide him. Never afraid of tackling unpopular themes, he passionately denounced war at the height of Victorian imperialism, and wrote indignantly of prostitution, the double standard, and religious hypocrisy during the heyday of Victorian respectability. At the outset his outspokenness was praised, as were his depiction of character, especially through dialogue, and his marvelous skill at evoking landscape. Like many of his contemporaries, however, he resorted to melodramatic shifts to resolve plot difficulties; and, also like many of them, he could not avoid the maudlin. Of his efforts on behalf of her sex Lynn Linton declared that he wrote "sentimental bunkum with splendid literary power." Only late in his career could he allow his heroine to be an attractive predator, in *Diana's Hunting* (1895), a novel now read, if read at all, for its "fancy sketch" of George Bernard Shaw.

Robert Williams Buchanan was born in Caverswall, Staffordshire, to Robert Buchanan, a Scottish socialist, and Mary Williams, daughter of a well-known radical lawyer of Stoke-on-Trent. He was brought up in Glasgow, where his father edited several newspapers, and attended Glasgow University, where he met David Gray, who became his closest friend. Both Gray and Buchanan published verse in the local press and aspired to literary careers. On Buchanan's father's financial collapse in 1859, the two friends resolved to try their fortune in London. Accustomed to middle-class comforts, and witnessing Gray's slow death from tuberculosis, Buchanan suffered much hardship during his first eighteen months there. By November 1861, however, he could afford to marry Mary Jay, whose sister Harriet (Buchanan's biographer) they subsequently adopted. In December Buchanan published *Storm-Beaten; or, Christmas Eve at the "Old Anchor" Inn* (1862), a collection of yarns of little merit written in collaboration with Charles Gibbon. His success thereafter, both critical and financial, was remarkable, especially with his verse.

London quickly came to represent to him a major corruptive influence, and as soon as he could afford it, he moved away: first to Sussex in 1866, where he wrote *London Poems* (1866); then to Oban in the Scottish highlands in 1870. He first wrote serious fiction while living in Scotland, and the short story "Eiradh of Canna," originally published in *The Land of Lorne* (1871) and republished in *A Poet's Sketch-Book* (1883), is among the best things he ever did. Experimenting with the dramatic monologue in his verse at the time, Buchanan wrote this poignant story of a Highland fisherman's daughter, orphaned by the sea and betrayed by her husband, as if told by a fellow villager who speaks only Gaelic. The story thus acquires an impressive and otherworldly Celtic quality; no less important, Buchanan avoids his besetting sin, an excess of sentimentality.

By this time, Buchanan's career appeared to be set. Conceited and aggressive, however, he became embroiled in a running battle with Algernon Charles Swinburne over the moral status of poetry. This led to his harsh reviews of Dante Gabriel Rossetti's *Poems* in October 1871, enlarged and republished as the notorious pamphlet *The Fleshly School of Poetry* in May 1872. However much they sympathized with his concern for literary morality, few dispassionate observers could forgive Buchanan for the ferocity of his attack, which resulted in Rossetti's attempted suicide in early June. Thereafter Buchanan became a "confirmed mutineer," and influential friends such as George Eliot and Robert Browning dropped away.

Buchanan moved again in 1874 to Rossport, County Mayo, Ireland, almost as far from London as he could get in the British Isles. Only when his verse sales began to diminish, and when desperate for a source of income, did he turn to writing novels in 1876. At first, jealous of his reputation, Buchanan took novel writing seriously, and *The Shadow of the Sword* (1876), published with much fanfare by Richard Gowing in the *Gentleman's Magazine*, remains one of his best. It tells of Rohan Gwenfern's refusal to be conscripted into Napoleon's army and his fugitive existence, hounded by the local militia, in the caves along the rugged Breton coast. Within three years the strapping young giant of 1812 is prematurely stooped and wizened. Written with a care unusual for Buchanan, the novel was praised highly when it appeared, ran to several editions, and remained in print for over fifty years.

After four years in Ireland he returned to London, maintaining for many years a home in Southend, Essex, as well. Within a few years of his return to London, Buchanan's reputation as a serious writer began to decline: his expensive tastes and his frantic efforts to cure his wife's cancer—from which she died in November 1881—drove him to desperate shifts to earn money; but his second novel, *A Child of Nature* (1881), less ambitious in scope and less didactic than *The Shadow of the Sword*, also remains readable. It is the first of many novels containing female protagonists. Surrounded by adoring women—his mother, his wife, and his adopted daughter—all his life, Buchanan understood and admired women more, perhaps, than most men do. Mina MacDonald, the orphaned protégée of a minister of the Church of Scotland, is an impressive prototype for a series of Buchanan heroines: intelligent, artless, at home in the harsh environment of the north coast of Scotland, quick to help those less fortunate than herself, she represents an ideal of womanhood not often found in Victorian fiction. Opposed to her are the absentee landowners—cynical, artificial, urban aristocrats. Although engaged to his cool, worldly, shallow cousin, Lord Arranmore falls in love with Mina; the pattern is completed by the cousin's falling in love with another Buchanan prototype, Mina's dour, brooding, uncommunicative yet powerful brother, Graham. Buchanan's penchant for authorial intrusion, which mars *The Shadow of the Sword*, is kept in abeyance in this novel, which is better, perhaps, than this brief description might suggest.

Buchanan, however, mounted his favorite hobbyhorse in his next novel, *God and the Man* (1881): that come what may we must strive to love one another. As an admission of his most glaring failure to live by this creed, the novel was dedicated

Largely overlooked by the general public in his own time—only one of his books, *Erewhon Revisited Twenty Years Later* (1901), was published without financial support from its author—Samuel Butler achieved fame soon after his death in 1902 and has ever since been recognized as a significant Victorian writer. His powerful critique of the family in the posthumously published *The Way of All Flesh* (1903), acclaimed in 1906 by an enthusiastic G. B. Shaw (whose comments, together with those of others, brought it wide attention), has aroused a strong response in many generations of readers and has been frequently imitated; his many-faceted appraisal of the whole human condition in his satire *Erewhon* (1872), in his books on evolution, and in his *Note-Books* (1912) still evokes shocked recognition; and his speculations concerning the unconscious give additional dimensions to the findings of psychoanalysis. Butler's clear, direct prose, contrasting sharply with Victorian "fine writing"; his startling use of irony and ambiguity; his iconoclastic attacks on the bigwigs of his time: all have aroused responses in creative and thoughtful people of the twentieth century.

Born on 4 December 1835 at Langar Rectory near Bingham, Nottinghamshire, England, Samuel Butler was the son of the Reverend Thomas Butler and the grandson of Dr. Samuel Butler, headmaster of Shrewsbury School and bishop of Lichfield, whose career and times his namesake later enthusiastically recorded in a two-volume biography. His mother was Fanny Worsley, the daughter of Philip John Worsley, a Bristol sugar refiner. Four children grew up in the Butler household: Samuel, his two sisters, and a younger brother; a fifth child died in infancy. Butler was not related to the seventeenth-century Samuel Butler, author of *Hudibras* (1663, 1664, 1678), with whom he is sometimes confused. Butler attended a private school at Allesley near Coventry and Shrewsbury School, traveled to Italy twice as a youngster with his family and once as a university student with a friend; after 1872, he vacationed in Italy annually. He never married but remained by deep conviction a bachelor. In 1858 he took a first-class degree in classics at St. John's College, Cambridge.

Butler's career as a publishing author began tentatively with occasional pieces in his college journal, the *Eagle* of St. John's. These include some telling comments on how to write, praising the clear, direct style of two hundred years earlier which Butler emulated; an account of his Easter trip to France, Switzerland, and Italy; and two articles de-scribing a voyage out to New Zealand and the life of a frontiersman. The voyage had come about as a result of a family quarrel. Because his family wished him to enter the ministry as his father had done before him, Butler, hoping to discover what he wanted to become, had worked for a time after his graduation from St. John's among the poor in London as an amateur lay assistant to a clergyman. Growing doubts about religion—from his own close reading of the Greek New Testament and from his observation that the boys in his evening class who had not been baptized were no worse than those who had been—and growing interest in art and music, especially the music of Handel, led him to decide against entering the church. After much heated discussion, his angered father, who firmly refused to support him in the art studies he now wished to undertake, advanced money (which eventually would have been his anyway since his grandfather had designated him as "tenant in tail" to a considerable estate) to allow him to emigrate from England and chart out a life of his own. On his initial night aboard the ship *Roman Emperor*, bound for New Zealand, Butler for the first time in his life failed to say his prayers, and he never said them again. During the three-month voyage he read Gibbons's *History of the Decline and Fall of the Roman Empire* (1776-1788), a book regarded with abhorrence by many orthodox Victorians and surely reading that would have been frowned upon at the rectory.

From 1859 to 1864 Butler lived in New Zealand, managing his own 8,000-acre sheep run and gradually building up a satisfactory mode of life, with new friends and plenty to do. He had a piano transported by bullock dray to the house he had built. (It was a two-day trip from the nearest town, Christchurch.) There in off hours he entertained himself and his infrequent visitors by playing Handel. In 1883, looking back on his life, Butler wrote: "Of all dead men Handel has had the largest place in my thoughts. In fact, I should say that he and his music have been the central fact in my life ever since I was old enough to know of the existence of either music or life. All day long—whether I am writing or painting or walking—but always—I have his music in my head."

Finally, when Butler's capital had been nearly doubled, he returned to London and took up residence at Fifteen Clifford's Inn, his home for the remainder of his life. While in New Zealand, in addition to the two articles for the *Eagle*, he had sent home letters of such interest that his father, now

Samuel Butler at Cambridge, mid-1850s

somewhat placated, combined the articles and the letters into a volume with the writer's approval and underwrote their publication. *A First Year in Canterbury Settlement* (1863) still makes interesting reading, although for reasons hard to fathom its author came to hate it and to wish it had never been published. Designed in part as a "how-to" manual to interest would-be emigrants, it vividly narrates the events of the three-month voyage from England, telling the reader how to equip himself for such a trip; describes the towns of Lyttleton and Christchurch; and, with considerable attention to financial details, explains how to go about acquiring a sheep run. It gives an account of explorations that eventually led Butler to the discovery of a mountain and a pass later named for him. Butler emphasizes the independence and self-reliance of frontier existence. He indeed remained a kind of intellectual "frontiersman" for the rest of his life.

More important for Butler's later career than *A First Year in Canterbury Settlement* were an indeterminate number of pieces he had published in the *Press*, the newspaper of Christchurch, under various pseudonyms, concerning the theory of evolution which Charles Darwin, a schoolfellow of Butler's father's at Cambridge, had recently formu-

Rendering of Butler's homestead in New Zealand by his friend and collaborator Henry Festing Jones
(St. John's College, Cambridge University)

lated. These pieces expressed views both for and against Darwinism and suggested, among much else, that machines had their own evolution and might someday take over the world. Back in England, Darwin somehow came into possession of the first of these articles. He liked it so much that he sought to have it reprinted in England. Later, Butler sent his pamphlet *The Evidence for the Resurrection of Jesus Christ* (1865) to Darwin, who wrote him a cordial note of acknowledgment to which Butler replied, sending him his second *Press* article on evolution. In 1872, Butler spent a weekend at Down, Darwin's home, at Darwin's invitation, and he later visited there again. One of the real tragedies of Butler's life is that this friendly relationship soon degenerated into bitterness as a result of misunderstandings for which neither Darwin nor Butler was solely to blame.

After his return from New Zealand, Butler devoted himself assiduously for thirteen years to the study of painting; several of his pictures were exhibited at the Royal Academy. The best known of these, *Family Prayers*, can sometimes be seen at the Tate Gallery in London. Butler continued writing in off-hours and on weekends, and immediately published at his own expense the pamphlet on the

conflicting accounts of the Crucifixion and Resurrection in the Gospels which he sent to Darwin. He then gradually completed a satirical fantasy called *Erewhon* based on his New Zealand experience, on his study of Darwin, and on his critical thoughts about religion and society. In this work as in much of his later writing, he was encouraged by Eliza Mary Ann Savage, a fellow art student, with whom Butler developed a warm friendship. She read each of Butler's manuscripts with delight and helped him with her intelligent comments and unfailing enthusiasm until her death in 1885. (Her many sprightly letters to Butler and some of his replies were published in 1935.)

In search of new pastures and possible wealth, the unnamed hero of *Erewhon* travels through the realistic mountain landscape of New Zealand to an imaginary topsy-turvydom on the other side of the range. On the top of the pass into Erewhon he encounters ten hollow statues which howl so in the wind as to scare off all would-be passersby—these statues clearly stand for the ten commandments. The hero, after losing his guide, almost in spite of himself gets past the statues, down a frightening ravine, and across a river, nearly losing his life. Then he enters the country of Erewhon, is jailed,

Family Prayers
"I did this in 1864 and if I had gone on doing things out of my own head instead of making Studies, I should have been all right." S.B.

Canvas 20 in. by 16 in.

Butler's best-known painting, now at the Tate Gallery

falls in love with the jail keeper's daughter Yram, is taken to the capital city where he is treated as a guest, and finds out about the looking-glass country where the hollowness of many of the "eternal verities" of Victorianism (and of today as well) is exposed.

On realizing that machines will take over the world, Erewhonians have banned them. Since they are convinced that being sick is a willful and wicked act, they impose long jail sentences for such things

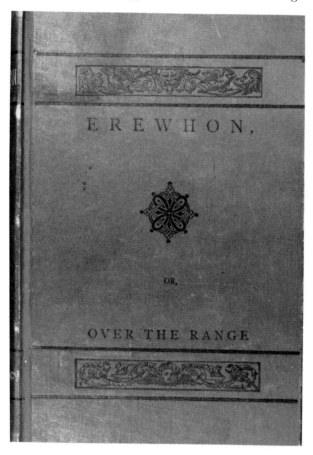

Front cover for the only book of Butler's that made a profit during his lifetime. It was written anonymously and published at Butler's expense. (Thomas Cooper Library, University of South Carolina)

as the common cold and pneumonia; but people who lie or steal are commiserated with and placed in the care of a "straightener" for cure since they are thought not to be blamed for their deeds. The Erewhonians have two currencies: one, the hard cash of commerce; and the other, the money of the Musical Banks (churches), which is reputed to lead to salvation but has no value at all in the real world. Their colleges are institutions of "unreason," where "hypothetical languages" of no conceivable use to

anyone are taught. After his experiences of these and other satirical transpositions of the European order, the hero escapes in a balloon to avoid punishment for his possession of a watch and returns to England.

This extravaganza has been criticized by some as too various in its scope, combining satire and utopianism in an inextricable mixture. But it is probably the most effective book of its kind in English literature since Swift's *Gulliver's Travels* (1726), which it resembles and which certainly influenced Butler. As Swift had done, Butler also makes the reader aware of the new perspectives from which any culture can be seen when reflected and distorted in an alien setting. Among his many telling suggestions, perhaps the most prophetic is that crime can be viewed as disease and illness as malingering: now there are specialists in the psychology of the criminal and in psychosomatic medicine. *Erewhon*, rejected by several publishers and then printed anonymously at its author's expense, was the only one of Butler's books that made a profit during his lifetime. Butler put his name on the fifth edition of *Erewhon* (1873).

Perhaps encouraged by the initially promising sales of *Erewhon*, Butler wrote and published at his own expense another book, again with satiric intent, building it around the substance of the pamphlet on *The Evidence for the Resurrection of Jesus Christ* which had gone almost unnoticed upon its publication eight years before. In response to Eliza Savage's urging that he write a novel, he dramatized his ideas in *The Fair Haven* (1873) by inventing an author, John Pickard Owen, who, before he dies insane, presents Butler's own analysis of the discrepancies in the Gospel accounts of Christ's death and resurrection; and he has the author's brother, William Bickersteth Owen, open the book with an extensive "Memoir" of John. This memoir, the most lively part of *The Fair Haven*, creates living pictures of Mr. and Mrs. Owen, culminating in a stream-of-consciousness daydream of the mother which ends with the martyrdom of her sons. In tone and detail it is a forerunner of *The Way of All Flesh*.

At the close of the memoir William gives passages from his brother's writings during the period when he had lost his faith. These passages are so convincing and effective that they tend to override the ostensible evangelizing of the body of the book. They sound like the notes Butler was writing for himself and kept on writing throughout the rest of his life, selections from which were later published as *The Note-Books of Samuel Butler*. John Pickard

Owen's argument, which commences after the memoir is done, is developed in an absolutely exasperating form, presenting material which grows more and more damaging to a literal faith in the Bible, meanwhile repeating over and over that all of this is leading up to a greater argument yet to come which will contradict it. When that greater argument finally arrives, it is that one must believe in spite of logical inconsistencies and flat contradictions. No wonder John fell into a state of idiocy and religious melancholy, and then died.

Some readers and reviewers thought the book a genuine defense of Christian faith, perhaps proving thereby that Butler's wish to make it a satire had not been fully realized. But when, upon reading Butler's preface to the second printing (the book had appeared anonymously at first, with no preface), they discovered that it was indeed intended as a satire and that they had been taken in, their dislike of Butler knew no bounds, and from that time they never forgave him. Indeed, some readers even today find the book too clever, arguing that when he wrote it Butler himself was unsure of his position and thus could not adequately control what he was doing. Since in 1873 even more than today an author dared not play fast and loose with religious faith, Butler's difficulty in finding an audience was surely increased by *The Fair Haven*.

Undeterred by its lack of success, Butler began work on *The Way of All Flesh*, which grew gradually into the sort of novel Eliza Savage had hoped he would write. Since its composition had been so closely related to his affection for her, he set it aside after her death in 1885, never to work on it again. Many of its details had been drawn from his own family experience, and so he also felt that publication would hurt the feelings of his closest relatives. The one book that might have been a commercial triumph in his lifetime thus did not appear until a year after his death. By 1953, it had appeared in sixty-eight editions in England, America, France, Germany, Spain, and Italy; there have been many others since, including one in the Houghton Mifflin Riverside series that restores the text of the 1885 manuscript, removing much of R. A. Streatfeild's (Butler's literary executor) editorial work. It is probably the most successful English novel of its era, both in numbers of readers and in influence on other writers, among them Shaw, Bennett, Maugham, Forster, and Joyce. Like Van Gogh and so many others, Butler could have been a wealthy and much-praised man had his fame not been posthumous.

More successfully than *The Fair Haven*, *The Way of All Flesh* also uses multiple perspectives. The principal narrator, Overton, belongs to the generation of Ernest Pontifex's father, but unlike Theobald Pontifex, he is a relaxed, worldly, imaginative man, though a trifle stuffy; thus he can interpret and to some extent empathize with the tense and sometimes tragic events he narrates and can take Ernest's side. But the novel does not adhere meticulously to Overton's perspective. Many passages have an omniscient narrator who reports inner thoughts and daydreams and has a wider view and greater knowledge than the thoughtful but complacent Overton: the book's implications reach beyond the ken of its elderly narrator.

Since *The Way of All Flesh* is about the evolutionary development of a family and about the unconscious but devastating influence of unexamined thoughts, Butler proceeds most deliberately, sketching in the simple and happy life of Ernest's great-grandfather John Pontifex (the name means "builder of bridges"), carpenter, organ maker, and amateur artist, and the eighteenth-century world in which he lived; then describing the gradual decay of this pastoral mode of life in the "successful" career of the grandfather, George Pontifex, whose one aim in life is money and achievement, and who becomes a big-city man. In the feeble attempt of his son, Theobald, to defy George Pontifex and not become a clergyman, the reader sees what Ernest's life would have been had he not reincarnated some of his great-grandfather's strength. Since Theobald is weak, his incipient rebellion leads nowhere. His entrapment into marriage—Christina becomes his wife through her luck at a game of cards—and the miserable honeymoon as well as the miserable career as a clergyman, a life for which he had no inner calling or talent, all are etched with acid and are quite unforgettable.

Well into the novel the "hero" Ernest appears, ganged up against by mother and father, who, thinking they are doing their duty, make his existence wretched. Theobald beats Ernest constantly for failing to learn his lessons, for saying "tum" instead of "come," and indeed for each and every expression of natural childhood. "All was done in love, anxiety, timidity, stupidity, and impatience," Overton says. "They [his parents] were stupid in little things; and he that is stupid in little will be stupid also in much." For a long time Ernest is sure that Theobald and Christina are right to blame him for everything, but another side of Ernest knows that he is surrounded by lies and must discover what he himself would be. Long before Sigmund Freud, Butler has the real Ernest say to Ernest: "The self of which you are conscious . . . will believe these lies. . . . This conscious self of yours, Ernest, is a prig. . . . Obey *me*, your true self, and things will go tolerably well with you. . . . I, Ernest, am the God who made you." But Ernest cannot hear.

To provide an outside force that will help Ernest discover his true self, Butler creates a sister of Theobald, Alethea (modeled on Eliza Savage), beloved by Overton (though they had too much good sense to marry), who befriends her nephew and for a time counteracts the misery of his life. Independently wealthy, she moves to the village where Ernest now attends prep school and quietly arranges for him to have lessons in carpentry so that he can learn to build an organ, as his great-grandfather had done before him (note the implication of sexual maturity in the term *organ*). She skillfully makes it seem that he does this because he wants to, not because he is told to. Having learned carpentry, he will have one thing he can do well because he loves it, and will begin to be proud of himself. Unfortunately, Alethea dies before her work is completed, but she leaves a large sum of money to come to Ernest when he is twenty-eight, though he is not to be told that this will happen. Theobald puts a quick end to the carpentry lessons, but Alethea's brief influence has given Ernest the strength to survive the deadly ordeals lying ahead.

In the next events of the novel, showing the unremitting tortures to which Christina and Theobald are eager to put their schoolboy son, all in the name of love, Butler dramatizes his conviction that each generation is ruined by too much conscious interference from the previous generation—by the demands of the superego, as Freud would say. Chapters thirty-eight through forty-four present such a string of disasters that some readers might think, "No parents could be so cruel!," while others might think, "This is the truth about parents!" Only Theobald's coachman, John, defends the browbeaten Ernest, declaring to Theobald, who is discharging him: "If you bear hardly on Master Ernest . . . I'll come back and break every bone in your skin." Unfortunately, he is unable to carry out this threat. Butler's uncanny ability to make the reader see the hidden, unconscious motives of both parents and child is the source of the power of this part of the novel.

Ernest survives the thumbscrews of parental inquisition, but just barely. At last he gets to Cambridge, where he has more freedom to grow. He takes an honors degree and, when he is twenty-two, comes into £5,000 left to him by his grandfather. Upon returning home a free and wealthy man, however, he still through habit defers to his father in all things and spends several hours a day studying the classics and his math. So wretchedly has he been molded. Back in Cambridge, he prepares for ordination. Unlike his father, who had felt his faith fading as this event approached, Ernest, upon hearing an evangelical preacher, suddenly becomes more passionately devoted to Christ than ever Christina or Theobald had been. They are frightened by his sudden zeal and regard him as a fool.

The newly ordained Ernest takes up his duties in central London where he becomes acquainted with a High Church curate, Pryer, who moves him rapidly toward Rome. Pryer persuades Ernest to turn his money over to him to invest in order, he says, to found a School of Spiritual Pathology to regenerate the Church of England. Overton apologizes for his godson, using an argument from biology: "The vagaries which it will now be my duty to chronicle," he says, are the result of "the shock of change," and are not surprising "when his antecedents are remembered." Butler's hero is definitely not heroic in these rapid changes but is nonetheless fascinating: a new type of hero-loser in the world of the novel. To put his ideas into immediate practice, Ernest rents a room in the slums of London from a landlady who sizes him up quite well: "He don't know nothing at all, no more than a unborn babe." Meeting Towneley, a classmate from Cambridge, by chance, he explains that he finds poor people fascinating. "Don't you like poor people?" he asks. Towneley answers "No, no, no," and "It was all over with Ernest from that moment." Towneley, wealthy, handsome, courteous, is Butler's portrait of what a man can be if he is as lucky in his parents (they died when he was two) as Ernest is unlucky, and if he has mastered life sufficiently to act without introspection and self-consciousness.

Doubts about what he is doing now haunt Ernest. He attempts to convert an atheist tinker, but instead is converted by him; then, with sensual—not spiritual—thoughts in mind, he goes to see a prostitute, one of two girls who live in his rooming house. Finding that Towneley already has an appointment with her, he rushes off to the other girl, who unfortunately for him is not a prostitute; he is arrested for assault, and sentenced to six months in jail because, as the judge says, he did not have "the common sense to be able to distinguish between a respectable girl and a prostitute." On his way to tell Theobald and Christina about their son's disaster, Overton speculates that no one is really to blame: neither Theobald for his treatment of his son, considering how badly his father treated him, nor Ernest for his actions, considering how he has been brought up. He puts the matter in a biological framework, reflecting his creator's *Life and Habit* (1878) theory (Butler was concurrently working on his next book): "If a man is to enter into the Kingdom of Heaven, he must do so, not only as a little child, but as a little embryo, or rather as a little zoosperm—and not only this, but as one that has come of zoosperms which have entered into the Kingdom of Heaven before him for many generations."

In prison, Ernest has an attack of brain fever, like John Pickard Owen before him, though unlike Owen he does not die. Having recovered, he is informed that his fellow curate, Pryer, has absconded with his wealth. Ernest learns to be a tailor and on leaving prison sets up an old-clothes shop. He marries Ellen, a servant girl who had been expelled from Theobald's house when she became pregnant. (The marriage turns out to be illegal because she is already married.) For a while real happiness comes to him. As he looks back, he sees that his school and university careers were "a lie" and "a sickly debilitating debauch" compared with life in prison and as a shopkeeper.

Now Ernest is approaching the age when his aunt's money will be his, and Overton, again using his creator's *Life and Habit* theory and feeling that "poverty is very wearing; it is a quasi-embryonic condition through which a man had better pass if he is to hold his later developments securely," persuades Ernest—who has separated from Ellen because she is an incurable alcoholic—to give up his tailor shop and become his secretary and steward. The novel moves rapidly to a close. Whether the climax is effective or not depends on each reader's perspective: can he believe that human fulfillment does not have to mean conventional recognition, success, and marriage?

To free the two children born to him and Ellen from the dangers of parental abuse, Ernest insists that they be brought up by others and is pleased when his son becomes a boatman and his daughter marries one of her playfellows. Ernest and Overton travel abroad; then Ernest, wealthy again, revisits his home to say farewell to his mother, who is dying. Theobald is shocked to see him looking so robust and well groomed: "This was not what he had bar-

gained for." At the reader's final glimpse of Ernest, he is a creative writer who insists on antagonizing people by his radical views concerning the family, evolution, and religion and will thus probably never win an audience.

Although many of the details in *The Way of All Flesh* closely parallel events in its author's life, it is nevertheless a genuine work of art, not merely an autobiographical novel: it presents a generalized case for all parent-child relationships. For this reason, those who argue that Butler distorted what had happened in his own family life because he had a chip on his shoulder miss the point. All children are in a way Ernest, and Ernest is no more identical with the historical Samuel Butler than Tom Jones is with his creator, Henry Fielding.

The Way of All Flesh, Butler's greatest work, became famous soon after it appeared in 1903 because Victorian smugness and traditional family relationships were ripe for questioning as Butler questioned them. The constructive side of the

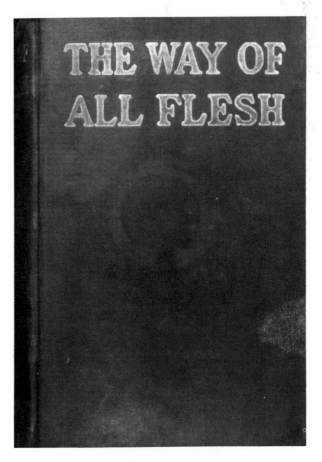

Front cover for Butler's posthumously published autobiographical novel, widely regarded as his greatest work (Thomas Cooper Library, University of South Carolina)

book—the way it illustrates theories of evolutionary memory and the development of unconscious learning, and the way it exposes the unconscious motives of its characters (even beyond the comprehension of Overton)—is its most enduring quality. It has not yet been fully explored. Can one understand an author who, after justifiably crucifying Theobald for his cruelty toward Ernest and saying when he dies that he had never been more than half alive, acknowledges the wisdom of a kind of racial learning by remarking: "This, however, was not the general verdict concerning him, and the general verdict is often the truest"? Butler is suggesting that the common view may possess a deeper wisdom, inherited over the centuries, than the critical judgment of the intellectual modern man.

When Butler had left New Zealand, he had paid the expenses of a friend, Charles Paine Pauli, to return to England with him for medical treatment. Ever since that time, and up to Pauli's death in 1898, Butler generously gave him a monthly allowance on his repeated claim that he was nearly destitute. He did not learn until Pauli's funeral that he had been lied to all those years. In addition to this continuous drain on his modest capital Butler failed to sell more than a few pictures or to make much money by writing and was soon perilously short of funds due to poor investments. In hope of higher dividends and on the advice of a banker friend, he had put his money into several new ventures, among them a Canadian tanning-extract company that soon showed signs of failure. In 1875, Butler traveled three times to Montreal to find out what was happening to this company (of which, because of his investment, he had been made a director) and to try to straighten out its affairs. From that time until his father's death in 1886, he had to worry continuously about money, so much so that he was forced to ask his father for help; nevertheless, he went on writing and publishing. In 1877 he gave up his nearly fruitless attempt to become a successful painter. He later blamed his lack of success on the academic style of the art schools. On the canvas of his *Family Prayers* he wrote in pencil across the ceiling of the room: "If I had gone on doing things out of my own head instead of making copies I should have been all right."

While in Montreal, and on Montreal Mountain for the first time, Butler had heard the bells of Notre Dame. Their sound as they echoed over the city gave him the idea that they were like ancestral selves in each of us calling out their messages. A

creature's "past selves," he wrote, "are living in unruly hordes within him at this moment and overmastering him. 'Do this, this, this, which we too have done, and found our profit in it,' cry the souls of his forefathers within him. Faint are the far ones, coming and going as the sound of the bells wafted on to a high mountain; loud and clear are the near ones, urgent as an alarm of fire. 'Withhold,' cry some. 'Go on boldly,' cry others. 'Me, me, me, revert hitherward, my descendant,' shouts one as it were from some high vantage-ground over the heads of the clamorous multitude. 'Nay, but me, me, me,' echoes another; and our former selves fight within us and wrangle for our possession."

This notion of ancestral voices became a key thought in his next book, *Life and Habit*, the most important of Butler's studies of evolution. In *Life and Habit* Butler examines the phenomenon of memory, relates it to heredity, and notes its paradoxical connection with consciousness and unconsciousness. What we really know, he observes, we cannot know that we know, just as a pianist must achieve unconscious command of all the infinite details of a passage if he is to play well. So the things we (that is, ourselves and our ancestors) have laboriously learned through eons of trial and error must now be performed without awareness—for example, digestion of food and the beating of the heart. This unconscious knowledge which has been handed on to us complete and perfect by our successful forefathers cannot be infringed upon by awareness without becoming problematical: "perfect knowledge and perfect ignorance" become "extremes that meet." Yet as we progress and acquire new abilities and knowledge we must go through an awkward stage before they can be perfected. "Beauty is but knowledge perfected and incarnate. . . . It is not knowledge, then, that is incompatible with beauty; there cannot be too much knowledge, but it must have passed through many people. . . . before beauty or grace will have anything to say to it."

In this book, one of the first to make extensive use of the concept of the unconscious and contemporary with his exploration of unconscious motives in *The Way of All Flesh*, Butler thus explains heredity as identical with memory—memory of practices so often repeated as to be unconscious. Life itself is also identical with memory: to say that a piece of matter lives is to say that it remembers, and what cannot remember is dead. Later, Butler came to believe that no hard line can be drawn between living and dead: "When people talk of atoms obeying fixed laws, they are either ascribing some kind of intelligence and free-will to atoms or they are talking nonsense," he writes. Some day, Butler thought, we will read and write as instinctively as we now circulate our blood. But if human records should be lost, it would take another Harvey to discover that we do so. Butler explores many of the implications of his ideas about memory and the unconscious, some full of humor, but none lacking seriousness as well. He indeed invented the term "unconscious humor" for people who give themselves away, as the unconscious unbeliever did who prayed to the Almighty "to change our rulers *as soon as possible*," or as Bacon did when he remarked that "reading good books on morality is a little flat and dead." Indeed, if this humor becomes excessive it distresses a healthy person. "Truly, if there is one who cannot find himself in the same room with the Life and Letters of an earnest person without being made instantly unwell, the same is a just man and perfect in all his ways."

In *Life and Habit* Butler argues that all living beings (who, in terms of their cells and thus in terms of their deeper memories, are identical with their ancestors) must have worked so long and so hard at such complex matters as digesting, breathing, hearing, and seeing, as to have acquired the ability to do them without conscious attention. "Is there anything," Butler asks, "in digestion, or the oxygenization of the blood, different in kind to the rapid unconscious action of a man playing a difficult piece of music on the piano?" He answers that there is not. Although we use the word "heredity" to explain our possession of such talents, he adds, the word explains nothing; whereas the analogy with memory and practice casts much light on what goes on. For example, accomplishments which we have in common with our remotest ancestors, such as digestion, are in us most unconscious and most beyond our control; whereas more recent acquisitions such as speech, the arts and sciences, and the upright position are much more within our control.

So obvious does Butler's interesting theory become to him that he argues that the burden of proof that his analogy is meaningless rests on those who think him wrong: "Shall we say, then, that a baby of a day old sucks (which involves the whole principle of the pump, and hence a profound practical knowledge of the laws of pneumatics and hydrostatics), digests, oxygenizes its blood (millions of years before Sir Humphry Davy discovered Oxygen), sees and hears . . . shall we say that a baby can do all these things at once . . . and at the same time

not know how to do them, and never have done them before?"

In discussing the problem of personal identity in *Life and Habit* Butler is at his most brilliant, handling, with the skill of a trained dialectician, the problem of where the self begins and ends. His conclusion that there are no clear demarcations between the present ego and the primordial spark of life in the original ooze is defended with a brilliance that would warm the heart of the teacher of logic; yet all the time he is ready to acknowledge the practical value of the demarcations set up in ordinary speech. To acquire the immense skill it possesses, the egg must be the chicken, must be the egg, must be the chicken for thousands of generations without gap in personal identity except for lapses into the unconscious as learning becomes perfected. Butler's book delights the thoughtful mind; still, to one (like most modern readers) who thinks only in terms of laboratory experiments and things that can be proved not by argument but by the microscope, it may all seem useless. What, one wonders, may be the connection between Butler's unconscious memory and the latest findings concerning DNA?

Butler's early support for Darwin's theory was now rapidly disappearing. His *Life and Habit* theory, he was convinced, got behind the back of natural selection by actually explaining how it works: namely, through memory in the individual and in the race and by ascribing a purpose to each individual being. "A chicken . . . is never so full of consciousness, activity, reasoning faculty, and volition, as when it is an embryo in the eggshell, making bones, and flesh, and feathers, and eyes, and claws, with nothing but a little warmth and white of egg to make them from . . . . Is it in the least agreeable to our experience that such elaborate machinery should be made without endeavour, failure, perseverance, intelligent contrivance, experience, and practice? . . . What is the discovery of the laws of gravitation as compared with the knowledge which sleeps in every hen's egg upon a kitchen shelf?" Butler now argued that the "natural selection" principle amounted to no more than saying that when variations arise, they will accumulate. He hoped that the Darwinians would respond to his theory. "Pitch into it and into me by all means" he wrote to Francis Darwin—but in vain. Although *Life and Habit* was fairly widely reviewed, no one confronted the thesis it set forth.

In the opening pages of *Life and Habit* Butler had warned his readers that he was not a scientist and had no wish to instruct, but rather to entertain and interest them. He also said, "Let no unwary reader do me the injustice of believing in *me*. In that I write at all I am among the damned." Developing his idea that no sharp line can be drawn between the individual and his ancestors or between the whole body and its parts, Butler had suggested that it is just as well that our cells do not know the larger life in which they participate. If a blood corpuscle should discover that it was part of a larger animal which would not die with its death, it would be introspecting too much. "I should conceive he served me better," Butler writes, "by attending to my blood and making himself a successful corpuscle, than by speculating about my nature." In this way this curious writer condemns his own work, since he at least refuses to be a complacent cell minding his own business and not asking questions. However, he found his work forcing itself upon him. "I never make them [his books]; they grow," he wrote; "they come to me and insist on being written."

Owning few books himself, Butler now, like Karl Marx, adopted the habit of working daily in the British Museum reading room where he could have access to an enormous library, a habit he continued for the rest of his life. He generally worked from 10:30 in the morning until 1:00, and found that he was happier in the British Museum than he was anywhere else, except in Italy. His search for material for *Life and Habit* had led him to discover Lamarck, Buffon, Erasmus Darwin, and other pre-Darwinian evolutionary theorists whom Charles Darwin had dismissed in a "brief but imperfect sketch" of previous speculations added to later editions of *On the Origin of Species by Means of Natural Selection* (1859).

In order to set before the general reading public a more complete picture of evolutionary theory and to show how his *Life and Habit* speculations fitted into it, Butler wrote *Evolution, Old and New* (1879). He came to link his memory theory with the purposeful evolutionary development of living forms, believing that it showed how the strivings of one individual were connected with those of other individuals and thus of the race and became latent in becoming intense. Butler succeeded in demonstrating that many passages in *On the Origin of Species* imply the necessity of use and disuse in evolution, and also that Buffon, Erasmus Darwin, and Lamarck had all stated the survival-of-the-fittest principle for which Charles Darwin and Alfred Russel Wallace were given credit.

In November 1879 an English translation of a German study of Erasmus Darwin, printed before *Evolution, Old and New* had appeared, was published with a foreword by Charles Darwin. In this book Butler found an attack upon himself, without his name being mentioned, and some of the same passages from Buffon he had used, translated by exactly the same words he had used in making his translation from the French. On checking the original German text (after hastily learning that language), he discovered to his amazement that this material had been added by the translator, although Darwin's foreword made no mention of the text's having been altered, and thus it would appear to predate Butler's book. He thereupon wrote Darwin inquiring what had happened, and Darwin replied that alterations in translations were so common a practice that he had not thought the changes worth mentioning in his foreword. Naturally this answer did not satisfy Butler, who then aired the whole matter in a letter to the *Athenaeum*. Darwin now recalled that the printer had inadvertently omitted a statement that the text was a revision, not merely a translation, and wished to inform Butler of this fact, but Darwin's friend Thomas Henry Huxley advised him not to do so; and later, after Butler had attacked Darwin again in his next book, *Unconscious Memory* (1880), and Darwin once more wished to reply, Leslie Stephen also advised silence. Thus Butler was never to learn that the misrepresentation was an error, compounded on Darwin's part by timidity and the taking of bad advice, and not really the commonplace of scientific behavior he came to believe it was.

In *Unconscious Memory*, the most quarrelsome book he ever wrote, Butler uncovers verbal subterfuges in Darwin and Huxley in a way that is both cruel to his opponents, who are less skilled in the use of language than he is, and also very funny. He attempts to explain the paradoxical fact that people had by now become converted to Darwinism when actually "natural selection" accounts for neither the arising of variations nor for their being handed on: this remarkable triumph of conversion, he believes, was brought about by a conspiracy to hoodwink the public by treating the key problems ambiguously and vaguely. He delights in proving that Darwin continually lets purposive concepts slip into his explanations while always denying that he is doing so. He points out again that his own *Life and Habit* theory deals effectively with the key issues on which Darwin, Huxley, and the others have to hedge. To give an example of scientific honesty as a contrast to what he thought was Darwin's shabby treatment of previous evolutionists, Butler carefully discusses the work of a certain Ewald Hering, a German scientist who in 1870 had set forth a memory theory similar to his own, and also explains the difference between his theory of the unconscious and that of Edward von Hartmann.

Butler's books on evolution aroused only moderate interest; they sold poorly and were discussed infrequently by reviewers and writers to the editors of various journals. Undaunted, Butler tried one more time, publishing *Luck or Cunning as the Main Means of Organic Modification?* (1886), in which he again stated the case for a revised Lamarckianism as opposed to what he regarded as the mindless mechanistic theory defended by the Darwinians. But now he is able to demonstrate by apt quotation that evolutionists such as Huxley, Romanes, Grant Allen, and even Darwin himself are coming to link heredity and memory as he had done, though without giving him credit for the idea. He traces the shifting statements on instinct in the various editions of *The Origin of Species* to show that Darwin reversed himself again and again, and he explores similar shifts and obfuscations in the other champions of the day. In *Luck or Cunning?* more than in the three other books on evolution, Butler discusses the psychology of persuasion, pointing out how prone the mind is to reject extreme change and how bound we are by what we want to know and want to believe. All knowledge is compromise with extremes, he says, whether of life or death, luck or cunning, design or absence of design. Grant Allen, writing in the *Academy*, rightly said of *Luck or Cunning?*: "Here is a work of consummate ingenuity, rare literary skill, and a certain happy vein of sardonic humour—a work pregnant with epigram, sparkling with wit, and instinct throughout with a powerful original fancy. . . . [Butler] stands by himself, a paradoxer of the first water, hopeless and friendless." But, typically, Allen considered none of the specific points Butler had raised. Perhaps some day there will be a reappraisal of Butler's strangely effective books on evolution.

While working on his books, Butler also carried out other literary projects, writing letters to magazines and newspapers, publishing book reviews and articles, and even, although he was really not fond of poetry except for Shakespeare and Homer, composing poems of his own. In "A Psalm of Montreal," which appeared in the *Spectator* in 1875, Butler humorously protests the failure of a Montreal museum to exhibit a plaster cast of the Discobolus because it had no clothes on, ending each stanza with the refrain "O God! O Montreal!" Later he wrote several sonnets, two moving ones about Eliza Savage and one about immortality which was printed in the *Athenaeum* in 1902. In this, the last of his sonnets, he wistfully denies the possibility of personal survival but celebrates instead the immortality of memory and fame: "Yet meet we shall, and part, and meet again, / Where dead men meet, on lips of living men."

In 1879, Butler published eight articles in the *Examiner* under the title "God the Known and God the Unknown," in which he speculates (as he had also done in *Life and Habit*) that as living cells make up our being, we and our ancestors and indeed all living forms, descended as we are from a common ancestor, may make up a larger being which we can call god, even though we are as unconscious of this being as our cells are of us. Henry Festing Jones says that Butler wished some day to revise these articles to show that inorganic matter must be included in this god as well as organic. Butler spoke of his theory as "a modest Pantheism." During the same year, Butler entertained himself and readers of letter columns by writing to the *Examiner*, under different names, a series of letters discussing the problems of an impoverished clergyman with a wife and five children who has come to doubt the literal truth of the Christian story he is paid to teach. In the opening letters he asks for help. Further letters in the series, purporting to be by other writers (and two or three of the sixteen actually were), propose different ways he might resolve his dilemma, either by dissembling his loss of faith or by courageously giving up his post and facing financial ruin and starvation for his family. Butler also occasionally lectured at the City of London College, the Working Men's College, and at the Somerville Club. Some of these lectures appeared in print at the time they were given; those for which manuscripts could be found are included in the Shrewsbury Edition of Butler's works. They explore Butler's biological theories, his Homeric speculations, and his general thoughts about life.

Even when his finances were at a low ebb, Butler had always insisted upon a summer vacation in Italy; in 1880 his publisher offered to pay him for an illustrated book about that country. He promptly wrote and made drawings for *Alps and Sanctuaries of Piedmont and the Canton Ticino* (1882), and when the publisher rejected it as not the sort of book he had had in mind, Butler published it at his own expense. Some of the drawings he included were by Henry Festing Jones, a close friend since 1876, who took

Samuel Butler and Henry Festing Jones

many vacation trips with him. The two men were united by their mutual love for Italy and for music—for Handel especially—and from 1887 on, Jones, like Pauli, received financial aid from Butler, who was nothing if not generous. Together they composed music in the style of Handel and published *Gavottes, Minuets, Fugues, and Other Short Pieces for the Piano* (1885) and a cantata called *Narcissus* (1888). Later, to remove some of the amateurishness from their work, they took lessons in harmony from two professional musicians.

Alps and Sanctuaries opens with a paean to Handel, who "is as much above Shakespeare as Shakespeare is above all others," and to London, especially the view down Fleet Street. Then, in a melange of biological philosophizing and general comment, following his ideas wherever they lead him, Butler describes his visits to Faido, San Michele, Lanzo, Varese, Locarno, and the other villages and towns of northern Italy which he loved so well. He discusses lies, pointing out that "lying is so deeply rooted in nature that we may expel it with a fork, and yet it will always come back again"; the difference between Catholics and Protestants, Englishmen and Italians, priests and other men; and

the radical changes in life to be expected from the advent of technology and advertising. Butler, who had a fluent command of Italian and could converse easily with many of the people he met, was able to fill the book with lively anecdotes and character sketches. In this work Butler reveals a mellow understanding of the paradoxes of life. He is especially kind to the Roman Catholicism of his Italian friends: the faith of the robust, beautiful, contented people of northern Italy must somehow be right since they themselves are so right. If Protestants understood Catholicism they "should find it to be in many respects as much in advance of us as it is behind us in others," he wrote.

Another expression of Butler's love for Italy appeared in 1888: *Ex Voto*, a study of the Sacro Monte at Varallo. But this time Butler was not so relaxed and casual as he had been in *Alps and Sanctuaries*. He had now developed an infatuation to match or even overtop his understandable devotion to Handel: this time it was for Tabachetti, who, he was convinced, had created in his *Journey to Calvary* "the most astonishing work that has ever been achieved in sculpture." Butler had acquired a camera; he illustrated this book with photographs he and Jones had taken. They do indeed show that the figures in the tableaux at Varallo are dramatic, full of motion and character, and surprisingly realistic, but they do not seem to justify Butler's fanatical enthusiasm. Was he longing to make the breakthrough as an art critic that the Victorian world had refused to admit that he had made in biological theory? In addition to *Ex Voto* he published several magazine articles on Tabachetti and on the Bellinis.

It is well to remember how completely Butler had come to trust intuitive insights. Having been so bitterly fooled as a young man by what he now regarded as pretensions, so that, for example, he had never questioned assumptions as diverse as religious literalism or the beauty of the St. Gothard Pass and had not learned to trust his conviction that Handel was the greatest composer, he now became at times a little ridiculous in championing private insights. He justifiably rejected any evaluation he found people making because it was "the right thing" and not because they really believed it. But he mercilessly extended this notion until he came to be convinced that all enthusiasms except his own were hollow and empty. His scorn for established "greats" can be withering and distressing to those with different insights from his, though often very funny in their hyperbole: for example, his attacks on Goethe, Bacon, Mendelssohn, Mozart, Bach, Beethoven, Raphael, George Eliot, and a host of others. Eventually, although enjoying the humor, one cannot help coming to question Butler's judgment. But then when one considers his often sly, skillful, thoughtful justifications of his idiosyncrasies, one is in a way won back to him again.

Between 1888 and 1890 Butler contributed eight articles to the *Universal Review* on art, Darwinism, and other topics, some in the loose-knit tradition of the personal essay. He speculates in "Quis Desiderio . . .?" that Wordsworth, in concert with Southey and Coleridge, probably murdered Lucy; with this thought in mind, he says, "there is not a syllable in the poem. . . . that is not alive with meaning." Quite unknowingly and in the spirit of fun, he is on the trail of the discovery made in 1922 of Wordsworth's love affair in France, which to some extent took him off the high moral pedestal he had occupied. In "A Medieval Girl School (Oropa)" he meditates on the unwillingness of the church to admit that it deals not with literal truth but with a kind of universal myth helpful to the well-being of mankind: "The cleric and the man of science (who is only the cleric in his latest development) are trying

to develop a throat with two distinct passages—one that shall refuse to pass even the smallest gnat, and another that shall gracefully gulp even the largest camel; whereas we men of the street desire but one throat, and are content that this shall swallow nothing bigger than a pony."

In 1888, Butler was asked to prepare a memoir of his grandfather, Dr. Samuel Butler (1774-1839). When he looked into Dr. Butler's voluminous unpublished correspondence, the material so fascinated him by its clarity and directness that he decided to write a book-length portrait of the man and his age, not just a memoir, and to put before his readers as much of the original material as he could. The biography rapidly grew into two large volumes, *The Life and Letters of Dr. Samuel Butler* (1896), published at the author's expense. Butler felt at home in the world of his grandfather; people then were genuine and honest, he thought, understood the value of common sense, and possessed a conviction of order. Science had not yet frightened them, and they loved the classical learning which Butler had lampooned in *Erewhon* but which he now saw that he loved, too. This work received the most favorable press accorded any book by Butler during his lifetime, but even then it did not sell.

In 1891, when Butler and Jones were composing their oratorio, *Ulysses* (1904), Butler, who wrote most of the lyrics, looked into the Greek text of the *Odyssey* once more and found the poem so delightful that he could not put it down. He thereupon set himself to make a translation of it which would be as much at home in contemporary English as the poem itself no doubt had been in the classical Greek of Homer's day. Later he translated the *Iliad* with the same objective in mind. He then built up an elaborate case for two intuitive convictions that came to him about the *Odyssey*: that it was written by a woman, and that the setting was Trapani and Mount Eryx in Sicily. Once again Butler had high hopes. "Nothing," he wrote, "has ever interested me (except, of course, Handel) so much as this *Odyssey* business has done; it is far the finest piece of good fortune that ever happened to me." He traveled to Sicily and later to the Troad to see for himself the relationship between the descriptions in the two poems and what he thought to be the actual places. But once again the professional world turned a deaf ear. It seemed that the courageous Butler could make no breakthrough, no matter how hard he tried. Reviewers were kinder to him, however, than they had usually been in the past. The *Saturday*

Clifford's Inn, London, where Butler lived the last thirty-eight years of his life

Butler's sitting room at 15 Clifford's Inn

Review said of *The Authoress of the "Odyssey"* (1897): "We do not disdain Mr. Butler's book. It is written with great vivacity, and if it takes a number of readers to the pure and beautiful text of the *Odyssey* . . . its action will not have been in vain." Later Butler published his two translations. They are still among the easiest to read and clearest available, though lacking in beauty and not to be compared with the best translations of recent decades.

A final adventure into literary detective work was *Shakespeare's Sonnets Reconsidered* (1899). Butler had long loved the sonnets, and now he learned them by heart. He did his utmost to rearrange the 128 separate poems into a coherent sequence, assuming, as others had before him, that they ought to tell a story. Unfortunately, the story that he makes them tell is unconvincing, involving as it does an all-too-literal interpretation of some of the sonnets to imply a degrading homosexual affair with someone far less sensitive than Shakespeare and quite capable of playing demeaning practical jokes at his expense. Still, like his other books of this period, his study of the sonnets sets one thinking, and as a result, although rejecting Butler's annoying literalism, one may come to know these amazing poems better.

In 1901 Butler completed *Erewhon Revisited Twenty Years Later*, a sequel he had been thinking about and planning for some time, and, with help from G. B. Shaw, for the first time in his life found a publisher willing to underwrite one of his books. The hero of *Erewhon* returns twenty years later to the topsy-turvy land he had discovered to find that the Erewhonians have started a new religion around his previous visit, based on his seemingly miraculous departure by balloon. In Hanky, Panky, and Downey, three leaders of the new religion, Butler attacks High Church and Jesuit and approves of Broad Church attitudes. The relationship of the hero with his son George, born after his departure from Erewhon as a result of his love affair with Yram, indicates Butler's realization that a good father-son relationship is possible, something he had not believed earlier in his life. George wants his father to announce that he and his balloon ascension were not miraculous, but his father takes a compromise course, telling the Erewhonians the truth about himself but urging them to change the new religion only gradually. If you wish, he says, you can "make me a peg on which to hang all your own best ethical and spiritual conceptions. . . . Better a corrupt church than none at all." Lacking the variety of the earlier *Erewhon*, this book is more

unified and, some have thought, better than its predecessor, though *Erewhon* is certainly more often read and more original.

One more achievement remained for Butler, this time one that was able to win an enthusiastic readership. As long ago as during his years in New Zealand he had begun jotting down each day in little black books, one of which he afterward always carried in his pocket, the thoughts that came to him. For at least a decade toward the end of his life he had commenced each working day by "posting" these notes, that is, revising, rewriting, and editing them, entering them into large volumes, and eventually preparing an index for each volume. He did this not because he expected them to be published and read ("they are not meant for publication," he noted) but because he found the work excellent practice and felt that every writer should keep a notebook: "One's thoughts fly so fast that one must shoot them; it is no use trying to put salt on their tails." Also, editing them was a creative process. "My notes always grow longer if I shorten them. I mean the process of compression makes them more pregnant, and they breed new notes." After Butler's death, his friend Henry Festing Jones, judging that Butler had really hoped for readers in spite of his statement to the contrary, selected from these books, edited the selections again, and made a sizable volume which appeared in 1912, after some of the notes had already been published in *New Quarterly Review* from 1907 to 1910. Many readers immediately came to regard the *Note-Books* as Butler's masterpiece. Since the Jones volume, several additional collections have been published from the same source, though much material still remains unpublished.

The notes are indeed a harvest of ideas; they probe and challenge. Many of them attracted early readers by what was at that time their shocking unconventionality; they attract the modern reader because they make him think. They search for the meaning of life, of religion, of philosophy; they reach pragmatic, mediating positions, deriding all extremism, whether of honesty or dishonesty, virtue or immorality. "American dishonesty," Butler notes, "refer it to their Puritan ancestry." "Ultimate triumph of Good. When we say that we believe in this, we mean that we are cocksure of our own opinions." "God as now generally conceived of is only the last witch." "Reason—if you follow it far enough, it always leads to conclusions that are contrary to reason."

Butler celebrates life and makes sport of those

too idealistic to see that it should be lived: "I have squandered my life," he reminisces, "as a schoolboy squanders a tip. . . . I do not squander it now, but I am not sorry that I have squandered a good deal of it. . . . Had I not better set about squandering what is left of it?" "A sense of humor," he observes, will keep a man from committing all sins "save those that are worth committing." "It is as immoral to be too good as to be too anything else." "To love God is to have good health, good looks, good sense, experience, a kindly nature, and a fair balance of cash in hand." From notes like these some readers came to think Butler a hedonist; surely that is an oversimplification, since his life obviously contained so much idealism.

"Man," Butler theorizes, "is but a perambulating tool-box and workshop, or office, fashioned for itself by a piece of very clever slime, as the result of long experience. . . . Hence we speak of man's body as his 'trunk,'" thus adumbrating in brief form much of *Life and Habit*. Again, he speculates that "all things are either of the nature of a piece of string or of a knife" for bringing things together or keeping them apart. But each kind contains its opposite; thus "in high philosophy one should never look at a knife without considering it also as a piece of string" and vice versa.

The *Note-Books* copiously illustrate Butler's unhappiness concerning what seemed to him the pretensions of science, literature, and religion. Like Whitman, he boasts: "I am the *enfant terrible* of literature and science. If I cannot, and I know I cannot, get the literary and scientific big-wigs to give me a shilling, I can, and I know I can, heave bricks into the middle of them." "Intellectual overindulgence," he writes, "is the most gratuitous and disgraceful form which excess can take, nor is there any the consequences of which are more disastrous." He notes that someone claims that the chattering of monkeys conveys ideas. With equal justice, he observes, monkeys might conclude "that in our magazine articles, or literary and artistic criticisms, we are not chattering idly but are conveying ideas to one another." "All philosophies," he writes, "if you ride them home, are nonsense; but some are greater nonsense than others." "Faith and authority are as necessary for [Euclid] as for any one else. True, he does not want us to believe very much; his yoke is tolerably easy, and he will not call a man a fool until he will have public opinion generally on his side; but none the less does he begin with dogmatism and end with persecution."

In March 1902, Butler set out for a trip to Sicily but fell ill on his arrival there and had to hurry back to London. His doctor put him in a nursing home, where his condition did not improve. On 18 June he died of what was diagnosed as pernicious anemia. His last words were to his servant: "Have you brought the cheque-book, Alfred?"

It is interesting to recall how this strangely stubborn writer, who published sixteen books in his lifetime, of which only slightly over 7,000 copies had been sold up to 1899, appeared to people who met him. He "never talked as if he was coming down to one's level." "His talk was always charming and full of fun," but "if there was one thing beyond all others he could not stand it was pretense of any sort." His "modest courtliness and gentleness. . . . [the] complete absence of anything that could be considered alarming or formidable" were striking. But as a young man he had been hot-tempered, and "anything approaching to ridicule where he was concerned was a mortal insult." Shaw thought him "a shy old bird," but others, such as a lady who met him in Greece, found him "delightfully simple and childlike" and very ready to reach out to others.

Butler's rise to fame after the comparative obscurity in which he had lived out his life makes an interesting chapter in the history of criticism. Obituaries reveal that in 1902 his work was not regarded as important, and *The Way of All Flesh* was hardly noticed on its publication in 1903; the *Times Literary Supplement* did not review it until 1919, by which time the novel's fame had finally forced it to do so. But slowly critics and writers began to speak out. Through the years he was studied, emulated, and praised by Arnold Bennett, Desmond MacCarthy, Arthur Clutton-Brock, George Bernard Shaw, Marcus Hartog, Augustine Birrell, Edmund Gosse, Gilbert Cannon, W. Bateson, C. E. M. Joad, and E. M. Forster. Butler was recognized for his "incessantly alive and stimulating mind" (Clutton-Brock) and was called "perhaps the most versatile genius of the Victorian age" (Hartog). When Shaw referred to him in the preface to *Major Barbara* (1906) as "in his own department the greatest English writer of the latter half of the XIX century," the tide turned in Butler's favor. From then on, increasing critical attention was given all aspects of his work, both in England and America, and when the *Note-Books* appeared in 1912, they received wide attention and were highly praised. The *Times Literary Supplement* gave them a glowing front-page review, calling Butler "a born writer." The *Athenaeum*

Samuel Butler, age sixty-five

blamed the reading public for having ignored Butler for so many years. Other reviewers compared Butler to Socrates, called *The Way of All Flesh* "masterly" and the *Note-Books* "perfect," and said that *Erewhon* and *Life and Habit* would not be forgotten. Several book-length studies of Butler soon appeared by Gilbert Cannan, John Harris, and Clara Gruening Stillman. Academic studies followed in France, the Netherlands, Germany, and the United States. Henry Festing Jones's two-volume biography (1919) provided a wealth of detail concerning Butler's life but did little to interpret his ideas. Negative reactions to Butler from religiously oriented writers such as May Sinclair (in *A Defence of Idealism*) culminate in Malcolm Muggeridge's onslaught in 1936 (*Earnest Atheist*). These attacks revealed that Butler's influence was great enough to merit fire from enemies of his liberal point of view. The Shrewsbury Edition of all of Butler's work in twenty volumes appeared in 1923-1926. The basis for this wide recognition is aptly put in the 1916

edition of *The Cambridge History of English Literature*, which rightly says that Butler is "very far from being a mere indiscriminating wit; he has, in the end, a constructive intention, not mockery, but the liberation of the spirit." More recently there have been fewer references to Butler in the general press, but academic studies continue. Formalistic criticism finds Butler hard to appraise; one recent writer says "the greater part of his writing is a formal disaster," and there is much skepticism concerning his constructive theories. In 1978 James A. Donovan, Jr., began issuing a *Samuel Butler Society Newsletter*.

This apparently lonely and unsuccessful but dedicated writer, who had so much trouble getting a hearing during his lifetime and yet kept courageously forging ahead, has thus earned a significant position in the literature of the country and the age he so energetically criticized but so deeply believed in. The spirit in which he wrote all of his books on such varied subjects is effectively expressed at the conclusion of *Life and Habit*: "I saw, as it were, a pebble upon the ground, with a sheen that pleased me; taking it up, I turned it over and over for my amusement, and found it always grow brighter and brighter the more I examined it. At length I became fascinated, and gave loose rein to self-illusion. The aspect of the world seemed changed; the trifle which I had picked up idly had proved to be a talisman of inestimable value, and had opened a door through which I caught glimpses of a strange and interesting transformation. . . . Will the reader bid me wake with him to a world of chance and blindness? Or can I persuade him to dream with me of a more living faith than either he or I had as yet conceived as possible?"

What readers think of him now, at the end of the twentieth century, is hard to ascertain. Many of his books do not circulate often in most libraries, except for *Erewhon* and *The Way of All Flesh*, but these two are available in mass-circulation reprints and are read by many others besides college students. Butler's work is surely less dated than that of most of his "successful" contemporaries. In the modern age of militant beliefs and ideologies, perhaps Butler's willingness to see life as a compromise rather than as a crusade alienates some readers, and they are not interested in his biological reasons for believing as he did. But his own crusade against the mindlessness of dogmatic science, against uncritical deferring to authority, and against the stultifying superego of his age, and his brilliant dialectical maneuvering and use of satire, should ensure that he will continue to live, as he hoped, "on lips of living men."

Other:

The Iliad of Homer, Rendered into English Prose, translated by Butler (London: Longmans, Green, 1898; New York: Dutton, 1921);

The Odyssey, Rendered into English Prose, translated by Butler (London: Longmans, Green, 1900; New York: Dutton, 1920).

Periodical Publications:

"On English Composition," *Eagle*, 1, no. 1 (1858): 41-44;

"Our Tour," *Eagle*, 1, no. 5 (1859): 241-255;

"Our Emigrant," *Eagle*, 2 (1861): 101, 149; 3 (1862): 18;

"Darwin on the Origin of Species: A Dialogue," *Press* (New Zealand), (20 December 1862);

"Darwin Among the Machines," *Press* (New Zealand), (13 June 1863);

"The Mechanical Creation," *Reasoner* (1 July 1865);

"Lucubratio Ebria," *Press* (New Zealand), (29 July 1865);

"A Psalm of Montreal," *Spectator* (18 May 1875);

"A Clergyman's Doubts," *Examiner* (February-June 1879);

"God the Known and God the Unknown," *Examiner* (May-July 1879);

"Quis Desiderio . . .?," *Universal Review* (July 1888): 411-424;

"A Medieval Girl School (Oropa)," *Universal Review* (December 1889);

"The Deadlock in Darwinism," *Universal Review* (April - June 1890);

"The Humour of Homer," *Eagle*, 17 (March 1892): 158-193;

"Not on Sad Stygian Shore," *Athenaeum* (4 January 1902): 18;

"The Note Books," *New Quarterly Review* (November 1907): 137-164; (March 1908): 295-324; (June 1908): 447-484; (October 1908): 613-632; (April 1909): 219-224; (February 1910): 109-128; (May 1910): 229-248.

Letters:

Samuel Butler and E. M. A. Savage, Letters 1871-1885, edited by Geoffrey Keynes and Brian Hill (London: Cape, 1935);

The Family Letters of Samuel Butler (1841-1886), edited by Arnold Silver (Stanford, Cal.: Stan-

ford University Press, 1962);

The Correspondence of Samuel Butler with His Sister May, edited by Daniel F. Howard (Berkeley: University of California Press, 1962).

Bibliographies:

Henry Festing Jones and A. T. Bartholomew, *The Samuel Butler Collection at Saint John's College Cambridge* (Cambridge: W. Heffer, 1921);

A. J. Hoppe, *A Bibliography of the Writings of Samuel Butler* (London: Bookman, 1925);

Carroll A. Wilson, *Catalogue of the Collection of Samuel Butler (of Erewhon) in the Chapin Library Williams College* (Portland, Maine: Southworth-Anthoensen, 1945);

Stanley B. Harkness, *The Career of Samuel Butler (1835-1902) A Bibliography* (New York: Burt Franklin, 1955).

Biographies:

Henry Festing Jones, *Samuel Butler, a Memoir* (2 volumes, London: Macmillan, 1919);

P. N. Furbank, *Samuel Butler (1835-1902)* (Cambridge: Cambridge University Press, 1948);

Philip Henderson, *Samuel Butler* (London: Cohen & West, 1953);

Lee E. Holt, *Samuel Butler* (New York: Twayne, 1964).

References:

Gilbert Cannan, *Samuel Butler: A Critical Study* (Folcroft, Pa.: Folcroft Library Editions, 1915);

Joseph Fort, *Samuel Butler, l'écrivain: Étude d'un style* (Bordeaux: J. Bière, 1935);

R. S. Garnett, *Samuel Butler and His Family Relations* (New York: Dutton, 1926);

John F. Harris, *Samuel Butler, Author of "Erewhon": The Man and His Work* (Folcroft, Pa.: Folcroft Library Editions, 1973);

C. E. M. Joad, *Samuel Butler* (London: Parsons, 1924; Boston: Small, Maynard, 1925);

Joseph Jones, *The Cradle of Erewhon* (Austin: University of Texas Press, 1959);

Paul Meissner, *Samuel Butler, der Jüngerer* (Leipzig: Tauchnitz, 1931);

Malcolm Muggeridge, *Earnest Atheist: A Study of Samuel Butler* (London: Putnam's, 1936);

Gerold Pestalozzi, *Samuel Butler der Jüngerer, Versuch einer Darstellung seiner Gedankenwelt* (Zurich: Universität Zürich, 1914);

Robert F. Rattray, *A Chronicle and an Introduction: Samuel Butler* (London: Duckworth, 1935);

May Sinclair, *A Defence of Idealism* (London: Macmillan, 1917);

Clara G. Stillman, *Samuel Butler: A Mid-Victorian Modern* (New York: Viking, 1932; London: Martin Secker, 1932);

Rudolf Stoff, *Die Philosophie des Organischen bei Samuel Butler* (Vienna: Phaedon Verlag, 1929).

Papers:
The Samuel Butler Collection of St. John's College, Cambridge, contains many Butler manuscripts, paintings, and books. The Carroll A. Wilson collection of Butler manuscripts, including the notebooks and first editions of most of his works, is at the Chapin Library at Williams College, Williamstown, Massachusetts. Many other Butler manuscripts and letters are in the British Museum.

Lewis Carroll
(Charles Lutwidge Dodgson)

Kathleen Blake
University of Washington

BIRTH: Daresbury, Cheshire, 27 January 1832, to Charles and Frances Jane Lutwidge Dodgson.

EDUCATION: Christ Church, Oxford, B.A., 1854, M.A. 1857.

DEATH: Guildford, Surrey, 14 January 1898.

SELECTED BOOKS: *A Syllabus of Plane Algebraical Geometry, Part I*, as Charles Lutwidge Dodgson (Oxford & London: Parker, 1860);

The Formulae of Plane Trigonometry, as Dodgson (Oxford & London: Parker, 1861);

A Guide to the Mathematical Student, Part I, as Dodgson (Oxford: Parker, 1864);

The New Method of Evaluation as Applied to π, anonymous (Oxford, 1865);

The Dynamics of a Parti-cle, anonymous (Oxford: Vincent, 1865);

Alice's Adventures in Wonderland (London: Macmillan, 1865; New York: Appleton, 1866);

An Elementary Treatise on Determinants, as Dodgson (London: Macmillan, 1867);

The Fifth Book of Euclid Treated Algebraically, as Dodgson (Oxford & London: Parker, 1868);

Phantasmagoria and Other Poems (London: Macmillan, 1869);

Through the Looking-Glass, and What Alice Found There (London: Macmillan, 1872; Boston: Lee & Sheppard/New York: Lee, Sheppard & Dillingham, 1872);

Lewis Carroll at age twenty-four (Morris L. Parrish Collection, Princeton University)

The New Belfry of Christ Church, Oxford, as D. C. L. (Oxford: Parker, 1872);

The Vision of the Three T's, as D. C. L. (Oxford: Parker, 1873);

The Blank Cheque: A Fable, as D. C. L. (Oxford: Parker, 1874);

Suggestions as to the Best Method of Taking Votes, as C. L. D. (Oxford: Hall & Stacy, 1874); revised as *A Method of Taking Votes on More than Two Issues*, anonymous (Oxford, 1876);

The Hunting of the Snark: An Agony in Eight Fits (London: Macmillan, 1876; Boston: Osgood, 1876);

Euclid and His Modern Rivals, as Dodgson (London: Macmillan, 1879; New York: Dover, 1973);

Doublets: A Word-Puzzle (London: Macmillan, 1879);

Rhyme? And Reason? (London: Macmillan, 1883);

Supplement to "Euclid and His Modern Rivals, as Dodgson (London: Macmillan, 1885);

A Tangled Tale (London: Macmillan, 1885);

Three Years in a Curatorship, by One Who Has Tried, as Dodgson (Oxford: Baxter, 1886);

The Game of Logic (London: Macmillan, 1886; New York: Macmillan, 1886);

Alice's Adventures Under Ground (London: Macmillan, 1886; New York: Macmillan, 1886);

Curiosa Mathematica, Part I: A New Theory of Parallels, as Dodgson (London: Macmillan, 1888);

The Nursery Alice (London: Macmillan, 1889);

Sylvie and Bruno (London & New York: Macmillan, 1889);

Eight or Nine Wise Words about Letter-Writing (Oxford: Emberlin, 1890);

Syzygies and Lanrick: A Word-Puzzle and a Game (London: Clay, 1893);

Curiosa Mathematica, Part II: Pillow-Problems, as Dodgson (London: Macmillan, 1893);

Sylvie and Bruno Concluded (London & New York: Macmillan, 1893);

Symbolic Logic, Part I: Elementary (London & New York: Macmillan, 1896);

The Lewis Carroll Picture-Book (London: Unwin, 1899); republished as *Diversions and Digressions* (New York: Dover, 1961);

Feeding the Mind (London: Chatto & Windus, 1907);

Further Nonsense Verse and Prose, edited by Langford Reed (London: Unwin, 1926; New York: Appleton, 1926);

The Collected Verse of Lewis Carroll (London: Macmillan, 1932; New York: Macmillan, 1933); republished as *The Humorous Verse of Lewis Carroll* (New York: Dover, 1960);

For the Train, edited by Hugh J. Schonfield (London: Archer, 1932);

The Rectory Umbrella and Mischmasch (London: Cassell, 1932; New York: Dover, 1971);

Lewis Carroll, Photographer, edited by Helmut Gernsheim (London: Parrish, 1949; New York: Dover, 1969);

Diaries of Lewis Carroll, edited by Roger Lancelyn Green, 2 volumes (London: Cassell, 1953; New York: Oxford University Press, 1954);

Useful and Instructive Poetry (London: Bles, 1954; New York: Macmillan, 1954);

Mathematical Recreations of Carroll, 2 volumes (New York: Dover, 1958; London: Constable, 1959);

The Annotated Alice: Alice's Adventures in Wonderland and Through the Looking-Glass, edited by Martin Gardner (New York: Potter, 1960);

Symbolic Logic, Parts I and II, edited by William Warren Bartley (New York: Potter, 1977).

COLLECTIONS: *The Complete Works of Lewis Carroll* (London: Nonesuch, 1939; New York: Modern Library, 1939);

The Complete Illustrated Works of Lewis Carroll, edited by Edward Guiliano (New York: Avenel, 1982).

Lewis Carroll (the Reverend Charles Lutwidge Dodgson) was a Victorian nonsense writer for children whose works hold enduring fascination for adults as well. His *Alice's Adventures in Wonderland* (1865) and *Through the Looking-Glass* (1872) are classics of the English language, vying with the Bible and Shakespeare as sources of quotation, and they have been translated into virtually every other language, including Pitjantjatjara, a dialect of Aborigine. Alice's story began as a piece of extempore whimsy spun out to entertain three little girls on a boating trip on the river Isis in 1862, and it continues to delight children and to excite the responses of psychoanalysts, philosophers, mathematicians, linguists, semioticians, and Victorianists; historians of children's literature and of childhood; those studying the sources of the parodies, the genre of nonsense, and the development of Victorian humor; along with biographers and literary critics of eclectic interests. Next to the Alice books, Carroll's *The Hunting of the Snark* (1876) attracts the most attention and admiration as a nonsense epic in verse, an absurdist quest poem, a *Moby-Dick* of the nursery. Carroll wrote a number of humorous works for children and some for his Oxford colleagues, as well as publishing many puzzles and games. Among these, the letters written over the years to his child-friends strike the classic nonsense note. The long, late novels *Sylvie and Bruno* (1889) and *Sylvie and Bruno Concluded* (1893) have risen in critical regard to the status of interesting failures for their mixture of fantasy and society-novel realism. Their high seriousness contrasts strikingly with the nondidacticism that makes the Alice books and *The Hunting of the Snark* seem light, dry, problematical, and "modern," even "post-modern." Interesting as period pieces, the *Sylvie and Bruno* novels also prefigure twentieth-century experimentations in form.

Quite different from these literary works are mathematical and logical studies by Carroll. These products of his career as a professor at Christ Church, Oxford, run the gamut from the purely academic—*An Elementary Treatise on Determinants* (1867)—to the wittily serious—*Euclid and His Modern Rivals* (1879), *The Game of Logic* (1886), and *Symbolic Logic, Parts I and II* (1896, 1977). They also cover a range of scholarly significance from negligible to considerable. The recovery of Carroll's last work, Part II of *Symbolic Logic*, confirms his claim to importance in his academic field. Of the academic studies, the most notable are not the most serious in tone but are leavened with humor, so that it is too simple to insist on any absolute split in style or character. However, another aspect of Carroll's work seems very separate and yet bears relation to the rest; the collection of his photographs in *Lewis Carroll, Photographer* (1949) demonstrates his excellence in this area. Yet the children who inspired the photographer inspired the storyteller and letter writer as well, and they kindled or rekindled the spirit which filled the logic text with nonsensical examples and an awareness that sense itself is a made-up thing, like a child's game.

Carroll divided himself up into two names, Lewis Carroll and the Reverend Charles Lutwidge Dodgson. He frequently insisted on the division because he detested lionization as the children's author while carrying on his very regular, donnish life at Oxford. He sometimes refused to receive fan mail addressed to Lewis Carroll at Christ Church. In one letter to a child-friend he gives an amusing account of the meeting of his two selves. Still, just as most of the letters to children and the major children's books are signed Lewis Carroll, so is *Symbolic Logic*. Some have viewed him as a split personality, and yet there is much that comes together in the life and works of Lewis Carroll; one may use a single name to refer to him.

A great deal is known about Carroll's life from *The Life and Letters of Lewis Carroll* (1899) compiled soon after his death by his nephew, and from im-

Photograph by Carroll of Alice Liddell, the inspiration for Alice's Adventures in Wonderland

portant editions of his extensive diaries and letters. But enough remains enigmatic about a man so varied in interests and output, whose best friends were little girls, to inspire new biographical interpretations. He was born in 1832, the eldest son in a clergyman's family of eleven children living in less than affluent circumstances at the parsonage of Daresbury, Cheshire. In 1843 the family moved to Croft in Yorkshire to enjoy a more capacious parsonage and a better living. The boy had a multitude of sisters, and he was the master of their ceremonies, inventor of games, magician, marionette theater manager, editor of the family journals. His mother was sweet, lovable, and much loved; she died just as her son turned nineteen. The letters make more reference to the father than to the mother. His father died when Carroll was thirty-six, and he called this the saddest blow he had known. The elder Reverend Charles Dodgson was an upstanding Christ Church and Church of England man and paterfamilias, who instilled in his son religious faith and a belief in earnest endeavor strong enough to make Carroll sometimes feel slack in his work and tardy in his progress despite his lifelong habits of discipline and labor. But his father was not only an earnest Victorian; he also had humor to pass on, judging from this letter to the seven-year-old Charles: "you may depend upon it I will not forget your commission. . . . I WILL have a file and a screw driver, and a ring, and if they are not brought directly, in forty seconds, I will leave nothing but one small cat alive in the whole town of Leeds. . . . Then what a bawling and tearing of hair there will be! Pigs and babies, camels and butterflies, rolling in the gutter together—old women rushing up the chimneys and cows after them—ducks hiding themselves in coffee cups, and fat geese trying to squeeze themselves into pencilcases."

Carroll was a writer from the earliest age. From the floorboards of the nursery at Croft has been recovered a cache he apparently left there for posterity when a new floor was laid, containing, among other things, a white glove, a child's left shoe, and the intriguing words, "And we'll wander through the wide world/ and chase the buffalo." More of the writer's funny juvenilia have survived, such as the poem "Rules and Regulations" from the family magazine *Useful and Instructive Poetry*:

> Don't push with your shoulder
> Until you are older.
> Lose not a button.
> Refuse cold mutton
> Starve your canaries.
> Believe in fairies. . . .
> *Moral*: Behave.

After his education at home and at Richmond and Rugby Schools (1844-1849), Carroll matriculated at Christ Church, Oxford, in 1850 and entered into residency in 1851. He passed from a studentship through bachelor and master's of arts degrees to a mathematical lectureship, and even after he resigned his teaching post in 1881, he functioned as curator of the Senior Common Room (1882-1892) and remained a member of the house for a total of forty-seven years until his death. In choosing Christ Church he followed in the footsteps of his father but did not, like him, go on to marry or to become a practicing minister. He became a deacon of the Church of England in 1861 but chose not to go further. After he had lost both parents he became the head of his family in that he provided a home for his unmarried sisters at Guildford in Surrey. His life came to be geographically defined by residency at Oxford, holiday visits to his family home, frequent trips to London, and summer seaside vacations most often at Eastbourne and San-

down. He departed from his usual track by making a trip to Russia with a friend in 1867. He had a gentle face and a thin erect figure and looked "as if he had swallowed a poker." He was abstemious in eating and drinking. His habits were extremely methodical: for instance, among his many other records, he maintained information on his dinner guests, what they had been served and where they had sat, so as to avoid repeating the same arrangements twice.

During the period of his studies and early teaching career, in the years leading up to the writing of *Alice's Adventures in Wonderland*, Carroll led a lively artistic and intellectual life, became a devoted playgoer, contributed to humorous journals, and created the pen name Lewis Carroll for the *Train* (in 1856). Based on a Latin translation of the author's first and second names, the pseudonym was chosen by the *Train*'s editor, Edmund Yates, from a list of four submitted. Also during this period Carroll took up his photographic hobby. This avocation was closely linked with his cultivation of child-friends, first and foremost of whom was Alice Liddell, instigator and auditor of the famous tale and the model for its heroine. Photography satisfied Carroll's artist's instincts and his love of gadgets and of children. It also provided an alternative to drawing: while he never gave up sketching, he became convinced of his limitations in this area. The great art critic John Ruskin took a discouraging view of his talent and persuaded him against pursuing this interest seriously. Many have felt, however, that Carroll's illustrations of early works and of the manuscript of *Alice's Adventures Under Ground* (1886) possess a grotesque, surreal power that offsets their lack of professional polish. For that matter, Carroll's aesthetic awareness was not so unformed as one might suppose. A Pre-Raphaelite influence is discernible in his drawings of Alice. He had purchased a painting by Arthur Hughes at about the time that he was illustrating his manuscript, and he was personally acquainted with such artists as Dante Gabriel Rossetti, John Millais, Holman Hunt, and G. F. Watts. He always took great interest in the decoration of his books and made many suggestions to his illustrators—John Tenniel, Henry Holiday, A. B. Frost, Harry Furniss, and Gertrude Thomson. Carroll found in photography the fullest expression of this strong visual interest. In addition, the technical challenge and advantages of the new collodian or wet-plate process helped attract him to the hobby. His invention-loving Uncle Skeffington Lutwidge introduced him to the camera in 1855,

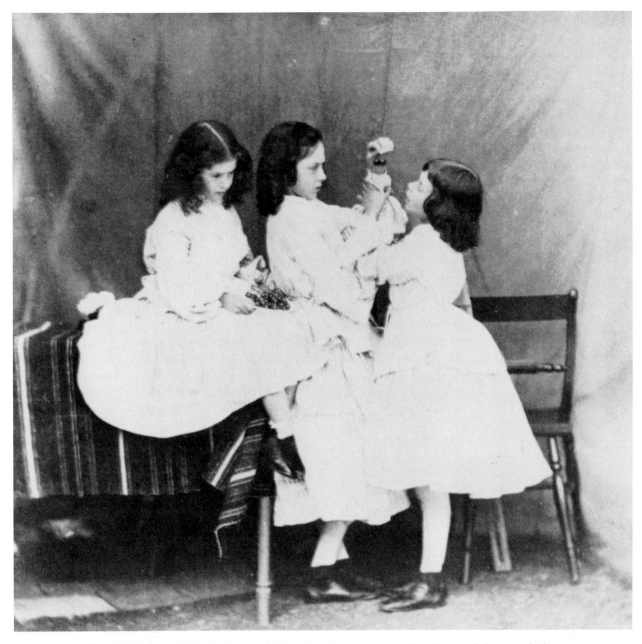

The Liddell sisters, Edith, Lorina, and Alice, for whose amusement Carroll created the story of Alice
(Morris L. Parrish Collection, Princeton University)

and Carroll was soon going to many lengths to capture distinguished sitters, such as Alfred Tennyson; he ran after the famous in a way that he came to dislike when he became famous himself. But it was not long before his interest shifted and settled on portraiture of children. Along with Julia Margaret Cameron, he has been hailed as one of the great portraitists in this new medium, "the most outstanding photographer of children in the nineteenth century." He lacked interest in landscape but could felicitously place a figure in a simple, expressive setting and excelled at composition. He made children look natural, despite the strain of having to hold still for a long time for the camera.

His camera brought him into contact with many young girls, most importantly Alice Liddell. She makes her first appearance in Carroll's diary in an entry of 25 April 1856, concerning a photographic venture. Carroll had sought to photograph Christ Church Cathedral from the deanery, where he had met the three little daughters of the dean of the college and had turned his lens on the girls. Alice was then almost four years old. The sisters were impatient sitters, but the entry concludes with the phrase Carroll reserved for his best times, "Mark this day with a white stone." On 5 June he is boating with two Liddells and marking the day as "Dies mirabilis." The entry for 14 November conveys an initial hint of the coolness from Mrs. Liddell which has intrigued biographers but eluded clear-cut interpretation: she wished the children to be photographed as a group, not separately. But photographing at the deanery continues to be noted. The diaries covering the period between 1858 and 1862 have disappeared, but they pick up in time to record the famous boating expedition of 4 July 1862 on which Carroll told Lorina, Alice, and Edith Liddell the story of Alice's adventures; Alice was ten years old. Here is an account by the grown-up Alice, Mrs. Hargreaves: "I believe the beginning of 'Alice' was told one summer afternoon when the sun was so burning that we had landed in

Photograph by Carroll of George MacDonald and his daughter Lily, who urged publication of Alice's Adventures in Wonderland

the meadows down the river, deserting the boat to take refuge in the only bit of shade to be found, which was under a new-made hayrick. Here from all three came the old petition, 'Tell us a story,' and so began the ever-delightful tale. Sometimes to tease us—and perhaps being really tired—Mr. Dodgson would stop suddenly and say, 'And that's all till next time.' 'Ah, but it is next time,' would be the exclamation from all three."

Carroll's method of composition for children followed one of the three ways described by C. S. Lewis. Like J. M. Barrie, Kenneth Grahame, and Beatrix Potter, he created for one or more particular children rather than for a child audience in the abstract, or, as Lewis himself did, for the sake of writing in a children's literary form. Carroll's particular child was Alice; she was the one who pressed him to put the story on paper. On the train the day after the river trip he wrote out headings, and while the work gestated he corrected proof sheets for his "Circular to Mathematical Friends." He met with the Liddell children for walks and croquet and heard them sing "Beautiful Star," which got into the book as the Mock Turtle's song on "Beautiful Soup," one of the many parodies of well-known songs and poems. Carroll records an all-day, all-night session grading exams, followed the next day by more work on *Alice's Adventures Under Ground*. At the same time he sensed some ebbing of his intimacy with the children. He suspected that Lorina would no longer be able to join their expeditions. By 21 November 1862, he records his surprise at an invitation by Mrs. Liddell to visit with the children. Yet 10 March 1863 was spent enjoying the wedding festivities of the Prince of Wales with the Liddells and was marked by a white stone.

The manuscript of *Alice's Adventures Under Ground* had been written out by 10 February 1863, and Carroll sent it to his friend, the writer George MacDonald. His children responded favorably, and the MacDonalds urged Carroll to publish the book. He took his time completing his illustrations for the manuscript, which was not sent to Alice until 26 November 1864. Meanwhile Carroll expanded *Alice's Adventures Under Ground* to form *Alice's Adventures in Wonderland* and arranged for Tenniel to illustrate it. By this time Carroll had registered Mrs. Liddell's desire that he keep his distance—no great hardship, it seems, for he found Alice much changed and hardly for the better, according to a diary entry of 11 May 1865. On 4 July 1865, three years after he first told the tale, he sent thirteen-year-old Alice Liddell a special vellum-clad copy of

60

at the Great Northern Hotel, & dined with the Burnetts —

July 29 (Sat.) From London to Croft.

Aug 2 (W). Finally decided on the re-print of "Alice," & that the first 2000 shall be sold as waste paper. Wrote about it to Macmillan, Combe & Tenniel — The total cost will be — drawing pictures — 138..
cutting ———————— 142
printing (by Clay) 240
binding & advertising (say) 80
———
600

i.e. 6/ a copy on the 2000 — If I make £500 by sale, this will be a loss of £100, & the loss on the first 2000 will probably be £100 leaving me £200 out of pocket.

But if a second 2000 could be sold it would cost £300, & bring in £500, thus squaring accounts: & any further sale would be a gain: but that I can hardly hope for.

A page from Carroll's diary, recording his decision to recall the first edition of Alice's Adventures in Wonderland *and republish it*

the first edition. This edition ran into difficulties due to the fastidiousness of illustrator and author. Tenniel complained about the printing of the pictures, and so Carroll insisted that the book be recalled. The unbound sheets were sold to Appleton of New York and published in 1866 as a second issue of the first edition. A second edition came out in 1865, though dated 1866. These complications have made early copies of *Alice's Adventures in Wonderland* rare items prized and paid royally for by later book collectors. This publishing history also illustrates Carroll's perfectionist standard and his concern for the beauty of the physical book.

The tremendous success of *Alice's Adventures in Wonderland* led to the writing of its sequel, *Through the Looking-Glass, and What Alice Found There*, begun in 1867 and published in 1872, also illustrated by Tenniel. Alice Liddell inspired this work only retrospectively, for by the time she received her copy she was a young lady with whom Carroll had virtually no contact. While these two novels are separate creations, they may be discussed together. *Alice's Adventures in Wonderland* concerns a seven-year-old Alice whose curiosity causes her to follow the White Rabbit down the rabbit hole into a dream world which she finds both wondrous and exasperating. In the course of her adventures she seeks out the key to the beautiful garden, nearly drowns in the pool of her own tears, eats and drinks one thing and then another, growing and shrinking, so that once she is so big she gets stuck in the White Rabbit's house and has to stick one foot up the chimney, and another time she is so small her chin strikes her foot. She does get into the garden, having encountered a gallery of eccentrics such as the Cheshire Cat with his grin, the Caterpiller on his magic mushroom who asks "Who are you?," the Mad Hatter gathered with the March Hare and the Dormouse at the Mad Tea-Party, and the Queen of Hearts presiding over a croquet game gone berserk and a trial that requires "Sentence first—verdict afterwards." This madcap world loses its appeal the more it becomes a downright mad one: Alice is not pleased to hear it when the Cheshire Cat says, "We're all mad here." She stands up for sense, finally condemning the nonsense of Wonderland, disrupting the trial of the Knave of Hearts, and waking from her dream. She may be seen as the sensible child not to be taken in by grown-up insanity; or, since she grows physically at the end, she may be seen as maturing to leave a childishly anarchic world behind her. Her character may seem unimaginative and priggish, or gallantly sane, depending on the reader's attitude toward sense and nonsense.

Sir John Tenniel

If Alice grows older in *Alice's Adventures in Wonderland*, she has to do it over again in *Through the Looking-Glass*, for she is no more than seven and a half in the later book, and she passes through the mirror to an analogous series of confrontations with anarchy, which she finally rejects and leaves. She finds herself a Pawn in a fascinating but mad game of chess, and as she passes across the board to the Eighth Square she meets up with the authoritarian Red Queen and the dissociated White Queen—she learns, among other things, to run as fast as she can to stay in place and to believe six impossible things before breakfast. She gets to know nursery-rhyme characters such as Tweedledum and Tweedledee, but she does not like it when they question whether even her tears make her a real child, rather than just a figment in a dream. Humpty-Dumpty gives her a lecture on languages, showing how made-up and confusing it really is. Throughout, Alice has trouble reciting songs and verses that won't come out right; "Jabberwocky" is the epitome of the nonsense poem

Specimen illustrations by Sir John Tenniel for the 1866 London edition of Alice's Adventures in Wonderland

that seems to mean something, though it is never clear quite what. This strange looking-glass land holds a charm for a very curious child, and Alice enjoys some companionship with the White Knight, a mad inventor, with anklets for his horse to keep off sharks and stakes for the head up which hair can be trained to grow to keep it from falling out. Yet, finally, Alice can stand no more a dream-game world she cannot comprehend, and she wakes. There is a subtle difference between this and the earlier *Alice's Adventures in Wonderland*: the reader is made more aware of the implications of loss and mortality in the growing-up process. In one chapter, Alice is likened to a flower whose petals have already begun to fade; and according to the dedication poem, the voice of time

> Shall summon to unwelcome bed
> A melancholy maiden!
> We are but older children, dear,
> Who fret to find our bedtime near.

Carroll suggests that maidenhood ends in the sexual bed, life in the bed of the grave. It seems likely that an Alice Liddell no longer a child somewhat saddened the tone of *Through the Looking-Glass*.

Other reflections of Carroll's personal experience appear in the books: the pool of tears no doubt derived from a wetting undergone by Carroll and the Liddell children on one of their outings, to give just one instance. Carroll—Dodgson—was the Dodo. Self-portraiture has also been seen in his characterization of the White Knight, the Gnat, and—since the rediscovery of a canceled sequence of *Through the Looking-Glass* known as "The Wasp in a Wig"—in the Wasp. Political and cultural allegory has been sought in the books: some evidence of veiled allusions to Oxford politics may be mustered; the likeness to Disraeli of the Man in White Paper brings the national political scene into view—though this caricature is Tenniel's, after all, not Carroll's. Some commentators recommend bearing in mind the Victorian context: for instance, remembering Darwin's ideas about evolution while considering the creatures emerging from the pool of tears. Carroll's work is placed in a historical context by those concerned with nonsense as a genre and with Victorian humor, and especially by historians of children's literature and of childhood. Growing interest in fairy tales and fantasy characterized the early nineteenth century and flowered in Carroll's writing. The Alice books marked an emancipation of children's literature from heavy-

handed didacticism. They also epitomized important developments in the concept of the child: Carroll expresses a romantic view of childhood in his introductory poem to *Through the Looking-Glass* dedicated to the "Child of the pure unclouded brow." At the same time the novels present a less-than-perfect heroine; not all readers like her. She has her good and bad points, plucky but also prim, polite but sometimes aggressive. This little girl likes to play "let's pretend" with her nurse—"Let's pretend that I'm a hungry hyaena and you're a bone!" Such a characterization of a girl in an age inclined to idealize the female is historically notable and of interest to feminists. Alice's brow is not conventionally unclouded: the dream adventures go on in *her* sleep and *her* head, and considerable darkness tinges tales told "all in the golden afternoon."

In their own time, the Alice books were mostly regarded as sparkling whimsy, and there are still those who decry an intellectual approach intent on discovering darker depths. But in this century, stress has fallen on those depths. William Empson's essay of 1935, "The Child as Swain," and Martin Gardner's 1960 edition of *The Annotated Alice* initiated consecutive waves of serious analysis. Freudian commentators have heightened awareness of the level of anxiety in the books, the eating and being eaten, the threats to body integrity implicit in radical size changes and such grotesque incidents as the lengthening of Alice's neck till it rises to the treetops and the near knocking of her chin on her foot as she shrinks. They have pointed out Alice's claustrophobia when she is stuck in the Rabbit's house, her frustration when she runs without getting anywhere, and, above all, the repeated crises of identity which she faces. She is unable to answer the Caterpillar's "Who are *you*?," she loses her name in the nameless woods, she is disquieted by a number of death jokes. At the extreme, Paul Schilder finds these tales too frightening to be fit fare for children. A Freudian approach also raises questions about the author's mental and emotional fitness. His interest in children and children's literature may signal nostalgia and regression. His devotion to Alice's real-life model may indicate sexual immaturity, if not perversion. His pleasure in nonsense may hint of escapism, or, alternately, his heroine's preference for sense may reveal anal-retentive compulsiveness. Carroll's exploration of assaults on life and identity raises questions about his control of his own aggressions and about his own wholeness as a man. At the extreme, Peter Coveney characterizes the author as "almost the case-book maladjusted

Lewis Carroll (Dodgson Family Collection)

so here," says Alice plaintively. Stability of being, consistency of rules to allow fair play, rational constructs, and even words themselves flow about amidst riddles, puns, conversational misconstructions, and constant plays upon semantic and grammatical anomalies. For the reader, like Alice, many statements seem to make no sense at all, and yet they are certainly English. Meaning threatens to dissolve in the flow.

It is worth turning to Carroll's personal attitude toward language, the vehicle of meaning. He had a lifelong attraction-repulsion to words. A letter written when he was a schoolboy shows his fascination and dismay; he had been reading Thomas B. Macaulay's *History of England from the Accession of James II* (1849-1861): "one passage struck me when 7 bishops had signed the invitation to the pretender, and King James sent for Bishop Compton (who was one of the 7) and asked him 'whether he or any of his ecclesiastical brethren had had anything to do with it?' He replied after a moment's thought, 'I am fully persuaded, your majesty, that there is not one of my brethren who is not as innocent in the matter as myself.' This was certainly no actual lie, but certainly, as Macaulay says, it was very little different from one. On the next day the King called a meeting of all the bishops. . . . He then for form's sake, put the question to each of them 'whether they had had anything to do with it?' Here was a new difficulty, which Compton got over by saying, when it came to his turn, 'I gave your majesty *my* answer yesterday.' It certainly showed talent, though exerted in the wrong direction." Carroll continued to find words problematical: he said it was their nature to be ambiguous. This was the reason why from 1861 until his death he kept a register of all letters received and sent, the last entry numbering 98,721. A precis allowed him to assure himself and sometimes his correspondent of what exactly had been said in case of later misunderstanding. By such recording he sought to secure verbal reliability, without altogether expecting to succeed. His *Eight or Nine Wise Words about Letter-Writing* (1890) humorously explores the proposition that if anything can misfire in communication, it will. Compared to natural language, mathematical/ logical symbol systems are a great deal more certain. In his revealing preface to *Curiosa Mathematica, Part I* (1888), Carroll praises pure mathematics for "the absolute certainty of its results: for that is what, beyond almost all mental treasures, the human intellect craves for. Let us only be sure of something." Concerning the uncertainty of language, it is interesting to compare Carroll to

neurotic." Reacting against a normative Freudian approach which stands in judgment of "unhealthy" aspects of the work or author are those who value Carroll's treatment of the integrity of self and world under radical stress; so viewed, Carroll seems to belong almost more to the twentieth century than to his own. Thus, the Alice books have been compared with the works of T. S. Eliot, James Joyce, Hermann Hesse, and Vladimir Nabokov; they have been analyzed in terms of game theory, linguistics, semiotics, and the philosophy of Ludwig Wittgenstein. A 1966 essay by Donald Rackin bears the characteristic title "Alice's Journey to the End of Night." Nightmare dissolution of coherence threatens Alice in a number of ways, for instance in the many identity problems, in the incoherence of the games—cards, croquet, chess—which figure in both books, in the logical conundrums, and in the many perplexities of language. "Things flow about

his friend and fellow writer of children's fantasies George MacDonald. MacDonald reveled in ambiguity, for in his view this increased suggestiveness, while Carroll was bothered as well as intrigued.

Carroll's decision not to proceed to full holy orders may be understood partly in terms of his doubts about language as a carrier of meaning. Religion offers the ultimate source and ground of meaning, and Carroll met with uncertainties here, too. A minister customarily advises members of the flock troubled in their faith, and Carroll once said he felt his utter incompetence in such a situation to convince anybody of anything. Furthermore, he had been a stammerer from childhood, which intensified his distrust of words. He did lecture and preach on occasion, but the occasions could be painful, and so it may be understandable that he never committed himself to a career of Sunday sermonizing and pastoral care and that he also gave up regular teaching at Christ Church when the sale of his books allowed him the privilege of lecturing as little as he liked. (He did do some teaching later; for instance, he presented a logic class at an Oxford senior girls' school.)

Other reasons have been proposed for Carroll's decision not to take full holy orders. These involve speculations about his unorthodoxy or even religious doubts. He had been advised by his bishop about the impropriety of playgoing in a clergyman, and this may have checked his advancement in the clergy, while it did not check his playgoing. Also, the preface to his *Curiosa Mathematica, Part II: Pillow Problems* (1893) contains the remark that mathematical puzzles may help divert the mind from irreverent thoughts on sleepless nights. No one knows what thoughts troubled him and how irreverent they were, but it is clear that he did not like to be troubled in this way. He sometimes complained about irreverent jokes. He had a better memory than was quite comfortable, for when some Biblical phrase he had heard used in a joke was cited in a sermon, he became the victim of verbal associations. However, when Carroll declared his faith, as in one letter to a young lady, he showed his real reverence at the same time that he revealed his sense of religious paradox: No realm, he says, is as certain as mathematics or logic. The letter indicates his awareness of contradictory views of God—if all-powerful, then how also all-good? He considers this problem as one incapable of rational resolution and explanation, yet resolvable in psychological terms: he says that one must simply choose the view that enables one to live a moral life, and so he chooses to

Self-caricature by Lewis Carroll

believe in a good God. Carroll lacked the flexibility of temperament to live at ease amid uncertainties; for that matter, Keats did not say it was easy either. He did what he could to live with certainties in his academic field and to minimize close encounters with religious uncertainties—he did not evade his own, but he could avoid the perplexities of parishioners. At the same time, he bowed out of careers demanding perpetual verbal explanation and did what he could to firm up the certainty of his own use of language. He chose his words carefully and kept a record of his correspondence.

In the Alice books certitude, linguistic and ontological-religious, remains unobtainable: Alice is not certain that Humpty-Dumpty can make words mean what he says they mean; neither is she sure of the status of the reality to which words so uncertainly refer. *Through the Looking-Glass* ends with an open question about the dreamer of the dream. Who dreamed it all, Alice or the Red King? What if he woke? The attitude expressed toward these

Specimen illustrations by Sir John Tenniel for the 1872 edition of Through the Looking-Glass, and What Alice Found There

quandaries—the degree of affirmation at the ends of *Alice's Adventures in Wonderland* and *Through the Looking-Glass*—remains a matter of dispute, though there is little reason to doubt Carroll's own affirmation of language despite everything. He was a writer, after all, glorying in words with all their unruliness, enjoying the giddy flirtation of sense with nonsense. One might as well be gleeful and rueful about the teetering of certitude. Nor is there reason to dispute Carroll's own religious affirmation. He was a devout member and deacon of the Anglican church and found a personal faith, even if he doubted his capacity to persuade others to believe. Still, his next major literary work, *The Hunting of the Snark*, ends in a way that is quite inconclusive and discomforting. Its last line came to Carroll first: "The Snark *was* a Boojum, you see." The meaning of this line is only darkly hinted at in the course of a long poem of eight parts, subtitled *An Agony in Eight Fits*. *The Hunting of the Snark* describes the voyage quest of a ship's company of incongruous characters linked only by the fact that their names all begin with a *B*. The Snark is an elusive prey:

> They sought it with thimbles, they sought it
> with care;
> They pursued it with forks and hope;
> They threatened its life with a railway-share;
> They charmed it with smiles and soap.

They have not much to go by. Having dispensed with merely conventional guidelines, they navigate by means of a blank map. Shipboard conflicts and foreboding dreams afflict them. The Barrister's dream resembles the "Mouse's Tale" and the courtroom scene of *Alice's Adventures in Wonderland*, for it involves a travesty trial, with the Snark as defense lawyer, jury, and judge, who eventually condemns and sentences his own client. Also carrying over from the Alice books is an obsession with assaults on identity: the success of the quest means the end of the Baker; upon discovering the Snark to be a Boo—, he vanishes in midword. This poem is gaining more and more attention and regard for its casting of certain characteristic themes of the Alice stories into a new, even more purely nonsensical and poetic form.

The Hunting of the Snark was dedicated to Gertrude Chataway, a little girl Carroll met in 1875, one of the many child-friends who took the place of Alice Liddell over the years. He met Gertrude at the seaside. This was one good place to strike up acquaintance with children; other opportunities came by way of railway journeys, backstage introductions to child actresses, and his photographic hobby, as well as meetings with the families of friends and colleagues. Carroll's letters to these child-friends offer nonsense in the best *Alice* and *Snark* veins, and they reveal his strange and very special relationship with children. Here is a letter concerning a visit to Carroll by a certain wax doll:

> she sat on my knee, and fanned herself with a penwiper, because she said she was afraid the end of her nose was beginning to melt.
>
> "You've no *idea* how careful we have to be, we dolls," she said. "Why, there was a sister of mine—would you believe it?—she went up to the fire to warm her hands, and one of her hands dropped right off! There now!"
>
> "Of course it dropped *right* off," I said, "because it was the *right* hand."
>
> "And how do you know it was the *right* hand, Mister Carroll?" the doll said.
>
> So I said, "I think it must have been the *right* hand, because the other hand was *left*."
>
> The doll said, "I shan't laugh. It's a very bad joke."

The letter is striking for its cleverness, its tinge of the grotesque in the joke about melting body parts, and the tartness of the response to the joke, suggestive of the teasing between Carroll and his young friends. The tone is unsentimental. In a real sense, Carroll communicated with children on their level; he did not confine himself to what a parent might entirely approve. For instance, one letter to Hallam Tennyson expresses regret that the knife given by Carroll should have been confiscated by the family authorities, " 'till you are older.' However, as you *are* older now, perhaps you have begun to use it by this time [and] I hope that if Lionel ever wants to have *his* fingers cut with it, you will be kind to your brother, and hurt him as much as he likes."

Perhaps symptomatically, Carroll pictures a brother at the receiving end of a sharp knife and a sharp-edged joke. He also gave Kathleen Tidy a penknife and advice about the convenient way it could be run into the hands and faces of her brothers. Carroll did have some friendships with boys, such as Hallam Tennyson, but his preference for girls was pronounced. One letter to a little girl concludes, "My best love to yourself—to your Mother my kindest regards—to your small, fat, impertinent, ignorant brother my hatred." Carroll explained that he was not impartial when it came to children: "With little *boys* I'm out of my element altogether." He did not like all little girls, nor too many at once, but he was not exclusive and kept up a variety of child contacts. Part of his interest was that of a collector. He sometimes expressed a generalized romantic notion of the purity of children as being closer to God than are adults. At other times he revealed more specific, personal tastes. He liked spontaneity, provided this combined with good manners. He applied physical standards and

A preliminary sketch made in 1887 by Carroll of a scene from Sylvie and Bruno Concluded *(1894)*
(Lilly Library, Indiana University)

looked for beauty in little girls to please his artist's and photographer's eye. A class bias occasionally appeared in remarks about the lesser looks of lower-class children.

Of course, one wonders whether this response to physical beauty implies a sexual element. None of the children or their families have left any record of being scandalized. This does not mean that all regarded Carroll's ways as quite conventional. He said of himself that he lived upon the frowns of Mrs. Grundy. He knew that he risked offending this mythical figurehead of respectability when it came to kissing girls who were not so young as they looked, or taking nude photographs of certain children, or inviting child-friends of rather advanced age—teenagers and even young ladies—to spend holidays with him at the seaside. He sought to avoid outraging Mrs. Grundy by doing nothing behind her back: he scrupulously discussed the kissability of daughters with their mothers, and also went over the family view of nude photographs and the particular child's attitude. Carroll did not wish to provoke the least bit of shyness in a girl. When he invited young ladies to spend time with him at the seaside, he declared his sense of propriety in doing so but asked them to make sure of their own feelings. Carroll could casually liken one such visit to a honeymoon and himself to a bachelor unused to tête-à-tétes with young females. It is hard to interpret the implications here. Is it important that he should raise the erotic issue, or unimportant in that he raises it so casually? Anne Clark's biography of Carroll suggests that he loved Alice Liddell in the romantic sense that he wanted to marry her. This idea remains controversial. There is no clear evidence of romance in his life, whether involving a girl or a woman. One may speculate about his affection for the actress Ellen Terry, which lasted from her childhood into her full adulthood. A number of his friendships did last in this way, and the older Carroll became, the more often a child kept him as a friend as she grew up. Sometimes Carroll joked about a girl's growing too old to be interesting, more often about her growing too old to care for him. The letters contain a great deal of byplay about gradually cooling forms of address and the evolution from intimacy to formality to be seen in ways of signing a name. Carroll certainly felt the loss of many friends to time, but he took his losses gracefully and found great satisfaction in his friendships with children, and he avoided catastrophe. Whatever one may make of Carroll's child-friendships in a post-Freudian age, one must recognize his own

freedom from conscious guilt or regret and admire his success in living as he chose to live. In any period it is unusual to care for children so much. It may be especially unusual to love them as children, without even a sexual element to explain it. Most people like only their own children and do not socialize with other people's. The romanticism of the nineteenth-century could glorify the rare ability to maintain the heart of a child, while today this may seem regressive and immature. Carroll joins J. M. Barrie as a children's writer open to such a range of praise and blame. C. S. Lewis would like to grant manhood to writers such as these: as he says, one need not lose touch with childhood in the process of also developing beyond it.

When Carroll gave up his photography and his lectureship in 1880-1881, the likely reason was his desire to devote all his time to his writing, and indicating the two main tracks of his interest are the two major works produced in this last portion of his life—the children's novels *Sylvie and Bruno* and *Sylvie and Bruno Concluded*, and the treatise *Symbolic Logic*. The inception of the Sylvie and Bruno books dates back to 1867 when Carroll published the story of "Bruno's Revenge." Several letters indicate his desire to write something of a more serious nature for children than the Alice books and *The Hunting of the Snark*. Over the years Carroll brought together various bits and pieces into his two-volume work of "litterature." These novels have struck most readers as overserious and disjointed. The story divides into two narrative lines, one realistic and edifying, the other fantastic. According to the first story line, the grown-up, real-life Lady Muriel Orme ends her engagement to her suitor Eric, who lacks religious faith, to marry another suitor, Arthur. He departs one hour after the wedding to risk his life doctoring epidemic-stricken villagers. Following a report of his death, it turns out that a reformed Eric has rescued Arthur, who reappears to be nursed back to health by his loving wife. The other narrative line tells of Lady Muriel's fairy double, the child Sylvie, and her adventures with her brother Bruno (Carroll *could* create a positive boy character) tracing their lost father and saving the throne of Outland from usurpation by the Vice-Warden and his son Uggugg. Linking these stories are the appearances and good works of Sylvie and Bruno amid the real-life characters and the knowledge of their doings in both England and fairyland by a narrator capable of "eerie" as well as ordinary states of unconsciousness. There is some interest in the narrative oddity here and in the interpenetration of dream and reality.

Fine nonsense enlivens the fairy sequences, such as this from "The Pig Tale":

> Little Birds are bathing
>   Crocodiles in cream,
>   Like a happy dream:
>   Like, but not so lasting—
> Crocodiles, when fasting,
>   Are not all they seem!

These lines provide the title for a one-actor dramatic rendering of Carroll's life by David Horwell and Michael Rothwell, *Crocodiles in Cream* (1976), and they signal the importance of aggression and the unimportance of righteousness in much of his nonsense. This is the Carroll who, when pressed to comment, said Alice was about malice. In the Sylvie and Bruno books Carroll notes that "live" spells "evil" backward. And yet these last books affirm life more decisively than anything earlier. The theme song about love strikes the serious note which Carroll sought. Some find it sentimental and "Victorian":

> For I think it is Love
> For I feel it is Love,
> For I'm sure it is nothing but Love!

Like the last children's work, Carroll's last academic work, *Symbolic Logic*, has been valued for good bits and historical interest more than for classic status. But with the recovery and publication of Part II by William Warren Bartley, its historical interest has grown and surpassed that of the Sylvie and Bruno books. The treatise has been persistently honored by quotation in later logic texts because of the ingenuity and charming presentation of its logical problems—the Jack Sprat problem, the Pig and Balloon problem, the problem of the Pork-Chop-Eating Logicians. According to Bartley, some innovation appears in Part I (enough to prompt the praise of Bertrand Russell), and Part II confirms and strengthens Carroll's standing as an original thinker. (For instance, his truth tables prefigure those developed by Wittgenstein in the 1920s.) Yet Carroll was not really a father of modern logic. Rather, his merit lies in synthesizing the Boolean logic of his day, an algebraic form which superseded syllogistic Aristotelian logic and has since been superseded by Russell's brand of mathematical logic. This synthesis is noteworthy first because Carroll went beyond anything being done in the logical backwater of Oxford to concern himself with the forefront of thought in his field, and second because he defined a logical system that was so soon revolutionized as to have left no other comprehensive text.

The volumes of *Symbolic Logic* reflect Carroll's lifelong attraction to certitude in the face of imponderables. According to a letter to his sister, he turned from a prospective book on religious difficulties to devote himself to this work, for which he felt more fitted. Thus in the works of his last years, Carroll affirmed as much as he could as clearly as he could—love in *Sylvie and Bruno*; in *Symbolic Logic*, sense. But, as Sylvie realizes that to love matters more than to be loved, Carroll's logic presents sense as something made, not given. As a logician he was very much a formalist. The earlier work, *The Game of Logic*, prepares the way for Carroll's statement in *Symbolic Logic* that "the rules, here laid down, are *arbitrary*." Throughout his life and works Carroll was concerned with the very difficult, very necessary task of making meaning enough to live by. He lived well by his own rules, loving little girls and God as he saw fit, as systematic in his mind and ways as

Lewis Carroll's grave, Guildford Cemetery

the uncertainty of things would allow. If he was eccentric or, more harshly, neurotic, he knew how to make the best of eschewing the norm. The Alice books strike most critics today as explorations of nightmare reaches beyond sense and security. And yet Alice does not lose her pluck or her mind (as she does in André Gregory's Manhattan Project dramatization of 1970). She perhaps grows or even triumphs; at least she emerges from her dreams. Mathematician, logician, photographer, the greatest nonsense writer in English and possibly any language, as indispensable to adults as to children, Carroll remained healthy and active to the end; in the last year of his life he thought nothing of an eighteen-mile walk. He died at the age of sixty-five at his sisters' home in Guildford of bronchitis taken after a cold.

Letters:

A Selection from the Letters of Lewis Carroll (The Rev. Charles Lutwidge Dodgson) to His Child-friends, edited by Evelyn M. Hatch (London: Macmillan, 1933);

The Letters of Lewis Carroll, edited by Morton Cohen with the assistance of Roger Lancelyn Green, 2 volumes (London: Macmillan/New York: Oxford University Press, 1979).

Bibliographies:

Sidney Herbert Williams, Falconer Madan, Roger Lancelyn Green, and Denis Crutch, *The Lewis Carroll Handbook* (Folkestone, U.K.: Dawson, 1979);

Edward Guiliano, *Lewis Carroll, An Annotated International Bibliography 1960-1977* (Charlottesville: University Press of Virginia/Sussex, U.K.: Harvester Press, 1980).

Biographies:

Derek Hudson, *Lewis Carroll: An Illustrated Biography* (London: Constable, 1976; New York: Potter, 1977);

Anne Clark, *Lewis Carroll: A Biography* (London: Dent/New York: Schocken, 1979).

References:

Nina Auerbach, "Alice and Wonderland, A Curious Child," *Victorian Studies*, 17 (1973): 31-47;

Kathleen Blake, *Play, Games, and Sport: The Literary Works of Lewis Carroll* (Ithaca & London: Cornell University Press, 1974);

Stuart Dodgson Collingwood, comp., *The Life and*

Letters of Lewis Carroll (London: Unwin, 1899);

William Empson, "Alice in Wonderland: The Child as Swain," in *Some Versions of Pastoral* (London: Chatto & Windus/New York: New Directions, 1935);

Martin Gardner, ed., *The Annotated Alice* (New York: Potter, 1960);

Jean Gattégno, *Lewis Carroll: Fragments of a Looking-Glass*, translated by Rosemary Sheed (New York: Crowell, 1976);

Donald J. Gray, "The Uses of Victorian Laughter," *Victorian Studies*, 10 (1966): 145-176;

Edward Guiliano, ed., *Lewis Carroll: A Celebration* (New York: Potter, 1982);

Guiliano, ed., *Lewis Carroll Observed: A Collection of Unpublished Photographs, Drawings, Poetry, and New Essays* (New York: Potter, 1976);

Guiliano and James R. Kincaid, eds., *Soaring with the Dodo: Essays on Lewis Carroll's Life and Art* (Charlottesville: Lewis Carroll Society of North America/University Press of Virginia, 1982);

Alice Hargreaves and Caryl Hargreaves, "Alice's Recollections of Carrollian Days," *Cornhill Magazine*, 73 (1932): 1-12;

Daniel Kirk, *Lewis Carroll, Semeiotician* (Gainesville: University of Florida Press, 1962);

Florence Becker Lennon, *Victoria Through the Looking-Glass* (New York: Simon & Schuster, 1945);

Cornelia Meigs, et al., *A Critical History of Children's Literature: A Survey of Children's Books in English*, revised edition (London: Macmillan, 1969);

Barry Moser, *Illustrations for "Alice in Wonderland"* (Berkeley: University of California Press, 1982);

Graham Ovenden, ed., *The Illustrators of Alice* (London: Academy/New York: St. Martin's, 1972);

George Pitcher, "Wittgenstein, Nonsense, and Lewis Carroll," *Massachusetts Review*, 6 (1965): 591-611;

Robert Phillips, ed., *Aspects of Alice: Lewis Carroll's Dreamchild As Seen Through the Critic's Looking-Glasses 1865-1971* (New York: Vanguard/London: Gollancz, 1971);

Robert M. Polhemus, "Carroll's *Through the Looking-Glass*: The Comedy of Regression," in *Comic Faith: The Great Tradition from Austen to Joyce* (Chicago & London: University of Chicago Press, 1980);

Elizabeth Sewell, *The Field of Nonsense* (London: Chatto & Windus, 1952);

Robert D. Sutherland, *Language and Lewis Carroll*

(The Hague: Mouton, 1970);

Warren Weaver, *Alice in Many Tongues: The Translation of Alice in Wonderland* (Madison: University of Wisconsin Press, 1964).

Papers:

Collections of Lewis Carroll's papers are held at the British Museum; the Castle Arch Museum, Guildford, England; the Christ Church College, Oxford, Library; Harvard University, Houghton Library; the National Portrait Gallery, London, Photographic Division; the New York Public Library, Berg Collection; New York University Library; Pierpont Morgan Library; Princeton University Library, Morris L. Parrish Collection; the Rosenbach Foundation, Philadelphia; and the University of Texas, Austin, Humanities Research Center.

Wilkie Collins

Ira B. Nadel
University of British Columbia

BIRTH: London, 8 January 1824 to William and Harriet Collins.

EDUCATION: Lincoln's Inn (1846-1851).

DEATH: London, 23 September 1889.

SELECTED BOOKS: *Memoirs of the Life of William Collins, Esq., R.A.* (2 volumes, London: Longman, Brown, Green & Longmans, 1848);

Antonina; or, The Fall of Rome (3 volumes, London: Bentley, 1850; 1 volume, New York: Routledge, 1897);

Rambles Beyond Railways; or, Notes in Cornwall Taken A-foot (London: Bentley, 1851);

Basil: A Story of Modern Life (3 volumes, London: Bentley, 1852);

Hide and Seek; or, The Mystery of Mary Grice (3 volumes, London: Bentley, 1854);

After Dark (2 volumes, London: Smith, Elder, 1856);

The Dead Secret (2 volumes, London: Bradbury & Evans, 1857; 1 volume, New York: Fifth Avenue, 1900);

The Queen of Hearts (3 volumes, London: Hurst & Blackett, 1859; 1 volume, New York: Harper, 1859);

The Woman in White (3 volumes, London: Low, Marston, 1860; 1 volume, New York: Harper, 1860);

No Name (3 volumes, London: Low, Marston, 1862; 1 volume, New York: Harper, 1863);

My Miscellanies (2 volumes, London: Low, 1863);

Armadale (2 volumes, London: Smith, Elder, 1866; 1

Wilkie Collins, circa 1851 (Oil Portrait by J. E. Millais at the National Portrait Gallery)

volume, New York: Harper, 1866);

The Moonstone (3 volumes, London: Tinsley, 1868; 1 volume, New York: Harper, 1868);

Black and White, by Collins and Charles Fechter (London: Whiting, 1869);

Man and Wife (3 volumes, London: Ellis, 1870; 1 volume, New York: Harper, 1870);

The Woman in White: A Drama in Prologue and Four Acts (London: Collins, 1871);

Poor Miss Finch: A Novel (3 volumes, London: Bentley, 1872; 1 volume, New York: Harper, 1872);

Miss or Mrs? And Other Stories in Outline (London: Bentley, 1873);

The New Magdalen (2 volumes, London: Bentley, 1873; 1 volume, Toronto: Hunter, Rose, 1873);

The New Magdalen: A Dramatic Story in a Prologue and Three Acts (London: Collins, 1873);

The Frozen Deep and Other Stories (2 volumes, London: Bentley, 1874);

Readings in America (Toronto: Hunter, Rose, 1874);

The Law and the Lady (3 volumes, London: Chatto & Windus, 1875; 1 volume, New York: Harper, 1875);

The Two Destinies (2 volumes, London: Chatto & Windus, 1876; 1 volume, New York: Harper, 1876);

My Lady's Money: An Episode in the Life of a Young Girl (New York: Harper, 1878);

The Haunted Hotel (London: Chatto & Windus, 1878; Toronto: Rose-Belford, 1878);

The Fallen Leaves (3 volumes, London: Chatto & Windus, 1879);

A Rogue's Life: From His Birth to His Marriage (London: Bentley, 1879);

Jezebel's Daughter (3 volumes, London: Chatto & Windus, 1880);

The Black Robe (3 volumes, London: Chatto & Windus, 1881);

Heart and Science (3 volumes, London: Chatto & Windus, 1883);

I Say No (New York: Harper, 1884; 3 volumes, London: Chatto & Windus, 1884);

The Evil Genius: A Domestic Story (3 volumes, London: Chatto & Windus, 1886);

The Guilty River (London: Arrowsmith, 1886; New York: Harper, 1886);

Little Novels (3 volumes, London: Chatto & Windus, 1887);

The Legacy of Cain (3 volumes, London: Chatto & Windus, 1889; 1 volume, New York: National, 1891);

Blind Love, by Collins and Walter Besant (3 volumes, London: Chatto & Windus, 1890; 1 volume, New York: Appleton, 1890).

"Make 'em cry, make 'em laugh, make 'em wait." This adage of Wilkie Collins epitomizes his success as the leading sensation novelist of Victorian England. Combining expert plotting with carefully described settings, Collins's novels define the excitement, attraction, and fascination with sensation fiction which had such a great impact on the reading public of the 1860s. Uniting a background in art with a legal education and a love of drama, Collins fashioned novels of immense popularity that resulted in his prominence as a literary celebrity. His estimated income of over £10,000 for 1862-1863 established a record for the highest yearly income of any writer of the nineteenth century, according to his most recent biographer. But more importantly, his development of the English detective novel initiated a tradition of extraordinary and continued appeal. His two classic examples of suspense and detection, *The Woman in White* (1860) and *The Moonstone* (1868), remain outstanding models of English crime fiction. Employing finely tuned plots, vivid descriptions, multiple narrative styles, and dramatic language, they have received critical praise from such writers as T. S. Eliot, Dorothy Sayers, and Julian Symons. Wilkie Collins was a novelist who took as his basic goal "the old-fashioned opinion that the primary object of a work of fiction should be to tell a story," as he stated in the preface to *The Woman in White*. But balancing his commitment to story was his realization that "not one man in ten thousand, living in the midst of reality, has discovered that he is also living in the midst of romance." The ambiguity of a reality which is both factual and mysterious is the foundation of his fictional world where crime lies hidden beneath the surface of the everyday. His world, as Dickens commented, is "wild yet domestic."

The studio life of the nineteenth-century artist provided a stimulating environment for the young William Wilkie Collins, eldest son of the respected and successful landscape painter William Collins, R.A., whose patrons included Sir Robert Peel and Lord Liverpool. Exhibitions, painting trips, celebrity visits, and drawing became common for the soon-to-be successful writer. Named after his godfather, the well-known painter Sir David Wilkie, R.A., Wilkie Collins studied painting for several years. At the age of twelve, he accompanied his family during a twenty-two-month sojourn to France and Italy, learning Italian to absorb the cultural and artistic life more thoroughly. Upon his return in 1838, he resumed his schooling but, shortly before his seventeenth birthday, decided against a career in the church or the study of classics at Oxford or mathematics at Cambridge in favor of a career in commerce. In 1841, he began as an apprentice in the tea trade at the London firm of Antrobus and Company, although he maintained his involvement with art, accompanying his father on painting tours to Scotland and the Shetland Islands. Bored by the tea trade, however, Collins began to write and had his first signed story published in Douglas Jerrold's *Illuminated Magazine* in August 1843: "The Last Stage Coachman" described the replacement of the stagecoach by the railroad. While in the tea business, Collins also wrote his first novel, set in Tahiti; it is now lost. In a letter he records that no British publisher would accept it.

Undaunted, Collins began to write a historical novel using his knowledge of Italy, setting the work in fifth-century Rome and focusing on the Gothic invasion. Visits to Paris, as well as his father's poor health, however, distracted Collins from his writing and interrupted his faltering commercial career. With his father's permission, Collins resigned in May 1846 to read law at Lincoln's Inn. He also reconsidered a career as a painter, which culminated in his showing a single painting at the Royal Academy in 1848. In February 1847, his father died and Collins put aside his historical novel to write a biography of him, long his father's wish. The two-volume *Memoirs of the Life of William Collins, Esq., R.A.* appeared in November 1848, dedicated to the former prime minister, Sir Robert Peel. Following the Victorian practice of biography, the work provides a detailed but uncritical account of his father's life with precise descriptions of his major paintings. The work was an apprenticeship for Collins's skill in landscape description and scene writing and, because of its accuracy and detail, was an admirable first book for the twenty-four-year-old writer. The reviews were generous and the sales respectable: within six weeks of publication more than half of the edition of 750 copies was sold.

Collins returned to work on the manuscript of his historical novel, encouraged by the reception of his father's biography. In mid-1848, he completed a revision of *Antonina; or, The Fall of Rome* and had it accepted by Richard Bentley, who published it in February 1850. With violence, mayhem, and villainy, the novel attempted, in the manner of Bulwer-Lytton, to recreate fifth-century Italy besieged by the Visigoths. Despite its complex plot, alien setting, and flamboyant style, reviewers reacted positively to the romance, calling it "a

richly-colored impassioned story, busy with life, importunately strong in its appeals to our sympathy." As a result of the biography and novel, Collins achieved the status of a minor celebrity.

A walking tour through Cornwall in the summer of 1850 became the focus of his third book, *Rambles Beyond Railways* (1851). In the company of a young artist friend, H. C. Branling, Collins sought to explore a world of traditional country life and customs. The book is a compendium of facts and details, anticipating the accuracy in describing events he was later to stress in his mature fiction. Local superstitions as well as graphic landscape descriptions fill the volume which was also a modest success with the reading public.

Rambles Beyond Railways appeared in January 1851; in March, Collins met Charles Dickens and the course of his literary career was altered. The mutual interest of Dickens and Collins in amateur theatricals was the initial reason for their association. Collins's pleasure in private theatricals and acting originated in his early friendship and juvenile productions with the painter E. M. Ward and others at his mother's home in Blandford Square, events which partially form chapters five and six of his novel *No Name* (1862). In February 1850, Collins had appeared on a public stage in a Soho theater when he played the lead in a French

Pencil sketch of Wilkie Collins by his father, William Collins (Collection of Douglas Ewing)

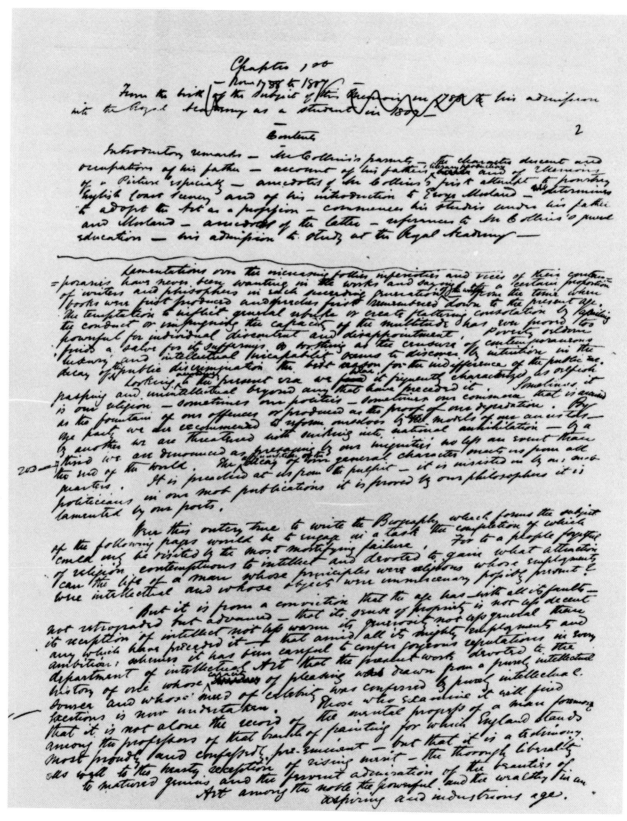

A page from the manuscript of Collins's biography of his father (Parke Bernet–1 December 1947)

play he translated and titled *A Court Duel*. Dickens, through the painter Augustus Egg, invited Collins to play the role of valet in Bulwer-Lytton's comedy, *Not So Bad As We Seem*, performed in May 1851 at Devonshire House in the presence of the queen and prince consort for the Guild of Literature and Art. So successful was the production that it was presented intermittently in London through the summer and, beginning in the fall of 1852, toured the major English cities with a cast that included Dickens, Mark Lemon (one of the founders of *Punch*), Douglas Jerrold, and, later, Egg and Collins.

When he met Dickens, Collins was twenty-seven—twelve years younger than the acclaimed author. Their friendship lasted almost twenty years and grew in intimacy through the 1860s, although they drew apart in about 1868 until a reconciliation occurred shortly before Dickens's death. When they met, Dickens had recently published *David Copperfield* (1849-1850), and was busy as editor of *Household Words*, which he had founded two years earlier, in addition to producing and acting in amateur theatricals and giving occasional reading tours. His prodigious energy soon began to affect Collins, who shortly afterward started to contribute to *Household Words*; his first publication there was a short story entitled "A Terribly Strange Bed," a Poe-like narrative of a four-poster bed designed to smother its occupants. The story initiated the fascination with the macabre and sensational aspects of everyday life that was to characterize his later writing. In 1856, at the age of thirty-two, Collins was appointed as a regular writer for *Household Words* and, as a sign of his attachment to Dickens, had all but one of his novels of the sixties appear first in Dickens's new journal, *All the Year Round*.

But what most completely united the two writers was the theater. Following the success of *Not So Bad As We Seem*, Collins moved up to share the lead as "Shadowy Softhead . . . Friend and Double to Lord Wilmot," played by Dickens. The description was prophetic. In January 1857, the two starred before the duke of Devonshire and the lord chief justice in their most famous play, *The Frozen Deep*, written by Collins with assistance from Dickens. This melodrama narrating the competing loves of two Arctic explorers ends with a climactic scene of the older hero, Richard Wardour, played by Dickens, sacrificing himself in the rescue of the younger, Frank Aldersley, played by Collins. The older dramatically carries the younger explorer to safety and to the woman they both love, who waits on the shores of Newfoundland. The scene suggests not only the nature of their relationship—Dickens protecting the developing career of Collins—but indicates the commitment of Collins to the theatrically startling and dramatic. Collins repeatedly adapted techniques of the theater to his fiction and, conversely, succeeded in dramatizing his novels for the stage. He was as much influenced by the melodramas of Dumas and Soulie which he saw in Paris, often in the company of Dickens, as he was by the Gothic novels he often read. At a rehearsal of the professional tour of *The Frozen Deep* in August 1857, Dickens first met Ellen Ternan, the eighteen-year-old actress with whom he was soon to fall in love.

Collins makes clear his strong attachment to the theater in the preface to the novel he was writing when he met Dickens, *Basil: A Story of Modern Life* (1852): "Believing that the Novel and the Play are twin-sisters in the family of Fiction; that the one is a drama narrated, as the other is drama acted; and that all the strong and deep emotions which the Play-writer is privileged to excite, the Novel-writer is privileged to excite also, I have not thought it either politic or necessary, while adhering to realities, to adhere to every-day realities only." Dickens responded to a presentation copy of the novel—about a young man's infatuation with a girl of inferior social position—with encouraging but not uncritical words, noting that the events in the story were highly unlikely, although he praised the writing and discrimination of character. He did not, however, comment on Collins's most important innovation, to be used later in his best works: the accumulation and synthesis into the narrative of private records such as journals and letters by various characters.

Balancing contributions to *Household Words* with a growing personal attachment to Dickens, Collins continued to flourish in the 1850s. He continued his law career and was called to the bar in November 1851, but he never practiced, preferring to maintain an identity with artists and authors with whom he cultivated numerous friendships started in his youth. Among his new friends was Edward Lear, who in 1855 attended a bachelor dinner given by Collins for the soon-to-be-married painter J. E. Millais (he was about to marry Effie Gray, whose six-year marriage to John Ruskin had been annulled in the summer of 1854). Lear and Collins remained lifelong friends, a fact noted by Lear's remark that he was frequently mistaken for Collins. During the 1850s, however, Collins's health began to deteriorate and in 1856 he had three periods of prolonged sickness that presaged the painful bouts of gout that were shortly and continuously to afflict him. However, the fifties were a time of great productivity for Collins: his short stories were collected in *After Dark* (1856) and *The Queen of Hearts* (1859); two novels appeared, *Hide and Seek* (1854) and *The Dead Secret* (1857); while various collaborations with Dickens began to be published regularly in *Household Words*. These included *The Lazy Tour of Two Idle Apprentices* and *The Perils of Certain English Prisoners*, published as Christmas extras.

Among Collins's own short stories that appeared during this period was a five-part novelette entitled *A Rogue's Life* (published in 1856 in *Household Words*; appeared in book form in 1879) with its master criminal, Dr. Dulcifer, prefiguring the suave but dangerous Count Fosco of *The Woman in White*. In "Anne Rodway," a short story from *The Queen of Hearts*, Collins published his first murder mystery, notable for its narrative technique since it is told completely in excerpts from a diary as the heroine tries to prove that her friend's "accidental" death was murder. Dickens admired the story tremendously. "The Biter Bit," from the same collection, tells—again in extracts, this time from letters exchanged by three policemen—of an amateur detective's bungling of his first case; it, too, anticipates the method of Collins's two later crime classics. By June 1857, the journalist and critic Edmund Yates could write in his periodical, the *Train*, that Collins ranked fourth among contemporary novelists after Dickens, Thackeray, and Charlotte Brontë. Such praise marked the growing popularity of Collins as a writer; and his next novel, *The Woman in White*, initiated a decade of extraordinary personal success for Collins. But that achievement followed his one clear-cut failure, his play *The Red Vial*, which opened in October 1858. The awakening of a supposed corpse in a morgue climaxed what all believed to be an outlandish and tedious play. Twenty years later, Collins rewrote the play as a novel, *Jezebel's Daughter* (1880); as a result of the play's failure, however, Collins for the next twelve years devoted himself almost exclusively to writing fiction.

During a moonlit night in the area of Regent's Park in early 1859, Collins, his younger brother Charles, and J. E. Millais were, in the words of Millais's biographer,

> suddenly arrested by a piercing scream coming from the garden of a villa close at hand. It was evidently the cry of a woman in distress; and while pausing to consider what they

should do, the iron gate leading to the garden was dashed open, and from it came the figure of a young and very beautiful woman dressed in flowing white robes that shone in the moonlight. She seemed to float rather than run in their direction, and, on coming up to the three young men, she paused for a moment in an attitude of supplication and terror. Then, suddenly seeming to recollect herself, she suddenly moved on and vanished in the shadows cast upon the road.

> "What a lovely woman!" was all Millais could say. "I must see who she is, and what is the matter," said Wilkie Collins, as, without a word, he dashed after her.

This unexpected encounter was not only the model for the opening scene of *The Woman in White*, but the beginning of Collins's intimate relationship with the woman, Caroline Graves, who had been fleeing a threatening man who kept her prisoner. She subsequently became Collins's mistress.

Fascinated by mental and physical imprisonment as well as by infirmity, Collins made all three important elements of dramatic action in *The Woman in White*. A passage from a letter written during a visit to Paris in 1856 anticipates his interest in asylums, which have a significant role in the novel. From his apartment window he describes the scene below: "A sober brown omnibus, belonging to a Sanitary Asylum . . . is full of patients getting their airing. I can see them dimly, and I fall into curious fancies about their various cases, and wonder what proportion of the afflicted passengers are near the time of emancipation from their sanitary prison on wheels." This interest in things medical and mental has a powerful fascination for Collins throughout his writing, although in *The Woman in White* and *The Moonstone* it achieves its most effective presentation.

The prominence of Collins among Victorian writers and readers might be said to have started on 29 November 1859, when the first installment of *The Woman in White* appeared in *All the Year Round*, Dickens's new weekly periodical. Applying a sensational melodrama to the background of middle-class Victorian life, first attempted in *Basil*, and then joining it to the mystery he proposed in *Hide and Seek* and the characterization and humor of *The Dead Secret*, Collins created a novel of startling impact and commercial success. Having started *All the Year Round* with the serialization of *A Tale of Two Cities*, Dickens needed an appropriate successor to maintain readership. He turned to his close friend Wilkie Collins, who was completing a novel partly

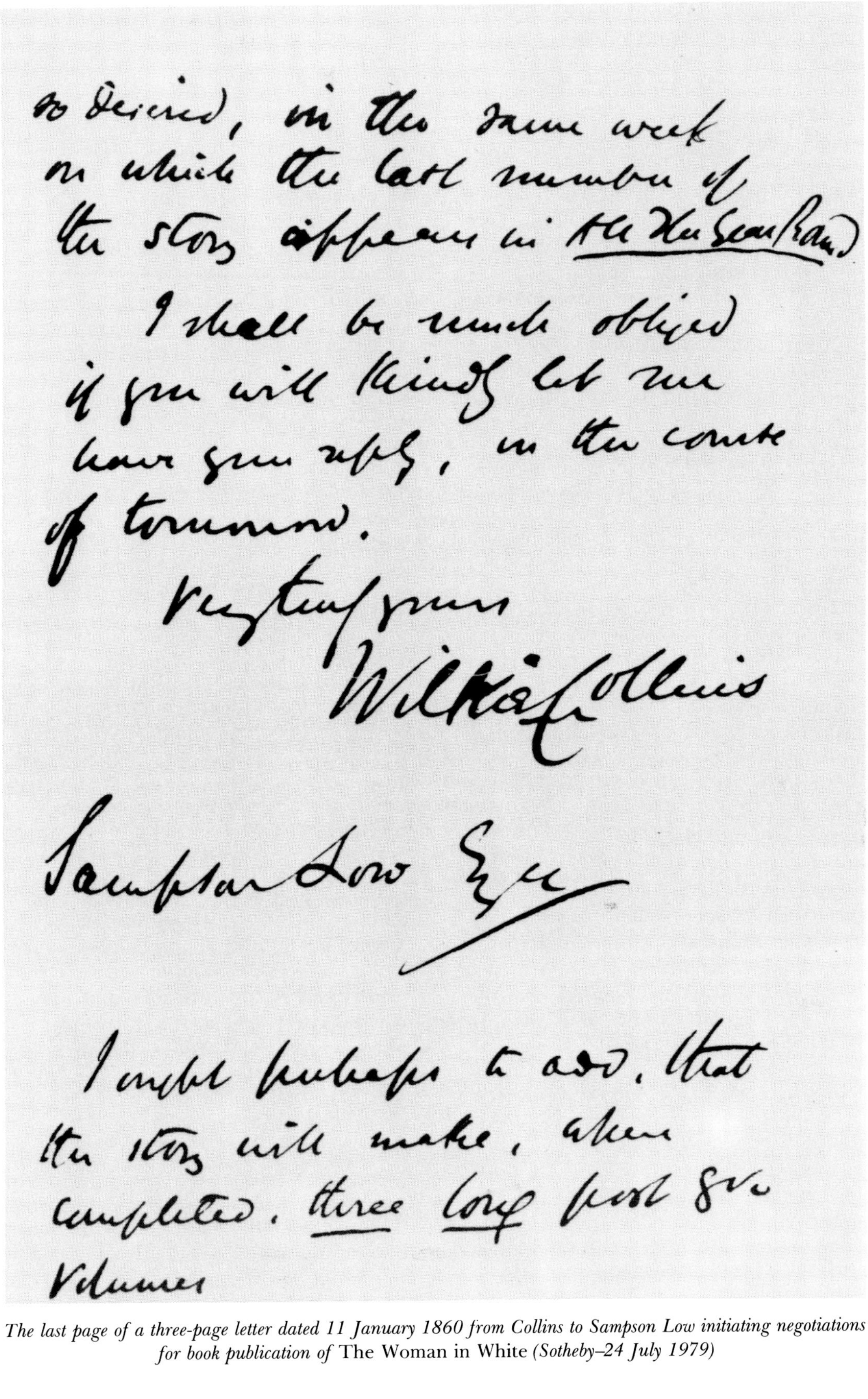

*so desired, in the same week
on which the last number of
the story appears in* All the Year Round

*I shall be much obliged
if you will kindly let me
have your reply, in the course
of tomorrow.*

Very truly yours

Wilkie Collins

Sampson Low Esq

*I ought perhaps to add, that
the story will make, when
completed, three long post 8vo
Volumes*

*The last page of a three-page letter dated 11 January 1860 from Collins to Sampson Low initiating negotiations
for book publication of* The Woman in White *(Sotheby–24 July 1979)*

originating in an incident reported in Maurice Méjan's *Recueil des Causes Célèbres*. Enroute to Paris to press charges against a brother who unscrupulously prevented her from an inheritance, a young woman was drugged, confined to a mental hospital, and declared dead. She escaped from the asylum wearing a white dress, but could not reestablish her legal identity and died penniless. These events, plus the accidental meeting with Caroline Graves in London, form the basic plot of *The Woman in White*, composed between August 1859 and July 1860.

The novel begins with a young drawing master, Walter Hartright, assuming a new post in Cumberland at Limmeridge House as art tutor to the blonde Laura Fairlie and her dark half sister, Marian Halcombe, both cared for by their hypochondriacal uncle, Frederick Fairlie. The night before he leaves for Cumberland, Walter encounters a mysterious woman in white reentering London. He accompanies her to the edge of the city, only to learn afterward that she has had some acquaintance with the Fairlies and that she has just escaped from an asylum. (Dickens bracketed this scene with the march of the women to Versailles in *The French Revolution*, 1837, by Carlyle as the two most dramatic moments in English literature.) At Limmeridge House Walter confides the details of his mysterious meeting with the woman in white to Marian Halcombe and they quickly guess her identity as Anne Catherick, a woman similar in appearance to the attractive Laura. In the graveyard at Limmeridge, Walter again meets the woman in white, mysteriously cleaning the gravestone of Laura's mother. In conversation with Walter, she creates suspicions over the behavior of Sir Percival Glyde, soon to marry Laura. Walter, himself in love with Laura, reluctantly leaves Limmeridge House after an emotional parting with Laura, who intends to continue with her marriage plans despite the mystery surrounding Sir Percival and the unanswered questions concerning the woman in white.

Marian Halcombe pursues the investigation and learns from Sir Percival that Anne Catherick, daughter of a woman in service to his family, required institutionalization; he produces a letter from Anne's mother to corroborate the details. The marriage between Sir Percival and Laura takes place, but upon their return from the honeymoon to live at Blackwater Park, an unsettling mood takes over. Marian, now living with them, notices this change; and the sudden appearance of the corpulent Count Fosco, husband to Laura's aunt, compli-

cates the situation while increasing her anxiety. Count Fosco, one of Collins's greatest inventions, is an urbane, intelligent, eccentric villain with a fondness for animals, good food, and his rival for power and knowledge, Marian Halcombe. Fosco and Sir Percival attempt to defraud Laura of a sizable fortune, but her refusal to sign a document until it can be studied halts their plan. As fear and suspense overtake Blackwater Park, Laura accidentally meets Anne Catherick and learns the secret involving Anne, Laura's mother, and Sir Percival. In reaction to discovering Laura's meeting with Anne, Sir Percival imprisons Laura and Marian and plans their murders. Both women become ill, but when Laura recovers, she is told that Marian has left for London. Before she realizes the lie, Laura is drugged by Count Fosco while searching for Marian in London, falsely declared insane, dressed in the clothes of Anne Catherick, and taken to the asylum from which Anne had escaped. Meanwhile, Sir Percival has discovered Anne near Blackwater and plans her murder, but she suddenly dies while in London; he cleverly falsifies her identity and buries her as "Laura, Lady Glyde."

The recovered Marian is told her sister is dead, but she does not believe it; seeking Anne in the asylum, she discovers the missing Laura and they arrange an escape. They return to Limmeridge to announce Laura's identity to their uncle but he does not believe them nor recognize his niece. In anger they leave and at the false grave of "Laura, Lady Glyde" encounter Walter, recently returned from Central America. His love for Laura renewed, Walter begins a quest to restore her true identity and proper position in the Fairlie family. Through accident and a parish register, he learns that Sir Percival is an impostor and that he is a baronet by fraud. In an effort to protect himself, Sir Percival sets fire to the church vestry, but is trapped in the burning building and dies. Mrs. Catherick, however, confirms that Laura's father, Mr. Philip Fairlie, had also been father to the illegitimate Anne. To clear Laura and reassert her identity, Walter returns to London to confront Count Fosco. With the aid of his old drawing instructor, Professor Pesca, Walter forces Fosco to reveal himself as a traitor to a secret Italian political society. Soon to be killed, the count confesses his complicity in the conspiracy to murder Laura and provides proof that she was still alive when Anne was buried as Lady Glyde. The novel concludes when Frederick Fairlie finally accepts the evidence of Laura's identity. At last, Walter and Laura marry—but only after Collins pro-

Drawing of Count Fosco from the first American edition of
The Woman in White

quirks and eccentricities that make them memorable. The overweight Count Fosco, whose pet mice "live in a little pagoda of gaily-painted wire-work, designed and made by himself," is a perfect example. His little pets perpetually crawl all over him, "popping in and out of his waistcoast," providing a complex figure of great appetites with a colossal paradox: a delicate sensibility and appreciation of animals combined with an evil and immoral mind. His equal in the novel, Marian Halcombe, is similarly engaging through her assertiveness, intellect, and "blunt, matter-of-fact nature" which the count admires. Even the honorable Walter Hartright is absorbing as he embodies those English virtues which combat fraudulent aristocrats and Continental deceivers. Collins furthermore establishes the convincing atmosphere necessary for the sensation novel, an atmosphere that makes the melodramatic incidents of plot appear inevitable. In this novel, scenic description and drama unite.

In his essay "How I Write My Books," published twenty-seven years after *The Woman in White*, Collins explains that the "destruction" of the heroine's identity "represents a first division of the story; the recovery of her identity marks a second division." The substitution of identities and their proper restoration are the central themes of the novel; the narrative style, characterization, and action—plus a plot complex enough to bear the suspense and fatality created by the action—account for its success. And unlike his previous novels where the villain was killed off (as in *Basil*) or revealed (as in *The Dead Secret*), too early, *The Woman in White* does not collapse at the end; instead, a constant succession of mysteries continues to unravel. The evenly matched antagonists, Fosco and Marian, Sir Percival and Walter, also provide a balance of tension and action.

The popularity of *The Woman in White* was immense and immediately propelled Collins forward as the leading writer of the time. On the day of publication each week, crowds surrounded the offices of *All the Year Round* waiting for the next installment of the story. Circulation of the magazine surpassed that set by *A Tale of Two Cities*. Within two months of the novel's publication in mid-August 1860, five editions were printed and by February 1861 seven editions had appeared. Perfumes, cloaks, bonnets, toiletries, and even waltzes labeled "Woman in White" capitalized on the success of the novel. (In 1871 Collins was himself to do so, successfully adapting the novel to the stage.) The praise of Thackeray, Edward Fitzgerald, Charles Reade,

vides a chilling description of the count lying in the Paris morgue before the eyes of the curious public.

The qualities that make *The Woman in White* so successful begin with its well-ordered but complex plot, where revelations lead to more questions and secrets to new discoveries. Yet, at the end, all is fully explained. Additionally, the experimental narrative style that allows various characters to tell the story insures reader interest, suspense, and development of character. Multiple narrators, writes Collins, "Forced me to keep the story constantly moving forward" and allowed the characters new opportunities to express themselves. It also prevented the secrets from being known too readily as the confusion of the narrators equals that of the reader. Collins renders his characters vividly, stressing the

Mrs. Oliphant, Gladstone, and Prince Albert, as well as Dickens, enhanced Collins's popularity and stature.

But as Collins's public life became the object of greater attention, his private life became more unorthodox. Except for an infatuation with a married woman three times his age when he was twelve, Collins had no serious involvement with women until 1859, when he pursued Caroline Graves. For a number of years she was his mistress, but he refused to marry her. In response she left Collins's household and married Joseph Clow, a plumber; the wedding took place on 4 October 1868, with Collins as a witness. At about the same time, he began a relationship with Martha Rudd, later known as Mrs. Dawson; in the next five years, she bore Collins three illegitimate children, two daughters and a son. The name in the registry of the father for the children is Collins's alias, "William Dawson, Barrister." He did, however, acknowledge the children in his will, and to his friends he often referred to his "morganatic family." Caroline Graves's marriage, however, did not succeed and she returned to Collins in the early 1870s, living with him as Mrs. Graves until his death in 1889. Of the two women, she exerted the greater influence. He adopted her daughter Harriet, who became his secretary and later married his solicitor. Supporting two illegitimate households and caring for three illegitimate children provided Collins with a private life outside the mainstream of Victorian domesticity throughout the remainder of his career. Yet his announced bachelorhood and independent style of living enhanced his reputation, in contrast to the scandal caused by Dickens's leaving his wife in the spring of 1858. The composition, publication, and success of *The Woman in White* coincided with the major changes and adjustments in the private life of Collins.

The decade following *The Woman in White* saw Collins's literary maturity, financial security, and social prominence increase. He frequented the musical Saturday afternoons of George Eliot and G. H. Lewes, spent weekends with Monckton Milnes, became a confident and much-requested after-dinner speaker. He also furthered his gourmet tastes by studying French cooking but explained to his friend Frederick Lehmann that "my style is expensive. I look on meat simply as a material for sauces." In January 1861, he resigned from the staff of *All the Year Round* and was hard at work on *No Name* (1862), his next novel. Expanding the social themes that earlier novels had referred

to—such as the fever hospitals in *Basil*, abuse of religious instruction in *Hide and Seek*, or the lack of public control over the asylums in *The Woman in White*—Collins focused on a new issue: the social and legal implications of illegitimacy. The story of Magdalen Vanstone's efforts to regain control of her father's fortune, now in the hands of her sickly cousin Noel Vanstone, involves problems of common-law marriage, the theater, and family plotting, issues that clearly reflected the concerns of Collins's private life. A scoundrel again created a large reader interest: Captain Wragge, an impudent, articulate, and well-educated swindler in constant combat with Mrs. Lecount, a woman fascinated by reptiles and science. However, the less definite lines of good and evil, less original plot, absence of mystery (Collins writes here with anticipation but not surprise), and explicit social criticism kept the book from equaling the success of *The Woman in White*.

No Name also did not please readers because of its conventional and epistolary narrative style, although the book temporarily rescued the falling sales of *All the Year Round*. Reviewers praised the storytelling skill but objected to the criticism of Victorian morality, especially the implicit approval of common-law marriage and the happy ending for Magdalen Vanstone after a career of deception. Dickens, however, thought the book better than *The Woman in White*. A hiatus in writing followed, but Collins kept his name in public view by publishing a collection of his journalistic pieces, *My Miscellanies* (1863). Bouts of illness and uncertain health, however, began to affect him seriously and he spent many months in Germany and Italy with Caroline Graves and her daughter. Upon returning to England in 1864, he began a new novel.

Armadale (1866) does not continue the social criticism of *No Name*. It explores, instead, the guilt associated with "Allan Armadale," a name shared by two men, although only one has true claim to it. The labyrinthine plot begins with the father of one young man confessing on his deathbed the murder of the father of another young man. The son of the murderer assumes the name "Ozias Midwinter"; his opposite falsely assumes the name of "Allan Armadale." "Ozias Midwinter" denies his true name (Allan Armadale) while struggling against the fatalism of a prophetic dream suggesting violence against the false Armadale. Lydia Gwilt, the missing maid of the true Allan Armadale's mother, returns after a life of crime including forgery, theft, adultery, and murder, and complicates an intended inheritance for the false Armadale through various criminal deeds. She is a quintessential sensationalist heroine, combining restraint and passion, gentility and hatred. But despite two attempts to murder the ineffectual and false Armadale, and a deceptive marriage to Ozias Midwinter, Lydia gallantly saves Midwinter from death before she commits suicide. Spying is the main occupation of the characters in the novel, including Jemmy Bashwood, a private detective. Fatalism, guilt, and expiation unite in *Armadale* to create a densely organized, thematically rich book.

Dreams play a prominent role in *Armadale*. Mr. Hawbury, a physician and dream analyst, provides an advanced theory for Midwinter: "A dream is the reproduction, in the sleeping state of the brain, of images and impressions produced on it in the waking state; and this reproduction is more or less involved . . . as the action of certain faculties in the dreamer is controlled more or less completely by the influence of sleep." These ideas were to be developed in *The Moonstone* (1868) and associated with the problem of sleepwalking and involuntary action. Dreams, behavior, and science are constant and important subjects in Collins's writing. *Armadale* took Collins longer to write than any other of his novels and is his largest book. The novel, however, was not a literary or critical success, straining, as it did, the sensationalist method. The prophetic dream of the hero at the opening becomes the sustained and even tedious outline of the entire complex plot. Swinburne and more recently, T. S. Eliot, however, thought favorably of the work while recognizing its limitations. With his novel finished and a production of *The Frozen Deep* performing in London, Collins went again to Italy before beginning his second major achievement, *The Moonstone*.

Early in 1867, Collins began to plan his eighth novel. He showed several installments to Dickens, who praised the "curious story, wild and yet domestic, with excellent character in it, and great mystery." But throughout the fall of 1867, Collins and Dickens became involved with one of their Christmas numbers published as *No Thoroughfare*; their collaboration brought them closer together than they had been for several years. Dickens then left for America and Collins returned to writing *The Moonstone*. But as he settled down to write the novel, Collins's mother became gravely ill. Worried over her impending death, he continued with the writing, although his own health weakened and he suffered from painful attacks of rheumatic gout requiring large doses of laudanum. In March, his

mother died, and his pains intensified as the disease worsened. In the preface to the revised edition, Collins recounts the difficulty and physical sacrifice required to compose the novel: only at intervals free from pain and grief was he able to dictate it, writing being too painful an exercise. (Virtually all of Miss Clack's narrative was written under these conditions.) In January 1868, the novel began to appear in *All the Year Round* and marked the return of Collins to Dickens's journal.

The plot of *The Moonstone* involves the mysterious Hindu diamond stolen by Colonel Herncastle in the battle of Seringapatam. He bequeaths the jewel to his niece, Rachel Verinder, on her eighteenth birthday. The diamond arrives at the Yorkshire estate of the Verinders in the care of Franklin Blake, a cosmopolitan young Englishman educated in Europe. At the same time, three Hindus disguised as jugglers appear in the neighborhood apparently in pursuit of the diamond. Franklin falls in love with Rachel but their idyll is disrupted by the disappearance of the diamond the morning after its presentation at a birthday dinner. Among the guests is the local physician and an Indian explorer, Mr. Murthwaite. The police arrive, led first by the officious and inadequate Superintendent Seegrave, and then by the renowned Sergeant Cuff, one of Collins's finest creations.

The opposite of Seegrave in every respect, Cuff is "a grizzled, elderly man, . . . miserably lean . . . dressed all in decent black . . . He might have been a parson, or an undertaker—or anything else you like, except what he really was"—one of England's most successful if unassuming detectives. Cuff proceeds to investigate the crime and after initial suspicions that Rachel herself stole the diamond, he concentrates on the disfigured Rosanna Spearman, a maidservant who has a criminal record and who is infatuated with Franklin. Tracing her to the Shivering Sands, an area of dangerous quicksand, Cuff deduces that something valuable is buried in the shallow waters; but before he can act, Rosanna commits suicide. Continued suspicions of Rachel's involvement, however, cause Cuff to be dismissed from the case, much to the satisfaction of Gabriel Betteredge, the elderly servant whose narrative begins the novel and who gradually falls victim to what he comically calls "the infernal detective fever." Betteredge is also a disciple of *Robinson Crusoe* and studies the book fervently.

Rachel becomes engaged to the philanthropist Godfrey Ablewhite, who soon proves himself to be untrustworthy. Franklin, who has been traveling, returns and, after seeing Rosanna's letter to him in which she made clear her love, recovers a box from the quicksand—only to discover his own paint-stained nightshirt, a crucial piece of evidence. Unable to explain the stolen nightshirt, Franklin suggests to the Verinder family lawyer, Mr. Bruff, that the jewel was somehow removed to a London bank. In a surprise meeting, Rachel tells Franklin she actually saw *him* remove the diamond from her room! Declaring his innocence but unable to prove it, Franklin returns to the Verinder estate and, with the aid of physician's assistant Ezra Jennings, learns that a doctor had secretly given him a dose of laudanum after an unsympathetic remark about medicine at the birthday dinner. The reaction to the drug and Franklin's worry over the diamond caused his unusual behavior. To prove his hypothesis and Franklin's innocence, Ezra Jennings restages the crime in the presence of witnesses. Franklin duplicates the theft but leaves unexplained how the diamond left the Verinder estate. Sergeant Cuff reenters and, as the scene moves to London, has a sailor followed after he visits the suspected bank. Breaking into a room rented by the sailor, Cuff and Franklin discover him dead—in disguise—and the diamond missing. The mystery partially explained but not solved, Rachel and Franklin restate their love and marry, learning several years later from Murthwaite, the Indian explorer, that the Moonstone has been rightfully restored to the moon god in India.

In the words of T. S. Eliot, *The Moonstone* is "the first, the longest, and the best of the modern English detective novels," an opinion echoed by Dorothy L. Sayers. Yet Collins's detective is wrong, only partially solves the case, and disappears for the major portion of the novel. The mystery is, in fact, solved in parts throughout the novel by a series of amateur detectives, the most important of whom are Franklin Blake and Ezra Jennings. Nonetheless, a number of conventions appear which became prototypes for later detective novels, including the unimpressive physical but outstanding mental qualities of the detective. The effort to reconstruct the crime scientifically and the summary explanation before the assembled suspects are also techniques used in later crime stories. Anticipating Agatha Christie's Hercule Poirot, who remarks that when a detail in solving a case "is completely unimportant that is why it is so interesting," Cuff declares that "in all my experience along the dirtiest ways of this dirty little world, I have never met with such a

thing as a trifle yet." The incompetent local police, shifting suspects, successful amateurs, and the sharing of clues with the reader are all features of modern detective fiction derived from *The Moonstone*. With the failure of logic to solve the crime, the subconscious is brought into play as the key to the solution.

Combined with its multiple narrative style, vivid descriptive sections, and engrossing characters, from the comic Miss Clack and Betteredge to the mysterious traveler Mr. Murthwaite and the secretive Ezra Jennings, *The Moonstone* sustains a suspenseful world of prolonged drama and revelation. The subject, divorced from social themes as found in *No Name*; the settings, more limited than in *Armadale* or *The Woman in White*; the plot, simpler than in Collins's earlier books, all display the fullest talents of Collins as a writer. The themes of the novel, such as English imperial aggression versus Indian self-determination, combine with the power of the unconscious to create a world very unlike the stereotype of the nineteenth century. Betteredge senses the contradiction: "here was our quiet English house suddenly invaded by a devilish Indian Diamond—bringing after it a conspiracy of living rogues, set loose on us by the vengeance of a dead man. . . . Who ever heard the like of it—in the nineteenth century, mind; in an age of progress, and in a country which rejoices in the blessings of the British constitution?" Surprise is everywhere in the novel, including the unique conception of making one of the narrators and the novel's hero the thief. Part of the originality of *The Moonstone* is in its focus on how the crime was committed and not on the capture of the criminal.

Only the extraordinary reception of *The Woman in White* exceeded that of *The Moonstone*. Willington Street in front of the offices of *All the Year Round* was thronged with eager readers as the weekly parts appeared. Dickens seems to have been affected by the novel and its technique; he incorporated a diary, the use of opium, an oriental atmosphere, a satire of philanthropy, and the practice of ending chapters on a suspenseful note in his last, unfinished novel, *The Mystery of Edwin Drood*, which appeared two years after *The Moonstone*. Collins—in his effort to trace "the influence of character on circumstances," as he wrote in the preface to *The Moonstone*—created a work that linked the sensational novel with the detective thriller.

Man and Wife (1870), the last major novel published by Collins, was begun during a period of upheaval in his private life as Caroline Graves left

Wilkie Collins, circa 1878

him to marry Joseph Clow, although her sixteen-year-old daughter chose to remain with Collins. *Man and Wife* concentrates on athleticism and the rigidity of marriage laws in England, Ireland, and Scotland. The result is a thesis novel, as the tone of this rhetorical passage illustrates: "Will his [the hero's] skill in rowing . . . his swiftness in running, his admirable capacity and endurance in other physical exercise, help him to win a purely moral victory over his own selfishness and his own cruelty?" The answer is clearly no! The complicated plot involves Geoffrey Delamayn, an athlete who seduces the heroine, then tries to leave her while he pursues a Scottish heiress. Murder seems the only solution, but at the end of the novel, Delamayn's plan backfires and he is killed, the victim of brandy

and the vengeance of an elderly woman: "The homicidal frenzy possessed her. She flew at his throat like a wild beast. The feeble old woman attacked the athlete! . . . Hester Dethridge pounced on his prostrate body—knelt on his broad chest—and fastened her ten fingers on his throat." In the novel, Sir Patrick Lundie expresses Collins's disdain for the excesses of athleticism and its effect on the morals of England: "There is far too much glorification in England, just now, of the mere physical qualities which an Englishman shares with the savage and the brute. And the ill results are beginning to show themselves already!" The attack on marriage laws in the book centers on their need for standardization and the importance of redefining the property rights of women. Critics found the novel worthy and praised it more highly than any other book by Collins except *The Woman in White*. But by 1870, Collins's work began to decline and in the remaining nineteen years of his life he never regained the commercial or artistic success of the 1860s. The reasons are varied and begin with the death of Dickens, his mentor, editor, and friend.

The Collins-Dickens association was a unique display of Victorian attachment between writers that created both a literary apprenticeship and a personal intimacy rarely matched in the period. Dickens clearly provided Collins with the encouragement, outlets, and support that sustained and advanced his writing. "Nobody," wrote Collins, "(my poor dear mother excepted, of course) felt so positively sure of the future before me in Literature, as Dickens did." Dickens advised, edited, negotiated publishing arrangements, and reinforced attitudes toward novel writing that Collins put forward. As critic and teacher to the younger writer, Dickens was invaluable. Collins, however, did not always assent to Dickens's suggestions. He refused to make Mr. Pendril comic in *No Name* and rejected the twenty-seven titles for the book suggested by Dickens in favor of his own. He similarly refused Dickens's offer to return from Paris to continue work on the novel when Collins's health threatened to prevent him from carrying on. But Collins did follow Dickens's technical and compositional advice designed to sustain reader interest, altering his tendencies to stretch probability, and to affront readers while dictating their responses. "I always contest your disposition to give an audience credit for nothing, which necessarily involves the forcing of points on their attention," Dickens wrote to Collins in commenting on *The Woman in White*. Following the death of Dickens in June 1870, Collins's novels became noticeably more strident in tone, social in subject matter, and belligerent in attitude. The tutelage of Dickens, however, may have limited the development of Collins's ability to construct an economical plot. In his anxiety to please, Collins followed Dickens's advice in elaborating details, varying suspense, and increasing comedy, all designed to make Collins a more popular writer.

The question remains: did Collins contribute anything to Dickens? Beyond friendship and support, especially in personal matters—the 1860s were when Dickens's small children were growing up after his marriage had failed following his involvement with Ellen Ternan—Collins provided Dickens with an intimate artistic as well as social colleague. Dickens collaborated more with Collins than with any other writer in the century, involving him in Christmas numbers, plays, and essays. Collins was also Dickens's most frequent travel companion, who helped him to reconcile the divisions in his life and to tolerate the pressures of writing. *The Mystery of Edwin Drood* most strongly reflects the immediate effect of Collins on Dickens's writing, although the novel was written when the two men had grown apart, partly over the marriage of Collins's sickly brother Charles to Kate, Dickens's third child. Another cause of their estrangement may have been Collins's self-congratulatory view of himself, when he became better known, as no longer a protégé of but a competitor with Dickens. The writing of *The Mystery of Edwin Drood* might possibly be understood as an attempt to improve *The Moonstone*, which Dickens found "wearisome beyond endurance" in construction and plagued by a "vein of obstinate conceit in it that makes enemies of readers." The very character of Edwin Drood, with his youthfulness, talent for sketching, attitude toward Rosa, and complacent, self-satisfied view of the future, parallels that of Collins. The uncle and guardian John Jasper's reaction to Drood may be similar to Dickens's association with Collins. But Collins's good humor, skeptical attitude, quest for pleasure and occasional exposition of "a code of morals taken from modern French novels," to quote Dickens, provided an important antidote to Dickens's often unhappy and earnest personal style. With his love of good food, crimson ties, champagne, blue-striped shirts, music halls, and Paris, where the two of them often reveled, Collins played an important part in the social, private, and artistic life of Dickens.

Poor health began to affect Collins's writing at the time of Dickens's death. His rheumatic gout increased his dependency on laudanum, which correspondingly intensified his determination to publish. One result was overproduction. During the 1870s, Collins turned more often to novels of protest and didacticism instead of relying on his successful blend of the sensational and realistic. His association with Charles Reade, a polemical novelist who used fiction for social criticism, encouraged Collins's excesses. In this last period, eleven novels plus volumes of short stories and plays appeared, which strained the imaginative as well as compositional talents of Collins. A confusion of purpose appears in these novels, a confusion over whether or not he was a sensational writer or social critic. During this period he also made a triumphant

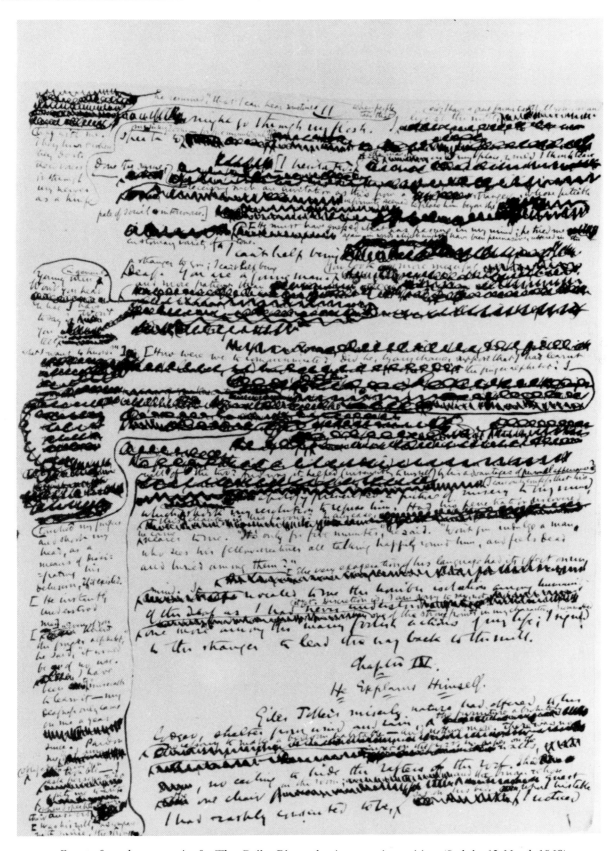

Excerpt from the manuscript for The Guilty River, *showing extensive revisions (Sotheby–12 March 1968)*

reading tour of the United States and Canada. He arrived in New York in September 1873 and was praised, celebrated, and feted. Mark Twain, Longfellow, Whittier, and Oliver Wendell Holmes attended a reception in his honor in Boston. Collins gave readings from a revised version of *The Dream Woman* and *The Frozen Deep* in Philadelphia, Boston, Toronto, and Chicago, and returned to England almost six months later with nearly £ 2,500.

Dominating his work in this period is the thesis novel. *The New Magdalen* (1873), *The Fallen Leaves* (1879), *The Black Robe* (1881), and *Heart and Science* (1883) all reflect this new approach. *The New Magdalen* argues for accepting the penitent, fallen woman; *The Black Robe* attacks the church, especially the Jesuits, while *Heart and Science* confronts the problem of vivisection. This last novel, his best of the 1880s, is a realistic novel of character and humor dealing with a brain surgeon and a modern, money-loving woman. It analyzes the replacement of feeling by science and attempts to restore a balance between the two. *The Evil Genius* (1886) deals with adulterous love and divorce, while his last completed work, *The Legacy of Cain* (1889), considers heredity and environment. During the early 1870s, however, he also continued to write the occasional sensation novel, such as *Poor Miss Finch* (1872) and *The Law and the Lady* (1875). The first novel deals with the rivalry of identical twins for the love of a blind girl and again involves advanced practices of medicine; the second provides the first English detective story with a female protagonist, Valeria Macallan, who tries to prove her husband guiltless of the murder of his first wife. Departing from the focus of *The Moonstone*, the book deals with murder, not theft; it also includes a variety of courtroom scenes, anticipating a convention of later crime stories. *My Lady's Money* (1878) and *I Say No* (1884) continued his detective and sensationalist interests. His last novel, completed by Walter Besant following Collins's explicit directions and detail, was *Blind Love* (1890).

In the last period of his life, Collins renewed his interest in the theater and had great success. In New York in January 1871, his dramatization of *No Name* opened; while in October of that same year, *The Woman in White* premiered at the Olympic Theatre in London and had a twenty-two-week run. *Man and Wife* opened in February 1873 and ran for over thirty-two weeks, becoming the hit of the season; *The New Magdalen* opened in May 1873, two days after the novel appeared, and played for nineteen weeks. This last work remained the most popular of his dramas, with performances given in France, Italy, and Austria as well as the United States. The dramatization of *Armadale*, called *Miss Gwilt*, opened in London in April 1876 with the actor-playwright Arthur Wing Pinero in the cast. *The Moonstone*, the last of his major novels adapted for the stage, premiered in September 1874 and had a nine-week run. His career as a dramatist ended, however, in 1883 with the failure of *Rank and Riches* in London, although it was a success in America. Nonetheless, the 1870s saw Collins reassert himself in the theater after a twelve-year absence, but at the expense of any lasting success in fiction.

In his last years, critics were mixed in evaluating Collins's writing, preferring his realistic fiction such as *Heart and Science* and *The Evil Genius* to the sensation novels such as *Poor Miss Finch* or *The Law and the Lady*. But he was always recognized as a master storyteller, ingenious creator of plots, and chief of the sensation school of novelists. He continued to find literature a profitable enterprise, declaring that he made more money from *The Evil Genius* than from any other novel. Translations of his work appeared in French, German, Dutch, Italian, and Russian. Although interest today centers almost exclusively on *The Woman in White* and *The Moonstone*, other works such as *No Name*, *Armadale*, *Man and Wife*, and *Heart and Science* deserve attention.

In January 1889 a collision between two London cabs threw Collins to the pavement and initiated his final year of poor health. In June he suffered a paralytic stroke the day before the first installment of *Blind Love* was to appear in the *Illustrated London News*. By mid-August he had recovered, but a month later he developed bronchitis and, on the morning of 23 September, he died quietly in his armchair, attended by his doctor, Frank Beard. At his funeral were not only old friends such as the painter Holman Hunt, Arthur Pinero, and Edmund Yates, but new ones, including the poet-critic Edmund Gosse and Oscar Wilde. Both George Meredith and Thomas Hardy participated on committees to secure a suitable memorial.

Swinburne oversimplified Collins's decline when he quipped, "What brought good Wilkie's genius nigh perdition? / Some demon whispered—'Wilkie, have a mission'"; the remark is more notable for the attention it drew to Collins's work than for its accuracy. The loss of a guiding mentor, failure of self-criticism, declining vitality, increasingly poor health, and distraction with the theater more clearly explain the decline in Collins's work in his last years. But despite this falling-off, his novels of detection and sensation, which combine crime with love and social criticism with humor, remain among the finest examples of the genre. For modern critics his work has not only illuminated the sensation novel but provided a new perspective on Victorian narrative technique and the psychological dimension of Victorian fiction.

References:

Robert Ashley, "Wilkie Collins," in *Victorian Fiction: A Guide to Research*, edited by Lionel Stevenson (Cambridge: Harvard University Press, 1966), pp. 277-284;

Ashley, "Wilkie Collins," in *Victorian Fiction: A Second Guide to Research*, edited by George H. Ford (New York: Modern Language Association, 1978), pp. 223-229;

Ashley, *Wilkie Collins* (London: Arthur Barker, 1952);

Kirk H. Beetz, *Wilkie Collins: An Annotated Bibliography, 1889-1976* (Metuchen, N. J.: Scarecrow Press, 1978);

Beetz, "Wilkie Collins and *The Leader*," *Victorian Periodicals Review*, 15 (Spring 1982): 20-29;

Bradford A. Booth, "Wilkie Collins and the Art of Fiction," *Nineteenth Century Fiction*, 6 (1951): 131-143;

Nuell Pharr Davis, *The Life of Wilkie Collins* (Urbana: University of Illinois Press, 1956);

T. S. Eliot, "Introduction," in *The Moonstone* (Oxford: Oxford University Press, 1928), pp. v-xii;

Eliot, "Wilkie Collins and Dickens," in *Selected Essays* (London: Faber & Faber, 1932), pp. 460-470;

Winifred Hughes, *The Maniac in the Cellar: Sensation Novels of the 1860s* (Princeton: Princeton University Press, 1980);

Sue Lonoff, "Charles Dickens and Wilkie Collins," *Nineteenth Century Fiction*, 35 (September 1980): 150-170;

William H. Marshall, *Wilkie Collins* (New York: Twayne, 1970);

Norman Page, ed., *Wilkie Collins: The Critical Heritage* (London: Routledge & Kegan Paul, 1974);

Kenneth Robinson, *Wilkie Collins: A Biography* (London: Bodley Head, 1951);

Dorothy L. Sayers, "Introduction," in *The Moonstone* (London: Dent, 1944), pp. i-xii;

Sayers, *Wilkie Collins: A Critical and Biographical Study*, edited by E. R. Gregory (Toledo, Ohio: Friends of the University of Toledo Libraries, 1977);

A. C. Swinburne, "Wilkie Collins," in *Studies in Prose and Poetry* (London: Chatto & Windus, 1894), pp. 110-128.

Sir Arthur Conan Doyle
(22 May 1859-7 July 1930)

George Grella
University of Rochester
and
Philip B. Dematteis

BOOKS: *A Study in Scarlet* (London: Ward, Lock, 1888; Philadelphia: Lippincott, 1890);

The Mystery of Cloomber (London: Ward & Downey, 1889; New York: Fenno, 1895);

Micah Clarke (London: Longmans, Green, 1889; New York: Fenno, 1895);

Mysteries and Adventures (London: Scott, 1890);

The Sign of the Four (London: Blackett, 1890; Philadelphia: Lippincott, 1893);

The Captain of the Polestar and Other Tales (London & New York: Longmans, Green, 1890; New York: Munro, 1894);

The Firm of Girdlestone (London: Chatto & Windus, 1890; New York: Lovell, 1890);

The White Company (3 volumes, London: Smith, Elder, 1891; 1 volume, New York: Lovell, 1891);

The Doings of Raffles Haw (New York: Lovell, 1891; London: Cassell, 1892);

The Great Shadow (Bristol: Arrowsmith, 1892; New

York: Harper, 1893);

The Adventures of Sherlock Holmes (London: Newnes, 1892; New York: Harper, 1892);

The Gully of Bluemansdyke (London: Scott, 1892);

The Great Shadow and Beyond the City (Bristol: Arrowsmith, 1893);

The Refugees (3 volumes, London: Longmans, Green, 1893; 1 volume, New York: Harper, 1893);

Jane Annie; or, The Good-Conduct Prize: A Comic Opera, by Conan Doyle and J. M. Barrie (London: Chappell, 1893);

The Memoirs of Sherlock Holmes (London: Newnes, 1893; New York: Harper, 1894);

Round the Red Lamp: Being Facts and Fancies of Medical Life (London: Methuen, 1894; New York: Appleton, 1894);

The Parasite (London: Constable, 1894; New York: Harper, 1895);

The Stark Munro Letters (London: Longmans, Green, 1895; New York: Appleton, 1895);

The Exploits of Brigadier Gerard (London: Newnes, 1896; New York: Appleton, 1896);

Rodney Stone (London: Smith, Elder, 1896; New York: Appleton, 1896);

Uncle Bernac: A Memory of the Empire (London: Cox, 1897; New York: Appleton, 1897);

Songs of Action (London: Smith, Elder, 1898; New York: Doubleday & McClure, 1898);

The Tragedy of the Korosko (London: Smith, Elder, 1898); republished as *A Desert Drama* (Philadelphia: Lippincott, 1898);

A Duet with an Occasional Chorus (London: Richards, 1899; New York: Appleton, 1899);

The Great Boer War (London: Smith, Elder, 1900; New York: McClure, Phillips, 1900);

The Green Flag and Other Stories of War and Sport (London: Smith, Elder, 1900; New York: Collier, 1900);

The Hound of the Baskervilles (New York: Collier, 1901; London: Newnes, 1902);

The War in South Africa: Its Cause and Conduct (London: Smith, Elder, 1902; New York: McClure, Phillips, 1902);

Adventures of Gerard (London: Newnes, 1903; New York: McClure, Phillips, 1903);

The Return of Sherlock Holmes (London: Newnes, 1905; New York: McClure, Phillips, 1905);

Sir Nigel (London: Smith, Elder, 1906; New York: McClure, Phillips, 1906);

Through the Magic Door (London: Smith, Elder, 1907; New York: Doubleday, Page, 1908);

The Case of Mr. George Edalji (London: Blake, 1907);

Arthur Conan Doyle in 1892

Round the Fire Stories (London: Smith, Elder, 1908; New York: McClure, Phillips, 1908);

The Crime of the Congo (London: Hutchinson, 1909; Garden City: Doubleday, Page, 1909);

Songs of the Road (London: Smith, Elder, 1911; Garden City: Doubleday, Page, 1911);

The Last Galley (London: Smith, Elder, 1911; Garden City: Doubleday, Page, 1911);

The Lost World (London: Hodder & Stoughton, 1912; New York: Doran, 1912);

The Case of Oscar Slater (London: Hodder & Stoughton, 1912; New York: Doran, 1913);

The Poison Belt (London: Hodder & Stoughton, 1913; New York: Doran, 1913);

The German War: Some Sidelights and Reflections (London: Hodder & Stoughton, 1914);

The Valley of Fear (New York: Doran, 1914; London: Smith, Elder, 1915);

A Visit to Three Fronts (London: Hodder & Stoughton, 1916; New York: Doran, 1916);

The British Campaign in France and Flanders, 6 volumes (London: Hodder & Stoughton, 1916-

1919; New York: Doran, 1917-1920);

The Origin and Outbreak of the War (New York: Doran, 1916);

His Last Bow: Some Reminiscences of Sherlock Holmes (London: Murray, 1917; New York: Doran, 1917);

Danger! And Other Stories (London: Murray, 1918; New York: Doran, 1919);

The New Revelation; or, What is Spiritualism? (London: Hodder & Stoughton, 1918; New York: Doran, 1918);

The Vital Message (London: Hodder & Stoughton, 1919; New York: Doran, 1919);

The Guards Came Through, and Other Poems (London: Murray, 1919; New York: Doran, 1920);

Spiritualism and Rationalism (London: Hodder & Stoughton, 1920);

The Wanderings of a Spiritualist (London: Hodder & Stoughton, 1921; New York: Doran, 1921);

The Evidence for Fairies (New York: Doran, 1921);

The Case for Spirit Photography (London: Hutchinson, 1922; New York: Doran, 1923);

The Coming of the Fairies (London: Hodder & Stoughton, 1922; New York: Doran, 1922);

Three of Them: A Reminiscence (London: Murray, 1923);

Our American Adventure (London: Hodder & Stoughton, 1923; New York: Doran, 1923);

Memories and Adventures (London: Hodder & Stoughton, 1924);

The Spiritualist's Reader (Manchester: Two Worlds, 1924);

Our Second American Adventure (London: Hodder & Stoughton, 1924; Boston: Little, Brown, 1924);

Psychic Experiences (London: Putnam's, 1925);

The Land of Mist (London: Hutchinson, 1926; Garden City: Doubleday, Doran, 1926);

The History of Spiritualism, 2 volumes (London: Cassell, 1926; New York: Doran, 1926);

The Case-Book of Sherlock Holmes (London: Murray, 1927; New York: Doran, 1927);

Pheneas Speaks (London: Psychic Press, 1927; New York: Doran, 1927);

The Maracot Deep and Other Stories (London: Murray, 1929; Garden City: Doubleday, Doran, 1929);

Our African Winter (London: Murray, 1929).

Of all the manifold literary achievements of the Victorian age, the most important and enduring may very well turn out to be those traditionally regarded as mere entertainment, as "light" and popular works. While authors such as Browning, Tennyson, Arnold, Dickens, and George Eliot occupy the center of the stage, and supporting players such as Rossetti, Swinburne, Meredith, and Butler wait eagerly in the wings, a numerous and ebullient crowd looks on from the cheap seats. Among that noisy and attractive group are such disparate figures as Edward Lear, Lewis Carroll, Rudyard Kipling, Robert Louis Stevenson, and, unquestionably, Sir Arthur Conan Doyle. Like his fellows, Conan Doyle has enjoyed great popularity and small critical success; like them, he toiled in fields distant from the capitals of high culture; like some of them, he espoused currently unfashionable views; like all of them, he sums up in his life, personality, and career a great many of the most significant truths of his rich and eventful era. Like so many of the great Victorians, he combined an immensely industrious artistic career with a rich and adventurous personal life; a keen sportsman, he also traveled widely all his life and served his country as a medical man during the Boer War. His devotion to literature, to his family, to public service, and to justice, as well as his personal generosity and decency, suggest that he was an altogether exemplary and admirable man. Of course, any sensitive reader of the Sherlock Holmes stories recognizes, among so much to admire, the magnanimity of their author, a marvelous largeness of mind and heart.

If he had done nothing else but those stories (and they will always be the works by which he is known), Conan Doyle would have entirely deserved the gratitude of his huge readership, which is not likely to diminish as long as English literature is read, enjoyed, and loved. In addition to his virtual reinvention of that major modern form, the detective story—whose elements he had inherited from Edgar Allan Poe—Conan Doyle contributed a great many other things to it. Endowing the characters, dialogue, and settings with a truly remarkable vividness and specificity, Conan Doyle cleansed Poe's tales of their characteristic juicy morbidity and fruity elegance. He imparted to the form his own special charm, wit, and energy, creating his best effects with considerable skill and economy, often with genuine brilliance. Perhaps most of all, he attained some of the rarest and most sought-after of all the goals of literature: he told some wonderful stories wonderfully well and created a whole world in such credible detail, with such richness of texture, with such authenticity of surface and atmosphere, that thousands of readers over almost a century have lost themselves inside it. The loving attention of passionate Sherlockians (especially those who call themselves the Baker Street Irregulars, with their "scion societies" all over the world) to what they term "the Conan" of the Holmes stories (also known as the Sacred Writings), manifested in innumerable books, essays, and notes of a mock-scholarly nature, testifies to Conan Doyle's literary powers and unending appeal. Appropriately, what distinguishes Sherlockian studies from far too much of the scholarly work it otherwise resembles is its great affection for the author and his creation; this is not the usual pedantic probing under stones better left unturned, but an act of love.

Arthur Conan Doyle was a descendant of an artistically talented Catholic family. His grandfather, John Doyle, was a prominent London caricaturist and illustrator who dined with the Prince of Wales and visited Queen Victoria; John Doyle's son, Richard—Arthur Conan Doyle's uncle—became a leading artist for *Punch*. Charles Altamont Doyle, Arthur's father, applied himself to architecture and building and became clerk of the Board of Works in Edinburgh, Scotland, supplementing his income by illustrating magazines and children's books. In 1855, Charles Doyle married seventeen-year-old Mary Foley, the daughter of his Irish lodging-housekeeper. Mary, who had gone to

Publications of some of the more than 150 Sherlock Holmes societies around the world
(Ronald Burt De Waal, The World Bibliography of Sherlock Holmes and Dr. Watson*)*

France at the age of twelve for her schooling, knew French thoroughly; her hobby was heraldry. Arthur Conan Doyle always called her "the Ma'am," and she was a strong influence on him. Even after she was widowed, she proudly declined his offer to live under his roof; but they corresponded and visited regularly until her death in 1921.

Arthur Conan Doyle (his middle name was taken from that of his great-uncle Michael Conan, a successful journalist who lived in Paris) was born 22 May 1859, one of five girls and two boys who grew up in genteel but shabby surroundings in Edinburgh. After attending Hodder House, the preparatory school for the Jesuit college at Stonyhurst in Lancashire, from ages seven to nine, he went on to Stonyhurst itself; he then spent a year at a Jesuit school in Feldkirch, Austria. In 1876, at his mother's urging, he entered Edinburgh University to study medicine. One of his professors was a tall, hawknosed Scotsman named Joseph Bell, who amazed the students with his ability not only to diagnose the diseases of his patients but to ascertain their occupations and other information merely by observing certain details about their appearance.

Dr. Joseph Bell of Edinburgh, the model for Sherlock Holmes

To help pay for his education, Conan Doyle worked during the summer of 1879 as an assistant to a physician in Birmingham. At about the same time, he began to try his hand at writing fiction; and in October, his first story, "The Mystery of Sasassa Valley," was published in *Chambers's Journal*. From February to September 1880 he acted as ship's surgeon on a sealing and whaling cruise to the Arctic, returning to take his bachelor of medicine degree in 1881. Almost immediately he took another post as ship's surgeon on a voyage to the west coast of Africa, returning in January 1882. Refusing to let his influential Catholic relatives set him up in a lucrative London practice—he felt that this would be hypocritical, since he had by then left the faith—Conan Doyle went into partnership in Plymouth with the eccentric Dr. George Budd, whom he had met at the university. The partnership lasted only a few months; Conan Doyle later fictionalized it in *The Stark Munro Letters* (1895), in which Budd appears as "Dr. Cullingworth." After his break with Budd, Conan Doyle went into practice on his own in July 1882 in Southsea, a suburb of Portsmouth on the south coast of England. His London relatives sent him letters of introduction to Catholic notables in the area, but Conan Doyle felt it would be dishonorable to use them, and his practice was never very successful. The first year, he earned only £ 154; he filled out his income-tax form to show that he owed no taxes, and it was returned with the notation "Most unsatisfactory." Conan Doyle wrote, "I entirely agree," and sent the form back to the authorities. Using his ten-year-old brother, Innes, as a page until he could afford a servant, Conan Doyle never made more than £ 300 a year in Southsea.

In the meantime, he published stories in *London Society*, *All the Year Round*, and the *Boys' Own Paper*. In January 1884 "Habakuk Jephson's Statement," based on the story of the mystery ship *Mary Celeste*, appeared anonymously in the prestigious *Cornhill* magazine, edited by James Payn; some reviewers thought it had been written by Robert Louis Stevenson, and a British official in Gibraltar—not realizing the story was intended as fiction—wrote angry letters to the newspapers denouncing it as a hoax. Conan Doyle now began to mingle with the London literary set; he was also working on his M.D. degree, which he received in July 1885. On 6 August, he married Louise Hawkins, the sister of one of his patients who had died of meningitis. By the following March, he had completed two novels: one was lost in the mail and never recovered; the other,

"Girdlestone & Co.," met with rejections from publishers.

It was at this point that Conan Doyle decided to try to write a detective story that would combine several of his interests: his early reading of Edgar Allan Poe's Dupin stories; his fascination with the American West; and the powers of observation of his old medical professor, Joe Bell. Using a plot perhaps suggested by the actual disappearance in London of a German baker named Stangerson (one of the victims in the story is named Stanger), Conan Doyle wrote a novel he at first titled "A Tangled Skein." His narrator was, like himself, a doctor; originally he was named Ormond Sacker, but Conan Doyle changed this to John H. Watson. His detective also underwent a name change from first draft to finished work, becoming Sherlock—instead of Sherrinford—Holmes. The novel was completed in April 1886 and, retitled "A Study in Scarlet," sent to the *Cornhill*. Payn pronounced it "capital," but turned it down because it was too long for one issue and too short to be serialized. After two rejections from book publishers, Ward, Lock paid Conan Doyle £25 for all rights to the novel, to be published the following year.

Early in 1887, Conan Doyle was introduced to the subject of spiritualism by one of his patients. He read more than seventy books on the topic and even held a number of séances, but remained skeptical. *A Study in Scarlet* finally appeared in December—not in book form, but as the lead feature in *Beeton's Christmas Annual*, published by Ward, Lock. The novel did not attract much attention from reviewers, but the annual was a sellout; in 1888, Ward, Lock published the novel separately, with six illustrations by Conan Doyle's father. These first publications are now among the rarest books in existence. *A Study in Scarlet* tells of the first meeting of Holmes and Watson ("You have been in Afghanistan, I perceive," says Holmes, to Watson's astonishment) and their decision to share rooms at Mrs. Hudson's establishment, 221B Baker Street. Watson gradually discovers that Holmes has set himself up in business as the world's first "unofficial consulting detective," and the two share their first case when Holmes is called on for help by inspectors Lestrade and Gregson of Scotland Yard. A dead man has been found in an abandoned house with no wound on his body but with a message written in blood on the wall. After another murder, Holmes is able to apprehend the killer, an American whose motive was revenge for the death of his sweetheart at the hands of Mormons in Utah (this story is told in the third person in a long central section of the novel).

A large and athletic man, Conan Doyle was by then captain of the Portsmouth Cricket Club and a back on the local football team. He was also involved in politics as a Liberal-Unionist, opposed—in spite of his ancestry—to Irish home rule. His first child, Mary Louise, was born in January 1889. The following month, his historical novel about Monmouth's Rebellion, *Micah Clarke*, was published and received enthusiastic reviews; a book of short stories, *The Mystery of Cloomber*, also appeared. At the request of the editor of *Lippincott's Magazine*, he wrote the second Sherlock Holmes novel, *The Sign of the Four* (1890), a tale of stolen treasure, an aboriginal dwarf, and murder by poison darts; at the end—after a thrilling chase down the Thames—Watson is engaged to be married to Holmes's client, Scotland Yard has gotten the credit for solving the case, and Holmes is left to turn for solace to the cocaine bottle. This novel, like *A Study in Scarlet*, attracted little critical notice. Also during 1890, Conan Doyle's earlier novel, retitled *The Firm of Girdlestone*, finally achieved publication, along with another volume of short stories. During much of this period, Conan Doyle was engaged in researching and writing what always remained his favorite novel, *The White Company* (1891), a tale of medieval chivalry featuring Sir Nigel Loring.

In October, Conan Doyle went to Berlin to investigate a reputed cure for tuberculosis, which he denounced in the press as holding out false hopes. In December, he returned to the Continent to study eye surgery in Vienna and Paris; and in March 1891, the family moved to London, where Conan Doyle opened a practice as an eye specialist. No patients ever came; and after a severe attack of influenza, he decided to give up medicine and make his living entirely by his writing. Between April and August he sent six Sherlock Holmes short stories to the new *Strand* magazine, receiving £35 for each; the first, "A Scandal in Bohemia," appeared in the July issue. The stories were enormously popular, and by October, the editors of the *Strand* were begging for more. Conan Doyle, who was working on *The Refugees* (1893), a historical novel set in Canada, was reluctant to continue the series; so he asked for £50 per story, thinking the demand would be rejected. It was eagerly accepted. Conan Doyle mentioned in a letter to "the Ma'am" that he was thinking about killing Holmes off in the twelfth and last story of the series, but she forbade it, and the detec-

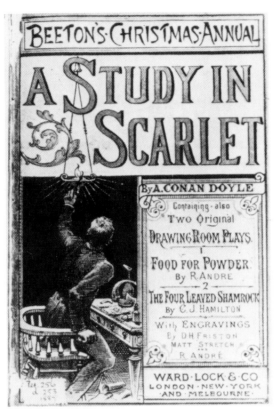

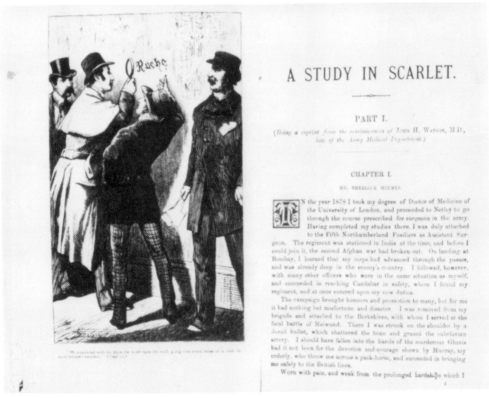

Cover and opening pages of the first publication of the first Sherlock Holmes novel, 1887

tive's life was spared. The stories were published in book form as *The Adventures of Sherlock Holmes* (1892).

Conan Doyle was now living in the London suburb of South Norwood with his wife, daughter, mother-in-law, and his sister Connie. Influenced by his friend J. M. Barrie, he wrote a play, *Waterloo*, which he sold to the actor Henry Irving. Once again, the editor of the *Strand* began "bothering me for more Sherlock Holmes tales," as he wrote to his mother early in 1892; he offered to write a dozen for £1,000, thinking the price ridiculously high—but it was immediately accepted. After completing a novel of the Napoleonic wars, *The Great Shadow* (1892), and taking a short vacation in Scotland, he began the new series with "Silver Blaze." (This is the story in which Holmes makes his famous remark about "the curious incident of the dog in the night-

time." "The dog did nothing in the night-time," replies another character. "That was the curious incident.") He spent August on vacation with Louise in Norway; in September he collaborated with Barrie on a light opera, *Jane Annie; or, The Good-Conduct Prize* (1893). His sister Lottie moved in with them in October, and in November, his son Kingsley was born. Early in 1893, Conan Doyle and Louise visited Switzerland and viewed the awesome Reichenbach Falls—and an idea began to take shape in his mind. In April, wearied by publishers' deadlines and the challenge of inventing new plots, and wishing to unburden himself once and for all of a character he felt was taking his time from more important work, Conan Doyle wrote "The Final Problem," killing Holmes by having him plunge into the Reichenbach Falls. The story did not appear in print until December.

Illustration by Sidney Paget for the 1892 short story "Silver Blaze" in the Strand *magazine*

In the lull before the storm that that publication would cause, *Jane Annie* failed at the Savoy Theatre in May. Later in the spring, Conan Doyle visited George Meredith at Meredith's home, Flint Cottage at Box Hill. While they were walking on a steep path, Conan Doyle heard Meredith—already feeling the effects of the spinal malady that would cripple him—slip and fall behind him. Not wishing to humiliate the proud old man, Conan Doyle pretended not to notice and walked on until Meredith caught up with him. During the summer, Connie Doyle married E. W. Hornung, later to become the author of the "Raffles" stories about a gentleman burglar. Conan Doyle's father died in October; shortly afterward, Louise was diagnosed as having tuberculosis. In an attempt to prolong her life, the Doyles moved to Switzerland in November; thus they were out of the country when "The Final Problem" appeared in the *Strand* in December. The plunge of Sherlock Holmes and the evil Professor Moriarty ("the Napoleon of crime"), locked in mortal combat, into the Reichenbach brought a

Paget's depiction of Sherlock Holmes's presumed death in "The Final Problem," Strand *magazine, December 1893*

tremendous outburst of public mourning for the sleuth. More than 20,000 readers cancelled their subscriptions to the *Strand*; Conan Doyle received an avalanche of hate mail; and City businessmen went to their offices wearing black crepe around their top hats.

Louise's health did improve in the Alpine climate, and Conan Doyle, his anxiety reduced, was able to write the autobiographical *Stark Munro Letters* and *The Parasite* (1894). He also introduced the Norwegian sport of skiing into Switzerland, predicting in the *Strand* that some day tourists would flock to Switzerland for skiing vacations. After a brief visit home, Conan Doyle—accompanied by his brother Innes, now an army officer—set out in September for an American reading tour. He scored triumphs in New York, Chicago, Indianapolis, Cincinnati, Toledo, and Milwaukee, and visited Kipling in Vermont, before rejoining Louise in Switzerland in December. There, by spring 1895, he completed a series of stories he had begun before the American tour about a French soldier in Napoleon's army; these stories were published in the *Strand* and in book form as *The Exploits of Brigadier Gerard* (1896). Etienne Gerard, one of Conan Doyle's most popular characters, was based on a real-life French soldier, General Baron de Marbot. Conan Doyle later wrote another series of stories about the heroic, comical, swaggering, boastful Gerard; these were collected as *Adventures of Gerard* (1903).

On a visit to England in May 1895, Conan Doyle met the writer Grant Allen, who told him that the Surrey climate had allowed him to keep his own tuberculosis under control. After communicating with Louise, who was, like her husband, anxious to return to England, Conan Doyle arranged for the building of a house at Hindhead. He then returned to Switzerland, where he wrote the prizefighting novel *Rodney Stone* (1896).

The Doyles spent the winter of 1895-1896 in Cairo; in January, they took a steamboat cruise up the Nile. Between Korosko and Wadi Halfa, they came upon a village which had recently been raided by the Mahdi's dervishes; Conan Doyle realized that it would be easy for a tourist party such as his to be kidnapped or massacred. Though nothing of the sort happened, Doyle later imagined such a situation in *The Tragedy of the Korosko* (1898). Two months after the cruise, when Major-General Kitchener moved to retake the Egyptian Sudan, Conan Doyle got himself appointed correspondent without pay for the *Westminster Gazette*; but when he reached the "front" at Wadi Halfa, he was told that no attack would be made for a month or more. In May 1896, the Doyles moved back to England, where they rented a house in Surrey while waiting for their own to be completed. There Conan Doyle wrote another novel about the Napoleonic wars, *Uncle Bernac* (1897).

In March 1897, Conan Doyle met Jean Leckie, a beautiful and talented twenty-four-year-old woman who could trace her ancestry back to Rob Roy MacGregor. They fell in love immediately and began seeing each other whenever they could; but due to Conan Doyle's sense of honor and feeling of obligation to his invalid wife, the relationship apparently remained platonic for the next ten years. Only "the Ma'am" was taken into their confidence; she enthusiastically approved of Jean, even allowing the two to meet in her home.

The Doyles moved into their new home, named Undershaw, in the fall of 1897. Shortly thereafter, Conan Doyle wrote a play about Sherlock Holmes, which he sent to the actor Beerbohm Tree; but Tree wanted the part of Holmes rewritten to better fit himself. Conan Doyle was ready to scrap the whole idea, but his agent sent the play to a New York impresario, who gave it to the American actor William Gillette. Gillette completely rewrote the play, with Conan Doyle's permission, and went on to star in it so successfully that he was identified with the role for the rest of his life. While Gillette was working on the play, Conan Doyle was collecting his poems into *Songs of Action* (1898) and writing a series of stories for the *Strand* that were later published as

American actor William Gillette as Sherlock Holmes

Undershaw, Conan Doyle's house at Hindhead, Surrey, from 1897 to 1907

Round the Fire Stories (1908). He also wrote *A Duet with an Occasional Chorus* (1899), a sentimental domestic story about the day-to-day experiences of an ordinary middle-class couple. Many readers, expecting a rousing adventure story, were disappointed, and some critics condemned the book as naive. But Swinburne and H. G. Wells admired it, and Conan Doyle always had a special fondness for it. *Halves*, Conan Doyle's dramatization of a novel by his old editor James Payn, was successfully produced in London in June 1899.

The Boer War broke out in the fall. Though he doubted the justice of the British cause—and quarreled with his mother over the matter—Conan Doyle patriotically tried to volunteer for service but was rejected because of his age (he was then forty and in robust health). Nevertheless, he did make it to the scene of action: from April to July 1900 he served without pay as senior civil physician with the privately-funded Langman Hospital near Bloemfontaine. While there, he wrote "Some Military Les-

Conan Doyle at the time of the Boer War

sons of the War" for the *Cornhill*, in which he made a number of proposals for modernizing British tactics. His suggestions—such as that artillery pieces should be concealed and dispersed instead of lined up in the open like sitting ducks, and that the cavalry should be equipped with rifles instead of swords—naturally caused outrage among the conservative military establishment. He also began his history *The Great Boer War* (1900), which he completed after his return to England. In the fall, he ran for a seat in Parliament from the Central District of Edinburgh as a Liberal-Unionist; but on election day, placards appeared around the polling places referring to his Roman Catholic origins and Jesuit education. Though he had left the church years before, this was enough to defeat him in strongly Protestant Edinburgh. Still, he came within 600 votes of being elected, while at the beginning of the ten-day campaign the Liberal candidate had been believed to have a 2,000-vote majority.

Returning to Surrey, he founded the Undershaw Rifle Club in accordance with his ideas about the value of civilian riflemen in case of an invasion of Britain. In the spring, he went on a golfing holiday with a friend, Fletcher Robinson, who recounted to Conan Doyle some of the legends of his native Dartmoor in Devonshire. After a tour of Dartmoor with Robinson, Conan Doyle began writing *The Hound of the Baskervilles* (1901). In his original conception, the novel was not supposed to involve Sherlock Holmes; but it became the most famous Holmes story of all. Set in 1886—before Holmes's death in the Reichenbach in 1891—the novel employs the traditional Holmes features: a Gothic setting, a seemingly inexplicable crime, the hero in disguise, the bungling of Watson (who carries out most of the investigation), and an unusual villain. Dr. James Mortimer arrives at Baker Street to reveal a legend involving a ghostly demon-dog and to describe the recent mysterious death of Sir Charles Baskerville on his estate. The only clues are footprints surrounding the body: "Mr. Holmes, they were the footprints of a gigantic hound!" He appeals to Holmes for protection for Sir Charles's nephew, the heir to the estate, soon to arrive from Canada. Pleading the press of other business, Holmes sends Watson to Devonshire to investigate. A variety of suspicious events and characters appear in the sinister landscape of the moor. By letting Watson carry on the lion's share of the inquiry, Conan Doyle builds the suspense, which climaxes with Holmes's unexpected appearance, the nick-of-time rescue of the young heir, and the unmasking of the villain. In a final chapter, Holmes, back at Baker Street, recapitulates the intricate plot to illegally secure the Baskerville inheritance. The story comes to a quick and cultured end, however, as Holmes invites Watson to relax with him by attending the opera after a delightful dinner at one of their favorite restaurants. The enduring popularity of this story can be seen in its transformation into the definitive Holmes movie: the 1939 *The Hound of the Baskervilles* introduced Basil Rathbone as Holmes and Nigel Bruce as Watson, initiating a series of successful Holmes films. While the novel was running in the *Strand*, Gillette's play *Sherlock Holmes* opened in London in September 1901; it was a huge success.

In South Africa, the Boer War dragged on. The British, now holding the upper hand, had adopted a scorched-earth policy. The European press, and some British papers as well, were filled with stories of British atrocities (bayoneting of babies, rape of Boer women) which Conan Doyle knew to be false, but to which the government would not deign to reply. So Conan Doyle wrote a reply: *The War in South Africa: Its Cause and Conduct* (1902). Without whitewashing the British, he presented voluminous amounts of evidence—much of it testimony from Boer soldiers and civilians and impartial foreign observers—to refute the atrocity charges. Using his own money and public donations, Conan Doyle had the book translated into nearly every European language and distributed throughout Britain, the Continent, and North America; it turned the tide of public opinion about British conduct of the war. As a result, he was knighted at the coronation of Edward VII on 9 August 1902.

In the spring of 1903, he received an offer from an American publisher of $5,000 a short story if he would bring Sherlock Holmes back to life; a British publisher offered more than half that much for the English rights. Conan Doyle, still unable to understand the fascination with what he considered some of his less important work, at last gave in. Realizing that he had fortunately provided no witnesses to the plunge of Holmes and Moriarty into the falls and that Holmes's body had never been found, Conan Doyle started the new series of stories with "The Adventure of the Empty House," set in 1894. Holmes reappears after an absence of three years (known to Sherlockians as "the Great Hiatus") and tells a shocked Watson that he never fell into the Reichenbach after all, but had decided that it would

be prudent for various (somewhat illogical) reasons if the world thought he had. Watson's wife has died in the interim, so the two friends move back into 221B Baker Street together, and all is as it was before. Or maybe not: some critics contend that the later Holmes stories are not up to the standard of the earlier ones, and it is true that most of the best-remembered tales are from the earlier group. Conan Doyle himself enjoyed telling about a Cornish boatman who said to him: "I think, sir, that when Holmes fell over that cliff he may not have killed himself, but he was never quite the same man afterward." But Conan Doyle did not agree with this assessment; and others have pointed out that the earlier stories also included some weak entries, while among the later ones are such classics as "The Adventure of the Dancing Men" (1903) and "The Adventure of the Devil's Foot" (1910), as well as *The Valley of Fear* (1914), which some consider to be one of the finest detective novels ever written.

Conan Doyle made another unsuccessful bid for Parliament from the Scottish border burghs of Hawick, Selkirk, and Galashiels in 1906, on a platform of preferential trade with the colonies. In the same year he published his novel *Sir Nigel*: it is what would now be called a "prequel," describing events in the life of Sir Nigel Loring prior to the action of *The White Company*. Doyle was disappointed in most of the reviews, which praised *Sir Nigel*—as they had *The White Company*—as a ripping adventure yarn, without noticing the pains he had taken to accurately recreate the milieu of the Middle Ages.

Louise Conan Doyle finally succumbed to her tuberculosis on 4 July 1906. While he had never been passionately in love with Louise, Conan Doyle was fond of her; he probably also felt guilty about his relationship with Jean Leckie. In any case, he was laid low for several months with depression and a series of apparently psychosomatic illnesses.

He was roused from his torpor at the end of the year by a letter from George Edalji, a young former solicitor of Indian descent. Edalji had been convicted in 1903 of a series of livestock mutilations in Staffordshire and sentenced to seven years imprisonment; then he had been suddenly released after three years, without explanation and without a pardon, his career in ruins. Still maintaining his innocence, he appealed to the creator of Sherlock Holmes for help. Conan Doyle saw from the newspaper clippings Edalji had sent that the evidence used to convict him was flimsy and contradictory; he met Edalji and realized that the man was practically blind with uncorrectable astigmatic myopia, making it virtually impossible for him to have skulked around a field in the middle of the night in a rainstorm, evading police patrols, to slash a pony. Conan Doyle worked on the case for eight months at his own expense, at the end of which he was able to demonstrate not only that Edalji was innocent and had been arrested due to racial prejudice but that another man who lived in the area was almost certainly the real slasher. The Home Office finally granted Edalji a pardon but refused to compensate him for the time he had spent in jail. Edalji was, however, readmitted to legal practice; and in large part because of the Edalji case, a court of criminal appeal was established in 1907.

A grateful George Edalji was a guest at Conan Doyle's wedding to Jean Leckie on 18 September 1907. The family moved to a new home, Windlesham, at Crowborough in Sussex. A son, Denis, was born in 1909. Later that year Conan Doyle published *The Crime of the Congo*, a documentation of mistreatment suffered by the natives at the hands of the Belgians. As with *The War in South Africa*, Conan Doyle never accepted any profit from the sale of the book.

Conan Doyle's interest in the theater was rekindled at this time. In the summer and fall of 1909, his dramatization of *The Tragedy of the Korosko* had a successful London run as *The Fires of Fate*. At the end of the year his prizefighting spectacle, *The House of Temperley*, opened; it was a huge hit at first, but the lack of any feminine interest in the story caused audiences to dwindle, and it closed after four months. Less than a month later, on 4 June, Conan Doyle's new play premiered: it was *The Speckled Band*, based on one of his Sherlock Holmes stories. He was able to more than recoup his losses on *The House of Temperley*, which he had backed with his own money. Even so, Conan Doyle swore off playwriting, feeling that his talents were better suited to the novel and short story.

In November 1910, another son, Adrian, was born; he grew up to become his father's literary executor and in the 1950s teamed up with John Dickson Carr to write a new series of Sherlock Holmes stories for *Collier's* magazine. In the summer of 1911, Conan Doyle—with Jean as passenger—took part in an Anglo-German automobile race around Germany and England; the British side won. They then traveled to Denmark for Innes's wedding to a Danish woman. At the reception, Innes—forced to make a speech—caused great hi-

larity and convinced the guests that he was indeed a true Englishman. His speech, in its entirety, was: "Well . . . I say, don't you know! By Jove! What!"

Back home in Sussex, Conan Doyle wrote another novel, inspired by some fossilized dinosaur footprints that had been found near his home. In *The Lost World* (1912), Prof. George Edward Challenger, the violent, eccentric adventurer recently returned from a mysterious South American expedition, shows a picture of a strange monster to Edward Malone, a journalist who narrates the story. A new expedition is soon organized, with Challenger and Malone being joined by Lord John Roxton and Professor Summerlee, all figures that soon captured the interest of the late-Victorian reading public. Conan Doyle provides vivid descriptions of the Amazon jungle through which the adventurers are led by Challenger. The novel's climax has Challenger lecturing to a rapt London audience which suddenly becomes terrorized when a captured pterodactyl escapes in the hall and flies about the city. Conan Doyle went on to write other Challenger stories, including *The Poison Belt* (1913), which describes the end of the world after the earth runs into a stream of poison gas. "BRING OXYGEN" is the ominous telegram that reunites the four explorers of *The Lost World* in this doom-filled but ironic work. Conan Doyle's pleasure in Challenger extended to his donning a black beard and dressing up as the professor for publicity photos and social engagements; he once visited his brother-in-law Hornung in this disguise and chatted with him for several minutes before Hornung recognized him.

The year 1912 was a busy one for Conan Doyle. He got involved in politics again—though not as a candidate this time—speaking and writing in favor of home rule for Ireland (a reversal of his earlier position) and reform of the archaic divorce laws, and against women's suffrage. He also led a fund-raising drive for training British athletes for the 1916 Olympics. In addition to all of this, he took up the cause of another wrongfully-convicted man. Oscar Slater had been sentenced to death in 1909 for the murder of an elderly woman in Glasgow, but his sentence had been commuted to life imprisonment. In *The Case of Oscar Slater* (1912), Conan Doyle ripped apart the evidence presented by the prosecution. He continued the fight for Slater for the next sixteen years; Slater's sentence was finally quashed in 1928, and he was paid £ 6,000 compensation.

First page of the manuscript of a 1911 Sherlock Holmes story, showing Conan Doyle's change of mind about the title
(Lilly Library, Indiana University)

The Doyles' third child, Lena Jean, was born in December 1912. At this time, Conan Doyle was beginning to worry about the possibility of war with Germany and about Britain's lack of preparedness. In articles and in a short story, "Danger! Being the Log of Captain John Sirius" (1914), he pointed out the danger of a submarine blockade of Britain and recommended the construction of a tunnel under the English Channel. As they had at the time of the Boer War, the military establishment scoffed at his ideas. It was unthinkable, they said, that any civilized nation would sink unarmed merchant ships carrying food.

Conan Doyle and Jean spent June 1914 in a tour of the Canadian Rockies as guests of the Canadian government and were back in England when World War I began in July. Conan Doyle immediately organized the first volunteer reserve company in England, the prototype of the later Home Guard. He volunteered his medical services at the front but was politely turned down. Jean opened a home for Belgian refugees in Crowborough, and they turned a wing of Windlesham into a club for Canadian officers. In articles, Conan Doyle proposed innovations to protect the fighting men, such as life belts and inflatable rafts for sailors and metal helmets and body armor for soldiers. On a visit to the front in 1916 at the request of the Foreign Office, he was asked by a French general whether Sherlock Holmes was in the British army; the surprised Conan Doyle stammered out that Holmes was too old to serve. (Holmes *did* serve, though, in the 1917 story "His Last Bow," in which the sixty-year-old detective comes out of retirement to capture a German spy.) Conan Doyle wrote several books about the conflict, including a six-volume history.

The war years were tragic ones for the Doyles, as they were for millions of others. Jean's brother Malcolm, an army doctor, was killed at Mons; Conan Doyle's sister Lottie's husband was also killed; his son Kingsley, weakened by wounds in the Somme campaign, died of pneumonia; a few months after the end of the war, his brother, Innes, also died of pneumonia; Jean's best friend, who had been staying with them, died after a short illness. Conan Doyle's interest in spiritualism—which he had maintained since being introduced to the subject in 1887—now became an obsession. His main objection to the claims of the spiritualists had been the triviality of the purported psychic phenomena—moving tables, floating trumpets, and so on. But he now decided that this was irrelevant, just as the ring of the telephone has nothing to do with the importance of the message. In late 1915 or early 1916, Conan Doyle believed he received a communication from Malcolm Leckie which contained personal information known to no one but the two of them; that completed his conversion. In 1918 he published *The New Revelation*, an argument for the existence of an intelligent force in nature; his *History of Spiritualism* appeared in 1926.

Conan Doyle, his wife Jean, and children Adrian, Lena Jean, and Denis
leaving Waterloo station in 1923 for a spiritualism lecture tour

Throughout his last decade, Conan Doyle became an ardent propagandist for spiritualism, even lobbying against English laws that persecuted mediums. In addition to his belief in communication with the dead, based on at least pseudoscientific experimentation, Conan Doyle was also inclined by his Celtic background to a belief in fairies and goblins. His speeches in support of psychic phenomena took him all over Europe, to Africa, and twice to America. He contributed £250,000 of his own money to the cause; he also turned down many opportunities to write short stories on other subjects which would have paid him ten shillings a word, the highest rate any writer could command at the time. He was removed from consideration for a peerage because of his unorthodox views. He was taken in by phony mediums and obviously faked photographs of fairies; his friend, the American magician Harry Houdini, exposed many of these frauds, causing a break between the two men. Conan Doyle injected his beliefs into some of his fiction: in *The Land of Mist* (1926), a skeptical Professor Challenger is finally converted to belief in communication with the dead. Remarkably, however, Conan Doyle never made Sherlock Holmes a believer, right through "The Adventure of Shoscombe Old Place" (1927), the last Holmes story he ever wrote. In fact, in "The Adventure of the Sussex Vampire" (1924), Holmes says: "This Agency stands flat-footed upon the ground, and there it must remain. The world is big enough for us. No ghosts need apply"—and the case does have a nonsupernatural solution.

Conan Doyle was stricken with angina pectoris on the way back from a speaking trip to Scandinavia in the autumn of 1929, but went on to speak at Armistice Day ceremonies in London, against medical advice. His health improved somewhat during the spring and summer, although he frequently had to be given oxygen to steady his heart rate. He died on the morning of 7 July 1930, sitting in a chair by the window of his bedroom, with Jean, Adrian, Denis, and Lena Jean around him. He was buried on the grounds of Windlesham under a headstone made of British oak, inscribed "Steel True, Blade Straight."

Besides those qualities which give the Holmes stories their lasting appeal, Conan Doyle's works (and, indeed, his life) embody some of the most characteristic attributes of his time and place; in both their tangible materiality and their underlying implications the stories provide what may be the best introduction to late-Victorian England. In them can be seen his ability to impart both meaning and magic to the most trivial details of everyday life—the tantalus and the gasogene, the deerstalker cap and the hansom cab, the cigars in the coal scuttle, the pipe tobacco in the Persian slipper, the hearth rug, the cozy fire, and the thick fog that hides some terrible crime and its perpetrator. The persistent polar tensions within his works suggest as well the powerful and paradoxical dualities of his era. A direct descendant of Poe and a contemporary of Robert Louis Stevenson, he shares their interest in doubling; Watson and Holmes constitute one of the great pairs of literature, in the tradition of Sancho Panza and Don Quixote, Boswell and Johnson, Mr. Pickwick and Sam Weller. The conjunction of the tall, thin, angular man with the short, stocky, rotund companion usually serves as the visual equivalent of two contrasting but essentially harmonious temperaments. That duality epitomizes the many others in Conan Doyle's works, marking them indelibly as the product of their temporal and cultural context.

In the figure of Sherlock Holmes, as many commentators have noted, a number of striking contradictions coexist. A brilliant rationalist

Conan Doyle in Paris for a spiritualists' congress, 1925

afflicted by chronic melancholia, he possesses the mind of the scientist and the soul of the artist. A strict logician who can deduce a life history from a hat, a pipe, a watch, he must mitigate the harsh discipline of reality by taking cocaine. Professing to despise the softer emotions and confessing ignorance of art, he often exercises profound compassion in his cases and loses himself for hours in the music of his beloved Stradivarius. Even stolid Dr. Watson betrays a certain dual personality: pretending to be an ordinary bourgeois, a placid general practitioner, he in fact appears to spend most of his time in wild adventures in detection and in composing romantic narratives of his friend's exploits. In some senses the Holmes stories are a perpetual allegory of the uneasy tension between appearance and reality—with enough concentration of intellect and imagination (themselves at times warring concepts), even the most humble and trivial objects can be forced to yield depths of meaning. Ultimately, for Holmes nothing is insignificant—or as he explains to Watson in *The Hound of the Baskervilles*, "the more outré and grotesque an incident is the more carefully it deserves to be examined. . . ."

Conan Doyle himself embodied a great many dualities, many of which appear as typically Victorian as those of Sherlock Holmes. He was a born poet who studied and practiced medicine, a prolific man of letters who served in the public sphere, a patriot with a deep ambivalence about his nation's actions in Ireland and South Africa, a rationalist who embraced spiritualism, a Victorian with a faith in British justice who defended men he felt were wrongly accused. Very much of a piece with his time, he yearned, in novels like *Micah Clarke*, *The White Company*, and *The Lost World*, for ever-more-distant ages and ever-more-exotic places. Those conflicting elements of thought and feeling within his own character must have proved fruitful for his career; they may, in fact, have provided the central source for the great energy that impelled his life and work. Containing within himself both Sherlock Holmes and Dr. Watson, he was gifted with the double vision that pervades his fiction and seems so much a part of his time.

In addition to the great beauty, charm, and originality of his works and the immeasurable amount of pleasure they have provided to millions of readers, Conan Doyle has exerted a powerful influence on the literary art that came after him. It is probably safe to say that the detective story, as an important and international literary genre of the twentieth century, owes both its existence and its

audience to the fiction of Sir Arthur Conan Doyle. His followers include the most distinguished contributors to the form: G. K. Chesterton, Agatha Christie, John Dickson Carr, Dorothy L. Sayers, and Ellery Queen. His influence is discernible even in those less traditional writers of detective fiction—Georges Simenon, Dashiell Hammett, Raymond Chandler, and Ross Macdonald—as well as among some experimental artists who are seldom regarded as authors of mystery stories—Jorge Luis Borges and Alain Robbe-Grillet, for example. *The Lost World* has been made and remade as a motion picture; its fantastic story of a journey to a remote region which becomes an excursion into the prehistoric past will no doubt continue to enchant reading and viewing audiences. The novel forms the essential basis for one of the most important American popular films, *King Kong* (1933), which itself has achieved the status of a classic.

Finally, by whatever standard literature is

The grave of Conan Doyle at Windlesham,
his last home in Sussex

measured, Conan Doyle must be seen not only as a great popular writer, a fascinating late Victorian "character," an inventor of remarkable artistic ingenuity, and an extraordinary teller of tales; he should be regarded more seriously by orthodox teachers, scholars, and critics. It remains a shame and a scandal that he is so little and so lightly studied within the professional academic and literary community. Like his colleagues in the popular arts, he ranks among the most significant creators of the Victorian Age. He and they will probably outlast most of the more highly acclaimed and seriously treated literature of his time.

Other:

H. Bayley, *The Undiscovered Country*, introduction by Conan Doyle (London: Cassell, 1918);

Arthur Hill, *Spiritualism*, preface by Conan Doyle (London: Cassell, 1918);

The Reverend G. Vale Owen, *Life beyond the Veil*, preface by Conan Doyle (London: Butterworth, 1919);

Life of D. D. Home, by His Wife, edited with a preface by Conan Doyle (London: Kegan Paul, 1921);

Leon Denis, *The Mystery of Joan of Arc*, translated by Conan Doyle (London: Murray, 1924).

Bibliographies:

Harold Locke, *A Bibliographical Catalogue of the Writings of Sir Arthur Conan Doyle, M.D., LL.D., 1879-1928* (Tunbridge Wells, U.K.: Webster, 1928);

Ronald Burt De Waal, *The World Bibliography of Sherlock Holmes and Dr. Watson* (New York: Bramhall House, 1974).

Biographies:

John Dickson Carr, *The Life of Sir Arthur Conan Doyle* (New York: Harper, 1949; London: Murray, 1949);

Hesketh Pearson, *Conan Doyle* (New York: Walker, 1961);

Pierre Nordon, *Conan Doyle*, translated by Frances Partridge (London: Murray, 1966; New York: Holt, Rinehart & Winston, 1967);

Charles Higham, *The Adventures of Conan Doyle: The Life of the Creator of Sherlock Holmes* (New York: Norton, 1976);

Ronald Pearsall, *Conan Doyle: A Biographical Solution*

(New York: St. Martin's, 1977).

References:

William S. Baring-Gould, ed., *The Annotated Sherlock Holmes* (2 volumes, New York: Potter, 1967);

H. W. Bell, ed., *Baker-Street Studies* (London: Constable, 1934);

T. S. Blakeney, *Sherlock Holmes: Fact or Fiction?* (London: Murray, 1932);

Gavin Brend, *My Dear Holmes: A Study in Sherlock* (London: Allen & Unwin, 1951);

T. S. Eliot, Review of *The Complete Sherlock Holmes Short Stories*, *Criterion*, 8 (April 1929): 552-556;

Trevor H. Hall, *Sherlock Holmes: Ten Literary Studies* (London: Duckworth, 1969);

Michael Harrison, *In the Footsteps of Sherlock Holmes* (London: Cassell, 1958; New York: Fell, 1960);

James Edward Holroyd, *Baker Street By-ways: A Book about Sherlock Holmes* (London: Allen & Unwin, 1959);

Holroyd, ed., *Seventeen Steps to 221B: A Collection of Sherlockian Pieces by English Writers* (London: Allen & Unwin, 1967);

H. R. F. Keating, "Arthur Conan Doyle," in *Twentieth-Century Crime and Mystery Writers*, edited by John M. Reilly (New York: St. Martin's, 1980), pp. 499-503;

Christopher Morley, ed., *Sherlock Holmes and Dr. Watson: A Textbook of Friendship* (New York: Harcourt, Brace, 1944);

S. C. Roberts, *Holmes and Watson: A Miscellany* (London: Oxford University Press, 1953);

Dorothy L. Sayers, *Unpopular Opinions* (London: Gollancz, 1946; New York: Harcourt, Brace, 1947);

Edgar W. Smith, ed., *Profile by Gaslight: An Irregular Reader about the Private Life of Sherlock Holmes* (New York: Simon & Schuster, 1944);

Vincent Starrett, *The Private Life of Sherlock Holmes* (Chicago: University of Chicago Press, 1960; London: Allen & Unwin, 1961).

Papers:

Various manuscripts by Conan Doyle are in the Berg Collection, New York Public Library; the Lily Library, University of Indiana, Bloomington; and the Humanities Research Center, University of Texas, Austin.

James Anthony Froude

(23 April 1818-20 October 1894)

Craig Turner
Texas A&M University

BOOKS: *Shadows of the Clouds*, as Zeta (London: Olliver, 1847);

A Sermon Preached at St. Mary Church on the Death of the Rev. George May Coleridge (Torquay, U.K.: Croydon, 1847);

The Nemesis of Faith (London: Chapman, 1849; Chicago: Belfords, Clarke, 1879);

The Book of Job (London: Chapman, 1854);

History of England from the Fall of Wolsey to the Death of Elizabeth, 12 volumes (London: Parker, 1856-1870; New York: Scribners, 1865-1870);

Short Stories on Great Subjects, 4 volumes (London: Longmans, Green, 1867-1883; New York: Scribners, 1871-1883);

Inaugural Address Delivered to the University of St. Andrews 19 March 1869 (London: Longmans, Green, 1869);

The Cat's Pilgrimage (Edinburgh: Edmonston & Douglas, 1870; New Haven, Conn.: East Rock Press, 1949);

Calvinism: An Address Delivered to the University of St. Andrews 17 March 1871 (London: Longmans, Green, 1871; New York: Scribners, 1871);

The English in Ireland in the Eighteenth Century, 3 volumes (London: Longmans, Green, 1872-1874; New York: Scribner, Armstrong, 1873-1874);

The Life and Times of Thomas Becket (New York: Scribner, Armstrong, 1878);

Caesar: A Sketch (London: Longmans, Green, 1879; New York: Scribners, 1879);

Science and Theology Ancient and Modern (Toronto: Rose-Belford, 1879; New York: The Truth Seeker, 188?);

Bunyan, English Men of Letters Series (London: Macmillan, 1880; New York: Harper, 1880);

Two Lectures on South Africa Delivered Before the Philosophical Institute (Edinburgh: Longmans, Green, 1880);

Thomas Carlyle: A History of the First Forty Years of His Life 1795-1835, 2 volumes (London: Longmans, Green, 1882; New York: Harper, 1882);

Luther: A Short Biography (London: Longmans, Green, 1883; New York: Scribners, 1884);

James Anthony Froude

Historical and Other Sketches, edited by D. H. Wheeler (New York: Funk & Wagnalls, 1883);

Thomas Carlyle: A History of His Life in London 1834-81, 2 volumes (London: Longmans, Green, 1884; New York: Harper, 1884);

Oceana; or, England and Her Colonies (London: Longmans, Green, 1886; New York: Scribners, 1886);

The Knights Templars (New York: Alden, 1886);

My Relations with Carlyle: Together with a Letter from the Late Sir James Stephen (London: Longmans, Green, 1886; New York: Scribners, 1903);

The English in the West Indies; or, The Bow of Ulysses (London: Longmans, Green, 1888; New York: Scribners, 1888);

Liberty and Property: An Address to the Liberty and Property Defence (London: Liberty and Property Defence League, 1888);

The Two Chiefs of Dunboy; or, An Irish Romance of the Last Century (London: Longmans, Green, 1889; New York: Munro, 1889);

Lord Beaconsfield (London: Low, Marston, Searle & Rivington, 1890; New York: Harper, 1890);

The Divorce of Catherine of Aragon: Being a Supplement

to the History of England (London: Longmans,
    Green, 1891; New York: Scribners, 1891);
The Spanish Story of the Armada and Other Essays (London: Longmans, Green, 1892; New York:
    Scribners, 1892);
Lectures on the Council of Trent (London: Longmans,
    Green, 1893; New York: Scribners, 1896);
Life and Letters of Erasmus (London: Longmans,
    Green, 1894; New York: Scribners, 1894);
English Seamen in the Sixteenth Century (New York:
    Scribners, 1894; London: Longmans, Green,
    1895);
A Siding at a Railway Station: An Allegory (London:
    Fifield, 1905).

James Anthony Froude is best known as a
controversial historian and the literary executor
and biographer of Thomas Carlyle. He was also,
however, an accomplished writer of fiction and
editor of *Fraser's Magazine* for more than a dozen
years. His autobiographical *The Nemesis of Faith*
(1849) was burned as heretical by the senior tutor
of Exeter College, and remains a remarkably honest—if somewhat sentimental—portrait of the spiritual trials of a nineteenth-century intellectual.

Anthony Froude was the last of eight children
born into the Devonshire household of Archdeacon
and Mrs. Robert Hurrell Froude. He was a sickly
child who at age three, in his own words, "was supposed to need bracing . . . was taken out of bed
every morning and dipped in the ice cold water
which ran from a spring into a granite trough in the
backyard." Such harsh, often well-intentioned but
ill-advised treatment Froude received from his
family throughout his life. Froude described his
father as "an excellent parish priest of the old sort"
who "had a taste for books, books especially of history and antiquities." Though "irregularly educated," the archdeacon had some talent as an
amateur artist—drawing in the vein of J. M. W.
Turner's early sketches—in addition to collecting a
valuable library. A country gentleman and a landowner of consequence, the Reverend Mr. Froude
was nevertheless a cold, hard, practical man who
never spoke of feeling or sentiment, even in his own
home. His wife, Margaret Spedding, died several
months before Anthony's third birthday, leaving
her youngest son to grow up in a stern, reserved,
very masculine environment.

Richard Hurrell, the eldest son fifteen years
Anthony's senior, was the family's acknowledged
genius: "We adored Hurrell. He was sparkling brilliant, moved as a sort of king in the element which

*Richard Hurrell Froude, J. A. Froude's older brother, as a child.
Hurrell grew up to become a leader of the Oxford Movement with
John Henry Newman.*

surrounded us." With John Henry Newman, John
Keble, and Edward Pusey, Hurrell Froude became
one of the chief figures in the conservative High
Anglican revival called the Oxford Movement.
Begun as a protest against what they considered an
increasing threat to the church from temporal politics, the movement developed an antiliberal, antirational credo asserting for the church authoritarianism in matters of faith. Published between 1833
and 1841, ninety *Tracts for the Times* set forth the
beliefs of its leading exponents based on appeals to
history and led to a second name for the
movement—Tractarianism. Hurrell's early death
proved a great disappointment to the father, who
desperately wanted his sons to achieve success in the
established professions—a desire which was never
to be fulfilled but which tainted his relationships
with his sons, especially Anthony.

Hurrell was a sort of chief aide in the household with the responsibility of looking after Anthony, and his harsh handling of his youngest
brother reflects something of the insensitivity and
narrowness Froude experienced during his early

years. Two such instances of Hurrell's concern for Anthony's lack of manliness Froude was never to forget: "A small stream ran along the fence which enclosed the garden, with newts, frogs, and other ugly things in it. I remember Hurrell once when I was very little taking me by the heels and stirring the mud at the bottom with my head. It had not the least effect which he desired. Another time I have a vivid recollection of being put overboard into deep water out of a boat in the river again to make me bold, which it didn't make me at all." Robert, one year Hurrell's junior, was the single member of the family who seems to have treated his youngest brother with compassion: he unfortunately died when Anthony was ten. "I have thought that had Robert lived to guide me, my own small career might have been a happier and more useful one," Froude was to write near the end of his own life.

Froude's early education began at Buckfastleigh School in Devonshire, where he was quite happy and demonstrated an early aptitude for Greek. His father unfortunately chose to send him at age eleven to Westminster College in the hope of seeing his youngest child at Christ Church with a scholarship at sixteen. Younger than the proper age and small as well, Anthony was by his own description "weak and nervous," with a hernia which curtailed his physical activities, a want of confidence, and suspicion rather than support from his father and oldest brother. His Westminster experience was to become the cornerstone for his earliest published novel, *Shadows of the Clouds*. Released pseudonymously under the name "Zeta" in 1847, this book actually consists of two separate stories—"The Spirit's Trials" and "The Lieutenant's Daughter"—united under a general title which reflects their thematic unity: the clouds of misfortune cast dark shadows over the lives of the characters. "The Spirit's Trials" tells the story of Edward Fowler's early life, education, and first love, which closely parallel Froude's: "He was undergrown for his age, infirm, and unhealthy; and a disposition might have been observed in him even then, in all his dealings with other boys and with his master, to evade difficulties instead of meeting them—a feature which should have called for the most delicate handling. . . . His nature required treatment the most delicate, it received the very roughest." At fifteen, Anthony Froude was summoned home from Westminster under the threat of apprenticeship to a tanner; his father met him with a beating for his supposed prodigality and with "the utmost coldness . . . never with a word of kindness or

encouragement." He was kept busy copying sermons and translating the letters of John of Salisbury for about two years, until his father sent him to a private tutor near Oxford in order to prepare for the university.

This period of private tutelage is characterized in "The Spirit's Trials" as sharply contrasting with his home life: "For the first time since he could recollect he found himself among people who were truly kind to him, and his frozen heart began to thaw in the warm atmosphere." Thus, when J. A. Froude enrolled at Oriel in 1836, he found himself a changing, if not a changed, young man. Little was expected of him at home, but he had grown tall and strong since recovering from his internal troubles and was beginning to feel that "at last I am like other people and am treated like a human being." Several of his sisters and brothers, including Robert and Hurrell, had died of consumption, and Anthony expected to follow them to an early grave. He thus determined to read what he chose and do as he chose—riding, boating, playing tennis, and attending wine and supper parties.

All was not frivolity, however, as Froude revived his interest in the classics and soon fell under the influence of John Henry Newman. But perhaps he most enjoyed the long vacations—the three months between the end of the summer term and the beginning of the fall term—when he would join a reading party of four or five undergraduates and a tutor in taking lodgings in the mountains or at the sea to read in the mornings and climb, sail, swim, or fish in the afternoons. On such a trip in 1838, Froude came to know intimately the family of the Reverend James Bush; more particularly, he fell in love with the eldest daughter, Harriet. The relationship that grew between the two substantially changed Froude's outlook; as late as the 1890s, he would remember: "The sense of being valued by another made me set a value on my own life. I had something to care for, something which made it worth my while to distinguish myself. I had an object in the future." After budding for almost a year—long enough to flower into the hopes of an engagement—the love of Anthony Froude and Harriet Bush was poisoned by their reverend fathers. In "The Spirit's Trials," Edward/Anthony feels honor bound to forward his father's vituperative letter to Mr. Hardinge/Bush about his future with Emma/Harriet: "he copied out his father's letter himself, and with a long one of his own, detailing most of his own history, he sent it off to Mr. Hardinge. . . . It was a thunder-train indeed which he

Oriel College, Oxford, where Froude studied from 1837 to 1842

had fired. . . . First there was a frightful silence; one terror-stricken letter came from poor Emma, saying her father was dreadfully agitated; and the next post the hurricane broke upon him in its brief fury one short stunning letter from himself, and one more of two lines from Emma, to say she could never be his wife." Half a century later, Froude recalled how "suddenly the sky clouded again, and the prospect which had opened so brightly was gone forever. . . . Months passed before I could throw off the leaden torpor into which I had been plunged." Though his fictional hero suffers a more immediate and melodramatic end—death from tuberculosis—by 1840 Froude had recovered sufficiently to continue his studies and to accept a private tutorship in the family of the Reverend William Cleaver, who held the living of Delgany in Wicklow, Ireland. Though Froude was impressed with the sincerity of the family's evangelical faith, the publication of Tract Ninety brought on attacks against Newman by Cleaver that Froude could not bear to listen to in silence; the tutorship was terminated, and Froude took a short tour of Ireland before returning to Oxford in 1842. His renewed work won for him the Chancellor's Prize for an English essay in the spring, and in the summer Froude was elected Fellow of Exeter.

About that same time, Froude first fell under the influence that was to affect so much of the rest of his life and career: he read Carlyle's *French Revolution* (1837). Already spurred by Newman and others into religious questionings, Froude's encounter with Thomas Carlyle deepened his perplexities and led him to explore Emerson, Goethe, Coleridge, Wordsworth, Lessing, Schiller, and others. Carlyle,

Emerson, and Goethe particularly fascinated him in their concern with actual phenomena, with things and people around them. There were no appeals to antiquity or tradition in their writings, but to nature and the intellect. Under their influence, Froude was asked by Newman to help prove the unbroken continuity of supernatural power working miracles throughout history by writing a saint's life. Froude chose to write about St. Neot who, according to tradition, began as a priest in Glastonbury before becoming a religious hermit in Cornwall. Froude began the work somewhat skeptically: "It is not pretended that every fact in the following Legend can be supported on sound historical evidence. . . . In other words, their Lives are not so much strict biographies, as myths, edifying stories compiled from tradition, and designed not so much to relate facts, as to produce a religious impression on the mind of the hearer." Having thoroughly explored Colgan's *Lives of the Irish Saints*, Froude returned to Ireland in 1845 and explored its "wild west"— reading, looking, and thinking. Finally, for Froude, "the individual figures of the great saints of Ireland dissolved into mist like the sons of Fingal on the rocks of Morven. . . . St. Patrick might be a myth. The living Ireland was a reality." Henceforth, his historical interests turned toward the Reformation and after in England, and much of his later work was either directly or indirectly aimed at Newman's teachings concerning the Reformation and the Tudors.

Before leaving for Ireland, Froude had somewhat tentatively agreed to be ordained, since church orders were necessary to become a fellow: "when I took Deacon's Orders in 1845 it was with no conscious doubt of the general truth of the Gospel history, but with my notions entirely vague as to how it was proved to be true." Froude was later to regard the taking of orders as the greatest mistake of his life.

In this state Froude began writing *Shadows of the Clouds*. "The Spirit's Trials" is ostensibly told by Arthur, friend of Edward Fowler, but a major portion of the narrative is conveyed by letters ascribed to Fowler, with Arthur filling in the gaps. *Shadows of the Clouds*—including the even more melodramatic and quasi-mystical dream vision "The Lieutenant's Daughter"—was briefly noted by the *Athenaeum*, but its chief result was to drive a wedge into the already considerable gap separating Froude from his father—a gap not to be bridged until six years later when he began publication of his *History of England* and began to redeem himself in his father's eyes.

(Margaret, Froude's oldest child, believed that the archdeacon attempted to suppress *Shadows of the Clouds* by buying all the copies he could and destroying them without ever having read a word of either story.)

Froude probably began work on *The Nemesis of Faith* shortly after the publication of this first novel in 1847. Also autobiographical, *The Nemesis of Faith* chronicles probably the most difficult crisis which Froude ever faced: he has described it as "an exact picture of my own mind. . . . It was a mood, not a treatise." And the mood in which Froude wrote his second book he recorded some forty-five years later: "It had always struck me as odd that, if to think rightly of religion was the thing of greatest moment to us, the principles on which we were ruled by Providence should not be found, like all other knowledge, in the present reality of our actual life and experience."

Markham Sutherland, Froude's autobiographical hero, struggles with a number of the intellectual, moral, and spiritual perplexities of the day—particularly the disintegration of the supernatural in his faith—but is finally convinced to take orders in the Church of England in spite of his skepticism. The novel ends with Sutherland full of

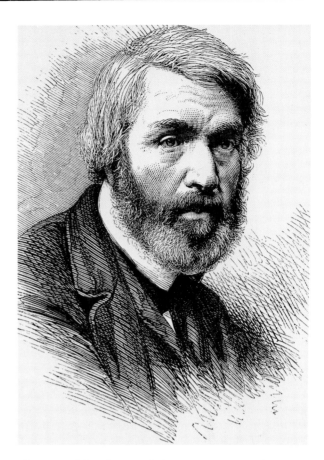

Thomas Carlyle, who exerted the most important influence on Froude's life

Harriet Bush, whose romance with Froude was broken up by their fathers. She served as the model for Emma Hardinge in Shadows of the Clouds *(1847).*

remorse over what he sees as the wasted ruins of his life and full of religious doubts even after a second commitment to another Christian church. Upon its publication in 1849, *The Nemesis of Faith* created quite a furor: Senior Tutor William Sewell of Froude's own college burned the book in College Hall, and Froude was roundly condemned as a heretic. He was called upon by the governing board of Exeter to resign his fellowship in February 1849, and, though he willingly abandoned the creed, he was abandoning his profession and his only means of livelihood as well. For until 1870, orders—even deacon's orders—were not retractable: priests and deacons were forbidden to enter any other learned profession or to sit in Parliament. With the passage of Bouverie's Act in 1870, Froude became one of the first to divest himself of orders and officially revert to the status of layman.

Froude's father became even more irate at his son and cut off his modest allowance entirely. Froude had considered resigning before the publication of *The Nemesis of Faith* and had therefore actively sought a teaching post at Hobart Town in Tasmania: the position was at first awarded to him, but was taken away because of the controversy. While he had also communicated with several friends about business possibilities, there were no realistic prospects for the resigned fellow when he left Oxford in 1849. Still, he did so with little regret: writing *The Nemesis of Faith* was, as Froude put it, "an extraordinary relief. I had thrown off the weight under which I had been staggering. I was free, able to encounter the realities of life without vexing myself further over the unanswerable problems."

Also in 1849, James Spedding took Froude to Cheyne Row and introduced him to the great Carlyle, with whom he discussed Ireland. Though Froude has recorded that he was treated "shortly and sternly," he immediately surmised "that no one need look for conventional politeness from Carlyle—he would hear the exact truth from him and nothing else." Neither could have guessed that their relationship would flower so that Froude would become literary executor and biographer of Carlyle. After leaving Oxford, Froude traveled around, visiting briefly with several friends before settling in Manchester at the insistence of solicitor Samuel Darbishire, who employed him as a private tutor for his son and daughters. Froude's state of mind at this time became the subject of his fable "The Cat's Pilgrimage," a tale of stoic determinism stressing the acceptance of one's duty in life. Even more momentous than the position with the Darbishires, however, was Froude's meeting with Charlotte Grenfell while visiting at Charles Kingsley's home in Ilfracombe in February 1849. After overcoming objections in both families, the two were married on 3 October 1849. Froude then settled rather comfortably—though finances were a bit tight—into domestic happiness. Soon he determined to try to make a living with his pen, and the couple moved to Plas Gwyant, North Wales, where he embarked on a writing career that was to lead him through numerous articles, his twelve-volume *History of England* (1856-1870), his four-volume biography of Carlyle (1882-1884), the editorship of *Fraser's Magazine* from 1861 to 1874, and volumes of other histories, biographies, and miscellanies.

Having suffered through much illness, an unusually severe winter, a prolonged cold spring, and a "wretched summer," the Froudes moved first to Babbicombe, near Torquay, and then to Bideford, primarily to attain proximity to the great libraries in London and at Oxford. In 1856, Anthony Froude

reached his thirty-eighth birthday, having lived approximately one-half of his total lifespan. He later felt that most of these first years were wasted: "I look back on my own life up to the time when I was thirty with nothing but disgust." But in the eight years after he had purged himself in *The Nemesis of Faith*, Froude had married, fathered three children, fallen under the spell of Carlyle, dedicated himself to historical writing, and published the first two volumes of his *History of England*.

The first—and possibly the ablest—major attack on Froude as a historian was leveled by Goldwin Smith, newly appointed Regius Professor of Modern History at Oxford (a position for which Froude had also been considered), in the July and October 1858 issues of the *Edinburgh Review*. Smith attacked Froude's examination of the character and reputation of Henry VIII, and established the major tactic employed by subsequent critics: he implied that "the beauty of Froude's style" and "the interesting character" of his narratives had deceived the public; Smith wrote that the first four volumes of Froude's *History of England* "cannot stand high in the estimation of those who look in a history above all things for truth." Similar volleys were fired at his histories by other critics, but the most virulent and persistent of Froude's deprecators proved to be Edward Augustus Freeman, a hardworking but rather dull, commonplace historian who became Regius Professor of Modern History in 1884. A man of strong opinions, Freeman—in the words of Froude's biographer, W. H. Dunn—"carefully created an impression that Froude was inaccurate and unreliable, an impression so often repeated and so widely circulated that its effects have continued even to this day." Examinations of the Freeman-Froude controversy have, on the one hand, cited Freeman's malignant public nature and his own historical inaccuracies; on the other hand, since Froude did all the research, translation, transcription, and writing for his highly original histories, occasional errors can be found—though, Froude's defenders insist, they are not so widespread as his critics have claimed. The major interpretations in Froude's historical writings must ultimately stand as their own advocates.

In addition to being a controversial novelist and historian, Froude also became the controversial literary executor and biographer of the Carlyles. Since their introduction in 1849, Froude's devotion to Carlyle and Carlyle's appreciation of Froude had steadily grown. After Jane Carlyle's death in 1866, Froude spent considerable effort in caring for the aging Sage of Chelsea. In June 1869, Carlyle presented his shocked disciple with a bundle of Jane's letters, journals, and miscellaneous writings, as well as his own abortive attempts at a commentary on her life and works, with the charge to deal with them as Froude saw fit after his death. In 1873, Carlyle formalized this request in his will, and the two volumes of their *Reminiscences* (1881) were edited and published by Froude exactly one month after Carlyle's death. Froude continued to work with the Carlyle papers—writing his four-volume biography of Thomas (1882-1884) and editing the *Letters and Memorials of Jane Welsh Carlyle* (1883)—in spite of the public attacks and legal proceedings of Mary Aitken Carlyle, a niece who, Dunn insists, was motivated to seek possession of the materials by her expectation of financial benefits.

Charlotte Grenfell Froude died in April 1860, leaving Froude with their three children: Margaret, Rose Mary, and Pascal Grenfell. He began his second marriage in September 1861 with Henrietta Elizabeth Warre, longtime acquaintance of his first wife who, in her final illness, had hoped for just such a union. Margaret remembered the twelve years of this marriage as the happiest of her father's life, and Henrietta's sudden death in 1874 was probably the greatest sorrow of Froude's life. He retreated with the children to Cragen House, Wales, to avoid the sad associations with London.

Fortunately for Froude's peace of mind and heart, Disraeli's government had just taken office, with Lord Carnarvon, an intimate of Froude's, as colonial secretary. Long an advocate of the confederation of the colonies, Froude proposed to make an unofficial trip to South Africa, ostensibly for his health, but in reality to assess the situation and report on a number of politically sensitive issues. His report led to Lord Carnarvon's suggesting a conference on native affairs, with Froude as his representative. Froude therefore returned to South Africa to present Carnarvon's position and found himself in the midst of a tempestuous political power struggle. He was censured by the House of Assembly, which resented the intrusion of the colonial secretary. In spite of Froude's arousing popular support for the confederation with his public speeches, the South African Conference was doomed before it convened by the personal and parochial interests of its representatives. Despite the controversy surrounding his South African visits, a decade later Froude made very pleasant unofficial trips to Australia and New Zealand (1884-1885) and to the British West Indies (1886-1887) that resulted in *Oceana* (1886) and *The English in the West Indies* (1888).

Froude's final novel, *The Two Chiefs of Dunboy*, grew out of his lifelong fascination with and appreciation of Ireland. In addition to tutoring there in 1840, he spent numerous extended holidays in Ireland—especially in Kerry—and wrote at length of Ireland, the Irish, and English-Irish relations: about 500 pages of his *History of England* were devoted to these subjects; his three-volume *The English in Ireland* was published from 1872 to 1874; and in 1872 he delivered five controversial lectures in America presenting a liberal English view of the Irish problem. Published in 1889 with the subtitle *An Irish Romance of the Last Century, The Two Chiefs* is the only extended fiction Froude wrote after his decision to support himself by writing. In a letter to his longtime friend, John Skelton, Froude reveals his exceptional interest in this book: "I had so bothered myself over the book that I could not tell whether it was good or bad, and was humbly prepared to hear that it was a dead failure." In the same letter Froude intimates that he had said more about the nature of the Irish and the Irish problem in the novel than he had yet said in his nonfiction: "I may say that Morty of *The Two Chiefs* is nearer the real article than the Morty of *The English in Ireland*."

This historical novel centers in Kerry on the southwestern coast of Ireland in the eighteenth century and deals with the characters and actions of Morty Sullivan and Col. John Goring. "Colonel Goring belonged to an order of men who," Froude wrote, "if they had been allowed fair play, would have made the sorrows of Ireland the memory of an evil dream; but he had come too late, the spirit of the Cromwellians had died out of the land, and was not to be revived by a single enthusiast." He is, of course, the real hero of the book and the embodiment of Froude's idea of proper Protestantism. His antagonist, Morty Sullivan, represents all that Froude admired in the Irish nature. The story is tragic—both Morty and the colonel ultimately fail: Morty leads a group that deceives and murders Goring, and Morty is in turn betrayed by one of his own and killed by English soldiers.

Though at times heavily political and overly didactic, *The Two Chiefs of Dunboy* is probably Froude's best fictional effort: his characterizations are more alive, and the descriptions of Kerry are presented more carefully and lovingly than the descriptions in any of his earlier novels. Also, he does an excellent job of weaving two strong narratives into a complex, interesting, and coherent plot.

Manuscript of the closing passage of Froude's inaugural lecture as Regius Professor of Modern History at Oxford, 1892

Lastly, *The Two Chiefs* contains historian Froude's unfettered final written reflections on Ireland, the Irish, and English Protestantism there.

The crowning irony of Froude's long and full career occurred in April 1892, when he was asked to succeed his archenemy Edward Freeman in the Regius Professorship of Modern History at Oxford. Finally, forty-three years after resigning an Oxford fellowship in disgrace, Froude returned to his university in distinction and triumph. He held the distinguished professorship proudly until his death on 20 October 1894.

Froude remains a controversial historian and biographer, but his infamy and importance in these areas will continue to decline with time. Though not among the best novels of the last century and ignored by the critics in the present century, his autobiographical fiction will continue to rank among the most honest and graceful prose which chronicles the spiritual and intellectual distress of mid-Victorian England. *The Two Chiefs of Dunboy* stands as one of the more interesting and sympathetic historical romances of the age and demonstrates Froude's three strengths as a fiction writer: he was an excellent, vivid storyteller; he was able to use varied and complex narrative structures with ease and grace; and he wrote with much genuine feeling. James Anthony Froude wrote to Charles Kingsley regarding *The Nemesis of Faith*, "There is something in the thing, I know, for I cut a hole in my heart and wrote with the blood."

Other:

"St. Neot," in *Lives of the English Saints*, 4 volumes (London: Freemantle, 1844-1845);

"Suggestions on the Best Means of Teaching English History," in *Oxford Essays, Contributed by Members of the University* (Oxford: Parker, 1855-1858);

William Thomas, *The Pilgrim: A Dialogue on the Life and Actions of King Henry the Eighth*, edited by Froude (London: Parker, Son & Bowen, 1861);

Thomas Carlyle, *Reminiscences*, edited by Froude, 2 volumes (London: Longmans, Green, 1881);

Letters and Memorials of Jane Welsh Carlyle, Prepared for Publication by Thomas Carlyle, edited by

James Anthony Froude in 1892

Froude (3 volumes, London: Longmans, Green, 1883; 1 volume, New York: Harper, 1883).

References:
Algernon Cecil, *Six Oxford Thinkers* (London: John Murray, 1909), pp. 156-213;

Waldo Hilary Dunn, *James Anthony Froude: A Biography*, 2 volumes (London: Oxford University Press, 1961-1963);
Robert Goetzman, *James Anthony Froude: A Bibliography of Studies* (New York: Garland, 1977);
Herbert Paul, *The Life of Froude* (London: Pitman, 1905).

George Gissing

Jacob Korg
University of Washington

BIRTH: Wakefield, Yorkshire, 22 November 1857, to Thomas Waller and Margaret Bedford Gissing.

EDUCATION: Owens College, Manchester, 1872-1876.

MARRIAGES: 27 October 1879 to Marianne Helen Harrison. 25 February 1891 to Edith Underwood; children: Walter Leonard, Alfred Charles.

DEATH: Ispoure, St.-Jean-Pied-de-Port, France, 28 December 1903.

BOOKS: *Workers in the Dawn: A Novel* (3 volumes, London: Remington, 1880; 2 volumes, Garden City: Doubleday, Doran, 1935);
The Unclassed: A Novel (3 volumes, London: Chapman & Hall, 1884; 1 volume, New York: Fenno, 1896);
Demos: A Story of English Socialism (London: Smith, Elder, 1886; New York: Harper, 1886);
Isabel Clarendon (2 volumes, London: Chapman & Hall, 1886);
Thyrza: A Tale (3 volumes, London: Smith, Elder, 1887);
A Life's Morning (3 volumes, London: Smith, Elder, 1888; 1 volume, Philadelphia: Lippincott, 1888);
The Nether World: A Novel (3 volumes, London: Smith, Elder, 1889; 1 volume, New York: Harper, 1889);
The Emancipated: A Novel (3 volumes, London: Bentley, 1890; 1 volume, Chicago: Way & Williams, 1895);
New Grub Street: A Novel (3 volumes, London: Smith,

George Gissing

Elder, 1891; 1 volume, Troy, N.Y.: Brewster, 1904);
Denzil Quarrier: A Novel (London: Lawrence & Bullen, 1892; New York: Macmillan, 1892);
Born in Exile: A Novel (3 volumes, London: Black, 1892);
The Odd Women (3 volumes, London: Lawrence & Bullen, 1893);
In the Year of Jubilee (3 volumes, London: Lawrence & Bullen, 1894; 1 volume, New York: Appleton, 1895);
Eve's Ransom (London: Lawrence & Bullen, 1895; New York: Appleton, 1895);
Sleeping Fires (London: Unwin, 1895; New York: Appleton, 1895);
The Paying Guest (London: Cassell, 1895; New York: Dodd, Mead, 1895);

The Whirlpool (London: Lawrence & Bullen, 1897; New York: Stokes, 1897);

Human Odds and Ends: Stories and Sketches (London: Lawrence & Bullen, 1898);

Charles Dickens: A Critical Study (London: Blackie, 1898; New York: Dodd, Mead, 1898);

The Town Traveller (London: Methuen, 1898; New York: Stokes, 1898);

The Crown of Life (London: Methuen, 1899; New York: Stokes, 1899);

By the Ionian Sea: Notes of a Ramble in Southern Italy (London: Chapman & Hall, 1901; New York: Scribners, 1905);

Our Friend the Charlatan (London: Chapman & Hall, 1901; New York: Holt, 1901);

The Private Papers of Henry Ryecroft (London: Constable, 1903; New York: Dutton, 1903);

Veranilda: A Romance (London: Constable, 1904; New York: Dutton, 1905);

Will Warburton: A Romance of Real Life (London: Constable, 1905; New York: Dutton, 1905);

The House of Cobwebs and Other Stories (London: Constable, 1906; New York: Dutton, 1906);

An Heiress on Condition (Philadelphia: Privately printed for the Pennell Club, 1923);

Critical Studies of the Works of Charles Dickens (New York; Greenberg, 1924);

Sins of the Fathers and Other Tales (Chicago: Covici, 1924);

The Immortal Dickens (London: Palmer, 1924);

A Victim of Circumstances and Other Stories (London: Constable, 1927; New York: Houghton Mifflin, 1927);

Brownie (New York: Columbia University Press, 1931);

Stories and Sketches, edited by A. C. Gissing (London: M. Joseph, 1938);

George Gissing's Commonplace Book (New York: New York Public Library, 1962);

Notes on Social Democracy (London: Enitharmon Press, 1968);

George Gissing: Essays and Fiction (Baltimore: Johns Hopkins, 1970);

My First Rehearsal and My Clerical Rival (London: Enitharmon Press, 1970);

London and the Life of Literature in Late Victorian England: The Diary of George Gissing, Novelist (Hassocks, U.K.: Harvester Press, 1978; Lewisburg, Pa.: Bucknell University Press, 1978);

George Gissing on Fiction (London: Enitharmon Press, 1978).

Although he was once best known as the au-

thor of a volume of essays, *The Private Papers of Henry Ryecroft* (1903), George Gissing is now recognized as one of the important novelists of the late Victorian period. His reputation rests on the long series of novels he wrote between 1880 and 1903, most of them realistic exposures of the injustices of modern industrial society. His early books, which often dealt with scenes of urban poverty, gave the impression that he was a slum novelist, but in the second part of his career he turned to middle-class settings and devoted his mature powers to a widely ranging criticism of ordinary society. Gissing had a special gift for linking private lives with public issues and for showing how sensitive young people were victimized by social forces. Using this approach, he dealt with such themes as poverty, the social disabilities of women, the problems of marriage, the vulgarity of contemporary civilization, and the commercialization of literature.

Gissing was an agnostic in religion and a skeptic with regard to social reform. He usually adopted an antidemocratic, pessimistic, and even fatalistic point of view toward the problems he dramatized. He felt that the nobler human capacities represented by art and learning were bound to be submerged by the mercenary drives and mass culture of democratic society. The social problems that afflicted the late nineteenth century provided him with material for showing how unlikely it was that a civilization free of passion and superstition and devoted to culture would ever emerge. His profound discontent with the conditions he observed led him to exceptional insights into the spiritual dilemmas of the time.

George Robert Gissing was of provincial and middle-class origin, the oldest of the five children of a pharmaceutical chemist who lived over his shop in the main square of Wakefield in Yorkshire. He attended the local school until his father's death, when George was thirteen; he was then sent to Lindow Grove School in Cheshire, and after two years entered Owens College in Manchester. His literary tastes became clear while he was at school and college: he wrote poetry as a child, and studied classical and modern languages and literature. During this time he gained the knowledge of Greek and Roman culture which became a lifelong interest and one of his deepest sources of pleasure. As a student he was a hard worker and compiled a brilliant record, earning high grades and winning numerous prizes and scholarships, and it seemed likely that he would continue his studies at Oxford or Cambridge after taking his degree.

But his career was interrupted in the spring of 1876, when he was eighteen and in his last year at Owens, by a shocking development. He had fallen in love with a seventeen-year-old girl named Marianne Helen Harrison (called "Nell") who was poor and without family and who frequented the pubs near the college, resorting to occasional prostitution to support herself. In an effort to keep her from the streets and enable her to earn an honest living, Gissing turned to the desperate expedient of stealing books, money, and clothes from the common room at the college. He was caught, arrested, expelled, and imprisoned for a month at hard labor. After his release he fled the scene of his disgrace by going to America in September 1876. This episode had a profound effect on the man and his work. It ended any possibility of an academic career; it forced him to begin life as a social exile and to regard himself as an outsider. More fundamentally, the indefensible violation of ordinary moral standards generated a sense of guilt which became one of the sources of his self-defeating behavior and his despairing vision of life.

Gissing spent a year in America, a time of restlessness and exile that was also, paradoxically, the time of his first modest literary successes. After a month in Boston, where he placed his first publication—a short article on some paintings in the museum—in a local periodical, he moved to Waltham, Massachusetts, to take a position in the high school as a teacher of French, German, and English. In March 1877 he left suddenly for Chicago and, in desperate need of money, wrote a number of short stories which he succeeded in selling to the *Chicago Tribune* and other periodicals. There is an accurate account of this and subsequent episodes in *New Grub Street* (1891), where many of Gissing's experiences in America are assigned to a character named Whelpdale. This was Gissing's real beginning as a writer of fiction. In July he moved to New York City, and then, finding that a newspaper in Troy, New York, had plagiarized one of his stories, he went there in the hope of being hired to write more. But he was rejected, and after drifting about New England for several months as an assistant to a traveling photographer, he returned to England in October 1877.

He lived in various poor lodging houses in London, where he was soon joined by Nell, whom he married in 1879. During this period, which is described in *The Private Papers of Henry Ryecroft*, he was in a state of precarious poverty and supported himself by teaching occasional pupils and taking

other irregular jobs while working seriously at a novel. When this first manuscript failed to find a publisher, he wrote another, but again met only with rejections. At last, in 1880, he published this second effort at his own expense with the title *Workers in the Dawn*, using some money from a legacy left by his father. The book attracted little attention and few copies were sold; but Gissing sent a copy to Frederic Harrison, the president of the Positivist Society. Gissing was at that time enthusiastic about Auguste Comte and his positivist philosophy and was an attentive reader of Frederic Harrison's articles. The heroine of his novel turns to positivism as one of several alternatives to conventional Christian faith, and Gissing no doubt hoped that Harrison might be interested in this aspect of his book. Harrison was strongly impressed by the novel, though he took exception to its ideas, and sent Gissing a letter praising it; he also introduced him to John Morley and other literary people and hired him as tutor to his two sons.

Workers in the Dawn is a rambling, heavy-handed novel of social protest that has far too many scenes, characters, and situations but nevertheless conveys a burning sense of indignation in its descriptions of poverty and exhibits a firm intellectual grasp of some of the contemporary theories of social reform. Gissing draws on his own experiences in telling the story of Arthur Golding, a youth born in the slums of London, who is torn between becoming a painter and devoting himself to political action on behalf of his fellow workers. His marriage to Carrie Mitchell, a young prostitute addicted to alcohol whom he rescues from the streets and tries to reform, is an obvious reflection of Gissing's own marital situation. Nell was an alcoholic, and her physical ailments, restlessness, and disobedience made Gissing's life miserable. It was characteristic of him to exploit these sufferings by making her the center of the most powerful scenes of his novel. Golding later falls in love with Helen Norman, a middle-class girl who teaches him that his artistic and political aims can be reconciled with each other. A number of solutions to the problems of the poor are investigated, but all seem futile, and the story ends as Golding, in a sequence that again follows Gissing's life, goes to America in the final chapter and after a time commits suicide by throwing himself into Niagara Falls. As Gissing later acknowledged, the form of his novel imitated George Eliot's, with their realistic descriptions, intricate psychological analyses, authorial comments, and multiple plots.

In spite of the failure of *Workers in the Dawn*,

Eduard Bertz, German socialist writer who was Gissing's friend and correspondent for over twenty years

Gissing's prospects seemed promising, for the people he had met through Harrison offered him work as a journalist. But he rejected most of these opportunities and clung to the life of a struggling novelist, writing industriously in poor lodgings, and supporting himself by tutoring. He had many handicaps to contend with, including the behavior of his wife, who often created crises in the slum neighborhoods where they lived. During this period, he formed two friendships that were to last for the rest of his life. One was with Eduard Bertz, a German socialist in exile who became a writer when he returned to Germany in 1884 and corresponded with Gissing until Gissing's death. The other was with Morley Roberts, a fellow student from Owens College, who was also a novelist and was to write a fictionalized biography of Gissing, *The Private Life of Henry Maitland* (1912).

By 1882, Gissing found that he could no longer live with Nell and sent her to live elsewhere, paying her a small regular allowance. In spite of the troubles he experienced at this time, he wrote several short stories and longer narratives but did not succeed in publishing any of them until he was fortunate enough to have his novel *The Unclassed*

(1884) evaluated by George Meredith, who was a reader for Chapman and Hall. Meredith saw the virtues of the original and rather uncertain story, advised Gissing to make some revisions, and approved the novel for publication in 1884.

In *The Unclassed*, Gissing, who had apparently made some progress while writing the many stories he had been unable to sell, demonstrates better control than he does in *Workers in the Dawn*; he limits himself to fewer themes and characters, embodies his protest in his story instead of expressing it directly, and arrives at a happy ending. Its hero, Osmond Waymark—a poor young intellectual living in the slums of London, the author of an unsuccessful novel, who shares Gissing's social theories and ideas about art and even resembles him closely in physical appearance—is the most autobiographical of Gissing's figures. He also shares Gissing's sexual dilemma, for he would like to marry the respectable middle-class Maud Enderby but is also attracted to Ida Starr, an implausibly intelligent and altruistic girl of the streets, who is no doubt an idealization of Nell. Through Waymark and his friends, Gissing attacks the competitiveness of modern society and its failure to make a place for gifted young people like himself. In the course of the story, Waymark, who begins as an idealist, learns that the slums and their people are beyond redemption, and turns to the view that art should be detached and objective, but insists that it must express misery because "misery is the key-note of modern life." Nevertheless, the novel ends optimistically as Ida Starr, after being imprisoned on a false charge, is discovered to be the granddaughter of a wealthy owner of slum houses, inherits his wealth, becomes a benefactress of the poor, and accepts Waymark when he turns to her.

In these first novels, Gissing denounces poverty but paradoxically expresses considerable hostility toward the poor themselves. He was recording the disillusionment he suffered during his first years in London as a social observer. He had romanticized the poor at first, but quickly learned that working people could not be taught to share his love of art, learning, and classical civilization; instead, they insisted on pursuing the way of life they had learned in the slums. Accordingly, he began to shift his stance as a social critic. He was now less interested in exposing poverty than in defending intellectual values against threats that arose both from the barbarism of the slums and the philistinism of the middle class. And he came to recognize that his true subject was not the proletariat but the intelligent young man who was not equipped to compete in industrial society. Some years later he wrote to Morley Roberts, "the most characteristic, the most important part of my work is that which deals with a class of young men distinctive of our time—well educated, fairly bred, *but without money*."

By 1884, Gissing's income had improved enough to enable him to lease a flat near Regent's Park, which became his first permanent home. He thought he had discovered the kind of environment congenial to cultural values on his visits to the country houses of the wealthy people whose children he tutored; and his next novels employed settings of this kind, turning on an interplay between the worlds of poverty and privilege. He wrote three stories in which young people plan to escape urban life by marrying into the landed gentry. *Isabel Clarendon* (1886) tells of a bookish young man who takes refuge from the turmoil of London in a country cottage and falls in love with a wealthy young widow who owns a mansion in the neighborhood. Instead of achieving his ideal of a life of the mind through marriage, however, he meets defeat and is forced to go into trade by making his living as a bookseller. In *A Life's Morning* (1888), a poor young governess discovers the beauty of country life as Gissing himself did, by teaching the children of wealthy parents. She experiences joy and serenity of mind when she leaves her narrow home life for the tasteful and orderly surroundings of a well-appointed mansion. Her engagement to a son of the family is disrupted when her father's employer seeks to force her into marriage by threatening to reveal a theft her father has committed and the father, unable to withstand the pressure of the scandal, kills himself. As a result, the heroine is unable to marry and to enter upon the life of cultivation for which she yearns until she meets her old lover by chance six years later.

Though it was completed in 1885, *A Life's Morning* was not published until 1888; by that time Gissing had written and published three other novels. The first of these, *Demos* (1886), boldly argues that plebeian life has a corrupting effect on character and follows the argument into its social, moral, and political implications. Richard Mutimer, a clever young socialist leader, comes into a fortune, converts the factory he owns to socialist methods of production, and marries into a higher social class. But he never overcomes the faults of character he brings from his proletarian origin and cannot hold the love of his wife, retain control of his socialist movement, or pass a moral test to which the plot subjects him. A newly found will deprives him of his property; he sinks into poverty and is killed by a stone thrown from a mob of his own followers. At the novel's end, the countryside, desecrated by his factory, reverts to its former beauty and quiet.

Demos is perhaps the first novel in which Gissing exhibits full confidence in his talent. It employs a wide range of skills, including realistic description, psychological analysis, and the creation of mood and atmosphere, and gives full development to a great variety of scenes and characters. The accounts of life among the poor of London are exceptionally authentic and intimate and express considerable sympathy. There are animated, colorful descriptions of socialist meetings based on actual observation. The novel as a whole makes a powerful, if somewhat eccentric, political statement: it condemns social democracy as a manifestation of the greed and egoism of the working-class mind and awards approval to patrician attitudes concerned with aestheticism and the preservation of cultural values. Because of the innate strength of its story and character-depiction and its controversial treatment of current social questions, *Demos* was a distinct success both with the public and with the critics. Though published anonymously, it soon became known as Gissing's work and established his position on the contemporary literary scene as a novelist who was to be taken seriously.

Meredith had warned Gissing not to abandon "low-life scenes," and his success with this material in *Demos* must have convinced Gissing that Meredith was right; for his next novel, *Thyrza* (1887), is set for the most part in a poor London neighborhood and depicts with insight and understanding the lives of working people. The heroine, an idealized figure of a working girl, is not convincing; but Gilbert Grail, the man who loves her—a factory worker with a devotion to books, who knows that he will never be able to free himself from a life of labor and monotony—is one of Gissing's most pathetic and authentic characters. The idea of the novel is embodied in the experience of its male protagonist, Walter Egremont, a member of the landed gentry who comes to the slums to spread culture and enlightenment and falls in love with the heroine. As in Gissing's earlier novels, the love that crosses class divisions proves to be destructive. Egremont finds that the poor cannot be redeemed, that it would be a mistake for him to marry Thyrza, and that, in effect, each segment of society should keep to itself and follow its own ways. As the novel ends, he decides to marry a girl of his own class; but the heartbroken

Thyrza, whom he has been forced to abandon, dies of grief.

As his diary shows, Gissing was an extraordinarily steady worker. Immediately after completing a novel, he turned to a new one and seldom went a day without either planning his work or actually writing. But he suffered from failures of motivation, indecision, and a lack of self-confidence. He often changed from one project to another, canceled many chapters of writing, and even left whole books unpublished. He had an especially trying period of indecision after completing *Thyrza* in January 1887. He wrote steadily as usual, completing or nearly completing four novels in the following fourteen months, but nothing written during that time achieved publication. This period of frustration came to an end in March 1888, when he was notified that Nell had died. He went to make the funeral arrangements and found that she had been living in desperate poverty. While he looked at her body lying in the squalid room where she had lived, he experienced a renewal of the resentment and despair with which he had responded to social injustice during his early years in London; immediately afterward, he wrote his last and most pessimistic novel of poverty.

There is no contrast between wealth and poverty in *The Nether World* (1889). It is an unrelieved accumulation of images from slum life, and while certain gradations of misery are evident, the ultimate effect is one of crushing hopelessness. The poor try to escape their plight by seeking employment, by crime, by politics; outsiders try to help with charity and education. But the vicious qualities of character bred in the slums cannot be extirpated, and the people make a hell of their environment with their drunkenness, violence, cruelty, and dishonesty. The characters who bring strength and courage to their struggle are submerged by the social forces raging in the slums. Gissing was powerfully motivated in writing this novel, but he displayed a new sophistication by channeling his feelings into literary workmanship instead of venting them in strident protest as he had when he first began to write. Slum scenes and people are rendered with an accuracy that shows patient observation, the effects of environment and experience on character are displayed in logical fashion, and the quality of lower-class life is projected through a number of eloquent descriptions.

In September 1888, Gissing took a vacation from his uninterrupted work of the last eight years and fulfilled a long-standing ambition by traveling on the Continent for five months. After a month in Paris with an uncongenial companion who had decided to join him, he went alone to Naples, Rome, Florence, and Venice. The main attractions of Italy for Gissing were the relics and ruins connected with Roman antiquity. He paid his respects to the art and architecture of the Renaissance but insisted that they had far less meaning for him than Roman remains. He also enjoyed observing contemporary Italian life, however, and recorded many details of street activities and daily behavior in the diary he kept.

The Italian visit had an immediate influence on his writing. He made use of some Italian scenes in his next novel, *The Emancipated* (1890), but the more important effect of the trip was to mark a sharp division between the two main phases of his career. After this journey, Gissing turned from the realistic treatment of poverty that had been his main strength up to this time to novels of middle-class life. He was still interested in social conditions, but he now focused on the psychological analyses of middle-class people who encountered the problems of an increasingly industrialized and democratic society. There was a parallel change in his style. He left behind the tones of fierce indignation and quiet despair that accompanied his treatment of poverty and began to cultivate an understated, objective style of neutral realism that varied from flat statement to quiet irony and could serve as a devastating medium of social criticism. *The Emancipated* deals with people who are wealthy enough to travel in Italy, and who rebel, in various ways, against conventional moral, aesthetic and religious standards. One of its central characters is a young widow who comes from a narrow Evangelical society and is taught, by the cultural experiences she has in Italy, to open herself to aesthetic feelings and to love. Placed in symmetrical opposition to her is an "emancipated" young woman who is well-educated and free to marry as she chooses, but uses this freedom unwisely. This dichotomy brings forward a theme that was becoming increasingly prominent in Gissing's novels, the problem of the social position of women.

He seems to have intended to deal with this theme in his next novel; for after completing *The Emancipated*, he planned a story called "The Headmistress" and read materials on women in the British Museum. Before completing the story, he left London in November 1889 for a second Mediterranean trip. This time he went first to Greece, and after a month in Athens, revisited

Naples, where he stayed until 20 February. While he was in Naples, he had the first touch of the lung disease that was to lead to his death and had to spend a week in bed in his lodging house. Soon after his return to London at the beginning of March 1890, he began to work not on "The Headmistress" but on the novel that ultimately turned out to be *New Grub Street*. For many months, however, he was unable to make any progress, switched from one plan to another, canceled many pages, and wrote in his diary that he felt "desperation" and even "madness." Although he had always cultivated seclusion, Gissing also suffered intensely from loneliness, and his unhappiness had become so intense that he was unable to work effectively. He often said, both in his novels and in letters about his own case, that a poor but educated man could not expect a woman who was his equal to share his poverty, and the idea dominated his thoughts about marriage. Consequently, when he decided to put an end to his frustration, he offered marriage—as he later admitted—to the first woman he met. This was Edith Underwood, a respectable but ignorant girl of proletarian background. Gissing thought she would be pliable and would adapt herself to his habits, but he could hardly have been more wrong. She turned out to be evil-tempered, incompetent, and violent, a cameo of all the qualities he hated in working people.

However, the first results of his friendship with her were favorable. A week after he met her he began to make progress with *New Grub Street*, even deciding on its title; a little more than two months later he completed it, in sharp contrast to the confused and ineffectual efforts of the preceding months. The book written at such speed is closely modeled on his own experiences, expresses some of his strongest personal convictions, and is generally considered his finest novel. There had been earlier books about novelists, such as Thackeray's *Pendennis* (1849-1850) and Dickens's *David Copperfield* (1850), but *New Grub Street* was the first to treat the occupational problems of the writer with candor. It describes the failure of a novelist who is unable to survive the competition of the literary marketplace or to fulfill the demands of a bourgeois marriage, and it exposes the way in which the mercenary standards of modern society corrupt literature and social life. When its protagonist, Edwin Reardon, finds that he is unable to continue writing, his wife advises him to produce whatever the publishers will accept. "Art," she says, "must be practiced as a trade, at all events in our time. This is the age of trade."

But Reardon cannot adjust himself to his age, and is forced to give up his claim to be a novelist, take a position as a clerk, and move to a humble flat. His wife refuses to follow him into poverty; and in an ironic conclusion, after Reardon has died, she marries the enterprising journalist who has always admired him but has made his fortune by practicing literature as a trade. Reardon's frustrations, fear of poverty, and feelings of helplessness are presented with a special intimacy; many of them were no doubt drawn from Gissing's own experiences. His mastery of realistic detail enabled him to sketch the general scene of working London writers, centering it in the reading room of the British Museum, and portraying a wide variety of types. The authenticity of these figures was widely recognized. "I know them all, personally," said one reviewer, ". . . and the fidelity of Mr. Gissing's portraits makes me shudder."

But *New Grub Street* is more than a lament over the commercialization of literature. It condemns the democracy of taste and the industrial standards that transform literature into a commodity through mass publication and shows how similar forces pervert human relations in love, marriage, and family life. Its people meet defeat not only in trying to defend the integrity of literature but also in their moral and spiritual conflicts. The London literary scene is only a setting in which a fate hostile to art, love, and idealism in general leads the characters to disaster. Contemporary reviewers sometimes complained that *New Grub Street* exaggerated the evils it described, and deplored its crushing pessimism; but they acknowledged its skillful realism, its honesty, and the sympathy with which Gissing entered into the lives of his characters. Since Gissing's death it has been recognized as his masterpiece; it has undergone many reprintings, and critical opinion places it far above his other novels. "Alone among Gissing's books," wrote Irving Howe, "*New Grub Street* survives as a classic, a work of abiding value and power." Modern critics value it not only for its penetrating insight into the pernicious influence of mass culture but for its translation of Gissing's personal resentments into a striking and plausible vision of life.

When he married Edith in February 1891, Gissing left the noise and turmoil of London behind and set up his new household in the placid little city of Exeter. Within six months of his marriage he wrote *Born In Exile* (1892), a novel which uses Exeter as a locale and is concerned with nineteenth-century moral issues on a more fundamental level than any

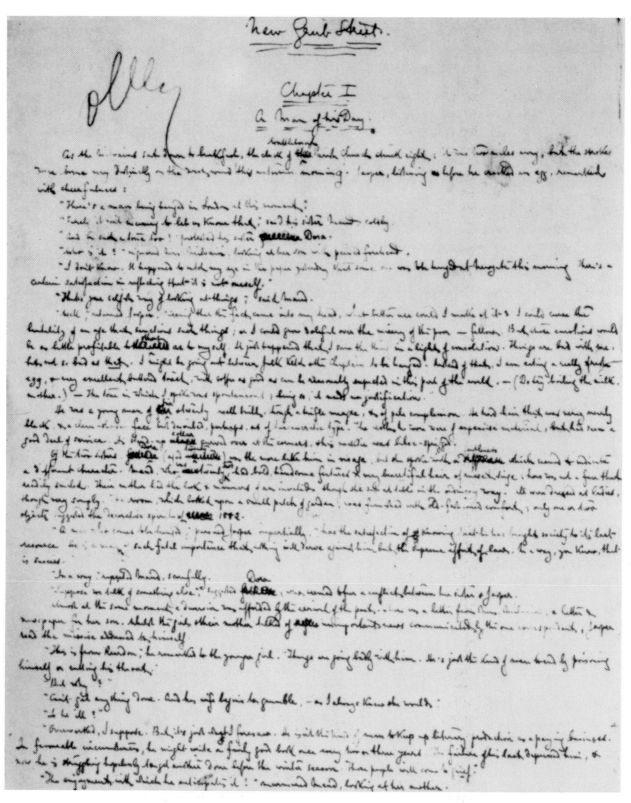

First page of the manuscript of New Grub Street *(1891), widely regarded as Gissing's masterpiece*
(Berg Collection, New York Public Library)

of Gissing's other works. Its protagonist, a boy of humble origins named Godwin Peak, leaves his college voluntarily in an episode that is a disguised version of Gissing's expulsion from Owens College. A freethinker of scientific interests, he falls in love with Sidwell Warricombe, a girl of good family, and in an effort to conceal his agnosticism, pretends to be a theological student. He justifies his dishonesty by telling himself that a man who has no principles is free to do as he pleases. In this way, Gissing opens the door to the existentialist vision of a world without authority, in which each man is allowed to create his own morality and must bear the responsibility for it. When his deception is exposed, Peak realizes that his crime has made him an "exile" from the class he tried to enter as surely as his birth did and blames his proletarian ancestry for his moral failure. *Born in Exile* is perhaps Gissing's most profound study of spiritual conflict and owes something to his admiration for Dostoevski, Turgenev, and other Continental authors.

In 1892, in response to a request from the new publishing firm of Lawrence and Bullen, Gissing broke with the tradition of the three-volume novel that had dominated Victorian fiction and for the first time wrote a novel in one volume. The new form naturally enabled him to employ a more unified and focused plot and fewer characters and also encouraged him to adopt the more objective or "dramatic" manner that was coming into fashion. *Denzil Quarrier* (1892), which is about a politician who has entered into an irregular union and suffers serious consequences when his secret is exposed, warns both of the repressive power of convention and of the danger of violating it. Quarrier is unable to marry Lilian, the woman he presents as his wife, because she was married earlier to a man who was arrested immediately after the wedding ceremony, and whom she has not seen since. The missing husband, Arthur Northway, is hired to turn up in the town and claim his wife in order to spoil Quarrier's chance of election. Because the secret is never actually made public, Quarrier wins his seat in Parliament, but fear of exposure drives Lilian to drown herself, and he is forced to admit the usefulness of such established customs as marriage.

Among his other views, the hero of *Denzil Quarrier* favors women's rights. This theme, which occupied a minor place in a number of Gissing's earlier novels, became the subject of his next book, *The Odd Women* (1893). He had always felt that the social inferiority of women was responsible for much suffering and injustice. In *The Odd Women* he deals—pessimistically, as usual—with women who try to cope with their difficulties in a variety of ways. At the center of the novel is a society set up to train women for work and prepare them for a moderate form of liberation. The heroine, Rhoda Nunn, is torn between her loyalty to this organization and a lover whom she is tempted to marry. The main plot is accompanied by a number of case histories, including those of two middle-aged sisters, Alice and Virginia Madden, who are forced to live at a level of bare survival because they are unemployable, and that of their pretty younger sister, Monica, who marries to escape the drudgery of working in a shop and reaps the consequences. The novel's verdict on life transcends the limits of the social problem, but it offers sensitive insights into the dilemmas women faced in striving for social and economic independence; it has become known as one of the most objective and penetrating treatments of the subject.

In 1893 Gissing, who was now the father of a son, moved his family to London. "I want the streets again," he wrote to Bertz. For nearly a year he was unable to make progress with a new novel, but another avenue was opened to him when an editor asked him to write some short stories for periodicals. Gissing had not written short stories for years, but he now found that he could succeed with them, while his efforts to write a full-length novel constantly failed. They were also a welcome source of income, for he was paid well for them, while the sales of his novels continued to be slow. At this time the public was beginning to demand shorter forms, as Gissing himself had noted in *New Grub Street*, and changing publishing conditions were leading to the disappearance of the three-volume novel.

In the Year of Jubilee, completed, after much labor, in April 1894, was the last of Gissing's novels to be published in three volumes. Its central character is a young woman who compromises her freedom by marrying, but is forced to bear her child and support herself while living apart from her equally independent-minded husband. The main story line is submerged by a large number of subordinate plots and characters loosely linked with each other in situations that expose the evils of modern society. Gissing calls special attention to the dangers of mass culture as they are exhibited in the behavior of the crowds at the celebrations of Victoria's jubilee year: illiterate democracy, vulgar advertising, unscrupulous opportunism, and coarse manners are all brought forward. But matrimonial dissension remains the center of the story. Married life is presented as a squalid trap; yet living separately, as the heroine does, has its own dangers.

Perhaps because he felt that as a married man he had to have a more secure income, perhaps because he accepted the view of the literary marketplace presented in *New Grub Street*, Gissing now began to adopt some of the methods of "the age of trade" and to approach his occupation with more professionalism. He joined the Society of Authors, employed a literary agent, and willingly accepted writing assignments, especially for short stories or shorter novels. His active participation in the publishing scene led him to open himself to friendships and social engagements, especially among writers and editors. He joined the Authors' Club and the Omar Khayyam Club, accepted dinner invitations, and even spent weekends with sociable groups; he saw the aged Meredith again, and formed friendships with H. G. Wells, Thomas Hardy, Edward Clodd, and other men of letters. Those who met him at this time found it hard to believe that he had ever been poor or a recluse.

Between 1894 and 1897 Gissing turned aside from his usual themes to write four short novels, *Eve's Ransom* (1895), *Sleeping Fires* (1895), *The Paying Guest* (1895), and *The Town Traveller* (1898). All were written to fulfill commitments to publishers or editors and were slight productions in which Gissing exhibited an unexpected gift for comedy and a deft touch for developing ironic situations. They could be marketed effectively and continued to be successful in reprints and translations. In *The Whirlpool* (1897), Gissing returned to a novel of serious social observation, undertaking to handle settings and situations that were entirely new to him. His characters are leisured, fashionable people and his protagonist is a bookish man who marries a talented but neurotic member of this group and takes her to live in the country. He cannot, however, escape the destructive influences that radiate from the turbulent centers of London society and feels the effects of financial disasters, suicides, and jealousy. Ultimately, his marriage fails and his wife dies. After these encounters with the blind forces that rage through the social world, the hero is glad to withdraw to a secluded life and to seek satisfaction in his relations with his little son—a conclusion that reflects Gissing's own concern for his older son. *The Whirlpool* is a powerful performance in which Gissing made excellent use of the skills he had acquired in writing the more dramatic and direct narratives of his short stories and short novels. Partly because his shorter books had caught the public's attention, partly because of its own merits, *The*

Whirlpool sold better than any of his previous works, and the critics belatedly discovered that he was a superb realist who was capable of depicting modern life with candor and authenticity.

In the meantime, his second marriage became as unhappy as his first had been. Edith, who eventually died in a lunatic asylum, began to show signs of her disorder a few years after the marriage. In his letters and diary Gissing complained that she neglected the children, quarreled with the servants—often driving them away—and disrupted the household with her fits of temper. She was abusive to Gissing, and there was so much turmoil and tension in the house that Gissing took his older son to live with his family in Wakefield, feeling pity for "this child, born of a loveless and utterly unsuitable marriage," as he wrote in his diary. He left Edith abruptly in February 1897, after a particularly violent dispute with her. There was a brief reconciliation, but a permanent separation took place as Gissing left for another visit to Italy in September 1897. The results of this trip were his first work of nonfiction, *Charles Dickens: A Critical Study* (1898), which was completed while he was living in Siena; and *By the Ionian Sea* (1901), a travel book written some years later with material gathered at this time. The book on Dickens was the first serious full-length study of its subject and has had a permanent influence on Dickens criticism. It offers a perceptive analysis of the divided motives behind Dickens's treatment of middle-class characters and excellent appreciations of his humor, characterization, and treatment of women. In subsequent years Gissing became known as an expert on Dickens and wrote a number of introductions to his novels for a collected edition; but only six of the novels appeared, and the remaining introductions went unpublished until 1924.

After completing *Charles Dickens*, Gissing traveled to southern Italy in order to spend some time in Calabria, the Magna Graecia of the ancient world, where the Greek and Roman civilizations had met. He went to sites few travelers had visited in order to capture their associations with classical personalities and events. After the Calabrian tour, he spent about a month in Rome, where he did research for the novel about ancient Rome that he was planning to write, and met a number of English friends, including Arthur Conan Doyle and H. G. Wells and his wife. On his way back to England he made a detour to Berlin to spend a few days with his old friend Eduard Bertz.

Gissing arrived in England in the middle of

Gissing, E. W. Hornung, Arthur Conan Doyle, and H. G. Wells in Rome in 1898

April 1898, rented a house in the town of Dorking, and resumed his writing. He lived alone, for Edith was established in London with his younger son, while the older one remained in Wakefield, where he had been sent to live with Gissing's mother and sisters. He was now occupied with the Dickens prefaces, short stories, and an abortive attempt to write a play, and saw something of H. G. Wells, who lived nearby. In June, a Frenchwoman named Gabrielle Fleury wrote to him for permission to translate *New Grub Street*. She came to see him the following month and visited him for a week in the fall. Gissing for the first time fell in love with a woman of refinement and intelligence who could sustain his idealistic conception of love. He was unable to secure a divorce and contract a formal marriage, but in the spring of 1899 moved to Paris to live with her. Both Gissing and Gabrielle were conservative enough to regard their union as a daring break with convention, although it was fully approved by Gabrielle's mother, who lived with them. Gissing now entered a new life, in which he had a few years of

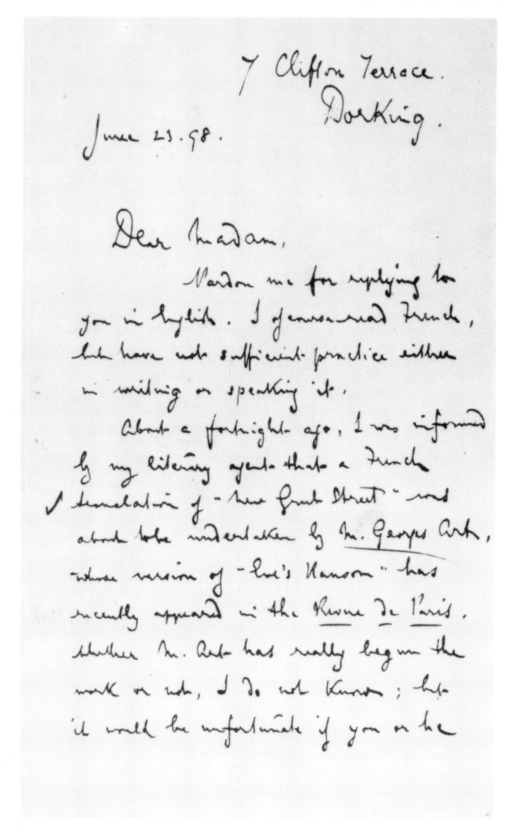

First page of Gissing's reply to Gabrielle Fleury, who had inquired about translating New Grub Street *into French*
(Berg Collection, New York Public Library)

comparative happiness. Before leaving England he had completed *The Crown of Life* (1899), a novel about a middle-class couple who agree to marry only after eight years of hesitation and misunderstanding; it expresses some of Gissing's idealistic views of love and reflects new concerns with international politics and British imperialism.

While Gissing was at last living with a woman he genuinely loved and who was his social and intellectual equal, the relationship was a troubled one. There were disagreements about meals and other domestic matters; Gissing did not like living in a Paris flat; and he was in ill health and pressed for money to support the family he had left in England. He now made use of the diary he had kept during his Calabrian trip to write *By the Ionian Sea*, which is one of the most direct expressions of his tastes and personality. This was followed by a novel, *Our Friend the Charlatan* (1901), a minor work with comic overtones which attacks the application of evolutionary theories to social questions. Then came another nonfiction work, *The Private Papers of Henry Ryecroft*, a series of short meditative essays on such subjects as nature, books, solitude, poverty, and Puritanism. Writing through a fictional figure closely resembling himself, Gissing was able to express the opinions about religion, democracy, leisure, and learning that he had formulated late in life. These sometimes correspond with the attitudes of his novels, and many of the essays reveal personal thoughts or experiences that are the bases of episodes in his books. But the most attractive element of the Ryecroft papers is the personality that speaks through them: that of a gentle old man who is conscious of his weaknesses and admits that he has accomplished little, yet is able to find serenity in his quiet life of books, observation of nature, and introspections about the past. *The Private Papers of Henry Ryecroft* became Gissing's most popular book; he was identified with it in the public mind, and its popularity ironically tended to obscure his reputation as a novelist.

Gissing had suffered for some years from a lung condition diagnosed as emphysema and became a semi-invalid compelled to give up his work for long periods of rest. In 1901 he spent a month at a sanatorium in Suffolk; and in 1902 he was forced to move to the neighborhood of St.-Jean-de-Luz in the south of France, which had a climate better suited to his health. He then wrote the last novel he was able to complete, *Will Warburton* (1905), a book which represents a return to some of his old interests but with a completely different emphasis. In it a

Gissing in 1901

middle-class businessman loses his money and is forced to become a grocer, a trade which allows him to escape the destructive competitiveness of commerce and to find an unexpected happiness. Gissing seems to have perceived that his old attachment to privileged leisure was deceptive, and that it is possible to find firmer grounds of love and friendship in a humble condition of life.

For a number of years, Gissing had been planning to write a book on a subject very different from his usual ones, a historical novel about sixth-century Rome. He had taken extensive notes for this, and during his last trip to Italy had visited the Abbey of Monte Cassino, where some of the scenes of the story were to take place. *Veranilda* (1904) is a story of adventure and intrigue that moves slowly, emphasizing the characters and their thoughts; its observations of scenes in the cities and countryside of ancient Rome include details that only close students of the period would appreciate. Gissing did not live to complete it, and it was published after his death with the last five chapters missing.

Gissing died as a result of his lung condition on 28 December 1903 at Ispoure in St.-Jean-Pied-de-Port, the town near St.-Jean-de-Luz, where he and Gabrielle were living. He lingered for a week, and H. G. Wells and Morley Roberts were summoned from England to his bedside. Roberts arrived the morning after he died, but Wells came in time to see the dying man and recorded the scene in his *Experiment in Autobiography* (1934). Gissing's death was surrounded by considerable controversy. Wells felt that Gabrielle was not caring for the sick man properly and had two nurses brought in, the first a

French nun, the second an Englishwoman. He thought that the light meals prescribed for the patient were insufficient and took it upon himself to give him more food, a step which Gabrielle declared led directly to his death. The English chaplain who had been asked to sit with Gissing published a report that he had embraced Christianity before his death. This was based on a misunderstanding of the dying man's delirious talk, and Roberts, after gathering information from Gabrielle and the English nurse, issued an energetic denial. Gissing was buried in the English cemetery at St.-Jean-de-Luz.

Two of Gissing's novels were published posthumously, the unfinished *Veranilda*, which appeared with a preface by Frederic Harrison, and *Will Warburton*, the last completed novel. His numerous short stories provided material for three collections, *The House of Cobwebs and Other Stories* (1906), *A Victim of Circumstances and Other Stories* (1927), and *Stories and Sketches* (1938), and the introductions written for the Rochester edition of Dickens's novels were collected in *Critical Studies of the Works of Charles Dickens* (1924) and *The Immortal Dickens* (1924). The stories Gissing had published in Chicago newspapers were identified and reprinted in *Sins of the Fathers* (1924) and *Brownie* (1931), and two stories, one unpublished and one reprinted, appeared in *My First Rehearsal and My Clerical Rival* (1970). Unpublished materials, including stories, essays, notes, and letters, have been brought out in *George Gissing's Commonplace Book* (1962), *George Gissing: Essays and Fiction* (1970), and *George Gissing*

Sketch of Gissing by H. G. Wells

on Fiction (1978), which also reprints two essays previously published. In 1978, the diary which Gissing kept for many years, and in which he recorded his writing and his travels, was published as *London and the Life of Literature in late Victorian England: The Diary of George Gissing, Novelist.*

Gissing's early novels, with their elaborate descriptions, passages of personal comment, and artificial, sometimes sensational plots, correspond to practices prevalent in the mid-century English novel. His development paralleled the shift in taste that accompanied the broadening of the reading public and the demise of the three-volume novel, and his later books are more economical, more objective, and more simply constructed. While his novels adhere closely to the spirit of realism dominant in Victorian fiction, he was never a dogmatic realist. He made his novels expressions of his own views, and many autobiographical elements appear in them. Far from denying that his work had a personal bias, he often insisted, in contradiction to the conception of realism that prevailed toward the end of the century, that a novel should be an expression of its author's attitudes. "No novelist," he wrote, "ever was objective or ever will be. His work is a bit of life as seen by *him*. It is his business to make us feel a distinct pleasure in seeing the world with *his* eyes." He rejected the idea that a novel should be an impersonal representation of reality, just as he rejected the notion that it should be written to please the public. He felt that what the novelist needed was not a capacity for reportorial accuracy but "the spirit of truthfulness," and he redefined realism as "artistic sincerity in the portrayal of contemporary life."

For Gissing, sincerity meant a vision of life that was, on the whole, pessimistic if not despairing. His world is blighted by injustice to the poor, to women, and to artists. It suffers from evils generated by competition, science, religion, commercialism, and egotism. None of the remedies proposed for eliminating social injustice seemed viable to him, and the industrialization and democratization which most people welcomed as signs of progress threatened the fragile humanism he valued. His own ideals offered no solution to the evils he lamented. But his sustained examination of the failure of society to encourage what he considered to be the best potentialities of human nature makes him one of the most sensitive and conscientious observers of social life among the English novelists.

Gissing's contemporaries often complained of his pessimism and his unsympathetic treatment of

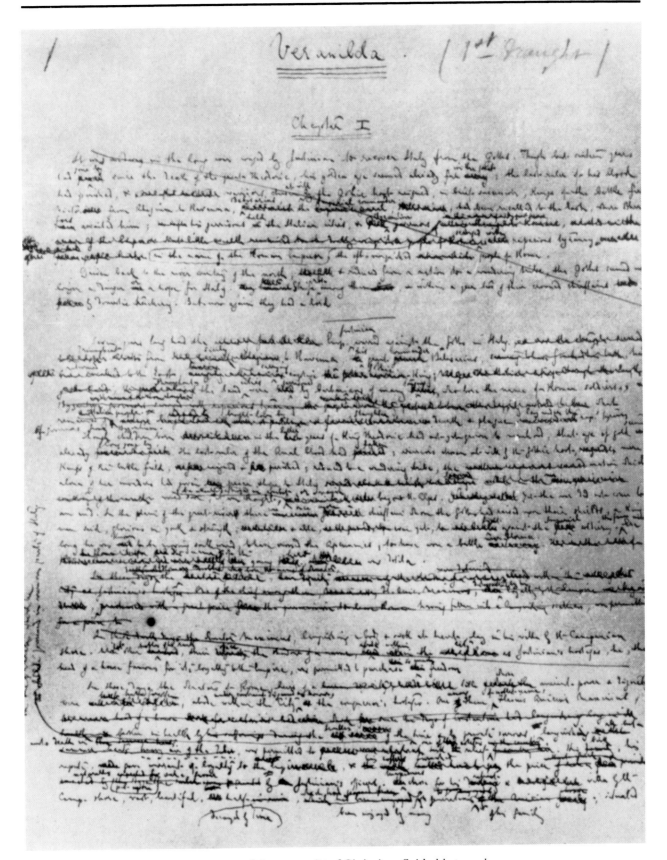

First page of the manuscript of Gissing's unfinished last novel

working-class characters, but they eventually recognized his technical mastery and the authenticity of his scenes of modern life. *The Private Papers of Henry Ryecroft*, which was mistakenly regarded as autobiographical, won much praise for its excellence of style and serenity of spirit and came to be his best-known book. More recent criticism often emphasizes Gissing's perceptive rendering of Victorian social life and examines the paradoxes involved in his effort to express his intense personal convictions through the medium of the realistic novel. In an article appearing in the *Times Literary Supplement* of 11 January 1912, Virginia Woolf wrote: "Naturally Gissing practised what is generally called the English method of writing fiction. Instead of leaping from one high pinnacle of emotion to the next, he filled in all the adjoining parts most carefully. It is sometimes very dull. The general effect is very low in tone. You have to read from the first page to the last to get the full benefit of his art. But if you read steadily the low almost insignificant chapters gather weight and impetus; they accumulate upon the imagination; they are building up a world from which there seems to be no escape. . . . He had a world of his own as real, as hard, as convincing as though it were made of earth and stone—nay, far more so—but it was a small world." P. J. Keating observes, in *The Working Classes in Victorian Fiction* (1971): "Gissing is the first Victorian novelist, whose efforts can be traced through a series of novels, to struggle seriously with the artistic problems involved in the presentation of the working classes in fiction." He adds that Gissing's novels, "when studied in chronological order . . . testify to a consistently serious attempt to break with static literary conventions; a struggle with the problem of how to establish a balance between a personal social viewpoint and artistic objectivity when writing about the working classes."

In spite of some differences of opinion, Gissing's critics give him a high ranking. George Orwell wrote in 1943 that "merely on the strength of *New Grub Street*, *Demos*, and *The Odd Women*, I am ready to maintain that England has produced very few better novelists." In *The English Novel* (1954), Walter Allen says: "Gissing is not a great novelist but he is considerably more than a minor one. He is one of those imperfect artists whose work inevitably leads one back to the writer in person. His fiction is not, except in perhaps three instances, sufficiently detached from its creator; it is too personal, the powerful expression, one cannot help feeling, of a grudge. The grudge expressed is a common one

Gabrielle Fleury, with whom Gissing lived for the last five years of his life

today, though Gissing was the first novelist directly to manifest it; and this in a way does universalize his work, in spite of its lack of objectivity." And John Halperin, in *Gissing: A Life in Books* (1982), after maintaining that Gissing wrote an unusually large number of excellent novels and one—*New Grub Street*—better than any but the best-known Victorian novels, declares, "Gissing is a major novelist; his themes are important ones, treated with sensitivity and intelligence; his perception of things is acute and detailed, his people and their problems real, 'relevant,' both for his time and for ours."

Other:

The Rochester Edition of the Works of Charles Dickens, introductions by Gissing (9 volumes, London: Methuen, 1900-1901);

Forster's "Life of Dickens," abridged and revised by Gissing (London: Chapman & Hall, 1903).

Letters:

Letters of George Gissing to Members of His Family, edited by Algernon & Ellen Gissing (London: Constable, 1927; Boston: Mifflin, 1927);

The Letters of George Gissing to Eduard Bertz 1887-1903, edited by Arthur C. Young (New Brunswick, N.J.: Rutgers University Press, 1961);

Gissing and H. G. Wells: Their Friendship and Correspondence, edited by R.A. Gettmann (Urbana: University of Illinois Press, 1961; London: Hart-Davis, 1961);

The Letters of George Gissing to Gabrielle Fleury, edited by Pierre Coustillas (New York: New York Public Library, 1964).

Bibliographies:

Joseph J. Wolff, ed., *George Gissing: An Annotated*

Bibliography of Writings about Him (Dekalb: Northern Illinois University Press, 1974);

Michael Collie, *George Gissing: A Bibliography* (Toronto: University of Toronto Press, 1975).

References:

Pierre Coustillas and Colin Partridge, eds., *Gissing: The Critical Heritage* (London & Boston: Routledge & Kegan Paul, 1972);

Mabel Collins Donnelly, *George Gissing: Grave Comedian* (Cambridge: Harvard University Press, 1954);

John Halperin, *Gissing: A Life in Books* (Oxford: Oxford University Press, 1982);

Jacob Korg, "George Gissing," in *Victorian Fiction: A Second Guide to Research*, edited by George Ford (New York: Modern Language Association, 1978);

Korg, *George Gissing: A Critical Biography* (Seattle: University of Washington Press, 1963);

Korg, "George Moore; George Gissing," in *Victorian Fiction: A Guide to Research*, edited by Lionel Stevenson (Cambridge: Harvard University Press, 1964);

Morley Roberts, *The Private Life of Henry Maitland* (London: Nash, 1912);

Gillian Tindall, *The Born Exile: George Gissing* (London: Temple Scott, 1974).

Thomas Hardy

Norman Page
University of Alberta

BIRTH: Higher Bockhampton, near Stinsford, Dorset, 2 June 1840, to Thomas and Jemima Hand Hardy.

MARRIAGES: 17 September 1874 to Emma Lavinia Gifford. 10 February 1914 to Florence Emily Dugdale.

AWARDS AND HONORS: Medal of the Royal Institute of British Architects for "On the Application of Coloured Bricks and Terra Cotta in Modern Architecture," 1863; LL.D., Aberdeen University, 1905; Order of Merit, 1910; Litt. D., Cambridge

University, 1913; honorary fellowship, Magdalene College, Cambridge, 1913; D. Litt., Oxford University, 1920; LL.D., St. Andrews University, 1922; honorary fellowship, Queen's College, Oxford, 1922; D.Litt., Bristol University, 1925.

DEATH: Dorchester, Dorset, 11 January 1928.

BOOKS: *Desperate Remedies: A Novel*, anonymous (3 volumes, London: Tinsley, 1871; 1 volume, New York: Holt, 1874);

Under the Greenwood Tree: A Rural Painting of the Dutch School, anonymous (2 volumes, London:

Thomas Hardy

Tinsley, 1872; 1 volume, New York: Holt &
Williams, 1873);

A Pair of Blue Eyes: A Novel (3 volumes, London:
Tinsley, 1873; 1 volume, New York: Holt &
Williams, 1873);

Far from the Madding Crowd (2 volumes, London:
Smith, Elder, 1874; 1 volume, New York:
Holt, 1874);

The Hand of Ethelberta: A Comedy in Chapters (2 volumes, London: Smith, Elder, 1876; 1 volume,
New York: Holt, 1876);

The Return of the Native (3 volumes, London: Smith,
Elder, 1878; 1 volume, New York: Holt,
1878);

The Trumpet-Major: A Tale (3 volumes, London:
Smith, Elder, 1880; 1 volume, New York:
Holt, 1880);

A Laodicean: A Novel (New York: Harper, 1881; 3
volumes, London: Low, Marston, Searle &
Rivington, 1881);

Two on a Tower: A Romance (3 volumes, London:
Low, Marston, Searle & Rivington, 1882; 1
volume, New York: Holt, 1882);

*The Mayor of Casterbridge: The Life and Death of a Man
of Character* (2 volumes, London: Smith, Elder,
1886; 1 volume, New York: Holt, 1886);

The Woodlanders (3 volumes, London & New York:
Macmillan, 1887; 1 volume, New York:
Harper, 1887);

Wessex Tales: Strange, Lively, and Commonplace (2 volumes, London & New York: Macmillan, 1888;
1 volume, New York: Harper, 1888);

A Group of Noble Dames (London: Osgood, McIlvaine, 1891; New York: Harper, 1891);

*Tess of the d'Urbervilles: A Pure Woman Faithfully Pre-
sented* (3 volumes, London: Osgood, McIlvaine, 1891; 1 volume, New York: Harper,
1892);

*Life's Little Ironies: A Set of Tales with Some Colloquial
Sketches Entitled "A Few Crusted Characters"*
(London: Osgood, McIlvaine, 1894; New
York: Harper, 1894);

Jude the Obscure (London: Osgood, McIlvaine, 1895;
New York: Harper, 1895);

The Well-Beloved: A Sketch of a Temperament (London:
Osgood, McIlvaine, 1897; New York: Harper,
1897);

*Wessex Poems and Other Verses, with Thirty Illustrations
by the Author* (London: Harper, 1898; New
York: Harper, 1899);

Poems of the Past and the Present (London: Harper,
1901; New York: Harper, 1901);

The Dynasts, Part First (London: Macmillan, 1904;
New York: Macmillan, 1904);

The Dynasts, Part Second (London: Macmillan, 1906;
New York: Macmillan, 1906);

The Dynasts, Part Third (London: Macmillan, 1908;
New York: Macmillan, 1908);

Time's Laughingstocks and Other Verses (London:
Macmillan, 1909);

A Changed Man, The Waiting Supper, and Other Tales
(London: Macmillan, 1913; New York:
Harper, 1913);

*Satires of Circumstance: Lyrics and Reveries with Mis-
cellaneous Pieces* (London: Macmillan, 1914);

Selected Poems (London: Macmillan, 1916);

Moments of Vision and Miscellaneous Verses (London:
Macmillan, 1917);

Collected Poems (London: Macmillan, 1919; enlarged, 1923, 1928, 1930);

Late Lyrics and Earlier with Many Other Verses (London: Macmillan, 1922);

The Famous Tragedy of the Queen of Cornwall (London: Macmillan, 1923; New York: Macmillan,
1923);

Human Shows, Far Phantasies, Songs and Trifles (Lon-

Hardy's drawing of his birthplace at Higher Bockhampton

don: Macmillan, 1925; New York: Macmillan, 1925);

Winter Words in Various Moods and Metres (London: Macmillan, 1928; New York: Macmillan, 1928);

Chosen Poems (London: Macmillan, 1929; New York: Macmillan, 1929);

Thomas Hardy's Personal Writings: Prefaces, Literary Opinions, Reminiscences, edited by Harold Orel (Lawrence: University of Kansas Press, 1966);

The Literary Notes of Thomas Hardy, edited by Lennart A. Bjórk (Göteborg: Acta Universitatis Gothoburgensis, 1974);

The Complete Poems, edited by James Gibson (London: Macmillan, 1976; New York: Macmillan, 1978);

The Personal Notebooks of Thomas Hardy, edited by Richard H. Taylor (London: Macmillan, 1978; New York: Columbia University Press, 1979);

The Variorum Edition of the Complete Poems of Thomas Hardy, edited by Gibson (London: Macmillan, 1979; New York: Macmillan, 1979).

COLLECTIONS: *The Wessex Novels* (18 volumes, London: Osgood, McIlvaine, 1895-1913);

The Works of Thomas Hardy in Prose and Verse, with Prefaces and Notes, Wessex Edition (24 volumes, London: Macmillan, 1912-1931).

In the later years of his long life, Thomas Hardy was probably the most famous English man of letters of his time, his reputation extending throughout the world. He is now generally regarded as both a major late-Victorian novelist and a major twentieth-century poet, and is the subject of

more intense scholarly, critical, editorial, and biographical attention than ever before; as a result, knowledge and understanding of his life, personality, and literary achievement are continually increasing and deepening. Nor is his appeal restricted to academics or students: he has long been one of the most widely read of English novelists; ten thousand people tramp every year through the modest cottage that was his birthplace; and he now reaches a mass audience through film and television adaptations of his books.

The time and place of his birth determined the early experiences on which he was to draw so heavily as a writer. In 1840 the county of Dorset was still relatively little touched by the sweeping changes that were transforming the rest of England: the railway, for instance, which had spread its network across the country in the 1820s and 1830s, did not reach Dorset until seven years after Hardy's birth, and the folk traditions of a small and scattered population thus survived longer there than in most other places. Higher Bockhampton, though within walking distance of the county town of Dorchester, was no more than a hamlet; Dorchester itself, though an ancient town dating back to Roman times and an important center for the surrounding agricultural region, was small. During his early years Hardy was to witness the hand of change at work on landscape and rural community at the same time that his own intellectual and emotional development was leading him in directions for which family history offered no precedent. Intensely individual, he was also in many respects a representative member of his generation.

His father and grandfather, alike named Thomas Hardy, were builders; the family was long settled in the district and, while certainly not affluent, lived comfortably enough at a time when Dorset was something of a byword for rural poverty and wretchedness. Thomas Hardy III, not a physically robust child, stayed at home until he was eight and then enjoyed only eight years of schooling, first in a nearby village and then in Dorchester. But he was zealous in pursuing a course of self-education after he left school at the age of sixteen and throughout his life retained a wide-ranging intellectual curiosity. As a young man, his interests were mainly literary, philosophical, and theological; and, like so many of his contemporaries, he underwent a crisis of faith—he was nineteen when Darwin's *Origin of Species* appeared, twenty in the year of the controversial theological symposium *Essays and Reviews*—that led him to abandon the Christianity in which he had been brought up. He retained for the rest of his life, however, his close knowledge of the Bible, his interest in church architecture, and his sense that something was missing in a godless world.

He had been apprenticed at sixteen to a Dorchester architect. During this period he came to know William Barnes, a Dorchester schoolmaster who was also a dialect poet of great distinction. Eventually the successful pursuit of his profession (to which he was to devote sixteen years of his life) took Hardy to London. During his years there (1862-1867) he read at the British Museum in his leisure hours, studied the pictures at the National Gallery, and began—with a total lack of success—to submit poems to the magazines. Back in Dorset as a result of ill health, he wrote his first novel, "The Poor Man and the Lady." The turning to fiction fairly clearly represented an acceptance of the realities of the contemporary publishing situation. The novelist's profession had by this time become lucrative and well-regarded: in 1863, for instance, George Eliot had been paid £ 10,000 for *Romola*; and Dickens had made a fortune as well as becoming a household name. Hardy accepted the fact that, whatever his poetic aspirations, he must turn to the novel if he were to succeed as an author.

His early novels show him attempting a variety

Hardy at age sixteen, about the time he began his architectural training (Hermann Lea Collection)

of kinds of fiction without any very strong conviction as to where his true gifts lay, and to some extent this lack of confidence persisted almost to the end of his career as a novelist. As late as 30 June 1891, for instance, he wrote in a letter that "much of my work hitherto has been of a tentative kind, and it is but latterly that I have felt any sureness of method." "The Poor Man and the Lady," unpublished and later destroyed, was evidently a social satire and episodic in structure; its title summarizes neatly a continuing preoccupation of his fiction and seems to reflect the social self-consciousness that continued to haunt him for the rest of his days. This early attempt was followed by *Desperate Remedies* (1871), a conscientious and still readable exercise in the "sensation novel" form that Wilkie Collins and others had made immensely popular during the previous decade. Hardy wrote it in the later months of 1869 and the opening months of 1870, having been advised by George Meredith (who, as a reader for Chapman and Hall, had rejected "The Poor Man and the Lady") to write a novel with a strong element of plot. Although it contains some melodramatic absurdities, there are also touches that can be recognized as characteristic—for example, in the sharply visualized quality of certain episodes—and that show Hardy in the process of devising an idiosyncratic technique of narration and description to convey a highly individual vision and sensibility.

Desperate Remedies was published anonymously in the conventional and expensive three-volume form, and its reception was unenthusiastic, though not actually as hostile as Hardy seems to have believed. The *Athenaeum* (1 April 1871) described it as "an unpleasant story . . . [but] undoubtedly a very powerful one"; the *Spectator* (22 April 1871) judged it "disagreeable, and not striking in any way," but praised the unknown author's "very happy facility in catching and fixing phases of peasant life"— approval that was to be echoed by critics of some subsequent novels. In his biography, *The Life of Thomas Hardy* (1962)—actually an autobiography, since it was largely ghostwritten by Hardy, though attributed to his second wife, Florence—Hardy describes his anguish at reading the *Spectator* review: "He remembered, for long years after, how he had read this review as he sat on a stile leading to the eweleaze he had to cross on his way home to Bockhampton. The bitterness of that moment was never forgotten; at the time he wished that he were dead." Commercially, the book was not a success: Hardy, who had contributed £ 75 of his modest savings toward the expenses of publication, recovered only part of his money, and within three months the book was remaindered.

By this time, however, he was at work on another novel of an entirely different kind. *Under the Greenwood Tree* is the shortest of Hardy's novels and arguably the least flawed—a minor classic, but assuredly a classic. It was written rapidly and incorporates material salvaged from "The Poor Man and the Lady." After a discouraging response from Alexander Macmillan, to whom he had first offered it, Hardy sent his manuscript in April 1872 to William Tinsley, who had published *Desperate Remedies*. Tinsley accepted it, and it was published, anonymously and in two volumes, in June. It was more favorably reviewed than its predecessor, and Hardy's friend Horace Moule praised it warmly in the influential *Saturday Review* (28 September 1872): "This novel is the best prose idyl that we have seen for a long while past. . . . the book is one of unusual merit in its own special line, full of humour and keen observation, and with the genuine air of the country breathing throughout it." The small edition was slow to sell, however, and it was more than a year before another edition was called for. At about the same time, it was published (June 1873) in New York by Holt and Williams—the first of Hardy's novels to be published in America, and the small beginning of what was eventually to become a considerable American readership. It could not be said, though, that Hardy, then in his thirties, had made a spectacular beginning as a novelist.

Moule's review of *Under the Greenwood Tree* makes a significant reference to *Silas Marner* (1861), and indeed the influence of George Eliot's early stories of rural life is apparent. Hardy's subtitle is *A Rural Painting of the Dutch School*, a phrase that recalls the famous defense of realistic portraits of peasant life and the analogy with seventeenth-century Dutch art in chapter 17 of *Adam Bede* (1859). Hardy can only have felt flattered at comparisons with a novelist who was not only a best-selling author but was venerated as an intellectual and a sage. At the same time, the influence of George Eliot on his work was not altogether happy and was not quickly to be shaken off; it probably helps to account for a habit of ponderous moralizing and a somewhat ostentatious display of learning (or at least information) that mar even Hardy's finest novels.

In *Under the Greenwood Tree*, however, his aims were far from grandiose. For the first time he was drawing on his own intimate knowledge of rural life, and the social world of this novel is presented with an authority that is impressive without being assertive. The novel is a love story that ends with the marriage of the heroine, Fancy Day, to the unassuming Dick Dewy. The course of true love has not run altogether smooth, however, for Fancy (whose name is significant) has been tempted by a rival suitor, Maybold, before finally returning to the faithful and unsuspecting Dick. Social distinctions are crucial in this situation: Fanny is a schoolteacher, Dick a countryman, Maybold a parson and thus the superior of them both in the local hierarchy. As it so often does in Hardy's subsequent fiction, the drama arises partly from social inequalities and social aspirations. Another theme of the novel is indicated by Hardy's original title, "The Mellstock Quire." The traditional church band (Hardy's father had played in a real-life counterpart) is in the process of being superseded by an organ: change has come to the village, the old is giving way to the new, the human to the mechanical. Here, again, is a theme which was to recur throughout Hardy's career as a novelist, and nowhere more potently than in his final works.

During the same busy summer of 1871, Hardy had conceived the idea of another novel, originally titled "A Winning Tongue Had He" and eventually known as *A Pair of Blue Eyes*. The favorable reviews of *Under the Greenwood Tree* led Tinsley to ask Hardy for a story to be published in the monthly magazine that was one of his enterprises; and in the summer of 1872, Hardy took up the outline of the novel he had sketched a year earlier and set to work on it. It was the first of his books to be serialized—a mode in which all his subsequent novels were to make their initial appearance. Tinsley's offer of £200 was an impressive advance on the terms he had offered for *Desperate Remedies* and *Under the Greenwood Tree*. (Hardy had accepted £30 for the copyright of the latter.) Serialization began in September 1872 and continued until July 1873; publication in three volumes at the end of May 1873 was no doubt timed to anticipate the final installments and to tempt impatient readers into purchasing the book, which is the first of Hardy's novels to bear his name as author. Its critical reception was generally favorable: the *Saturday Review* (2 August 1873) again invoked the name of George Eliot ("Mr. Hardy has . . . developed, with something of the ruthlessness of George Eliot, what may be called the tragedy of circumstance") and concluded that, although the author had "much to learn, and many faults yet to avoid," he was "a writer who to a singular purity of thought and intention unites great power of imagination."

Social differences, and their impact on love relationships, are again prominent in *A Pair of Blue Eyes*. The heroine, Elfride Swancourt, is loved by two men: Stephen Smith, "a rural builder's son" and architect engaged in church restoration, bears a strong resemblance to Hardy; Henry Knight, a metropolitan intellectual who contributes to the reviews, has something in common with Horace Moule. The plot makes a somewhat excessive use of coincidence, but there is one famous and impressive scene which, for all its contrivance, possesses a haunting imaginative power. When Knight, hanging from a cliff and apparently about to plunge to his death, looks at the cliff face a few inches from his eyes, he sees "an imbedded fossil, standing forth in low relief from the rock. It was a creature with eyes. The eyes, dead and turned to stone, were even now regarding him. It was one of the early crustaceans called Trilobites. Separated by millions of years in their lives, Knight and this underling seemed to have met in their place of death." The awed Victorian awareness of the immensity of geological time and the corresponding insignificance of human life is dramatized in a vivid fictional moment.

Horace Moule, a Dorchester friend and a Cambridge man, had acted as a tutor or mentor to Hardy during Hardy's slow process of self-education; and his suicide on 21 September 1873 was a great blow to Hardy, whose biographer, Robert Gittings, has suggested that the influence of Moule's death was both profound and far-reaching: "we can date the emergence of Hardy as a fully tragic artist, an expounder of man's true miseries, from the suicide of his friend, and the appalling revealed ironies of that personal history."

The autobiographical element in *A Pair of Blue Eyes* owes much to recent experiences of a happier kind. In 1870 Hardy had traveled down to St. Juliot on the coast of Cornwall on architectural business; there he had met Emma Lavinia Gifford, sister-in-law of the local clergyman. It was only after a lengthy courtship, and in the face of opposition from both families, that they were able to marry (17 September 1874), for Hardy's earning capacity was limited. The success of his next novel, *Far from the Madding Crowd* (1874), enabled him to marry as well as to quit architecture for the precarious—but, in the event, highly successful—profession of full-time writer.

Leslie Stephen, distinguished critic and editor, had been impressed by *Under the Greenwood Tree* and

wrote to Hardy in November 1872 to invite him to contribute a novel to the *Cornhill* magazine, a prestigious monthly that had published the work of such established authors as Anthony Trollope and Mrs. Gaskell. Hardy replied that he was busy with *A Pair of Blue Eyes*, which was already promised to Tinsley, but that "the next should be at Mr. Stephen's disposal." He added that "the chief characters would probably be a young woman-farmer, a shepherd, and a sergeant of cavalry." The title had already been settled on. Stephen responded enthusiastically, and in June 1873 Hardy sent him "a few chapters..., with some succeeding ones in outline"; more followed in September, Stephen accepted the work, and publication began in January 1874, continuing for the rest of that year. Hardy finished writing the novel in July 1874, and it appeared in volume form in November.

It was widely reviewed in England and also marked an important stage in the growth of Hardy's international reputation: the famous Paris journal *Revue des deux mondes*, for example, made it the occasion for a long survey-article on Hardy's work to date. After the appearance (anonymously) of the first installment, the *Spectator* observed that "If *Far from the Madding Crowd* is not written by George Eliot, then there is a new light among novelists." The portrayal of rustic life received especial praise, though one can well imagine that the feelings of the socially ambitious Hardy, painfully aware of his modest origins, were distinctly mixed when he read Henry James's comment in the *Nation* (24 December 1874): "Mr. Hardy describes nature with a great deal of felicity, and is evidently very much at home among rural phenomena. The most genuine thing in his book, to our sense, is a certain aroma of the meadows and lanes—a natural relish for harvesting and sheep-washings." Although he had achieved success on a scale unprecedented in his short career, Hardy was to show no enthusiasm to be typecast as a chronicler of rural life.

The outline of the novel as originally submitted to Stephen makes no mention of Boldwood; his introduction was presumably an afterthought. In its final version the story is constructed around a quartet of characters: the attractive young woman-farmer Bathsheba Everdene and the three men who, in their quite different ways, all love her. The story is thus, among other things, a study in the various faces and aspects of love. Bathsheba is vivacious and independent, even headstrong, like so many of Hardy's heroines, from Fancy Day in *Under the Greenwood Tree* to Sue Bridehead in *Jude the*

Obscure (1895) more than twenty years later. Gabriel Oak, the shepherd, is the faithful, noble, deep-feeling, and long-suffering type of hero that Hardy was to present again in Giles Winterborne in *The Woodlanders* (1887); his surname suggests something of his unpretentious dependability, and his work identifies him with the timeless world of the countryside, with its traditional skills and values. Sergeant Troy is his opposite: an outsider, rootless and restless, a striking and colorful figure in his scarlet uniform, a Victorian version of the soldier-seducer to be found in many popular ballads and folk songs. Boldwood is a farmer whose passion for Bathsheba, stimulated by an irresponsible joke, turns into an obsession and leads to madness and death. At this stage in his career Hardy is still prepared to bring about a happy ending, and the faithful Gabriel is eventually rewarded by marriage with Bathsheba; but this is only attained by a route which involves much suffering and sorrow and three deaths. A subplot deals with the innocent maiden Fanny Robin, who has been seduced by Troy and dies bearing his child. Rural life is invaded by violence and tragedy; and the title, taken from Gray's *Elegy Written in a Country Churchyard* (1751), is obviously intended ironically.

In writing *Far from the Madding Crowd*, Hardy encountered a problem that was to become much more acute as his career continued. His desire to write novels about the relations of the sexes and the problems of love and marriage brought him into head-on collision with the watchful forces of propriety and with the censorship that was exercised, in fact if not in name, by readers, circulating libraries, and editors and publishers. Study of Hardy's manuscript has shown that he had to make extensive alterations in the portions of the novel referring to Fanny Robin and her illegitimate child. In a revealing letter, Stephen wrote to him that he thought that "the cause of Fanny's death is unnecessarily emphasized" and added that he would "somehow be glad to omit the baby"—pointing out also, however, that "I object as editor, not as critic, i.e. in the interest of a stupid public, not from my own taste." In the event, the serial version omitted virtually all references to the baby. Not for the last time Hardy was forced to effect a compromise between the kind of novel that he wanted to write and what his editor, acting on behalf of a conservative public, was prepared to tolerate. As one who hoped to make a living by his pen, he could not afford to sacrifice the additional profits that accrued from serialization.

During these early years, however, Hardy may

not have found the censorship of his work particularly irksome: he was still seeking to establish himself as an author and seems to have been prepared to listen patiently to an experienced editor and to abide by his suggestions. A few years later (12 April 1877) he was to write to the publisher John Blackwood, in sending him part of the manuscript of *The Return of the Native* (1878), that "should there accidentally occur any word or reflection not in harmony with the general tone of the magazine, you would be quite at liberty to strike it out if you chose. I always mention this to my editors, as it simplifies matters." Later in his career, however, as the divergence between the kind of novel Hardy wanted to write and the kind his editors and publishers would tolerate became wider, and the required bowdlerization damaged the fabric of his work more extensively, Hardy became less easygoing and chafed more bitterly at the burden of censorship.

What renders the suppression of such details as the dead baby doubly absurd is that in chapter 28 of *Far from the Madding Crowd* ("The Hollow amid the Ferns"), Hardy wrote one of the most erotic scenes in the whole of his fiction. Both the physical setting and the vivid account of Sergeant Troy's swordplay are fraught with sexual symbolism; but because the eroticism is symbolic and not explicit, its effectiveness belonging to the whole scene and situation rather than being located in any specific word or detail that might be deemed overtly offensive, it seems to have aroused less excitement than a reference to a dead child lying in a coffin.

In a preface he wrote when *Far from the Madding Crowd* was republished in a collected edition of his works (1895), Hardy recalled that it was in that novel that he first used the term *Wessex* to delineate a fictional region that nevertheless bore a close resemblance to actuality: "I first ventured to adopt the word 'Wessex' from the pages of early English history, and give it a fictitious significance as the existing name of the district once included in that extinct kingdom. The series of novels I projected being mainly of the kind called local, they seemed to require a territorial definition of some sort to lend unity to their scene." At the same time, Hardy drew a map to illustrate his fictional territory. Wessex extends well beyond the bounds of his native Dorset, east into Hampshire and north into Somerset and Wiltshire. In the novels, he usually modifies place-names, so that (for instance) Salisbury becomes Melchester, Dorchester becomes Casterbridge, and Bournemouth becomes Sandbourne. In this way he can create a fictional world that is

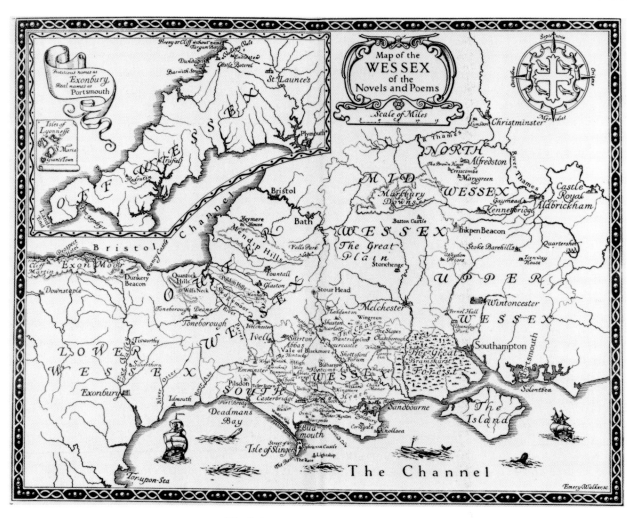

The fictional county created by Hardy

authentic without being bound by a slavish realism. Today thousands of enthusiasts explore "the Hardy country" in quest of places made interesting for them by incidents in the novels; but it is important to remember that the world of the novels is, after all, a *fictional* world, however closely at times it may resemble that on the map or in a book of photographs.

Hardy's wedding, which took place in London while *Far from the Madding Crowd* was appearing in the *Cornhill*, was attended by no member of his own family. He was conscious that he had married above the social level into which he had been born; for Emma came of a middle-class family and had an uncle who was an archdeacon. The marriage that was later to cause such heartache and bitterness began brightly; and for the first ten years or so, the couple lived in a series of rented houses and furnished lodgings in Dorset and London. Hardy had

at that point given up the practice of architecture and depended on his writings for a livelihood. His next novel, *The Hand of Ethelberta*, also appeared in the *Cornhill* but did not repeat the success of its predecessor. The new novel is subtitled *A Comedy in Chapters* and resolutely turns its back on the pastoral world of *Far from the Madding Crowd*—somewhat perversely, indeed, for Hardy must have been aware of the grounds of that book's success. At this stage in his career, Hardy seems to have had aspirations to write an entirely different kind of fiction, dealing with fashionable life rather than rustics and with ideas rather than homely incidents. Perhaps he was also feeling some discontent at being launched on a career as a novelist when his real desire was to succeed as a poet; such seems to be the implication of the remark in *The Life of Thomas Hardy*: "*finding himself committed to prose*, he renewed his consideration of a prose style" (italics added).

Emma Lavinia Gifford, who became Hardy's first wife
(Dorset Natural History and Archeological Society)

Hardy wrote the early chapters of *The Hand of Ethelberta* at the beginning of 1875 in prompt response to Leslie Stephen's request for another serial, and publication began in July. Composition was completed in January 1876, serialization the following May, and volume-publication was in April. Reviewers were lukewarm; R. H. Hutton, for instance, one of the most perceptive of Victorian critics, found the characters unconvincing. The novel contains ingredients that were becoming familiar in Hardy's fiction. The heroine is a girl of spirit and energy seeking to make her way in the world in spite of her modest background; for her father is a butler, and on one occasion she undergoes the painful experience of being served by him when she dines at the fashionable house where he is employed. The suitors between whom she must choose (after she comes to accept that marriage is a woman's only road to security) include Christopher Julian, a faithful and self-effacing musician, and Lord Mountclere, a dissipated aristocrat old enough to be her grandfather. She marries the latter, and the

novel limps to a somewhat unconvincing conclusion. Comparison with *Far from the Madding Crowd* suggests that what is missing is a social and physical world presented with confidence and authority: Hardy is dealing with themes close to his heart but attempts to present scenes and characters that for the most part he knows only as an outsider.

His last two novels having been of entirely different kinds, Hardy seems to have been uncertain in which direction to move after completing *The Hand of Ethelberta*; and in a letter dated 5 March 1876, he wrote to a publisher that "I do not wish to attempt any more original writing of any length for a few months, until I can learn the best line to take for the future." His next novel, *The Return of the Native*, returns to a Wessex setting.

The title of *The Return of the Native* suggests a theme that recurs in his fiction and also reflects the fact that during this period of his life Hardy spent a good deal of his time away from Dorset. Much of the novel was written at Sturminster Newton, where he and Emma seem to have been happier than they ever were again; but it was finished in London. It was probably started in the summer of 1877, and serialization in the monthly magazine *Belgravia* began in January 1878, continuing until the end of the year. Hardy had first offered it to Leslie Stephen for the *Cornhill*, but Stephen had been dismayed by the potentially explosive situation involving Eustacia, Wildeve, and Thomasin, and had prudently declined the offer. It was published in three volumes in November 1878, and its reception was mixed. Some reviewers praised the graphic descriptions, but others found Hardy's writing strained and pretentious and objected that his peasants talked more like Shakespearean clowns than nineteenth-century Englishmen.

From the portentous and celebrated opening description of Egdon Heath to the drowning (whether accidental or suicidal) of Eustacia Vye and Damon Wildeve, this was Hardy's most somber and tragic novel to date. Its structure has been compared to the five acts of a Shakespearean tragedy (the sixth book is in effect an epilogue, the deaths of Eustacia and Wildeve occurring at the end of the fifth book). Hardy's preoccupation with time—geological as well as historical—and his vision of human life against a backdrop of millenia are clear from the outset; equally apparent is his anxious awareness of the unprecedentedly difficult lot of contemporary man, faced with the intellectual and spiritual upheavals of the nineteenth century: "to know that everything around and underneath had

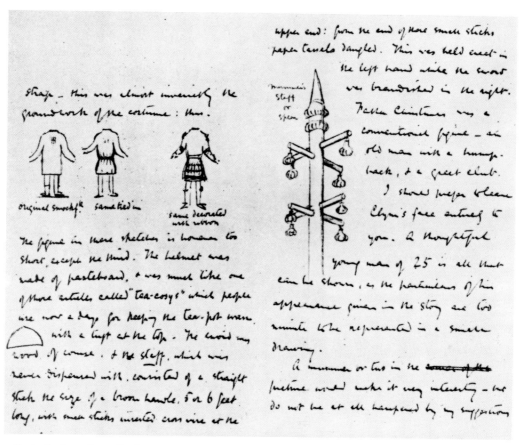

Part of a letter from Hardy suggesting illustrations for the serialization of The Return of the Native

been from prehistoric times as unaltered as the stars overhead, gave ballast to *the mind adrift on change, and harassed by the irrepressible New*" (italics added). The story is based upon a number of character contrasts of a kind by then familiar in Hardy's fiction. The gentle, undemanding Thomasin Yeobright is the antithesis of the restless, egotistical, and ambitious Eustacia; Diggory Venn the "reddleman" (itinerant dealer in dye), loyal and undemanding, contrasts with the dashing and heartless Damon Wildeve (as so often in Hardy, the names carry symbolic implications, though not always of the most obvious kind). Eustacia's passionate nature finds no satisfaction in a marriage to Clym Yeobright, the returned native; she resumes her premarital affair with Wildeve, flees with him, and—at the same time accomplishing a tragic destiny and satisfying the moral expectations of the reader—they die together. Eustacia has been compared to Emma Bovary, though Hardy claimed that he had not read Flaubert's 1856 novel at this time.

The setting of the story possesses a unity that may derive from a conscious attempt to follow the Aristotelian prescription for tragic drama. Hardy made this point in suggesting, in a letter to the publisher of the book version (1 October 1878), that a map might be provided (a suggestion that was taken up): "Unity of place is so seldom preserved in novels that a map of the scene of action is as a rule impracticable: but since the present story affords an opportunity of doing so I am of opinion that it would be a desirable novelty, likely to increase a reader's interest." The sense of place is intensified by the numerous references to local folk customs (for example, the mummers' play, and the scene in which a peasant woman, regarding Eustacia as a witch, makes a wax effigy of her). Such allusions also emphasize the contrast between two worlds—the traditional way of life (represented by the reddleman) and "the irrepressible New," manifested by Eustacia's cravings for independence. Clym Yeobright's rejection of the city (he has worked for a jeweler in Paris) and his return to Wessex to embrace successively the occupations of schoolmaster, furze cutter, and itinerant preacher, represent an impulsive turning back from the new to the old.

The shaping of the novel gave Hardy a certain amount of trouble. Thomasin seems originally to have been intended to play a fuller role than she does in the final version; but, some way into the task of writing the novel, Hardy changed his mind and made Eustacia the tragic heroine. The happy ending, with Thomasin united at last to Diggory Venn, was a concession to the readers of the serial: Hardy's original intention had been to make Venn disappear and to leave Thomasin in her widowhood.

The Return of the Native was followed by three minor novels. *The Trumpet-Major* (1880) represents Hardy's attempt at historical fiction; it is set in the Napoleonic period, which always held a great fascination for him and a generation later became the setting for his grandiose epic-drama *The Dynasts* (1904, 1906, 1908). A notebook in which he recorded material for use in the novel has been recently published and provides the fullest surviving evidence of Hardy's preparations for writing fiction: his painstaking research in the British Museum reveals his concern for authenticity, not only of historical events but of details of costume and manners. The novel seems to have been written in 1879-1880, when Hardy was living in London, and was serialized in the magazine *Good Words* during the twelve months of 1880; publication in three volumes was in October 1880.

The Trumpet-Major is set against a background of public events and, like Tolstoy's *War and Peace* (1864-1869), introduces into the fiction historical characters, such as King George III and that Admiral Hardy (as he later became) with whom Thomas Hardy claimed kinship. But the heart of the novel is concerned with private experience in times of crisis and uncertainty, and the love story has similarities to that of *Far from the Madding Crowd*. The heroine, Anne Garland, is loved by three men: the modest and self-sacrificing John Loveday (the trumpet-major of the title), his insensitive and shallow sailor-brother Bob, and the loutish Festus Derriman, a cruder version of Sergeant Troy. The novel has charm but lacks the solidity, the suggestiveness, and the power of Hardy's major fiction; the texture is thin and the writing lacks resonance; but a good word must be said for the poignancy of the conclusion. The modesty of Hardy's aims in *The Trumpet-Major* is suggested by his statement in a letter dated 9 June 1879 that the novel he was engaged on would be "above all things a cheerful story, without views or opinions, and . . . intended to wind up happily"—a promise that was not entirely kept.

During this period, Hardy's fame was growing steadily. He had established himself in a London suburb so as to be near the literary circles of the metropolis; he joined a club, dined out regularly, and met celebrities. He also formed friendships which lasted for the rest of his life—for example, with the critic Edmund Gosse. Hardy and his wife took occasional holidays on the Continent; as yet, they had no permanent home. Toward the end of 1880, while Hardy was at work on his next novel, *A Laodicean*, a serious blow fell: he became seriously ill with an internal hemorrhage and spent months in bed. He continued work on the novel, dictating it to Emma, though his pain and anxiety must have been considerable. Soon after his recovery in the spring of 1881, they set about looking for a house in Dorset. They eventually made a temporary home at Wimborne Minster—the first stage in what was to turn out to be a permanent return to Hardy's native county.

The circumstances of its composition make it unsurprising that *A Laodicean* is one of Hardy's least successful books, labored and unconvincing. Nevertheless, like everything he wrote, even the

Hardy about the time of the publication of
The Trumpet-Major *(1880)*

shortest poem, it is stamped with his individuality. It appeared in monthly installments from December 1880 to December 1881 and was serialized almost simultaneously in America. Book publication in both countries was toward the end of 1881. That Hardy, who usually preserved his manuscripts, should have destroyed that of *A Laodicean* suggests that he was not satisfied with the novel.

The hero is an architect, the heroine an heiress: in other words, the reader is offered yet another version of "the poor man and the lady." There is a certain desperation about the plotting of the latter half of the book, and many of the conventional trappings of Victorian fiction and melodrama are resorted to—a bastard son and other guilty secrets, overheard conversations, coincidental meetings, and blackmail. The painful circumstances of its production, with Hardy anxious to complete what he must at times have thought of as meager financial provision for his widow, account for its weakness. But there remains the larger problem of why the period of about five years from 1879 should be so barren of major creative achievement. At about forty, Hardy might have been expected to be at the height of his powers; but the greatest works still lay ahead. He always insisted that he was a late developer, and a happy corollary of this was that he retained his creative powers into extreme old age. Perhaps the fact that he was still, in middle life, without a settled home or a place in any community caused a deep discontent. Certainly, the flowering of his genius that followed the decision to settle permanently in Dorchester is very striking.

Meanwhile, the third of the minor novels of this period came in rapid succession to *A Laodicean*. In September 1881, while that novel was still running its course, the editor of the *Atlantic Monthly* invited Hardy to write a serial for his magazine. The result was *Two on a Tower*, serialized from May to December 1882 and published in book form at the end of October 1882. The dates of composition are unclear, but Hardy admitted in a letter to Gosse (21 January 1883) that "though the plan of the story was carefully thought out, the actual writing was lamentably hurried—having been produced month by month. . . ." It looks as though Hardy was conscious of paying a heavy artistic price for the insatiable demands of serialization.

The universe that had opened up so disconcertingly for the Victorians required a radical readjustment to new concepts of space as well as time: not only had the earth been shown to be immensely more ancient than had usually been be-

lieved, but the discoveries of nineteenth-century astronomy revealed a universe of boundless space. Hardy said in another letter (4 December 1882) that his aim in his new novel had been "to make science, not the mere padding of a romance, but the actual vehicle of romance." The hero of *Two on a Tower* is a young astronomer; his romantic entanglement with a high-born lady (yet again the theme of social inequality is prominent) takes place against a background of what Hardy calls "the stellar universe." Lady Constantine is ten years older than Swithin St. Cleeve—a drop in the ocean of astronomical time, but woefully significant in human lives. She is also married; but an erroneous report of her husband's death enables her to love and marry Swithin without moral turpitude but with complex consequences. Again, the latter part of the novel resorts to a huddle of melodramatic incidents. But the initial conception has genuine imaginative power—an idea of strength and originality that, in working out, falls victim to the demand for strong plotting generated by the serial mode, as well as (perhaps) to the haste imposed on the serious novelist catering to an eager public.

It would have been surprising if reviewers had been wildly enthusiastic about these three minor novels. But Hardy was by then an established author, and his work sold steadily. The first edition of *Two on a Tower*—1,000 copies—sold quite quickly, and a reprinting was called for. His royalties on volume sales were, of course, in addition to the fees he received from the magazines that serialized his work; and this double profit was no doubt what kept him at work as a serial novelist even though the task was often irksome and in violation of his artistic conscience.

After settling at Wimborne Minster in 1881, Hardy seems to have attempted to put down some roots in Dorset: for instance, he joined the Dorset Natural History and Antiquarian Field Club. But he still spent considerable periods in London during the social "season," mixing freely with other literary personalities in clubs and salons and at dinner tables. The urge to settle was strong, however; and by this time his financial position justified him in taking a major step—building a house, to his own designs. He considered various sites and eventually selected a piece of land just outside Dorchester. From the upstairs windows of the house he built, his old home could be seen across the fields; and the homecoming—the return of the native—seems to have been in a sense a symbolic act. In June 1883, Hardy and his wife moved into temporary accommodations in Dorchester so as to be on hand to supervise the building of the house, which he decided to call Max Gate (after Henry Mack, a former toll-gate keeper of the neighborhood). The move into Max Gate was made in June 1885, and apart from visits to London and elsewhere, Hardy remained there for the rest of his life.

The move to Dorchester initiated a major period of Hardy's creative life as a novelist, and it is surely significant that the first novel he wrote after returning to Dorchester is set in "Casterbridge," the fictional equivalent of that ancient borough. *The Mayor of Casterbridge* seems to have been begun early in 1884 and, in spite of numerous interruptions, was finished in April 1885. Unusually, composition was complete before serialization began, for it was not until 2 January 1886 that its first installment appeared in the weekly *Graphic*, where it continued until 15 May. Volume publication was only a few days in advance of the completion of serialization. In America, the novel appeared simultaneously in *Harper's Weekly*.

Weekly serialization no doubt helps to account for the high proportion of dramatic and sensational incident in this novel, some of it contrived and inessential; but unity is ensured by the dominant presence of the hero, Michael Henchard. His impulsive and ultimately self-destructive nature is evident in the opening incident, the bizarre but historically authentic wife-selling (scholars have unearthed a number of comparable cases reported in nineteenth-century newspapers); it is also emphasized by being set in contrast with the cautious, rational character of Farfrae, the outsider ("from far," as his name indicates) and new man whose scientific methods render outdated the traditional, largely intuitive business methods of Henchard. As with *The Return of the Native*, the novel invites comparison with Shakespearean tragedy, especially *King Lear*; a parallel with the Old Testament story of Saul and David has also been suggested.

The dating of the action remains rather obscure, and manuscript evidence suggests that Hardy may have changed his mind on this point. It has been suggested that the *Mayor of Casterbridge*, like *Tess of the d'Urbervilles* (1891), is concerned with the plight of English agriculture and the agricultural laborer during the crisis years toward the end of the nineteenth century. Another interpretation holds that Hardy had an earlier period in mind. The reference to a royal visitor may allude to Prince Albert's visit to Dorchester in 1849, but not all the other incidents and allusions are chronologically

Hardy's sketch from memory of the Three Mariners Inn, Dorchester, the model for the inn of the same name in The Mayor of Casterbridge *(Dorset County Museum)*

consistent with this. What is fairly clear is that the bulk of the action takes place around the mid-century, and that, like so many Victorian novelists, Hardy is therefore going back a generation before the date of composition, to the period of his own youth. The first two chapters of the novel form a prologue, with a gap of eighteen years between the second and third chapters. The work, like so much elsewhere in his prose and verse, is permeated by an aching sense of loss: Hardy is aware of the irrevocable destruction of a way of life which involves both an epoch of history and a precious part of his own early memories.

A note of discontent with the constraints of serialization makes itself heard from Hardy at this time—a discontent that was to be exacerbated rather than relieved as time went on. Hardy later wrote in *The Life of Thomas Hardy* that *The Mayor of Casterbridge* was "a story which [he] fancied he had damaged more recklessly as an artistic whole, in the interest of the newspaper in which it appeared serially, than perhaps any other of his novels, his aiming to get an incident into almost every week's part causing him in his own judgment to add events to the narrative somewhat too freely." Consideration of the fight in the loft and the encounter with the bull is likely to lead the reader to endorse this view. Before volume publication, Hardy took pains to tone down some of the more sensational incidents; and his subtitle, *The Life and Death of a Man of Character*, insists that the stress must fall on what Henchard is rather than what he does or suffers. (The pathetic incident in which Henchard returns to Elizabeth-Jane with his wedding present, a caged goldfinch, was omitted but subsequently restored to the text.) Though flawed, it remains one of the great tragic novels of the nineteenth century and Henchard one of Hardy's finest characters. The professional reviewers were disappointingly unappreciative of *The Mayor of Casterbridge*, though its reputation now stands high among Hardy's major fiction. Three writers, however, all praised it privately—George Gissing and Robert Louis Stevenson in letters to Hardy, and Gerard Manley Hopkins in a letter to Robert Bridges praising the wife sale.

In the new burst of creativity that followed the return to Dorchester, Hardy was at work on his next novel even before *The Mayor of Casterbridge* began to appear. He started *The Woodlanders* in November 1885, having undertaken to provide a serial in twelve installments for *Macmillan's Magazine*; serialization began in May 1886, but composition proceeded rather slowly, and the book was not completed until February 1887. Volume publication followed in March. Once again, there was editorial interference with Hardy's creative intentions: Mowbray Morris, the editor of the magazine, suggested that Fitzpiers's sexual escapade with Suke Damson needed tactful handling.

In the 1895 preface to *The Woodlanders*, Hardy notes that what he rather pedantically calls "the question of matrimonial divergence" was raised in the novel but not pursued with any thoroughness or boldness. It is, however, a topic that was to constitute one of the major themes of his later fiction; and his portrayal of Grace Melbury's unhappy marriage to Fitzpiers is followed by other and more searching studies of failed marriages. A 1912 postscript to the preface touches on another matter, that of the location of Little Hintock. Hardy declares that "I do not know myself where that hamlet is more precisely than as explained above and in the pages of the narrative," adding ironically that "tourists assure me positively that they have found it without trouble." The reminder that Hardy's landscapes are

partly real and partly fictional—that he laid a map of the imagination over the map of Dorset and the surrounding areas, and that "Wessex" exists fully only within the novels—is one that is still often disregarded.

The opening of this novel is highly characteristic: the reader is shown an empty road, then an unidentified and solitary figure, joined by other figures, their identities and purposes emerging only gradually from the account given by a narrator who is watchful and perceptive but certainly not omniscient. It is one of the most striking of Hardy's openings and displays a narrative technique both assured and original. The anticipation by Hardy of what later came to be thought of as cinematic techniques is well illustrated: one has the sense of a camera moving and registering the scene and its visual peculiarities. The first chapter ends with another characteristic motif: an outsider looks through the window of a cottage and observes the scene within. Hardy's novels are full of such moments of multiple spying: the reader watches the narrator watching a character who watches another. The scene inside the cottage—Barber Percomb's purchase of Marty South's hair, to be used to adorn the head of Mrs. Charmond—hints at one of the themes of the novel: naturalness versus artificiality. After her marriage, Grace is to feel this contrast very poignantly when she sees Giles Winterborne, "Autumn's very brother," and contrasts him with her effete husband.

The relationships of the characters are mainly on familiar lines. Grace is caught between two impulses: her long-standing commitment to her childhood friend, the faithful Giles, and her fascination with the elegant doctor, Edred Fitzpiers. As usual, the choice is between one belonging to the rural community and in harmony with its traditions, and one who is an exotic outsider unattached to the rural world by any ties of affection or loyalty; and, inevitably, social differences underscore the problem of a choice of husband, for Fitzpiers promises to lift her into another social sphere, whereas Giles can offer to share with her only the life of a working man. Hardy also introduces the theme of education: Grace's well-meaning and ambitious father has sent her away to school, with the result that she has lost touch with her old home (in Hardy's phrase, "fallen from the good old Hintock ways"). For one who had himself made such heroic—and successful—efforts at self-education and self-improvement as a path to social advancement, Hardy had a curiously ambiguous attitude toward education and was conscious of the losses as well as the gains it brings.

This outline suggests that the plot of the novel has much in common with *Far from the Madding Crowd* a dozen years earlier, and even with *Under the Greenwood Tree* earlier still. But there are differences: Fitzpiers's sexual immorality is dealt with more fully and involves not only a country girl, Suke Damson, whose frank carnality contrasts strikingly with the sentimental pathos attached to Fanny Robin, but the wealthy Mrs. Charmond—another outsider and exotic. Moreover, this time there is no question of a happy ending: Gabriel's patience and long-suffering had been rewarded, but Giles dies miserably, a quixotic victim of the proprieties. As for Grace, Hardy later pointed out to a correspondent (19 July 1889) that "the *ending* of the story, as hinted rather than stated, is that the heroine is doomed to an unhappy life with an inconstant husband. I could not accent this strongly in the book; by reason of the conventions of the libraries &c." A subplot concerns the unrequited love for Giles of the simple country girl Marty South, and one of the finest scenes in the novel shows them working side by side planting young trees: an occupation both traditional and creative, involving a communion between them that requires no words and contrasts strikingly with the middle-class world into which Grace is so unhappily drawn.

The Victorian reviewers were troubled by certain aspects of *The Woodlanders*. Richard Holt Hutton, in the *Spectator* (26 March 1887), announced that "this is a very powerful book, and as disagreeable as it is powerful"—and "disagreeable" was one of the favorite epithets used of Hardy by contemporary critics. Hutton found the strength of the novel to consist in its pictures of rural life, but was disturbed by the moral implications of the story ("written with an indifference to the moral effect it conveys"). Like many others, he would obviously have been happier if Hardy had been content to remain a chronicler of quaint country ways; Hardy's determination to tackle highly controversial moral and social issues in his later fiction must be seen as going willfully against the tide of critical approval. It is only fair to add, however, that some critics were genuinely appreciative: the *Athenaeum* (26 March 1887), for instance, found the construction of the story "simply perfect," and urged "all who can tell masterly work in fiction when they see it" to read the book—though at the same time adding significantly that "the novel is distinctly not one for the young person of whom we have lately heard." Much earlier

Hardy's revised draft of the title page of his controversial 1891 novel, with subtitle and quotation from The Two Gentlemen of Verona *added (Dorset County Museum)*

in his career, Hardy had been warned by Leslie Stephen to "remember the country clergyman's daughters"; and during the next few years his refusal to conform to the "young person" standard was to involve him in greater difficulties, and to lay him open to more severe attack, than ever before.

The Woodlanders had followed very quickly on the heels of *The Mayor of Casterbridge*; but there was to be a considerable interval before the appearance of his next novel, *Tess of the d'Urbervilles*. This is to some extent accounted for by the fact that Hardy was busy writing short stories based on the history of various Dorset families (published in various magazines and collected in 1891 as *A Group of Noble Dames*). But it is also true that *Tess of the d'Urbervilles* occupied him for a long time, partly because of the difficulties he underwent in finding a publisher and the necessity he eventually accepted of radical revisions to render the novel acceptable as a serial. *Tess of the d'Urbervilles* was begun in the autumn of 1888 and was intended for Tillotson and Son, a Lancashire newspaper syndicate with strongly Christian associations. At that time its title was "Too Late, Beloved!" In September 1889, Hardy sent portions of his manuscript (probably about one-half of the completed novel) to Tillotson's, who were considerably dismayed by such scenes as the seduction of Tess and the improvised baptism of her dying baby. Hardy refused to agree to their suggestion that certain scenes should be omitted, and the contract between them was canceled by mutual consent. The novel, still incomplete, was offered to *Murray's Magazine* and then to *Macmillan's Magazine*; both turned it down. Hardy thereupon set to work to "dismember" the story (his own vivid word) and produced a version that would not cause offense. This was accepted by the *Graphic*, and Harper accepted it for publication in America. There was still much work to be done, however, and the novel was not completed until the latter part of 1890. Serialization began in the weekly *Graphic* on 4 July 1891 and continued until 26 December. Two passages removed from the novel were published as separate sketches in other periodicals: "Saturday Night in Arcady," dealing with the seduction of Tess, and "The Midnight Baptism, A Study in Christianity."

Hardy's story was severely mangled for serialization: for example, he was obliged to introduce a mock marriage, staged by Alec to make Tess believe that she was his wife, and to omit the illegitimate baby. For volume publication (November 1891) Hardy carefully restored his original text, omitting the interpolations and restoring most of the omissions.

While he was engaged in the protracted attempts to find a publisher for *Tess of the d'Urbervilles*, Hardy wrote an essay published in the *New Review* in January 1890 as "Candour in English Fiction." The essay exposes the "fearful price" that a self-respecting artist has to pay for "the privilege of writing in the English language": thanks to the pressures imposed upon contemporary fiction by editors and librarians, and the prevalence of the "young person" standard, the literature of the day is largely "a literature of quackery," and it has become impossible to depict life as it really is. "Life being a physiological fact," writes Hardy, "its honest portrayal must be largely concerned with, for one thing, the relations of the sexes"; but to the frank treatment of this subject "English society imposes a well-nigh insuperable bar."

Tess of the d'Urbervilles received more attention than any of Hardy's previous books, though much of the discussion was of a moral rather than a critical kind. On the literary side, approval and disapproval were mixed in various proportions. The *Athenaeum* (9 January 1892) found the book "not only good,

but great"; the *Academy* (6 February 1892) called it "a tragic masterpiece"; and in America the *Atlantic Monthly* gave it a long review, praising it as Hardy's greatest achievement. The *Saturday Review* (16 January 1892), on the other hand, spoke of "the terrible dreariness of this tale"; some critics objected to Alec as melodramatic and Angel as priggish; and the *Quarterly Review* (April 1892), in familiar terms, declared that "Mr. Hardy has told an extremely disagreeable story in an extremely disagreeable manner." Hardy, always much more affected by criticism than by praise, was so hurt by this last review that he declared: "Well, if this sort of thing continues no more novel-writing for me. A man must be a fool to deliberately stand up to be shot at."

One result of the controversy surrounding *Tess of the d'Urbervilles* was that it sold better than any of Hardy's previous novels. It comes as a surprise to find that, when Hardy's novels appeared in volume form, usually only 1,000 copies of the first edition were printed; but it is important to remember that the three-volume novel was an expensive luxury. In the case of *Tess of the d'Urbervilles*, the 1,000 copies were soon sold, and another 1,000 were printed within a few months; when a cheap reprint in one volume appeared in September 1892, it quickly ran into five impressions and sold 17,000 copies. The novel was also widely translated.

For many readers *Tess of the d'Urbervilles* is Hardy's greatest novel, and part of its richness derives from the different layers of interest that interpretation can uncover. It includes some of the archetypal situations of old ballads and folk songs—for instance, the ruined maid who murders her seducer—and at many points in the story Hardy invites the reader to see it as folk tale or morality play (Alec, for instance, is repeatedly identified with Satan). Yet it is also a novel of nineteenth-century life and is rooted in a highly specific landscape. When, in chapter 30, Tess stands at the railway station beside the "gleaming cranks and wheels," or when later in the novel she is obliged to work according to the mechanical rhythms of the steam-driven harvester, she belongs unmistakably to a rural world invaded by the results of the Industrial Revolution. The schooling she has received, insufficient to make her a really educated person, is enough to cut her off from the world to which her mother belongs; so that the "generation gap" is measurable in centuries rather than years. (Again, Hardy shows a distrust of the effects of popular education.) Tess speaks two languages, the dialect of her home and a standard form of speech ac-

The end of the manuscript for Tess of the d'Urbervilles *(Dorset County Museum)*

quired from her London-trained teacher; the result is a discontent with the sphere of life into which she has been born, and when, in the second chapter, Angel Clare has briefly passed into her life and (for the time being) out again, she has no time for the village lads, who "did not speak so nicely as the strange young man had done." Part of the social background of the novel is that depopulation of the countryside and breakdown of the old stable communities of which Hardy had written in an essay, "The Dorsetshire Labourer," printed in *Longman's Magazine* in July 1883; Hardy drew on his essay for certain passages in *Tess of the d'Urbervilles*, such as the account of the Lady-Day moving in chapters 51 and 52.

The various settings of the action to a large extent reflect the structure of the novel. Tess begins in her symbolically named native village of Marlott (her lot or destiny is from the outset marred or spoiled); she moves to the Durberville home at Trantridge; works successively at Talbothays and Flintcomb-Ash; and eventually murders Alec at Sandbourne, is arrested at Stonehenge, and is executed at Wintoncester (this list of her wanderings is selective). Although the geographical range of her experiences is not extensive, Hardy skillfully uses settings to contrast with each other and to symbolize her mood at various phases of her existence. The lush fertility of Talbothays is associated with the period of her growing love for Angel; the harsh life of Flintcomb-Ash (another significant name) harmonizes with her mood of despair after Angel has left her; the middle-class seaside resort of Sandbourne is the apt setting for her reunion with the shallow, pleasure-loving Alec; and, arrested at Stonehenge, she becomes a sacrifice to conventional morality and the victim of a barbaric system of justice. Tess's wanderings are also assigned to particular seasons of the year: she is at Talbothays in summertime, but Flintcomb-Ash is associated with winter and death. In many ways this is Hardy's most poetic novel, and his evocation of the natural world and of his heroine, in all their concrete, detailed, and often sensuous physicality, recalls the odes of Keats.

Tess possesses an intensely physical presence and an unconsciously radiated sexuality that make her almost unique in Victorian fiction. (For somewhat later parallels, one may turn to the work of D. H. Lawrence, who studied Hardy's novels carefully, wrote about them, and probably owed them a good deal.) Her physical attractiveness is, however, a curse: when, in chapter 46, she asks Alec, "What have I done!," he tells her, "Nothing intentionally.

But you have been the means—the innocent means—of my backsliding. . . ." It is true that Tess does "nothing intentionally," and this passivity or unconsciousness is a limitation of her character: there are numerous comparisons of her to a shy animal, she moves through scenes and experiences as if in a dream, and the reader is given virtually no sense of an inner life; when she finds herself involved in moral action or moral debate, as in the scene after her marriage to Angel, she is shown as naively and almost childishly lacking in worldly wisdom or even peasant common sense. The highly self-conscious and ironically named Angel is her antithesis in this respect: he reflects too much and obeys his instincts too little. As for Alec, he is both a figure out of Victorian melodrama and the occasion for satire on the rapid social advancement of the urban middle classes. Alec's father has made a fortune in the North of England, and in one generation the family has attempted to obtain gentility by purchase, not only moving into Wessex and buying land there but actually adopting the name of one of the old local families—that ancient name of which Tess's is itself a corruption. Hardy was much preoccupied by the decline of old families; then in his fifties, he probably felt deeply his own childlessness (in the event, none of his generation producing any issue, the family line died out). Tess's misfortunes begin on the day that her father, John Durbeyfield, learns that he is a descendant of the once-great family of d'Urbervilles; from that point—the thoughtless imparting of a piece of antiquarian information by a character who then disappears from the story—subsequent events move forward with a relentless logic, as her father's foolish notions of gentility drive Tess into service with Alec's family and eventually into Alec's arms.

Tess of the d'Urbervilles contains some of Hardy's best writing—surprisingly, when one recalls the frustrating and exasperating circumstances in which much of the novel was written. The recurrent imagery (one pattern throughout the novel associated with the color red, for instance, and another with the sun and the moon) gives it great density of texture; there is correspondingly less of the generalizing and moralizing that are among Hardy's defects as a prose writer and that must in part, at least, be laid at the door of the serial novel with its requirement of a specified length and its consequent encouragement of padding. Certain passages (chapter 20, for example) have a poetic intensity rare in the late-nineteenth-century novel.

Hardy's next novel was to be poetic in conception but curiously schematic in structure and as thin in texture as *Tess of the d'Urbervilles* is rich. Hardy himself seems to have felt no great enthusiasm for *The Well-Beloved*: he described it in a letter to his American publishers as "short and slight, and written entirely with a view to serial publication," and he seems to have been in no hurry to see it appear in volume form. It is the product of an interlude of much less intense creative activity between the two major novels, *Tess of the d'Urbervilles* and *Jude the Obscure*. Begun toward the end of 1891, as the serialization of *Tess of the d'Urbervilles* drew to a close, it was serialized in the weekly *Illustrated London News* from 1 October to 17 December 1892. In view of the trouble that *Tess of the d'Urbervilles* had caused him, it is interesting to find Hardy assuring his publishers that in this new novel "There is not a word or scene . . . which can offend the most fastidious taste; and it is equally suited for the reading of young people, and for that of persons of maturer years." After serialization, Hardy put the novel aside for nearly four years; in 1896 he revised it and changed the ending, and it appeared in volume form in March 1897.

The Well-Beloved (originally titled "The Pursuit of the Well-Beloved") is subtitled *A Sketch of a Temperament* and bears on the title page a quotation from Shelley ("One shape of many names"). The story blends Shelleyan idealism with preoccupations that a knowledge of Hardy's temperament suggests may be autobiographical. His hero is an artist: Pierston is a sculptor who seeks perfection both in art and in life. The implausible plot shows him falling in love successively with three women belonging to three generations of the same family: time passes, he grows older, but his desire for the ideal remains as fresh as ever. None of his loves brings happiness. The tone of the novel is light, but the underlying conception is wistful and even melancholy. This short novel shows Hardy as haunted by the idea of time and growing old—"a time-torn man," as he describes himself in one of his poems. Although so much in the book is fanciful and insubstantial, the setting (on Portland Bill, referred to in the book as the "Isle of Slingers") has an admirable solidity.

Between the serialization and the volume publication of *The Well-Beloved*, Hardy wrote and published his last novel, *Jude the Obscure*. This work seems to have occupied him for longer than any other of his novels. As early as 1887, before *Tess of the d'Urbervilles* was even begun, he had begun making notes for the novel that was to become *Jude the Obscure*; in 1890 he "jotted down" its "scheme"—presumably a plot outline; in 1892-1893 he visited the village of Great Fawley in Berkshire (formerly the home of his grandmother and the prototype of Marygreen in the novel, as well as the source of the hero's surname), and also spent some time in Oxford (the Christminster of the novel); during the same period he wrote the story "in outline"; and in 1893-1894 he wrote it in full. It was serialized in *Harper's New Monthly Magazine* from December 1894 to November 1895 and published in volume form in November 1895.

Once again Hardy found himself forced to make extensive compromises with his original intentions in order to win acceptance for his novel as a serial. His early assurance to his editor that the story "could not offend the most fastidious maiden" was not justified by events and suggests that, in the course of composition, the novel underwent a radical shift of direction. The germ of the novel may be contained in a note Hardy made in his diary on 28 April 1888: "A short story of a young man—'who could not go to Oxford'—His struggles and ulti-

mate failure. Suicide. There is something [in this] the world ought to be shown, and I am the one to show it to them. . . ." The theme, that is, was to be a poor man's quest for an education and the tragic outcome of his failure to storm the bastions of educational privilege. This theme survives in the completed novel, but it has become subordinate to the central discussion of marriage. Jude's tragedy is only partly caused by his unsuccessful struggles to gain admission to the university: his entanglements, first with the country girl Arabella and then with the intellectual Sue, occupy a dominant position in the novel. It is true that "the marriage question" was topical in the 1890s, and *Jude the Obscure* is not the only novel in which it is debated; but the state of Hardy's own childless marriage surely influenced his attitude toward the subject. His relationship with the snobbish, foolish, but not unlikable, Emma Hardy deteriorated as they grew older; and by this time, although they continued to live under the same roof, the couple were leading virtually separate lives.

The effects of change and the breakdown of a

Hardy's study at Max Gate

Hardy's second wife, the former Florence Emily Dugdale

Thomas and Florence Hardy at Max Gate with their dog, Wessex, in 1914

traditional order had always been a major theme of Hardy's fiction; and in *Jude the Obscure* the note is sounded in the opening sentence: "The schoolmaster was leaving the village. . . ." Jude, an orphan, feels rootless and unwanted: Hardy presents a hero who is from the outset deprived of a place in the community. The short opening chapter moves ahead with great economy and assurance; its final paragraph briefly evokes the destruction of the past that is changing the face of rural England—thatched cottages have been pulled down, and the medieval church has been "restored" by some such well-meaning architect as Hardy himself had been a generation earlier.

Hardy declared that there was no autobiography in the novel, but the claim is transparently false. Like the young Hardy, Jude works painfully but patiently to educate himself, concentrating (as Hardy had done) on the traditional academic disciplines of the classics and theology. Since he must earn a living, he becomes a stonemason (recalling the occupation of Hardy's father and grandfather). His ambition takes him to Christminster, the great university town whose colleges are monopolized by the sons of the well-to-do rather than by the poor scholars for whom they were originally founded, and Hardy moves his hero outside the familiar Wessex world. Jude is the most restless of Hardy's protagonists, and his wanderings mirror the unsatisfied longings of his heart.

Jude's slow progress toward his distant goal is interrupted, and eventually frustrated, by his encounters with two women of contrasting types. Arabella, first seen washing a pig's innards and repeatedly associated with pigs, recalls the sorceress Circe who turned Odysseus's companions into swine. She seduces Jude, traps him into a disastrous marriage, and then leaves him to begin his life afresh. In Christminster he meets his cousin Sue Bridehead, a study in the "new woman"—a boyish or androgynous figure, intellectual and skeptical, and a representative of the demand for female emancipation and equality of the sexes. Sue marries Phillotson, Jude's old schoolmaster—another disastrous marriage—even though she and Jude are in love; later Sue and Jude live together, but their children die tragically, they part, and Jude dies within a stone's throw of the colleges to which he has, to the very end, been denied admission. Hardy's treatment of marriage is bleakly uncompromising, and on one level *Jude the Obscure* is a propaganda novel, eloquently pleading a case—or, more precisely, two cases: one holding that marriage can only be binding for life at the expense of considerable human misery, the other advocating opportunities of higher education for the workingman. But it is also a work of poetic resonance that uses recurring symbols and allusions to unify the episodic narrative and shifting scenes. Jude, who dies at thirty, is a Christ-figure; and the novel contains numerous biblical allusions, including the association of Jude and Arabella with Samson and Delilah. Hardy makes much use of contrast: Christian and pagan beliefs, Gothic and classical styles of architecture, scholarship and manual labor, sexuality and frigidity. The patterning of the plot involves some fairly complex interrelationships between the four principal characters; Hardy remarked in this connection (in a letter dated 4 January 1896) that "the rectangular lines of the story were not premeditated, but came by chance." The tasks of mangling the original novel for serialization and subsequently restoring it to its original form seem to have wearied him, and he wrote in 1895 that "I have lost energy for revising and improving the original as I meant to do." Nevertheless, though there are unsatisfactory passages—the dialogues between Jude and Sue and the murder of their children by Jude and Arabella's son, who then commits suicide, have come in for frequent criticism—the novel is deeply impressive.

Hardy declared that he felt sure that the book "makes for morality," but this was not the opinion of many of its reviewers; and *Jude the Obscure* was more savagely attacked than any of its predecessors. One reviewer said that it was "almost the worst book I have ever read"; another described it as "steeped in sex"; and Hardy was accused of "wallowing in the mire" and "attacking the fundamental institutions of society." It was nicknamed "*Jude the Obscene*," a bishop attacked it in the press, and a leading circulating library withdrew it from circulation. Some, however, were not too blinded by prejudice to perceive its merits; and before Hardy's death it had been widely translated and was recognized as a masterpiece.

Though Hardy lived for another thirty-two years after the publication of *Jude the Obscure*, he never wrote another novel; and this silence has given rise to varied explanations. The traditional belief that he was so disgusted by the reception of *Jude the Obscure* that he declined to expose himself again to the same kind of treatment is hard to accept; there is evidence in his letters that he had thoughts of writing another novel several years later, though he never did so. The end of his novel-writing career was not abrupt or dramatic, and it can have dawned on the reading public only gradually that they were to have no more novels from his pen. From the last years of the nineteenth century, his energies went into the writing and publication of verse; although he had devoted a quarter of a century to fiction, his sense of a poetic vocation had never left him, and he had gone on writing poems (though not publishing them). In 1898 there appeared the first volume of his verse, *Wessex Poems*, and for the rest of his life he published poems frequently and in large quantities. He had long been impatient with the constraints of serialized fiction; in any case, the success of *Tess of the d'Urbervilles* and *Jude the Obscure* brought him financial security, and he died a rich man. But it would be wrong to suppose that he lost all interest in his novels: the first collected edition (*The Wessex Novels*, 1895-1913) was followed by the *Wessex Edition* (1912-1931), for which Hardy not only wrote a

Hardy at Max Gate with the Prince of Wales in 1923

Mem:

Vol II. might begin here — if 2 vols.

[Number of typoscript pages in the whole, probably about 650 or under, when finished, which at 250 words each page makes 150,000 - (a fair length for a biography.)]

PART V.

Tess, Jude, and the end of Prose.

Chapter XX.

The Reception of the Book.

1892. Aet. 51 - 52.

Tess of the d'Urbervilles

As ~~the novel~~ got into general circulation it attracted an attention that Hardy had apparently not foreseen, for at the time of its publication he was planning something of quite a different kind, according to an entry he made:

"Title:- 'Songs of Five-and-Twenty Years'. Arrangement of the songs: Lyric Ecstasy inspired by music to have precedence."

However, reviews, letters, and other intelligence speedily called him from these casual thoughts back to the novel, which the tediousness of the alterations and restorations had made him weary of. From the prefaces to later editions can be gathered more or less clearly what happened to the book as, passing into great popularity, an endeavour was made *by some critics* to change it to *scandalous* notoriety — the latter kind of clamour, raised by a certain small section of the public and the press, being quite inexplicable to *its just* ~~any fair~~ judge, and to the writer himself. It would have been amusing if it had not revealed such antagonism at the back of

The sub-title of the book, added as a casual afterthought, seemed to be especially exasperating. All this

Typescript of the first page of The Later Years of Thomas Hardy, 1892-1928, *showing Hardy's revisions. The biography is credited to his second wife, but it was largely written by Hardy (Dorset County Museum).*

"General Preface" (1911) but meticulously revised his text.

Apart from his fourteen novels, Hardy was a prolific writer of short stories, most of which were collected in four volumes. They were written for magazine publication and are of uneven quality; the best, however, are not mere potboilers but are excellent specimens of their kind. Comparison of the ballad-like "The Three Strangers" with the realistic stories of modern life such as "The Son's Veto" or "On the Western Circuit" will illustrate the range of Hardy's art in this genre.

Hardy's nonfictional prose also calls for mention. At various times he wrote nearly forty prefaces for his volumes of fiction and verse; and although these cannot be said to present any fully articulated aesthetic, they include interesting comments on specific novels and sometimes raise questions of general import. Among Hardy's essays, "The Dorsetshire Labourer" and "Candour in English Fiction" have already been mentioned; others of interest include "The Profitable Reading of Fiction" (1888) and "Memories of Church Restoration" (1906). Hardy's notebooks and commonplace books have been published and offer many insights into his reading and his intellectual interests. He was a prolific though not a self-revealing letter writer, but most of the surviving letters belong to his later years, and the first volume of the collected edition now in course of publication covers the years 1840-1892.

Hardy's fame increased steadily in his later years; and although he remained more and more at Max Gate, he received there a stream of distinguished visitors, including the Prince of Wales, who came to pay homage to the most famous English writer of his age. After declining the offer of a knighthood, he accepted the Order of Merit—bestowed by the sovereign and the highest honor that can be accorded to an English author—in 1910. Fifteen months after the death of Emma Hardy on 27 November 1912, Hardy married Florence Emily Dugdale, a teacher who was some forty years his junior. The volume of criticism devoted to his work increased steadily and he was the subject of several full-length studies during his lifetime. He died at Max Gate on 11 January 1928 at the age of eighty-seven.

Other:

Florence Emily Hardy, *The Early Years of Thomas Hardy, 1840-1891*, and *The Later Years of*

Thomas Hardy, 1892-1928, ghostwritten by Hardy (London: Macmillan, 1928, 1930; New York: Macmillan, 1928, 1930); republished in one volume as *The Life of Thomas Hardy, 1840-1928* (London: Macmillan, 1962; New York: St. Martin's, 1962).

Letters:

The Collected Letters of Thomas Hardy, edited by Richard Little Purdy and Michael Millgate (3 volumes, Oxford: Clarendon Press, 1978-1982).

Bibliography:

Richard Little Purdy, *Thomas Hardy: A Bibliographical Study* (Oxford: Clarendon Press, 1954).

Biographies:

Robert Gittings, *Young Thomas Hardy* (London: Heinemann, 1975);

Gittings, *The Older Hardy* (London: Heinemann, 1978);

Gittings, *The Second Mrs. Hardy* (London: Oxford University Press, 1980);

Michael Millgate, *Thomas Hardy: A Biography* (New York: Random House, 1982).

References:

John Bayley, *An Essay on Hardy* (Cambridge: Cambridge University Press, 1978);

Douglas Brown, *Thomas Hardy* (London: Longmans, Green, 1954);

R. G. Cox, ed., *Thomas Hardy: The Critical Heritage* (London: Routledge & Kegan Paul, 1970);

A. J. Guerard, *Thomas Hardy: The Novels and Stories* (Cambridge: Harvard University Press, 1949);

Irving Howe, *Thomas Hardy* (New York: Macmillan, 1967);

J. T. Laird, *The Shaping of "Tess of the d'Urbervilles"* (Oxford: Clarendon Press, 1975);

J. Hillis Miller, *Thomas Hardy: Distance and Desire* (Cambridge: Belknap Press, 1970);

Michael Millgate, *Thomas Hardy: His Career as a Novelist* (London: Bodley Head, 1971);

Millgate, "Thomas Hardy," in *Victorian Fiction: A Second Guide to Research*, edited by George H. Ford (New York: Modern Language Association of America, 1978), pp. 308-332;

Norman Page, *Thomas Hardy* (London: Routledge & Kegan Paul, 1977);

Page, ed., *Thomas Hardy Annual No. 1* (London: Macmillan, 1982);

Page, ed., *Thomas Hardy: The Writer and His*

Background (London: Bell & Hyman, 1980);

F. B. Pinion, *A Hardy Companion* (London: Macmillan, 1968);

George Wing, *Hardy* (Edinburgh: Oliver & Boyd, 1963).

Papers:

The manuscripts of many of Hardy's novels survive, complete or in part, and provide interesting evidence of his methods of composition and revisions.

Jude the Obscure is in the Fitzwilliam Museum, Cambridge; *The Mayor of Casterbridge*, *The Woodlanders*, and *Under the Greenwood Tree* in Dorset County Museum; *The Return of the Native* at University College, Dublin; *Tess of the d'Urbervilles* in the British Library; *The Trumpet-Major* at Windsor Castle; *Two on a Tower* in the Houghton Library at Harvard; and a portion of *A Pair of Blue Eyes* in the Berg Collection at New York Public Library. *Far from the Madding Crowd* is in private hands.

G. A. Henty
(8 December 1832 - 16 November 1902)

Patrick A. Dunae
University of Victoria

BOOKS: *A Search for a Secret* (3 volumes, London: Tinsley, 1867);

The March to Magdala (London: Tinsley, 1868);

All but Lost (3 volumes, London: Tinsley, 1869);

Out on the Pampas; or, The Young Settlers (London: Griffith & Farran, 1871; New York: Burt, n.d.);

The Young Franc-Tireurs, and their Adventures in the Franco-Prussian War (London: Griffith & Farran, 1872; New York: Hurst, n.d.);

The March to Coomassie (London: Tinsley, 1874);

Seaside Maidens (London: Tinsley, 1880);

The Young Buglers: A Tale of the Peninsular War (London: Griffith & Farran, 1880);

In Times of Peril: A Tale of India (London: Griffith & Farran, 1881; New York: Dutton, 1881);

The Cornet of Horse: A Tale of Marlborough's Wars (London: Low, Marston, Searle, & Rivington, 1881; Philadelphia: Lippincott, 1881);

Winning His Spurs: A Tale of the Crusades (London: Low, Marston, Searle, & Rivington, 1882); republished as *The Boy Knight, Who Won His Spurs Fighting with King Richard of England: A Tale of the Crusaders* (Boston: Roberts, 1883);

Facing Death; or, The Hero of the Vaughan Pit: A Tale of the Coal Mines (London: Blackie, 1882; New York: Scribner & Welford, n.d.);

Under Drake's Flag: A Tale of the Spanish Main (London: Blackie, 1883; New York: Blackie-Scribner, 1883);

Friends, though Divided: A Tale of the Civil Wars (Lon-

don: Griffith & Farran, 1883);

Jack Archer: A Tale of the Crimea (London: Low, Marston, Searle, & Rivington, 1883); republished as *The Fall of Sebastopol; or, Jack Archer in the Crimea* (Boston: Roberts, 1884);

By Sheer Pluck: A Tale of the Ashanti War (London: Blackie, 1884; New York: Blackie-Scribner, n.d.);

With Clive in India; or, The Beginnings of an Empire (London: Blackie, 1884; New York: Scribner & Welford, 1884);

True to the Old Flag: A Tale of the American War of Independence (London: Blackie, 1885; New York: Blackie-Scribner, n.d.);

St. George for England: A Tale of Cressy and Poitiers (London: Blackie, 1885; New York: Blackie-Scribner, n.d.);

The Young Colonists (London: Routledge, 1885);

In Freedom's Cause: A Story of Wallace and Bruce (London: Blackie, 1885; New York: Scribner & Welford, n.d.);

Through the Fray: A Tale of the Luddite Riots (London: Blackie, 1886; New York: Scribner & Welford, n.d.);

For Name and Fame; or, Through the Afghan Passes (London: Blackie, 1886; New York: Blackie-Scribner, 1886);

The Dragon and the Raven; or, the Days of King Alfred (London: Blackie, 1886; New York: Scribner & Welford, n.d.);

The Lion of the North: A Tale of the Days of Gustavus Adolphus (London: Blackie, 1886; New York: Blackie-Scribner, n.d.);

With Wolfe in Canada; or, The Winning of a Continent (London: Blackie, 1887; New York: Scribner & Welford, 1887);

The Young Carthaginian (London: Blackie, 1887; New York: Scribner & Welford, 1887);

A Final Reckoning (London: Blackie, 1887; New York: Scribner & Welford, 1887);

The Bravest of the Brave; or, With Peterborough in Spain (London: Blackie, 1887; New York: Scribner & Welford, n.d.);

In the Reign of Terror: The Adventures of a Westminster Boy (New York: Scribner & Welford, 1887; London: Blackie, 1888);

For the Temple: A Tale of the Fall of Jerusalem (London: Blackie, 1888; New York: Scribner & Welford, n.d.);

Bonnie Prince Charlie: A Tale of Fontenoy and Culloden (London: Blackie, 1888; New York: Blackie-Scribner, n.d.);

Gabriel Allen, M.P. (London: Blackett, 1888);

Sturdy and Strong; or, How George Andrews Made His Way (London: Blackie, 1888; New York: Blackie-Scribner, n.d.);

Orange and Green: A Tale of the Boyne and Limerick (London: Blackie, 1888; New York: Blackie-Scribner, 1888);

The Curse of Carne's Hold: A Tale of Adventure (2 volumes, London: Spencer, Blackett & Hallam, 1889);

The Plague Ship (London: Society for the Propagation of Christian Knowledge, 1889; New York: Young, 1889);

The Cat of Bubastes: A Tale of Ancient Egypt (London: Blackie, 1889; New York: Blackie-Scribner, n.d.);

The Lion of St. Mark: A Tale of Venice (London: Blackie, 1889; New York: Blackie-Scribner, n.d.);

Captain Bayley's Heir: A Tale of the Gold Fields of California (London: Blackie, 1889; New York: Scribner & Welford, 1889);

One of the 28th: A Tale of Waterloo (London: Blackie, 1889; New York: Scribner & Welford, 1890);

Tales of Daring and Danger (London: Blackie, 1890; New York: Scribner & Welford, n.d.);

With Lee in Virginia: A Story of the American Civil War (London: Blackie, 1890; New York: Blackie-Scribner, n.d.);

By Pike and Dyke: A Tale of the Rise of the Dutch Republic (London: Blackie, 1890; New York: Scribner & Welford, n.d.);

Those Other Animals (London: Henry, 1891);

Maori and Settler: A Story of the New Zealand War (London: Blackie, 1891; New York: Scribner & Welford, 1891);

A Hidden Foe (2 volumes, London: Low, Marston, 1891; 1 volume, New York: National Book Company, n.d.);

By Right of Conquest; or, With Cortez in Mexico (London: Blackie, 1891; New York: Blackie-Scribner, 1891);

By England's Aid; or, The Freeing of the Netherlands (1585-1604) (London: Blackie, 1891; New York: Blackie-Scribner, n.d.);

A Chapter of Adventures; or, Through the Bombardment of Alexandria (London: Blackie, 1891; New York: Scribner & Welford, 1891);

Held Fast for England: A Tale of the Siege of Gibraltar (New York: Scribners, 1891; London: Blackie, 1892);

Beric the Briton: A Story of the Roman Invasion (New York: Scribners, 1891; London: Blackie, 1892);

The Dash for Khartoum: A Tale of the Nile Expedition (New York: Scribners, 1891; London: Blackie, 1892);

Redskin and Cow-Boy: A Tale of the Western Plains (New York: Scribners, 1891; London: Blackie, 1892);

The Ranche in the Valley (London: Society for the Propagation of Christian Knowledge, 1892; New York: Young, 1892);

Condemned as a Nihilist: A Story of Escape from Siberia (New York: Scribners, 1892; London: Blackie, 1893);

In Greek Waters: A Story of the Grecian War of Independence (1821-1827) (New York: Scribners, 1892; London: Blackie, 1893);

Rujub, the Juggler (3 volumes, London: Chatto & Windus, 1893); republished as *In the Days of the Mutiny: A Military Novel* (New York: Ogilvie, 1893);

Through the Sikh War: A Tale of the Conquest of the Punjaub (New York: Scribners, 1893; London: Blackie, 1894);

Saint Bartholomew's Eve: A Tale of the Huguenot Wars (New York: Scribners, 1893; London: Blackie, 1894);

A Jacobite Exile: Being the Adventures of a Young Englishman in the Service of Charles XII of Sweden (New York: Scribners, 1893; London: Blackie, 1894);

Wulf the Saxon: A Story of the Norman Conquest (New York: Scribners, 1894; London: Blackie, 1895);

In the Heart of the Rockies: A Story of Adventure in Colorado (New York: Scribners, 1894; London: Blackie, 1895);

When London Burned: A Story of Restoration Times and the Great Fire (New York: Scribners, 1894; London: Blackie, 1895);

Dorothy's Double (3 volumes, London: Chatto & Windus, 1894; 1 volume, Chicago: Rand McNally, 1895);

A Knight of the White Cross: A Tale of the Siege of Rhodes (New York: Scribners, 1895; London: Blackie, 1896);

The Tiger of Mysore: A Story of the War with Tippoo Saib (New York: Scribners, 1895; London: Blackie, 1896);

A Woman of the Commune: A Tale of Two Sieges of Paris (London: White, 1895); republished as *Two Sieges of Paris; or, a Girl of the Commune* (New York: Fenno, 1895);

Through Russian Snows: A Story of Napoleon's Retreat from Moscow (New York: Scribners, 1895; London: Blackie, 1896);

Surly Joe: The Story of a True Hero (London: Blackie, 1896);

White-Faced Dick: A Story of Pine-Tree Gulch (London: Blackie, 1896);

On the Irrawaddy: A Story of the First Burmese War (New York: Scribners, 1896; London: Blackie, 1897);

At Agincourt: A Tale of the White Hoods of Paris (New York: Scribners, 1896; London: Blackie, 1897);

With Cochrane the Dauntless: A Tale of the Exploits of Lord Cochrane in South American Waters (New York: Scribners, 1896; London: Blackie, 1897);

The Queen's Cup: A Novel (3 volumes, London: Chatto & Windus, 1897; 1 volume, Chicago: Donahue, 1898);

Among Malay Pirates: A Tale of Adventure and Peril (New York: Hurst, 1897);

With Moore at Carunna (New York: Scribners, 1897; London: Blackie, 1898);

A March on London: Being a Story of Wat Tyler's Insurrection (New York: Scribners, 1897; London: Blackie, 1898);

With Frederick the Great: A Story of the Seven Years' War (New York: Scribners, 1897; London: Blackie, 1898);

Both Sides the Border: A Tale of Hotspur and Glendower (New York: Scribners, 1898; London: Blackie, 1899);

Colonel Thorndyke's Secret (London: Chatto & Windus, 1898; New York: Hurst, 1901);

Under Wellington's Command: A Tale of the Peninsular War (New York: Scribners, 1898; London: Blackie, 1899);

At Aboukir and Acre: A Story of Napoleon's Invasion of Egypt (New York: Scribners, 1898; London: Blackie, 1899);

On the Spanish Main (London: Chambers, 1899);

The Golden Canon (New York: Mershon, 1899);

A Roving Commission; or, Through the Black Insurrection of Hayti (New York: Scribners, 1899; London: Blackie, 1900);

No Surrender! A Tale of the Rising in La Vendee (New York: Scribners, 1899; London: Blackie, 1900);

Won by the Sword: A Tale of the Thirty Years' War (New York: Scribners, 1899; London: Blackie, 1900);

The Lost Heir (London: Bowden, 1899);

Do Your Duty (London: Bowden, 1900);

Out with Garibaldi: A Story of the Liberation of Italy (New York: Scribners, 1900; London: Blackie, 1901);

In the Irish Brigade: A Tale of War in Flanders and Spain (New York: Scribners, 1900; London: Blackie, 1901);

With Buller in Natal; or, A Born Leader (New York: Scribners, 1900; London: Blackie, 1901);

In the Hands of the Cave-Dwellers (New York: Harper, 1900; London: Blackie, 1903);

At the Point of the Bayonet: A Tale of the Mahratta War (New York: Scribners, 1901; London: Blackie, 1902);

To Herat and Cabul: A Story of the First Afghan War (New York: Scribners, 1901; London: Blackie, 1902);

John Hawke's Fortune: A Story of Monmouth's Rebellion (London: Chapman & Hall, 1901);

Queen Victoria: Scenes from Her Life and Reign (London: Blackie, 1901);

With Roberts to Pretoria: A Tale of the South African War (New York: Scribners, 1901; London: Blackie, 1902);

The Sole Survivors (London & Edinburgh: Chambers, 1901); republished as *Redskins and Colonists* (New York: Stitt, 1905);

With the British Legion: A Story of the Carlist Wars (New York: Scribners, 1902; London: Blackie, 1903);

The Treasure of the Incas: A Tale of Adventure in Peru (New York: Scribners, 1902; London: Blackie, 1903);

With Kitchener in the Soudan: A Story of Atbara and Omdurman (New York: Scribners, 1902; London: Blackie, 1903);

Through Three Campaigns (New York: Scribners, 1903; London: Blackie, 1904);

With the Allies to Pekin: A Tale of the Relief of the Legations (New York: Scribners, 1903; London: Blackie, 1904);

By Conduct and Courage: A Story of Nelson's Days (New York: Scribners, 1904; London: Blackie, 1905);

Gallant Deeds (London & Edinburgh: Chambers, 1905);

In the Hands of the Malays and Other Stories (London: Blackie, 1905);

A Soldier's Daughter and Other Stories (London: Blackie, 1906).

G. A. Henty once described himself as "a fierce and truculent Briton, ready to defy the whole world." It was an exaggerated yet appropriate description, given Henty's character and appearance. He was a tall, powerfully built man, with a large head and a long, flowing, dark beard. He was a noted pugilist and had once disarmed four stiletto-wielding Italian bandits; he was a skilled wrestler who single-handedly disposed of a gang of Irish roughs who had insulted his wife; he was a crack shot, as he demonstrated in a duel with a Spaniard who had cast aspersions on Queen Victoria. He was in many ways a personification of the military power and imperial zeal which characterized late-Victorian/Edwardian Britain. Henty's faith in the British Empire was evident in the dispatches he wrote during his long and distinguished career as a war correspondent for the London *Standard*; his imperial creed was also apparent in the editorials he wrote for the *United Services Gazette* (1884-1885). His imperial ideas and enthusiasms found fullest expression, though, in the eighty-odd adventure tales he wrote for adolescent boys.

George Alfred Henty was born in Trumpington, near Cambridge, but was raised near Canterbury, where his father, a successful stockbroker and coal-mine owner, established a home. In contrast to the singularly robust youths he portrayed in his boys' books, Henty was a sickly child and until the age of fourteen was "practically a confirmed invalid." Thanks to a regimen involving repeated doses of magnesia, salts, and senna, his health improved, and in 1847 he was sent to Westminster School in London. Five years later he went up to Caius College, Cambridge, to read for a degree in Classics. Yet while he excelled in varsity sports, such as cricket, rowing, and boxing, Henty did not enjoy academic life, and in 1853, after only a year's study, he left the university. He returned to London, where he drifted aimlessly through an assortment of odd jobs; he also spent a bleak period working for his father's collieries in South Wales. In 1855, however, his fortunes improved, for in October of that year he was commissioned a lieutenant in the army purveyor's department. He subsequently served with the hospital commissariat at Scutari during the Crimean War and was awarded the Turkish Order of Mejidie. Prior to resigning his commission in February 1858, as a captain Henty was also stationed in Belfast, Portsmouth, and Italy. In 1860 Henty married Elizabeth Finucane, the sister of a fellow army officer. She bore him two daughters, Maud and Ethel, and two sons, Hubert and Charles.

Their marriage was happy, but tragically short, for Mrs. Henty died in 1865, probably of consumption. Henty's daughters also died of consumption in the 1870s. He remarried in 1889, but did not have any children by his second wife (and former house-keeper), Elizabeth Keylock.

While serving in the Crimea, Henty had written a number of letters to his father, describing and criticizing conditions at the front. He was particularly concerned with sanitary conditions, since his brother Frederick had died of cholera at Scutari and he himself was invalided home with enteric fever. Henty's letters, which were published in the *London Morning Advertiser*, initiated his career as a journalist and war correspondent. He wrote for several papers, but from the mid-1860s was most closely connected with the *Standard*, a leading Tory daily.

Henty witnessed almost every major conflict of the period, including the Austro-Italian War and Garibaldi's Tyrolean campaign (1864), Lord Napier's Abyssinian expedition (1867), the Franco-Prussian War (1870), the Second Ashanti War in West Africa (1874), the Turko-Serbian War (1876), and the North West Rebellion in Canada (1885). During these various wars he earned a reputation for physical strength, audacious tenacity, and a disregard for personal safety. While reporting on Napier's Abyssinian campaign, for example, he was involved in fierce hand-to-hand fighting and was instrumental in capturing a battery of the enemy's field guns; during the Austro-Italian War Henty, who had disguised himself as a naval engineer in order to witness an important sea battle, was nearly hanged as a spy. While covering these conflicts and while reporting on other major events such as the opening of the Suez Canal and the Dreyfus trials, Henty also met and became friends with some of the leading men of the day, including George Meredith, Archibald Forbes, George Augustus Sala, H. M. Hyndman, H. M. Stanley, and Viscount Wolseley. Henty's stature as a war correspondent and his reputation as a social and political commentator, however, have been eclipsed by his fame as a writer of popular literature.

Henty wrote for both adult and juvenile audiences. His adult novels—the first being a three-decker (three-volume novel) entitled *A Search for a Secret* (1867)—were not successful, even though they incorporated romance, intrigue, high society, and other elements of the fashionable novels of the day. Nor did he have much success with the two weekly periodicals he owned and managed—the *Union Jack* (1880-1883) and a resurrected version of S. O. Beeton's *Boys' Own Magazine* (1889-1890). But Henty's boys' books and the adventure stories he penned for popular weeklies such as the *Boy's Own Paper*, *Chums*, and *Young England* more than compensated for his disappointments.

Henty's first boys' book, *Out on the Pampas*, was written in 1868 but was not published until 1871. He wrote the book in order to raise money to support his family and to pay the debts he had contracted while trying to develop an unsinkable boat, an advanced spar torpedo, and other unsuccessful "inventions." Henty guessed that W. E. Forster's Elementary Education Act (1870) would prompt a tremendous growth in the field of juvenile literature, as millions of newly educated adolescents began swelling the ranks of the reading public. It was a perceptive guess, and during the decades that followed Henty enjoyed great popularity and prosperity. Under contract to write at least three books per year, Henty was Blackie and Son's most successful author. By the early 1890s his books were selling 150,000 copies annually in Britain and between 25,000 and 50,000 copies in Canada and the United States. His books were also in great demand in elementary schools (where they were used as supplementary readers), in Mechanics' Institute reading rooms, and in public lending libraries. In fact, so popular were the books that some libraries limited borrowers to three "Henty's" per week.

Despite their phenomenal popularity, Henty's historical adventure tales have many weaknesses: the narrative rambles, the dialogue is stilted, and the historical sections are not always accurate. The defects stem mainly from the fact that Henty wrote his books with such haste: about 6,500 words, set down during the course of a five-hour working day, was average for Henty. To speed up production further, he allowed his amanuensis, E. Petit Griffith, to fill in the historical sections in many of the books; Henty merely supplied the settings, characters, and plot. The result was less than perfect, since the factual sections often stood independently from the fiction. "The Boys' Own Historian" was not concerned, however, with meeting high literary standards in his juvenile tales: he was more interested in providing readers with an appreciation of their imperial heritage and, as he put it, with encouraging "manly and straight living and feeling amongst boys."

Henty's books were set in all parts of the world and ranged, chronologically, from ancient times to the present century. But his best-known and most popular works are those which deal with imperial history. Most of these books follow a uniform pattern. Usually, they chronicle the adventures of a well-born orphan, about seventeen years old, who is compelled to leave Britain and seek a competence in the overseas empire. Henty's boys reach their destination just before the start of a war or a native rebellion. At the outbreak of hostilities, the young heroes join an irregular troop of cavalry or carry out undercover operations for the senior British commander—a device (and Henty's trademark) which allowed young readers to meet Clive, Wolfe, Wellington, Roberts, and a host of other Victorian heroes. At the end of these tales, Henty's young men often return to England to marry their childhood sweethearts. With prize money they have won during their colonial adventures, they retire to a country estate. Henty's heroes are abstractions, meant simply to personify contemporary ideals of manliness and muscular Christianity; thus, they are all hearty, honest, resourceful, and athletic. His young heroes are also anti-intellectual, even though most are portrayed as being graduates of prestigious public schools like Eton and Rugby. "What do the natives care for our learning? It is pluck and fighting power that has made us their masters," one of Henty's characters declares in *With Clive in India* (1884). "Give me a lad with pluck and spirit and I don't care a snap of my fingers whether he can construe Euripides or solve a problem in higher mathematics." In this regard Henty's boys closely resemble the hero of Thomas Hughes's *Tom Brown's School Days* (1857). Henty's boys are, however, more conservative, xenophobic, and ethnocentric. While they are not bellicose jingoists, they are nevertheless committed to the idea of Anglo-Saxon superiority and to a faith in Britain's imperial mission.

Henty's juvenile books not only reflected certain ideas and values in Victorian/Edwardian Britain; they also helped to stimulate and reinforce popular opinion. Principally, they fanned patriotic ardor and helped inculcate imperial enthusiasms in millions of impressionable young readers. It is for this reason that Henty has been bracketed with Alfred Austin and Rudyard Kipling as one of the "prime movers of the national spirit." But like Austin and Kipling, Henty has been the subject of considerable debate among critics. He has, on the one hand, been dismissed as a "trash merchant" who purveyed cardboard characters and implausible plots; on the other hand, he has been credited with sensing public moods and interests and with nurturing in later generations a spirit that sustained

Britain through two world wars. Even during his lifetime he was a figure of controversy, so much so that in 1888 the critic Edward Salmon felt obliged to launch a counteroffensive aimed at absolving Henty from the sins of militarism and chauvinism.

Henty's work has also been scrutinized by historians such as A. P. Thornton, Godfrey Davis, and Robert Huttenback. They have found that Henty was not always accurate in conveying historical details, that he oversimplified complex international issues, and that, on occasion, he was guilty of plagiarism. Henty's most recent biographers—William Allan and Guy Arnold—concede that he adopted a rather "slap-dash" approach to his historical fiction. Even so, most students agree that Henty's books help to clarify the age and the society for which they were written. Straightforward, unabashed, and uncomplicated, his boys' books illuminate—with a bright, naked light—the kind of world in which so many English-speaking youths were encouraged to believe.

Although imperial enthusiasms have virtually disappeared, G. A. Henty remains an important figure in nineteenth-century literature. He played a major role in the development of the popular press and in refining the genre of romantic, historical fiction. He was never condescending, and his books, for all their faults, were always entertaining and topical. Unlike his first biographer, George Manville Fenn, and his principal rivals—R. M. Ballantyne, W. H. G. Kingston, and Dr. Gordon Stables—he was never saccharine, never unduly sentimental, never blatantly didactic or moralistic. Moreover, unlike Robert Leighton and some of the other popular writers of the day, Henty was not an armchair adventurer. Rugged, innovative, well-traveled, and well-informed, he was much like the paternal characters who befriend and tutor the young heroes in his books.

Henty's principal means of relaxation was sailing, an appropriate diversion for someone who had spent so much time following army campaigns. He owned a number of boats during his life, the last being his beloved "Egret," a twenty-ton ketch. He was aboard his yacht in Weymouth Harbor when he died on 16 November 1902. Obituaries appeared immediately in the *Times*, the *Athenaeum*, and a host of other magazines and newspapers in Britain. All paid tribute to his reputation as a journalist, although most predicted—correctly—that he would be remembered principally as a writer for boys. Approximately a dozen of his boys' books are still in print, while earlier editions of his books are sought eagerly by collectors throughout the world. Regrettably, Henty's role as a war correspondent and "friend of the famous" has received little attention; however, he is still very much a figure of interest and controversy among biographers, historians, and literary critics.

Bibliography:

Robert L. Dartt, *G. A. Henty: A Bibliography* (Cedar Grove, N.J.: Dar-Web, 1971; Altrincham, U.K.: Sheratt, 1971).

Biographies:

George Manville Fenn, *George Alfred Henty: The Story of an Active Life* (London: Blackie, 1907);

Guy Arnold, *Held Fast for England: G. A. Henty, Imperialist Boys' Writer* (London: Hamish Hamilton, 1980).

References:

William Allan, "G. A. Henty," *Cornhill*, no. 1082 (Winter 1974-1975): 71-100;

Godfrey Davis, "G. A. Henty and History," *Huntington Library Quarterly*, 17 (May 1955): 159-167;

Patrick A. Dunae, "Boys' Literature and the Idea of Empire, 1870-1914," *Victorian Studies*, 24 (Autumn 1980): 105-121;

Robert A. Huttenback, "G. A. Henty and the Vision of Empire," *Encounter*, 35 (July 1970): 46-53;

Edward Salmon, *Juvenile Literature As It Is* (London: H. J. Drane, 1888);

John Cargill Thompson, *The Boys' Dumas. G. A. Henty: Aspects of Victorian Publishing* (Cheadle Hulme, U.K.: Carcanet Press, 1975);

A. P. Thornton, "G. A. Henty's British Empire," *Fortnightly Review*, 175 (February 1954): 97-101.

Thomas Hughes

(20 October 1822-22 March 1896)

George J. Worth
University of Kansas

SELECTED BOOKS: *Tom Brown's School Days*, anonymous (Cambridge: Macmillan, 1857); republished as *Schooldays at Rugby* (Boston: Ticknor & Fields, 1857);

The Scouring of the White Horse; or, the Long Vacation Ramble of a London Clerk (Cambridge: Macmillan, 1858; Boston: Ticknor & Fields, 1859);

Tom Brown at Oxford (17 monthly parts, Boston: Ticknor & Fields, 1859-1861); republished as *Tom Brown at Oxford, by the Author of "Tom Brown's School Days"* (3 volumes, London: Macmillan, 1861);

Tracts for Priests and People, No. 1: Religio Laici (Cambridge: Macmillan, 1861);

The Cause of Freedom: Which is Its Champion in America, The North or the South? (London: The Emancipation Society, 1863);

Alfred the Great (3 parts, London: Macmillan, 1869; 1 volume, Boston: Osgood, 1871);

Memoir of a Brother (London: Macmillan, 1873; Boston: Osgood, 1873);

The Old Church: What Shall We Do with It? (London: Macmillan, 1878);

The Manliness of Christ (London: Macmillan, 1879; Boston: Osgood, 1880);

Rugby, Tennessee: Being Some Account of the Settlement Founded on the Cumberland Plateau by the Board of Aid to Land Ownership (London & New York: Macmillan, 1881);

Memoir of Daniel Macmillan (London: Macmillan, 1882);

James Fraser, Second Bishop of Manchester: A Memoir, 1818-85 (London: Macmillan, 1887);

David Livingstone (London: Macmillan, 1889);

Vacation Rambles (London: Macmillan, 1895).

In *Tom Brown's School Days* (1857), Thomas Hughes celebrated one school and founded another. This extremely popular novel brought to the attention of a large audience the great work Thomas Arnold had achieved in reforming Rugby and, more generally, the education of the future leaders of the English nation and the British Empire. It also created a significant new subgenre of English fiction: as John R. Reed has written in his definitive *Old School Ties: The Public Schools in British Literature* (1964), *Tom Brown's School Days* "established permanently the traditional characters, topics, and situations of the public school novel," which has survived for a century and a quarter, even while undergoing some profound changes. Curiously, however, Hughes's first novel, which was at least as important in forming public attitudes as it was in shaping a particular fictional form, was not the work of a professional storyteller. Not quite thirty-five years old when *Tom Brown's School Days* was published anonymously, Hughes brought out two more novels in rather rapid order, *The Scouring of the White Horse* (1859) and *Tom Brown at Oxford* (1859-1861), and then went on to devote the remaining three and a half decades of his busy life to other pursuits.

Like his Tom Brown, Hughes was born in the Berkshire Downs, some sixty miles west of London. His father, John Hughes, had attended Westminster school and Oriel College, Oxford, but returned to live near his parents at Uffington, where he married Margaret Wilkinson. They had eight children, Thomas being the second son. George, thirteen months older than Thomas, was a formative and lasting influence on his brother. After George's

Thomas Hughes

death in 1872, Thomas Hughes published a tribute to him in *Memoir of a Brother* (1873). The two brothers attended a private school at Twyford, near Winchester, from 1830 to 1834; in 1834, when Thomas was eleven, they were sent to Rugby, an old public school then taking on new life under the energetic and imaginative leadership of Dr. Arnold. Preferring physical to intellectual or spiritual exertions, Hughes never belonged to the inner circle of that memorable headmaster's most fervent young disciples. Nonetheless, he was profoundly and permanently influenced by Arnold's ideas, especially by his firm commitment to upright thought and virtuous action permeated by Christian principles, and by his belief that his privileged young charges must make themselves responsible for bringing together the people of the nation—rich and poor, educated and unschooled, powerful and powerless—when they assumed the positions of authority for which Rugby was preparing them.

In 1842, Thomas Hughes joined his brother George at Oriel College, Oxford, where they lived off the same staircase. Dr. Arnold's precepts must have been very much in Hughes's mind when—having taken his degree in 1845 and been admitted to the bar in January 1848—he joined such men as Frederick Denison Maurice, Charles Kingsley, and John Malcolm Ludlow in founding the Christian Socialist movement in 1848. Amid the revolutions and rumors of revolutions that were convulsing Europe in that fateful year, it was their conviction that the best hope for the English worker lay not in confrontation and competition but in cooperation: cooperation among the classes, but also cooperation among the workers themselves, in the spirit of Christ. Christian Socialism ceased for all practical purposes to exist as a coherent force after half a dozen years, though the term has been revived from time to time; but Hughes continued to dedicate himself to its ideals: as a lawyer and (after 1882) as a county-court judge; as an advocate for the emerging cooperative and trade-union movements; as an organizer of the London Working Men's College and its principal from 1872 to 1883; as a member of Parliament from 1865 to 1874; as a polemicist for the increasingly beleaguered Church of England; and as the tireless author of a succession of pamphlets and articles about the organization of labor, of religious tracts, of biographical studies, and of autobiographical reminiscences.

A significant event of the year 1847 for Hughes was his marriage to Frances Ford, the daughter of a clergyman and the niece of Richard

Ford, the author of the then-famous *Handbook for Travellers in Spain* (1845). The couple moved into a house on Upper Berkeley Street in London, where George Hughes lived with them briefly. In 1853, Thomas Hughes and J. M. Ludlow built a house in Wimbledon, where Ludlow and the Hughes family lived in what Ludlow called a "communistic experiment" until 1857. Thomas and Frances Hughes ultimately had nine children; two died in childhood.

Hughes turned to novel writing more or less by accident. In the summer of 1856, he gave much thought to the future of his eight-year-old son, who was about to go off to school for the first time. What could he do to prepare the boy for the challenges and opportunities he would encounter in this new setting? As he pondered the question, he recalled later, "I took to writing a story, as the easiest way of bringing out what I wanted." When Ludlow saw the completed manuscript, he urged Hughes to publish this "story," and Hughes sent it to Alexander Macmillan, like Ludlow a fellow Christian Socialist, who was equally impressed with its virtues. *Tom Brown's School Days* was brought out by Macmillan's firm in April 1857 and scored an instant success, running through six English and two American editions in less than a year. By 1890, nearly fifty editions or reprints had appeared in England alone. At a time when education—and, in England, public-school education in particular—was a subject of intense interest, Hughes dealt with it in a highly attractive way and in a form, the novel, that was bound to appeal to a wide readership. As Mack and Armytage have written in their biography of Hughes, *Tom Brown's School Days* "was literally the first work of fiction to present a real world of boys in the setting of a real English public school." As Hughes depicts Rugby in the novel, it is more than an educational institution: Rugby is a community, a civilizing force, a microcosm anticipating the real world the schoolboys will encounter as men. Tom Brown, a youngster who has been used to the freedom of rural life, is subjected at this famous school to the discipline of a venerable establishment rich in tradition. He has to be tamed; or, rather, he must learn to curb his exuberant animal spirits in the service of causes larger and more significant than his own pleasure: his team, his house, his school, and the Christian church.

During his first year, Tom falls in with a set of troublemakers and gets into numerous scrapes: staying out after hours, defying a ban against going into town at fair time, poaching, defacing the great clock on the school tower. As a result of such misad-

ventures, he incurs the wrath of Dr. Arnold and the masters and comes very close to expulsion. For the headmaster, the issue is clear: a good Rugbeian must learn to restrain his boyish impulses and conform to the rules, which, he explains, are not "made capriciously" but rather "for the good of the whole School, and must and shall be obeyed." Team sports at Rugby serve the same purpose of teaching boys to subordinate themselves to an entire community: a game like cricket "merges the individual into the eleven; he doesn't play that he may win, but that his side may." Arnold, a great believer in the monitorial system, brings out Tom's latent virtues, not by subjecting him to corporal punishment but rather by making him responsible for a frail new boy, the spiritually inclined George Arthur, and the rest of Tom's school career becomes everything the doctor could have hoped for. By the time Tom leaves Rugby at the age of nineteen, he occupies honored positions as prepostor and captain of the cricket team.

The Scouring of the White Horse, a little book that Hughes published for the Christmas trade in 1858 (although the date on the title page is given as 1859), seems to have little connection with the Tom Brown novels that preceded and followed it. A London clerk by the name of Richard spends a September holiday in the Berkshire countryside where Hughes had grown up and that he always remembered with great affection, observing an ancient local ritual, learning all he can about the history and folklore dealing with that event, and, incidentally, falling in love. But Hughes's preface makes it clear that he intended *The Scouring of the White Horse* to be more than an idyll, just as he intended his other two novels to be more than juvenile fiction. "We are sure," he wrote, "that reverence for all great Englishmen, and a loving remembrance of the good deeds done by them in old times, will help to bring to life in us the feeling that we are a family, bound together to work out God's purposes in this little island, and in the uttermost parts of the earth. . . ."

Tom Brown at Oxford carries Tom's fortunes through his university days. Tom finds himself attracted to all the pleasures available to a well-to-do undergraduate at St. Ambrose's College, especially carousing, mischief-making, and participating in sports. But he also discovers, largely through his friendship with the poor servitor Hardy, that there are important causes in urgent need of attention at his university and in the society at large and that there are higher purposes than mere mindless diversion to be served by physical activity. *Tom Brown*

THE

SCOURING OF THE WHITE HORSE;

OR, THE

LONG VACATION RAMBLE OF A LONDON CLERK.

BY

THE AUTHOR OF "TOM BROWN'S SCHOOL DAYS."

ILLUSTRATED BY RICHARD DOYLE.

BOSTON:
TICKNOR AND FIELDS.
M DCCC LIX.

Frontispiece and title page of first U.S. edition of Hughes's second novel

at Oxford contains a fine exposition of "muscular Christianity," the mid-nineteenth-century doctrine often associated with Hughes that praises the use of bodily strength for "the protection of the weak, the advancement of all righteous causes, and the subduing of the earth which God has given to the children of men." Tom's views undergo a somewhat confused evolution while he is an undergraduate. He has little sympathy for the Oxford Movement, led by John Henry Newman, whose growing defiance of the Church of England is the talk of the town. Aware that what Thomas Carlyle called the "condition-of-England" problem is reaching a critical phase at a time of widespread unemployment and starvation, he is deeply moved by that Scottish sage's newly published *Past and Present* (1843). For a

time he even becomes a revolutionary, bearing the nickname "Chartist Brown," but he subsides in the face of opposition from family and friends. Despite structural weaknesses, *Tom Brown at Oxford* at its frequent best conveys a vivid sense of what life at the university must have been like in the early 1840s for a vigorous, stouthearted, sensitive, and certainly not remarkably intellectual young man—a young man, one can be fairly sure, very much like the Thomas Hughes who had been an undergraduate at Oriel College at this same period.

Hughes's lifelong interest in the United States grew from the same essentially religious roots as his endeavors on behalf of social justice and social harmony in England. He abhorred slavery as a sinful institution and, partly under the influence of James

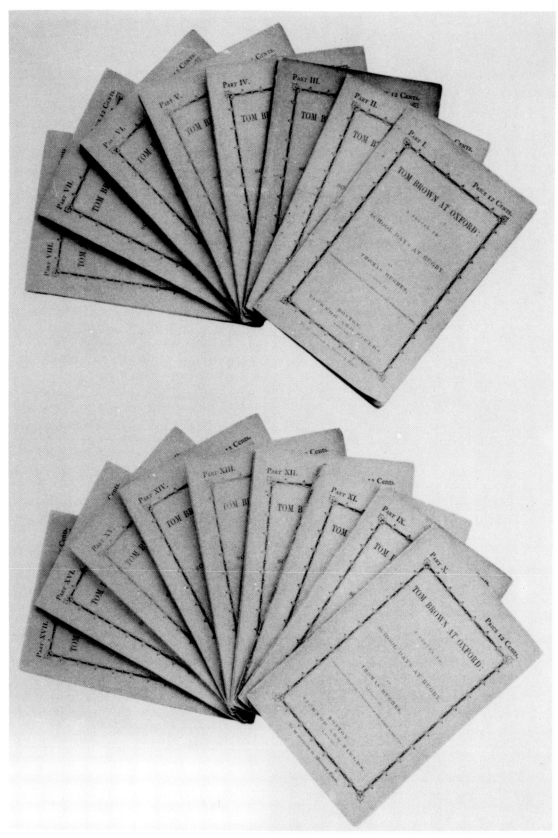

First publication, in parts, of Hughes's second Tom Brown novel

Russell Lowell's poetry, aligned himself with the American abolitionists in the 1850s. During the Civil War, he spoke out forthrightly for the Northern cause, while most of those who shaped public opinion in his country were siding with the Confederacy or maintaining a strict neutrality in their public utterances. After the cessation of hostilities, he worked tirelessly for close and cordial relations between England and the United States. Lowell invited Hughes to visit him in 1870, and this first American trip turned into a triumphal tour that took Hughes as far west as Omaha. A decade later, he was the prime mover in establishing a Christian and cooperative settlement, which he named Rugby, on the Cumberland plateau of northeastern Tennessee. Gradually disease, unproductive land, and poor management led to its collapse.

After his appointment as county-court judge in July 1882, Hughes moved to Chester, where he spent the rest of his life. He died in Brighton on 22 March 1896.

The idea that human existence has a divinely ordained purpose to be vigorously pursued suffuses not only Hughes's three novels but all of his writings and indeed his entire career of service to mankind. Though he was sometimes inconsistent in his thought and often unsuccessful in his action, Hughes remains an engaging figure, embodying much of the best in the social activism and spiritual

questing of the Victorian era. Regarded as a minor classic for generations, *Tom Brown's School Days* has never gone out of print; however, for the past decade or two, little of substance has been written about it, and the rest of Hughes's output has received even less attention. Modern critics tend to find his preaching offensive and his idealism quixotic, but it should be recalled that in his own lifetime Hughes was able to command a large and by no means unsophisticated following. That fact alone should earn his work at least a modest revival of interest.

Biography:
Edward C. Mack and W. H. G. Armytage, *Thomas Hughes* (London: Benn, 1952).

References:
Asa Briggs, *Victorian People* (Chicago: University of Chicago Press, 1955), pp. 140-167;
Bruce Haley, *The Healthy Body and Victorian Culture* (Cambridge, Mass.: Harvard University Press, 1978), pp. 141-155;
Mortimer Proctor, *The English University Novel* (Berkeley & Los Angeles: University of California Press, 1957), pp. 105-113;
John R. Reed, *Old School Ties: The Public Schools in British Literature* (Syracuse, N.Y.: Syracuse University Press, 1964), pp. 17-27.

Eliza Lynn Linton
(10 February 1822-14 July 1898)

Dorothea M. Thompson
Carnegie-Mellon University

SELECTED BOOKS: *Azeth the Egyptian* (3 volumes, London: Newby, 1847);
Amymone: A Romance of the Days of Pericles (3 volumes, London: Bentley, 1848);
Realities: A Tale (3 volumes, London: Saunders & Otley, 1851);
Witch Stories (London: Chapman & Hall, 1861);
The Lake Country, Illustrated by W. J. Linton (London: Smith, Elder, 1864);
Grasp Your Nettle: A Novel (3 volumes, London: Smith, Elder, 1865);
Lizzie Lorton of Greygrigg: A Novel (3 volumes, London: Tinsley, 1866; 1 volume, New York: Harper, 1866);
Sowing the Wind (3 volumes, London: Tinsley, 1867; 1 volume, New York: Harper, 1890);
The Girl of the Period and the Fashionable Woman of the Period, anonymous (New York: Redfield, 1869);
Ourselves: A Series of Essays on Women (London & New York: Routledge, 1869);
The True History of Joshua Davidson, Christian and Communist, anonymous (London: Strahan, 1872; Philadelphia: Lippincott, 1873);

Eliza Lynn Linton

Patricia Kemball: A Novel (3 volumes, London: Chatto & Windus, 1874; 1 volume, Philadelphia: Lippincott, 1875);

The Mad Willoughbys and Other Tales (London: Ward, Lock & Tyler, 1875);

The Atonement of Leam Dundas: A Novel (3 volumes, London: Chatto & Windus, 1876; 1 volume, Philadelphia: Lippincott, 1876);

The World Well Lost (2 volumes, London: Chatto & Windus, 1877; New York: Munro, 1877);

At Night in a Hospital (London: Fisher, 1879);

Under Which Lord? A Novel (3 volumes, London: Chatto & Windus, 1879; 1 volume, New York: Munro, 1890);

The Rebel of the Family (3 volumes, London: Chatto & Windus, 1880; 1 volume, New York: Harper, 1880);

With a Silken Thread and Other Stories (3 volumes, London: Chatto & Windus, 1880);

My Love: A Novel (3 volumes, London: Chatto & Windus, 1881; 1 volume, New York: Harper, 1881);

The Girl of the Period and Other Essays from the "Satur-

day Review" (2 volumes, London: Chatto & Windus, 1883);

The Autobiography of Christopher Kirkland (3 volumes, London: Bentley, 1885);

Stabbed in the Dark: A Tale (London: White, 1885; New York: Munro, 1886);

The Rift in the Lute: A Tale (London: Simpkin, Marshall, 1885);

Paston Carew, Millionaire and Miser: A Novel (3 volumes, London: Bentley, 1886; 1 volume, New York: Harper, 1886);

Through the Long Night (3 volumes, London: Hurst, 1888-1889; 1 volume, New York: Harper, 1888);

About Ireland (London: Methuen, 1890);

An Octave of Friends; with other Silhouettes and Stories (London: Ward & Downey, 1891);

About Ulster (London: Methuen, 1892);

The One Too Many (3 volumes, London: Chatto & Windus, 1894; 1 volume, New York: Neely, 1894);

In Haste and at Leisure (3 volumes, London: Heinemann, 1895);

Dulcie Everton (2 volumes, London: Chatto & Windus, 1896);

Twixt Cup and Lip (London: Digby & Long, 1896);

My Literary Life; with a Prefatory Note by Beatrice Harraden (London: Hodder & Stoughton, 1899);

The Second Youth of Theodora Desanges, with an Introduction by G. S. Layard (London: Hutchinson, 1900).

Eliza Lynn Linton, novelist and journalist, continues in importance today because of her role as one of the first women to earn a living as a journalist. Between 1860 and 1867, she wrote more than 200 articles for such journals as *All the Year Round*, the *Cornhill*, *Temple Bar*, *London*, the *Saturday Review*, and the *Athenaeum*. Her subjects—the social and political ramifications of the woman question, literary criticism, and contemporary social customs—provide the modern social historian with information about a conservative yet independent woman's views on such diverse issues as the emancipation of women and social Darwinism.

Eliza Lynn, the youngest of twelve children, was born at Keswick on 10 February 1822. After their mother died when Eliza was an infant, the older children shared in the nurture of the younger ones. Deprivation of love and benign neglect in her early years influenced Linton for the rest of her life. In her autobiography, *My Literary Life* (1899), she states that the dominant circumstances of her life were loneliness and loss; she blames her clergyman father, well-educated himself and holding two Church of England livings, for ignoring his children's education because he was extremely lazy. Thus largely self-taught, Linton read extensively in her father's library and mastered the rudiments of several languages well enough to read them. But it was her reading of many mythologies that set her on a path that made her different from her peers.

A religious struggle, not uncommon to young people at that time, lasted many years and was an outstanding feature of her written work all her life and eventually coalesced into a form of deism or humanitarianism. Her writings for most of her life bear witness to her attempt to reconcile her early religious upbringing with the intellectual and scientific theories of the century. As she tells it in her autobiography, a flash of insight one day showed her the analogies between several well-known myths and the stories in the Bible and revealed to her the need, common to all peoples, for a supernatural belief. She describes this important episode: "I was digging away at the myths of Nisus and Scylla, and the purple lock wherein the old king's strength lay, when for the first time, I was struck by the likeness of this story to that of Samson and Delilah." Her first published work, in *Ainsworth's Magazine* in 1845, demonstrated to her family that she intended to be a writer. For this work, a poem entitled "The National Convention of the Gods," she was paid the munificent sum of two guineas. Having won permission and a year's allowance from her skeptical father, and chaperoned by the family solicitor, she arrived in London in 1845. She found a job on the *Morning Chronicle* to help support herself while researching and writing her first two novels.

Azeth the Egyptian (1847) was a product of her research in the British Museum in the field of Egyptology. She had to pay £50 to have the novel published but was richly rewarded by the favorable review in the *Times*. For *Amymone* (1848), a novel situated in the age of Pericles, she received the sum of £100. This novel's publication was even more important than her first because it called her to the attention of the poet Walter Savage Landor, who wrote a very favorable review in the *Examiner*.

During her six years in London, Lynn was an active member of a small social group of which the literary Thornton Hunts and the George Leweses were a part. Although she met and dined with Charles Dickens early in her career, their paths did not cross again until she, as her father's executrix, sold to Dickens in 1855 Gad's Hill, one of her

father's properties. In these first years in London she also became the staunch friend of Landor, calling him "Father" while he called her "Daughter." She revered his work and considered him a great intellect; he was her personal hero. In her visits to Landor at Bath, she often met John Forster, Landor's literary executor, at social events. Forster resented Lynn, and in his subsequent biography of Landor, he left out any mention of her in the circle of Landor's friends. In *My Literary Life*, Linton wrote that Forster denied her a place in the Landor biography, but that she had the satisfaction of reviewing Forster's book, and "I took the skin off him."

A serious quarrel in 1851 with John Douglas Cook, editor of the *Morning Chronicle*, precipitated Lynn's move to Paris, where she was a correspondent for several years. In 1858, a few years after her return to England, Eliza Lynn married William James Linton, engraver, author, and widower with seven children. The marriage lasted only nine years. After living together in London for seven years, the couple separated, with William Linton retiring to his house, "Brantwood," in Coniston in the Lake District. His wife spent summers with him and his children until 1867, when William went to Connecticut in the United States for what was at first only a visit. He never returned to England to live, and Brantwood was eventually sold to John Ruskin. Eliza Linton's autobiography states that the marriage foundered on money problems which served to exacerbate the couple's innate incompatibility. William Linton was unworldly, always initiating new altruistic, impractical endeavors, while Eliza Linton, infinitely practical and hardworking, was forced to work doubly hard to earn money for the ménage. Although obliged to live apart, the Lintons remained good friends for the rest of their lives and corresponded regularly until William's death a few months before her own.

Eliza Linton launched into her literary career when she returned to London from Brantwood in 1867, after the breakup of her marriage. Layard, her biographer, states that "she was as yet little more to the public than one of the great nameless band of literary hacks." She began writing for the *Saturday Review* in 1868 a series of articles on women which caused a literary furor. The titles of the thirty-seven essays give a fair indication of the stereotypic portraits: "Foolish Virgins," "Husband-Hunting," "Plain Girls," and "What is Woman's Work?" Many of the essays exhibit a confused line of reasoning between the need to develop better use of women's talents through better training and education and society's need to keep women dependent on men, ostensibly for their own moral good. She once said that "a public and professional life for women is incompatible with the discharge of their highest duties or the cultivation of their noblest qualities." The other side of the dichotomy is particularly noticeable in "The Goose and the Gander," which illustrates Linton's belief that society pays a price for keeping its women subjugated to the rule of men in the form of the large number of women condemned to poverty because they do not marry. She wrote, "It remains to be proved that it is wise to teach and train the sex to fix all their views in life . . . on the chance of the one rare thing—a lucky mat-

rimonial choice." The unsigned articles, collectively known as "The Girl of the Period" (the title of one of them), were not claimed by Linton for sixteen years. During that time, controversy over their authorship was extensive; a *Girl of the Period* journal was started; comedies and farces derived ideas from the stereotypical essence of womanhood portrayed by Linton in her essays. The author, widely believed to be a man, was roundly taken to task for the harsh attitude toward the emancipation of women in the essays. Linton, forever unrepentant, later declared, "I neither soften nor retract a line of what I have said."

Eliza Linton was herself an emancipated woman, fiercely independent and proud of it. Her

A caricature of the writer of "The Girl of the Period" articles, as imagined by Matt. Morgan before Linton's authorship became known

workbook indicates that in 1858, the year of her marriage, she wrote ninety-seven journal articles. One may discover the reason for her satirical attacks on women in her later publication, *The Autobiography of Christopher Kirkland* (1885). In this work, she states that her position on women's rights was misunderstood. She says that she always maintained that women should be educated separately but equally as well as men; that women should have the right to hold their own property free of their husbands' or trustees' control; and that women should have equal rights to their children. What she could not condone and therefore satirized was the effort made by strident extremists for women's political rights. Nevertheless, one of Linton's biographers indicates that her stand on the emancipation of women may have gone too far for credibility with her public: Beatrice Harraden says that Linton was always in favor of a liberal education for women, but that she had overstated her case against the "Wild Women" and the "Shrieking Sisterhood." In her later life, more than one person charged Linton with cheap journalism and writing for effect. Another series of essays on a similar theme by Linton, "Ourselves," also were published in the *Saturday Review*; these essays present a much softened approach to the role of women.

However secret was the identity of the author of "The Girl of the Period," Linton's repute as a reviewer and general writer for the *Saturday Review* increased, as did her output in a variety of genres including short stories, literary criticism, and travel books. But it was the publication, at first anonymously, in 1872 of *The True History of Joshua Davidson, Christian and Communist* that made her famous. Within three months, a third edition was printed, and by 1890 the work was in its tenth edition. Later it became a part of William T. Stead's "Penny Series" (Masterpiece Library of Penny Poets, Novels and Prose Classics).

The work is a religious tract thinly disguised as a biography. Linton describes through her protagonist, Joshua, son of David, the progress of her own religious thoughts. Joshua, the carpenter, befriends two sinners—Mary, a girl of the streets, and Joe, a drunkard—and reforms them. Progressing through stages of religiosity from blind acceptance of Scripture (by literally trying to fly), through involvement in established church ritual, to political activism, Joshua is ultimately kicked to death by a maddened "Christian" crowd at a political meeting. This trenchant satire was a strong attack for the times on the inability of organized religion to live up

to its tenets. Linton appeals at the end of the book for enlightenment on the question that she feels her age must answer: "I cannot, being a Christian, . . . reconcile modern science with Christ. . . . Which is true—modern society . . . or the brotherhood and communism taught by the Jewish carpenter of Nazareth?"

From 1875 to 1879, when Linton spent most of her time on the Continent, she published her better novels, many of which appeared serially in periodicals such as *Temple Bar* and the *Cornhill*. Among these works were *Patricia Kemball* (1874), *The Atonement of Leam Dundas* (1876), and *Under Which Lord?* (1879). *The Atonement of Leam Dundas* was considered by Linton to be her best novel to date. Victorian readers did not take kindly to the Spanish heroine, who had clearly transgressed all moral law when she poisoned her stepmother. Her suicide after her rejection by her suitor satisfied the Victorian audience's need for statements of conventional outward morality. However, Linton's obvious preference for her heroine, drawn with much greater skill than she had shown in any of her previous novels, ended in confusing her ordinary reader.

In a later novel for which she received more notoriety, Linton reverted to a complete inability to draw characterizations or to develop a plot successfully. *Under Which Lord?* presents as its hero a saintly agnostic, Fullerton, whose wife and daughter fall under the fatal influence of a High Church clergyman. Exaggerated traits of personality turn all the characters into stereotypes. The novel, like many written at that time, is heavily padded to flesh out the required three volumes of nine hundred pages. For instance, by page twenty-nine, the author has rapidly narrated in a terse, journalistic style all previous actions of the main characters and set them in place. But nothing much happens to move or change the characters and the rest of the book is little more than an overgrown tract. As reviewers pointed out, the moral lesson that she always drew in the development of her plots lowered the dramatic and literary quality of the work.

Linton's finest work, *The Autobiography of Christopher Kirkland*, which she wrote when in her sixties and near the end of her active literary life, constitutes a rich source of information about the women of the time. More than 900 pages long, it would be of greater interest if it were shorter and less repetitive. It was not popular when it appeared and never reached a second edition. The curious feature of this thinly-disguised autobiography is that Linton makes her fictionalized "persona" a man. Christopher Kirkland, a male journalist, interacts with women as a man, but is portrayed as having outstandingly feminine sensibilities. The aura of transvestitism pervades the work, making it both bizarre and incomprehensible. Moreover, the protagonist appears flat and one-dimensional; he is little more than Linton's mouthpiece for long discussions of her religious struggles.

Nevertheless, Eliza Linton used her sharpened journalistic skills in *The Autobiography of Christopher Kirkland* to describe the literary and social circles in which she moved. In addition to describing her friendship with Landor, she delineates in what is nearly a roman à clef, the group of greats and near-greats that revolved around the Thornton Hunts, George Lewes, George Eliot, Douglas Cook, and many others. Book three is the most interesting because of Linton's discussion of the intellectual ferment of her times. After her failed marriage, when she took up again her former trade of journalism, it was to Darwin's theory of the "unity of nature" that she felt she owed her reawakened intellectual life. She says in *The Autobiography of Christopher Kirkland* that the emancipation of human intellect from superstition "was all in the air."

Both a journalist and novelist all her life, Linton continued to write up to her death from pneumonia on 14 July 1898. Many of her novels were successful and went through more than one edition; many others failed due to flimsy, trite plots and flat characterizations that failed to support the excessive padding required by the three-volume format so popular in the Victorian era. But it was in the essays that she wrote for the major journals of her day that Linton made her greatest contribution to literature. Vineta Colby summed up Linton's appeal to her public in her lifetime: "Whatever her limitations as a novelist, she understood the needs of her public. . . . A radical conservative, a militantly feminine antifeminist, a skeptical idealist and a believing atheist, Mrs. Linton consistently mirrored the inconsistencies of her times."

References:

Vineta Colby, *The Singular Anomaly: Women Novelists of the Nineteenth Century* (New York: New York University Press, 1970), pp. 15-43;

Beatrice Harraden, "Mrs. Lynn Linton," *Bookman*, 14 (August 1898): 124-125;

George Somes Layard, *Eliza Lynn Linton: Her Life, Letters and Opinions* (London: Methuen, 1901);

"Mrs. Lynn Linton" (obituary), *Athenaeum*, 112 (23 July 1898): 131-132.

George MacDonald

(10 December 1824-17 September 1905)

Marjory Lang
University of British Columbia

BOOKS: *Within and Without: A Poem* (London: Longman, Brown, Green & Longmans, 1855; New York: Scribner, Armstrong, 1872);

Poems (London: Longman, Brown, Green, Longmans & Roberts, 1857; New York: Dutton, 1887);

Phantastes: A Faerie Romance for Men and Women (London: Smith, Elder, 1858; New York: Munro, 1885);

David Elginbrod (3 volumes, London: Hurst & Blackett, 1863; Boston: Loring, 1872);

Adela Cathcart (3 volumes, London: Hurst & Blackett, 1864; 1 volume, Boston: Loring, 1875);

The Portent: A Story of the Inner Vision of the Highlanders Commonly Called the Second Sight (London: Smith, Elder, 1864; New York: Munro, 1884);

Alec Forbes of Howglen (3 volumes, London: Hurst & Blackett, 1865; 1 volume, New York: Harper, 1867);

Annals of a Quiet Neighbourhood (3 volumes, London: Hurst & Blackett, 1867; 1 volume, New York: Harper, 1867);

Dealings with the Fairies (London: Strahan, 1867; New York: Routledge, 187?);

The Disciple and Other Poems (London: Strahan, 1867);

George MacDonald in 1870, photographed by Lewis Carroll

Unspoken Sermons (3 volumes, London: Strahan, 1867-1869; 1 volume, New York: Routledge, 1871);

Guild Court (3 volumes, London: Hurst & Blackett, 1868; 1 volume, New York: Harper, 1868);

Robert Falconer (3 volumes, London: Hurst & Blackett, 1868; 1 volume, Boston: Loring, 1876);

The Seaboard Parish (3 volumes, London: Tinsley, 1868; 1 volume, New York: Routledge, 1872);

England's Antiphon (London: Macmillan, 1868; Philadelphia: Lippincott, 1869);

The Miracles of Our Lord (London: Strahan, 1870; New York: Routledge, 1871);

At the Back of the North Wind (London: Strahan, 1871; New York: Routledge, 1871);

Ranald Bannerman's Boyhood (London: Strahan, 1871; Philadelphia: Lippincott, 1871);

The Princess and the Goblin (London: Strahan, 1872; Philadelphia: Lippincott, 1872);

The Vicar's Daughter (3 volumes, London: Tinsley, 1872; 1 volume, Boston: Roberts, 1872);

Wilfred Cumbermede (3 volumes, London: Hurst & Blackett, 1872; 1 volume, New York: Scribners, 1872);

Gutta Percha Willie: The Working Genius (London: King, 1873; New York: Dutton, 1875);

Malcolm (3 volumes, London: King, 1875; 1 volume, Philadelphia: Lippincott, 1875);

The Wise Woman: A Parable (London: Strahan, 1875);

Exotics: A Translation of the Spiritual Songs of Novalis, the Hymn Book of Luther, and Other Poems from the German and Italian (London: Strahan, 1876);

Thomas Wingfold, Curate (3 volumes, London: Hurst & Blackett, 1876; 1 volume, New York: Routledge, 1876);

St. George and St. Michael (3 volumes, London: King, 1876; 1 volume, New York: Munro, 1880);

The Marquis of Lossie (3 volumes, London: Hurst & Blackett, 1877; 1 volume, Philadelphia: Lippincott, 1877);

Sir Gibbie (3 volumes, London: Hurst & Blackett, 1879; 1 volume, New York: Munro, 1879);

Paul Faber, Surgeon (3 volumes, London: Hurst & Blackett, 1879; 1 volume, New York: Munro, 1879);

Mary Marston (3 volumes, London: Low, Marston, Searle & Rivington, 1881; 1 volume, New York: Appleton, 1881);

A Book of Strife, in the Form of the Diary of an Old Soul (London: Hughes, 1882; London & New York: Longmans, Green, 1898);

Castle Warlock: A Homely Romance (3 volumes, London: Low, Marston, Searle & Rivington, 1882; New York: Munro, 1882);

Orts (London: Low, Marston, Searle & Rivington, 1882); enlarged as *A Dish of Orts* (London: Low, Marston, 1893);

Weighed and Wanting (3 volumes, London: Low, Marston, Searle & Rivington, 1882; 1 volume, New York: Harper, 1882);

The Gifts of the Child Christ and Other Tales (2 volumes, London: Low, Marston, Searle & Rivington, 1882; 1 volume, New York: Munro, 1883);

Donal Grant (3 volumes, London: Kegan Paul, Trench, 1883; 1 volume, Boston: Lothrop, 1883);

The Princess and Curdie (London: Chatto & Windus, 1883; New York: Munro, 1883);

The Tragedie of Hamlet, with a Study of the Text of the Folio of 1623 (London: Allen & Unwin, 1885);

What's Mine's Mine (3 volumes, London: Kegan
Paul, Trench, 1886; 1 volume, New York:
Harper, 1886);

Home Again: A Tale (London: Kegan Paul, Trench,
1887; New York: Appleton, 1888);

The Elect Lady (London: Kegan Paul, Trench, 1888;
New York: Appleton, 1888);

Cross Purposes, and The Shadows: Two Fairy Stories
(London: Blackie, 1890);

A Rough Shaking: A Tale (London: Routledge, 1890;
New York: Burt, 1890);

The Light Princess and Other Fairy Stories (London:
Blackie, 1890; New York: Macmillan, 1926);

*A Cabinet of Gems, Cut and Polished by Sir Philip Sid-
ney, Now for the More Radiance Presented without
their Setting by George MacDonald* (London:
E. Stock, 1891);

There and Back (3 volumes, London: Kegan Paul,
Trench, Trübner, 1891; 1 volume, Boston:
Lothrop, 1891);

The Flight of the Shadow (London: Kegan Paul,
Trench, Trübner, 1891; New York: Appleton: 1891);

The Hope of the Gospel (London: Ward, Lock, 1892;
New York: Appleton, 1892);

Heather and Snow (2 volumes, London: Chatto &
Windus, 1893; 1 volume, New York: Harper,
1893);

The Poetical Works of George MacDonald (2 volumes,
London: Chatto & Windus, 1893);

Lilith: A Romance (London: Chatto & Windus, 1895;
New York: Dodd, Mead, 1895);

*Rampolli: Growths from a Long-Planted Root, Being
Translations Chiefly from the German, along with A
Year's Diary of an Old Soul* (London & New
York: Longmans, Green, 1897);

Salted with Fire: A Tale (London: Hurst & Blackett,
1897; New York: Dodd, Mead, 1897).

COLLECTION: *George MacDonald: An Anthology*,
edited by C. S. Lewis (London: Bles, 1946).

Although George MacDonald began his literary career as a poet and considered poetry to be the
highest literary calling, he made his mark in Victorian literature as a novelist and fantasist. In his own
day his realistic novels were popular and controversial critiques of materialistic society and Calvinist
theology. But MacDonald's enduring reputation
rests on the fairy tales which evince his poetic aspirations, his romantic imagination, and his religious
mysticism. In tribute to his acknowledged master,
C. S. Lewis observed of MacDonald: "What he does

best is fantasy—fantasy that hovers between the allegorical and the mythopoeic. And this in my opinion he does better than any man."

MacDonald's best work recalled the personal
and cultural experiences of his childhood and
youth. Though his father, a tenant farmer, was a
fair and generous man, he was also strict and un-
demonstrative. He was no substitute for the loving
mother who died when George was still a child. In
the highly charged and symbolic father-son relationships of his novels and the maternal divinities
of his fairy tales, MacDonald worked out his complex feelings of mixed gratitude and resentment
toward his father and his yearning for his mother.
The impressions of a boy growing up in a small
Scottish village formed the background of his most
successful novels, where his ability to recreate the
character, landscape, and folklore of his native land
made a unique contribution to Scottish literature.

At fifteen, MacDonald left his native Huntly in
West Aberdeenshire to attend King's College,
Aberdeen. Though he excelled in chemistry and
natural philosophy, it was the literature of German
romanticism that made the most abiding impression
upon him. The short, tragic life of Novalis had a
morbid fascination for the similarly delicate young
MacDonald. In 1845 MacDonald received a master's degree and became a private tutor in London,
where he met his future wife, Louisa Powell, his
cousin's sister-in-law. He enrolled in the Independent theological college at Highbury in 1848, but
before he completed his training, he was ordained
at Trinity Congregational Church, Arundel. On the
strength of this appointment, he married in 1851.
Soon, however, the unorthodox theology of this
youthful mystic alarmed the prosaic congregation.
His sermons, bereft of doctrine and promising salvation to heathens and even animals, plus his privately published translation of twelve of Novalis's
Spiritual Songs, convinced the Arundel congregation that their minister was a heretic tainted with
German philosophy. The antagonism of his flock
prompted MacDonald to resign his post in 1853.

He found no other pulpit, yet he never ceased
to preach. As an itinerant lecturer and man of letters he broadcast his philosophy of divine love and
struggled to support a burgeoning family. Poverty
and ill health plagued the years after Arundel as he
moved first to Manchester and then to Hastings.
Nevertheless, he had already begun to attract the
support of friends and patrons which would become his financial mainstay throughout his career.
A subscription raised on his behalf by his loyal audi-

ence of Mancunian workingmen, plus a contribution from Lady Byron, allowed MacDonald to recuperate in Algiers during the winter of 1856-1857.

It was his verse drama, *Within and Without* (1855), that attracted Lady Byron's attention and also won recognition from Tennyson and Charles Kingsley. But his first prose work, *Phantastes* (1858), a fairy romance for adults, firmly established his literary reputation. The dream world of animated flora and fauna where Anodos, the hero, discovers his true spiritual self betrayed MacDonald's debt to Novalis. To the English audience, however, *Phantastes* seemed perfectly original and its publisher, George Smith, compared it to the classic *Undine* by Fouque (1811), MacDonald's own favorite fairy tale. Smith also convinced MacDonald to seek more concrete rewards writing realistic novels. Henceforth, MacDonald alternated between the mystical romances which satisfied his poetic impulses and the conventional Victorian three-volume novels which found a ready market.

The 1860s and 1870s were the most happy and productive years of MacDonald's life. Moving to London in 1859, he took a prominent place in literary and intellectual circles. His home, The Retreat, later to become William Morris's Kelmscott Manor, welcomed such luminaries as Matthew Arnold, Burne Jones, Browning, Ruskin, and Tennyson. In Frederick Dennison Maurice, MacDonald found a mentor and kindred spirit. Maurice had helped MacDonald find a publisher for *Phantastes*, he secured MacDonald a post as professor of English literature at Bedford College, and he led the renegade Congregationalist into the Church of England. A fictional portrait of Maurice appears in MacDonald's first novel of real life, *David Elginbrod* (1863).

David Elginbrod describes the influence of a humble Scottish saint on the spiritual evolution of an autobiographical hero, Hugh Sutherland. While working as a tutor to a laird's family, Hugh is attracted to the original theological views of David Elginbrod, the estate manager. Though Hugh does not see Elginbrod after the first volume, Elginbrod's impression endures as Hugh, now a tutor in England, struggles with his infatuation for the flirtatious Euphrasia Cameron and with the wicked mesmerist who has entranced her. It is Elginbrod's daughter, Margaret, who steers Euphrasia toward salvation in death, and it is for Margaret that Hugh discovers real love in the end.

In this as in all his novels, MacDonald aimed to broaden religious ideals. Hell, he preached, was but another facet of divine love which cleansed all sinners and prepared them for salvation. Though dogmatic Calvinists opposed him, MacDonald won a wider audience as a novelist than he could ever have gathered as a Nonconformist minister.

Along with *David Elginbrod*, *Alec Forbes of Howglen* (1865), *Robert Falconer* (1868), and *Malcolm* (1875) were his most acclaimed novels, in which his humor and sympathy for Scottish culture transcended the polemical diatribes and melodramatic plots that might otherwise have condemned them to deserved oblivion. *Alec Forbes* follows another autobiographical hero from childhood innocence through forsaken love, a descent into drunkenness and depravity, to eventual conversion and return to his childhood home and love. *Robert Falconer*'s odyssey revolves around Falconer's quest to find and redeem his wayward father. MacDonald's faith in the spiritual purity of children surfaced in *Malcolm*, the story of a saintly fisherboy who altruistically relinquishes his rightful inheritance in favor of his beloved half-sister, the marchioness of Lossie.

Vivid portraits of Highland characters illuminate the narratives of MacDonald's Scottish novels and leaven his sermonizing; the English novels lack this dimension of local color and hence retain little enduring interest. *Wilfred Cumbermede* (1872) is a tale of passionate boyhood friendship which ends in tragic misunderstanding when the boys meet girls. Wilfred's effort to reclaim his ancestral inheritance from a dissolute usurper complicates the already convoluted plot. Following the Victorian fashion for sequels, MacDonald frequently used familiar characters to tie groups of novels together. The Reverend Mr. Walton united as a series *Annals of a Quiet Neighbourhood* (1867), *The Seaboard Parish* (1868), and *The Vicar's Daughter* (1872). The title character in *Thomas Wingfold, Curate* (1876) is a hero when he helps his beloved manage the crisis arising from her Indian half-brother's crime of passion. He reappears in a minor role in *Paul Faber, Surgeon* (1879), as the savior of an atheist doctor driven to despair when his wife reveals the guilty secret of her unchaste past.

The novels, nearly thirty in all, furnished MacDonald with a living and, moreover, a substitute for the pulpit he had resigned. But the mystical and romantic Macdonald poured his soul into his fairy tales, the best of which became classics of children's literature. Contemporaries judged him to be far more original than his friend Lewis Carroll, who only agreed to publish *Alice's Adventures in Wonderland* (1865) after the insistent encouragement of the

MacDonald family. MacDonald's novels and fairy tales for children were the mainstay of the brilliant but short-lived periodical *Good Words for the Young*, which he edited from 1869 to 1872.

Despite his association with children's literature, MacDonald insisted that "I do not write for children, but for the childlike, whether five, or fifty, or seventy-five," and, indeed, his best fairy stories offer far more than nostalgic interest. "The Golden Key," first published in a collection of short romances entitled *Dealings with the Fairies* (1867), was one of MacDonald's most beautiful creations. Two children, Mossy and Tangle, cross an allegorical landscape to reach "the land whence shadows fall," exemplifying MacDonald's conviction, expressed earlier in *Phantastes*, that life is a dream and death a waking into more life.

The same theme runs through *At the Back of the North Wind* (1871). This was MacDonald's only attempt to merge the real and fantasy worlds in one story. His hero, Diamond, the son of a London cabdriver, is a mystically sensitive child in transition between the two worlds. During recurring bouts of illness, Diamond becomes aware of a maternal spirit, North Wind. Traveling in her bosom, Diamond sees how North Wind is always at work in the everyday world, though none but he can detect her presence. Diamond also gains a preview of the heavenly landscape when North Wind takes him to the regions at her back. Unlike other writers of children's fantasy, MacDonald did not try to rationalize Diamond's spiritual visions as dreams or hallucinations. Again, his confidence that "the child is not meant to die but to be forever freshborn" saves Diamond's inevitable death from being lachrymose.

The "Curdie" books—*The Princess and the Goblin* (1872), generally regarded as MacDonald's finest story, and *The Princess and Curdie*, published in book form in 1883 but serialized in 1877—had purely fairy-tale settings, yet they evinced MacDonald's rejection of the hypocritical, materialistic society of his day. In both stories the pure and valiant Curdie, a miner boy, battles the enemies of his beloved Princess Irene and, with the help of Irene's immortal grandmother, another mother-spirit, vanquishes first the Goblins and then the corrupt inhabitants of the kingdom of Gwyntystorm.

In his own life, MacDonald kept faith with the unworldly, antimaterialistic values he propounded in his books. In many ways his poverty was self-inflicted. For instance, in 1873, after a triumphant

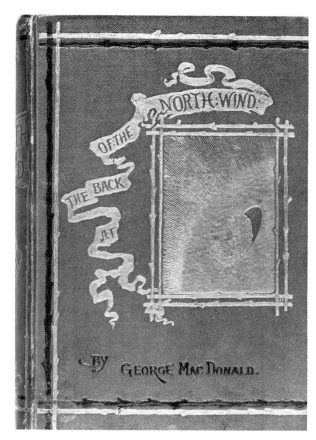

The cover of MacDonald's 1871 novel, in which he combined realism and fantasy

lecture tour of America, where he charmed Emerson, Whittier, and Longfellow, among others, he turned down the entreaties of the congregation of a Fifth Avenue church to become their minister at a salary of $20,000 a year. Like his heroes, MacDonald was holy in his poverty; but his influential admirers supported him and his family of eleven children with gifts, and secured him a civil list pension of £100 a year from Queen Victoria in 1877. Donations from friends also enabled MacDonald to build "Casa Corregio" in Bordighera, Italy, where he wintered from 1877 onward as tuberculosis began to ravage his own and his children's health.

Throughout his tragic last decades, when four of his children succumbed to the family disease, MacDonald continued to lecture and write but produced nothing of lasting significance except *Lilith*, which he labored over from 1890 until its publication in 1895. Like his first important work, *Phantastes*, his last was a fantasy for adults which illustrated his conception of resurrection. Through a mirror the hero, Henry Vane, moves between the seen and unseen worlds with the protean Mr. Raven, his guide to a mystical realm of good and evil spirits, grotesque adults, and heavenly children. W. H. Auden considered *Lilith* to be "equal if not superior to the best of Poe."

Though MacDonald never lost his faith in divine goodness, a darker vision of humankind permeated his later work as depression and despair clouded his old age. After the death of his wife in 1902, he lapsed into total silence and waited for the death into new life which was the reward he promised his heroes. In his last days, MacDonald feared the falling away of his public; and for MacDonald the novelist, those fears were justified. But as a fantasy writer, MacDonald heads a tradition followed by C. S. Lewis, Charles Williams, and J. R. R. Tolkien. G. K. Chesterton, in his obituary notice of MacDonald, summed up his place in Victorian liter-

George MacDonald in old age

Illustration by Arthur Hughes for At the Back of the North Wind, *showing North Wind carrying Diamond away*

ature: "If we test the matter by originality of attitude, George MacDonald was one of the three or four greatest men of the nineteenth century."

References:

Greville MacDonald, *George MacDonald and His Wife* (London: Allen & Unwin, 1924);

Colin N. Manlove, "George MacDonald's Early Scottish Novels," in *Nineteenth-Century Scottish Fiction*, edited by Ian Campbell (New York: Harper, 1979), pp. 68-87;

Manlove, *Modern Fantasy: Five Studies* (Cambridge, London, New York & Melbourne: Cambridge University Press, 1975);

Stephen Prickett, *Romanticism and Religion* (Cambridge, London, New York & Melbourne: Cambridge University Press, 1976);

Prickett, *Victorian Fantasy* (Hassocks, U.K.: Harvester Press, 1979);

Robert Lee Wolff, *The Golden Key* (New Haven: Yale University Press, 1961).

W. H. Mallock

(7 February 1849-2 April 1923)

Barry V. Qualls
Rutgers University

BOOKS: *The Isthmus of Suez* (Oxford: Shrimpton, 1871);

Every Man His Own Poet; or, The Inspired Singer's Recipe Book (Oxford: Shrimpton, 1872; Boston: DeWolfe, Fiske, 1878);

The New Republic; or, Culture, Faith, and Philosophy in an English Country House (2 volumes, London: Chatto & Windus, 1877-1879; 1 volume, New York: Scribner & Welford, 1878);

Lucretius (Philadelphia: Lippincott, 1878; Edinburgh & London: Blackwood, 1898);

The New Paul and Virginia; or, Positivism on an Island (London: Chatto & Windus, 1878-1879; New York: Scribner & Welford, 1878);

Is Life Worth Living? (London: Chatto & Windus, 1879; New York: Putnam's, 1879);

Poems (London: Chatto & Windus, 1880; Rochester, N.Y.: Fitch, 1880);

A Romance of the Nineteenth Century (2 volumes, London: Chatto & Windus, 1881; 1 volume, New York: Putnam's, 1881);

Social Equality: A Short Study in a Missing Science (London: Bentley, 1882; New York: Putnam's, 1882);

Atheism and the Value of Life: Five Studies in Contemporary Literature (London: Bentley, 1884);

Property and Progress; or, A Brief Enquiry into Contemporary Social Agitation in England (London: Murray, 1884; New York: Putnam's, 1884);

The Landlords and the National Income: A Chart Showing the Proportion Borne by the Rental of the Landlords to the Gross Income of the People (London: Allen, 1884);

The Old Order Changes: A Novel (3 volumes, London: Bentley, 1886-1887; 1 volume, New York: Putnam's, 1886);

In an Enchanted Island; or, A Winter Retreat in Cyprus (London: Bentley, 1889);

A Human Document: A Novel (3 volumes, London: Chapman & Hall, 1892; 1 volume, New York: Cassell, 1892);

Labour and the Popular Welfare (London: Black, 1893);

Verses (London: Hutchinson, 1893);

The Heart of Life: A Novel (3 volumes, London: Chapman, 1895; 1 volume, New York: Putnam's, 1895);

Studies of Contemporary Superstition (London: Ward & Downey, 1895);

Classes and Masses; or, Wealth, Wages, and Welfare in the United Kingdom: A Handbook of Social Facts for Political Thinkers and Speakers (London: Black, 1896);

Aristocracy and Evolution: A Study of the Rights, the Origin, and the Social Functions of the Wealthier Classes (London & New York: Macmillan, 1898);

W. H. Mallock

164

The Individualist: A Novel (London: Chapman &
    Hall, 1899);
*Doctrine and Doctrinal Disruption: Being an Examina-
    tion of the Intellectual Position of the Church of
    England* (London: Black, 1900);
Lucretius on Life and Death (London: Black, 1900);
*The Fiscal Dispute Made Easy; or, A Key to the Principles
    Involved in the Opposite Policies* (London: Nash,
    1903);
Religion as a Credible Doctrine (London: Chapman &
    Hall, 1903; New York: Macmillan, 1903);
The Veil of the Temple; or, From Night to Twilight (Lon-
    don: Murray, 1904; New York: Putnam's,
    1904);
The Reconstruction of Belief (London: Chapman &
    Hall, 1905; New York: Harper, 1905);
A Critical Examination of Socialism (New York & Lon-
    don: Harper, 1907);
An Immortal Soul (London: Bell, 1908; New York:
    Harper, 1908);
*The Nation as a Business Firm: An Attempt to Cut a Path
    through Jungle* (London: Black, 1910);
*Social Reform as Related to Realities and Delusions: An
    Examination of the Increase and Distribution of
    Wealth from 1801 to 1910* (London: Murray,
    1914; New York: Dutton, 1915);
The Limits of Pure Democracy (London: Chapman &
    Hall, 1918; New York: Dutton, 1918);
Capital, War, and Wages: Three Questions in Outline
    (London: Blackie, 1918);
Memoirs of Life and Literature (London: Harper,
    1920; New York: Harper, 1920).

W. H. Mallock is the "exemplary" crisis-of-
faith nineteenth-century writer, enacting in the late
Victorian and Edwardian periods the careers of the
sages of the preceding generation. He set as his
task—in essays, treatises, novels, and poetry—the
work of "reducing this chaos of revolutionary
thought to order." But unlike Thomas Carlyle and
John Ruskin and George Eliot, he made no accommodations with the changes science had brought to
man's physical and metaphysical landscapes. His
"order" was absolutely traditional: Mallock spent
his career proclaiming the necessity of orthodox
belief, if human beings were to be more than animals and any civilized life were to be possible. And
he died asking, characteristically, the question that
he had asked throughout his life, "whether the
Church of Rome was not perhaps the one true religion, after all."

Born in 1849 into a Church of England family
(his father was a rector, his maternal grandfather an
archdeacon; his maternal uncles were Richard
Hurrell Froude, the Tractarian, and James A.
Froude, the historian and Carlyle biographer/
disciple), William Hurrell Mallock quite simply
never doubted the faith of his fathers. He went up
to Balliol College, Oxford, in 1869; won the Newdi-
gate Prize in 1871 for a poem on the Suez; and
earned himself the reputation of a dilettante. He
also found himself repulsed by the liberal theology
of Benjamin Jowett and others: "Their denials of
everything which to me had been previously sacred," he wrote in his *Memoirs of Life and Literature*
(1920), "appalled me like the overture to some approaching tragedy. Their confident attempts at
some new scheme of affirmations affected me like a
solemn farce." Out of this repulsion came Mallock's
writing career—inaugurated in 1872 by an anonymously published satire on poetry, *Every Man His
Own Poet; or, The Inspired Singer's Recipe Book*; then
established triumphantly by those satires which
still maintain his reputation, *The New Republic* (1877)
and *The New Paul and Virginia* (1878-1879). The
remainder of his life was, he asserted, uneventful,
"spent in alternations of solitude and society," the
latter—lived mainly at the country houses and London dwellings of the aristocracy—"naturally agreeable," the former necessary for his writing.
Throughout his career he championed traditional
conservative values, even standing for Parliament
from a Scottish constituency in the 1880s (he later
withdrew his candidacy) and writing books such as
Social Equality (1882); *Aristocracy and Evolution*
(1898); *Religion as a Credible Doctrine* (1903); and *A
Critical Examination of Socialism* (1907), a collection
of lectures Mallock had delivered on a speaking
tour of America in 1907. He died in Somerset 2
April 1923, with a Catholic priest in attendance.

*The New Republic; or, Culture, Faith, and
Philosophy in an English Country House* focuses on one
question, "What is the Aim of Life?" Using the
works of Plato, Petronius, and Thomas Peacock as
models for presenting the clash of ideas, Mallock
offers the "answers" available to his contemporaries
from their chief sages, facsimiles of whom he as-
sembles at an English country house for a weekend
of civilized "talk." Heard, among others, are
Thomas Henry Huxley (presented as Mr. Storks,
"great on the physical basis of life and the imaginative basis of God"), Bishop Jowett (Dr. Jenkinson,
"the great Broach-church divine who thinks that
Christianity is not dead, but changed by himself and
his followers in the twinkling of an eye"), W. K.
Clifford (Mr. Saunders, the champion of a "Science

[which] will drain the marshy grounds of the human mind, so that the deadly malaria of Christianity, which has already destroyed two civilisations, shall never be fatal to a third"), Matthew Arnold (Mr. Luke, "great critic and apostle of culture"), Walter Pater (Mr. Rose, whose "two topics are self-indulgence and art"), and—for the truth—Ruskin (Mr. Herbert, whose voice "seemed as if it came from a disconsolate spirit, hovering over the waters of Babylon, and remembering Sion"). *The New Republic* establishes the essential questions of the Victorian debate about the nature of God and religion in a scientific age and, through Ruskin, provides the answers Mallock urged in more than twenty books in the next four decades.

The New Paul and Virginia; or, Positivism on an Island (the title refers to Bernardin de Sainte-Pierre's 1787 romance, *Paul et Virginie*) is a slighter work, but still great fun, employing the same technique of reductio ad absurdum and pushing the arguments of its targets—Clifford, Huxley, John Tyndall, Frederic Harrison, and Harriet Martineau—"to some consequence more extreme, but more strictly logical, than any which those who proclaimed them either realised or had the courage to avow." In a treatise which he wrote at the same time and dedicated to Ruskin, *Is Life Worth Living?* (1879), Mallock declared that "scientific negation" was "decomposing religious belief," and he damned the scientists' "enthusiasm of humanity" as a pale and silly alternative to a belief in God. In his satire on "Positivism" (by which he means the rationalist and materialist ideas of the period), Mallock offers Paul Darnley, a positivist professor preaching "the Gospel of the kingdom of man": "There is no heaven to seek for; there is no hell to shun. We have nothing to strive and live for except to be unspeakably happy." Darnley is stranded on an island with Virginia St. John, a Ritualist convert on her way to join her husband, the bishop of Chasuble Islands. Their discussions, and the clashes of their passions with their ideas, constitute a compendium of nineteenth-century intellectual controversies (Mallock quoted his adversaries with often devastating effect) and problems and illuminate Mallock's essential idea that "supernatural religion was implicit in all civilized life," which life would collapse into ruin if such faith were eliminated. In his *Memoirs of Life and Literature* he lamented how English life had become more and more intolerable, less and less civilized, as it had abandoned the "cardinal doctrines of religious orthodoxy" for any

will-o'-the-wisp that Huxley, Tyndall, Harrison, Jowett, Arnold, or Mrs. Humphry Ward might recommend. Their voices and a thousand more would, he asserted, "establish in [orthodoxy's] place some purely natural substitute, such as the 'enthusiasm of humanity,' a passion for the welfare of posterity, or a godless deification of domestic puritanism for its own sake"; they refused to see that it is on belief in "a God . . . who is interested in the fortunes of each soul individually" that a civilized nation's "moral, emotional, and intellectual values" depend. Life itself is absurd if founded on no real faith.

Mallock's subsequent books illustrate these same ideas and apply them to English social problems of the latter part of the century. Alarmed by the effect of the writings of Karl Marx and others on "the minds of certain English malcontents," Mallock began issuing treatises and novels that dealt with "extreme democracy or Socialist Radicalism" in the same way as he had before considered "atheism in religion and morals." His novel *The Old Order Changes* (1886) focuses with nostalgia on a vanishing feudal England and celebrates the aristocracy, "with its natural position, with its memories, with its historic consciousness," as the very "body" of the nation. This is all opposed by the radical and socialist positions argued by the novel's less exalted characters and by the frightening visions of "an East End mob" which Mallock offers. The novel, like his others, is witty in its dialogue, but there is little if any psychological probing of character; and it interests now only as a late-Victorian social-problem novel taking the Conservative position. John Lucas has significantly discussed this novel and Mallock's social writings in the context of Henry James's *The Princess Casamassima* and George Gissing's *Demos*, which appeared in the same year and share similar emphases.

Other treatises and novels followed, including a debate (1907-1909) about socialism with Bernard Shaw (who asserted that "any Socialist over the age of six could knock Mr Mallock into a cocked hat"). The title of his 1905 volume, *The Reconstruction of Belief*, aptly summarizes Mallock's career (and suggests why Raymond Williams, in 1958, called him "perhaps the most able conservative thinker of the last eighty years"). For Mallock the notion of "the physical basis of life," which had constituted a principal idea for so many of the century's sages, was in the end a brutish appeal to the appetites because no "natural" man could possibly be fully, creatively human, or even civilized, without a belief in God and in the order, social and moral, derived from orthodox religion. The "Gospel of the kingdom of man" was for him the gospel of man as preying animal, and Mallock spent a career repeating mid-Victorian debates about this gospel, fighting with energy and wit and absolute conviction all the signs of the times. If he is read now only for the fun of his satires on famous Victorians and for the cogency of his exposures of their excesses, one might also witness in him the last Victorian voice of orthodoxy, arguing even beyond the Great War and into the wasteland of the twentieth century that "supernatural religion was implicit in all civilised life."

Bibliography:

Charles C. Nickerson, "A Bibliography of the Novels of W. H. Mallock," *English Literature in Transition*, 6 (1963): 190-198.

References:

Amy Belle Adams, *The Novels of William Hurrell Mallock* (Orono, Maine: University Press, 1934);

John Lucas, "Conservatism and Revolution in the 1880s," in *Literature and Politics in the Nineteenth Century*, edited by J. Lucas (London: Methuen, 1971), pp. 173-219;

J. Max Patrick, "Introduction," *The New Republic* (Gainesville: University of Florida Press, 1950);

Osbert Sitwell, *Laughter in the Next Room* (Boston: Little, Brown, 1948);

Raymond Williams, *Culture and Society 1780-1950* (London: Chatto & Windus, 1958), pp. 162-166;

P. M. Yarker, "W. H. Mallock's Other Novels," *Nineteenth Century Fiction*, 14 (1959): 189-205.

Henry Mayhew

(25 November 1812-25 July 1887)

Anne Humpherys

Herbert H. Lehman College, City University of New York

BOOKS: *The Wandering Minstrel: A One-Act Farce* (London: Miller, 1834; Philadelphia: Turner, 1836);

But, However–: A One-Act Farce, by Mayhew and Henry Baylis (London: Chapman & Hall, 1838);

What to Teach and How to Teach It: So that the Child May Become a Wise and Good Man, Part I (London: Smith, 1842);

The Prince of Wales's Library: No. I–The Primer (London: Illuminated Magazine, 1844);

The Greatest Plague of Life; or, The Adventures of a Lady in Search of a Good Servant, by Mayhew and Augustus Mayhew (London: Bogue, 1847; London & New York: Routledge, 1859);

The Good Genius That Turned Everything into Gold; or, The Queen Bee and the Magic Dress, by Mayhew and Augustus Mayhew (London: Bogue, 1847);

Whom to Marry and How to Get Married! or, The Ad-

Henry Mayhew

ventures of a Lady in Search of a Good Husband, by Mayhew and Augustus Mayhew (London: Bogue, 1847-1848; New York: New World, 1848);

The Image of His Father; or, A Tale of a Young Monkey, by Mayhew and Augustus Mayhew (London: Hurst, 1848; New York: Harper, 1848);

The Magic of Kindness; or, The Wondrous Story of the Good Huan (London: Darton, 1849; New York: Harper, 1849);

Acting Charades; or, Deeds Not Words, by Mayhew and Augustus Mayhew (London: Bogue, 1850);

The Fear of the World; or, Living for Appearances, by Mayhew and Augustus Mayhew (New York: Harper, 1850); republished as *Living for Appearances* (London: Blackwell, 1855);

Low Wages: Their Causes, Consequences, and Remedies, parts 1-4 (London: Woodfall, 1851);

London Labour and the London Poor, Nos. 1-63 (volume 1 and parts of volumes 2 and 3, London: Woodfall, 1851-1852; 4 volumes, London: Griffin, Bohn, 1861-1862; 4 volumes, New York: Dover, 1968);

1851; or, The Adventures of Mr. and Mrs. Sandboys and Family, by Mayhew and George Cruikshank (London: Bogue, 1851);

The Story of the Peasant-Boy Philosopher; or, A Child Gathering Pebbles on the Sea Shore (London: Bogue, 1854; New York: Harper, 1855);

The Wonders of Science; or, Young Humphry Davy (London: Routledge, 1855; New York: Harper, 1856);

The Rhine and Its Picturesque Scenery (London: Bogue, 1856; New York: Bangs, 1856);

The Great World of London, Parts 1-9 (London: Bogue, 1856); completed by John Binny as *The Criminal Prisons of London and Scenes of Prison Life* (London: Griffin, Bohn, 1862);

The Upper Rhine (London: Routledge, 1858; London & New York: Routledge, Warne & Routledge, 1860);

Young Benjamin Franklin; or, The Right Road through Life (London: Blackwood, 1861; New York: Harper, 1862);

The Boyhood of Martin Luther (London: Low, 1863; New York: Harper, 1864);

German Life and Manners as Seen in Saxony at the Present Day (2 volumes, London: Allen, 1864);

Report Concerning the Trade and Hours of Closing Usual among the Unlicensed Victualling Establishments at Certain So-Called "Working Men's Clubs" (London: Judd, 1871).

COLLECTION: *The Unknown Mayhew*, edited by E. P. Thompson and Eileen Yeo (New York: Pantheon, 1971).

Henry Mayhew is best known today for his four-volume survey of London street life at mid-century, *London Labour and the London Poor* (1851-1852; 1861-1862), the best and perhaps the only extensive glimpse available of this fascinating underside of Victorian life. In his own day, however, his reputation rested primarily on his investigation of the exploited pieceworkers in London's skilled and unskilled trades. He wrote these articles as the metropolitan correspondent for the *Morning Chronicle* from late 1849 through late 1850. The value of all his surveys is in the number and scope of the personal interviews Mayhew conducted with his subjects. In his decision to seek out these interviews, to rely on the information gleaned from them to project a picture of "Labour and the Poor" in London at mid-century, and to print as many full-length interviews as space and time would allow, Mayhew was unique as a social investigator and journalist in the Victorian period.

Mayhew was the fourth son of a very well-to-do London solicitor, Joshua Dorset Joseph Mayhew. Family tradition has it that he was the most brilliant of all the seven Mayhew brothers, but he had an erratic and disappointing career from the beginning. He was sent to a good school, Westminster, but ran away. He went to sea—probably to India, where his brother Alfred was working—as a midshipman; he worked in his father's law office, but that came to an end, so the family story goes, when he forgot to file some papers and almost caused his father to be arrested at his own dinner table. In the late 1820s, he entered the new field of popular journalism, founding magazines with an investment of five pounds (*Figaro in London* was the best), writing for others, collaborating with his friends on ephemeral farces for the nonlicensed stage, and in general enjoying himself very much. Somewhere along the way he developed an interest in chemistry and experimental science in general, an unusual direction for an upper-middle-class Englishman in the early 1800s. This interest was to affect the subjects of a few journalistic pieces (for example, a scientific, albeit comic, classification of voters in *Punch* in 1842) and in his boys' books (biographies of Humphry Davy [1855] and Benjamin Franklin [1861]). But most importantly it resulted in the deductive and empirical

An illustration for a reprint of one of Mayhew's 1849 Morning Chronicle *articles on "Labour and the Poor,"*
a survey of life in a London slum

intentions that lay behind his social surveys.

In the 1840s, his life began to take a more serious turn, as one would expect of a man entering his thirties. After a decade of miscellaneous journalism and farce writing, he and his associates founded the venerable *Punch* in 1841, though Mayhew had only a tenuous connection with the magazine after its first year. He tried various projects on his own, including an abortive series on education. In 1844 he married Jane Jerrold, the daughter of the writer Douglas Jerrold; the couple had two children, Amy and Athol. Shortly after his marriage, financial disaster struck; Mayhew went bankrupt in 1846. It was a blow from which he never recovered; his father disinherited him as a result and the rest of his life was marked by the precariousness of his financial situation. Between 1846 and 1850, he and his youngest brother, Au-

gustus, wrote a series of six comic novels on standard *Punch* themes of silly women and middle-class pretensions. They are good novels of their kind, but slight. Mayhew also took on a variety of journalistic assignments to make ends meet. One of these was from the *Morning Chronicle*—after the *Times* the most prestigious newspaper in England—to investigate the conditions in a notorious slum in south London where there had been a severe outbreak of cholera in 1848 and 1849; it led Mayhew almost immediately to his major work, the social surveys of London's working population.

Mayhew's series of eighty-odd articles for the *Morning Chronicle* was part of the paper's national survey on "Labour and the Poor." Mayhew investigated the clothing industry in London most thoroughly, and his exposé of the brutal conditions among pieceworkers in the East End made him famous. He also touched at varying lengths on furniture makers, sailors, toy makers, dockworkers, and "hucksters." This last led to his three-volume work on street folk, *London Labour and the London Poor*, which he began publishing on his own in weekly installments in December 1850 after he and the *Morning Chronicle* had come to an unfriendly parting of the ways.

In *London Labour and the London Poor*, volumes one and two, Mayhew surveyed a vast array of street sellers, buyers, and "finders" (those who picked up items on the streets and sold them). His interviews with this shifting population are sensitive, probing, and fascinating to read. Due to pressures of space and his respect for the empirical scientific method, which he thought required him to publish all his data before he drew any conclusions, he gives long "autobiographical" statements by his informants in which the questions are absorbed into the answers and each informant seems to be speaking in his own voice. His informants told him about their backgrounds, but the most fascinating parts to a

modern reader are their descriptions of their "trades," such as that of a sixty-year-old "pure" (dogs' dung, used in tanning) finder: "If we only gathered a pail-full in the day, we could live very well; but we couldn't do much more than that, for there wasn't near so many at the business then, and the Pure was easier to be had. For my part I can't tell where all the poor creatures have come from of late years; the world seems growing worse and worse every day. They have pulled down the price of Pure, that's certain; but the poor things must do something, they can't starve while there's anything to be got. Why, no later than six or seven years ago, it was as high as 3*s.* 6*d.* and 4*s.* a pail-full, and a ready sale for as much of it as you could get; but now you can only get 1*s.* and in some places 1*s.*2*d.* a pail-full; and, as I said before, there are so many at it, that there is not much left for a poor creature like me to find."

Due to a lawsuit in which his publisher sued Mayhew over some unjustified expenditures, *London Labour and the London Poor* stopped publication

HENRY MAYHEW.
[From a Photograph.]

LONDON LABOUR AND THE LONDON POOR:

THE CONDITION AND EARNINGS OF

THOSE THAT WILL WORK, CANNOT WORK, AND WILL NOT WORK.

BY

HENRY MAYHEW.

Vol. II.

LONDON STREET-FOLK.

LONDON:
CHARLES GRIFFIN AND COMPANY,
STATIONERS' HALL COURT.

Frontispiece and title page for the second volume of Mayhew's four-volume work on the "street folk" of London

in February 1852 toward the end of volume two. Mayhew was never to get to the theoretical stage of his survey, though he did try to draw some weak analogies between the Kaffirs of Africa and the London street folk. His importance is as an observer and reporter, not as a theoretician. When he picked up the project again in 1856, he did a survey of "street entertainers" at the same time that he was engaged in a new work, a look at the London prisons, published as *The Great World of London* in 1856. Mayhew surveyed the different prison regimes and found them all wanting, but was not able to offer any substantive suggestions before both projects were stopped in mid-sentence by the death of his publisher. In 1861-1862 all the surveys were published in book form: volume four of *London Labour and the London Poor* was finished by John Binny and others; Binny also completed the prison book, which was published as *The Criminal Prisons of London and Scenes of Prison Life* (1862). There appears to have been little, if any, critical reception of these volumes; they came too long after the fact.

Mayhew's life after 1852 is marked by a sad decline. He went to Germany several times to live cheaply; there he wrote three ill-tempered travel books (1856, 1858, 1864) plus an undistinguished one on the life of the young Martin Luther (1863). He embarked on a series of children's books of mediocre quality and a few short-lived journalistic projects. He and his wife separated, though he visited her weekly at the home of their daughter and her husband. After 1865 he disappears from view until he died, forgotten and obscure, in 1887. His son, Athol, wrote a small volume vindicating his father's role in founding *Punch*; then he, too, disappeared.

Other:
Figaro in London, volumes 4-8, edited by Mayhew (London: Strange, 1835-1839);
The Comic Almanac, edited by Mayhew (London: Bogue, 1850-1851);
The Shops and Companies of London and the Trades and Manufactories of Great Britain, parts 1-7, edited by Mayhew (London: Strand, 1865);
London Characters, second edition, contributions by Mayhew (London: Chatto & Windus, 1874).

Periodical Publications:
"London and the Poor," letters 1-82, London *Morning Chronicle* (19 October 1849-12 December 1850);
"The Great Exhibition," parts 1-9, Edinburgh *News and Literary Chronicle* (1851).

References:
John L. Bradley, Introduction, *Selections from "London Labour and the London Poor"* (London: Oxford University Press, 1965);
Gertrude Himmelfarb, "The Culture of Poverty," in *The Victorian City: Images and Realities*, edited by H. J. Dyos and Michael Wolff (2 volumes, London: Routledge & Kegan Paul, 1973), II: 707-736;
Anne Humpherys, *Travels into the Poor Man's Country: The Work of Henry Mayhew* (Athens: University of Georgia Press, 1977);
Athol Mayhew, *A Jorum of Punch* (London: Downey, 1895);
F. B. Smith, "Mayhew's Convict," *Victorian Studies*, 22 (1979): 431-448;
E. P. Thompson, "Mayhew and the 'Morning Chronicle,'" in *The Unknown Mayhew*, edited by E. P. Thompson and Eileen Yeo (New York: Pantheon, 1971), pp. 11-50;
Eileen Yeo, "Mayhew as a Social Investigator," in *The Unknown Mayhew*, pp. 51-95.

George Meredith

Michael Collie
York University

BIRTH: Portsmouth, Hampshire, 12 February 1828, to Augustus and Jane Eliza Macnamara Meredith.

MARRIAGES: 9 August 1849 to Mary Ellen Nicolls; child: Arthur Gryffydh. 20 September 1864 to Marie Vulliamy; children: William Maxse, Marie Eveleen.

AWARDS AND HONORS: Presidency of the Society of Authors, 1892; vice-presidency of the London Library, 1902; Order of Merit, 1905; Gold Medal of the Royal Society of Literature, 1905.

DEATH: Mickleham, Surrey, 18 May 1909.

BOOKS: *Poems* (London: Parker, 1851; New York: Scribners, 1898);

The Shaving of Shagpat: An Arabian Entertainment (London: Chapman & Hall, 1856; Boston: Roberts, 1887);

Farina: A Legend of Cologne (London: Smith, Elder, 1857);

The Ordeal of Richard Feverel: A History of Father and Son (3 volumes, London: Chapman & Hall, 1859; 1 volume, Boston: Roberts, 1887);

Evan Harrington; or, He Would Be a Gentleman (New York: Harper, 1860; 3 volumes, London: Bradbury & Evans, 1861);

Modern Love, and Poems of the English Roadside, with Poems and Ballads (London: Chapman & Hall, 1862); edited by E. Cavazza (Portland, Maine: Mosher, 1891);

Emilia in England (3 volumes, London: Chapman & Hall, 1864); republished as *Sandra Belloni* (London: Chapman & Hall, 1886; Boston: Roberts, 1887);

Rhoda Fleming: A Story (3 volumes, London: Tinsley, 1865; 1 volume, Boston: Roberts, 1886);

Vittoria, 3 volumes (London: Chapman & Hall, 1866; Boston: Roberts, 1888);

The Adventures of Harry Richmond (3 volumes, London: Smith, Elder, 1871; 1 volume, Boston: Roberts, 1887);

Beauchamp's Career (3 volumes, London: Chapman & Hall, 1876; 1 volume, Boston: Roberts, 1887);

The House on the Beach: A Realistic Tale (New York: Harper, 1877);

The Egoist: A Comedy in Narrative, 3 volumes (London: Kegan Paul, 1879; New York: Harper, 1879);

The Tragic Comedians: A Study in a Well-Known Story (2 volumes, London: Chapman & Hall, 1880; 1 volume, New York: Munro, 1881);

Poems and Lyrics of the Joy of Earth (London: Macmillan, 1883; Boston: Roberts, 1883);

Diana of the Crossways (3 volumes, London: Chapman & Hall, 1885; 1 volume, New York: Munro, 1885; Boston: Roberts, 1887);

Ballads and Poems of Tragic Life (London: Macmillan, 1887; Boston: Roberts, 1887);

A Reading of Earth (London: Macmillan, 1888; Boston: Roberts, 1888);

The Case of General Ople and Lady Camper (New York: Lovell, 1890);

The Tale of Chloe: An Episode in the History of Beau Beamish (New York: Lovell, 1890);

One of Our Conquerors (3 volumes, London: Chapman & Hall, 1891; 1 volume, Boston: Roberts, 1891);

Poems: The Empty Purse, with Odes to the Comic Spirit, to Youth in Memory and Verses (London: Macmillan, 1892; Boston: Roberts, 1892);

Jump to Glory Jane (London: Swan Sonnenschein, 1892);

The Tale of Chloe; The House on the Beach; The Case of General Ople and Lady Camper (London: Ward, Lock & Bowden, 1894);

Lord Ormont and His Aminta: A Novel (3 volumes, London: Chapman & Hall, 1894; 1 volume, New York: Scribners, 1894);

The Amazing Marriage, 2 volumes (London: Constable, 1895; New York: Scribners, 1895);

An Essay on Comedy and the Uses of the Comic Spirit (London: Constable, 1897; New York: Scribners, 1897);

Selected Poems (London: Constable, 1897; New York: Scribners, 1897);

The Nature Poems (London: Constable, 1898);

George Meredith

Odes in Contribution to the Song of French History (London: Constable, 1898; New York: Scribners, 1898);

The Story of Bhanavar the Beautiful (London: Constable, 1900);

A Reading of Life, with Other Poems (London: Constable, 1901; New York: Scribners, 1901);

Last Poems (London: Constable, 1909; New York: Scribners, 1909);

Chillianwallah (New York: Marion Press, 1909);

Love in the Valley, and Two Songs: Spring and Autumn (Chicago: Seymour, 1909);

Poems Written in Early Youth, Poems from "Modern Love," and Scattered Poems (London: Constable, 1909; New York: Scribners, 1909);

Celt and Saxon (London: Constable, 1910; New York: Scribners, 1910).

COLLECTIONS: *The Works of George Meredith*, De Luxe Edition (39 volumes, London: Consta-

ble, 1896-1912); Library Edition (18 volumes, London: Constable, 1897-1910); Boxhill Edition (17 volumes, New York: Scribners, 1897-1919); Memorial Edition (27 volumes, London: Constable, 1909-1911; New York: Scribners, 1909-1911).

Between 1856 and 1895, George Meredith published fifteen novels and a number of long short stories or novellas, taking as his special subject the instability of human relationships within a sharply conceived but usually arbitrary social context. As a novelist, he was interested in the individual, not in the crowd, the events which affected his individuals occurring more in the head than in the daily traffic of exterior existence. He was, or during the course of his career became, a psychological novelist, seeming to some idiosyncratic but to others profoundly right in his rejection of the moral standards his contemporaries took for granted.

Born in Hampshire in 1828, Meredith was the grandson of Melchizedek Meredith, a well-established Portsmouth tailor; he was the son of Augustus Meredith, who took over the business when the "Great Mel" died, and of Jane Macnamara, the daughter of an innkeeper. Meredith was educated at St. Paul's (a small, probably not very distinguished, private school in nearby Southsea), at an as-yet-unidentified country boarding school (which may, however, have been near Lowestoft), and in 1843-1844 at the Moravian Brothers school in Neuwied on the Rhine; the cost of his education was met by a small legacy from his mother's side of the family. Various attempts, none of them conclusive, have been made to assess this rather eccentric education. On the positive side, some say, was the escape from the more repressive features of the English educational system at that time. At the Protestant school in Neuwied he acquired the tolerance, self-discipline, and cosmopolitan awareness that infused all his later actions. But the circumstances of his being sent to school, first away from his own locality, then to a boarding school in another part of the country, then to a boarding school in a different country, have never been fully explained. Nor has Meredith's early family life been satisfactorily described and analyzed. His mother died in 1833. His father went bankrupt in 1838 and, moving from Portsmouth to London, married his housekeeper, Matilda Buckett, with whom he had in effect been living for a number of years. Meredith absolutely refused in later life to talk about his youth, so it is not known whether he regarded it as happy and normal or as turbulent and unhappy, though various theories have been spun in which his feelings, indeed his traumas, are deduced from his fiction. He may have been disturbed by the realization that his father was sleeping with his housekeeper and may have been sent to boarding school because of this. He may have been upset by the social airs and snobbish manner said to have been adopted by his father. He may have been ashamed to have been the son of a tailor, albeit a tailor with pretensions. He may have had the early but traumatic love affairs some critics say must be deduced from love affairs in his novels. There is in fact little direct evidence about what Meredith felt or thought during the first eighteen years of his life. It is important to say this if Meredith's fiction is to be enjoyed, because his novels, if autobiographical at all, are not naively so. He did not work out his own problems through his fiction; rather his fiction explored with keen insight the problems of humanity, not independent of but over and above his own formative experiences.

His modest capital had been held in chancery between his father's bankruptcy and his eighteenth birthday, but in February 1845 a significant part of it was pried loose when approval was given to his being articled to a London solicitor, Richard Charnock. Although he never intended to become a solicitor himself, he was at the age of eighteen guaranteed room and board for five years, together with a small salary. During this period he began to write.

Meredith adopted as quite obviously correct those nineteenth-century assumptions about the greatness of literature which allowed an aspiring writer, without bothering overmuch about the writer's social function, to dedicate his or her life to the making of "modern" works—that is, books and poems appropriate to the times but matching in quality the masterpieces of the past. Meredith always thought of himself as a poet and indeed published more volumes of poems than novels, as well as many occasional pieces, including translations. Poetry in its nature did not require justification, thought Meredith's peer group; nor did Meredith ever provide one. But Meredith was also determined to be a novelist, because the novel was regarded, by others as well as by himself, as the literary form most appropriate to the times in which he lived. His high ambition was eventually satisfied. Among the novels he produced during his long career, some were masterworks, the fruit of his distinctive genius and a unique achievement that was

marked in many ways: by three important collected editions; by a very unambiguous recognition of his greatness in North America from 1885 on; by the plaudits of suffragettes and feminists who were well placed to see that he had written about sexual relations, matrimony, matrimonial law, and woman's position in society in a daring but essentially clearheaded way; by the admiration of his fellow writers, who elected him president of the Society of Authors after the death of Tennyson; and by the award, late in his life, of the Order of Merit, which recognized him for what he then was—a great national figure.

Although Meredith took for granted the importance of writing a good poem or a good novel, he did not immediately know how to do this. He was an extremely intelligent, sensitive creative artist given to experimentation while a particular work was being written or revised, rather than to either a slavish imitation of what others had already done or a repetitious provision of what the public was supposed to want. He never tried to be popular. In order to be free to write, he earned his living as best he could. The struggle to establish himself as a completely independent writer was a long one. In fact, he would have to be described as a struggling author throughout the greater part of the period from roughly 1850 to 1880, and it was not until 1885, when he published *Diana of the Crossways*, that he enjoyed full public acclaim. Meredith was not the morose type of writer who separated himself from existence in order to write about it; on the contrary, he had great vitality, a zest for life, a love of good company, and a high regard for health, fitness, and physical activity. Meredith never lacked friends, least of all literary friends who recognized his remarkable talents, enjoyed his conversation—even his monologues—and (with only one or two exceptions) gave him strong support when he needed it. It was in the company of such friends that he met his attractive, high-spirited first wife, Mary Ellen Nicolls, the widow of Lt. Edward Nicolls and daughter of Thomas Love Peacock. Life was worth living: Meredith never really doubted this, though from the beginning he was an unbeliever, at least an agnostic, probably an atheist.

It may be that Meredith contributed significantly to the failure of his first marriage by expecting it to survive both the low standard of living that was sustained on the hope that first this, then that novel would be sufficiently well received to generate an income, and his own low tolerance of foolishness in other people—in this case, his wife. George

Meredith's first wife, the former Mary Ellen Nicolls, the daughter of Thomas Love Peacock

Meredith and Mary Nicolls were married in London in August 1849; Thomas Love Peacock was there, but Augustus Meredith was not. (In London he had recovered something of his prosperity as a tailor and on his savings had recently immigrated to South Africa.) With the duns at the door, as Meredith cheerfully put it, the young couple lived in various lodging houses and cottages in London, Surrey, Sussex, and Kent, and for a short while with Peacock. Their only child, Arthur Gryffydh, was born in June 1853. Whatever may have gone wrong with this marriage was, of course, expressed only in transmuted form in *The Ordeal of Richard Feverel* (1859) and in *Modern Love* (1862), the two works readers have thought most bear the marks of autobiographical pressure. Meredith never gave a clear account of what caused a once carefree relationship to go sour, or at least none has survived. Edith Nicolls, Mary Meredith's daughter, who was five years old when her mother remarried, did not very much like Meredith and he, it seems, did not very much like her. Nor did Mary like her husband's

preference for male companionship and his habit (which turned out to be lifelong) of disappearing on long pedestrian expeditions with his friends. Visitors to the Meredith home reported that in domestic talk Meredith's tongue was sometimes waspish and hurtful. At the same time, evidence has come to the surface that Mary was often insensitive, coquettish, and hysterical; she once had to be restrained from throwing herself into the Thames. Gradually she became more and more impatient of his long absences and his long periods at work, while he became testy at having to labor for hours at a small table in the corner of the bedroom. Neither gave what the other wanted or needed. This was compounded when Mary became pregnant with a child Meredith knew could not be his. It has always been assumed that the father was the painter Henry Wallis, with whom she traveled in Wales in 1857 before going to live with him in Italy. She took Meredith's refusal to reply to her letters as the pretext for believing that he was indifferent to what she did. Perhaps by the time of her last known letter to him—in September 1857—he was indeed indifferent. He at any rate refused to attempt a reconciliation, as he refused to allow her to see their son until just before her death.

The breakdown of his first marriage affected Meredith in an extraordinary way: it hardened his heart, but it also made him sensitive to the position of women in Victorian society. His determination to write did not meanwhile slacken. Throughout the years of his first marriage and during the years which immediately followed its breakdown, Meredith was sustained by his own massive ego, by his equally massive intellect, by many strong and lasting friendships with literary contemporaries, and by his reading, which was extensive. Like George Gissing, that other omnivorous reader among Victorian novelists, Meredith read Latin, Greek, German, French, and Italian with equal ease, to some extent compensating for his lack of sympathy with British taste by developing a cosmopolitan awareness of what writers were thinking and doing in other places. This was reinforced by frequent expeditions to France, to Germany (where he eventually sent Arthur to school), to Switzerland, and to Italy. He brought up his son by himself, managed without help, was a survivor. His independence was above all the independence of intellect, a fact which informed everything he wrote as a particular sort of perception about what mattered in life. In a godless world, people matter; and if people matter, how they get on with each other matters. For Meredith, this getting on or not getting on was personal, not social. Because the individual human being had always to exist as an independent, self-contained, private entity, at issue was how such an individual could relate to other individuals, if he could at all. The individual human being had to manage as best he could by himself, never as part of a group. Meredith explored this problem in novel after novel, compulsively filling the imaginative space between John Stuart Mill's *On Liberty* (1859)—where self is the basic premise—and Émile Durkheim's *On Social Method* (1895)—where society is the basic premise—with fascinating, subtle, and sometimes terrifying explorations of human instabilities, both individual and social.

Meredith discovered, as he wrote, what he could do with the novel form—not starting with a theory and applying it, but learning through trial and error what would work and what would not. In this long process, there were setbacks as well as gratifying successes. His first two novels were lightweight pieces, not calculated to alert the reading public to the arrival on the scene of a genius. *The Shaving of Shagpat*, written during the two years after the birth of his son, was published in December 1855 (though dated 1856) and affects a mock-oriental tone that perhaps reflects the lively but frivolous quality of Meredith's conversation with his friends. Remote from life, the young intellects sported with words and ideas. Meredith concocted a tale about a tyrannical clothier whose power over a city derives solely from the denseness of his hair and beard and a young barber, Shibli Bagaray, who acts the part of a social reformer, eventually cutting off the hair that was the source of authority. In a loosely-constructed plot, Meredith tests Bagaray's resourcefulness as he attempts to overcome, in a series of episodes, his own gullibility and pride, which he eventually does with the help of a woman, Noorna bin Noorka. This type of laughter at the absurdity of egoism later, in more subtle forms, was to become one of the hallmarks of Meredith's genius. As social allegory, however, the book's main drift was too obscure for it to be taken seriously, while it was too precious in manner to be enjoyed as a joke at the expense of orientalists. In any case, a great novel-writing career cannot very well be launched with a joke. *Farina: A Legend of Cologne* (1857) was an equally insignificant bit of storytelling: it is little more than a mannered caricature of the stock characters of romantic fiction and represents just the first stage in Meredith's disengagement from the romance convention. In what

is now the standard biography, *The Ordeal of George Meredith* (1953), Lionel Stevenson said that "in this fairly brief tale Meredith was attempting a difficult type of art—the grotesque, or comic-gruesome," but that at the same time the plot of *Farina*, which concerns a "young tradesman who defies entrenched privilege and wins honour by performing great public service," reveals Meredith's lifelong preoccupation with the problem of class.

Then came two important novels which, bearing the marks of a powerful imagination at work, still hold their place among the acknowledged masterpieces of Victorian fiction, despite the fact that they were not at first well received or understood. *The Ordeal of Richard Feverel* and *Evan Harrington* (1860) represent in different ways Meredith's first serious engagement with the novel form as it had been fashioned by early Victorian novelists; by middle-class family publishers such as Frederic Chapman of Chapman and Hall; by the editors of magazines who wanted serialized fiction for family reading; and by the proprietors of circulating libraries, notably the all-powerful Charles Edward Mudie. By 1859, the multivolume novel, shaped by these forces, had come to dominate the literary scene as the medium that would best accommodate a number of disparate factors: the novelist's independent grasp of the social reality he created for his characters, the publisher's moral and literary predispositions, the magazine editor's nervous responsiveness to weekly or monthly sales, and the public's pleasure in new fiction that might challenge but would always eventually reinforce the reader's own values. These factors in turn represented the taste of the particular social subset that read novels; that is, part of the literate middle class. Often the accommodation was achieved by means of the novelist's strategy of allowing his reader to believe that narrator, character, reader, and, by implication, novelist all subscribed to the same social values, despite interesting, even alarming, deviations from the norm by some characters. In *The Ordeal of Richard Feverel*, however, Meredith disturbed this détente. Instead of subscribing to the values of his readers, he let the narrator be ironic at the expense of the characters to the extent that the uneasy reader came to realize the author was being ironic at his expense as well. This problem of tone and style was compounded by the suspicion that the author was also withholding, somewhat maliciously, information that the reader needed. In writing about the tortured relationship between father and son, for example, Meredith made only oblique references to

Richard Feverel's mother, despite the fact that the novel is about the boy's growth into consciousness in an unusual family environment; it is unusual because of the harshness with which Sir Austin Feverel imposes his strict, emotionally debilitating educational "system" on his son, who reacts by refusing to play the role his father has prescribed, by rebelling to the point of criminality (he burns down a neighbor's stack of wheat), and by marrying for love

Drawing of Meredith circa 1860 by Dante Gabriel Rossetti

a woman of whom his father does not approve.

Not only does *The Ordeal of Richard Feverel* confirm Meredith's interest in the divisiveness of class and in the forces of "nature" which compensate to some degree for the inadequacies of "society," it also demonstrates, again, the author's antiromantic tendencies. Richard Feverel falls in love with Lucy in poignant early episodes that are written with a marvelous lyricism; but Richard is not represented as being an admirable person and Meredith prevents the reader from identifying with his hero in an unthinking way. While the novel on one level is a lively, perfectly intelligible depiction of a conflict between father and son, on another it is a complex verbal exploration of human relations, the

surface tensions of which imply more than is directly stated. In *The Ordeal of Richard Feverel*, Meredith adopts the technique which in later novels he refined; that is, he engages the reader's mind in a complexity of style which is an analogue of the complexity of character that is his subject.

This technique was not immediately understood by Meredith's contemporaries. Did these cryptic comments refer to a matrimonial situation that could have been described in plain terms? Was it part of Meredith's art to make the mother as elusive to the reader as to Richard Feverel? Or was Meredith disturbing the surface of plain narration for some other reason? The contemporary reader was upset by this sort of thing. He could not simply dismiss a book that was so powerfully written; on the other hand, he could not immediately cope with the techniques of subtle evasiveness, structural irony, and delayed explanation. Meredith had had to accept the constraints of the three-volume form and the expectations associated with it but made imaginative elbowroom for himself by being ironical about the story he was telling, about the characters involved, and, in effect, about the nature of fiction itself. This anarchic attitude to a well-established, well-liked institution was not well received. One reviewer commented on the "quaint sarcastic style" and said that Meredith had "overstepped the legitimate boundaries of what is known by the adjective 'proper.'" Another spoke of the "extreme licence the author allows his pen." And in the *Athenaeum*, the reviewer wrote: "The only comfort the reader can find in closing the book is—that it is not true." An atheistic, freethinking, witty, socially disengaged and therefore irresponsible writer, as the moralist took him to be, had collided with the full force of mid-Victorian morality. Mudie refused to circulate *The Ordeal of Richard Feverel*, which, partly in direct consequence, fell dead.

This cause célèbre helped determine Meredith's attitude to the writing of fiction for the next few years. He was upset by the reception of *The Ordeal of Richard Feverel* and, in one sense, devoted much energy in later work to finding ways of neutralizing the reader's apparent appetite for a romantic story simply told. This did not mean, however, that he was willing to write the type of socially and morally acceptable fiction some middle-class readers may have wanted. It meant, rather, that he became technically devious in writing the sort of book that would satisfy his own standards, this technical virtuosity resulting in important advances in the art of fiction. Meanwhile, it must be noted that

Garden and rear of house at 16 Cheyne Walk, Chelsea, where Meredith lived with Rossetti and Algernon Charles Swinburne in 1862

when Meredith revised *The Ordeal of Richard Feverel* for the important second edition published by Kegan Paul (1878), he did not simplify it, or alter those parts of the novel that had been judged offensive to the British matron.

Fortunately, Meredith was already committed to the writing of *Evan Harrington* well before he experienced the public's negative reception of *The Ordeal of Richard Feverel*. After living with Arthur for about two years in Hobury Street in London, Meredith settled at Copsham Cottage in Esher in the late summer of 1859. Here he wrote his only novel that was intended primarily for magazine publication, though before the serialization in *Once a Week* had ended, he had sold the novel to Harper in the United States and to Bradbury and Evans in England. Meredith had difficulty while writing *Evan Harrington* in devising a plot appropriate to his sense of character ("To invent probabilities in modern daily life is difficult," he said), although he succeeded in writing a good story about a young man who has to come to terms with his own pretentious-

ness, snobbery, and false standards, and in creating a number of racily drawn and memorable characters (notably Evan's two uncles). The story concerns the adventures of a young man who leaves his home in the provinces to avoid a life of trade in the tailor's premises of his widowed mother, who expects him to stay with her, pay off his father's debts, and restore the family's reputation. Instead, he aspires to transcend social circumstances by becoming a "gentleman," so giving Meredith the opportunity to criticize, satirically, the class system within which Evan is trapped. Once again, and not for the last time, the novelist devises a plot in which the tough experiences of life knock some sense into a hero preoccupied with a foolish dream, experience always being preferred by Meredith to the fanciful notions with which he filled his characters' heads. He said that when the novel was finished, it disgusted him, so he passed over the opportunity to revise *Evan Harrington* when it was being prepared for book publication: "I should have had to cut him to pieces, put strange herbs to him and boil him up again—a tortuous and a doubtful process." In retrospect one can see that Meredith would have had at least two reasons for disliking a novel that others regarded as a successful comedy of manners. First, as the story of a tailor's son, it too overtly gave the impression of being autobiographical. Second, in making his characters comic, he had rendered psychological analysis impossible (comedy assumes social norms and does not need psychology; psychology questions social norms and does not think deviations are fun). Once again, the writing of a novel brought Meredith face to face with a set of problems he did not immediately solve.

His next novels, *Emilia in England* (1864), *Rhoda Fleming* (1865), *Vittoria* (1866), *The Adventures of Harry Richmond* (1871), and *Beauchamp's Career* (1876), represent his attempt to satisfy at least some of his readers' desires and expectations, a problem to which he frequently referred in his correspondence. Was it possible to be a serious novelist who wrote what he felt had to be written, popular or not, *and* satisfy what Meredith regarded as the public's craving for romance? Because Meredith knew that his ideas about life were radical by comparison with those of his readers, he became somewhat obsessed by the difficulty of satisfying both himself and the general reader. Meredith did not believe life to have the type of coherence a coherent plot implies; he did not think human beings enjoyed the psychological stability that orthodox characterization in moral terms would have the reader assume. Therefore, the kind of fiction in which the narrator, the reader, and some of the characters subscribe to the same value system was, for him, impossible: less because he himself was radical, iconoclastic, and perversely out of the common mold than because he observed that individuals did not invariably get on with one another. Was there not a fiction that dealt with broken friendship, alienation, bad faith, and human failure or inadequacy, as well as the romantic kind that dealt with harmony, reconciliation, forgiveness, and matrimonial stability? Did people meet and live in harmony, or did they sometimes meet, believe they could live in harmony, yet fail? Meredith thought failure as likely as success, but in the novels he wrote between 1861 and 1879 he tended to gloss this over, attempting by expedients to satisfy both the reader and himself: the reader by feeding him romance, or what might be taken as romance; himself by means of a covert antiromantic ironical style.

This means that a mere plot summary tells one very little about a Meredith novel because events are rarely represented as being important in themselves, while a sequence of events (plot) becomes only a device which demonstrates that a character's mental existence is independent of circumstance; Meredith never subscribed to the types of determinism which flourished during his lifetime. That *Emilia in England* (republished in 1886 as *Sandra Belloni*) is the story of an Italian émigré singer whose art, simplicity of manner, and democratic convictions are contrasted with the vapid social aspirations of the three daughters of Mr. Pole, a city businessman whose money, partly embezzled, supports their sentimental deviations from commonsense, tells one little about a novel remarkable for its critique of materialism and its insight into the mentality of characters whose social position is parasitic and false. In his next novel, *Rhoda Fleming*, Meredith tried to devise a plot, a "plain story" as he called it, that would satisfy the less sophisticated members of his public—"the seduction of a pretty country girl by an unscrupulous gentleman, and her rescue by her heroic sister" (this is the formula to which one critic reduced the book)—but this only convinced him as well as his readers that plots were not his forte, for this is the weakest of his novels. In *Vittoria* (a sequel to *Sandra Belloni*, though independent of it) he tried to compensate for the lack of a convincing plot line by placing his artistic but politically engaged heroine in the exotic setting of nineteenth-century Italian politics; this served only to underscore the fact that, while he remained interested throughout his writing career in the interface between character and politics, his mode of expression was never in the telling of a story, but in narrative structures that permitted a shift in emphasis away from "plot" toward an analysis of a character's interior existence. This is true even in *Harry Richmond*, an adventure story in which a boy travels abroad in search of his father; and it is true, remarkably, in *Beauchamp's Career*, where Meredith weakens a brilliant analysis of the dilemmas of politics as they affect both engaged and disengaged individuals, both radicals and Tories, by artificially committing his characters to an absurd sequence of events which may have added to the book the "romantic" element which Meredith despised but which certainly distracted attention from the book's center of interest. Plots, in the conventional meaning of the word, are not observable in life, and Meredith did not believe in them. But the reader discovered that he was being patronized, while, by becoming a patronizer, Meredith somewhat sacrificed his position as artist. As a result, none of these books is entirely successful, though they contain fine sections and passages no other novelist could have written. The critique of materialism in *Emilia in England* is masterly, as is Meredith's depiction of Mr. Pole's nervous breakdown and disintegration of character, both of which themes anticipate later work; many scenes in *Harry Richmond* are marvelously and humorously inventive; the spirit of antiestablishment, revolutionary European politics is almost, in *Vittoria*, adequately incorporated into a plot that sustains the reader's interest; and *Beauchamp's Career*, a much stronger (because it is less squeamish) Second Reform Bill novel than George Eliot's *Felix Holt* (1866), and the most brilliant novel of Meredith's middle period, only falls short of complete success because Meredith did not allow his hero to be as socially disruptive as he would have been if his political ideas had been implemented, but instead, implausibly, killed him off.

Although in these middle years Meredith was still in the process of discovering for himself what could be done with the novel as Victorians understood it, the period was nonetheless one of real, if modest, achievement. Meredith's financial problems have perhaps been exaggerated. He was not wealthy, but nor was he poor, though like many an author he gave the impression of being in difficulties, expecting that everything he wished to do he should be able to afford. From 1860, he had a combined income from at least three part-time jobs: reading once a week for Mrs. Benjamin Wood, the cultured and wealthy widow of a member of Parliament; writing two columns and a leading article each week for the *Ipswich Journal* (without, however, having to go to Ipswich); and reading the manuscripts of aspiring authors for Chapman and Hall (this necessitated staying in London one night every week, for which purpose he for a short time shared a house with Swinburne and Rossetti in Cheyne Walk). To these activities he added jobs as he could. Without telling Frederic Chapman, he secretly worked for Saunders and Otley, a new publishing house; he increased the amount of work he did for Chapman and Hall; he contributed to and became involved in the organization of various magazines and journals, notably the *Pall Mall Gazette* and the *Fortnightly Review* (of which he was editor for a three-month period in the absence of John Morley); and he even accepted an assignment as special war correspondent for the *Morning Post* in Italy, despite the difficulty of getting friends to do his other work while he was away. With Arthur at boarding school in Norwich, Meredith could buckle down to work as

he saw fit, and this work soon included the preparation of new editions of his earliest work. During the 1860s, there were second editions of *The Shaving of Shagpat* (1861), *Farina* (1865), and *Evan Harrington* (1866); *The Ordeal of Richard Feverel* was serialized in *Revue des deux mondes* (1865); and *Farina* went to a third edition (1868).

Whatever he may have said to friends about the difficulties he had with each new novel—and these difficulties were, of course, real—he was nonetheless an established writer and man of letters. He mixed with the most distinguished literary people of his day and enjoyed himself prodigiously in their company, particularly in after-dinner talk and in long cross-country rambles which often lasted several days and involved convivial overnight stays at remote country pubs. He was witty, full of anecdotes and zest for existence, and always happy when out of doors with male friends of equal intelligence. Mary Meredith, whom he had seen only very occasionally since their separation, died in October 1861, leaving him free to put his life in order, to come to terms with the experience of his first marriage, and to consider how he would manage in the future. This last question was answered when he met Marie Vulliamy, the young daughter of a retired, anglicized French businessman. They were married on 20 September 1864, after protracted negotiations about Meredith's income and respectability. They lived in a number of temporary homes, including (for about three years) Kingston Lodge in Kingston-on-Thames, before moving in 1868 to Flint Cottage at the foot of Box Hill, where Meredith remained for the rest of his life. Because Marie had brought to the marriage a small income of her own, the Merediths' future was reasonably secure. Though Flint Cottage was small and cramped, he now had what he wanted: a garden of his own; the marvelous woodland; the famous beauty spot, Box Hill itself, to climb before sunrise; and the still unspoiled countryside, conveniently bisected by the railway that let him travel to London but with its lanes not yet replaced by roads.

As Meredith consolidated his position during the 1860s and early 1870s, he found that because of the critique of the British way of life his ironical mode implied, his creative genius was as quickly appreciated overseas as in England. *Evan Harrington* in book form was first published in America, as was *The House on the Beach* (1877); *Emilia in England* (as *Sandra Belloni*) and *The Ordeal of Richard Feverel* were serialized in France; and *The Ordeal of Richard Feverel* was included in Tauchnitz's Collection of British Authors. This trend was to continue. Of course, other British authors were also published or republished overseas, but it was an important aspect of his career that Meredith came to feel that it was chiefly foreigners, particularly Americans, who fully appreciated and understood what he did. This feeling later on had a highly beneficial, liberating effect. Also during the 1860s and 1870s, a pattern was established: Meredith almost invariably revised a novel when a new edition was prepared, not only to remedy flaws and infelicities but also to strengthen the action by insisting upon its complexity. He corrected, added, and deleted, but he never simplified. By far the best example of the creative artist in the process of revision is the second edition of *The Ordeal of Richard Feverel*, which Meredith prepared for Tauchnitz. During the course of this revision the novel first assumed its true character, though there were further minor changes when Kegan Paul published the novel in one volume, and major ones when Chapman and Hall included it in their first collected edition in 1885. Meredith was experimental in approach; his skill developed as his career proceeded; his attitude to the novel was plastic, not rigid. He

was truest to himself, as artist, in the very activity of the pen on the page, the countless corrections, deletions, and additions representing an idea of the novel as a never-ending process that actively engaged the attentive reader in the turbulence of verbal activity, rather than as a fixed entity that locked the reader into one and only one response. The second English edition of *The Ordeal of Richard Feverel* (1878) is a much better book than the first of 1859; Meredith was learning as he wrote. While Marie brought up their two young children, William and Marie, in Flint Cottage, Meredith, in the little two-room wooden cabin he had had built as his writer's den in their idyllic garden, began to imagine to himself those major works that added distinction to his later years.

The period between 1877 and 1884 was a turning point in Meredith's career, albeit a turning point open to various interpretations. Two long short stories or novellas, *The House on the Beach* and *The Case of General Ople and Lady Camper*, were published in the *New Quarterly Magazine* in 1877; in the same year *An Essay on Comedy* was published in the same magazine; *The Egoist* appeared in three volumes in 1879. The traditional view of Meredith has

Flint Cottage, Box Hill, Meredith's home for the last forty years of his life

An Essay on Comedy and *The Egoist*, taken together, as so typical of his art that his other books can best be understood in the terms they establish. In this view, *The Case of General Ople and Lady Camper* is a direct reflection, through the way in which Lady Camper makes fun of her neighbor General Ople, of what Meredith thought was the purpose of fiction. Another view is that in *An Essay on Comedy*, as well as in the fiction contemporary with it, Meredith thought out something which he then largely put behind him: the idea of society as something that did not change because human nature did not change, an idea that could have little appeal for a late Victorian who could not avoid noticing the impact on behavior of science, industry, empire, education, population growth, and wealth.

An Essay on Comedy, first delivered as a lecture entitled "On the Idea of Comedy and the Uses of the Comic Spirit" at the London Institution on 1 February 1877 (published in book form in 1897), is a classic statement of the beneficial social effects of the great comedies of the Western tradition, such as Molière's: comedy rectifies the excesses of human behavior by allowing an audience to laugh at them and, in the process of enjoyment, to achieve a sort of

sanity or equipoise, a return to normality. *The Egoist*, by common consent one of the most brilliant of Meredith's novels, is a highly original, but, in an important sense, orthodox comedy of manners with many theatrical features, just as *Evan Harrington* had been twenty years earlier. It is a novel, written in the spirit of *An Essay on Comedy*, about the excessive egoism of Sir Willoughby Patterne within the enclosed "society" of Sir Willoughby's own extensive estate. If the reader can believe that the aristocratic and upper-middle-class characters who occupy the stage that Willoughby's house and park represent are a credible microcosm of some other, real society, that reader can enjoy the absurdly conceited behavior of the egoist as a foible of character which is eventually revealed for what it is and redressed. Meredith now had the inventiveness with character, the sure touch with dialogue, the control of plot, to write this kind of book with considerable virtuosity.

Meredith, however, called *The Egoist* a "potboiler." This was because he saw that the "society" of Patterne Hall was not a microcosm of England in 1879, where the stresses caused by class, poverty, urbanization, and industry were too obvious to ig-

Meredith's study in the garden chalet at Box Hill

nore, and because he clearly understood the options in theory open to a late-nineteenth-century novelist. If the serious writer was not preoccupied with social change, he could remain within the romance tradition, as Meredith's friend, Robert Louis Stevenson, consciously chose to do. If he was preoccupied with social change, he had either to be a naturalist like Zola (someone who concentrated on the surface detail of existence) or a psychological novelist (someone who tried to penetrate beneath surface appearance to the underlying, perhaps unconscious, springs of behavior)—character in this latter case being no longer a fixed moral entity and behavior being no longer a question of complying or not complying with a social norm. In England in 1880, there were no social norms, perhaps, or those that existed many regarded with suspicion; people did not behave as they had been made to behave in the novels of George Eliot; both men and women were more complex than the traditional stereotypes to be found in a play by Molière. Meredith wanted to write a modern novel, one in which the emphasis was psychological rather than moral, and devoted the next fifteen years to trying to do so. During this fifteen-year period, he published *The Tragic Comedians* (1880), *Diana of the Crossways* (1885), *One of Our Conquerors* (1891), *Lord Ormont and His Aminta* (1894), and *The Amazing Marriage* (1895), despite illness and bereavement finding the energy in his fifties and sixties for a new set of experiments with the novel form. He also wrote *Celt and Saxon* (1910), which remained unfinished but expressed Meredith's growing conviction that the Celt, particularly the Welsh, was uncontaminated by the snobbery, prudery, haughtiness, and insensitivity that characterized the Anglo-Saxon.

The Tragic Comedians, a failure, effectively brought to an end the type of novel in which Meredith was ironical at the expense of his principal characters. Here he tried what he had tried before: to combine within the same plot an actual political concern (the career of the European socialist Ferdinand Lassalle) and an imagined love relationship (Lassalle's unconsummated, abortive affair with a young Jewess). Meredith failed to give substance and credibility to his depiction of socialism, and he trivialized both it and the relationship between the two main characters by making fun, at their expense, of the romantic convention in which he had chosen to place them. This exploration of the connection between the political and the personal, the public and the private, was one of Meredith's preoccupations. He had conducted it in *Vittoria* and in

Beauchamp's Career; he was to renew it more subtly in *Diana of the Crossways*, as well as, obliquely, in his last three novels. He continued to write as though there *ought* to be a connection between the behavior of the individual and the political crosscurrents of the time in which that individual lived, though his sense of political reality altered as he grew older, as did his definition of individuality. *The Tragic Comedians* also placed an emphasis on a second preoccupation, that by making fun of romantic love (relationships between people based more on vague feeling than clearheadedness), he could create an opportunity of analyzing what actually went on between people, and in particular between men and women for whom the intellectual and sexual were intermingled or confused. In *The Tragic Comedians*, however, the analysis (if that is the right word for a novel in which the characters are unskillfully denied the meeting at which they might have resolved their difficulties) is quite superficial, while its banal resolution is expressed in negative terms. The characters do not overcome the barrier of race. They do not prevail over social convention. Alvan's career is not proof against the scandal of an affair. Clotilde does not have the strength of character to act upon her deepest feelings. The novel is therefore, at one and the same time, a disappointment and a clear statement of a set of as-yet-unsolved novelistic problems. Only after a long struggle did Meredith find solutions to these problems that satisfied him.

In the very difficult period between the publication of *The Tragic Comedians* in December 1880 and the serial publication of *Diana of the Crossways* in the second half of 1884, Meredith began, wrote substantial sections of, but failed to complete *Celt and Saxon, One of Our Conquerors, Lord Ormont and His Aminta*, and *The Amazing Marriage*. By 1884, multiple, partial manuscripts of these novels, as well as of *Diana of the Crossways*, filled the limited shelf space of his garden chalet, becoming so mixed up that even now passages that clearly belong in a particular book turn up in one of the others. Meredith was thinking hard about the nature of fiction, about how he could avoid the pitfalls encountered in the writing of *The Tragic Comedians*, and about how he could modify the novel form in a way that would more satisfy his sensibility than did the traditional three-decker. Although Meredith insisted on living in the Home Counties rather than in London, he was by no means out of touch. He knew that Thomas Hardy was beginning to produce his strongest work; he knew that George Gissing was beginning to write what, in England, was a new type of fiction; he knew both men personally and exchanged books with them. He also knew as much as anyone about Continental European fiction and the troubles and excitement caused by the work of writers like Zola, Ibsen, Turgenev, Alphonse Daudet, Bourget, and others. He knew, in other words, that he was far from being alone in his desire to liberate the novel from its mid-century mold. But he did not immediately find his way. He had domestic problems and problems of health. His wife began to feel the effects of the cancer that eventually killed her (on 17 September 1885); he began to be affected by the spinal malady that later crippled him. He had been working too hard at too many things. He had to slow down; he had to give things up, including his long walks and his wine. So a few years slipped by without his being able to publish a new work.

Out of the confusion of these years, though, Meredith found the strength to take up the manuscript of *Diana of the Crossways* and during 1884 to finish it. The novel was based on the story of Mrs. Caroline Norton, a wit and beauty, granddaughter of the Irish dramatist Richard Brinsley Sheridan: her husband had accused Lord Melbourne, the prime minister, of having seduced her and had taken him to law; later it was rumored that Mrs. Norton was the person who had betrayed the secret of the cabinet's decision to repeal the Corn Laws to the *Times* in December 1845, causing a crisis that obliged Peel to resign as prime minister, and that she had gotten the news from Sidney Herbert, who was her lover. In the novel, Caroline Norton became Diana Warwick and Sidney Herbert became Percy Dacier. This sort of thing interested Meredith because it permitted exploration of public and private motive, the interrelationship of politics and love, and the impingement of feeling upon practical intelligence. Also, the story existed as a set of rumors: no one knew precisely what had happened. Lord Melbourne had been acquitted; Sidney Herbert had not been openly accused of treachery. Here, then, was the basis in real life for a story in which motive could be sharply analyzed at a point of crisis. Because Meredith introduced into the novel recognizable portraits of other real people, some of whom were still alive (notably his old friends Sir Alexander and Lady Duff Gordon), he later had to issue the disclaimer which is now to be found at the beginning of the novel: "A lady of high distinction for wit and beauty, the daughter of an illustrious Irish House, came under the shadow of calumny. It has latterly been examined and exposed as baseless. The story of *Diana of the Crossways* is to be read as

fiction." This disclaimer, written to appease Meredith's friends, is of little interest now because Meredith, as usual, had transcended his source material. *Diana of the Crossways* cannot be understood by reference to the actual historical situation on which it was based. The novel is powerfully—if sometimes obscurely—written, and the characters are drawn with great vitality; in addition, Meredith at last found a means of uniting plot with the analysis of character, so that the plot could not be disposed of by the reader as mere melodrama, or the analysis of character be condemned as complexity for complexity's sake. Here the motives were complex and Meredith's disposition of events was correspondingly subtle. So in *Diana of the Crossways* there is a necessary connection between motive and event, captured with both power and sophistication.

Meredith did not immediately see the full potential of his material: as usual, he discovered what he had to do in the course of doing it. He had the partial manuscript he had put aside a few years earlier; during the winter of 1883-1884, he took this up and tried to write the serial version for the *Fortnightly Review*. The early parts of the novel appeared in eight issues of the magazine beginning in June and ending in December 1884, at which point the reader was abruptly told: "Thus was the erratic woman stricken; and those who care for more of Diana of the Crossways will find it in the extended chronicle." In other words, the serial version would not be continued, so the reader would have to buy the novel in book form. There is no more striking example than this of a Victorian novelist breaking with a convention that had shackled him. The novel, however, had not yet been completed; indeed, Meredith had immediately started to give it a new shape as he rewrote the early magazine parts in order to create a new manuscript for his publisher. This meant that for many months different parts of the novel were not consistent with each other, Meredith having a strenuous time refashioning his material and giving it the unity it now has. Thus one can see the stages by which his imagination moved away from clever reportage to a type of fiction full of insight and compassion. Broadly speaking, in the winter of 1883-1884 Meredith wrote a novel about a woman who compromises herself with a cabinet member, a novel in which he could raise topical questions about marriage, as he said was his intention. And *Diana of the Crossways* remains one of the most challenging, disturbing marriage novels of the Victorian period. In 1884-1885, he rewrote the book, reducing the importance of the allusions to the repeal of the Corn Laws and reducing the emphasis on the moral dilemma of the woman compromised by a foolish action, but increasing the psychological interest by not concluding with her consequent breakdown and death, so that the implications of her action could be thoroughly examined. Meredith, in rewriting *Diana of the Crossways*, had achieved a breakthrough. Not only had he written a novel whose whole spirit was compatible with the recently passed "Married Woman's Property Act" and the public feeling associated with it, he had also convincingly moved his focus from the moral to the psychological, so that Diana became a person to be understood rather than to be judged. The novel was an immediate success.

With *Diana of the Crossways*, Meredith had finally achieved independence from the Victorian magazine. *Evan Harrington* had been written for *Once a Week*; *Vittoria* and *Beauchamp's Career* had both been serialized in the *Fortnightly Review*; *The Egoist* had appeared in the Glasgow *Herald*, but not on Meredith's initiative. Now with *Diana of the Crossways* he had actually written a novel that defied serialization; that is, it lacked the episodic character appropriate to a serial, having instead the unity and flow of an action that occurred much more within the heads of the characters than in sensational events. The success of *Diana of the Crossways* also coincided with Chapman and Hall's decision to publish a collected edition of Meredith's works in 1885. Technological and commercial factors had combined to reduce the unit cost of a book, with the consequence that the reader could buy the book for himself, rather than borrow it one volume at a time from a circulating library. *The Egoist* sold at thirty-one shillings and sixpence, the standard price for a three-volume novel: the volumes in Chapman and Hall's collected edition sold at six shillings or three shillings and sixpence, depending upon the quality of the paper. These volumes could be purchased separately or together. More people could afford to buy Meredith's work, and they did. This collected edition of 1885 was bought by Roberts Brothers of Boston and brought to the attention of a wide American readership by a mail-order sales technique, so much so that, having at first merely sold the copies they had bought in sheets from Chapman and Hall, Roberts Brothers began to print copies of their own and to sell large numbers. Meredith saw that he was no longer at the mercy of British moral prejudice and the cult of respectability. His popularity in the United States increased rapidly to the extent that, a few years later, Ameri-

Lady Duff Gordon, the model for Lady Dunstane in Diana of the Crossways

can publishers' agents, stimulated by impending changes in American copyright law, began to bid for the first refusal of his new work and for the right to republish his old. Because he had work on the shelf, as well as in his head, he was able to respond to this changed situation.

Meredith had for so many years attempted to accommodate the middle-class reader that it was a great relief no longer to have to do so; now he could write as he wished. He had always avoided the explicit: very few characters in a Meredith novel fully understand the situation in which they find themselves; nor is the author often willing to offer a simple explanation for a complex situation. He did not believe in simple explanations: a character motivated only by the desire for money, position, or political power, or one guided exclusively by moral principle, would not become the subject of a Meredith novel, or if he did, his position would be represented as complicated by other factors, not all of which he would himself understand. This technique of Meredith's often left readers exasperated. "If he knows what is happening, why does he not tell us?," some would say. In the novels of the 1880s and 1890s, Meredith took this technique several stages further by writing not about what characters did, but about what other characters thought they did; not about what was understood, but what was thought to be understood; not about total and clear explanations of behavior, but about partial and opaque explanations; not about absolutes, but about that shifting, unstable, difficult world in which the relationship between one person and another is rarely fixed or totally comprehensible. In order to transfer to the page his sense of the instability of human relationships, Meredith became interested in what he frequently (in these last novels) called gossip. (In *The Amazing Marriage* one of the narrators is Dame Gossip.) The reader gets to know, not what the novelist thinks is true, but what the character thinks is true. The character, while not necessarily completely mistaken, is rarely completely right, for what people say about other people is inevitably gossip: opinion based upon insufficient evidence. By letting a novel consist of sets of half-understood events, impingements, and collisions and by letting the emphasis rest on what the characters do not understand, the novelist can remove himself from the novel, no longer disguising himself as the narrator who knows everything before it has happened. Thus is created the illusion of the characters having to thread their way through a maze of half-truth and inaccurate report, in a world in which separation, alienation, and breakdown are at least as likely as their opposites. In *The Egoist* the narrator was supremely ironical at the expense of Sir Willoughby Patterne, who could not understand the defects of his position; in *Diana of the Crossways* the reader does not have to cope with the narrator's irony to nearly the same extent, but is made to share Diana's bewilderment as she tries to relate to the people in her life. In the novels which followed *Diana of the Crossways*, Meredith further accentuated this flight from the absolute by adopting techniques of multiple narration, two or more narrators giving quite different accounts of the same events, as—famously—in *The Amazing Marriage*. In this way, Meredith made a radical advance in the art of fiction, discovering a technique more appropriate for the analysis of unconsciously motivated behavior than for the depiction of behavior itself. Always a psychological novelist in intention, he had now found out how to be one.

A reader who believes life to be informed by moral principle will probably not enjoy Meredith's creation of an essentially secular, unstable world in

these later novels, especially because of the emphasis upon acts of bad faith, breakdown, doubt, and confusion. But though his outlook was secular, antireligious, and intellectual, Meredith was not unprincipled, was not merely playing with what other people took seriously; on the contrary, he used the new type of multiple narrative to explore even more rigorously those matters which had always deeply concerned him: the springs of human character as they found expression in behavior and in relationships. On three particular concerns his emphasis was always deadly serious: the individuality which tended always to the isolation of a terribly exclusive egoism; the irredeemable nature of an action once it had been committed; and the concealed motive which could operate without its full force being understood. These three concerns were at the heart of Meredith's entire corpus, and now in his last novels he gave them a new, brilliant treatment.

First, the egoist: Meredith had given deadly portraits of egoists in *The Ordeal of Richard Feverel*, where the suffering of both Sir Austin and Richard Feverel derived from their belief in self, from their being confined within themselves, and from their inability to relate, fully or honestly, to people outside themselves. Neville Beauchamp, in *Beauchamp's Career*, had been another egoist, trapped within his consciousness of self, believing in independence of individual action rather than in the interdependence of people. Sir Willoughby Patterne, in *The Egoist*, was, of course, the supreme exemplum, the sun around which all other things in life were forced to circulate. Under attack here, though only implicitly in these early novels, was that mid-century, liberal idea of the freestanding individual whose rights vis-à-vis "society" were codified by J. S. Mill in *On Liberty*. Meredith's egoists would very much have agreed with the proposition that, provided they did no harm to others, they should be free to think and do as they wished—an attitude which disastrously cut them off from other people, both individually and in the mass, while creating, in effect, a new type of harm. The egoist is represented as being simply incapable of accepting the legitimacy of a contrary opinion: he knows how to dominate, but intimacy based upon reciprocal understanding eludes him. In the extreme case, this condition of the ego trapped within itself would give way to mental breakdown, as in the case of Mr. Pole in *Emilia in England*. In the later novels, Meredith presents a terrifyingly uncompromising psychological analysis of the tragedy of the ego. The businessman Victor

Radnor in *One of Our Conquerors*, confident, ebullient, virile, masterful, marvelous in so many ways, sees only with his own eyes and, as a human being, fails: he fails to respond to his wife's love, fails to try to understand her, fails to examine his own actions and motives critically, and fails to recollect why it was so important to be a "conqueror." He loses control, goes insane, and dies. The Earl of Fleetwood, in *The Amazing Marriage*, provides an equally deadly example. Total egoism is shown in these novels to be an alienating force: Fleetwood holds himself back from his wife, tragically preferring an intact ego to the give-and-take of a love in which neither person is dominated or wholly possessed.

Meredith saw, second, that if much in life is relative, an action is not. Richard in *The Ordeal of Richard Feverel* burns down a stack of wheat and by doing so unwittingly enters the world of other people's standards, the world in which crime will be punished and good actions rewarded. Meredith rarely let his characters exist only on the level of talk, even though it was mostly through their talk that the reader got to know them. In *Beauchamp's Career* the conflict of personal and political opinion is interrupted by the brute fact of one character horsewhipping another. Diana in *Diana of the Crossways* sells a cabinet secret brought to her by her lover: the public and the private are locked together; what does such an action mean and can one recover from it? In *The Amazing Marriage*, the Earl of Fleetwood deliberately insults and degrades his wife on their wedding day and, in effect, rapes her. Can a human relationship survive such an atrocity, and if so, how? Actions of this kind are irredeemable in Meredith's novels because the characters are not allowed to behave as though the action never occurred: Meredith was a nineteenth-century psychological novelist who probed human motives in relation to events, not a twentieth-century novelist who probes personality disconnected from "real world" occurrences. Diana never recovers her ground with Dacier, whom she betrayed; and it is only as a much changed woman, after a debilitating nervous breakdown, that she can to some extent repair her life in a relationship with a different man, who distinctly requires of her some surrender of egoism. In *The Amazing Marriage*, Fleetwood remains unforgiven; although the reader knows that he has come to love his wife, not everything can be talked away or repaired. (The different treatment given to Diana and the Earl of Fleetwood in these two important novels did not, of course, escape the feminist eye.)

Third, the concealed motive: Meredith understood that what motivated men and women in many if not all of their more profound relationships with each other was their sexuality, though the exterior might be moral or intellectual. But whether because of Meredith's own reserve, or because of the conventions of his time, the sexual is rarely given explicit statement. The narrator does not give explicit explanations to his reader. His characters do not give explicit explanations to themselves or to each other. Indeed they mostly do not know why they behave as they do, though they can observe easily enough that their behavior is not completely rational. They can observe their behavior, but they have no way to be articulate about the hidden springs of action. Meredith did not have the conceptual framework and the vocabulary of twentieth-century psychology, but he knew that what a man said to a woman or a woman said to a man could rarely be taken at face value, even, for example, when they believed themselves to be talking rationally about the events of the day. Thus, when Diana and Dacier talk late at night about the repeal of the Corn Laws, they are in fact making love, any subject of conversation being a possible vehicle for an intimacy that convention required should not be openly stated. Obviously Meredith was being characteristically Victorian, albeit in a masterly way, in making an art of what could not be said openly; and his predicament was not without its advantages, since his psychological insights could be expressed metaphorically, without simplification. Richard Feverel conceals his true feelings behind an expressionless face and, with an expressionless face, the Earl of Fleetwood conceals from his companions that one of his oldest friends has blown his brains out. This mask is in Meredith the image of the repressed self. Fleetwood is incapable of breaking down and sharing his grief with his friends; in the same way, he is incapable of expressing his growing love for his wife.

The last novels significantly confirm the direction that Meredith had all the time been taking, despite his forays into the comedy of manners. They all show a heightened social awareness, an increased tendency to take a humane view of human stupidity and error, a strong preference for psychological rather than moral analysis, and a sharp focus on the underprivileged position of women. *Diana of the Crossways* is the story of a woman who thinks she can carry all before her by virtue of her wit, her beauty, her energy, in an independent existence which allows her to flout convention, prize eccentricity, and patronize others. Victor Radnor in *One of Our Conquerors*, a man who early in life married a woman for her money and then deserted her for a younger, more spirited companion, believes that he can dominate existence, manipulate it to his own ends, and ride roughshod over other people's feelings, for their own good as well as his own. In *Lord Ormont and His Aminta*, Lord Ormont considers that he can possess his wife as a chattel without bothering to get to know her as a person in her own right. And in *The Amazing Marriage*, Meredith shows brilliantly how the arrogant, excessively wealthy aristocrat, who had been brought up to take for granted the fruits of others' labor, by a painful process learns (though too late) that his values had been ill-founded—were, in fact, wrong values. These characters are Meredith's typical egoists, but in his treatment of them there is a new emphasis: a somewhat right-wing author has moved significantly to the left; he makes his privileged characters become aware of the predicament of ordinary people, including the poor. In *The Amazing Marriage*, Carinthia Jane takes refuge in Whitechapel, where the sympathy and understanding her husband withheld are found in a greengrocer's shop. In the same novel, much hinges on her identifying with the plight of Welsh coal miners who are on strike and without means to support themselves. As the reader sympathizes with Carinthia Jane, he is moved to a democratic, not an autocratic, appreciation of events. Also, in each novel the debilitating arrogance of the egoist is counterbalanced by milder characters who, though by no means lacking in sensibility or intelligence, have settled for a more limited existence within the bounds of good sense and good feeling. So Diana is balanced by Emma Dunstane in *Diana of the Crossways*; Victor Radnor by his daughter, Nesta, in *One of Our Conquerors*; Lord Ormont and his sister by Matthew Weyburn in *Lord Ormont and His Aminta*; and Fleetwood by Gower Woodseer in *The Amazing Marriage*. Meredith addresses the psychological health of his characters, ignoring the merely moral aspects of the situations he creates for them. Diana's treachery, Victor Radnor's bigamy, Lord Ormont's incest, Fleetwood's abuse of his wife are not the subjects of the novels: the subject is in each case what happens in the mind of the human being trapped by events. Further, Meredith ascribes to the women characters a remarkable independence, in that they are not defined in these novels by social position or by their subservient relation to a man. Diana, Nesta Radnor, Aminta, and Carinthia Jane

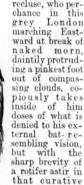

element of humour. It was a failure, but still passed with the public.—The Judge: A kind of elephantine humour?—The Witness: Quite so. I did not like it, but one would have to object to so much."

There the report of Mr. MEREDITH's evidence ends. Exigencies of space apparently caused the omission of a great deal of it. Fortunately it is in our power to supply this deficiency.—ED.]

The Judge. Quite so, Mr. MEREDITH. I may say for myself that I fully understand you. But perhaps it would be well to explain yourself a *leetle* more clearly for the benefit of the jury.

Mr. George Meredith. My Lord, I will put it with a convincing brevity, not indeed a dust-scattering brevity fit only for the mumbling recluse, who per-chance in this grey London marching East-ward at break of naked morn, daintily protrud-ing a pinkest foot out of compas-sing clouds, co-piously takes inside of him doses of what is denied to his ex-ternal bat- r e-sembling vision, but with the sharp brevity of a rotifer astir in that curative compartment of a homœopathic globule—so I, humorously purposeful in the midst of sallow——

The Judge. One moment, Mr. MEREDITH. Have you considered——

Mr. G. M. Consideration, my Lord, is of them that sit revolving within themselves the mountainously mouse - productive problems of the overtoppingly catastrophic backward ages of empurpled brain - distorting puzzledom : for puzzles, as I have elsewhere said, come in rattle - boxes, they are actually children's toys, for what they contain, but not the less do they buzz at our under-standings and insist that they break or we, and, in either case, to show a mere foolish idle rattle in hollowness. Nor have the antic bobbings——

Sir Charles Russell (cross-examining). Really, Mr. MEREDITH, I fail to follow you. Would it not be possible——

Mr. G. M. Ay, there you have it. In truth, the question looks like a paragraph in a newspaper, upon which a Leading Article sits.

Caricature from Punch *of Meredith testifying in an 1891 libel suit against Chapman and Hall. A man named Pinnock thought a dishonest character in a story Meredith had approved for publication was based on him. Pinnock won £ 2000 from the publishers.*

all break with convention or are outside it: Diana abandons her first husband; Nesta is illegitimate; Aminta clearheadedly opts for adultery; Carinthia Jane abandons her child, as well as her husband, to go to Spain with her brother. In each case, the woman defines herself not in the moral terms that would represent the opinion of others, but existentially in what she discovers to be her own personal response to whatever befalls her, irrespective of the outcome. When full understanding is at length achieved, Diana agrees to marry, as does Nesta Radnor, but Aminta chooses to live with Matthew in Switzerland while still married to Lord Ormont (symbolizing, incidentally, Meredith's emancipation from his titled characters), while Carinthia Jane rejects marriage outright and goes to Spain to work as a nurse. Meredith's contemporaries well understood that the restrictive or negative type of middle-class morality had been dealt a severe blow. He had successfully made himself a "modern" novelist.

Between 1885 and his death in 1909 Meredith enjoyed immense popularity. The collected editions—Constable's Deluxe Edition in thirty-nine volumes which began to appear in 1896, the Library Edition and its equivalent in America published by Scribners—allowed readers to assess his work as a whole. His later novels were recognized as brilliant. It was seen, retrospectively, not only that he had championed women's rights but that he had done so in a subtle and telling way. It was seen that he had espoused radical causes without resorting to a strident type of protest. It was seen that he had not only rejected the Evangelical morality of the period of

his youth but that he had moved his fiction toward an extremely humane but unsentimental appraisal of change, instability, uncertainty in both personal and social affairs. And it was seen that, though he had throughout his life been European in outlook and cosmopolitan in thought, he had remained a patriot, with an unquenchable love of the English countryside and an abiding concern for all matters (except party politics) that involved the welfare of the nation. Suffragettes cycled down to Box Hill to take his advice. Newspaper editors sent down messengers to obtain his views on international events. Aspiring authors sat outside his house on the lower slopes of Box Hill just to catch sight of him. Writers such as Paul Valéry came from overseas in homage and out of interest. Although Meredith in his later years went deaf, was confined to a downstairs room in Flint Cottage, and could eventually only venture out of doors in a donkey cart, with Cole the gar-

Meredith, crippled by a spinal condition, being taken for his daily ride in a donkey cart on Box Hill

dener and Miss Nicholls the nurse in attendance, he was nonetheless lionized, fussed over, and admired, at long last recognized for the cantankerous, willfully independent genius he had always been. Because of his lifelong agnosticism, which incorporated a pronounced abhorrence of the Church of England, he could not be buried in Westminster Abbey; a plaque was placed there as a compromise and his ashes were buried in Dorking churchyard, next to his wife's grave.

Finally, a word must be said about Meredith's extraordinary engagement with the English language. From the beginning, he had shown an immense liking for the well-turned phrase, the witty expression, and the complex sentence. He collected aphorisms and allowed his characters to collect them; he used them at the dinner table and made his characters do likewise. For a character to cap another character's witty remark with one that was wittier was represented as a sign of intelligence, something that distinguished him or her from lesser mortals. Sir Austin Feverel, somewhat ponderously, was addicted in this way; so, more lightheartedly, was Diana of the Crossways; so, philosophically, was Gower Woodseer in *The Amazing Marriage*. What Meredith's characters considered to be witty has often, by his readers, been considered meretricious and affected, especially when aphoristic fine talk is extended through a chapter or two until the reader longs for plain words, plain explanations. But although Meredith too often let his love of the neatly turned phrase get the better of him, it is only a small part of a mastery of the English language so complete that what sometimes seemed to others convoluted, difficult, and wordy, was for him the essential verbal instrument for the type of psychological analysis he was practicing. When the revision of *One of Our Conquerors* would have allowed him to alter those crucial passages that critics had found obscure, impossible to work out, perversely complex, Meredith not only declined to simplify but introduced new complexities. The complexities were not merely verbal, as perhaps they had been in some of his early novels; on the contrary, they were an integral part of the delineation of his introverted characters' minds. While he was popular, Meredith was recognized as one of the great masters of prose style; and attentive readers, prepared to engage themselves with the difficulties of the text, discovered with pleasure that he had not, after all, been merely verbose. Late in the twentieth century fewer readers, maybe, make the attempt; but for those who do, the rewards are just as great.

Letters:
The Letters of George Meredith, edited by C. L. Cline (3 volumes, Oxford: Clarendon Press, 1970).

Bibliographies:
Michael Collie, *George Meredith: A Bibliography* (Toronto: University of Toronto Press, 1974);
John C. Olmsted, *George Meredith: An Annotated Bibliography of Criticism 1925-1975* (New York: Garland, 1978).

Biography:
Lionel Stevenson, *The Ordeal of George Meredith: A Biography* (New York: Scribners, 1953).

References:
Gillian Beer, *Meredith: A Change of Masks; A Study of the Novels* (London: Athlone Press, 1970);
Ian Fletcher, ed., *Meredith Now: Some Critical Essays* (London: Routledge & Kegan Paul, 1971);
V. S. Pritchett, *George Meredith and English Comedy* (London: Chatto & Windus, 1970);
Mohammad Shaheen, *George Meredith: A Reappraisal of the Novels* (London: Macmillan, 1981);
Ioan Williams, ed., *Meredith: The Critical Heritage* (London: Routledge & Kegan Paul, 1971);
Judith Wilt, *The Readable People of George Meredith* (Princeton, N.J.: Princeton University Press, 1975).

George Moore

Susan Dick
Queen's University

See also the Moore entry in *DLB 10, Modern British Dramatists, 1900-1945*.

BIRTH: Moore Hall, County Mayo, Ireland, 24 February 1852, to George Henry and Mary Blake Moore.

DEATH: London, England, 21 January 1933.

BOOKS: *Flowers of Passion* (London: Provost, 1878);

Martin Luther: A Tragedy in Five Acts (London: Remington, 1879);

Pagan Poems (London: Newman, 1881);

A Modern Lover (3 volumes, London: Tinsley, 1883; 1 volume, Chicago: Laird & Lee, 1890);

A Mummer's Wife (London: Vizetelly, 1885); republished as *An Actor's Wife* (Chicago: Laird & Lee, 1889);

Literature at Nurse, or Circulating Morals (London: Vizetelly, 1885);

A Drama in Muslin: A Realistic Novel (London: Vizetelly, 1886);

Parnell and His Island (London: Sonnenschein, Lowrey, 1887);

A Mere Accident (London: Vizetelly, 1887; New York: Brentano, 1887);

Confessions of a Young Man (London: Sonnenschein, Lowrey, 1888; New York: Brentano, 1888);

Spring Days: A Realistic Novel–A Prelude to Don Juan (London: Vizetelly, 1888); republished as *Shifting Love* (Chicago: Wilson, 1891);

Mike Fletcher: A Novel (London: Ward & Downey, 1889; New York: Minerva, 1889);

Impressions and Opinions (London: Nutt, 1891; New York: Brentano, 1913);

Vain Fortune (London: Henry, 1891; New York: Collier, 1892);

Modern Painting (London: Scott, 1893; New York: Scribners, 1893);

The Strike at Arlingford: A Play in Three Acts (London: Scott, 1893; New York: Scribners, 1893);

Esther Waters: A Novel (London: Scott, 1894; Chicago & New York: Stone, 1894);

The Royal Academy 1895 (London: New Budget, 1895);

Celibates (London: Scott, 1895; New York: Macmillan, 1895);

Evelyn Innes (London: Unwin, 1898; New York: Appleton, 1898);

The Bending of the Bough: A Comedy in Five Acts (London: Unwin, 1900; Chicago & New York: Stone, 1900);

Sister Teresa (London: Unwin, 1901; Philadelphia: Lippincott, 1901);

The Untilled Field (London: Unwin, 1903; Philadelphia: Lippincott, 1903);

The Lake (London: Heinemann, 1905 ; New York: Appleton, 1906);

Memoirs of My Dead Life (London: Heinemann, 1906; New York: Appleton, 1907);

George Moore

Reminiscences of the Impressionist Painters (Dublin: Maunsel, 1906);

The Apostle: A Drama in Three Acts (Dublin: Maunsel, 1911; Boston: Luce, 1911);

Hail and Farewell: A Trilogy, 3 volumes (London: Heinemann, 1911-1914; New York: Appleton, 1911-1914);

Elizabeth Cooper: A Comedy in Three Acts (Dublin: Maunsel, 1913; Boston: Luce, 1913);

Muslin (London: Heinemann, 1915; New York: Brentano, 1915);

The Brook Kevith: A Syrian Story (Edinburgh: Laurie, 1916; New York: Macmillan, 1916);

Lewis Seymour and Some Women (London: Heinemann, 1917; New York: Brentano, 1917);

A Story-Teller's Holiday (London & New York: Cumann Sean-eolais na h-Eireann, 1918; 2 volumes, revised, London: Heinemann, 1928);

Avowals (London: Cumann Sean-eolais na h-Eireann, 1919; New York: Boni & Liveright, 1919);

The Coming of Gabrielle: A Comedy (London: Cumann Sean-eolais na h-Eireann, 1920; New York: Boni & Liveright, 1921);

Héloïse and Abélard (2 volumes, London: Cumann Sean-eolais na h-Eireann, 1921; 1 volume, New York: Boni & Liveright, 1921);

In Single Strictness (London: Heinemann, 1922; New York: Boni & Liveright, 1922); republished as *Celibate Lives* (London: Heinemann, 1927; New York: Boni & Liveright, 1927);

Conversations in Ebury Street (London: Heinemann, 1924; New York: Boni & Liveright, 1924);

Peronnik the Fool (New York: Boni & Liveright, 1924; London: Heinemann, 1933);

Pure Poetry: An Anthology (London: Nonesuch, 1924; New York: Boni & Liveright, 1924);

Ulick and Soracha (London: Nonesuch, 1926; New York: Boni & Liveright, 1926);

The Making of an Immortal: A Play in One Act (New York: Bowling Green Press, 1927);

A Flood (New York: Harbor Press, 1930);

The Passing of the Essenes: A Drama in Three Acts (London: Heinemann, 1930; New York: Macmillan, 1930);

Aphrodite in Aulis (London: Heinemann, 1930; New York: Fountain Press, 1930);

The Talking Pine (Paris: Hours Press, 1931; Tempe, Arizona: Hill, 1948);

A Communication to My Friends (London: Nonesuch, 1933).

COLLECTIONS: Carra Edition (21 volumes, New York: Boni & Liveright, 1922-1924);
Uniform Edition (20 volumes, London: Heinemann, 1924-1933).

George Moore occupies a central position in the transition period between Victorian and modern literature. He challenged many of the ruling assumptions of his day about the subjects and methods suitable to the novel. Because of his success in winning new freedoms for the writer and his introduction of innovative narrative methods, he is an important precursor of later writers such as James Joyce, D. H. Lawrence, and Virginia Woolf. After the turn of the century, Moore played an influential role in the Irish Literary Renaissance. In his last years, as the sage of Ebury Street in London, he welcomed and encouraged many younger writers. The focus of this article is on the first stage of Moore's career, during which he worked with great skill and energy to establish himself as a writer who could not be ignored.

The eldest of five children, George Augustus Moore spent the earliest years of his life at Moore Hall in County Mayo. He was not a precocious child; he learned so little at Oscott, the Jesuit boys' school to which he had been sent, that his father was persuaded by J. Spencer Northcote, the president of the school, to remove him. (Moore later liked to claim that he had been expelled after flirting with a maidservant.) In 1868, Moore's father was elected to Parliament, and the family moved to London the following year. Moore, who was then seventeen, had decided that he wanted to be a painter and attended evening classes at the school of art in the South Kensington Museum. Hoping to give his son at least the rudiments of a formal education, Moore's father sent him to an army tutor named Jurles. With the death of his father in 1870, Moore inherited the family estate, which would provide him with an income of £500 a year when he came of age. Then, Moore declared, he would go to Paris and study painting. He spent the three intervening years in London, where he painted in studios and worried his mother with his extravagant spending.

On 21 March 1873—less than a month after his twenty-first birthday—Moore set out for Paris, accompanied only by his valet, William Moloney. The six and a half years Moore spent in Paris were seminal years in his life, as his autobiographical novel, *Confessions of a Young Man* (1888), would show. For a time he studied painting and then, in

Moore's ancestral estate, Moore Hall, County Mayo, Ireland, as seen from across Lough Carra.
The house was burned out in 1923 by the Irish Republican Army.

1875, decided instead to become a writer. His interest in both arts led to his acquaintance with many of the painters and authors who made up the French avant-garde. Through Bernard Lopez, with whom he collaborated on a play called *Worldliness* (c. 1874; no copy has been found) and another called *Martin Luther* (1879), Moore was introduced to the writers and painters who were engaged in the struggle to establish new artistic movements and to free the artist from constraints imposed by society: Leconte de Lisle and Catulle Mendés, Parnassian poets; Stéphane Mallarmé, the symbolist poet; Édmond Duranty, a novelist of the realist school; Émile Zola, Edmond and Jules de Goncourt, and Joris Karl Huysmans, all naturalists when Moore knew them; and Edouard Manet, Edgar Degas, and Camille Pissarro, Impressionist painters. It is no wonder that Moore found the Parisian atmosphere so invigorating. When he was forced to return to London and Ireland in 1879 to look after his estate, he cast himself in the role of a returning pilgrim. Now he would give English readers the benefit of his sojourn among the French artists whom he had come to admire so much.

After spending some time in Dublin and at

Moore Hall, where the activities of the newly established Land League were making it difficult for his agent to collect the rents, Moore settled in London in the spring of 1881. In *Confessions of a Young Man*, he dramatizes the determination with which he now worked to establish himself as a writer. His second volume of verse, *Pagan Poems* (1881), was as bad and as outrageous as his first volume, *Flowers of Passion* (1878), had been, and it earned him for a time the nickname "Pagan Moore." Both volumes (which Moore later wisely disowned) are filled with echoes of the poetry of Baudelaire, Gautier, and Swinburne. His themes (paganism; incest; lesbianism; hopeless, and even necrophagous, love) were outlandish, his rhymes forced, his diction archaic, and his rhythms mechanical. *Pagan Poems* was abused so vehemently in the press that Moore withdrew the volume.

Moore soon realized that his talents were best suited to prose, not to poetry. He wrote to Zola, whom he then saw as his mentor, and visited him in 1882. He would become, he proudly informed the French author, Zola's "ricochet" in England. He was by this time publishing reviews, articles, short stories, and even a few poems in the journals; and

Moore in his early days in Paris, about 1875

he was working hard on a novel, *A Modern Lover*, which was published the following year. The title of Moore's first novel (which D. H. Lawrence later borrowed for a short story) heralds his intention to be both innovative and daring. The novel is, as later critics have shown, highly eclectic. Moore draws on his reading of Balzac in particular, as well as on his own experiences as an aspiring painter, to portray a young man who is amoral, ambitious, and—worst of all—successful. The novel is both a study of character and a dramatization of some of the ideas then current among artists and their critics. Moore's hero, Lewis Seymour, uses three women to further his career. The gentle and innocent Gwynnie Lloyd is a poor maidservant who loves Seymour and agrees to model for him when he appears to be on the brink of ruin. Seymour accepts her sacrifice quite placidly, and when she disappears out of shame, he is too preoccupied with the wealthy woman whom he has just met to make much effort to find her. This woman is Mrs. Bentham. She becomes Seymour's benefactress and, like Gwynnie

Lloyd, falls in love with him. She takes him to decorate her house in the country, her profligate husband being conveniently in Paris. Moore is cautious in his handling of their relationship, and the reader (like Mr. Bentham) suspects but cannot prove that they are having an affair. While staying with Mrs. Bentham, Seymour meets Lady Helen, whom he eventually marries. In one scene late in the novel, the three women gather to discuss their "modern lover." Gwynnie Lloyd, badly disfigured by smallpox, is now Lady Helen's maid; Mrs. Bentham is visiting them. The women are resigned to accepting Lewis Seymour as he is: "He was the same beautiful, soft creature, bad only because he had not strength to be good." The novel ends with Seymour, now a successful academy painter, gaining lucrative commissions through the calculated flirtations of the reluctant but acquiescent Lady Helen. Early in his career Seymour championed the Moderns, a group of painters who, like the French Impressionists, scorn the academicians and seek a "new aestheticism," a way to render modern life in their paintings. However, once he becomes successful as a fashionable painter, he renounces the Moderns completely. Unlike the other artists who appear in Moore's later novels, Seymour is an opportunist without any real commitment to art; his success comments on the gullibility of society.

A Modern Lover is an interesting beginning but not a good novel. Published in three volumes, it strikes the reader as padded and verbose. The picaresque plot meanders with little momentum and no form. Nevertheless, some individual scenes are effective and show that Moore could develop characters, and the events through which they reveal themselves, with considerable skill. The critic of *Spectator* praised *A Modern Lover*, but both circulating libraries, Smith's and Mudie's, banned it. Moore reported that he was told by Smith that his book was considered immoral by two ladies from the country, who wrote to object to the scene in which Gwynnie Lloyd sits as the model for Venus (the scene, Moore enjoyed pointing out, that the *Spectator*'s critic had singled out for praise). Moore already saw himself as the champion of new freedoms for writers in England, and this ban was a direct challenge that he soon welcomed. His campaign to eliminate the monopoly of the circulating libraries had now begun.

Smith's and Mudie's had exercised a strong influence over popular literature since the 1840s. They bought novels (typically published in three volumes and priced at thirty-one shillings six pence)

and lent them to their subscribers, who paid a guinea a year. The libraries refused to buy any novels that their readers, whose taste tended toward sentimental romances, would not like. Thus writers depended on the libraries for their sales, and the libraries were as powerful as censors. Close on the heels of the publication of his second novel, *A Mummer's Wife*, in the autumn of 1884 (dated 1885), Moore published an article in the *Pall Mall Gazette* entitled "A New Censorship of Literature" (December 1884), in which he recounted his troubles with Smith and Mudie. To his delight, an article appeared in the *Saturday Review* (13 December) in support of his position.

A Mummer's Wife would certainly have displeased the two ladies in the country had Smith and Mudie circulated it. In this novel Moore showed the lessons he had learned from Zola and the other naturalists by chronicling in detail the slow disintegration of his heroine's character. No Victorian writer before him had dared (or cared) to be so explicit in his dramatization of physical and moral decay. At the opening of *A Mummer's Wife*, Kate Ede is nursing her ill-tempered husband Ralph through one of his frequent attacks of asthma. Kate's life in this northern pottery town where she helps Ralph run a linen-draper shop is boring and confining. Dick Lennox, a member of a touring acting company, has rented a room in the Edes' house. His large, sensuous presence and easygoing, flirtatious manner appeal to Kate, and before long, she has eloped with him. They join the other actors, who soon discover that Kate has a good singing voice. She goes on stage and becomes a great hit. Soon, however, Kate must pay the wages of sin. Strikes in the north where the company is on tour diminish their audiences, and the company is forced to break up. Now pregnant, Kate (who has been divorced from Ralph) marries Dick. After the birth of their child, Kate's doctor prescribes a little brandy as a stimulant, and Kate becomes an alcoholic. Then the three-week-old baby dies of neglect. Kate's bad temper grows worse as she becomes bitterly jealous and accuses Dick of unfaithfulness. He puts up with her continuing cycles of drunken abuse and sober remorse for a time but eventually is driven away. Ralph remarries, Dick finds a bluestocking named Mrs. Forest who will look after him, but Kate has nothing to anticipate but a slow death. Moore records the stages of her decline with a precision worthy of Zola. Unlike Lewis Seymour, Kate is punished for breaking society's laws. While challenging Victorian sensibilities, Moore nevertheless upheld Victorian moralities.

Moore's intention in *A Mummer's Wife* was not so much to show punishment for moral transgressions as to illustrate the influence of environment upon character, one of the central tenets of the naturalists. For the epigraph, he used a quotation from Victor Duruy's *L'Introduction Générale à l'Histoire de France* (1881): "Change the surroundings in which man lives, and, in two or three generations, you will have changed his physical constitution, his habits of life, and a goodly number of his ideas." Yet the alteration in Kate is caused not only by a radical change in her surroundings but also by her character. Like Emma Bovary in Flaubert's *Madame Bovary* (1856), Kate has read a good deal of sentimental fiction, and this has determined her assumptions about life; Dick Lennox appears to offer her the way to the pleasure-filled existence of which she has dreamed. Kate cannot accommodate the inevitable

Pastel by Manet of Moore as he looked just before his return to Ireland from Paris (Metropolitan Museum of Art, New York)

return from dream to familiar and difficult reality. Circumstances, environment, and her character all contribute to her degeneration.

A Mummer's Wife quickly gained notoriety and even some praise, though often reviewers commended Moore for succeeding at writing a kind of novel of which they strongly disapproved. For example, the reviewer for the *Graphic* wrote: "It is the first thoroughgoing attempt, at any rate of importance, to carry out the principles of realism in fiction to their final, and possibly their only logical, result. Regarding Mr. George Moore as intentionally representing a school to which we are opposed, root and branch, we must nevertheless, bear witness, however unwillingly, to the remarkable fidelity and ability with which his work is done." The reviewer for *Society* singled out for special praise the scene in which Kate's child dies and added that "if all the book were as powerful as this, Mr. Moore might fairly claim the title of the English Zola." This was, of course, a title that Moore hoped to claim. Not only had Zola inspired much of his narrative, he had also, according to Moore, counseled him to publish the novel in a cheap single volume rather than in three and thus to undercut the monopoly of the circulating libraries. Moore assumed that the circulating libraries would not have bought his novel in any case, and he announced proudly in the fourth edition (1885) of *A Mummer's Wife*: "This book has been placed in the Index Expurgatorius of the Select Circulating Libraries of Messrs. Mudie and W. H. Smith and Son."

Moore had found a publisher, Henry Vizetelly and Company, who would aid him in his campaign against the circulating libraries. Early in 1885, Vizetelly published a revised one-volume edition of *A Modern Lover*. Moore included an advertisement for this "New and Cheaper Edition" in the pamphlet also published by Vizetelly in 1885, *Literature at Nurse, or Circulating Morals*. Like Henry James, whose "The Art of Fiction" had appeared the previous year, Moore argued in his pamphlet that English novelists could no longer be obliged to write for an audience composed mainly of young women. The novelist must be free, Moore stated, as James had done, "to describe the moral and religious feeling of his day as he perceives it to exist, to be forced no longer to write with a view of helping parents and guardians to bring up their charges in all the traditional beliefs." Moore included extracts from novels circulated by Smith and Mudie which were, he felt, far more risqué than the scenes in his two books to which the libraries had objected. After

each quotation he asks Mudie if "this doll" is not showing "just a bit too much bosom?" His spirited pamphlet was persuasive and a journalist for the *World* wrote an article called "Mudie and Nude-y," in which he defended Moore's argument in *Literature at Nurse*.

Moore had written much of *A Mummer's Wife* during the winter of 1883-1884 in Dublin, where he had gone to collect material for his next novel, *A Drama in Muslin*. (Earlier he had traveled in the north of England with the operatic touring company of *Les Cloches de Corneville*—a light comic opera, published in 1883, with lyrics translated by Moore—collecting material for *A Mummer's Wife*.) He was gathering information on the grand balls given at Dublin Castle, where young unmarried women found themselves on display in the annual marriage market. *A Drama in Muslin* was published by Vizetelly (in one volume) in 1886. In an author's note, Moore explained that this was the story of a group of girl friends, with the men merely silhouettes. He planned, he said, to write another book about a group of young men, in which the women would be decorative background. Taken together, the two books would picture completely, he asserted, "the young of my own time." The second book Moore foresaw here may be *Spring Days* (1888); in any case, the note makes clear Moore's intention to draw a portrait in his novel of individuals who would also be representative.

The "muslin martyrs" at the center of Moore's story are Alice and Olive Barton and Violet Scully. On leaving the convent where they have been schoolgirls together, they must face the inevitable question of marriage. Like Jane Austen, Moore skillfully dramatizes a society in which young girls have scarcely any choices to make in shaping their futures. The three friends must endure the boring and humiliating ordeal of the annual balls, where their mothers embarrass them with their attempts to put eligible men in their way. During the first season, Alice, the most sensible of the three and the main character in the story, meets and is attracted to John Harding, a novelist Moore's readers had met in *A Modern Lover*. Unfortunately for Alice, Harding is only visiting Ireland, and he does not return, as she must, for the second season. Alice shows her independent spirit by writing short stories which she sells to journals and also by secretly giving some of the money she has earned to her friend May Gould, who must go off to London to have her illegitimate child. Eventually Alice marries the intelligent Dr. Reed, lives in a house in London, has two children, and writes novels. In the preface to a largely rewritten version of the novel, *Muslin* (1915), Moore congratulates himself on having chosen "instinctively" the subject that Ibsen had dramatized a few years before in *A Doll's House* (1879). Though Alice settles down in her home instead of leaving it as Ibsen's Nora does, Alice has, like Nora, asserted her individuality within a society that seeks rigid conformity to its limiting rules. In *A Drama in Muslin*, Moore juxtaposes the domestic dramas with the political events of the early 1880s, the period in which the novel is set. The reader is reminded periodically of the Land League agitation, of the acts of violence against landlords, and of the suffering and poverty of the peasants. Moore takes sides with neither the landlords nor the tenants, for he is critical of the excesses on both sides in the bloody dispute, as he will be again in *Parnell and His Island* (1887).

As later critics have demonstrated, *A Drama in Muslin* is, like Moore's other early novels, highly eclectic. He has borrowed narrative methods or details from a variety of writers, including Balzac, Zola, Flaubert, and the de Goncourts. In the novel one finds not only passages in which the scene is presented in vivid detail (as the realists would have done it) but also passages which show Moore exploring the lyrical resources of prose. Probably the most frequently quoted example of the latter is Moore's description of the fabrics in a Dublin dressmaker's shop: "Lengths of white silk clear as the notes of violins playing in a minor key; white poplin falling into folds statuesque as the bass of a fugue by Bach; yards of ruby velvet, rich as an air from Verdi played on the piano. . . ." This is just the opening of a long cascade of similes. Moore is not giving his readers photographic realism here; he is evoking an atmosphere and a mood by appealing to their senses.

A Drama in Muslin angered many Irish readers who appreciated neither Moore's portrait of their society nor the anti-Catholic sentiments voiced by some of his characters. He was even threatened with a libel suit by the nuns of the convent portrayed in the opening scene: "their sex asserting itself through all their vows of celibacy, they gloried," Moore wrote, "in having been, at least, the providers of the brides of men." Moore cut the offending scene from later editions. In England, *A Drama in Muslin* was less popular than *A Mummer's Wife* had been; but, though banned by the circulating libraries, it sold well, and Moore felt that he had arrived as a writer.

In January 1886, Moore visited Paris with Edward Martyn, a young Irishman who became one of his dearest friends and served as one of the models for John Norton, the hero of Moore's next novel, *A Mere Accident*. Moore spent the summer of 1886 in Sussex, where he stayed with his old friends, the Bridgers, and completed a series of articles on Ireland which were published in July and August in *Le Figaro*. Moore referred to these articles, originally entitled *Lettres sur Irlande*, in a letter published in the *Times* on 12 August 1886. In his letter Moore begins by describing the censorship his books have been subjected to; he then declares with great gusto his intention to write from now on for a French audience and thus to "no longer expose myself to the risk of insult by having my books again refused by Messrs. Mudie and Smith." Librarians will not object to what he writes, he says sarcastically, "so long as I do not write it in English."

Lettres sur Irlande was expanded and published in 1886 in France as *Terre d'Irlande* and as *Parnell and His Island* in England in June 1887. Like *A Drama in Muslin*, it presents a far from flattering portrait of Ireland. The narrator describes, with the realist's attention to detail, the poverty and suffering of the Irish peasants. He accompanies a young landlord, newly returned from Paris, as he collects rents from his hostile tenants. The landlord anticipates Edwin Dayne of *Confessions of a Young Man*: he is an aesthete, still dressed for the boulevard, and his only response to the poverty he sees is to write a poem, "the chief merit of which," the narrator notes satirically, "lay in the ingenuity of rhyming Lilith with lit."

Parnell and His Island illustrates, as had *A Drama in Muslin*, Moore's movement away from the narrative methods of the naturalists. In it he experiments with the first-person point of view as a means to evoke the inner life of his character. He would carry these experiments further in *Confessions of a Young Man*. Moore wanted to draw his critics' attention to his reformation, and he published an article in *Time* in March 1887, "Defensio pro Scriptis Meis," in which he claimed that he had now abandoned naturalism and was concerned with creating complex character studies. This shift of focus from the external to the internal world is apparent in *A Mere Accident*, published in the summer of 1887.

A Mere Accident is set in Sussex, and Moore's description of the land reflects his love of the English countryside. Nevertheless, Sussex is merely the backdrop against which the story of John Norton is told. The forces directing Norton's life are internal ones and owe little to his environment. Though based in part on Edward Martyn, the character of John Norton owes a great deal to Des Esseintes of Huysmans's *A Rebours* (*Against the Grain*, 1884) and to Marius, the hero of Walter Pater's novel *Marius the Epicurean* (1885). In *Confessions of a Young Man*, Moore hails Pater as the fourth "echo-augury" in his life (following Shelley, Gautier, and Balzac, or Shelley, Moore's experiences in France, and Zola, depending on how one tallies them up). Pater's aestheticism, his focus on the inner life, and his exploration of the subtle nuances of sensation, all appealed to Moore, who had begun to recognize the limitations of naturalism. John Norton says his decision to write a history of Christian Latin was made after reading *Marius the Epicurean*; Pater's book has changed his life. "It seemed to me that for the first time I was made known to myself," Norton claims. Norton does not, however, know himself as well as this statement, made early in the novel, suggests. He has come home having turned contemptuously away from the world and will now convert his house into a monastery and devote his life to his history of Christian Latin. His mother, understandably upset by his plans, invites their neighbor's attractive young daughter, Kitty, to visit them soon after Norton's return. Before long, Norton finds that, quite against his will, he has fallen in love. He overthrows his earlier attitudes and becomes engaged. Moore then introduces a daring event into the novel: walking home alone on the downs one evening, Kitty is raped by a tramp. Moore dramatizes this event and its consequences with considerable skill by focusing on Kitty's thoughts and dreams. In these, one sees the abhorrence of the flesh that Norton had overcome in himself now drive the frenzied Kitty to fall from a window to her death. This is the "mere accident" that confirms Norton's belief in the "inherent misery of existence." He declares at the end of the novel that "the world shall be my monastery." Norton reappears in *Mike Fletcher* (1889).

A Mere Accident was not a success. The ending displeased many readers—including Pater, who, Moore recorded in *Avowals* (1919), said something to the effect that "the object of art is to enable us to forget the crude and the violent." Moore was disappointed by this critical reception but was too busy at work on *Confessions of a Young Man* to let it trouble him very much. During 1887 he divided his time between London, where he had rooms in Danes Inn, and Sussex. *Confessions of a Young Man* began to

appear serially in *Time* in July of that year and was published in book form in March 1888. In February he had sent a review copy to his friend, Edouard Dujardin, editor of *La revue indépendante*, and *Confessions of a Young Man* began appearing (in translation) in that magazine in March. A French edition, *Confessions d'un jeune Anglais*, appeared in 1889.

In *Confessions of a Young Man*, Moore combines fact and fiction to present a lively account both of his own life and career up to that point and of the artistic milieux of France in the 1870s and London in the 1880s. His hero, "Edwin Dayne" in the first edition, "George Moore" in all subsequent ones, suffers the same humiliations and disappointments that Moore had experienced, just as he voices with satirical excess the enthusiasms that had shaped Moore's career. Dayne returns from Paris proudly displaying the literary movements he has encountered there: "Naturalism I wore round my neck, Romanticism was pinned over the heart, Symbolism I carried like a toy revolver in my waistcoat pocket, to be used on an emergency." Naturalism, romanticism, and symbolism are also proudly displayed within the narrative of *Confessions of a Young Man*. Moore would later suggest that his portrait of "awful Emma," the maid of all work in Dayne's lodging house, foreshadowed Esther Waters, the heroine of the 1894 novel in which Moore again showed that he had absorbed a great deal from the naturalists and realists. From romanticism, and, to an even greater extent, the writing of the symbolists, Moore had learned to explore the lyrical and evocative potentialities of prose. Moore's reading of Edouard Dujardin's experimental works, *Les Hantises* (1886) and *Les Lauriers sont coupes* (1887) contributed to his own experimentation in *Confessions of a Young Man* with the method Dujardin later called *"le monologue interieur."* Moore excluded several of his early novels from later collected editions, but he remained firmly loyal to *Confessions of a Young Man* throughout his career (publishing nine distinct versions of it between 1888 and 1923). In it he had dramatized the period of his career which he continued to view as seminal. All that he had written after it, he would later say, was anticipated in *Confessions of a Young Man*. Moore's critics share his assessment of its importance.

As soon as he had completed *Confessions of a Young Man*, Moore began work on another novel. *Spring Days* (1888) was written in Sussex, where he was living on a rabbit farm with his friend Colville Bridger. Moore told his correspondent Clara Lanza that *Spring Days* was "the tale of a city merchant who is worried about his daughters—a sort of comic King Lear." Joseph Hone refers to it as an English suburban variant of *A Drama in Muslin*. Moore's intention, he later said, was to "recreate Jane Austen's method in *Spring Days*." Unfortunately, he failed to do that (as the unfavorable reviews told him): he lacked Austen's wit and her exquisite sense of pacing. Nevertheless, the book was not a complete failure. At the beginning of the novel the reader meets the Brookes family: Mr. Brookes, a widower; his three unmarried daughters, Grace, Sally, and Maggie; and his son, Willy. Questions of marriage direct the action, as they did in *A Drama in Muslin*. But after the introduction of Willy's friend, Frank Escott, into the story, the plot loses its sense of direction, for the focus shifts to Frank and his life in London. Willy's life intersects with Frank's enough to keep the Brookes family in the story, but Moore fails to integrate the two parts into a coherent whole. His real interest is in Frank Escott, who is a recurring type in Moore's early novels. A sensitive, self-centered young man who is something of an aesthete and a dilettante, Frank is extravagant and without any clear purpose in life. He dresses too well, indulges a belligerent bulldog, relies on the uncertain charity of his rich uncle, and proves to be more interested in decorating his studio than in painting or writing in it.

As in his other early novels, Moore is better at creating interesting characters, such as Frank Escott, than at shaping a lively and compelling story. One suspects that the failure of *A Mere Accident*, where the tensions of John Norton's inner life are central, led Moore to try his hand again at a realistic novel where action and dialogue are prominent. Unfortunately, Moore's failure to focus his attention sharply on a single line of action was a serious failure, and the book was not well received. Moore was disappointed by the cool reception given his *Spring Days*, but the success of various critical articles that he was publishing at that time in several journals kept up his self-confidence. He began work on his next novel; this one, he felt certain, would be a triumph.

In later years, Moore refused even to discuss *Mike Fletcher* (1889). (It is the only novel from this period that Moore never republished.) His ambitions for the book had been great: *Spring Days* was to have been the first novel in a trilogy, he later said, *Mike Fletcher* the second. Harding, the novelist from *A Drama in Muslin*, and Mike Fletcher had both appeared in *Spring Days* as friends of Frank Escott; now Moore would tell the story of these young men

who were trying to establish themselves as writers in London. Though a failure as a novel, *Mike Fletcher* is still an extremely interesting work. Fletcher is modeled in part on Moore's conception of the Don Juan figure: amoral, sensuous, restless, self-destructive. Through Fletcher and some of the other characters, Moore explores various ideas which were in the air in the 1880s, in particular the philosophy of Schopenhauer. Early in the story, Lady Helen (from *A Modern Lover*) commits suicide, and her death prompts recurring discussions among the characters about the rights and wrongs of taking one's own life. In the end, Fletcher kills himself, believing that in destroying himself he is destroying the world. *Mike Fletcher* is written in an energetic, nervous style, but the pacing of the story is, as in Moore's other early novels, far too slow. No principle of selection seems to have guided his choice of incidents. One can see why Moore's friends had been encouraging when he read them separate parts of the novel and then dismayed when they

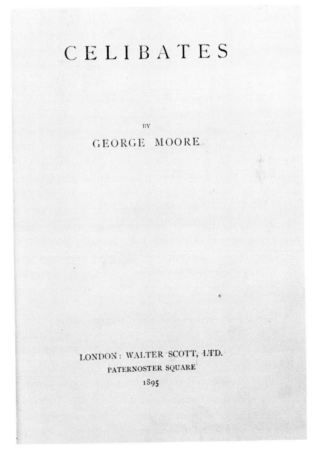

CELIBATES

BY

GEORGE MOORE

LONDON: WALTER SCOTT, LTD.
PATERNOSTER SQUARE
1895

Title page of Moore's 1895 collection of three character sketches. He published a revised version of this work as In Single Strictness *in 1922.*

read it as a whole. He succeeds in recreating the texture of the lives of young writers like himself, but he fails to produce a coherent and convincing novel.

After he finished *Mike Fletcher*, Moore again tried his hand at playwriting. *The Strike at Arlingford* was written in the spring of 1890 but was not produced or published until 1893. He then began to write a novel "all about servants," as he told Clara Lanza. "The human drama is the story of the servant girl with an illegitimate child. . . ." Moore was forced to put aside this novel (it would become *Esther Waters*, 1894) because of money problems. He wrote a short novel, *Vain Fortune*, which was published serially in *Lady's Pictorial*, July through October 1891; and he revised some of his critical essays and published them in *Impressions and Opinions* (1891), which was very well received. Moore revised the serial version of *Vain Fortune* and published it in 1891. He revised the novel again for the second American edition (1892), and then yet again for the second English edition (1895). These reworkings of his novel following so closely on the heels of one another indicate Moore's dissatisfaction with it. Moore may have felt that he had allowed "the senseless cruelty of nature" which, as Hone says, the story was meant to illustrate, to play too heavy-handedly with his characters, who are perhaps too much at the mercy of fate. Emily Watson falls in love with Hubert Price, an aspiring writer who has inherited the money that should have gone to Emily. Hubert falls in love not with Emily, but with Julia Bentley, Emily's older companion. Hysterical with jealousy, Emily kills herself, and Julia and Hubert receive the news of her death on their wedding night. Her act makes Hubert see the limitations in himself. He will never be a first-rate writer; all he can hope to do is to make Julia happy. Though in *Vain Fortune* Moore had not yet succeeded in joining the separate parts of his story into a single, coherent line of action, he had achieved here a more refined and restrained style than in *Mike Fletcher*. The novel has had its admirers, including James Joyce.

During the winter of 1891-1892, Moore returned to *Esther Waters*. At this time he was also the art critic for the *Speaker*, and in 1893 he published a selection of his articles on contemporary art and artists in *Modern Painting*. Moore was then friendly with a number of the painters associated with the New English Art Club, and he championed their work as he had that of the French Impressionists. Both groups, like Moore, stood opposed to any form of commercialism in art. The club welcomed,

he wrote, all those "who paint for the joy of painting."

Moore devoted a great deal of time to the writing of *Esther Waters*. The encouraging success of *Impressions and Opinions* had led him to wonder, as others did, if his strengths as a writer might not lie more in critical than in fictional works; but *Esther Waters* soon showed that Moore was still a novelist of importance. The critics were generally pleased with the book, and though Smith banned it, Mudie did not. Some compared the novel to Hardy's *Tess of the d'Urbervilles*, which had been published three years before and which also told the story of a young girl and her illegitimate child. Moore, like most readers, could see little resemblance between the two works aside from the basic situation. Through Tess's story, Hardy explores the harsh workings of fate; through Esther's, Moore anatomizes the hypocrisies and injustices of contemporary English society.

In several of his earlier novels Moore had experimented with narrative methods for dramatizing the inner lives of intense, sensitive, intellectual characters. With the exception of *Confessions of a Young Man*, these novels had not won him much praise. This may be one reason for his decision to write a book "about servants" in a simpler, more straightforward, realistic manner. Also he would avoid the weaknesses of *Spring Days* by writing, as he had in *A Mummer's Wife*, about one main character. *Esther Waters*'s drama is external; she must find a way to survive in a society that offers her negligible encouragement or support. The novel opens with Esther settling into her new position as housemaid at Woodview, a country house where racehorses are bred. There she is seduced by William, another servant, and when her pregnancy is discovered, she is dismissed from her job by the kindly but stern Mrs. Barfield. Esther returns home but cannot stay there long because her drunken stepfather bullies her and spends her money. She moves to a shabby rooming house and then to a lying-in hospital where her son, Jackie, is born. Upon leaving the hospital, she takes a job as a wet nurse for a vain, wealthy woman. Jackie is left with another wet nurse who nearly allows him to die. Esther gives up her job, rescues her son, and then finds work again as a maid. When William reenters her life, she breaks her engagement with a kind but colorless man named Fred and goes off to live with William. In the last part of the novel Moore dramatizes the hazards of illegal betting, for William and Esther run a pub where William doubles as a bookie. Moore drew upon his early memories of horseracing in Ireland to create vivid scenes of Derby Day. In the end, Esther is poor and husbandless again, William having died of consumption after a lengthy illness. Moore used to draw readers' attention to the scene near the end of the novel in which Esther returns to Woodview to work again for Mrs. Barfield, for it mirrors the opening scene. Esther's life has come full circle. Jackie appears wearing an army uniform and Esther proudly introduces him to Mrs. Barfield.

In *Esther Waters*, Moore generally refrains from intruding into the narrative to comment on its implications. The description of settings is skillfully done, the dialogue is sure, and though the events in the story do not display the inevitability one expects in a carefully designed plot, the novel is shaped with more care than Moore's earlier ones had been. The echo of the opening scene in the later one indicates that Moore is developing a greater sense of the importance of structure. Moore would always point to *Esther Waters* as proof that he had a social conscience. He had earned a reputation in the 1880s as an iconoclast and even a threat to public morals; yet here was a novel which led, he later boasted, to the establishment of homes for unwed mothers. In *Esther Waters* Moore criticizes society not only for failing to provide for girls in Esther's plight but also for allowing employers to impose inhuman working conditions on their domestic servants: in one house Esther must work eighteen hours and more each day. Moore had shown some sympathy for "awful Emma's" life in *Confessions of a Young Man*; in *Esther Waters* he dramatizes the servant's life from the servant's point of view. Esther is a significant achievement, for she shows that Moore can create convincing central characters who are not in some ways reflections of himself.

Moore published a dozen short stories during this period, only three of which were later reprinted (in *The Untilled Field*, 1903). It may have been his experiments with this genre which led him to write three separate character sketches and publish them together in his book *Celibates* (1895). One of the portraits in *Celibates*, "John Norton," is a revision of *A Mere Accident*. Moore condensed the story somewhat and altered the rape scene (perhaps with Pater's comment in mind) to make it shorter and less explicit. The other two stories are new. "Mildred Lawson," the longest and most ambitious of the three stories, is also the most disappointing. James Joyce told his brother that he was translating

"Mildred Lawson" into Italian, and the opening scene in which Mildred lies in bed thinking about the events of the past day probably contributed to Joyce's experiments with quoted and narrated monologue. One wishes that Moore had gone further with his own explorations into the potentialities of this narrative method. "Mildred Lawson" disappoints because after beginning it in this promising way, Moore shifts his attention too often away from Mildred's thoughts to her actions. As in some of his other early novels, Moore fails to develop a plot with any momentum or shape. He includes too many incidents developed at too great length. Also, Moore seems uncertain in his treatment of Mildred: is she a woman who cannot love, a woman capable of love if she can find the right man, or a femme fatale who enjoys making men unhappy? At various points in the story each of these descriptions of her is appropriate. "Agnes Lahens" raises fewer questions in the reader's mind. Agnes Lahens resembles some of Henry James's young heroines in that she is caught between the emotional demands of her parents and is required to make a choice before she is old enough to understand its consequences. Agnes is brought home at sixteen from the convent where she has been educated. There she finds herself in the company of her worldly mother, her mother's lover of ten years, and their decadent friends. When she can, she sneaks upstairs to the garret, where her father, who must depend upon the meager charity of his wife, does typewriting for money. In the end, Agnes escapes back to the convent; her father has asserted his place in the household, but Agnes has seen enough of domestic life to know that it is not for her. Unlike Mildred Lawson and John Norton, Agnes Lahens is not so much a natural celibate as one whose celibacy has been imposed by circumstances.

"Mildred Lawson" is the most interesting story in *Celibates* because of the skill with which Moore portrays the unresolved tensions of Mildred's inner life. "Agnes Lahens," though offering less scope for the rendering of complex emotional states, is the most carefully structured of the three. The reviewers were not enthusiastic about *Celibates*, but it continued to interest Moore, and he published a revised version, *In Single Strictness*, in 1922 (republished as *Celibate Lives* in 1927). By the time the reviews came out, Moore was deeply engaged in writing his next novel, *Evelyn Innes* (1898), the last one he would have published in the nineteenth century.

Evelyn Innes was the most ambitious novel that

Moore and W. B. Yeats at Coole Park, the home of Yeats's friend Lady Gregory

Moore had yet undertaken. Evelyn would be first an opera singer and then a nun, and Moore had to learn about both of these very different occupations. Already an enthusiast of Wagner, Moore turned to his new friend, the poet and critic Arthur Symons, to supplement his knowledge of opera. Through another friend, Moore met Mrs. Virginia Crawford, who was able to help him to write accurately and sympathetically (as he had not done in *A Drama in Muslin*) about convent life. Moore dedicated *Evelyn Innes* to Symons and W. B. Yeats, "two contemporary writers with whom I am in sympathy." Moore had met Yeats in London earlier in the 1890s at the Cheshire Cheese restaurant and was now reacquainted with him. He was also seeing his old friend Edward Martyn, who in 1897 was planning the Irish Literary Theatre, a group which both Yeats and Moore would help to direct. The influence of his Irish friends, Yeats in particular, is reflected in *Evelyn Innes* in the character of Ulick Dean, a musician who, like Yeats, is interested in Celtic mythology and the poetry of Blake, and who believes in "continuous revelation." Joseph Hone sees the two strands in Moore's life at this time represented in the two men with whom Evelyn is in love: Sir Owen Asher, a self-centered, educated, worldly man who lacks "the religious instinct" and is puzzled by Evelyn's Catholicism, reflects the social phase of Moore's life in London; Ulick Dean, who counters Owen's materialism with his spiritualism,

anticipates, Hone feels, Moore's return to Ireland.

Moore eventually split *Evelyn Innes* into two novels, *Evelyn Innes* and *Sister Teresa* (1901). In the first, he traces Evelyn's life from the time that she meets and falls in love with Sir Owen and goes away with him to study singing in Paris to the period of crisis which comes several years later when Evelyn must decide whether she will marry and whether she will give up her successful career. In the sequel, Evelyn follows the impulse which is beginning to develop at the end of the first novel and gives up both marriage and career to become Sister Teresa. In *Evelyn Innes* Moore portrays, with considerable skill, the conflict within his characters between intellect and emotion. He also speaks far more openly than he has done before of sexual passion. While he was writing *Evelyn Innes*, Smith's finally agreed to circulate *Esther Waters*, admitting as they did so that they had lost a large sum of money by banning Moore's popular book. This triumph may have encouraged Moore to be as open in his dramatization of Evelyn's passions as he wished to be. Moore has been praised for the knowledge of both opera and early Christian music (Evelyn's father's enthusiasm) that he displays in this novel; he makes especially good use of his familiarity with Wagner's operas. Evelyn often stages episodes in her own life as if they were scenes from the operas in which she sings. As she seeks to discover what she really wants in life, she slowly frees herself from her habit of playing roles, offstage as well as on. The inconsistencies one finds in Evelyn's character are essential to it; Moore has made great strides since "Mildred Lawson" in creating a complex female character.

As the century came to an end, so did a stage in Moore's career. In 1898 and 1899 he became increasingly involved in the activities of the Irish Literary Theatre. He reworked Edward Martyn's play *The Tale of a Town* (with some help from Yeats), and it was published, as *The Bending of the Bough*, in January 1900 and produced by the Irish Literary Theatre in February. Early in the following year, Moore, who was deeply upset by England's role in the Boer War, decided to move to Dublin. He settled in a house in Ely Place and lived there for the next ten years, a period brilliantly recounted in his autobiography, *Hail and Farewell* (1911-1914). This phase of Moore's career, as well as the twenty years following it when he again lived in London, is outside the scope of this volume. Moore continued to be a prolific writer: he would publish over two dozen more works—novels, short stories, memoirs, plays, critical essays, and revised versions of earlier works—before his death at the age of eighty. Though Moore's later prose style is far more

Moore in 1908

polished than his earlier one, his later works (and his revisions of the earlier ones) lack the energy and immediacy, along with some of the weaknesses, of his early writing. When Oscar Wilde noted that "Moore conducts his education in public," he was correct, if not kind. Each early novel was a new departure for him; after the turn of the century, he experimented less with new narrative methods and concentrated more on perfecting a distinctive prose style. Present-day readers must turn to the flawed but fresh first versions of Moore's early works if they wish fully to appreciate the important contributions that he made to the evolution of both nineteenth- and twentieth-century fiction. These contributions have been studied in detail by literary critics, for though not as popular as they once were, Moore's works are still read, and his role as a central figure in the history of modernism has come to be clearly recognized. "If we want to find out what the literary scene looked like to a young man of advanced tastes in the eighties and nineties," Graham Hough has written, "we can hardly do better than look at [Moore's] early works." Jean C. Noël's thoroughly researched critical biography, *George Moore: L'homme et l'oeuvre* (1966); Helmut Gerber's annotated collection of letters, *George Moore in Transition* (1968); and Edwin Gilcher's excellent bibliography (1970) have provided expanded knowledge of Moore's life and work. Two collections of essays, *George Moore's Mind and Art* (1968) and *The Man of Wax* (1971), contain a number of useful studies of Moore's early works, including essays on his literary debts to other writers, on the importance of Wagnerism in his work, on his short stories, and on his role as spokesman of the 1880s and 1890s. Recent reprints of some of his early books, including the infamous poems, testify to Moore's enduring appeal to both readers and scholars.

Other:

Emile Zola, *Piping Hot! (Pot-Bouille)*, preface by Moore (London: Vizetelly, 1885);

Zola, *The Rush for the Spoil (La Curée)*, preface by Moore (London: Vizetelly, 1886);

"The Fool's Hour, the First Act of a Comedy by John Oliver Hobbes and George Moore," in *The Yellow Book*, volume 1 (London: Elkin Mathews & John Lane, 1894; Boston: Copeland & Day, 1894);

Fedor Dostoevski, *Poor Folk*, introduction by Moore (London: Elkin Mathews & John Lane, 1894; Boston: Roberts, 1894).

Letters:

John Eglinton, ed., *Letters from George Moore to Ed. Dujardin, 1886-1922* (New York: Gaige, 1929);

Rupert Hart-Davis, ed., *George Moore: Letters to Lady Cunard, 1895-1933* (London: Hart-Davis, 1957);

Helmut E. Gerber, ed., *George Moore in Transition: Letters to T. Fisher Unwin and Lena Milman, 1894-1910* (Detroit: Wayne State University Press, 1968).

References:

Susan Dick, ed., *Confessions of a Young Man* (Montreal & London: McGill-Queen's University Press, 1972);

Edwin Gilcher, *A Bibliography of George Moore* (Dekalb: Northern Illinois University Press, 1970);

Joseph Hone, *The Life of George Moore* (London: Gollancz, 1936);

Douglas Hughes, ed., *The Man of Wax: Critical Essays on George Moore* (New York: New York University Press, 1971);

Jean C. Noël, *George Moore: L'homme et l'oeuvre* (Paris: Didier, 1966);

Graham Owens, ed., *George Moore's Mind and Art* (Edinburgh: Oliver & Boyd, 1968).

Papers:

There are collections of Moore's papers in the British Library, National Library of Ireland, Brotherton Collection (Leeds), University of London Library, Fitzwilliam Museum (Cambridge), Bibliothèque nationale (Paris), University of Washington Library, Academic Center Library (University of Texas), Beinecke Library (Yale), Boston Public Library, Houghton Library (Harvard), Library of the State University of New York at Buffalo, Princeton University Library, New York Public Library, and the Berg Collection (New York Public Library).

William Morris

(24 March 1834-3 October 1896)

Joseph R. Dunlap

BOOKS: *The Defence of Guenevere and Other Poems* (London: Bell & Daldy, 1858; Boston: Roberts, 1875);

The Life and Death of Jason: A Poem (London: Bell & Daldy, 1867; Boston: Roberts, 1867);

The Earthly Paradise: A Poem, 3 volumes (London: Ellis, 1868-1870; Boston: Roberts, 1868-1870);

The Lovers of Gudrun: A Poem (Boston: Roberts, 1870);

Love is Enough; or, the Freeing of Pharamond: A Morality (London: Ellis & White, 1873; Boston: Roberts, 1873);

The Story of Sigurd the Volsung and the Fall of the Niblungs (London: Ellis & White, 1876; Boston: Roberts, 1876);

Hopes and Fears for Art: Five Lectures Delivered in Birmingham, London, and Nottingham 1878-81 (London: Ellis & White, 1882; Boston: Roberts, 1882);

A Summary of the Principles of Socialism Written for the Democratic Federation, by Morris and H. M. Hyndman (London: Modern Press, 1884);

Textile Fabrics: A Lecture (London: Clowes, 1884);

Art and Socialism: A Lecture; and Watchman, What of the Night? The Aims and Ideals of the English Socialists of Today (London: Reeves, 1884);

Chants for Socialists: No. 1. The Day is Coming (London: Reeves, 1884);

The Voice of Toil, All for the Cause: Two Chants for Socialists (London: Justice Office, 1884);

The God of the Poor (London: Justice Office, 1884);

Chants for Socialists (London: Socialist League Office, 1885; New York: New Horizon Press, 1935);

The Manifesto of the Socialist League (London: Socialist League Office, 1885);

The Socialist League: Constitution and Rules Adopted at the General Conference (London: Socialist League Office, 1885);

Address to Trades' Unions (The Socialist Platform–No. 1) (London: Socialist League Office, 1885);

Useful Work v. Useless Toil (The Socialist Platform–No.

2) (London: Socialist League Office, 1885);

For Whom Shall We Vote? Addressed to the Working-Men Electors of Great Britain (London: Commonweal Office, 1885);

What Socialists Want (London: Hammersmith Branch of the Socialist League, 1885);

The Labour Question from the Socialist Standpoint (Claims of Labour Lectures–No. 5) (Edinburgh: Co-operative Printing Co., 1886);

A Short Account of the Commune of Paris (The Socialist Platform–No. 4) (London: Socialist League Office, 1886);

The Pilgrims of Hope (London: Buxton Forman, 1886; Portland, Maine: Mosher, 1901);

The Aims of Art (London: Commonweal Office, 1887);

The Tables Turned; or, Nupkins Awakened: A Socialist Interlude (play) (London: Commonweal Office, 1887);

True and False Society (London: Socialist League Office, 1888);

Signs of Change: Seven Lectures Delivered on Various Occasions (London: Reeves & Turner, 1888; New York: Longmans, Green, 1896);

A Dream of John Ball and A King's Lesson (London: Reeves & Turner, 1888; East Aurora, N.Y.: Roycroft, 1898);

William Morris

A Tale of the House of the Wolfings and All the Kindreds of the Mark (London: Reeves & Turner, 1889; Boston: Roberts, 1890);

The Roots of the Mountains Wherein is Told Somewhat of the Lives of the Men of Burgdale, Their Friends, Their Neighbours, Their Foemen, and Their Fellows in Arms (London: Reeves & Turner, 1890; New York: Longmans, Green, 1896);

Monopoly; or, How Labour is Robbed (The Socialist Platform–No. 7) (London: Commonweal Office, 1890);

News from Nowhere; or, An Epoch of Rest: Being Some Chapters from a Utopian Romance (Boston: Roberts, 1890; London: Reeves & Turner, 1891);

Statement of Principles of the Hammersmith Socialist Society, anonymous (Hammersmith: Hammersmith Socialist Society, 1890);

The Story of the Glittering Plain Which Has Been also Called the Land of Living Men or the Acre of the Undying (Hammersmith: Kelmscott Press, 1891; London: Reeves & Turner, 1891; Boston: Roberts, 1891);

Poems by the Way (Hammersmith: Kelmscott Press, 1891; London: Reeves & Turner, 1891; Boston: Roberts, 1892);

Address on the Collection of Paintings of the English Pre-Raphaelite School (Birmingham: Osborne, 1891);

Under an Elm-Tree; or, Thoughts in the Country-side (Aberdeen: Leatham, 1891; Portland, Maine: Mosher, 1912);

Manifesto of English Socialists, anonymous, by Morris, Hyndman, and G. B. Shaw (London: Twentieth Century Press, 1893);

The Reward of Labour: A Dialogue (London: Hayman, Christy & Lilly, 1893);

Concerning Westminster Abbey, anonymous (London: Women's Printing Society, 1893);

Socialism: Its Growth and Outcome, by Morris and E. B. Bax (London: Sonnenschein, 1893; New York: Scribners, 1893);

Help for the Miners: The Deeper Meaning of the Struggle (London: Baines & Searsrook, 1893);

Gothic Architecture: A Lecture for the Arts and Crafts Exhibition Society (Hammersmith: Kelmscott Press, 1893);

The Wood beyond the World (Hammersmith: Kelmscott Press, 1894; London: Lawrence & Bullen, 1895; Boston: Roberts, 1895);

The Why I Ams: Why I Am a Communist, with L. S. Bevington's Why I am an Expropriationist (London: Liberty Press, 1894);

Child Christopher and Goldilind the Fair (2 volumes, Hammersmith: Kelmscott Press, 1895; 1 volume, Portland, Maine: Mosher, 1900);

Gossip about an Old House on the Upper Thames (Birmingham: Birmingham Guild of Handicraft, 1895; Flushing, N.Y.: Hill, 1901);

The Well at the World's End: A Tale (Hammersmith: Kelmscott Press, 1896; 2 volumes, London: Longmans, Green, 1896);

Of the External Coverings of Roofs, anonymous (London: Society for the Protection of Ancient Buildings, 1896);

How I Became a Socialist (London: Twentieth Century Press, 1896);

Some German Woodcuts of the Fifteenth Century, edited by S. C. Cockerell (Hammersmith: Kelmscott Press, 1897);

The Water of the Wondrous Isles (Hammersmith: Kelmscott Press, 1897; London: Longmans, Green, 1897);

The Sundering Flood (Hammersmith: Kelmscott Press, 1897; London: Longmans, Green, 1898);

A Note by William Morris on His Aims in Founding the Kelmscott Press, Together with a Short Description of the Press by S.C. Cockerell and an Annotated List of the Books Printed Thereat (Hammersmith: Kelmscott Press, 1898);

Address Delivered at the Distribution of Prizes to Students of the Birmingham Municipal School of Art on 21 February 1894 (London: Longmans, Green, 1898);

Art and the Beauty of the Earth (London: Longmans, Green, 1899);

Some Hints on Pattern-Designing (London: Longmans, Green, 1899);

Architecture and History, and Westminster Abbey (London: Longmans, Green, 1900);

Art and Its Producers, and the Arts and Crafts of Today (London: Longmans, Green, 1901);

Architecture, Industry, and Wealth: Collected Papers (London: Longmans, Green, 1902);

Communism (Fabian Tract No. 113) (London: Fabian Society, 1903);

The Unpublished Lectures of William Morris, edited, with an introduction, by Eugene LeMire (Detroit: Wayne State University Press, 1969);

Icelandic Journals of William Morris (Fontwell: Centaur Press, 1969);

A Book of Verse by William Morris Written in London 1870 (London: Scolar Press, 1980);

Socialist Diary, edited by Florence Boos (Iowa City: Windhover Press, 1981);

The Novel on Blue Paper, edited by Penelope Fitzgerald (London: Journeyman Press, 1982); edited by Michael Timko, Fred Kaplan, and Edward Guiliano, *Dickens Studies Annual Essays on Victorian Fiction*, volume 10 (New York: AMS Press, 1982), pp. 153-220;

The Juvenilia of William Morris, edited by Boos (New York: William Morris Society, 1983).

COLLECTIONS: *The Collected Works of William Morris*, edited by May Morris, 24 volumes (London; Longmans, Green, 1910-1915; New York: Russell & Russell, 1966);

William Morris: Artist, Writer, Socialist, edited by May Morris, 2 volumes (Oxford: Blackwell, 1936; New York: Russell & Russell, 1966).

William Morris was a man of abundant energy and many talents which he devoted to art, literature, and social justice. His life was one of constant creativity as designer, craftsman, writer, translator, lecturer, calligrapher, merchant, medievalist, socialist, typographer, printer, environmentalist, and pioneer in architectural preservation. His contributions to these fields were significant and frequently influential. In all of his endeavors Morris showed his devotion to beauty in nature and in the works of mankind and to the creation of a society in which mastery had given way to fellowship. He hated ugliness, the economic exploitation of human beings and of the environment, and the poor quality often associated with profitable mass production. He was best known in his day as the author of the long narrative poems in *The Earthly Paradise* (1868-1870), as the designer of attractive wallpapers and fabrics which were sold from his shop in London, as a lecturer on art and socialism, as a revolutionary socialist, and ultimately as the designer and printer of unique books at his Kelmscott Press. In his expository writings Morris used vigorous, straightforward prose. In his romances, however, he developed a style that enhanced the adventures of medieval men and women in distant lands and times by introducing archaisms, using many monosyllabic words, and employing a high proportion of words with Old English roots. Indeed, Morris maintained that the great influx of words derived from Latin and French had weakened the English language.

William Morris's father, of Welsh descent, was a bill broker in Lombard Street, London, to which he commuted by stagecoach from suburban Essex. He and his wife, Emma Shelton Morris, had a family of five boys and four girls, of which William was the

and lives. In his first lecture, "The Lesser Arts" (also called "The Decorative Arts"), he pointed out the social relevance of art and stated bluntly: "I do not want art for a few, any more than education for a few, or freedom for a few." This was "art made by the people and for the people, a joy to the maker and the user." "It is the province of art," he maintained years later, "to set the true ideal of a full and reasonable life before [men], a life to which the perception and creation of beauty . . . shall be felt to be as necessary to man as his daily bread." During the 1880s Morris published two collections of selected lectures, *Hopes and Fears for Art* (1882) and *Signs of Change* (1888), which gave reviewers a chance to commend or condemn Morris's opinions; the second book drew censure even from the Fabian Society reviewer in its journal *Today*. Cheaply printed copies of a number of the lectures were sold on the street and at socialist gatherings for a penny each.

Henry Mayers Hyndman had founded the first English Socialist party, the Democratic Federation (later the Social Democratic Federation) in 1881. Morris joined it early in 1883 and worked enthusiastically for it by speaking and by contributing to its newspaper, *Justice*, which began

publication in January 1884; but late in 1884 he and his supporters withdrew from the federation because of differences with Hyndman and founded the Socialist League. To its publication, *Commonweal*, which he edited, Morris contributed comments on current events, articles, poetry, and two works of fiction: *A Dream of John Ball* (1888) and *News from Nowhere* (1890). A series of articles entitled "Socialism from the Root up," written by Morris and E. Belfort Bax, appeared in *Commonweal* during 1886 and 1887, and in book form as *Socialism: Its Growth and Outcome* in 1893. It is a survey of social history from primitive society to "the full expression of the commercial period" and the works of Karl Marx. A "gradual shifting of the opinions and aspirations of the masses for bringing about the beginning of the Socialistic system" is, they feel, basic to any change for the better. "Armed revolt or civil war" could in no case "supplant the . . . change in popular feeling, and it must, at all events, follow rather than precede it." For the authors "the Socialism which we can foresee . . . promises to us the elevation of mankind to a level of intelligent happiness and pleasurable energy unattained as yet."

Outdoor meetings in various parts of London,

Kelmscott Manor, Morris's country home on the Thames near Oxford

especially on Saturday afternoons or Sunday mornings, were a recognized method of acquainting people with the aims of socialism. Morris participated in many of these meetings and would often bail out speakers seized by the police. On one occasion in 1885, while attending the sentencing of a socialist tailor for "obstruction" in the street, Morris joined the cry of "Shame!" and was arrested for disorderly conduct. The judge let him go when he identified himself as "an artist and a literary man"—an example of the unequal treatment caricatured by Morris in his play *The Tables Turned* (1887).

By 1890 tensions within the Socialist League and the dominance of its irresponsible anarchist section caused Morris to withdraw and form the Hammersmith Socialist Society from the league's Hammersmith branch; socialist activities continued, especially the Sunday evening lectures at which many notable persons spoke.

In the course of the 1880s the Arts and Crafts Movement, embodying many of Morris's ideals, came into being. The first exhibition of the Arts and Crafts Exhibition Society took place in London in November 1888. A lecture on printing given at the exhibition by Morris's friend and neighbor Emery Walker—a printer and photoengraver—included slides of fifteenth-century pages which resulted in Morris's designing a roman and a black-letter typeface inspired by incunabula of Venice and Germany; he used them at his Kelmscott Press to print fifty-three titles, from duodecimos to the monumental *Works* of Chaucer, on hand presses between 1891 and 1898. He devised over 600 decorative borders, initials, title pages, and ornaments for his pages, and the wood-engraved illustrations were designed by Burne-Jones, Walter Crane, and others. The unique appearance of these books inspired both enthusiasm and distaste, but in either case his example of meticulous printing could not be ignored. In articles and lectures he insisted that the current level of printing be raised by the use of good materials, intelligent typography, and coherent design. Since his time Morris's influence, directly or indirectly, on the book arts has been great.

When *A Dream of John Ball* began to appear in *Commonweal* in 1886, Morris entered upon a decade during which he wrote ten works of imaginative fiction in addition to all his other activities. In these works, dream, vision, fantasy, and adventure in known and unknown lands are given reality by the vividness with which Morris transmits to his reader the colorful pictures moving before his eyes. In two

of the tales Morris himself ventures into past and future England; in two others, free Germanic tribesmen and women resist incursions of Romans and Huns; and the remainder tell of journeys, quests, encounters, dangers, witchcraft, heroism, and love in realms of fantasy.

In *A Dream of John Ball*, Morris finds himself near a village in Kent in the summer of 1381 as Wat Tyler's rebellion is in progress. He hears John Ball, the hedge priest who was a leader of the insurrection, speak from the village cross about their cause and the future based on brotherhood they hope to bring about: "Forsooth, brothers, fellowship is heaven and lack of fellowship is hell; fellowship is life and lack of fellowship is death: and the deeds that ye do upon the earth, it is for fellowship's sake that ye do them, and the life that is in it, that shall live on and on for ever." "Man shall help man, and the saints in heaven shall be glad, because men no more fear each other." The approach of armed men brings about a battle, and the oppressors are defeated by the men of Kent. John Ball and the narrator spend the summer night conversing in the church near the bodies of the slain. In their double dream, the man from the future assures the man of the past that the fight against the unjust system will eventually be won, but that it will be replaced by the pervasive injustice of wage slavery: "Ye, forsooth, are fighting against villeinage which is waning, they shall fight against usury which is waxing." They both take comfort in the assurance that "the Fellowship of Men shall endure, however many tribulations it may have to wear through," and John Ball's name and deeds will not be forgotten. As the day dawns, Morris wakes on a wintry morning in nineteenth-century London. *A Dream of John Ball* was written amid Morris's most active agitation for social justice, and a message he gives both to John Ball and to himself is expressed in his meditation during a pause in Ball's speech: "Men fight and lose the battle, and the thing that they fought for comes about in spite of their defeat, and when it comes turns out not to be what they meant, and other men have to fight for what they meant under another name."

When *A Dream of John Ball* was published in book form, the last ten pages of the volume contained "A King's Lesson," a short medieval tale by Morris that had appeared in *Commonweal* in September 1886 as "An Old Story Retold." Matthias Corvinus, king of Hungary, demonstrates the harsh monotony of peasant toil to his shallow courtiers by compelling them to labor several hours in a vine-

Morris in the 1870s

yard. Afterward the king and a companion agree that they of the upper class live by robbing the poor, and that this injustice "is safe for many and many a generation."

Morris's commitment to socialism caused him to express himself in verse as well as in prose. His *Chants for Socialists* (1884, 1885) were set to well-known tunes for the most part and sung at league gatherings. In the pages of *Commonweal* between March 1885 and July 1886 he published a series of poems which, when collected and printed by Buxton Forman, formed his last verse narrative: *The Pilgrims of Hope* (1886). In it an earnest young man attending a socialist meeting is filled with the "love of the day to be" by Morris himself. Later, rather anachronistically, the young man, his wife, and her lover fight for the commune in Paris. The young man survives the conflict but the other two do not.

Though Morris had very little interest in the theater, he wrote a short play in the autumn of 1887 to be performed for the benefit of *Commonweal*. *The Tables Turned; or, Nupkins Awakened* consists of two acts—one before and one after the socialist revolution. Morris and his daughter May were in the cast. It was greatly appreciated in socialist circles, earn-

ing kind words from George Bernard Shaw, and was performed four times. The title indicates Morris's attachment to the works of Dickens. The first act, which takes place in Nupkins's courtroom, caricatures a scene with which the socialists, including Morris, had become familiar, in which the judge's sentences are conditioned by the social status of the prisoner; but the scene is interrupted by the outbreak of the social revolution. In the second act England has become a socialist country of cooperative communes. Nupkins fears for his life but is set to doing *useful* work—digging potatoes. The significance of this piece lies in the glimpse of the England Morris desired to see after the revolution had cleared away the powers of class, money, the courts, and the state to allow everyone a life of freedom, neighborliness, and rewarding work.

Morris gave a fuller picture of his vision of the future in *News from Nowhere*, which was published in *Commonweal* during 1890. As in *A Dream of John Ball*, Morris wakes, not in wintry London but in midsummer—this time in the twenty-first century—to find that his home in Hammersmith has become a guest house where he meets handsome, healthy young men and women in garments "somewhat between that of the ancient classical costume and the simpler forms of the fourteenth century." Money is no longer used, architecture with a medieval flavor is more attractive, social-class distinctions have disappeared, people live longer and healthier lives and enjoy the work that they do. London is greatly changed—the country has invaded the city, rather than the reverse. Morris, now called Guest, learns the details of the revolution and the subsequent changes from "Old Hammond," a vigorous centenarian who may be Morris's descendant. They discuss the great contrast between the evils of Victorian England and the stimulus of living in socialist England, where ugliness, anxiety, exploitation, and poverty have been replaced by happiness attained by doing useful, rewarding work in attractive surroundings. The latter part of the book details a four-day trip taken by Guest and a young couple up the Thames in a rowboat, with the object of assisting in the haymaking at a place on the river's upper reaches which turns out to be the village of Kelmscott. The manor, in its rural surroundings, is still standing, in significant contrast to the change undergone by his city home. During the trip they are joined by Ellen, who embodies the new life of the new age. What she says or does is "all done in a new way, and always with [an] indefinable interest and pleasure of life." She attracts Guest strongly

The Oxford Street showrooms of Morris's firm, opened in 1877

and her remarks often echo his own feelings, as in her frequently-quoted exclamation: "How I love the earth, and the seasons, and weather, and all things that deal with it, and all that grows out of it!" Guest-Morris's visit to the future ends as he is about to participate in a feast with a merry band of haymakers. Suddenly his friends can no longer see him and awareness of his presence fades from their faces. Sorrowfully he turns away, finds himself in nineteenth-century Kelmscott, and thereupon wakes in dingy Hammersmith. Yet Ellen's last mournful look seems to encourage him to continue to "build up little by little the new day of fellowship, and rest and happiness," and he adds: "If others can see it as I have seen it, then it may be called a vision rather than a dream."

News from Nowhere, perhaps Morris's best-known book of fiction, derives its title from More's *Utopia* (1516)—Greek, meaning "nowhere"—and shares it with Butler's *Erewhon* (1872). His view of England in the future differs widely from that of Richard Jefferies's *After London* (1885), with which Morris was acquainted, but it owes a good deal to W. H. Hudson's *A Crystal Age* (1887). The im-

mediate occasion of its writing, however, was Morris's distaste for the picture of the future given in Edward Bellamy's *Looking Backward* (1888). Bellamy described an urban utopia: a highly mechanized Boston in which the economy is nationalized, labor is done by a "workers' army," and life is organized to an extent that repelled Morris—hence his utopia of joy in work on the fruitful earth. *News from Nowhere* is subtitled *An Epoch of Rest*, indicating that Morris realized that changes might take place even in his happy land. For Morris, however, rest did not mean inaction but the full use of one's powers unhampered by the anxieties, discontents, and injustices of modern civilization. In regard to eventual change he wrote in *Socialism: Its Growth and Outcome*: "Socialism denies the finality of human progress, . . . any particular *form* of Socialism of which we can now conceive must necessarily give way before fresh and higher developments, of the nature of which, however, we can form no idea."

Opinions of *News from Nowhere* are numerous and are likely to coincide with the reader's hope for, or fear of, fundamental social change. Literalists who consider it to be a blueprint judge it severely. Others look upon it as a presentation in personal terms of Morris's often-repeated ideals for art, nature, and human life. Maurice Hewlett, in an early review, accused *News from Nowhere* of having no soul and of proposing "that Instinct should govern Reason." More recently, Lionel Trilling has held that the book states "the case against mind," that is, "that mind in its traditional authoritative and aggressive character" was not "in the service of mankind" but "that the authority accorded to mind leads to the negation of social equality" and that "mind works a personal deformation in those who commit themselves to its service." In reply to Trilling's expression of anxiety at the disappearance of the aggressive individualism necessary for excellence, art, and freedom, Patrick Brantlinger points out that "it is Morris's great strength to be able to imagine the forms which art and freedom might take in a world without aggression because [it is] without the scarcity and hardship which makes aggression necessary." "Morris is . . . willing to envision . . . an art not based on misery." Frederick Kirchhoff feels that Morris assumes that "a life style largely subservient to cycles of Nature can answer to the claims of the Imagination." "*News from Nowhere* is both an expression of Morris' visionary ideal and the record of his inability, as a man of the late nineteenth century, to achieve it." At the conclusion of his detailed study, *William Morris: The Marxist Dreamer*, Paul Meier

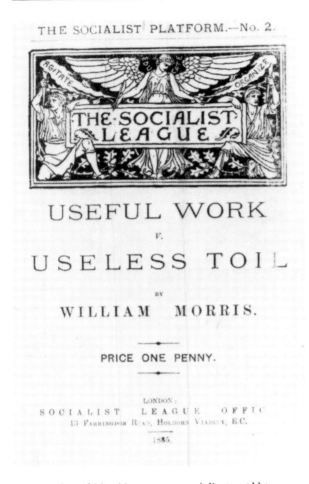

One of Morris's numerous socialist pamphlets

Morris in the mid-1880s, about the time he became a committed socialist

writes that in Morris's eyes "his utopia is neither a visible certainty nor an intangible ideal." "It is Morris's humanism, more than the detail or the general line, which makes *News from Nowhere* a lasting work. Utopia supports a scale of values."

A Tale of the House of the Wolfings (1889) and *The Roots of the Mountains* (1890), written between *A Dream of John Ball* and *News from Nowhere*, are set in less defined, yet still recognizable, times and places. In *A Tale of the House of the Wolfings*, a Gothic clan of about the first or second century A.D., living a free, healthy, uncomplicated life in northern Europe, is threatened by the approach of Roman legions who represent the forces of urban and imperial enslavement and corruption. Thiodolf, leader of the Wolfings, receives from his woodland love Wood-Sun a hauberk to protect him in battle. But the enchanted armor will save his life at the expense of his honor, so he rejects it, is killed in battle as his forces defeat the Romans, and lives on in the life of his people as one of their heroes—thus attaining the kind of immortality Morris promised to John Ball. The communal life of the clan, symbolized by their great hall, is of fundamental importance to this people, who live in a state of "upper barbarism" between savagery and civilization, as defined by Lewis H. Morgan in *Ancient Society* (1877). The idea of such an open, yet fully responsible, society attracted Morris, who disliked both anarchism and the "civilization" of the nineteenth century. As Carole Silver points out: "Morris found, in barbarian society, a culture in which human rights were not separated from human duties, a world without class exploitation." In *A Tale of the House of the Wolfings*, Morris experimented with the use of fourteen-syllable couplets as the form in which leading personages made significant speeches, thus making a transition from his metrical narratives of myths to his prose fantasy.

The Roots of the Mountains takes place in the fifth century A.D., when both Goths and Romans had to deal with the Huns. Face-of-god, known also as Gold-mane, a member of the House of the Face, dwelling in rural Burgdale near the Italian Alps, goes into the upland forests and meets there the beautiful Sun-beam and her brother Folk-might of the Kindred of the Wolf, whose home area, Silverdale, has been taken over by the cruel Huns. Despite his betrothal to the Bride, a girl of Burgdale, Gold-mane shifts his affections to Sun-beam. After leading the Burgdalers, the men of the Wolf, and other folk—including some female warriors—in a successful campaign of extermination against the

Manuscript page for an essay on printing by Morris

Huns, Gold-mane marries Sun-beam, Folk-might marries the Bride, and the tribes, who have discovered that they are kin, are united. In *A Tale of the House of the Wolfings*, several clans had united to defeat the Romans and thus evolved into a tribe; in *The Roots of the Mountains*, the tribe joins other tribes to become a people. Though some aspects of the earlier organization remain, prominent families are influential now in the government of the communities. Burgdale, lying between the upland forests and the cities of the plain, is lovingly described by Morris: its pastoral abundance and its cheerful folk who "trod its flowery grass beside its rippled streams amidst its green tree-boughs proudly with goodly bodies and merry hearts." "Thus then lived this folk in much plenty and ease of life, though not delicately nor desiring things out of measure. They wrought with their hands and wearied themselves; and they rested from their toil and feasted and were merry: tomorrow was not a burden to them, nor yesterday a thing which they would fain forget: life shamed them not, nor did death make them afraid." This passage indicates the relationship of the life of Burgdale to that of England in *News from Nowhere*, and it also is an example of the style which Morris adopted for these tales.

The romances which Morris wrote in the last years of his life, like the stories of his youthful days, have a medieval flavor but are laid, for the most part, in the far lands of fantasy, where mingled normal and magical events are expected and experienced. They are like tales told by a minstrel to responsive audiences who delight in folk stories and folk art, and who might weave them into tapestries or picture them on their walls. Following a different path from the science fiction of Verne and H. G. Wells, they have strongly influenced writers of fantasy such as C. S. Lewis, J. R. R. Tolkien, and many others. All of these novels share with legends and medieval romances the theme of a journey or quest, a device Morris had used most prominently in *The Earthly Paradise* and *Love is Enough*.

The Story of the Glittering Plain (1891) opens in a tribal community in northern Europe. Hallblithe of the House of the Raven searches for his beloved, the Hostage, who has been captured by sea raiders. On the Isle of Ransom, "a land of lies," he undergoes many trials. Eventually he accompanies an old chieftain, Sea Eagle, to the Glittering Plain, also known as the Land of Living Men or the Acre of the Undying—a land where the inhabitants gain immortality, permanent youth, and easy living; all desires are granted, all is harmonious; there is no adventure, no growth, no change. Hallblithe detests this slothful utopia (which is seen by some commentators as countering the England of *News from Nowhere*) and eventually leaves to rescue the Hostage from the Isle of Ransom and return to his home. Rolf and the Wanderers in *The Earthly Paradise* were baffled by reality in their search for a deathless land where they might live merrily, but when Hallblithe, also from the north coast of Europe, reaches it, his values cause him to loathe it and leave it.

In *The Wood beyond the World* (1894), Golden Walter has a recurring vision of two fair women and a dwarf. When he leaves his seaport home and his unfaithful wife, he comes eventually to the Wood, where he finds the persons of his dream. The Wood is dominated by the Lady, an enchantress who lures men to her bower but destroys them when she tires of them. Walter becomes her lover but is saved by the Maid, who also possesses magic powers. They escape via the valley of the People of the Bears, a primitive stone-age tribe, whom they assist in evolution from savagery to barbarism. Thence they go to the city of Stark-wall, where Walter and the Maid become king and queen and reign well and long. Thus instead of going forth and returning home, the pattern Morris employs in his other romances, Walter uses his talents where they are needed at the farthest reach of his journey.

Child Christopher and Goldilind the Fair (1895) is a shorter book based on the thirteenth-century English metrical romance *Havelock the Dane*. A prince and a princess flee from captors who are keeping them from their rightful thrones. After a time in the woodland, Christopher overcomes his enemies and gains the throne of his father.

Mention should be made of four romances which Morris translated from Old French. They are representative of the medieval tales which delighted and inspired him. He published them first at his Kelmscott Press in three attractive little volumes: *The Tale of King Florus and the Fair Jehane* (1893), *Of the Friendship of Amis and Amile* (1894), and *The Tale of the Emperor Coustans* in the same volume with *The History of Over-Sea* (1894). Morris recounted the doings and adventures of valiant knights and noble ladies in a style he considered appropriate to their time: "So King Florus of Ausay dight his departure and went his ways with a right great folk to come to the country of the fair lady; and when he was come thither, he took her and wedded her, and had great joy and great feast thereof."

Morris's longest and most elaborate romance, one that H. G. Wells called "stout oaken stuff," is *The Well at the World's End* (1896). The water of the well quenches sorrow, clears the vision, and confers long life, healing, wisdom, wholeness, and love. Sought by many and found by few, it has been described as a pagan Grail. Ralph, youngest son of a "kinglet," leaves his home, Upmeads (Kelmscott Manor), to see the world and is soon involved in the quest for the well. The towns through which he passes symbolize various tyrannies. One of them is Goldberg, devoted to moneymaking, "half marble and half slums," ruled by a queen who suggests Victoria. He is loved by the Lady of Abundance, a Great Mother figure who can create and destroy but who is soon killed. Ralph is joined by Ursula, a perfect companion; their adventures take them to the corpse-strewn desert of the Dry Tree and its poison pool, then over mountains called the Wall of the World to the well by the edge of the ocean. Strengthened and revitalized, Ralph and Ursula return to Upmeads, finding on their way improved conditions in formerly evil places. They reign long and usefully thereafter.

In *The Water of the Wondrous Isles* (1897), Morris follows the fortunes of an intelligent, resourceful young woman, Birdalone, who was stolen as an infant by a cruel witch and raised near a grim forest and a great lake. In the wood one day Birdalone meets Habundia, a supernatural "wood mother," who educates Birdalone and encourages her to flee from the witch. Birdalone sails in a self-propelled boat to the Isle of Increase Unsought, ruled by the evil sister of the witch, where three maidens are imprisoned. The maidens send Birdalone to their three knights at the Castle of Quest on the mainland. On her way, the boat takes her to four other islands where natural life is arrested. After the knights rescue the maidens, Birdalone and the knight Arthur are mutually attracted. She solves this triangle temporarily by going to Utterhay, the city in which she finds her mother and lives usefully as an embroiderer. When her mother dies, Birdalone travels in the magic boat by way of the Wondrous Isles, now revitalized, to her former home and discovers that the witch is dead. Habundia reunites Birdalone and Arthur, and the friends settle in Utterhay in a community of friendship, "their love never sundered, and . . . they lived without shame and died without fear."

The Sundering Flood (1897) is a mighty torrent which divides Osberne and Elfhild, who love each other as children. The story is derived from an Icelandic novel, and much of the tone of Morris's

Cover and first page of the Kelmscott Press edition of Chaucer's Works

romance is Norse. Osberne is instructed by the wise, immortal Steelhead (a masculine Habundia), who provides him with the sword Boardcleaver. When Elfhild is captured by raiders, Osberne leaves his rural home in search of her. She escapes from her captors and, accompanied by a magic foster mother, seeks Osberne. The latter follows the river downstream, passing through several stages of civilization, learning the lessons of fellowship and justice, until he reaches the City of the Sundering Flood, where he aids the Lesser Craft Guilds in defeating the king and the merchants, and in forming a socialist society. Eventually the lovers meet and return to the communal "upper barbarism" of Osberne's origins. Morris dictated the last pages of this book during the final days of his life, so it lacks the revision and amplification he would have given it. Nevertheless, it is one more clear presentation of the development in understanding and the integration of character that Morris's heroes and heroines achieve in his romances.

After a severe attack of gout and kidney disease in 1891, Morris gradually lost the robust health that had characterized him. His last illness was diagnosed as diabetes with other complications resulting in "general organic degeneration." However, Mackail quotes an eminent physician as saying: "The disease is simply being William Morris, and having done more work than most ten men." He died on 3 October 1896 in Kelmscott House, Hammersmith, and was buried three days later in the churchyard near Kelmscott Manor. Philip Webb, who had designed Red House for him, designed his gravestone.

For many years reviewers and commentators on the late romances of Morris tended to treat them as his furlough from reality, as agreeably adventurous fairy stories, or as tedious tales told in a needlessly archaic style. George Bernard Shaw remarked that Morris was attempting the "resuscitation of Don Quixote's burnt library." In their biographies of Morris, Mackail and Henderson pay the tales scant attention, while as late as 1967 Paul Thompson in *The Work of William Morris* spoke ill of "the silly language of the later romances." Others, who have looked beneath the surface, have seen things differently. In the *Spectator* of July 1895, the reviewer of *The Wood beyond the World* stated: "Mr. Morris preaches his Socialism in the most seductive and poetic form." H. G. Wells, reviewing *The Well at the World's End* in 1896, wrote: "His dreamland was no futurity but an illuminated past." W. B. Yeats, reviewing the same book in the same year, asserted:

"Almost alone among the dreamers of our time . . . he saw amid its incompleteness and triviality, the Earthly Paradise that shall blossom at the end of the ages."

As interest in Morris waned between the world wars, superficial clichés about his work became common, and his admirers felt isolated, according to C. S. Lewis, writing in 1936. In the same year, May Morris wrote: "I think that some day these romances will take their right place among Morris's writing," and it seems as though her prediction has come about with the rise of scholarly attention to them, plus the extensive spread of fascination with fantasy literature due in large measure to the influential books of Tolkien. Between 1969 and 1973 Morris's last four books were reprinted in paperback in the Ballantine Adult Fantasy series with appreciative introductions by Lin Carter, who considers *The Wood beyond the World* to be "the first great masterpiece of the imaginary-world tradition." In this way the late romances (the others have also been reprinted) have reached a wider public than have any other works of Morris. In 1976 the U.S. branch of the William Morris Society published *Studies in the Late Romances of William Morris*, the first collection of essays on this subject, and in 1978 appeared *Worlds Beyond the World* by Richard Mathews, an in-depth study of both the early tales and the late romances.

"In his romances," writes Roderick Marshall, "Morris created a world of exciting accomplishment [in a] world of purposeful adventure." The hero or heroine undertakes a quest in the course of which he or she experiences personal growth and renewal and becomes a force for liberation and justice both on the journey and in the place where he or she finally settles. "[A] process of personal and social rebirth lies at the heart of the last romances," states Carole Silver, and Barbara Bono sees personal growth as a microcosm for social development; the successful achievement of the goals of the quest gives strength for social regeneration. Current critics contrast the often deadly terminations of his early tales with the hopeful endings of his late romances. Peter Faulkner attributes this change of attitude to Morris's commitment to socialism, with which he gained "a renewed confidence in the ability of man eventually to liberate himself from the inequalities and injustices of existing types of society, and to achieve the 'society of equals.'" These stories "convey, through the adventures of their central characters, a clear sense of values which relates to Morris' most deeply held beliefs." It may be noted in passing that the styles adopted by Morris

Kelmscott House, Hammersmith, purchased by Morris in 1878 and his home for the rest of his life

to express himself in these and other works bother persons who dislike the works but are considered suitable modes of expression by those who favor them—if, indeed, they think to mention his style at all.

The prose of William Morris begins in his Pre-Raphaelite youth with colorful stories of love, deeds, and death at the same time as he was writing equally colorful and vivid verse. It continues with his lectures and articles on art, crafts, and social concerns and with his translations of Icelandic sagas and medieval French tales. In his own narratives Morris illuminates his social vision with visits to the past and future of England; describes the resistance of pastoral European tribes to incursions on their way of life; then, moving beyond the world, he traces the journeys of heroes and heroines in lands of fantasy and recounts their *deeds* (a very important word for Morris) leading to maturity for themselves and social regeneration for others.

The interest of the reading public in Morris's poetry and prose was fairly constant until the time of World War I. His *Collected Works*, edited by his daughter May, were published in twenty-four volumes from 1910 to 1915. Even during the subsequent decline of his literary reputation, however, a number of publications appeared at the time of the Morris centennial in 1934, and in 1936 May Morris published *William Morris: Artist, Writer, Socialist* in two volumes.

Indications of renewed interest came in 1950 with Philip Henderson's publication of a selection of Morris's letters and with the opening of the William Morris Gallery in Walthamstow. The William Morris Society was founded in London in 1955, and it soon spread to North America. Before 1960 Peter Floud of the Victoria and Albert Museum was bringing exact knowledge to the study of Morris's pattern designs; A. C. Sewter had begun his monumental work on the stained glass of Morris and Company; E. P. Thompson's immense biography stressing the socialist side of Morris had been published; and an exhibition of Morris's book arts, originating in London, had been seen in museums in England and on the Continent.

A rapid rise in the attention paid to Morris

became evident in the middle of the 1960s with the increasing numbers of books, articles, and dissertations written about him, his works, and his circle; by the republication of his *Collected Works* in 1966; by exhibitions and displays of his works; and by the soaring prices of Kelmscott Press volumes. Current methods of literary criticism applied to Morris's imaginative writings have increased the understanding of works formerly dismissed as ornamental escapism. Studies such as Silver's "Myth and Ritual in the Last Romances of William Morris," showing the effect on Morris of anthropological studies of mythology and folklore, have proved particularly enlightening. A comprehensive collection of Morris's letters in three volumes, edited by Norman Kelvin, is in process of publication.

Other:

"Mural Decoration," by Morris and J. H. Middleton in the *Encyclopaedia Britannica*, 9th ed., volume 17 (Edinburgh: Black, 1884; New York: Allen, 1888);

John Ruskin, *The Nature of Gothic*, preface by Morris (London: Allen, 1892; New York: Garland, 1977);

Thomas More, *Utopia*, foreword by Morris (London: Reeves & Turner, 1893);

Robert Steele, ed., *Medieval Lore*, preface by Morris (London: Stock, 1893; Boston: Luce, 1907);

Arts & Crafts Exhibition Society, *Arts and Crafts Essays*, preface and three articles by Morris (London: Rivington, Percival, 1893; New York: Scribners, 1893).

Translations:

The Story of Grettir the Strong, translated from the Icelandic by Morris and Eiríkr Magnússon (London: Ellis, 1869; New York: Longmans, Green, 1901);

The Story of the Volsungs and Niblungs, translated from the Icelandic by Morris and Magnússon (London: Ellis, 1870; New York: Longmans, Green, 1901);

Three Northern Love Stories and Other Tales, translated from the Icelandic by Morris and Magnússon (London: Ellis & White, 1876; New York: Longmans, Green, 1901);

The Aeneids of Virgil, translated by Morris (London: Ellis & White, 1876; Boston: Roberts Bros., 1875);

The Odyssey of Homer, translated by Morris, 2 volumes (London: Reeves & Turner, 1887; New York: Longmans, Green, 1897);

The Saga Library, translated from the Icelandic by Morris and Magnússon (6 volumes, London: Quaritch, 1891-1905);

"The Ordination of Knighthood," translated by Morris from William Caxton's translation of *The Order of Chivalry* (London: Reeves & Turner, 1892);

The Tale of King Florus and the Fair Jehane, translated from the Old French by Morris (Hammersmith: Kelmscott Press, 1893);

Of the Friendship of Amis and Amile, translated from the Old French by Morris (Hammersmith: Kelmscott Press, 1894);

The Tale of the Emperor Coustans and of Over Sea, translated from the Old French by Morris (Hammersmith: Kelmscott Press, 1894);

The Tale of Beowulf, translated from Old English by Morris and A. J. Wyatt (Hammersmith: Kelmscott Press, 1895; New York: Longmans, Green, 1898);

The Story of Kormak, the Son of Ogmund, translated by Morris, edited by Grace Calder (London: William Morris Society, 1970).

Letters:

Philip Henderson, ed., *The Letters of William Morris to His Family and Friends* (London: Longmans, Green, 1950; New York: AMS Press, 1978);

Norman Kelvin, ed., *The Collected Letters of William Morris*, 3 volumes projected (volume 1, 1848-1880, Princeton: Princeton University Press, 1983).

Bibliographies:

H. Buxton Forman, *The Books of William Morris* (London: Hollings, 1897; Chicago: Way & Williams, 1897);

Theodore G. Ehrsam, et al., *Bibliographies of Twelve Victorian Authors* (New York: Wilson, 1936);

William E. Fredeman, *Pre-Raphaelitism: A Biblio-critical Study* (Cambridge: Harvard University Press, 1965).

Biographies:

John W. Mackail, *The Life of William Morris* (2 volumes, London & New York: Longmans, Green, 1899);

Margaret R. Grennan, *William Morris, Medievalist and Revolutionary* (New York: King's Crown Press, 1945);

Philip Henderson, *William Morris, His Life, Work and Friends* (London: Thames & Hudson, 1967;

New York: McGraw-Hill, 1967);

Jack Lindsay, *William Morris, His Life and Work* (London: Constable, 1975; New York: Taplinger, 1979);

E. P. Thompson, *William Morris: Romantic to Revolutionary* (London: Merlin Press, 1977; New York: Pantheon Books, 1977).

References:

J.-M. Baissus, "Morris and the *Oxford and Cambridge Magazine*," *Journal of the William Morris Society*, 5, no. 2 (Winter 1982): 2-13;

Patrick Brantlinger, " 'News from Nowhere': Morris's Socialist Anti-Novel," *Victorian Studies*, 19 (September 1975): 35-49;

Blue Calhoun, *The Pastoral Vision of William Morris* (Athens: University of Georgia Press, 1975);

Lin Carter, *Imaginary Worlds* (New York: Ballantine, 1973);

Fiona Clark, *William Morris, Wallpapers and Chintzes* (London: Academy Editions, 1974; New York: St. Martin's, 1974);

Peter Faulkner, *Against the Age* (London & Boston: Allen & Unwin, 1980);

Faulkner, ed., *William Morris: the Critical Heritage* (London & Boston: Routledge & Kegan Paul, 1973);

John Hollow, ed., *The After-Summer Seed; Reconsiderations of William Morris's "The Story of Sigurd the Volsung"* (New York: William Morris Society, 1978);

Frederick Kirchhoff, *William Morris* (Boston: Twayne, 1979; London: Prior, 1979);

Kirchhoff, et. al., *Studies in the Late Romances of William Morris* (New York: William Morris Society, 1976);

C. S. Lewis, "William Morris," in his *Rehabilitations and Other Essays* (London: Oxford University Press, 1939; New York: Folcroft, 1973);

H. C. Marillier, *History of the Merton Abbey Tapestry Works Founded by William Morris* (London: Constable, 1927);

Roderick Marshall, *William Morris and His Earthly Paradises* (Tisbury: Compton Press, 1979);

Richard Mathews, *Worlds Beyond the World* (San Bernardino: Borgo Press, 1978);

Paul Meier, *William Morris: The Marxist Dreamer*, 2 volumes (Hassocks: Harvester Press, 1978; Atlantic Highlands: Humanities Press, 1978);

Charlotte Oberg, *A Pagan Prophet: William Morris* (Charlottesville: University Press of Virginia, 1978);

Linda Parry, *William Morris Textiles* (London: Weidenfeld & Nicolson, 1983; New York: Viking Press, 1983);

A. Charles Sewter, *The Stained Glass of William Morris and His Circle* (New Haven & London: Yale University Press, 1974-1975);

Carole Silver, ed., *The Golden Chain; Essays on William Morris and Pre-Raphaelitism* (New York: William Morris Society, 1982);

Silver, *The Romance of William Morris* (Athens: Ohio University Press, 1982);

H. Halliday Sparling, *The Kelmscott Press and William Morris, Master-Craftsman* (London: Macmillan, 1924; New York: Gordon Press, 1976);

Paul Thompson, *The Work of William Morris* (London: Heinemann, 1967; New York: Viking, 1967);

Lionel Trilling, "Aggression and Utopia, A Note on William Morris's 'News from Nowhere,'" *Psychoanalytic Quarterly*, 42 (1973): 214-225;

Trilling, "Mind in the Modern World," *Times Literary Supplement* (17 November 1972);

Aymer Vallance, *The Art of William Morris* (London: Bell, 1897); republished as *William Morris; His Art, His Writings and His Public Life* (London: Bell, 1897; revised 1898; Kennebunkport, Maine: Milford House, 1971);

Victorian Poetry, special Morris issue, 13, nos. 3-4 (Fall-Winter 1975);

Ray Watkinson, *William Morris as Designer* (London: Studio Vista, 1967, 1979; New York: Macmillan, 1967, 1979);

William B. Yeats, "The Happiest of Poets," in his *Ideas of Good and Evil* (London: Bullen, 1903).

Papers:

The largest collection of Morris's manuscripts, letters, and other papers belongs to the British Library in London. Other important collections are located at the Bodleian Library, Oxford University; the Fitzwilliam Museum, Cambridge University; the Victoria & Albert Museum, London; the William Morris Gallery, Walthamstow; and the International Institute of Social History, Amsterdam. Significant collections in the United States include the Tinker Collection at Yale University; the Pierpont Morgan Library, New York City; the Huntington Library, San Marino, California; the University of Texas; and the Sanford Berger Collection in Carmel, California, which contains the Dearle Collection especially concerned with Morris and Company's stained glass and other products of the firm.

John Henry Newman

(21 February 1801-11 August 1890)

Lionel Adey
University of Victoria

SELECTED BOOKS: *Memorials of the Past* (Oxford: King, 1832);

Tracts for the Times, by Members of the University of Oxford, nos. 1-3, 6-7, 8, by Newman and R. H. Froude; nos. 10-11, 15, by Newman and Sir W. Palmer; nos. 19-21, 31, 33-34, 38, 41, 45, 47, 71, 73, 74, by Newman and B. Harrison; nos. 75-76, 79, 82, 83, 85, 88, 90, by Newman (6 volumes, Oxford: 1833-1841);

Loss and Gain, anonymous (London: Burns, 1848; Boston: Donahoe, 1854);

Discourses on the Scope and Nature of University Education, Addressed to the Catholics of Dublin (Dublin: Duffy, 1852); revised and republished as *The Idea of a University Defined and Illustrated* (London: Pickering, 1873);

Callista: A Sketch of the Third Century, anonymous (London: Burns, Oates, 1856; New York: Sadlier, 1856);

Apologia pro Vita Sua: Being a Reply to a Pamphlet Entitled "What, Then, Does Dr. Newman Mean?" (London: Longman, Green, Longman, Roberts & Green, 1864; New York: Appleton, 1865); republished as *History of My Religious Opinions* (London: Longman, Green, Longman, Roberts & Green, 1865);

The Dream of Gerontius (London: Burns, Lambert, 1866; Philadelphia: McKay, n.d.);

Verses on Various Occasions (London: Burns, Oates, 1868).

COLLECTIONS: *Works of John Henry Newman*, Uniform Edition (41 volumes, London: Longmans, Green, 1908-1918);

Newman: Prose and Poetry, edited by Geoffrey Tillotson (London: Hart-Davis, 1957; Cambridge, Mass.: Harvard University Press, 1957).

John Henry Newman

Newman's continuing influence depends primarily upon his spiritual autobiography and his ideal of a Christian humanist education. In his own day, he was famous for his hymn "Lead, Kindly Light" (1833) and his poem *The Dream of Gerontius* (1866); for his preaching and theological writing; above all for his leading role in the Oxford Move-ment and subsequent Catholic revival. His two novels, *Loss and Gain* (1848) and *Callista* (1856), have been read because of their author's attainments in other fields. As Edward Wagenknecht says, Newman can be fairly judged only from his spiritual autobiography, *Apologia pro Vita Sua* (1864), written as a counterblast to an attack by Charles Kingsley, the Anglican "Broad Church" clergyman and bitterly anti-Catholic novelist and historian.

The eldest child of a London banker, John Henry Newman spent his early years mainly in a house at Ham, Richmond, that in old age he dreamed of as "paradise." Educated at Ealing (private) School, he grew up deeply attached to his violin playing, to Scott's novels, and to the Arabian

Nights stories. During 1816, in succession, his father's bank failed; he suffered an illness; and under a schoolmaster's influence, he became a Calvinistic Evangelical, aware of two "luminously self-evident beings, myself and my Creator." In that year, also, he felt called to live a celibate life. The following year, he entered Trinity College, Oxford, winning a scholarship in 1818. Four years later, despite having barely passed his degree examination owing to exhaustion, he secured a fellowship at Oriel College, then dominated by the liberal divines known as "Noetics." At first his mentor was Richard Whately, but between 1826, when Hurrell Froude joined Oriel as fellow, and 1833, when John Keble's sermon *National Apostasy* launched the Oxford Movement, Newman became a High Churchman. Another serious illness in 1827, and his sister Mary's death in 1828, intensified the otherworldliness so largely responsible for his extraordinary power to inspire the poor of St. Clement's parish and the university congregation of St. Mary's Church. Until 1839, when his study of the Donatist heresy raised grave doubts in his mind about the validity of the Anglican position, Newman exercised an unparalleled influence over Oxford undergraduates. Matthew Arnold and J. A. Froude, the historian, among many others, later described his famous sermons.

From 1833, as editor and frequent author of *Tracts for the Times* (1833-1841), Newman led the Oxford (or "Tractarian") Movement to reform the Church of England by asserting its independence of Parliament and reviving its Catholic traditions. In 1841, his Tract 90, a Catholic interpretation of the Thirty-Nine Articles (the basic statement of Anglican doctrine), incurred censure by the assembled heads of colleges, and the bishop of Oxford advised him to discontinue the series. During the next two years he resigned his cure of St. Mary's, retracted his criticisms of Rome, and withdrew to a religious house he set up at Littlemore, where in 1845 the Passionist Father Dominic received him into the Roman church.

In 1847, while Newman was studying in Rome prior to reordination, a fellow convert heard him laughing over the manuscript of *Loss and Gain*, which he was writing to help the publisher James Burns, who since being converted had gotten into financial difficulties. Newman preferred to use the novel form rather than, as Archbishop Wiseman had suggested, write a direct account of his conversion (as he later did in the *Apologia*) to answer J. A. Froude's "preposterously fanciful" fictional account of the Tractarians in *Shadows of the Clouds*

(1847) and a then best-selling novel, *From Oxford to Rome* (1847), by Elizabeth Harris. Although both Newman and Miss Harris, who apparently regretted her conversion from the Anglican to the Roman faith, published anonymously, they were soon identified, and a fashion set in for tracing Newman's characters to participants in the conflict between the leaders of the Oxford Movement and the college and ecclesiastical establishments. Despite the obvious parallels between author and hero traced in Robert Lee Wolff's notable account, Newman's lifelong friend and fellow convert Ambrose St. John rightly claims that "the great leader was absent from the picture." Charles Reding (pronounced "reading") has his creator's agonized doubts, love of a sister, and instinctive celibacy, but lacks his drive and passionate imagination. Although Reding resembles Newman in seeking religious authority, in losing his father while at Oxford, and in rejecting the worldliness of the collegiate establishment, the novel is not merely autobiographical. Reding, son of a country parson, does brilliantly in his examinations but leaves without a degree to be received into the Roman church at Father Dominic's monastery in London. Despite recognizable portraits, notably of Blanco White as the rationalist Sheffield, the characters are representatives of theological standpoints rather than credible personalities. Moreover, Charles's unexplained choice of celibacy, his derisive view of a young clergyman and wife, and his inability to "take full unrestrained pleasure in anything" could never have endeared the book to the common reader. Newman's ascetic strain, however, underlies the irony and invective that largely redeem *Loss and Gain*. A college tutor observes a fast-day by breakfasting on "plain beefsteak and saddle of mutton."

Newman's desk in his room at the Birmingham Oratory, which he founded in 1848

John Henry Newman   **DLB 18**

Charles complains of college heads, "ministers of Christ with large incomes, living in finely furnished houses, with wives and families, and stately butlers and servants in livery, giving dinners all in the best style . . . without anything to make them clergyman but a black coat and a white tie." Here and in his satirical account of Charles's inquisition by Jennings, the vice-principal, Newman took revenge on Edward Hawkins, provost of Oriel, and other anti-Tractarian members of the Oxford establishment.

While generally endorsing the judgment of Ambrose St. John and other "actors in the drama" of the movement that *Loss and Gain* is "a perfect representation of the Oxford society of those days," critics have usually condemned it as a novel. Lionel Stevenson says only that this and Froude's novel "serve to induce a more favourable opinion of [Charles Kingsley's] *Yeast* [1851]," and Wagenknecht says that "Newman was no novelist." Robert Lee Wolff, however, praises its "many comic passages," its "vivid series of portraits," and its "unsparing account of Newman's own spiritual travails leading to his conversion." After discussing, with a sympathy nowadays rare, its themes of sexual abstinence and spiritual anxiety, Wolff concludes: "the secularist would be well advised to reflect that there are obviously decisive forces in some men's lives that fail to prove decisive in others'."

World-and-life denial also permeates Newman's more readable novel, *Callista*, first published anonymously. This he began in 1848, but broke off from "inability to devise personages or incidents." Early in 1848, he founded at Birmingham the Oratory of St. Philip Neri, and in 1849 he opened the London Oratory. The Oratorians were an order of secular priests devoted to teaching, scholarship, and missionary endeavors in large cities. Early members of the English branch included the hymn translator Edward Caswall of the Birmingham and the hymn writer Frederick Faber of the London Oratory. Newman also founded at Birmingham the St. Philip's Boys' School, at which the poet Gerard Manley Hopkins taught briefly after Newman had received him into the Roman Catholic church. Two further preoccupations that delayed the completion of *Callista* were the founding at Dublin of a Catholic university, of which Archbishop Cullen invited him to become the first rector, and an unpleasant libel suit. After constant difficulties with Cullen and other Irish prelates, Newman resigned the rectorship and in 1857 returned to Birmingham for good. In 1852, he delivered at Dublin his fa-

mous series of lectures later republished as *The Idea of a University* (1873). These constitute one of the most eloquent and persuasive arguments for a liberal, yet also a Christian, education ever penned. In 1851, when lecturing at the Birmingham Corn Exchange on "The Present Position of Catholics," Newman had repeated accusations of immoral conduct that Wiseman had leveled against the former Dominican Giacinto Achilli, then engaged in a personal crusade against the Catholic church. When Achilli sued for libel, an anti-Catholic judge and jury found for him in the face of overwhelming evidence. The appeal court judge showed similar bias when confirming the verdict and fining Newman £100. While Catholics generously paid Newman's fine and costs by subscription, and the *Times* called the proceedings "indecorous . . . unsatisfactory . . . and little calculated to increase . . . respect . . . for the administration of justice," the trial and the disputes in Ireland sapped Newman's energies.

He was prompted to complete *Callista* in 1855 by Charles Kingsley's attack in *Hypatia* (1853) upon monasticism and Catholicism generally. In the

Charles Kingsley, whose writings called forth Newman's novel Callista *(1856) and his spiritual autobiography,* Apologia pro Vita Sua *(1864)*

Catholics of Alexandria in the fifth century, Kingsley represented Tractarians and English Catholics under the thinnest of disguises. A further stimulus was Wiseman's *Fabiola* (1854), intended as the first in a series of propagandist novels by Catholics. Set in the imaginary North African city of Sicca, the action of *Callista* consists of the Christian farmer Agellius's rejection by the beautiful Greek sculptress Callista; his pursuit by a mob blaming Christians for a plague of locusts; her wrongful arrest, final conversion, and martyrdom. The shift of interest from Agellius to Callista deprives the story of its inner conflict between faith and love, for once she has read St. Luke's Gospel, given her by the priest Caecilius (St. Cyprian), her martyrdom is never in doubt. While its account of her conversion is moving, the novel suffers from Newman's tendency to address the reader and treat characters as mouthpieces. It succeeds best in its declared aim of conveying the pagan ethos during the Decian persecution and in its descriptions of the locust-swarm and subsequent riots, the latter reflecting Newman's disgust at the drunkenness and unreasoning fury of the mob.

Described by Baker as "of small literary importance," *Callista* has attracted more critical attention of late than *Loss and Gain*. Stevenson has called it "as neatly counterbalanced" against *Hypatia* as Newman's earlier novel was against *Yeast* and *Shadows of the Clouds*, pointing to Kingsley's beautiful, intellectual heroine and thrilling mob scenes. While Stevenson confines his criticism to the propagandism and absence of love interest, Andrew Sanders calls *Callista* a "disappointing novel" that, like *Hypatia*, fails "to probe the heart of the problem it investigates." Reminding readers of Newman's love for Scott's Waverley novels, Sanders thinks him "far better at describing landscapes than . . . at characterization or at picturing normal human activity" and praises his "precision" and "imaginative creation" in describing the locust-swarm. Finally, he judges *Callista* a "dramatized thesis," its city of Sicca almost like the Oxford of *Loss and Gain*, and its heroine, for a provincial girl, too steeped in the literature and politics of her age. Wolff expounds the novel as both "a considerable work of art" and a "clever satire on Newman's own day." Sicca, for example, means "dry" and stands on a height. Being "high and dry," it could typify one facet of old-style Anglicanism, while localities within it typify others, for example, Evangelicalism. Without going so far as reviewers of Newman's time who read it as autobiographical, he considers that the author "turned

Newman at about seventy years of age

inwards" for the conversion account.

Newman wrote best in response to an external need or an attack such as Kingsley's accusation of intellectual dishonesty which called forth the great *Apologia*. Kingsley had refused Newman's request for an unconditional retraction of a charge in a book review that Newman had preached with the "cunning . . . Heaven has given to the Saints . . . to withstand the brute male force of the wicked world which marries or is given in marriage." When Newman published this correspondence in a pamphlet, Kingsley rejoined by accusing him of equivocation and idolatry. Writing at white heat, Newman produced first a *History of My Religions Opinions* in seven weekly pamphlets, issued on Thursdays from 21 April to 2 June 1864, with an appendix on 16 June. All were included in the first book edition, *Apologia Pro Vita Sua: Being a Reply to a Pamphlet Entitled "What, Then, Does Dr. Newman Mean?"* By its so-called "1865 edition," actually finalized in 1886, Newman had removed all references to Kingsley's name and softened its original anger and scorn. As

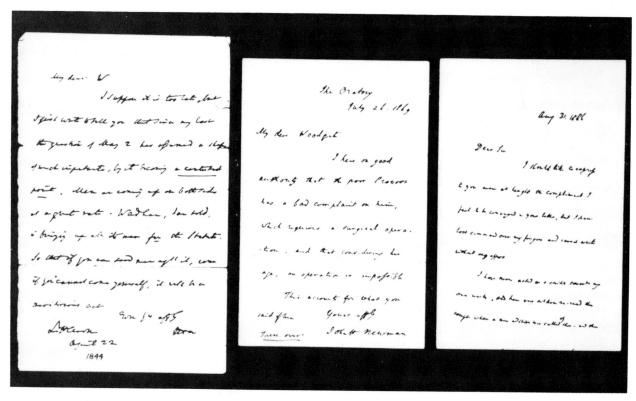

Three letters written by Newman over a period of forty-two years. The latest one both mentions and demonstrates the difficulty he had in writing in old age.

so modified, the *Apologia* stands comparison with the *Confessions* of St. Augustine as among the grandest works of its kind. Relating essentially the same events as *Loss and Gain*, it far transcends the novel in its directness, breadth of vision, and passionate aspiration. While these, and Newman's mastery of the periodic sentence, reach their climax in the famous paragraph on the human condition without God, a briefer example of both his romanticism and his power to depict his spiritual quest in prose at once supple, rhythmic, and vitally metaphorical occurs shortly before: "I am speaking for myself only; and I am far from denying the real force of the arguments in proof of a God, drawn from the general facts of human society and the course of history, but these do not warm me or enlighten me; they do not take away the winter of my desolation, or make the buds unfold and the leaves grow within me, and my moral being rejoice."

As a fiction writer, Newman stands in a line of gifted Victorian amateur novelists beginning with Disraeli. His underlying theme in the novels, *Apologia*, and *The Dream of Gerontius* alike is the spiritual journey: from unbelief to Christianity, from Anglican to Roman Catholic faith, from this

An etching by H. R. Robertson of Newman at age eighty-two (Newman Preparatory School Collection, Boston)

world to the next. Created cardinal in 1879, Newman, who died in 1890, is presently being considered for canonization.

Letters:
Charles Stephen Dessain, Ian Ker, Thomas Gornal, eds., *Letters and Diaries of John Henry Newman* (31 volumes, Oxford: Clarendon Press, 1961-).

Bibliography:
J. Rickaby, *Index to All Works of John Henry Cardinal Newman* (London: Longmans, Green, 1914).

Biographies:
Wilfrid Ward, *The Life of John Henry Cardinal Newman, Based on His Private Journals and Correspondence* (2 volumes, London: Longmans, Green, 1921);
Meriol Trevor, *Newman* (2 volumes, London: Macmillan, 1962).

References:
Ernest Baker, *History of the English Novel* (New York: Barnes & Noble, 1950);
A. Dwight Culler, *The Imperial Intellect* (New Haven:

Yale University Press, 1955);
Charles Frederick Harrold, *John Henry Newman: An Expository and Critical Study of His Mind, Thought and Art* (London: Longmans, Green, 1945);
Americo D. Lapati, *John Henry Newman* (New York: Twayne, 1972);
Andrew Sanders, *The Victorian Historical Novel 1840-1880* (London: Macmillan, 1978), pp. 137-148;
Lionel Stevenson, *The English Novel* (London: Constable, 1960);
Stevenson, *The Victorian Historical Novel* (London: Macmillan, 1978);
Edward Wagenknecht, *Cavalcade of the Victorian Novel* (New York: Holt, Rinehart & Winston, 1954);
Robert Lee Wolff, *Gains and Losses: Novels of Faith and Doubt in Victorian England* (New York: Garland, 1977).

Papers:
Newman's correspondence, diaries, and other autobiographical material; unpublished sermons and notes; and manuscripts of articles and lectures are in the archives of the Birmingham Oratory, Birmingham, England.

Laurence Oliphant

(? 1829-23 December 1888)

Tom Winnifrith
University of Warwick

BOOKS: *A Journey to Katmandu with the Camp of Jung Bahadoor, Including a Sketch of the Ambassador at Home* (London: Murray, 1852; New York: Appleton, 1852);
The Russian Shores of the Black Sea in the Autumn of 1852, with a Voyage down the Volga, and a Tour through the Country of the Don Cossacks (Edinburgh & London: Blackwood, 1853; New York: Redfield, 1854);
The Coming Campaign (Edinburgh & London: Blackwood, 1855);
Minnesota and the Far West (Edinburgh & London: Blackwood, 1855);
The Trans-Caucasian Provinces the Proper Field of Op-

eration for a Christian Army (Edinburgh & London: Blackwood, 1856);
The Trans-Caucasian Campaign of the Turkish Army under Omar Pasha: A Personal Narrative (Edinburgh & London: Blackwood, 1856);
Narrative of the Earl of Elgin's Mission to China and Japan in the Years 1857, 58, 59 (2 volumes, Edinburgh & London: Blackwood, 1859);
Patriots and Filibusters: Incidents of Political and Exploratory Travel, Reprinted from "Blackwood's Magazine" with Corrections and Additions (Edinburgh & London: Blackwood, 1860);
Universal Suffrage and Napoleon the Third (Edinburgh & London: Blackwood, 1860);

On the Present State of Political Parties in America (Edinburgh & London: Blackwood, 1866);

Piccadilly: A Fragment of Contemporary Biography (Edinburgh & London: Blackwood, 1870; New York: Harper, 1884);

The Land of Gilead, with Excursions in the Lebanon (Edinburgh & London: Blackwood, 1880; New York: Appleton, 1881);

The Land of Khemi: Up and down the Middle Nile (Edinburgh & London: Blackwood, 1882);

Traits and Travesties, Social and Political (Edinburgh & London: Blackwood, 1882);

Altiora Peto (2 volumes, Edinburgh & London: Blackwood, 1883; 1 volume, New York: Harper, 1883);

Sympneumata; or, Evolutionary Forces Now Active in Man (Edinburgh & London: Blackwood, 1885);

Masollam: A Problem of the Period (3 volumes, Edinburgh & London: Blackwood, 1886);

Haifa: or, Life in Modern Palestine (London: Blackwood, 1887; New York: Harper, 1887);

Episodes in a Life of Adventure; or, Moss from a Rolling Stone (Edinburgh & London: Blackwood, 1887; New York: Harper, 1887);

Fashionable Philosophy and Other Sketches (Edinburgh & London: Blackwood, 1887);

Scientific Religion; or, Higher Possibilities of Life and Practice through the Operation of Natural Forces, with an Appendix by a Clergyman of the Church of England (Edinburgh & London: Blackwood, 1888; Buffalo, N.Y.: Wenborne, 1889).

Laurence Oliphant's works are rarely read, although they are quite unlike other Victorian novels. His life, fascinating in its complexity and with a tragic gap between his promise and his achievements, has recently been the object of a sympathetic study, and he would seem to be worth investigating in order to show some of the more unusual and hidden sides of the Victorian character.

Oliphant was born in Capetown, South Africa, in 1829. His father and mother were both members of old Scottish families and both were fervent evangelicals in religion. In 1839 his father was made chief justice of Ceylon and knighted. Oliphant traveled widely in his youth, but his education was much interrupted. He did not go to a university but accompanied his parents on a prolonged tour of Europe, witnessing some of the revolutions of 1848. He joined the colonial bar in Ceylon and visited Nepal. He wrote an account of this trip which was published in 1852 while he was reading for the bar in England. His studies were interrupted by visits to Russia and by being appointed secretary to Lord Elgin, governor-general of Canada, who made Oliphant superintendent of Indian affairs. Returning to England in 1855, Oliphant then revisited Russia, about which he had written two books (published in 1853 and 1855), and was briefly at the siege of Sebastopol during the Crimean War before plunging further south into the Caucasus. In this campaign he had been acting as correspondent for the *Times* and in 1856 was invited by the editor of that newspaper to visit the southern United States. From here, after many adventures, he returned briefly to England before accompanying Lord Elgin, again as private secretary, on his visit to China. He wrote an account of the mission, *Narrative of the Earl of Elgin's Mission to China and Japan*, which was published in 1859. In 1860 he visited Italy and in 1861 Montenegro, before being appointed first secretary to the legation in Japan. Here he was badly wounded and returned home via Korea. The year 1862 was relatively quiet, with visits to Corfu, Italy, and Herzegovina; and in 1863 he made short expeditions to the rebellion in Poland, to Romania, and to the war in Schleswig-Holstein. Then, at the age of thirty-four, having visited every continent except South America and Australia and having had a fairly major hand in the affairs of more than a dozen countries, he was anxious to settle down.

In 1864 he started a journal entitled the *Owl*, contributing to the first ten numbers, and in 1865 wrote a short novel, *Piccadilly* (1870). This novel, highly praised by Michael Sadleir, has little plot but some amusing dialogue mildly reminiscent of Peacock. It tells of the efforts of Lord Frank Vanecourt to woo and win Lady Ursula Newlyte in spite or because of the mercenary and hypocritical society around him. The world-weariness and the religious sincerity of Lord Frank are no doubt autobiographical. In the same year that he wrote *Piccadilly*, Oliphant was elected member of Parliament for the Stirling Burghs; but his meteoric career, which appeared to have reached its zenith, was about to take a peculiar, if not a tragic, turn. In *Piccadilly* he had praised, as the greatest poet of the age, Thomas Lake Harris, the leader of an obscure religious community in America. In 1867 he resigned his seat in Parliament and joined this community at Brocton, New York, near Lake Erie, making over his money to them. The next year Oliphant's mother joined the community but was not allowed much contact with her son. In 1870 Harris permitted Oliphant to return to Europe to act as *Times* correspondent in the Franco-Prussian War. While in Paris in 1871, he met Alice Le Strange and married her the next year; but there were difficulties when she, too, was forced to join Harris's community. In 1873 all three Oliphants returned to Brocton. While Oliphant was allowed to engage in commercial enterprises for the community, his wife and mother were given menial tasks, and for long periods he was kept away from them. Oliphant was involved in schemes to colonize Palestine for the Jews and visited Egypt. In 1881 Lady Oliphant died, and Oliphant began to be troubled by doubts about Harris, whom he had always called Father. Accompanied by his wife, he visited the Near East in 1882 and at Haifa wrote a second novel, *Altiora Peto* (1883), which is another statement of Oliphant's religious views. (The title means "I seek higher things.") As in *Piccadilly*, the heroine, oddly named Altiora, tries to find true religion in the middle of the frenzied folly of the smart social set. By this time the break with Harris was fairly severe, and in 1886 Oliphant published a hostile portrait of him in *Masollam*, which Sadleir calls an "enfeebled" novel. Alice Oliphant died in 1887, and Oliphant believed that she showed herself to him in spiritual manifes-

tations. Autobiographical papers he had published in *Blackwood's Magazine* were collected in a volume appropriately entitled *Episodes in a Life of Adventure; or, Moss from a Rolling Stone* (1887), and he continued to write religious books and pamphlets. Oliphant married again in 1888, but shortly afterward he became ill and died on 23 December.

Few men can have done so much and achieved so little as Laurence Oliphant. Contemporary accounts and the publication in 1891 by Margaret Oliphant (a distant relative) of *Memoir of the Life of Laurence Oliphant and of Alice Oliphant, His Wife*, attest to the charm of his personality and the brilliance of his intellect. One's regret at his strange religious delusions is tempered by an awareness that even when under the influence of Harris he showed both energy and efficiency. His novels are hard to appreciate in an age when there is little interest in religious enthusiasm or life in high society, and the combination of the two seems almost impossible. Oliphant's clever assault on the Wholly Worldlies and the Worldly Holies is not understood by those who have never associated worldliness with holiness. The ephemeral nature of journalism is re-

Thomas Lake Harris, religious leader who dominated Oliphant's life for almost twenty years

flected in the novels, which have become badly dated; and somehow the novels, though full of spiritual fervor, lack the vigor which Oliphant showed in his life. Nevertheless, they are still worth reading as insights into an unusual and exciting Victorian character.

Biographies:

Margaret Oliphant, *Memoir of the Life of Laurence Oliphant and of Alice Oliphant, His Wife*, 2 volumes (Edinburgh & London: Blackwood, 1891; New York: Harper, 1891);

Anne Taylor, *Laurence Oliphant, 1829-1888* (New York: Oxford University Press, 1982).

Margaret Oliphant

(4 April 1828-25 June 1897)

Tom Winnifrith
University of Warwick

BOOKS: *Passages in the Life of Mrs. Margaret Maitland* (3 volumes, London: Colburn, 1849; 1 volume, New York: Appleton, 1851);

Caleb Field (London: Colburn, 1851; New York: Harper, 1851);

John: A Love Story (2 volumes, London: Bentley, 1851; 1 volume, New York: Harper, 1870);

Merkland: A Story of Scottish Life (3 volumes, London: Colburn, 1851; 1 volume, New York: Stringer & Townsend, 1854);

Memoirs and Resolutions of Adam Graeme of Mossgray (3 volumes, London: Colburn, 1852; 1 volume, New York: Munro, 1885);

Katie Stewart (New York: Harper, 1852; Edinburgh & London: Blackwood, 1853);

Harry Muir: A Story of Scottish Life (3 volumes, London: Hurst & Blackett, 1853; 1 volume, New York: Appleton, 1853);

Quiet Heart: A Story (Edinburgh & London: Blackwood, 1854; New York: Harper, 1854);

Magdalen Hepburn: A Story of the Scottish Reformation (3 volumes, London: Hurst & Blackett, 1854; 1 volume, New York: Riker, Thorne, 1854);

Lilliesleaf: Conclusion of "Margaret Maitland" (3 volumes, London: Hurst & Blackett, 1855; 1 volume, Boston: Burnham, 1862);

Zaidee: A Romance (3 volumes, Edinburgh & London: Blackwood, 1856; 1 volume, Boston: Jewett, 1856);

The Athelings; or, The Three Gifts (3 volumes, Edinburgh & London: Blackwood, 1857; 1 volume New York: Harper, 1857);

The Days of My Life (3 volumes, London: Hurst &

Blackett, 1857; 1 volume, New York: Harper, 1857);

Sundays (London: Nisbet, 1858);

The Laird of Norlaw (3 volumes, London: Hurst & Blackett, 1858; 1 volume, New York: Harper, 1859);

Orphans: A Chapter in Life (London: Hurst & Blackett, 1858; New York: Munro, 1880);

Agnes Hopetown's Schools and Holidays (Cambridge: Macmillan, 1859; Boston: Gould & Lincoln, 1859);

Lucy Crofton (London: Hurst & Blackett, 1860; New York: Harper, 1860);

The House on the Moor (3 volumes, London: Hurst & Blackett, 1861; New York: Harper, 1861);

The Last of the Mortimers (3 volumes, London: Hurst & Blackett, 1862; New York: Harper, 1862);

The Life of Edward Irving (2 volumes, London: Hurst & Blackett, 1862; 1 volume, New York: Harper, 1862);

The Rector and the Doctor's Family, anonymous (3 volumes, Edinburgh & London: Blackwood, 1863);

Salem Chapel, anonymous (2 volumes, Edinburgh & London: Blackwood, 1863; 1 volume, New York: Munro, 1884);

Heart and Cross (London: Hurst & Blackett, 1863; New York: Gregory, 1863);

The Perpetual Curate, anonymous (3 volumes, Edinburgh & London: Blackwood, 1864; 1 volume, New York: Harper, 1865);

A Son of the Soil (New York: Harper, 1865; 2 volumes, London: Macmillan, 1866);

Agnes (3 volumes, London: Hurst & Blackett, 1866; 1 volume, New York: Harper, 1866);

Miss Marjoribanks, anonymous (3 volumes, Edinburgh & London: Blackwood, 1866; 1 volume, New York: Harper, 1867);

Madonna Mary (New York: Harper, 1866; 3 volumes, London: Hurst & Blackett, 1867);

Francis of Assisi (London: Macmillan, 1868);

The Brownlows (3 volumes, Edinburgh & London: Blackwood, 1868; 1 volume, New York: Harper, 1868);

Historical Sketches of the Reign of George II (2 volumes, Edinburgh & London: Blackwood, 1869; 1 volume, Boston: Littell & Gay, 1869);

The Minister's Wife (3 volumes, London: Hurst & Blackett, 1869; 1 volume, New York: Harper, 1869);

The Three Brothers (3 volumes, London: Hurst & Blackett, 1870);

Squire Arden (3 volumes, London: Hurst & Blackett, 1871; 1 volume, New York: Harper, 1874);

At His Gates (3 volumes, London: Tinsley, 1872; 1 volume, New York: Scribner, Armstrong, 1873);

Memoirs of the Count of Montalembert: A Chapter of Recent French History (2 volumes, Edinburgh & London: Blackwood, 1872);

Ombra (3 volumes, London: Hurst & Blackett, 1872; 1 volume, New York: Harper, 1872);

May (3 volumes, London: Hurst & Blackett, 1873; 1 volume, New York: Scribner, Armstrong, 1873);

Innocent: A Tale of Modern Life (London: Low, Marston, Low & Searle, 1873; New York: Harper, 1873);

A Rose in June (2 volumes, London: Hurst & Blackett, 1874; 1 volume, Boston: Osgood, 1874);

For Love and Life (3 volumes, London: Hurst & Blackett, 1874; 1 volume, New York: Munro, 1879);

The Story of Valentine and His Brother (3 volumes, Edinburgh & London: Blackwood, 1875; 1 volume, New York: Harper, 1875);

Whiteladies (3 volumes, London: Tinsley, 1875; 1 volume, New York: Munro, 1882);

Phoebe Junior: A Last Chronicle of Carlingford, anonymous (3 volumes, London: Hurst & Blackett, 1876; 1 volume, New York: Harper, 1876);

The Curate in Charge (2 volumes, London: Macmillan, 1876; 1 volume, New York: Harper, 1876);

The Makers of Florence: Dante, Giotto, Savonarola, and Their City (London: Macmillan, 1876; London & New York: Macmillan, 1888);

Carita (3 volumes, London: Smith, Elder, 1877; 1 volume, New York: Harper, 1877);

Dante (Edinburgh & London: Blackwood, 1877; Philadelphia: Lippincott, 1877);

Mrs. Arthur (3 volumes, London: Hurst & Blackett, 1877; 1 volume, New York: Harper, 1877);

Young Musgrave (3 volumes, London: Macmillan, 1877);

Dress (London: Macmillan, 1878; Philadelphia: Porter & Coates, 1879);

The Primrose Path: A Chapter in the Annals of the Kingdom of Fife (3 volumes, London; Hurst & Blackett, 1878);

Molière, by Oliphant and F. Tarver (Edinburgh & London: Blackwood, 1879; Philadelphia: Lippincott, 1879);

Within the Precincts (3 volumes, London: Smith, Elder, 1879; 1 volume, New York: Harper, 1879);

The Greatest Heiress in England (3 volumes, London: Hurst & Blackett, 1879; 1 volume, New York: Harper, 1880);

A Beleagured City (New York: Munro, 1879; London: Macmillan, 1880);

Cervantes (Edinburgh & London: Blackwood, 1880; Philadelphia: Lippincott, 1881);

He that Will Not when He May (3 volumes, London: Macmillan, 1880; 1 volume, New York: Harper, 1880);

Harry Joscelyn (3 volumes, London: Hurst & Blackett, 1881; 1 volume, New York: Harper, 1881);

A Little Pilgrim in the Unseen (London: Macmillan, 1882; Boston: Roberts, 1882);

In Trust: The Story of a Lady and Her Lover (3 volumes, London: Longmans, Green, 1882);

Literary History of England in the End of the Eighteenth and Beginning of the Nineteenth Century (3 volumes, London: Macmillan, 1882; 1 volume, New York: Macmillan, 1882);

Hester: A Story of Contemporary Life (3 volumes, London: Macmillan, 1883; 1 volume, New York: Harper, 1884);

It was a Lover and his Lass (3 volumes, London: Hurst & Blackett, 1883; 1 volume, New York: Harper, 1883);

The Lady's Walk (New York: Munro, 1883; London: Methuen, 1897);

Sheridan, in the English Men of Letters series (London: Macmillan, 1883; New York: Harper, 1883);

The Ladies Lindores (3 volumes, Edinburgh & London: Blackwood, 1883; 1 volume, New York: Harper, 1883);

Sir Tom (New York: Harper, 1883; 3 volumes, London: Macmillan, 1884);

The Wizard's Son (New York: Lovell, 1883; 3 volumes, London: Macmillan, 1884);

Madam (New York: Harper, 1884; 3 volumes, London: Longmans, Green, 1885);

Two Stories of the Seen and Unseen (Edinburgh & London: Blackwood, 1885);

The Prodigals and Their Inheritance (New York: Munro, 1885; 2 volumes, London: Methuen, 1894);

Oliver's Bride: A True Story (New York: Lovell, 1885; London: Ward & Downey, 1886);

A Country Gentleman and His Family (3 volumes, London: Macmillan, 1886; 1 volume, New York: Harper, 1886);

Effie Ogilvie (2 volumes, Glasgow: MacLehose, 1886; 1 volume, New York: Harper, 1886);

A House Divided against Itself (3 volumes, Edinburgh & London: Blackwood, 1886; 1 volume, New York: Harper, 1886);

A Poor Gentleman (New York: Munro, 1886; 3 volumes, London: Hurst & Blackett, 1889);

The Son of His Father (New York: Harper, 1886; 3 volumes, London: Hurst & Blackett, 1887);

The Makers of Venice: Doges, Conquerors, Painters, and Men of Letters (London & New York: Macmillan, 1887);

Memoir of the Life of John Tulloch (Edinburgh & London: Blackwood, 1888);

The Land of Darkness, along with Some Further Chapters in the Experience of the Little Pilgrims (London & New York: Macmillan, 1888);

Joyce (3 volumes, London: Macmillan, 1888; 1 volume, New York: Harper, 1888);

The Second Son (3 volumes, London: Macmillan, 1888; 1 volume, Boston & New York: Houghton, Mifflin, 1888);

Cousin Mary (London: Partridge, 1888);

Neighbours on the Green: A Collection of Stories (3 volumes, London & New York: Macmillan, 1889);

Lady Car: The Sequel of a Life (London: Longmans, Green, 1889; New York: Harper, 1889);

Kirsteen: A Story of a Scottish Family Seventy Years Ago (3 volumes, London: Macmillan, 1890; 1 volume, New York: Harper, 1890);

Royal Edinburgh: Her Saints, Kings, Prophets, and Poets (London: Macmillan, 1890; New York: Mershon, 1890);

The Duke's Daughter and the Fugitives (3 volumes, Edinburgh & London: Blackwood, 1890);

Sons and Daughters (Edinburgh & London: Blackwood, 1890);

The Mystery of Mrs. Blencarrow (London: Hurst & Blackett, 1890; Chicago: Donohue, Henneberry, 1894);

Janet (3 volumes, London: Hurst & Blackett, 1891);

Jerusalem: Its History and Hope (London & New York: Macmillan, 1891);

Memoir of the Life of Laurence Oliphant and of Alice Oliphant, His Wife (2 volumes, Edinburgh & London: Blackwood, 1891; New York: Harper, 1891);

The Railway Man and His Children (3 volumes, London: Macmillan, 1891; 1 volume, New York: Lovell; 1891);

The Heir Presumptive and the Heir Apparent (New York: Lovell, 1891; 3 volumes, London:

Macmillan, 1892);

The Marriage of Elinor (New York: United States Book Company, 1891; 3 volumes, London: Macmillan, 1892);

Diana Trelawney: The Story of a Great Mistake (2 volumes, Edinburgh & London: Blackwood, 1892); republished as *Diana: The History of a Great Mistake* (New York & Chicago: United States Book Company, 1892);

The Cuckoo in the Nest (3 volumes, London: Hutchinson, 1892; 1 volume, New York & Chicago: United States Book Company, 1892);

The Victorian Age of English Literature, by Oliphant and F. R. Oliphant (2 volumes, London: Percival, 1892; New York: Dodd, Mead, 1892);

Lady William (3 volumes, London & New York: Macmillan, 1893);

The Sorceress (3 volumes, London: Chatto & Windus, 1893; 1 volume, New York: Taylor, 1893);

Thomas Chalmers, Preacher, Philosopher, and Statesman (London: Methuen, 1893; Boston & New York: Houghton, Mifflin, 1893);

A House in Bloomsbury (2 volumes, London: Hutchinson, 1894; 1 volume, New York: Dodd, Mead, 1894);

Historical Sketches of the Reign of Queen Anne (London: Macmillan, 1894);

Sir Robert's Fortune: A Story of a Scotch Moor (New York: Harper, 1894; London: Methuen, 1895);

Who Was Lost and Is Found (Edinburgh & London: Blackwood, 1894; New York: Harper, 1895);

Two Strangers (London: Unwin, 1894);

A Child's History of Scotland (London: Unwin, 1895);

The Makers of Modern Rome (London & New York: Macmillan, 1895);

Old Mr. Tredgold (New York: Longmans, Green, 1895; London: Longmans, Green, 1896);

Jeanne d'Arc: Her Life and Death (London & New York: Putnam's, 1896);

The Two Marys (London: Methuen, 1896);

The Unjust Steward; or, The Minister's Debt (London & Edinburgh: Chambers, 1896; Philadelphia: Lippincott, 1896);

Annals of a Publishing House: William Blackwood and His Son, Their Magazine and Friends (2 volumes, Edinburgh & London: Blackwood, 1897; 3 volumes, New York: Scribners, 1897-1898);

The Ways of Life: Two Stories (London: Smith, Elder, 1897; New York & London: Putnam's, 1897);

The Autobiography and Letters of Mrs. M. O. W. Oliphant, edited by Mrs. H. Caghill (Edinburgh & London: Blackwood, 1898);

That Little Cutty; and Two Other Stories (London & New York: Macmillan; 1898);

A Widow's Tale and Other Stories (Edinburgh & London: Blackwood, 1898; New York: Fenno, 1899).

Margaret Oliphant is an underrated figure in the history of the Victorian novel. Her enormous output is worth studying as a barometer of Victorian taste, although she did eventually fail to keep up with contemporary fashions. Most of her novels are entertaining, and one or two of them aspire to greatness even if they do not achieve it. Her life has a certain tragic dignity about it.

Margaret Oliphant Wilson was born in Musselburgh, Scotland, 4 April 1828. Her father, Francis Wilson, was an inefficient businessman, but her mother, Margaret, was energetic; this pattern was repeated in Mrs. Oliphant's own marriage, and her brothers and sons followed this unfortunate tradition. Curiously, Mrs. Oliphant's novels do not reflect as much bitterness to the male sex as might be expected, although the heroine is very often both dynamic and managing. At the age of twenty-one, she produced her first novel: *Passages in the Life of Mrs. Margaret Maitland* (1849) is a Scottish regional tale about a quiet, virtuous woman who adopts a motherless relative, protects her from her unscrupulous father, and sees a romance develop between the girl and her nephew. *Lilliesleaf* (1855) was a sequel to this story. The Scottish novel enjoyed a certain popularity at the time, but *Passages in the Life of Mrs. Margaret Maitland* did not create much of a stir.

On 4 May 1852, she married her cousin, Francis Wilson Oliphant, an artist. She began writing for *Blackwood's Magazine* in 1853 and produced four novels for them in the next four years, as well as giving birth to two children. In 1859 her husband's health failed, and at great expense the family moved to Italy, where Francis Oliphant died—leaving his wife heavily in debt, pregnant, and with nothing but her indefatigable energy to support her. Blackwood was very helpful, and between 1862 and 1865 there were published anonymously in *Blackwood's Magazine* four "Chronicles of Carlingford," tales of English provincial life revolving around the church and the chapel, starting with *The Rector and the Doctor's Family* (1863). The most famous was *Salem Chapel* (1863). This is a melodramatic tale full of schemes that go astray, brain fever, kidnappings, and attempted murder, all revolving around the unlikely Dissenting clergyman Mr. Vin-

Mrs. Oliphant at her home in Windsor in 1874 with (left to right) her sons, "Cecco" and Cyril, and her nephew, Frank Wilson, whom she raised after her brother's death. All three died as young men.

cent. In 1866 *Miss Marjoribanks* was published as a book, and in 1876 Mrs. Oliphant returned to Carlingford with *Phoebe Junior: A Last Chronicle of Carlingford*. This title is consciously modeled on Anthony Trollope's *The Last Chronicle of Barset* (1867); and the novels (which have attractive heroines but not a great deal of action) stand comparison with Trollope, although contemporary readers frequently assumed they were written by George Eliot. In fact they lack the breadth of Trollope and the depth of George Eliot, although Mrs. Oliphant's careful and not wholly unsympathetic portrait of English Dissenters, a group which does not figure very prominently or creditably in the Victorian novel, is a remarkable achievement in view of her ignorance of the subject. She had been brought up in the Scottish Free Church, and in 1862 wrote a life of Edward Irving, with whose sect (the Catholic Apostolic Church, or "Irvingites") she mingled; but this hardly gave her a firsthand knowledge of the rich and varied fabric of Dissent or the Church of England. Yet her novels provide valuable and objective insights into religious quarrels of the time. As fiction they are less impressive, as her characters are

uninteresting and predictable, although the energy of Miss Marjoribanks and of the young Phoebe Tozer is surprising, and old Tozer both in *Salem Chapel* and *Phoebe Junior* is a good portrait of the narrowly commercial, yet essentially righteous Dissenter.

In 1864 Mrs. Oliphant's daughter died, and an additional burden was put upon her by the arrival of her widowed brother and his three children from Canada. Heroically but unwisely she took upon herself the task of supporting these additions to her family and of educating her own two sons at Eton, moving to Windsor for this purpose. Her sons did not achieve great academic success and tragically predeceased her. Mrs. Oliphant's efforts to earn money to pay for her sons' education resulted in a flood of novels and a series of biographical and historical works; she was also constantly in demand as a reviewer. A facile pen, a talent for describing scenery, and a happy sympathy with the views of the average well-read reader made her an admirable servant to Blackwood, but they hardly made her a master of the novel. In any case the sheer labor of producing so much so rapidly must have diminished the talent she had shown in the "Chronicles of Carlingford." Nevertheless, some of her later novels are interesting—especially those, like *A Beleaguered City* (1879), dealing with historical subjects and the occult.

Mrs. Oliphant's sons died in 1890 and 1894; but, though crushed by grief and still not free from financial cares, she continued to produce important work in the last decade of her life, writing a sympathetic portrait (1891) of her distant relative Laurence Oliphant and the history of Blackwood's publishing house (1897). She was aware that her fiction was no longer fashionable, and in her posthumously published letters and autobiography (1898), some bitterness about this change in taste is evident. Her death on 25 June 1897 at her home in Windsor did not elicit much response; today, perhaps, its lonely pathos can be appreciated.

In her autobiography, Mrs. Oliphant refers to her talent as "the equivocal virtue of industry." One must sympathize with her bitterness that this virtue was not recognized when she was alive. Posterity has hardly been kinder to her reputation, although *Salem Chapel* has occasionally been reprinted. Recently, the publication of a full-length biography and the inclusion of Mrs. Oliphant as an important author in a series of novels on Victorian religion may indicate some minor revival, and modern readers may find even in an average Oliphant novel both a valuable insight into Victorian behavior and some moving scenes of pathos.

Biography:
Vand R. Colby, *The Equivocal Virtue* (New York:

Archon, 1966).

Reference:
Robert Lee Wolff, *Gains and Losses: Novels of Faith and Doubt in Victorian England* (New York: Garland, 1977).

Ouida
(Marie Louise de la Ramée)
(1 January 1839-25 January 1908)

Roy B. Stokes
University of British Columbia

BOOKS: *Held in Bondage* (3 volumes, London: Tinsley, 1863; 2 volumes, Philadelphia: Lippincott, 1864);

Strathmore (3 volumes, London: Chapman & Hall, 1865; 1 volume, Philadelphia: Lippincott, 1866);

Chandos (London: Chapman & Hall, 1866; Philadelphia: Lippincott, 1867);

Under Two Flags (3 volumes, London: Chapman & Hall, 1867; 1 volume, Philadelphia: Lippincott, 1867);

Idalia (3 volumes, London: Chapman & Hall, 1867; 1 volume, Philadelphia: Lippincott, 1867);

Tricotrin (2 volumes, London: Chapman & Hall, 1869; 1 volume, Philadelphia: Lippincott, 1869);

Cecil Castlemaine's Gage and Other Novelettes (London: Chapman & Hall, 1870);

Puck (3 volumes, London: Chapman & Hall, 1870; 1 volume, Philadelphia: Lippincott, 1871);

Folle Farine (3 volumes, London: Chapman & Hall, 1871; 1 volume, Philadelphia: Lippincott, 1871);

A Dog of Flanders and Other Stories (London: Chatto & Windus, 1872);

Pascarel (3 volumes, London: Chapman & Hall, 1873; 1 volume, Philadelphia: Lippincott, 1873);

Two Little Wooden Shoes (London: Chapman & Hall, 1874; Philadelphia: Lippincott, 1897);

Signa (3 volumes, London: Chapman & Hall, 1875; 1 volume, Philadelphia: Lippincott, 1875);

In a Winter City (London: Chapman & Hall, 1876; Philadelphia: Lippincott, 1876);

Ariadne: The Story of a Dream (3 volumes, London: Chapman & Hall, 1877; 1 volume, Philadelphia: Lippincott, 1877);

Friendship (3 volumes, London: Chatto & Windus, 1878; 1 volume, Philadelphia: Lippincott, 1878);

Moths (3 volumes, London: Chatto & Windus, 1880; 1 volume, Philadelphia: Lippincott, 1880);

Pipistrello and Other Stories (London: Chatto & Windus, 1880; New York: Munro, 1880);

A Village Commune (2 volumes, London: Chatto & Windus, 1881; 1 volume, New York: Munro, 1881);

In Maremma (3 volumes, London: Chatto & Windus, 1882; 1 volume, Philadelphia: Lippincott, 1882);

Bimbi: Stories for Children (London: Chatto & Windus, 1882; Philadelphia: Lippincott, 1882);

Frescoes: Dramatic Sketches (London: Chatto & Windus, 1883; New York: Munro, 1883);

Wanda (3 volumes, London: Chatto & Windus, 1883; 1 volume, New York: Lovell, 1883);

Princess Napraxine (3 volumes, London: Chatto & Windus, 1884; 1 volume, New York: Lovell, 1884);

A Rainy June (London: Maxwell, 1885; New York: Lovell, 1885);

Othmar (3 volumes, London: Chatto & Windus, 1885; 1 volume, Philadelphia: Lippincott, 1885);

Don Gesualdo (London: Routledge, 1886; New York: Munro, 1886);

A House Party (New York: Lovell, 1886; London: Hurst & Blackett, 1887);

Guilderoy (3 volumes, London: Chatto & Windus, 1889; 1 volume, New York: Lovell, 1889);

Ruffino (London: Chatto & Windus, 1890; New York: United States Book Company, 1890);

Syrlin (3 volumes, London: Chatto & Windus, 1890; 1 volume, Philadelphia: Lippincott, 1890);

Santa Barbara (London: Chatto & Windus, 1891; New York: Lovell, 1891);

The Tower of Taddeo (3 volumes, London: Heinemann, 1892; 1 volume, New York: Hovendon, 1892);

The New Priesthood: A Protest against Vivisection (London: Allen, 1893);

Two Offenders and Other Tales (London: Chatto & Windus, 1894; Philadelphia: Lippincott, 1894);

The Silver Christ, and A Lemon Tree (London: Unwin, 1894; New York & London: Macmillan, 1894);

Toxin (London: Unwin, 1895; New York & London: Stokes, 1895);

Views and Opinions (London: Methuen, 1895);

Le Selve and Other Tales (London: Unwin, 1896);

An Altruist (London: Unwin, 1897; London & New York: Neely, 1897);

The Massarenes (London: Low, Marston, 1897; New York: Fenno, 1897);

La Strega and Other Stories (London: Low, Marston, 1899);

The Waters of Edera (New York: Fenno, 1899; London: Unwin, 1900);

Street Dust and Other Stories (Philadelphia & New York: Biddle, 1899; London: White, 1901);

Critical Studies (London: Unwin, 1900; New York: Cassell, 1900);

Helianthus (London & New York: Macmillan, 1908).

If Ouida is now remembered at all, three-quarters of a century after her death, it is probably only as the author of *Under Two Flags* (1867). Even that small measure of fame owes something to the dramatized versions of the story rather than to the original novel. The lack of serious modern critical regard, however, cannot obscure the picture of a popular late-nineteenth-century writer. She lived for most of her career and died in Italy, a few miles from Pisa, surrounded by the dogs whose company she came to enjoy more than that of many humans. When Wilfrid Scawen Blunt and Sydney Cockerell went to visit her, their driver could only find his way when he realized that they wished to see "the lady with the many dogs." Her main monument in England was a drinking fountain for dogs and horses in Bury St. Edmunds, the town of her birth; but in 1909, a fountain which boasted an inscription written especially for the occasion by Lord Curzon of Kedleston, the most eminent patrician figure of the age, was scarcely an ordinary trough.

She was born on the first day of 1839 to an English mother and a French father. Louis Ramé, middle-aged, small, and ugly, had arrived in Bury St. Edmunds in the 1830s; he was reputed by some to be a Bonapartist agent, a suspicion supported by his frequent absences from home. It is difficult to see what role he could have played in Bury St. Edmunds, in spite of its being a garrison town; but his airs of gallantry made him a figure for speculation in this small provincial community. Louise adored her father and when, two years before her death, she was annoyed by plans to put a plaque on her birthplace, she referred to "this tomfoolery in Suffolk" and said that she identified herself with her "father's French life and blood." Her distaste for East Anglia was carried into her writing: "Norfolk we voted . . . unanimously as the most infernally slow and hideous county going; and so, with the exception of its twin province, Suffolk, I still hold it is." M. Ramé had come to Bury St. Edmunds, ostensibly at least, to teach French, but he was a man of much wider interests than that alone. Although Louise attended a normal "Young Ladies" school where she learned the useful arts of needlework, painting, and deportment, her father added breadth to the program. He taught her history and mathematics, instilled in her a love of literature and, on their long walks together, gave her an intense feeling for nature. It is small wonder that she hero-worshipped him, and as his visits home became less and less frequent until they finally ceased altogether, she carried a romanticized memory of him all her life. This early hero worship of her father can be seen as the genesis of all the later typical Ouida heroes. Tall, handsome, romantic, mysterious, they were the embodiment of all that her father was not; but in her imagination they flaunted the attitudes and graces of her idealized portrait of him.

No other influence was so strong as that one from her early years. Bury St. Edmunds in the mid-nineteenth century enjoyed no circumstances which could put it into a relationship with the world of high society. It boasted little of the horsey camaraderie of the hunting shires; yet Louise was drawn toward the glamour of the military and fashionable worlds. Perhaps it was as the distant line of the Shropshire hills was to A. E. Housman, "a sentimental feeling for . . . [the] horizon." There is no reason to believe that the Ramé family ever had contact with the population of the garrison. Beside the house in which she was brought up were the gates of Hardwick House, the park and grounds of which were open to the public and in which she walked with her family; but it is unlikely that the family would have penetrated the society of the big house itself. Twice, and each time with remarkable effect, she broke out of the confines of her limited society. In 1850, M. Ramé, then abroad, invited his wife and daughter to spend a part of their summer holiday with him in Boulogne. In spite of an appalling channel crossing the stay opened up to her new vistas of life. As she recorded in her diary, "You can have a ball any night you please. . . . I went last Wednesday to the ball, I danced a great deal, I had five beaux. . . . I went to the theatre. . . ." It was so different from her hometown where, she said, "the inhabitants are driven to ring their own door-bells lest they rust from disuse." In 1851 she traveled up to London for the Great Exhibition, which she

The Villa Farinola in Scandicci, Italy, where Ouida lived from 1874 to 1888 with her mother and her dogs. She was evicted because—evidently believing plants to have feelings—she refused to keep the garden hedges trimmed.

found to be a "noble idea"; the exhibits on display were of an unbelievable beauty.

Luck played a part in the launching of Ouida's career. By the age of twenty she was living in Hammersmith, where her neighbor and medical adviser was Dr. Francis W. Ainsworth, cousin to William Harrison Ainsworth. An introduction to W. H. Ainsworth led to his encouragement of Ouida and to his invitation to her to write for *Bentley's Miscellany*, of which he was then editor. Ainsworth was the first of many literary figures who saw first promise and then fulfillment in her career. Her first story, "Dashwood's Drag; or, The Derby and What Came of It," appeared in 1859, and thereafter the pace remained as hectic as her prose. Six more stories were published in 1859, ten in 1860, eight in 1861, five in 1862; then there was a slackening in periodical publication. So much exposure in a popular, well-regarded journal allowed her to feel that what she had to offer was in keeping with an appreciable segment of the taste of her day. It is also a large enough body of work for some of her dominant themes and attitudes to be apparent. The stories, when told in the first person, are narrated by men; many are set in a very masculine world: an army mess, rooms in the Inns of Court, chambers in the fashionable bachelor establishment of the Albany along Piccadilly, Cambridge colleges—all locations which, in Ouida's day, were male preserves and, in the society which she depicted, the world of a particular type of male. They were splendid fellows, "cool, proud, plucky as a terrier, strong as a bruiser, and generous as the winds"; a typical example was "a young Greek, with his gay debonnaire air, long chestnut hair, and languid hazel eyes."

These marionettes dominated her stories as they cynically and nonchalantly dominated the women in their lives. Ouida's view of her fashionable sisters, as seen through the eyes of her heroes, is unflattering but consistent. "I've made love to no end of women in my time; but when one love was died out I took another, as I take a cigar, and never wept over the quenched ashes." The women themselves paint an equally depressing picture and one example seems to evoke a picture of Ouida's ordinary mother clipping the wings of her extraordinary father: "If you marry me, sir, you'll give up latch-keys, Epsom, bals d'Opéra, loo parties, and all the cognac of life, and be ironed down into a model husband forthwith." None of this can prove that Ouida disliked her own sex, but invariably unflattering comments do not indicate a very high regard. Perhaps in this lay one reason for her choosing the

pseudonym under which she wrote from her very first story. "Ouida" was her interpretation of a childish mispronunciation of "Louise" and, on one occasion at least, she used it to put down a false trail. There was the "dear, dashing little widow (who was perusing *Bentley*, and asked me if I did not think 'that fellow Ouida had been jilted by some woman, he was so spiteful on the beau sexe's shortcomings')."

Ouida's first novel was published in 1863 by Tinsley. It had first appeared in the *New Monthly Magazine* under the title of "Granville de Vigne" but in book form was changed to *Held in Bondage*. With this novel Ouida began as she intended to continue; all the marks of a typical Ouida romance were there from the start. It is the story of a group of cavalry officers and the adventures which befall them. Their leader, and the book's main character, is Granville de Vigne, who becomes involved with a "fast lady" and marries her; but luckily in the end she turns out to be a bigamist. Ouida's settings are opulent and gave to her imagination-starved readers the sensations of having touched the fringes of high society. From this time until the end of the century, there was scarcely a year without an offering from Ouida to her public; novels, short stories, essays, tracts on vivisection poured from her pen. Her own eccentricities and somewhat flamboyant personality heightened the general public's awareness of her presence and her work. Her appearance was strangely striking. William Allingham described her in his diary: "in green silk, sinister, clever face, hair down, small hands and feet, voice like a carving knife." She was renowned for her rudeness, her snobbery, her bitter tongue (especially when expressing dislike of her own sex), her extravagance. She talked approvingly, and loudly, of her own work and was the natural center of any party. Even though many members of the general public had not penetrated her pseudonym, there could be no mystery in literary circles. It was in these circles that she wished to be recognized and known, and she left no doubt whatsoever of her own worth. "As I talk better than others," she said, "I ought to be listened to even if singing is going on." Some largely fortuitous circumstances played a part in her success. Her novel *Strathmore* (1865) was parodied by Francis Burnand in ten issues of *Punch* in 1878 under the title "Strapmore! A Romance by 'Weeder.'" Perhaps even more helpful to her reputation was a savage attack on her work by Lord Strangford in the *Pall Mall Gazette*, an influential and established magazine. Notoriety, then as now,

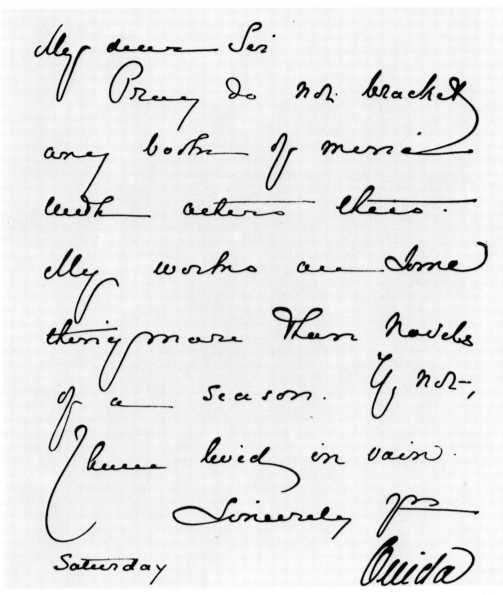

Letter from Ouida to publisher T. Fisher Unwin in 1900, showing her high opinion of her own work and her low regard for other authors

was a splendid spur to sales.

As her fame began to grow, she insisted that the family should call itself "de la Ramée" instead of simply Ramé. This did not meet with her mother's approval, but Ouida used this more fashionable version for the rest of her life in spite of some embarrassing moments. On one occasion she was staying at Knebworth as the guest of Lord Lytton and had irritated most of the house party with her intolerable manners. The Lyttons' governess also was from Bury St. Edmunds, and when Ouida was talking of her father's aristocratic descent, the gov-

erness addressed her as Miss Ramé and asked her whether she remembered the parties at her grandmother's house at No. 1, Union Terrace. Ouida began to make extended trips to Italy and in 1874 settled with her mother at a house in Florence. She later moved to Scandicci, three miles outside Florence, and lived in or near Florence for twenty-three years. For many years the income from her writing enabled her to live up to the standards which she depicted in her novels. The best chefs in Italy, the choicest wines, the finest clothes by Worth, the most expensive furs surrounded her with luxury. She once said that she never received more than £1,600 for any one novel but that she found America "a mine of worth." She had assuredly been well treated by American publishers, much better than many of her contemporaries. Her books were very popular there, and Lippincott paid her £300 for advance sheets for each of her books until pirated editions forced a reduction of the payment. This led her to write a letter to the *Times* complaining about piratical publishing.

Ouida's pictures of high-society life can in no sense be regarded as accurate accounts. They do not have the same touch of personal involvement as did some of the writings of the "silver-fork" school. Although she added society figures to her list of friends and acquaintances throughout her life, Ouida was never truly a part of that scene. Her view was largely an external and mainly an admiring one. Tinsley recorded a rumor that she invited young guards' officers to dinner and asked them to talk and behave as if she and her mother were not present; this may have been her nearest approach to realism in regard to society. Her pictures of peasant life and character, on the other hand, which she introduced into a number of her stories written during the Florence years, were drawn from her close and acute observation. The country population around her home in Italy provided the necessary raw material and here, more than anywhere else in her writing, are some closely and carefully drawn characters.

There are, nevertheless, positive characteristics in her writing which have had as much appeal to a number of critics as they did to her general readers. The sheer exuberance of her style, the vitality of her action did much to counterbalance the somewhat puppetlike poses of her heroes and heroines. She endowed her basically simple story lines with larger-than-life figures, backgrounds, and emotions. Inevitably, the "theatrical" quality which she created was seized upon by many contemporary critics as an outstanding attribute. If the term resists precise interpretation, its appropriateness can be judged partially by the relationship between her works and the theater and cinema. Several of her novels were adapted for dramatic presentations and Ouida herself embarked on one attempt, admittedly abortive, to write a play for the actors Sir Squire and Marie Wilton Bancroft. But serious critics also held her in some esteem. Max Beerbohm compared her with George Meredith, "the only living novelist in England who rivals Ouida in sheer vitality," and spoke of her as "that unique, flam-

boyant lady, one of the miracles of modern literature. After all these years, she is still young and swift and strong, towering head and shoulders over all the other women (and all but one or two of the men) who are writing English novels." Many other critics and public figures paid tribute to her work. Bulwer-Lytton wrote an eight-page letter praising *Folle Farine* (1871) as a triumph of modern English romance; Lady Dorothy Nevill, Sydney Cockerell, Norman Douglas, and Wilfrid Scawen Blunt were among those who regarded her as an important figure on the literary scene.

It is not easy now to judge this enthusiasm. Few of the novels are readily available, and, even if they were, it would be necessary to read them against the background of a society which is imaginatively difficult to recreate. *Under Two Flags*, her most enduring novel, is deeply rooted in its contemporary morals and attitudes. It tells the story of the Honorable Bertie Cecil of the First Life Guards. His father, Lord Royallieu, owns an estate which is mortaged to the hilt and has encouraged his sons to adopt the same mode of life. Bertie leads an existence surrounded by fast friends, fast women, and fast horses. He shoulders the blame for a horse-doping incident in order to protect a lady's name. By a throw of the dice he decides to join the French Foreign Legion. His power over women remains a dominant part of his character and, in particular, he is the object of the love of Cigarette, a singer, dancer, and fierily independent woman. She rescues him from certain death at the hands of a group of drunken Arabs and nurses him back to health after he has been wounded in battle. Finally, when Bertie is condemned to face a firing squad for striking a superior officer who had insulted a lady, Cigarette saves his life for the last time. As the volley of shots rings out, Cigarette flings her body in front of his and dies—but Bertie is saved. This kind of melodramatic romance is common to all her stories and sustained her well. G. K. Chesterton was the reader of *The Waters of Edera* (1899) for Unwin and his report commenced: "This is, of course, a picturesque, animated, poetic, eloquent and supremely nonsensical story; it is by Ouida: and age does not wither nor custom stale her infinite lack of variety." By the early 1890s, however, her publishers warned her that her novels were losing popularity, but she remained as willful and as financially reckless as ever, with the result that her fortunes rapidly declined. She blamed much of it on "dishonest lawyers and absconding bankers," but most of the trouble lay within herself. Her poverty became so acute that when her mother died in 1893 she was buried in a pauper's grave.

The late years of the nineteenth century witnessed much agonizing and writing over the state of the book trade in England and, in particular, the part played by the three-decker (three-volume) novel. Ouida entered this controversy with an article in the *North American Review* of February 1895 in which she saw the circulating library as an important element in the rise in publication of "works which should have been put on the fire, which should indeed never have been written at all." The circulating librarian, however, needed "box-stuffers—i.e., any amount of trash so long as it is new." Many of these novels were badly produced and compared unfavorably with their counterparts in France, but the libraries could absorb enough of them to make their publication profitable. Ouida's increased distaste for many things English also came to the fore: her writing expressed her support for the Boers during the South African War and a vehement dislike of Colonial Secretary Joseph Chamberlain and his imperialist policies. She saw the lamentable literary and artistic taste of the English lying at the base of many of the problems of publishing. "Books are the things which English people, gentle and simple, can do without most easily. They read, also, in a muddle-headed kind of way. They read when they are tired, when they are travelling, when they are alone after dinner, and when they want to go to sleep. When they can do anything better or more amusing they seldom read."

At last, after years of abject poverty but with no lessening of her self-esteem, Ouida died of pneumonia. She was buried, as she wished, in Italy at Bagni di Lucca with a tombstone paid for by an admirer. It carries a recumbent figure of herself with a dog lying at her feet.

Ouida was a writer of marked individuality in her work as well as in her life, where she strayed happily into eccentricity. She was not a sufficiently good craftsman to rank as an outstanding writer, and her stern hostility to women's suffrage makes her unacceptable to many modern tastes; but she cannot be ignored if one wishes to study the growing effect of women novelists on British letters during the nineteenth century. She claimed for herself the right to be different, to speak her mind on a variety of topics, to be subservient to no one. Prickly, yet capable of feeling and of kindling great affection for and in a wide variety of people, Ouida

Ouida's tomb in the English cemetery at Bagni di Lucca, Italy, paid for by an anonymous admirer. The sculpture shows Ouida with one of her beloved dogs lying at her feet.

cannot be omitted from the story of the nineteenth-century novel.

Biographies:

Elizabeth Lee, *Ouida: A Memoir* (London: Unwin, 1914);

Monica Stirling, *The Fine and the Wicked: The Life and Times of Ouida* (London: Gollancz, 1957).

References:

Max Beerbohm, *More* (London: John Lane, 1899);

Eileen Bigland, *Ouida, The Passionate Victorian* (London: Jarrolds, 1950);

Yvonne ffrench, *Ouida, A Study in Ostentation* (London: Cobden-Sanderson, 1938);

Rose Macauley, "Eccentric Englishwomen: Ouida," *Spectator* (7 May 1937): 855-856.

James Payn

(28 February 1830-25 March 1898)

R. C. Terry
University of Victoria

BOOKS: *Stories from Boccaccio and Other Poems* (London: Wright, 1852);

Poems (Cambridge: Macmillan, 1853);

Stories and Sketches (London: Smith Elder, 1857);

Leaves from Lakeland (London: Hamilton, Adams, 1858);

Furness Abbey and Its Neighbourhood (Windermere: Garnett, 1858);

A Handbook to the English Lakes (London: Simpkin, Marshall, 1859);

The Foster Brothers (London: Hall, Virtue, 1859);

The Bateman Household (London: Hall, Virtue, 1860);

Richard Arbour; or, The Family Scapegrace (Edinburgh: Edmonston & Douglas, 1861);

Meliboeus in London (Cambridge: Macmillan, 1862);

Lost Sir Massingberd: A Romance of Real Life (2 volumes, London: Low, Marston, 1864; 1 volume, Philadelphia: Peterson, 1870);

Married beneath Him (3 volumes, London: Macmillan, 1865; 1 volume, New York: Munro, 1879);

People, Places, and Things (London: Beeton, 1865);

Mirk Abbey (3 volumes, London: Hurst & Blackett, 1866);

The Clyffards of Clyffe (3 volumes, London: Hurst & Blackett, 1866; 1 volume, Philadelphia: Peterson, 1871);

The Lakes in Sunshine: Being Photographic and Other Pictures of the Lake District of Westmoreland and North Lancashire (2 volumes, Windermere: Garnett, 1867-1870);

Lights and Shadows of London Life (2 volumes, London: Hurst & Blackett, 1867);

Carlyon's Year (1 volume, New York: Harper, 1867; 2 volumes, London: Bradbury, Evans, 1868);

Blondel Parva (2 volumes, London: Bradbury, Evans, 1868);

Bentinck's Tutor, One of the Family: A Novel (2 volumes, London: Low, 1868);

Maxims by a Man of the World (London: n.p., 1869);

A Perfect Treasure: An Incident in the Early Life of Marmaduke Drake, Esq. (London: Tinsley, 1869);

A County Family: A Novel (3 volumes, London: Tinsley, 1869; 1 volume, Boston: Littell & Gay, 1870);

Found Dead (3 volumes, London: Tinsley, 1869);

Gwendoline's Harvest: A Novel (2 volumes, London: Bungay, 1870; 1 volume, New York: Harper, 1870);

Like Father, like Son: A Novel (London: Chapman & Hall, 1871);

Not Wooed but Won: A Novel (London: n.p., 1871);

A Woman's Vengeance (3 volumes, London: Bentley, 1872; 1 volume, New York: Harper, 1872);

Cecil's Tryst: A Novel (3 volumes, London: Tinsley, 1872; 1 volume, New York: Harper, 1872);

Murphy's Master and Other Stories (2 volumes, London: Tinsley, 1873; 1 volume, New York: Harper, 1873);

The Best of Husbands (3 volumes, London: Bentley, 1874; 1 volume, New York: Harper, 1874);

At Her Mercy (3 volumes, London: Bentley, 1874; 1 volume, New York: Harper, 1874);

Walter's Word: A Novel (3 volumes, London: Tinsley, 1875; 1 volume, New York: Harper, 1875);

Halves: A Novel, and Other Tales (3 volumes, London: Tinsley, 1876; 1 volume, New York: Harper, 1876);

Fallen Fortunes (3 volumes, London: Tinsley, 1876; 1 volume, New York: Munro, 1880);

What He Cost Her (3 volumes, London: Chatto & Windus, 1877; 1 volume, New York: Harper, 1877);

By Proxy: A Novel (2 volumes, London: Chatto & Windus, 1878; 1 volume, New York: Harper, 1878);

Less Black than We're Painted: A Novel (3 volumes, London: Chatto & Windus, 1878; 1 volume, New York: Harper, 1878);

Under One Roof: An Episode in a Family History (3 volumes, London: Chatto & Windus, 1879; 1 volume, New York: Harper, 1879);

High Spirits: Being Certain Stories Written in Them (3 volumes, London: Chatto & Windus, 1879; 1 volume, New York: Harper, 1879);

A Confidential Agent (3 volumes, London: Chatto & Windus, 1880; 1 volume, New York: Harper, 1880);

From Exile: A Novel (3 volumes, London: Chatto & Windus, 1881; 1 volume, New York: Harper, 1881);

A Grape from a Thorn: A Novel (3 volumes, London: Smith, Elder, 1881-1882; 1 volume, New York: Harper, 1881);

Some Private Views: Being Essays from the "Nineteenth Century Review" with Some Occasional Articles from the "Times" (London: Chatto & Windus, 1881);

For Cash Only: A Novel (3 volumes, London: Chatto & Windus, 1882-1884; 1 volume, New York: Harper, 1882);

Thicker than Water: A Novel (3 volumes, London: Longmans, Green, 1883; 1 volume, New York: Harper, 1883);

Kit: A Memory (3 volumes, London: Chatto & Windus, 1883; 1 volume, New York: Harper, 1882);

The Canon's Ward: A Novel (3 volumes, London: Chatto & Windus, 1884; 1 volume, New York: Harper, 1884);

Some Literary Recollections (London: Smith, Elder, 1884; New York: Harper, 1884);

The Luck of the Darrells: A Novel (3 volumes, London: Longmans, Green, 1885; 1 volume, New York: Harper, 1885);

In Peril and Privation: Stories of Marine Disaster Retold (London: Chatto & Windus, 1885; New York: Harper, 1885);

The Heir of the Ages: A Novel (3 volumes, London: Smith, Elder, 1886; 1 volume, New York: Harper, 1886);

Glow-Worm Tales (3 volumes, London: Chatto & Windus, 1887; 1 volume, New York: Harper, 1881);

Holiday Tasks: Being Essays Written in Vacation Time (London: Chatto & Windus, 1887);

The Eavesdropper: An Unparalleled Experience (London: Smith, Elder, 1888);

A Prince of the Blood: A Novel (London: Ward & Downey, 1888; New York: Harper, 1888);

The Mystery of Mirbridge (3 volumes, London: Chatto & Windus, 1888-1889; 1 volume, New York: Harper, 1888);

Notes from the "News" (London: Chatto & Windus, 1890; New York: Lovell, 1890);

The Word and the Will: A Novel (3 volumes, London: Chatto & Windus, 1890; 1 volume, New York: Lovell, 1890);

The Burnt Million (3 volumes, London: Chatto & Windus, 1890; 1 volume, New York: Lovell, 1890);

Sunny Stories and Some Shady Ones (London: Chatto & Windus, 1891; New York: Lovell, 1891);

A Stumble on the Threshold: A Novel (2 volumes, London: Cox, 1892; 1 volume, New York: Appleton, 1892);

A Modern Dick Whittington; or, A Patron of Letters (2 volumes, London: Cassell, 1892; 1 volume, New York: Taylor, 1892);

A Trying Patient (London: Chatto & Windus, 1893);

Humorous Stories about People, Places, and Things (London: Chatto & Windus, 1893);

Gleams of Memory with Some Reflections (London: Smith, Elder, 1894);

In Market Overt: A Novel (London: Cox, 1895; Philadelphia: Lippincott, 1895);

The Disappearance of George Driffell (London: Smith, Elder, 1896);

Another's Burden (London: Downey, 1897);

The Backwater of Life; or, Essays of a Literary Veteran, biographical introduction by Sir Leslie Stephen (London: Smith, Elder, 1899).

James Payn was among the brightest disciples of Dickens, to whom he dedicated *Mirk Abbey* (1866). He found fame with his thriller *Lost Sir Massingberd* (1864) and for many years thereafter delighted his public with a blend of romance, intrigue, adventure, and comedy. The key phrase for him is *High Spirits*, the title of one of his collections of short stories published in 1879. Mysteries and family stories flowed easily from his pen for nearly forty years. He was a brilliant writer of vignettes and the tidbits that the public demanded as the century wore on. But he had gifts as a novelist, particularly in plotting, and brought the art of the comedy thriller into prominence. He was also adept at drawing credible characters whom he placed in impossible fixes against vividly realized backgrounds drawn from the length and breadth of Britain and from overseas. He should perhaps be classified among the sensational writers, but he brought his own flair to the apparatus of lost wills and ingenious deaths and branched out in other fields, notably the exotic adventure that became the staple of Kipling, Rider Haggard, and Conrad. Payn is the prime example of the later Victorian appetite for entertaining fiction or "light literature," as he himself called it, and the embodiment of the professional man of letters. He was, said Leslie Stephen simply,

the best of the journalists, among whom most of his working life was spent.

James Payn was born on 28 February 1830 at Cheltenham, Gloucestershire, and spent his childhood in Maidenhead, Berkshire, where his father was clerk to the Thames Commissioners and kept the Berkshire harriers. He attended Eton, where a talent for storytelling kept bullies at bay. He also had a brief, unhappy spell at the Royal Military Academy, Woolwich. At Trinity College, Cambridge (1849-1854), he began his literary career with *Stories from Boccaccio and Other Poems* (1852) and contributions to *Household Words* and other periodicals. In 1854 he married Louisa Adelaide Edlin. They had seven children; the eldest daughter, Alicia, married G. E. Buckle, editor of the *Times*. From 1859 to 1874 Payn successfully edited *Chambers's Journal*, which published many of his novels in serial form. In 1861 he took a house at Maida Vale, London, where he remained until his death on 25 March 1898.

His first prose work, *Stories and Sketches* (1857), stands comparison with Dickens's work in a similar vein; it was followed by his first novel, *The Foster Brothers* (1859), which established a pattern of unremitting labor resulting in forty-six novels, seven volumes of short stories, several books of essays, and two fine autobiographical studies, *Some Literary Recollections* (1884) and *Gleams of Memory* (1894), both useful diaries of events and personalities of the Victorian heyday.

Payn had all the gifts of the born journalist—lively curiosity, abundant energy, retentive memory, and a friendly disposition; above all, he had an eye for the telling detail of a scene and the distinguishing trait of character, both of which guaranteed his success as novelist as well as journalist. His reputation for fairness and his thorough knowledge of the book trade made him a much-loved figure in literary circles. For many years he was reader for the publisher George Smith and also an active collaborator with Walter Besant in the cause of authors' rights. Succeeding Leslie Stephen as editor of Smith's ailing *Cornhill Magazine* (1883-1896), he helped launch the career of Arthur Conan Doyle. In later years, much crippled with rheumatism, he still contributed a regular column to the *Illustrated London News*. Although nearly all his novels contain distinctive bits of action and acute observation of character, he remains within the limits he set for himself: a minor novelist, but of the better sort. Critics in the *Saturday Review* and *Spectator* showed remarkable unanimity in greeting each new work of fiction as readable and amusing, while lacking the ultimate care and deliberation of which Payn was capable.

It was with *Lost Sir Massingberd* that Payn joined the ranks of best-selling authors. Publication in *Chambers's Journal* raised the circulation by 20,000 copies, and the young author recalled with pride that "Dickens touched my trembling ear with praise." The story, spiced with Payn's high-spirited humor, is a sensational tale in a romanticized country-house setting. It was Payn's trademark to invest a thriller with a touch of the fantastic and supernatural that made it a Victorian version of Gothic romance. The central episode concerning the disappearance of an outrageously wicked baronet is what caught the public interest; even Wilkie Collins confessed he had been baffled by the

mystery. Payn's ingenuity had been to make his villain fall down inside a hollow tree; his arms pinioned and far from help, Sir Massingberd stuck fast and starved to death. Although not the best of Payn's novels, *Lost Sir Massingberd* illustrates his careful plotting and journalistic flair for the arresting detail. In novel after novel he dreamed up original ways of putting his heroes in awkward predicaments or disposing of his villains, and in this respect made a contribution to the sensational novel which has not been sufficiently explored. In *The Clyffards of Clyffe* (1866), for example, one villain is cut off by the tide, traps his arm in a rock fissure, and drowns. In *Like Father, like Son* (1871), a man traps a rival in an old mine shaft, removes a ladder, and leaves him to be eaten by rats. In *The Bateman Household* (1860), the hero discovers a missing man while skating on a lake in Westmoreland by seeing

Yellow-back editions of two of Payn's novels

the frozen features staring up at him from beneath the ice. Quicksand, drownings, madness, prussic acid, rooms with secret apartments are the very stuff of a Payn plot. One of his most outlandish deaths occurs in *Not Wooed but Won* (1871), in which a tyrant is in the habit of throwing his bulldog violently at the door until it eventually turns on him and bites him, giving him hydrophobia.

Like other sensationalists, Payn is partial to characters in pairs—betrayer and betrayed, the good and bad cousins, the hobbledehoy and the false friend—and their love and legacy entanglements; in *Cecil's Tryst* (1872), the involved plot concerns identical twins. Often Payn relies on the lost-and-found motif with the presumably lost heir or lover reappearing at the appropriate moment to confound the villain, claim his inheritance, console his parents, or win the heroine. But however close in outline to the sensationalism of Collins and Miss Braddon, Payn's has a playful self-consciousness that makes it all his own. In *The Clyffards of Clyffe*, for example, his exuberant style is splendidly manifest in a farrago of secret passages, shrouded figures, and cliff-hanging suspense; the book amounts to a parody of serious sensational novels. The setting is Donnerblick Scars in West Yorkshire, where the Boggart (evil spirit) walks, and the plot concerns a wicked woman's attempt to defraud the true heir of the Clyffard estates by impersonating a ghostly ancestor. Contemporary reviews generally agree that Payn was reviving a cheerful Gothicism that gave new life to current sensationalism. As the *Saturday Review* observed of *A Woman's Vengeance* (1872), "he does not scruple to go to the very verge of possibility."

Fantasy and comic invention are Payn's chief assets in his best stories. *A Perfect Treasure* (1869), one of his own favorites, concerns the mysterious hold a certain Indian servant has over his master. The hero unravels the secret only when the Indian is recovered from a shipwreck and a diamond surgically removed from his body turns out to be the legacy due the young man. *By Proxy* (1878), Payn's most popular tale after *Lost Sir Massingberd*, is another bravura work, in which a romantic setting in China exactly suits the extravagant nature of the plot. Again the story concerns a valuable diamond, but this time it is stolen from a Chinese temple; and the narrative blends rather nicely the suggestion of supernatural retributive processes at work with the psychological breakdown by conscience of the thief.

Besides novels, Payn enjoyed considerable success with short stories and essays, both early and late in his career. Some of these are collected in *Meliboeus in London* (1862), *People, Places, and Things* (1865), *Maxims by a Man of the World* (1869), and *Some Private Views* (1881). Among his short stories, "High Spirits" is a charming futuristic tale of the year 1979, which forecasts television, super air conditioning, a tunnel under the English Channel, concentrated foods in pills, air fleets, and twice-daily postal deliveries between Australia and England; the *Times* is the only surviving high-priced newspaper.

His longtime friend Leslie Stephen described Payn as a "Scheherazade of fiction," a thoroughly professional writer who knew his limits and was entirely without jealousy, a fine, witty conversationalist, "the simplest and most transparent of men." In an early novel, *Married beneath Him* (1865), Payn offered an illuminating view of authorship. His hero aspires to be a writer and Payn says of him: "Experience of life, of course, he had not; but he had wonderful intuition in place of it; while high spirits—inestimable gift, almost always denied to a well-seasoned writer; that virtue to which Dickens owed so much of his charm . . . illumined every page." It was Payn's good fortune to combine high spirits with experience.

Reference:
R. C. Terry, *Victorian Popular Fiction, 1860-80* (London: Macmillan, forthcoming).

Papers:
Some of Payn's manuscript materials are at the University of Chicago and the Humanities Research Center, University of Texas at Austin. A complete collection of his works is at the University of Victoria, British Columbia.

Anne Thackeray Ritchie

(9 June 1837-26 February 1919)

Barbara J. Dunlap
City College, City University of New York

BOOKS: *The Story of Elizabeth* (London: Smith, Elder, 1863; New York: Gregory, 1864);

The Village on the Cliff (London: Smith, Elder, 1867; New York: Harper, 1873);

Five Old Friends; and a Young Prince (London: Smith, Elder, 1868);

To Esther and Other Sketches (London: Smith, Elder, 1869);

Old Kensington (London: Smith, Elder, 1873; New York: Harper, 1873);

Bluebeard's Keys and Other Stories (London: Smith, Elder, 1874; New York: Harper, 1875);

Toilers and Spinsters and Other Essays (London: Smith, Elder, 1874);

Miss Angel (London: Smith, Elder, 1875; New York: Harper, 1875);

Out of the World, and Other Tales (Leipzig: Tauchnitz, 1876; New York: Munro, 1880);

Fulham Lawn and Other Tales (Leipzig: Tauchnitz, 1877);

From an Island: A Story and Some Essays (Leipzig: Tauchnitz, 1877; New York: Munro, 1880);

Da Capo (New York: Harper, 1878);

Madame de Sévigné (London: Blackwood, 1881; Philadelphia: Lippincott, 1881);

Miss Williamson's Divagations (London: Smith, Elder, 1881; New York: Harper, 1881);

A Book of Sibyls: Mrs. Barbauld, Miss Edgeworth, Mrs. Opie, Miss Austen (London: Smith, Elder, 1883; New York: Harper, 1883);

Mrs. Dymond (London: Smith, Elder, 1885; New York: Harper, 1885);

Jack Frost's Little Prisoners (London: Skeffington, 1887);

Records of Tennyson, Ruskin, and Robert and Elizabeth Browning (London: Macmillan, 1892; New York: Macmillan, 1892);

Alfred, Lord Tennyson and His Friends: A Series of 25 Portraits from the Negatives of Mrs. Julia Margaret Cameron and H. H. H. Cameron. Reminiscences by Anne Thackeray Ritchie (London: Unwin, 1893);

Lord Amherst and the British Advance Eastwards to Burma, by Ritchie and R. Evans (Oxford: Clarendon Press, 1894);

Chapters from Some Memoirs (London: Macmillan, 1894; New York: Macmillan, 1894);

A Discourse on Modern Sibyls (London: English Association, 1907);

Blackstick Papers (London: Smith, Elder, 1908; New York: Putnam's, 1908);

From the Porch (London: Smith, Elder, 1913; New York: Scribners, 1913);

From Friend to Friend, edited by Emily Ritchie (London: Murray, 1919; New York: Dutton, 1920).

COLLECTION: *Works of Miss Thackeray* (10 volumes, London: Smith, Elder, 1875-1890).

Her father wrote *Vanity Fair*; she became the aunt of Virginia Woolf. In her multitude of

Anne Thackeray Ritchie

251

friendships, Lady Ritchie was a link between the great Victorians of her father's era and such modern phenomena as the Bloomsbury group. Her use of impressionistic detail and concern for capturing moments of consciousness anticipate Woolf's own work. After an unconventional marriage, Anne Ritchie combined a literary career and a fully attentive maternal role with a success few of her sister writers enjoyed.

Anne Isabella ("Anny") Thackeray was born in London and spent the first few years of her life in Bloomsbury. Shortly after the birth of her sister, Harriet Marion ("Minny"), their mother, Isabella, began to exhibit signs of the mental illness which finally forced her to live apart from her family until her death in 1894. The girls stayed with their paternal grandmother in Paris for several years while William Makepeace Thackeray traveled with Isabella in hope of finding a cure for her. This sojourn in Paris during the 1840s, and a later one in 1852-1853, made Anny equally at home with French and English life. In 1846 Thackeray made a home for his children and himself in Kensington. His relationship with his elder daughter was very close, perhaps intensified by her early manifestation of literary talent and ambition. Her first ap-

Drawing by William Makepeace Thackeray of himself and "Anny" discussing a drawing of Thackeray in Punch *by John Leech*

pearance in print came in May 1860; Thackeray, who was then editor of the *Cornhill* magazine, had accepted "Little Scholars," an article about her visits to several charity or "ragged" schools for very young, poor children. Anne Thackeray later said that her father had provided the title and corrected the punctuation. She related how she had "written several novels and a tragedy by the age of fifteen, but then my father forbade me to waste my time any more scribbling, and desired me to read *other* people's books."

With *The Story of Elizabeth*, serialized in the *Cornhill* during 1863 and published in book form the same year, she obtained real literary success. Henry James refers to this novel in "The Art of Fiction" (1884), where he describes how a writer of his acquaintance, "a woman of genius," had used a passing impression of several French Protestant youths seated at a meal and her knowledge of French life to create a vivid picture of life in the family of a French Protestant *pasteur* (pastor). He did not add that in 1853 Anne and her sister had been taken by their grandmother to a series of confirmation classes conducted by the *pasteur* Sylvère Monod. *The Story of Elizabeth* begins with Caroline Gilmour's despair over Sir John Dampier's dislike of her; jealousy prompts her to tell a lie which prevents him from proposing to her daughter, Elizabeth. Mrs. Gilmour then marries a *pasteur*, and Elizabeth finds life in her stepfather's household extremely uncongenial. After a period of wretchedness, she is united with Sir John. The milieu of the novel was new to most English readers, the heroine charming, and the slight story deftly handled; amid an almost universal chorus of praise, the book went into five editions. From this book and some of her other writings, Anne Thackeray earned a considerable sum in her lifetime, but her benevolence and extravagance assured those connected with her perpetual frets over money.

Thackeray made close companions of his daughters during the last decade of his life, taking them on Continental travels, and introducing them to his wide range of literary and artistic friends. Anne's unpunctuality and financial irresponsibility sometimes irritated him, and memories of her failings in this regard added to her misery after his sudden death on Christmas Eve 1863. To their unexpected pleasure, the sisters found that Thackeray's friends remained theirs. Anne's extraordinary gift of empathetic friendship caused that circle to expand until, in the words of Howard Sturgis, "there was hardly a name famous in the art and literature of England during the last half-century that does not occur in her reminiscences." So many of her essays and memoirs mention or allude to the author of *Vanity Fair* that "Thackeray's daughter" is not merely a description of Anne Thackeray's parentage but a persona.

In 1867 Minny Thackeray married Leslie Stephen, who moved into their house, using the top floor for his work while Anne wrote and received friends in her own sitting room. During the previous year she had made an extended stay in Normandy and prior to the marriage published *The Village on the Cliff* (1867). The novel is infused with her knowledge of French life. Catherine George, a poor young governess in London, falls in love with the dilettante artist Dick Butler, a nephew of her employer. As a result, Catherine is sent off to Normandy to work for relatives of her employers. Dick has visited these DeTracys and fallen passionately in love with Reine Chrétien, the capable manager of a prosperous farm. When Dick revisits Reine, Catherine feels her own passion is hopeless and in reaction accepts the suit of the middle-aged mayor of Pettiport, M. Fontaine. The plot unwinds as Catherine is suddenly widowed. Dick moves hesitantly toward her, as his social pride makes him wary of marriage with Reine. Catherine, recognizing the depth of their mutual attachment, indirectly brings Dick and Reine together. The novel's originality and interest lie in its concern with capturing the essence of a moment or a feeling and in the use of external objects as correlations of relationships and states of mind. The author's favorite scene was that in which Catherine plays the piano while M. Fontaine inharmoniously accompanies her on the cornet—a perfect emblem of their lack of union. These techniques would be taken up and developed by Anne Thackeray's niece, Virginia Stephen Woolf.

The other major work of this period was *Old Kensington* (1873). The story first examines Dorothea Vanborough's relationship with her brother George and her stern but loving aunt, Lady Sarah Francis. Denied an affectionate father by his early death and deserted for years by her frivolous mother, Dorothea has an overwhelming need to find a secure and strong emotional center. She makes a serious mistake in engaging herself to the priggish Robert Henley. He fortunately frees her by marrying Rhoda Parnell—a character closely resembling William Makepeace Thackeray's own Becky Sharpe. Eventually Dorothea finds an appropriate husband in Frank Raban, a man who re-

The house at 27 Young Street, Kensington, where the Ritchies lived for the first seven years of their marriage. As a girl, Anne Thackeray had lived directly across the street at number 13.

spects her individuality and her intelligence as Robert did not. Atmosphere and technique, rather than the plot, make the novel interesting. Anne Thackeray recreates the Kensington of her childhood and further develops her attempts to capture the sensations, fleeting impressions, and associations which impinge on Dorothea Vanborough at crucial moments in her life. The often rhapsodic style anticipates some of the flights of Virginia Woolf.

Exposure to the paintings of Angelica Kauffmann aroused Anne Thackeray's interest in the problems faced by Kauffmann as a woman artist; the result was her only historical novel, *Miss Angel* (1875). The happy life of writing, visits, and frequent trips to the Continent altered when Minny died in childbirth in October 1875 while Anne was away visiting the novelist Margaret Oliphant. The loss of this "tenderest, faithfullest and unspeakably loving sister" shattered Anne and drove Stephen into more than usual moroseness. They continued to keep house, and their totally dissimilar personalities—he solemn and anxious, she full of chatter and quick impressions—had a bond of union in their devotion to Stephen's retarded daughter, Laura. The "gorilla" and the "dove," as Stephen named them, remained on such intimate terms that to Virginia Stephen Woolf and the other children of his second marriage she was always "Aunt Anny."

Anne Thackeray's friendship with her second cousin Richmond Thackeray Ritchie had grown more intense during the months following Minny's death. Their engagement and marriage in August 1877 startled some of their circle, as Ritchie was seventeen years her junior. (George Eliot was not unmindful of Thackeray's precedent when in 1880 she married the much younger John Cross.) The Ritchies had two children, Hester Helena Thackeray, born in 1878, and William Makepeace Denis, born in 1880. Ritchie went directly from Cambridge to the India Office, where he rose to become permanent under secretary of state for India; he was knighted in 1907.

In 1862 Anne Thackeray had made the first of many trips to the Isle of Wight. She had gone as the guest of the noted photographer Julia Margaret Cameron and had begun during that memorable visit her close friendship with Tennyson. Anne Thackeray swiftly became a vital part of the Cameron circle, which also included Lewis Carroll. The Isle of Wight became for her a source of spiritual and physical refreshment for over fifty years. Appropriately, the novel which fictionalizes persons and situations from the Cameron circle, *From an Island* (1877), was composed during the emotional months of her engagement. This novella should be read in connection with Virginia Woolf's *To the Lighthouse* (1927) and *Freshwater: A Comedy* (1976), both of which are heavily dependent on the same milieu.

In addition to her novels, Anne Thackeray Ritchie wrote numerous short stories. In the collection *Miss Williamson's Divagations* (1881), Miss Williamson, the persona she had created in *The Village on the Cliff*, narrates many of the tales and sometimes intervenes in the action. In the same year *Madame de Sévigné*, her only full-length biography, appeared; the subject, another literary woman with a genius for friendship, was most congenial. She had accepted this commission from her good friend Mrs. Oliphant, who was editing the Foreign Classics for English Readers series.

Anne Thackeray Ritchie's last novel was *Mrs. Dymond* (1885). In the marriage of Susanna Dymond, she reworked a situation in *The Village on the Cliff*, just as the situation of the mother and daughter reunited after a long absence is another variation of those in *The Story of Elizabeth* and *Old Kensington*. For obvious reasons, the figure of the absent mother haunted her. Both Elizabeth Gilmour and Dorothea Vanborough had yearned for affectionate sympathy and expected to find it when reunited with their mothers; Dorothea's mother was merely selfish, but Caroline Gilmour was actively jealous of the daughter who appeared on her return from boarding school to be a social rival. In *Mrs. Dymond*, Susanna had been sent to live with her grandfather in the Lake District when her widowed mother married a worthless Irish journalist and moved to Paris. When the now adult Susanna returns after the grandfather's death, her mother is loving but so harassed by household cares and keeping up appearances that she cannot be a companion to her daughter. As had Catherine George before her, Susanna tries to escape from her distasteful circumstances by marrying a kindly older man for whom she can feel only friendship. Again like Catherine, she is conveniently widowed and has to learn to trust the authority of her own emotions and live according to her own values. Her achievement of emotional authenticity is represented by her marriage to Max du Parc, a young French artist who is in every respect the opposite of the conventional, tradition-bound Colonel Dymond.

During 1885 and 1886 Anne Ritchie undertook the furnishing and staffing of a new house on such a lavish scale that Richmond Ritchie soon found he could not afford to maintain it and moved his family to his mother's large house at Wimbledon in 1886. Although the household was a happy one, Anne came to recognize that her fecklessness had dealt a severe blow to her husband's pride—in addition to giving him a lengthy journey back and forth to the India Office each working day. Yet her spending proclivities were by no means always directed to her own comfort. She contributed heavily to the upbringing of two Thackeray cousins and to the support of her mother until Isabella Thackeray's death in 1894.

In 1885 Anne Ritchie wrote an article on her friend Elizabeth Barrett Browning for *The Dictionary of National Biography*. Stephen, the editor, made several "savage criticisms" of her propensity for "sentimental reflection" but allowed to stand one such passage which illustrates Anne Thackeray Ritchie's belief that "the now is not with us as we hold it, nor is the moment all over that is past."

Anne Thackeray Ritchie about 1891

Commenting on the young Elizabeth's love of white roses, Anne Ritchie remarks, "The roses are still blooming for the readers of 'Lost Bower,' clear as once beneath the sunshine."

In 1893 Anne Ritchie contributed a long memoir to a book of photographic portraits of Tennyson and his circle taken years earlier by Julia Margaret Cameron. Along with her *Records of Ten-*

nyson, Ruskin, and Robert and Elizabeth Browning (1892), it is a rich source of primary material about these figures. The friendship with John Ruskin dated from 1876, when she and Stephen had spent the summer near his home in the Lake District.

In the 1890s Anne Ritchie devoted her literary efforts entirely to the writing of memoirs. Her culminating work was the series of long introductions

*Charcoal portrait of Ritchie by John Singer Sargent,
commissioned by 139 of her friends*

she prepared in 1897 and 1898 for the Biographical Edition of her father's works. While keeping to the letter of his command that no biography be written, she used these introductions to correct published charges of heartlessness and excessive cynicism which had been brought against Thackeray by his enemies. She won widespread praise for her recreation of Thackeray's domestic life and of the circumstances surrounding the composition of each of his novels. Lady Ritchie revised the introductions for the Centenary Edition published from 1910 to 1911 and, despite increasing ill health, frequent changes of address, and the unexpected loss of her husband in 1912, published three more volumes of essays in the two decades before her own death.

In 1914 a group of her friends raised the money to commission John Singer Sargent to paint her portrait. Henry James was one of the warmest proponents of this scheme and in writing to her about it, addressed her as "Dearest Anne, admirable old friend and illustrious confrère!" When, early in March 1918, her house in Chelsea was struck by a

bomb, she and her daughter removed to The Porch, their cottage on the Isle of Wight. She died there early in 1919.

Virginia Woolf had regarded her aunt with a mixture of admiration and exasperation which found outlet in her portrait of Lady Ritchie as Mrs. Hilbery in *Night and Day* (1919). In her obituary tribute Woolf praised the memoirs and biographical writings, maintaining that their author "will be the unacknowledged source of much that remains in men's minds about the Victorian age. She will be the transparent medium through which we behold the dead." In her brief mention of Lady Ritchie's fiction, Woolf stressed Ritchie's ability to create atmosphere and her power "of an apparently simple and yet inevitably right sense of the use of language." While the impressions conveyed may be slight or transient, they have been perfectly realized: "But every sentence is formed: they cohere together; and invariably at the end of a chapter or paragraph there is a sense that the melody has found its way through one variation and another to its natural close."

These remarks are as close as Mrs. Woolf comes to attempting an analysis of "Aunt Anny's" style and techniques. Joanne Zuckerman, a Virginia Woolf scholar who has provided the only detailed critical assessment of Lady Ritchie's fiction to appear since the obituary tributes, notes that both novelists confront the "same problem of reconciling the recording of experience, as it actually passes through the mind, with the demands of the conventionally structured novel. . . ." This "vivid recording of impressions, the handling of structural motifs in such a way that they almost supercede plot as the basic structural feature of a novel" constitute Lady Ritchie's originality as a novelist and make her a precursor of the fiction of her niece Virginia Woolf. Perhaps in 1919 Mrs. Woolf was unable either to recognize or admit to these affinities, especially in an obituary article which appeared without her signature; but as far as is now known, she never did come to terms with the influence of Anne Thackeray Ritchie on her own work.

Henry James was alluding to *The Story of Elizabeth* when he mentioned "an English novelist, a woman of genius" who "was blessed with the faculty which when you give it an inch takes an ell, and which for the artist is a much greater source of strength than any accident of residence or of place in the social scale." He goes on to say: "If experience consists of impressions, it may be said that impressions *are* experience. . . ." The line of descent from

James to Virginia Woolf has been traced more than once in studies of the modern novel; the student of these two seminal figures clearly should not overlook the work of Virginia Woolf's "Aunt Anny" and Henry James's "intimately associated old friend," Anne Thackeray Ritchie.

Other:

"Elizabeth Barrett Browning," in *The Dictionary of National Biography*, volume 3 (London: Smith, Elder, 1885), pp. 78-82;

Mary Russell Mitford, *Our Village*, introduction by Ritchie (London: Macmillan, 1893; New York: Macmillan, 1893);

Maria Edgeworth, *Ormond, Castle Rackrent, Helen, Popular Tales*, introductions by Ritchie (London: Macmillan, 1895-1896; New York: Macmillan, 1895-1896);

Maria Edgeworth, *The Parents' Assistant*, introduction by Ritchie (London: Macmillan, 1897; New York: Macmillan, 1897);

Elizabeth Cleghorn Gaskell, *Cranford*, introduction by Ritchie (London: Macmillan, 1898; New York: Macmillan, 1898);

Works of William Makepeace Thackeray with Biographical Introduction by His Daughter, 13 volumes (London: Harper, 1898-1899; New York: Harper, 1898-1899);

Centenary Edition of Thackeray's Works, with expanded introductions by Ritchie, 26 volumes (London: Harper, 1910-1911; New York: Harper, 1910-1911).

Periodical Publications:

"Little Scholars," *Cornhill*, 1 (May 1860): 549-559;

"The Boyhood of Thackeray," *St. Nicholas for Young Folks*, 18 (December 1889): 99-112;

"Robert and Elizabeth Barrett Browning," *Harper's Monthly*, 84 (May 1892): 832-855.

Biographies:

Hester Thackeray Fuller and Violet Hammersley, *Thackeray's Daughter: Some Recollections of Anne Thackeray Ritchie* (Dublin: Euphorion, 1951);

Winifred Gerin, *Anne Thackeray Ritchie: A Biography* (London: Oxford University Press, 1981; New York: Oxford University Press, 1981).

References:

Elizabeth French Boyd, *Bloomsbury Heritage: Their Mothers and Their Aunts* (New York: Taplinger, 1976), pp. 77-93;

Edmund Gosse, *Books on the Table* (New York: Scribners, 1921), pp. 291-298;

Jennie Huie, "Anne Thackeray Ritchie," dissertation, University of London, 1961;

Peter Mornay, *The Best Years of Their Lives* (London: Centaur Press, 1955), pp. 189-194;

Ove Jacob Hjort Preus, "Anne Thackeray Ritchie and the Victorian Literary Aristocracy," dissertation, University of Minnesota, 1959;

Gordon N. Ray, *Thackeray: The Uses of Adversity (1811-1840)* (New York: McGraw-Hill, 1955; London: McGraw-Hill, 1955);

Ray, *Thackeray: The Age of Wisdom (1841-1863)* (New York: McGraw-Hill, 1958);

Howard Overing Sturgis, "Anne Isabella Thackeray (Lady Ritchie)," *Cornhill* (November 1919): 449-467;

Virginia Woolf, "The Enchanted Organ," in *The Moment and Other Essays* (New York: Harcourt, Brace, 1948), pp. 193-196;

Woolf, "Lady Ritchie," *Times Literary Supplement* (6 March 1919): 123;

Joanne P. Zuckerman, "Anne Thackeray Ritchie as the Model for Mrs. Hilbery in Virginia Woolf's *Night and Day*," *Virginia Woolf Quarterly*, 1 (Spring 1973): 32-46.

Mark Rutherford
(William Hale White)
(22 December 1831-14 March 1913)

Catherine Harland
Queen's University

BOOKS: *An Argument for the Extension of the Franchise: A Letter Addressed to George Jacob Holyoake, Esquire* (London: F. Farrah, 1866);

A Letter Written on the Death of Mrs. Elizabeth Street (London: Griffith, 1877);

The Autobiography of Mark Rutherford, Dissenting Minister, Edited by His Friend, Reuben Shapcott (London: Trübner, 1881; New York: Putnam's, 1881);

Mark Rutherford's Deliverance: Being the Second Part of His Autobiography; edited by His Friend, Reuben Shapcott (London: Trübner, 1885);

The Revolution in Tanner's Lane, by Mark Rutherford; edited by His Friend, Reuben Shapcott (London: Trübner, 1887; New York: Putnam's, 1887);

Miriam's Schooling and Other Papers, by Mark Rutherford; edited by His Friend, Reuben Shapcott (London: Kegan Paul, Trench, Trübner, 1890);

Catharine Furze, by Mark Rutherford; edited by His Friend, Reuben Shapcott (2 vols., London: Unwin, 1893; 1 vol., New York: Macmillan, 1893);

Clara Hopgood, by Mark Rutherford; edited by His Friend, Reuben Shapcott (London: Unwin, 1896; New York: Dodd, Mead, 1896);

An Examination of the Charge of Apostasy against Wordsworth (London: Longmans, Green, 1898);

Pages from a Journal, with Other Papers, by Mark Rutherford (London: Unwin, 1900);

John Bunyan (New York: Scribners, 1904; London: Hodder & Stoughton, 1905);

More Pages from a Journal with Other Papers (London: Oxford University Press, 1910);

The Early Life of Mark Rutherford by Himself (London: Oxford University Press, 1913);

Last Pages from a Journal with Other Papers, edited by Dorothy V. White (London: Oxford University Press, 1915);

Letters to Three Friends, edited by Dorothy V. White (London: Oxford University Press, 1924).

William Hale White ("Mark Rutherford") felt, along with countless other Victorians, that he had been born "a hundred years too late" to commit himself wholly to a religious creed. His crisis of faith and subsequent reevaluation of life are therefore familiar to students of Victorian literature, but both his quest for moral and religious freedom and his fictional exploration of that process are unique. Satisfied neither with wholesale rejection of his Calvinist heritage nor with the more attractive paths of the various substitute faiths of his time, White turned slowly to the faith of his ancestors and reinterpreted the vital center of sixteenth- and seventeenth-century Puritanism for a modern and secular age. Throughout his life White found that the attempt to penetrate to the living spirit and original necessity of Calvinism was precisely the "reaching after a meaning ... which constituted heresy." White's "heretical" formulation is that the reconciliation of the human and divine is the fundamental

Mark Rutherford (William Hale White)

religious experience; he is then significant as the historian and interpreter of nineteenth-century nonconformity. His examination of this territory also encompasses the experience of melancholic dread and the problems of moral freedom. Finally, the beauty and power of White's prose are unparalleled in Victorian fiction. His fiction combines sincerity, intensity, and uncompromising psychological realism with an extraordinary stylistic purity.

Hale White did not begin to write fiction seriously until he was fifty years old, when he published under the pseudonym "Mark Rutherford." Born in 1831, "just before the Liverpool and Manchester Railway was opened," his first memory was "the coronation of Queen Victoria and a town's dinner in St. Paul's Square." His father, William, was a printer and bookseller; his mother was the former Mary Anne Chignell. White always loved his native town of Bedford, the home of John Bunyan, and recalled a happy childhood swimming and boating in the River Ouse in summer and skating on it in winter, roasting potatoes over open fires and eating gooseberries from a neighbor's garden. But these "perfect poetic pleasures" of a rural childhood were eclipsed each week by Sunday, which White describes as a "season of unmixed gloom."

White's family had been Independents—now commonly known as Congregationalists—since the mid-eighteenth century. The Independents were a sect of Dissenters or Nonconformists, so called because they refused to conform to the dogmas and practices of the established Church of England. As Calvinists, the Independents regarded their basic doctrines as those of St. Paul. White attended Bunyan Meeting, the Independent chapel in Bedford, until he was a young man. His wish to become an artist was overruled by his mother, who wanted him to become a Dissenting minister. Consequently, after testifying to his conversion and being "admitted" to the congregation of Bunyan Meeting, he matriculated into the Countess of Huntingdon's College at Cheshunt. Here he remained until 1851, when he transferred to New College, St. John's Wood, London. White later condemned the education he received; he found it academically superficial and spiritually pernicious. In *The Autobiography of Mark Rutherford, Dissenting Minister* (1881), "Rutherford" describes the classical instruction as "inefficient" and the biblical study as "a sham." He was unmoved by anything he studied and was alienated from a genuine spiritual life. The "terrible invention" of Calvinist doctrine seemed irrelevant, belonging to a world "totally disconnected from my

own." "I learnt nothing at Cheshunt," he writes, "and did not make a single friend."

This sterile existence was shattered in his final year by the influence of the *Lyrical Ballads* (1798) by Samuel Taylor Coleridge and William Wordsworth, which "excited a movement and a growth which went on till, by degrees, all the systems which enveloped me like a body decayed from me and fell away into nothing." His vital growth resulted, however, in White's dismissal from New College on the ground that his views were heretical. Deprived of a clerical vocation, White found work with the well-known publisher of heretical books and editor of the *Westminster Review*, John Chapman ("Wollaston" in *The Autobiography of Mark Rutherford, Dissenting Minister*). In spite of the friendship of Mary Ann Evans (George Eliot—"Theresa" in *The Autobiography of Mark Rutherford, Dissenting Minister*), who was then assistant editor of the periodical, White disliked the job intensely. In 1854, refusing Chapman's offer of a partnership, he took a job as a clerk in the registrar general's office in Somerset House. At this time White was courting Harriet Arthur, whom he married in 1856 when he was twenty-five years old. Not long after the marriage came the terrible discovery that his wife had disseminated sclerosis, an incurable disease of the nervous system. This distressing fact irrevocably altered White's life and contributed directly to his becoming a writer. As his domestic situation inevitably became more difficult and frustrating, White's need for mental freedom intensified. His wife's illness and White's consequent isolation also help to explain his insistent fictional exploration of unhappy marriages. In 1857, White was appointed registrar of births, deaths, and marriages for Marylebone, and a year later he was transferred to the Admiralty. He rose to the position of assistant director of naval contracts in 1879, but in the twenty-odd years between these appointments he experienced much emotional and financial anxiety. Initially, White supplemented his ill-paid civil service job by preaching in Unitarian pulpits. In 1861, however, he became a House of Commons reporter, and wrote weekly London columns for provincial newspapers. He remarked years later of his work in the Admiralty, "I never liked it," but he remained there until his retirement in 1892, a year after his wife's death. Journalism he liked even less, and he refused in later life to have any of his newspaper pieces of twenty years reprinted. His first separately printed work, written in these strenuous years, was a pamphlet entitled *An Argument for the Extension of the*

Franchise: A Letter Addressed to George Jacob Holyoake, Esquire (1866). In this piece White argues with wit and eloquence for universal manhood suffrage. During 1857-1866 he also made various contributions to *The Imperial Dictionary of Universal Biography*. In his early thirties, White completed (though he did not publish until 1883) the first major intellectual project since his marriage: a translation of the *Ethic* of Spinoza, the seventeenth-century pantheist philosopher who continued to be a profound, shaping influence on White's life. This work was done in the early morning hours prior to his departure for work at the Admiralty, the only leisure time White had for reading and writing.

At a time of life when other writers are at the peaks of their creative powers and are engaged in the production of their major works, Hale White felt that he had accomplished nothing. Fifty years old, he struggled under immense daily pressure, trying to finish his office duties in time to go to the House of Commons, then home to write his reports at night. These he sometimes completed in the waiting room of Victoria Station the following morning. Since 1858, he had also been writing articles for various journals on a range of subjects from literature to astronomy. White came home to an invalid wife and an atmosphere of joyless gloom, but he nevertheless performed his duty stoically. A personal intrusion into his fine essay "Notes on the Book of Job" (1885), however, powerfully suggests the bitterness he felt as he saw his life being slowly eroded by arduous, uncongenial work and by the "mean, miserable and sordid cares" of his domestic situation. Despite these difficulties, in 1880 the early morning work became suddenly productive. Four significant essays appeared in the *Secular Review*: "The Genius of Walt Whitman" (20 March), "Marcus Antoninus" (3 July), "Ixion" (11 September), and "Heathen Ethics" (27 November).

Further, in 1881, *The Autobiography of Mark Rutherford, Dissenting Minister*, was completed—written, as he said later, "at extraordinary high pressure" at four-thirty each morning. Through this confessional fiction White was able to extend the boundaries of his daily existence and affirm the freedom of his spirit. Although it alters many external facts, Rutherford's autobiography is the true story of White's mental and spiritual life. White confirmed, in his nonfictional *The Early Life of Mark Rutherford by Himself* (1913), that much of what he was now writing had been said before "under a semi-transparent disguise." The pseudonym and the additional mask of the fictitious editor, Reuben

Shapcott, who purports to be publishing his friend's work posthumously, ensured confessional freedom. Rutherford gives expression not to a life of success and triumph, but to one of humiliation and loneliness. He writes, "Mine is ever the tale of a commonplace life, perplexed by many problems I have never solved; disturbed by many difficulties I have never surmounted; and blotted by ignoble concessions which are a constant regret." His apologia is similar to that of seventeenth-century spiritual autobiographers: he shares his experience of suffering with anonymous readers so that they may be "freed from the sense of solitude which they find so depressing." Toward the end of his life White remarked to his second wife, Dorothy, that he wished he had never written novels: "If I had been given you as a wife when I was thirty I would never have let the public hear a syllable from me." This remarkable statement is best understood not as a repudiation of what he had written but as an explanation of why he wrote at all. If he had known the accepting love of Dorothy, his confessional would not have been the reading public.

The Autobiography of Mark Rutherford, Dissenting Minister and its sequel, *Mark Rutherford's Deliverance* (1883), chart the movement from depression and self-hatred to reconciliation and self-acceptance. Rutherford, like his creator, initially rejects orthodoxy and then begins a process of reexamination. Central experiences in these two novels also suggest the thematic direction of all White's subsequent fiction. An event which Rutherford (and White) considered the source of later anguish and the impetus of his quest was the youthful conversion and admission to Bunyan Meeting. Public testimony was expected of all converts. White later wrote that the genuine experience of conversion—"a kind of miracle wrought in the heart by the influence of the Holy Spirit, by which a man becomes altogether different to what he was previously"—was almost impossible by the time he was initiated in 1848. His own experience was "uneventful," although he testified that the "witness of God in me to my own salvation was as clear as noon-day." The episode is condemned by Rutherford as psychologically damaging. He felt that he had inadvertently participated in hypocrisy. Self-deceived, he had taken external assent for the active response of the heart. His profession of individual election eventually fostered guilt and self-consciousness. Moreover, religion became increasingly something external and unreal to his feeling self. This sense of unreality continued through Rutherford's time at college.

Rutherford's characterization of his encounter with Wordsworth's poetry as a *genuine* spiritual rebirth is therefore significant. The poetry conveyed "no new doctrine," he writes, but "the change it wrought in me could only be compared with that which is said to have been wrought on Paul himself by the Divine Apparition." The immediate consequence of this experience was renewed intellectual curiosity, most strikingly manifested in a deepening interest in his Puritan heritage. But as in White's own case, the issue of Rutherford's attempt to "reach through to that original necessity" which had inspired Christian doctrine was an ignominious reprimand from his college.

The Autobiography of Mark Rutherford, Dissenting Minister also recreates with intense realism an experience that followed on the heels of the expulsion. This was the onset of what White variously calls "melancholia," "hypochondria," "the ancient enemy." It haunted him ever afterward and became a central theme of his fiction. His initial encounter with melancholia occurred in Stoke Newington, where, some months after his expulsion from New College, White had obtained a position as a schoolteacher. At this period, White was

psychologically vulnerable. He felt himself to be "adrift, knowing no craft, belonging to no religious body." Reflecting years later on what he then suffered, White finds it difficult to explain "the worst of all calamities, the nameless dread, the efflux of all vitality, the ghostly haunting horror so nearly akin to madness." His descriptions of this "nameless dread" are similar to those of such writers as Donne, Bunyan, Carlyle, Kierkegaard, Sartre: he feels utterly abandoned, alienated from God and his fellow man, and a stranger to himself. While others have found a position, an occupation, a home in the world, he alone is worthless and powerless. "The pit opens under me," he writes, when he confronts, unprepared, questions of ultimate purpose, identity, and worth. This depression can be seen to originate at least partly in his youthful experience of conversion. That early participation in a faith which he now felt was bankrupt intensified the self-hatred which is closely related to melancholia. The early creed, he writes, "had as evil consequences that it concentrated my thoughts upon myself, and made me of great importance. God had been anxious about me from all eternity, and had been scheming to save me." A sense of being one of God's chosen

Independent chapel in Bedford, attended by White as a youth

lapsed along with his faith, leaving him with a continual feeling of worthlessness and abandonment. During attacks of melancholia, these feelings, in addition to a sense of guilt, intensified. The experience of Stoke Newington was, White remarks, "the beginning of a trouble which has lasted all my life." Fictional dramatization and resolution of complex life experiences is typical of White's art, however, and in the quasi-fictional *Autobiography of Mark Rutherford, Dissenting Minister* and *Mark Rutherford's Deliverance*, Rutherford goes on to find work, friendship, and marital affection. Gradually, he learns what his creator struggled a lifetime to realize: to shift the center of existence "from self to what is outside self, and yet is truly self."

The need for love and sympathy almost devoured White, as it did Mark Rutherford. The loss of a spiritual community contributed to his melancholia and disorientation. The far-reaching consequences of this alienation can be seen in the numerous references in *The Autobiography of Mark Rutherford, Dissenting Minister* to the feeling of being out of touch with the inner self, and living, in Yeats's phrase, where "motley is worn." As a young minister, Rutherford continually feels repulsed by his congregation; as a reporter, he has no sense of his audience ("I wrote for an abstraction; and spoke to empty space"); at Wollaston's publishing house, the work is antagonistic to his temperament. Because of this lack of a vital human connection, he falls "a prey to self-contempt and scepticism." Rutherford's deliverance from this anguish comes through his love of his wife, Ellen. He had initially broken off his engagement to Ellen, but years later he finds her and proposes again. A marriage is now possible because both have changed and matured through suffering. He describes their love as a "revelation of the relationship in which God should stand" to man. Thus human love both gives him back the self from which he had been separated and reveals the potential relationship of the self to God. When genuine reconciliation occurs, he experiences freedom from egocentric suffering and limiting self-definition.

The insight of *Mark Rutherford's Deliverance*, that individual value is revealed by means of relationship, is an idea explored in all White's later work. A notebook entry records an extraordinary and emblematic event: one morning, as he was looking at a great oak tree, suddenly, "it seemed no longer a tree away from me and apart from me. The enclosing barriers of consciousness were removed and the text came into my mind, 'Thou in me and I in thee.' The distinction of self and not-self was an illusion." He feels the sap rising in the tree and in himself senses an equivalent fountain of joy. This is the "religion of the Reconciliation," occurring both through human love and by means of the natural world. The early effect of Wordsworth's poetry had been to recreate Rutherford's deity, "substituting a new and living spirit" for the old which had "gradually hardened into an idol." As White matured, his sense of the regenerative power of nature grew and became another source of deliverance from melancholia and daily anxiety. Mark Rutherford reflects on the vastness of the cosmos in which he suffers, and is comforted: as he looks up at the stars a man is freed "from the tyranny of the senses" and ceases to make his limited mind "the measure of the universe." In two holidays which he shares with his family before his death, Rutherford experiences this momentary liberation. Beautiful weather, clouds, the stillness of the ocean, the intensity of the sunlight, all contribute to the creation of a day that is "perfect in its beauty," in which "everything breathed one spirit." In these brief moments, imaginatively realized and preserved in his fiction, self-consciousness and melancholia were forgotten in the presence of what White calls "actual joy."

Mark Rutherford dies suddenly of a stroke at the end of *Mark Rutherford's Deliverance*, but his creator lived on. Although writing his spiritual autobiography in these first two novels (and in the two personal essays published in 1885, "Notes on the Book of Job" and "Principles") purged White of much frustration and pain, the central issues which they explored remained with him. In 1887, in spite of intense depression, he published *The Revolution in Tanner's Lane*, perhaps his most popular novel, and again questioned the meaning of his religious heritage. Many readers have felt that the novel is "broken-backed," two separate stories tenuously connected. Indeed, White felt, as a novelist, that he could "supply conversation and description" but that "it was very difficult to invent a plot." Nevertheless, the two plots of the novel are significantly interrelated by the unifying central theme, the historical transformation of nineteenth-century Calvinism. White's fiction, while not all directly autobiographical, is nonetheless intensely personal, and his presentation of Calvinism in decay is a reflection of his own experience of it. In fact, the first half of the nineteenth century, the period of the novel's action, was one of major growth and expansion for Independency. White's evaluation of the liberalism that characterized this expansion is, however, usually negative. He felt that the "moderate Calvinism" taught in Bunyan Meeting during his youth was really Calvinism in decay. The "New System" was midway between traditional Calvinist doctrine and the Arminian (antipredestination) emphasis of Independency in the latter part of the century. If "moderate Calvinism" had any meaning, he writes, "it was that predestination, election, and reprobation were unquestionably true, but they were dogmas about which it was not prudent to say much." White thought that although the nineteenth-century reevaluation of Calvinist doctrine might be finally beneficial, the divorce of dogma from experience encouraged mental dishonesty and spiritual hypocrisy. Yet while recognizing that by mid-century Calvinism had lost the power it originally possessed, White nevertheless realized that the decay was necessary: the original spirit of Puritanism had become the dead letter. *The Revolution in Tanner's Lane* traces this devolution.

The novel opens in 1814, when Calvinism was, for some, still dynamic. The original Puritan temper is represented by the Reverend Thomas Bradshaw, whose energy and fervor belong to a passing generation. His second wife recalled that White had once remarked to her that he had "never *created* a character in his life, never set down to write without having somebody before his mind's eye." Bradshaw's actual counterpart was the Reverend Samuel Hillyard, who had been minister of Bunyan Meeting during White's father's time and in White's own youth. He was succeeded by the Reverend John Jukes, who, in White's memory at least, was a shallow and unimaginative man. White is drawing upon his own memory in recreating Jukes as the fictional John Broad of his novel. The second story, set a generation after the first, shows how Calvinism has decayed. Whereas men like Bradshaw are seen as "bold and uncompromising," Broad is weak and ingenuous, a canting hypocrite. The protagonist, Zachariah Coleman, is a man caught between these two worlds. As he attempts to live the letter of Calvinist dogma, he comes into conflict with his human compassion and innate sense of justice. He participates in the famous march of the Blanketeers from Manchester to London in 1817 and becomes friendly with people who share his political but not his religious sympathies. In a forceful scene Zachariah tries to enlighten his infidel friends, but his sincere if embarrassed effort at conversion is a sorry failure. The narrator remarks that Zachariah "was a century and a half too late" and failed "not through want of courage, but because he wanted a

deeper conviction." The conflict becomes impossible for him, and friendship defeats dogma.

Although Zachariah is incapable of complete commitment to Calvinism, the novel explores and vindicates the original power of that tradition. Here White again uncovers the experiential truth beneath religious doctrine: "Even if Calvinism had been carved on tables of stone and handed down from heaven by the Almighty Hand, it would not have lived if it had not been found to agree more or less with the facts. . . . the Epistle to the Romans serving as the inspired confirmation of an experience." The "facts" are described throughout White's work. For most of us, he writes, the "facts" are "a dark street, crowds, hurry, commonplaceness, loneliness, and worse than all, a terrible doubt which can hardly be named as to the meaning and purpose of the world." These facts of his own experience are those he demanded that a real faith confront. Mr. Bradshaw, in his magnificent sermon on Jepthah, suggests what that original faith was. He argues that election may well be to suffering rather than to happiness, to the renunciation of the heart's dearest possession. Zachariah Coleman personally experiences this election to suffering. He is tested by political persecution, unemployment, and also by an incompatible marriage. (White's interest in the latter subject, which provides a second unifying theme of the novel, had also been apparent in the first two novels: Rutherford breaks off his youthful engagement with Ellen when he discovers that he no longer loves her; the elderly Miss Arbour reveals the anguish of her early marriage; and Rutherford's friend M'Kay is married to a gentle but unintellectual woman whose value he learns only when she becomes fatally ill.) Zachariah is the first, but certainly not the last, of White's protagonists to make the discovery that they have missed "the great delight of existence." Even the late marriage of Rutherford and Ellen needed "perpetual cherishing" to continue happily, and the celebration of marital delight is much less frequent than White's fictional insistence on mistaken choices. In the fiction there are generally two kinds of unhappy marriages: the first kind concerns the unhappiness which results when one of the partners is cold and unfeeling; the second kind is the consequence of a self-centered and intellectually proud spouse who eventually learns to value the human qualities of the neglected mate. Zachariah's wife, Jane, is the coldest and most mentally rigid of all the characters who repel their partners. She is also the most complex. She has sympathy with neither

Zachariah's religious doubts nor with his infidel friends. Zachariah is finally moved to cry out, "Your home is no home to me. My life is blasted, and it might have been different." White's life might also have been different if his wife had been healthy and if there had been greater intellectual sympathy between the two. Yet the narrator of the novel is just: he allows that with another man, Jane Coleman would have been a better woman. Zachariah gets another chance: his first wife dies, and he marries Pauline Caillaud, the brilliant and attractive daughter of his radical and agnostic friend Jean. His happiness is short-lived, however. As the second plot begins, Zachariah and his daughter are alone; Pauline presumably has died in childbirth.

In the second half of the novel, George, the son of Zachariah's friend Isaac Allen, also mistakes his feelings and marries Priscilla, the pretty but insipid daughter of the Reverend Thomas Broad. George's life changes as he gradually learns how totally incapable his wife is of understanding anything that concerns him deeply. Both Zachariah and George Allen, essentially because of their mistaken marriages, learn the meaning of renunciation. White redefines heroism in this novel: Martyrdom, he argues, is easy enough. Dying for an idea, assured that one will live on in others' memories as a saint, is an insufficient ideal for the modern world. Zachariah, a poor unhappily married printer, with forty more years before him, "determined to live through them . . . without a murmur, although there was to be no pleasure in them." But the narrator adds that an even "diviner heroism" is to do in these days "what Zachariah did, and without Zachariah's faith." White here sees the highest duty as self-renunciation and endurance.

In 1890, three years after the publication of *The Revolution in Tanner's Lane*, another volume edited by the fictitious Reuben Shapcott appeared, containing the short but beautiful novel *Miriam's Schooling*. Miriam is "schooled" by suffering and despair. The lessons are by now familiar, but the character who learns them is of a new type. Miriam Tacchi is the daughter of a Cowfold watchmaker. (White's fictional towns—Cowfold, Fenmarket, Eastthorpe—are all his native Bedford.) Unlike Zachariah, Miriam has no religion to direct her impulses. She is a character innately generous, honest, and passionate, who acts from intuition or feeling rather than abstract principle. Because of her father's remarriage, Miriam and her brother Andrew are sent to London. In the great metropolis Andrew becomes an alcoholic, and Miriam falls desperately in love with George Montgomery, a dissolute music-hall singer. Two crises are central to her spiritual growth. The first takes place in London: as she looks out a window one evening after her brother has lost his job through drink, she sees Montgomery stagger drunkenly into the house of a prostitute. Realizing that the man she loves is lost to her forever, Miriam rapidly descends into the valley of the shadow of death, like Mark Rutherford and Zachariah Coleman before her. She soon stands before the Thames considering suicide. The narrator describes her attack of melancholia as the experience below which humanity cannot go, "when all life ebbs from us, when we stretch out our arms in vain, where there is no God. . . . Satan we might conquer, . . . but what can we do against this leaden 'order of things' which makes our nerves ministers of madness?" All of White's melancholy sufferers are overwhelmed by the "phantom foes" that he himself knew so intimately.

Miriam does not kill herself: she "held back and passed on." At home she soon becomes seriously ill. As she recovers, she is sent to stay with friends in Salisbury, and one day during her recuperation sees Stonehenge for the first time. Her experience is richly ambiguous and takes her closer to a less egocentric relationship with the universe. In her fragile state, the sight of that mysterious monument, and the ideas that it suggests, cause her to feel "oppressed with a sense of her own nothingness and the nothingness of man." Immediately, this sudden awareness of the fact of human transience and her own insignificance in the light of forgotten cultures brings another idea into her mind: "she must do something for her fellow creatures." In White's fiction, suffering and salvation are inextricably united. In *The Early Life of Mark Rutherford*, White criticizes the conversion experiences related by the elect in Bunyan Meeting as being "very often picturesque, and . . . framed after the model of the journey to Damascus." But since the central concern of his fiction is the secular experience of the shattering of the old self and the birth of the new, in his novels and short stories White himself evokes the original model as the appropriate metaphorical parallel to the lives of his characters. In so doing, he makes the feeling and the spirit of the original idea once more vital. Miriam's sudden urge toward new life takes the form of a desire to become a nurse. With characteristic narrative reticence, White refuses to offer a psychological explanation for her change of heart. He appeals rather to the genuineness of the ar-

Harriet Arthur, White's first wife

chetype: "It may be urged that no sufficient cause is shown for Miriam's determination. What had she undergone? A little poverty, a little love affair, a little sickness. But what brought Paul to the disciples at Damascus? A light in the sky and a vision." Miriam's nursing career is short-lived, but she remains in a hospital long enough to witness the death of Montgomery owing to a drunken accident. With nothing to keep her in London, she returns to Cowfold and, after severe internal debate, marries Didymus Farrow, a good-hearted but commonplace basket maker. Miriam soon escapes from the boredom of her life by reading old books she finds in an upstairs cupboard. She grows increasingly self-absorbed and detached. Eventually she is helped out of the egoism of despair by Mr. Armstrong, the vicar of a nearby parish. It is, however, the vicar's love of astronomy and not his doctrine that comes to her aid.

White also found healing power in astronomical observation. Although his childhood love of the natural world had deepened through contact with Wordsworth's poetry, it was only in July 1889 that he wrote excitedly to a friend of a recent purchase,

an astronomical telescope. The stars became a means by which he could escape the tyranny of his imagination. It is splendidly ironic that impersonal natural laws, the "forces which maintained the universe" and had replaced a benevolent God in White's young mind, became in his maturity a source of deliverance. The predictability of the stars and the necessary motion of the planets he now saw as the glorious manifestation of those laws. In the novel, Mr. Armstrong encourages Miriam to look through his telescope not so that she may gape in astonishment, but so that she may glimpse universal order. Miriam learns that the firmament, "instead of being a mere muddle . . . had a plan in it." Her growing understanding of planetary motion frees her from preoccupation with her own unhappiness. At first she is unable to grasp the celestial processes which her despised husband understands at once. The narrator comments ironically that although she could imagine "Verona and Romeo with such intense reality . . . she could not perform such a simple feat as that of portraying to herself the revolution of an inclined sphere." Her husband helps her by constructing an orrery. Among the aspects of Miriam's schooling, then, are a transformed perception of her place in the cosmos and a new appreciation for her husband's character.

Appended to the novel were four short fictions. The first three are provocative recreations of biblical stories, narrated from unusual points of view. "Gideon" is the story "Jotham told his children on the day before his death concerning the achievements of his father Gideon." "Samuel" is told by Samuel himself, and "Saul" is a moving view of the events of "Samuel" from the perspective of Saul's Horite wife, Rizpah. In all the stories, White imaginatively reenters the spirit of the original events. His profound love of the Bible, constant throughout his life, is celebrated here. To his father he wrote that in the Bible he embraced "no clothed, disguised man but . . . [felt] the blood beating and the touch of warm flesh." White explores the complex feelings of these characters and encourages readers to apprehend the opposed views of Rizpah and Samuel. Two aspects of "Saul" are especially noteworthy. First, White is particularly interested in Saul's experience of "the Terror" and the feeling of dread he comes to associate with David, and in Saul's anguish because he feels God has forsaken him. Second, he emphasizes the erotic dimension of the marriage of Rizpah and Saul. "Michael Trevanion," the final piece in the volume, is a potent story about a father's exceptional devotion to his only son. The tale examines the complex and peculiar nature of Michael's Puritan mind, the possessiveness he feels for his child, the error he commits in relation to him, and his final reconciliation with him.

After thirty years of worsening pain, Harriet White died on 1 June 1891. A year later, White retired from the Admiralty, receiving from the Lords the highest praise for his work and "their regret at parting with so valuable an officer." With his daughter, he moved in the same year to a new home in Hastings. There he wrote his next novel, *Catharine Furze* (1893), which also depicts self-renunciation and conversion. The heroine of this beautiful, lyrical novel is a remarkable young woman who, like many of George Eliot's protagonists, is obliged to struggle in a narrow and oppressive environment. The daughter of an Eastthorpe ironmonger, Catharine, like Miriam Tacchi, has neither religion nor culture to direct her questing nature. As a young woman, Catharine is sent to a finishing school run by two Calvinist spinsters. She despises her vacuous and trivial schoolmates, but her education begins when she meets—and falls in love with—the brilliant and eloquent Reverend Cardew, who gives religious instruction in the school. Like both Mark Rutherford and Zachariah Coleman, Catharine is emotionally in exile in her environment. The narrator suggests that she was born too late to have been molded by the faith of her ancestors, and too soon to be influenced by the new education of the later nineteenth century. She falls in love with Cardew inevitably, for it is he who provides her with a spiritual home.

For much of the novel, Catharine struggles to overcome her passionate love for Cardew, who is incompatibly married and who has fallen in love with her as well. Finally, however, like White's other protagonists, she descends into the abyss and cries out to be delivered from "the body of this death." Melancholia, "terrors vague and misty," contributes to her growing despair. Soon consumption is diagnosed; her depression is so profound that she has no will to live. Knowing that Cardew is unattainable, and having rejected the simple workingman, Tom Catchpole, who worships her, Catharine recognizes that "her life would be spent without love, or, at least, without a love which could be acknowledged." The man who brings Catharine to the brink of death is neither a sentimentalist nor a hypocrite. On the contrary, at least in his eloquence and in the content of his sermons, Cardew is modeled after the Independent minister Caleb Morris, who was the

inspiration of White's youth and one of the most enduring of all the influences upon him. White first knew him in 1849, just before Morris left Fetter Lane Chapel in London. More than fifty years later White said of Morris: "He *made* me." Without Morris, White claimed, he would "either have settled down as a mere partisan in the church, or else broken away from creeds altogether." White perceived in this Welsh minister what he called "an indwelling of the Christ of the Gospels, shaping thought, speech and life." White believed that this gracious activity of the Spirit within the human dimension constituted the richest and most genuine freedom.

Catharine Furze renounces Cardew because she loves him, and this positive action bears fruit. She initially turns from him through a power "not her own." After she leaves him, Cardew also feels something come to him: "it smote him as the light from heaven smote Saul of Tarsus journeying to Damascus. His eyes were opened; he crept into an outhouse in the fields and there in an agony he prayed." An enlightened Cardew now sees with new eyes his wife's virtues and his duty toward her. His love for Catharine is denied fulfillment, yet it transforms his life. The continuing vision of Catharine's face before her death "controlled and moulded him with an all-pervading power more subtle and penetrating than that which could have been exercised by theology or ethics." Shortly before she dies, Catharine and Cardew meet for the last time. He wishes to tell her that she has saved him. She smiles and replies, "You have saved *me*." The narrator continues, "By their love for each other were they both saved. The disguises are manifold which the Immortal Son assumes in the work of our redemption." Cardew's earlier sermon on the prodigal son (a favorite parable of White's and Caleb Morris's) foreshadows this reconciliation. The parable, Cardew suggests, exhibits not only "the magnificence of the Divine Nature, but of human nature—of that Nature which God assumed." The parable, as Cardew preaches it, is an example of the "indwelling Christ," for the power of God moving in the son opens his eyes and allows him to realize both his error and the meaning of his relationship with the father. The father's forgiveness is complete: a loving embrace welcomes the son back to life. The sermon illuminates the theme of *Catharine Furze*, as does Cardew's story about Charmides, a Roman sculptor who dies the death of a Christian martyr because the woman he loves is a Christian. In various dimensions, the novel explores the interrelatedness of divine and human love.

Mark Rutherford at the age of seventy-seven

When White's final novel, *Clara Hopgood*, was published in 1896, many critics condemned it, mainly because of the controversial subject matter. Yet this novel is the culmination of White's imaginative and intellectual achievement. In his excellent analysis of the work, Irwin Stock suggests that *Clara Hopgood* "has a character often associated with a master's late works, the character of an ultimate distillation." The quality of the prose and the compact structure of the novel reveal White at his purest and most austere. The story concerns the differing characters and perspectives of two sisters, Madge and Clara Hopgood. Madge relies on instinct, whereas Clara is characterized by rational insight. In the opening dialogue, the two sisters sit playing chess. Their remarks effectively suggest their differing natures and also serve to introduce the principal theme and method of the novel. Madge declares that she is unable to play chess well because she does not possess the "gift" or "instinct" which makes a good player. Clara responds that her sister is overfond of the word "instinct" and points out that Madge is a poor player because she refuses to anticipate logically her opponent's next move. The two attitudes express dominant and often conflicting aspects of White's own character. The claims of principle and reasonable dogma were often in conflict with the prompting of what he described as "the inner light." Both attitudes are examined in the novel, and neither is dismissed. Rather, they are held in delicate equipoise, for each has valid claims. Through her instinct Madge falls in love with Frank Palmer, the attractive son of a friend of her late father. Although during the courtship she begins to doubt their compatibility, she becomes engaged to him. The couple are intensely attracted to each other, and Madge is able to deceive herself for a long while because of her physical response to Frank. She finally rejects him, but soon discovers that she is pregnant. Because she realizes that she does not love the father of her child, she refuses to marry him. She defends her personal morality: intuitively she understands that to marry for conventional and expedient reasons would be more sinful than her original error. The family removes to London, where Clara meets and falls in love with Baruch Cohen. In this character White pays his greatest tribute to Spinoza, for Baruch is not only the philosopher's namesake but also his voice. Throughout the work, Baruch expresses many of Spinoza's central ideas. (In 1894 White had published his amended translation of Spinoza's *Ethic*, followed in 1895 by a translation of *Tractatus de Intellectus Emendatione et de Via*.)

Clara falls in love through the principles and attitudes that she espoused early in the story, yet at the moment when an answering look to Baruch's tentative questions would secure her a loving husband and a useful, joyful future, she refrains: "Something fell and flashed before her like lightning from a cloud overhead, divinely beautiful, but divinely terrible." The narrator does not reveal at this point what she has seen. Only later does it become apparent that she has recognized the potential for a relationship between Baruch and her sister Madge. A man of Baruch's temperament would ignore convention and her sister's history. An illegitimate child would create no problems for him. One day Clara sees Baruch and Madge together, obviously beginning to care for each other. "The message then was authentic," she says to herself, "I thought I could not have misunderstood it." Significantly, when Madge refused to marry Frank she had used similar language: "It is not the first time in my life that the truth has been revealed to me suddenly, supernaturally . . . and I know the revelation to be authentic." Clara goes to Italy as a spy in the service of Mazzini, the Italian patriot, and Madge and Baruch marry. Eighteen months later the happily married couple learns from Mazzini that Clara is dead. He points to the nature and meaning of her action: "The theologians represent the Crucifixion as the most sublime fact in the world's history. It was sublime, but let us reverence also the Eternal Christ who is forever being crucified for our salvation." Ten years later Baruch tells his daughter of her aunt Clara, who died, he says, "because she wanted to free the poor people of Italy who were slaves." The ending is sad and profoundly ironic. Neither Madge nor Baruch ever comprehends what Clara did. In White's finest novel, his quest for personal freedom is imaginatively concluded. Freedom is here expressed as the love which is perfect service. Clara sacrifices herself not for love of God in the abstract but for love of her sister. This is White's point: unselfish love actively pursued in the human sphere is love of God. Thus the concluding irony is more subtle and pervasive than Baruch's ignorance of Clara's love and the action that defines her nature. The central word is "freed." Those Clara frees are not only in Italy but in England. Madge is freed not only from her former bondage to the old life and its penalties; she is literally freed through Clara's love into new life.

In the following years White wrote several critical works, of which the most important was a biography of John Bunyan (1904), for whom White always had a deep affection. In 1907, when he was seventy-five years old, he met Dorothy Horace-Smith, then thirty, who became his second wife. His description of their meeting is immensely revealing: "When I first saw Dorothy I loved her. . . . Something was wrought in me instantaneously. It was spiritual regeneration answering to what is known as conversion in the language of religion." White's love for Dorothy was the most complete and the happiest of all his conversions. When they were married on 8 April 1911 and she became a permanent resident of the household, many of White's hypochondriacal fears disappeared. He told Dorothy that what he had seen in Caleb Morris as a young man and had been seeking for fifty years he had seen again in her. In both he recognized the perfect freedom which was the expression of a felt sense of the "indwelling Christ."

In 1900 Hale White published the first of his three volumes of miscellaneous pieces, *Pages from a Journal.* The journals are remarkable works, each containing short fiction, occasional essays, and diverse notes on an extraordinary range of subjects taken from his private notebooks. In the first volume, "The Governess's Story," "James Forbes," and "Mrs. Fairfax" all concern questions of conscience and love. The most impressive story is entitled "Atonement" and is perhaps the best illustration of White's attempt to realize in fiction a focus for amorphous guilt and create imaginatively a means of expiation. "Letters From Aunt Eleanor" is the brilliant and moving account of a woman's grief over the deaths of her husband and daughter. In 1910 White published *More Pages from a Journal.* In addition to essays on Shakespeare, Wordsworth, the nature of faith, and other subjects, the volume contains substantial short stories. The most interesting illuminate White's inner life at earlier stages of his career. "Mr. Whittaker's Retirement" explores the ambivalent feelings White experienced upon his own retirement: Mr. Whittaker enjoys his freedom for the first few weeks and then longs to be again part of the bustling life of "the City." At length he joyfully returns to work as a mere office clerk. "Confessions of a Self-Tormentor" describes the profound self-hatred of the protagonist, whose feelings of worthlessness foster a wretched pride that causes him to reject the compassionate friendship of Mrs. A. The circumstances of the story suggest that the model for Mrs. A is George Eliot, and that White is here expressing the remorse he felt for his self-punishing response to her kindness. In *The Early Life of Mark Rutherford*, White writes that "it was a lasting sorrow to me that I allowed my friendship with her to drop, and that after I left Chapman I never called on her." The story "Esther" is an exchange of letters between a loving mother and her unhappily married daughter; "Kate Radcliffe" also examines the intensity of parental affection.

The nonfictional *Early Life of Mark Rutherford*, written at the request of White's children and published posthumously in 1913, confirmed the authenticity of the earlier *Autobiography of Mark Rutherford, Dissenting Minister.* In that year White also published two stories in the *Nation*, "The Fire at Milldeep Manor" and "The Love of Woman," which were subsequently reprinted in the posthumous *Last Pages from a Journal* (1915), edited by Dorothy White. This volume, much of it written during the last years of White's life, includes some of his best essays and four short works of fiction. The astonishing essay "Captain James's 'Strange and Dangerous Voyage' " reveals White's fascination with extraordinary adventures and with the ability of the human spirit to endure against ferocious odds; pieces on Samuel Johnson, George Eliot, and Caleb Morris testify to his continuing affection for these major influences on his life and work; and his essay "How Can We Tell?" is a provocative vindication of Galileo.

Two of the stories in *Last Pages from a Journal*, "The Sweetness of Man's Friend" and "The Fire at Milldeep Manor," treat incompatible love relationships. White's most extraordinary piece of short fiction on this theme, however, is "The Dream of Two Dimensions," which had been printed anonymously for private circulation in 1884 and was reprinted in this volume. This fantasy is a subtle exploration of the author's ambivalent feelings toward his first wife. The narrator dreams he is in a world of colored shadows, where he alone of the inhabitants has three dimensions. His wife disappears each evening along with the other shadows, and the protagonist is left in solitude. He continually wishes that his gentle shadow wife were "something different" and shared his third dimension. The narrator's egoism, resentment, frustration, and profound remorse are described, but the story offers no resolution of the problems it raises.

Hale White died in 1913, in Groombridge, Kent. Although he eagerly encountered new ideas and events until his death, and although his writing sometimes expresses the pessimism characteristic of many later nineteenth-century writers, intellectually and temperamentally he belongs with the great earlier Victorians, with Tennyson and Carlyle and George Eliot. His work has always commanded a small but dedicated group of admirers, readers as diverse as Swinburne, Arnold, Conrad, and André Gide. D. H. Lawrence spoke for many of these admirers when he remarked that White's writing was "so thorough, so sound and so beautiful." The process of White's intellectual life, toward a greater moral and emotional freedom, is mirrored in the development of his fiction. The movement toward clarity of vision and unadorned purity of expression culminates in *Clara Hopgood*, but the reinterpretation of religious truths is central to his entire literary achievement. In all his work White imaginatively recreates and revitalizes a personal faith that arises out of and addresses itself to the facts of experience in all their complexity. In "reaching after a meaning" he encountered both melancholic dread and joyful reconciliation. He is one of the finest and the most courageous of the minor Victorian novelists.

Other:

Benedict Spinoza, *Ethic*, translated from the Latin by White (London: Trübner, 1883);

Spinoza, *Tractatus de Intellectus Emendatione et de Via, qua Optime in Veram Rerum Cognitionem Dirigitur*, translated by White, revised by Amelia H. Stirling (London: Unwin, 1895);

William White, *The Inner Life of the House of Commons*, introduction by White (2 volumes, London: Unwin, 1897);

A Description of the Wordsworth and Coleridge MSS. in the Possession of Mr. T. Norton Longman, edited by White (London: Longmans, Green, 1897);

Coleridge's Poems, A Facsimile Reproduction of the Proofs and MSS. of Some of the Poems, edited by James Dykes Campbell, preface and notes by White (Westminster: Archibald Constable, 1899);

Selections from Dr. Johnson's "Rambler," edited with preface and notes by White (London: Henry Froude, Oxford University Press, 1907).

Periodical Publications:

"The Genius of Walt Whitman," *Secular Review*, 12 (20 March 1880): 180-182;

"Marcus Antoninus," *Secular Review*, 1 (3 July 1880): 5-6;

"Ixion," *Secular Review*, 11 (11 September 1880): 164-165;

"Heathen Ethics," *Secular Review*, 22 (27 November 1880): 347;

"Dr. John Chapman," *Athenaeum*, 3502 (8 December 1894): 790-791;

"Mark Rutherford," *British Weekly* (Letter signed "Reuben Shapcott"), 20 (30 July 1896): 232;

Review of *The Poetical Works of William Wordsworth*, edited by William Knight, *Athenaeum*, 3609 (26 December 1896): 893-894;

"An Ancestor of Emerson," *British Weekly*, 23 (17 March 1898): 521-522.

Bibliographies:

W. Eugene Davis, "William Hale White (Mark Rutherford), An Annotated Bibliography," *English Literature in Transition*, 10 (1967): 97-117, 150-160;

Simon Nowell-Smith, *Mark Rutherford: A Short Bibliography of the First Editions* (Darby, Pa.: Folcroft Library Editions, 1973).

References:

Valentine Cunningham, *Everywhere Spoken Against: Dissent in the Victorian Novel* (Oxford: Clarendon Press, 1975);

David Daiches, *Some Late Victorian Attitudes* (London: Deutsche, 1969);

Linda K. Hughes, "Madge and Clara Hopgood: William Hale White's Spinozan Sisters," *Victorian Studies*, 18 (1974): 57-75;

Catherine Macdonald Maclean, *Mark Rutherford* (London: Macdonald, 1955);

E. S. Merton, *Mark Rutherford (William Hale White)* (New York: Twayne, 1967);

Gamini Salgado, "The Rhetoric of Sincerity: *The Autobiography of Mark Rutherford* as Fiction," in *Renaissance and Modern Essays*, edited by G. R. Hibbard (London: Routledge & Kegan Paul, 1966), pp. 159-168;

Irwin Stock, *William Hale White (Mark Rutherford)* (London: Allen & Unwin, 1956);

Wilfred H. Stone, *Religion and Art of William Hale White* (Stanford: Stanford University Press, 1954);

Patricia Thomson, "The Novels of Mark Rutherford," *Essays in Criticism*, 14 (1964): 256-267;

Dorothy Vernon White, *The Groombridge Diary* (London: Oxford University Press, 1924);

Basil Willey, *More Nineteenth Century Studies: A Group of Honest Doubters* (New York: Columbia University Press, 1969).

Papers:
There are collections of White's papers in the Colbeck Collection, the University of British Columbia; in the Bedford Public Library, Bedford, England; and in the Bodleian Library, Oxford.

Olive Schreiner
(24 March 1855-11 December 1920)

Joyce Avrech Berkman
University of Massachusetts-Amherst

BOOKS: *The Story of an African Farm: A Novel*, as Ralph Iron (2 volumes, London: Chapman & Hall, 1883; 1 volume, Boston: Little, Brown, 1883);

Dreams (London: Unwin, 1890; Boston: Roberts, 1891);

Dream Life and Real Life: A Little African Story, as Ralph Iron (London: Unwin, 1893; Boston: Roberts, 1893);

The Political Situation in Cape Colony, by Schreiner and S. C. Cronwright-Schreiner (London: Unwin, 1896);

Trooper Peter Halket of Mashonaland (London: Unwin, 1897; Boston: Roberts, 1897);

An English-South African's View of the Situation: Words in Season (London: Hodder & Stoughton, 1899);

Closer Union: A Letter on the South African Union and the Principles of Government (London: Fifield, 1909);

Woman and Labour (London: Unwin, 1911; New York: Stokes, 1911);

Thoughts on South Africa (London: Unwin, 1923; New York: Stokes, 1923);

From Man to Man; or, Perhaps Only (London: Unwin, 1926; New York: Harper, 1927);

Undine (London: Benn, 1928; New York: Harper, 1928).

With the publication of *The Story of an African Farm* in 1883, Olive Emilie Albertina Schreiner became the first major South African writer in the English language. Lyndall, the novel's female protagonist, was the most outspoken feminist to appear until then in British fiction. Schreiner's unique empathy in detailing the loss of faith suffered by her male protagonist, Waldo, elicited lavish praise from such distinguished Victorians as Herbert Spencer, Sir Charles Dilke, Cecil Rhodes, John Galsworthy, and William Gladstone. The directness, simplicity, and immediacy of Schreiner's prose also won it broad popularity, characterized by this response from a Lancashire working-class woman: "I read parts of it over and over.... About yon poor lass [Lyndall] ... I think there is hundreds of women what feels like that but can't speak it, but *she* could speak what we feel."

Schreiner's writing spanned diverse genres. Her allegories and short stories further develop the lyricism and social understanding of *The Story of an African Farm*. One allegory, "Three Dreams in a Desert," inspired imprisoned early-twentieth-century British suffragettes in their staunch resistance to forced feedings. Her various political and social treatises and essays on South African society and politics offer trenchant criticisms of British imperialism and racism and abundant insights into the history and character of the multiple cultural groups inhabiting South Africa. These writings establish Schreiner as a singular prophet, first of the Anglo-Boer War (1899-1902), then of the violent and barbaric consequences both of the war and of the South African constitution adopted in the war's aftermath.

Schreiner's most influential writing on women's lives, *Woman and Labour* (1911), touted as "the Bible" of the early twentieth-century women's movement, carved a position rare among feminists of her time. Invoking evidence from both the animal world and women's history, Schreiner argued that sex traits and roles were neither universal nor

innate. She envisioned a time when "new women" and "new men" would populate the earth and work and love one another on a basis of complete equality and shared labor.

Throughout Schreiner's writing, including her prodigious correspondence, the guiding vision is of integrated being: she rejected such Victorian dualisms as mind and body, emotions and reasons, and "male" and "female" traits. In place of racial, social-class, and sexual antagonisms, she championed egalitarian cooperation with full respect for racial and ethnic plurality. Such a vision of comprehensive integration prefigures mid- and late-twentieth-century intellectual movements, but in a Victorian society oriented to sharply dualistic and hierarchical modes of thought, Schreiner was a lonely rebel.

Until Schreiner's arrival in England in 1881, her intellectual isolation was nearly total. She was born on 24 March 1855 in a remote, mud-floored Wesleyan mission house in Wittebergen on the border of Basutoland. The ninth child of Rebecca Lyndall and Gottlob Schreiner, she was one of the seven of their twelve offspring to survive childhood. Survival did not come easily: Schreiner almost died of a lung inflammation when she was nine months old. The meager salary of missionaries was insufficient to feed and clothe the growing Schreiner family, so Gottlob Schreiner resorted to private trading, an infraction of missionary regulations for which he was expelled. Within a few years, still unable to provide for family needs, he was obliged to send his youngest two children, eleven-year-old Olive and nine-year-old Will, to live with their older brother Theo, the headmaster of a school in Cradock. An older sister, Ettie, kept house for Theo and together with him assumed parental responsibilities. From that point until she took positions as governess for up-country Boer families, Schreiner resided for varying lengths of time with different relatives and family friends.

The central drama of Schreiner's South African youth was her gradual and painful repudiation of the upbringing of her missionary parents and of the beliefs of her older siblings, relatives, and family friends. Initially, she shared her family's convictions, recalling, "I started in life with as much insular prejudice and racial pride as is given to any citizen who has never left the little Northern Island to possess." As a child she fantasized herself as Queen Victoria, decreeing that "all black people in South Africa . . . be collected and put into the desert of the Sahara, and a wall built across Africa shutting it off; I then ordained that any Black person returning south of the line should have his head cut off. . . ." Her parents instilled in her feelings of ethnic superiority to the neighboring African Dutch, the Boers. The mere use of Dutch words was taboo in the Schreiner household; her mother once whipped her severely for exclaiming "*Ach!*" The young Schreiner so absorbed evangelical doctrines on heaven and hell that she was beset with nightmares of throngs of sinners doomed to hell fire. She accepted, as well, her parents' Victorian attitudes toward gender roles, believing that the virtuous woman was above all self-denying for the sake of others.

Despite her adherence to family values, young Schreiner was restive. She described herself as *köppig*, a Cape Dutch word meaning heady, headstrong, perverse; and she likened herself to the Basuto pony, the spirited, nimble-footed, and daring pony of native blacks. Intensely emotional, she had trouble conforming to the modulated temperament expected of proper young ladies. Further, her inquisitive mind fastened upon existential and social dilemmas, especially after the death of her beloved younger sister Ellie. Between the ages of ten and eleven, Schreiner lost faith in Christianity. For increasingly conscious defiance of family strictures, her relatives called her "wicked," "odd," and "queer," and she came to view herself as an outcast.

During her childhood, chastised for her "deviant" behavior—from playing with snakes to refusing to attend church—Schreiner turned for solace to nature. Amid the glories of the landscape, the unimpeded stretches of the dry South African tableland, or karoo, she found freedom and affection: the sparse solitary plants seemed to reciprocate her love, and the vast horizon suggested infinite human possibility. Schreiner traced her visions of an integrative model of the universe and of human community to these periods of ecstatic meditation on the karoo.

Unlike her brothers, Schreiner had no formal schooling. Apart from the tutoring she received from her mother, Theo, and Ettie, she was self-educated. During her early adolescence, she discovered writers whose outlook was akin to hers: chief among these were Herbert Spencer, John Stuart Mill, Darwin, Goethe, and Emerson. Her reading of these authors was unsystematic, interrupted by much traveling and a tumultuous love affair. When Schreiner was fifteen she accompanied her brother Theo to the diamond fields in Griqualand West. (As

a temporary miner, Theo vainly nourished the hope of extracting enough wealth to send his sister to an American women's college.) After Schreiner's stay in the diamond fields came a series of extended visits with South African relatives and family friends. She ultimately settled in Dordrecht with the Reverend Zadoc Robinson and his family, where she met Julius Gau, a representative of a Swiss insurance company. She fell deeply in love with him. The precise nature of their relationship, long shrouded in secrecy and only disclosed fairly recently, remains elusive. Enough evidence exists to suggest that Schreiner, fearing herself pregnant, elicited Gau's willingness to marry her. Once her fears proved groundless, resurfacing areas of mutual unsuitability ended the engagement, leaving Schreiner severely despondent. The long-term effects of her thwarted love for Gau and the complex nature of her sexual and emotional needs and attitudes emerge in veiled ways in her fiction, shaped her feminist outlook, and set the boundaries of her adult intimate relationships.

However fragmentary, Schreiner's informal education sufficed to enable her to earn wages as a governess. After the Gau episode, from 1875 to 1881 she instructed children within various Boer family homes. Although her work was often frustrating—income paltry, children unruly, employers occasionally temperamental and bigoted—she had time for long walks on the karoo and for forming close friendships with some of her employers and their children. Boer women struck her as preferable alternative models of female possibility to those paraded by British society. Sharing with men heavy agricultural labor, the Boer women possessed not only physical strength and daring but also economic self-reliance (holding property in their own right) and indomitable will. At the same time, unlike Schreiner's mother, they were warmly affectionate and exuberant in humor. Her friendships with Boer women helped her shed her ethnocentrism. During her years as governess, Schreiner mastered oral Afrikaans. Later, she became a leading public advocate of the preservation of the threatened Boer language, the Taal. Although a less-than-flattering portrayal of a Boer woman appears in *The Story of an African Farm*, subsequent characterizations of Boer women in her fiction and nonfiction vaunt their admirable traits as protofeminist.

The rigors of Schreiner's duties as governess left only late night hours for reading and writing. Often working well into the early morning, she managed to complete her first two novels, *Undine* (published posthumously in 1928) and *The Story of an African Farm*, as well as begin a third one, later titled *From Man to Man* (1926). The two completed novels incorporate much of her childhood and adolescent experience. *Undine*, begun during her stay at the diamond fields, introduces themes more fully and intricately developed in *The Story of an African Farm*. Whereas *Undine* follows the life of one central individual in linear, narrative fashion, *The Story of an African Farm* focuses upon several primary figures, mingling linear sequences with flashbacks, extended allegories, and introspective passages. Through the wayward eponymous Undine and through Waldo, the young poetic spirit of *The Story of an African Farm*, both novels depict a young person's loss of faith in Christianity and search for spiritual and moral direction within a world of natural and human cruelty side by side with goodness and beauty. It is a second major protagonist in *The Story of an African Farm*, the orphan Lyndall, who permits Schreiner to carry further Undine's struggle for female identity and integrity in the face of social ridicule and expulsion, of male privilege and domination, of the sexual double standard, of meager work options for single women, and of the characters' inner battle between submissive love and independent selfhood. Throughout both novels the formidable structure of colonialism and racial and social class hierarchies intensify the isolation, vulnerability, and futility of the social rebel's quest for self-realization. Both Undine and Lyndall meet tragic deaths, while Waldo's fate is more ambiguous.

Despite the considerable autobiographical matter in her two early novels, Schreiner omitted one essential experience of her adolescence—the onset of asthma, a condition of such crippling magnitude that much of Schreiner's adult life was spent combating its attacks and accompanying respiratory viruses. Occasional chest spasms, a foreshadowing of her fatal heart disease, compounded her ill health. With nineteenth-century medical knowledge of asthma haphazard at best, Schreiner experimented with an array of drugs, some of which had debilitating side effects. Chronic illness and nervous strain periodically plummeted her into deep depression.

With her novels in hand and with earnings patiently saved as a governess, Schreiner in 1881 traveled from South Africa to England. While she had long nurtured the dream of becoming a writer, it was not primarily to peddle her fiction that she left her homeland. As a child and adolescent, she had

yearned even more to become a doctor. Unable to study medicine in South Africa, where even nursing remained the preserve of women in religious orders (and unpaid at that), Schreiner devised a plan, with encouragement from highly supportive friends, Dr. John and Mary Brown, to enter medical studies initially through nurses' training at the Royal Infirmary at Edinburgh, Scotland, one of only three hospitals in the British Isles with such programs for women. Unfortunately, Schreiner's respiratory ailments sabotaged her medical ambitions: she lasted at the Royal Infirmary a shocking three days. Though England was conducive to her intellectual growth, the impact of its cold and damp climate wrecked her health. Steady work on her writing also became impossible. She moved from residence to residence in hopes of breathing more easily (though some shifts were prompted by landladies opposed to Schreiner's entertaining men in her rooms). During her stay in England (1881-1889) such writing as she did complete was limited in scope— allegories and short stories—and most of these were finished while she sojourned in Italy on two separate extended trips.

Schreiner's income derived primarily from the successful publication in 1883 of *The Story of an African Farm*, originally printed under the pseudonym Ralph Iron, though her identity as author was soon disclosed. Widespread acclaim for her novel helped to cushion the blow to her medical aspirations, but she remained torn between her sense of obligation to alleviate the suffering of others and her duty to her art and her intellectual self. Ultimately, she channeled her medical-career impulses into social and political directions. While in England, she began her research for a full-scale, multidisciplinary study of women's lives. At one point she collected cosigners for a letter she wrote and had published in support of William Stead's expose of the brutal prostitution of young girls. At the same time, she deepened her understanding of modern capitalism and formed close relationships with leading socialists such as Eleanor Marx, Edward Carpenter, and Karl Pearson.

Since adolescence Schreiner had idealized a comradeship of equals with her male friends and a combined sexual, emotional, and intellectual intimacy with those men she felt she could marry. During her English years she was constantly disappointed in both ideals. Her intense intimate relationship with the psychologist Havelock Ellis foundered for lack of sexual and temperamental compatibility, though they remained close friends.

Schreiner had met Ellis in 1884 after an exchange of letters he had initiated following his reading of *The Story of an African Farm*. A medical student at the time, as well as literary essayist for the *Westminster Review*, he was wrestling with many of the same issues which preoccupied Schreiner—the rejection of Christianity, the nature of sexuality and gender, and the dynamics of social progress. Through Ellis, Schreiner entered sophisticated circles of British intellectual life, such as the Fellowship of the New Life (the womb of the Fabian Society). Ellis and Schreiner met frequently, traveled together (primarily within England), and wrote to each other daily, sometimes several letters in a single day. Even their eventual marriages to others did not diminish the depth of their mutual commitment.

No less passionate but much shorter-lived were Schreiner's feelings for Karl Pearson. With Pearson, however, she ardently sought a purely platonic friendship, but one rich in emotional expressiveness. Pearson, highly cerebral and re-

served, feared Schreiner's flamboyance and spurned her attempts at more open communication. Their mutual friends interpreted her passion for friendship with Pearson as a camouflage for erotic intentions. So muddled and agonized had their relationship become by the winter of 1886-1887 that Schreiner, on the verge of nervous collapse, fled to Europe and severed their contact. By 1889, Schreiner despaired of ever realizing in her lifetime her ideals of heterosexual friendship and love. She projected these ideals into the future and resolved to pave the way for subsequent generations of "new women" and "new men."

The combination of emotional despair and ill health spurred her decision in 1891 to return to South Africa, where she focused her healing attention on the condition of African Boers and blacks. By the early 1890s, her brother Will was a prominent Cape political leader (Prime Minister Cecil Rhodes's attorney general), and by the end of the decade Will became the first South African-born

A letter from Schreiner to Havelock Ellis, 1892. The "enclosed cutting" is an article from the Pall Mall Gazette *about "two literary ladies—one of whom is widely famous"—who had entered into a suicide pact, and one of whom had reneged without telling the other. Schreiner thinks the article refers to her and Amy Levy, a poet and novelist who killed herself in 1889.*

prime minister of the Cape Colony. As Will's sister and as a celebrity in her own right, Schreiner could exert an influence upon South African political life.

After a brief romantic attraction to the charismatic Cecil Rhodes, Schreiner became his most articulate foe. Incensed by Rhodes's support of military and economic expansion, with native blacks consequently dispossessed and exploited and the autonomy of the two Boer republics imperiled, Schreiner issued fiery diatribes against English racism and imperialism. Schreiner's most excoriating attack on conventional British ethnic assumptions, her novella *Trooper Peter Halket of Mashonaland* (1897) unleashed a tornado of abuse from her pro-English family and friends. Peter Halket is an English soldier who, as a member of Cecil Rhodes's Chartered Company, is engaged in efforts to suppress the Mashonaland rebellion. His moral upbringing in human decency and fair play haunts him in a dream one night while he sleeps in the veld: Christ appears in disguise and through an inquiring dialogue impels Peter to assess the Chartered Company's atrocities, the rape, murder, and looting of native Africans. Peter, guilt-stricken, resolves to redeem himself. The novella climaxes when he cleverly aids an African prisoner of his company to escape, an action which results in Peter's being shot to death.

In her anti-imperial agitation Schreiner had the hearty cooperation of Samuel Cron Cronwright, whom she had met in 1892 and married the following year. A successful cattle breeder, Cronwright shared many of Schreiner's convictions, and, in accord with her wishes, took Cronwright-Schreiner as his married name. Though Schreiner's marriage to Cronwright fell short of her adolescent yearnings, it approximated her ideals more closely than any male relationship hitherto. There were difficulties. Schreiner's asthma necessitated that her husband sell his thriving farm at Krantz Plaats to enable them to move to more salutary surroundings in Kimberly, a wrenching experience for Cronwright-Schreiner, who then became impatient with his wife's continued inability to complete *From Man to Man*. The tragic and inexplicable death in 1895 of their apparently healthy daughter only sixteen hours after birth, followed by a series of miscarriages, further strained their marriage. After Schreiner's death, Cronwright-Schreiner wrote a biography of his wife and published an edition of her letters and speeches as well as her first novel, *Undine*, and her unfinished novel, *From Man to Man*. The biography is filled with startling omissions and

Schreiner's husband, Samuel Cron Cronwright-Schreiner

Olive Schreiner in 1897, the year she published her anti-British novel, Trooper Peter Halket of Mashonaland

distortions along with passages of both unabashed reverence for and resentment of his wife. Similarly, the letters are sloppily edited, occasionally involving flagrant word and sentence changes. During Schreiner's lifetime, however, despite the tensions in their marriage, they were deeply attached to one another, bolstering each other's moral fortitude in the face of relentless social criticism, especially during the Anglo-Boer War.

The war confirmed Schreiner's forebodings. She experienced its horror directly, interned in Hanover for almost a year without her husband; their home in Johannesburg was looted, her manuscripts destroyed. After the war she labored for a democratic constitution for the new South African republic. In *Closer Union* (1909) she presented her case for a decentralized, federated, culturally plural nation. She helped to form the South African Women's Enfranchisement League and spoke in defense of persecuted Jews and striking trades-union women. Her political proposals for the new constitution went unheeded. Disheartened by the racist political evolution of South Africa, even resigning from the Women's Enfranchisement League when racial exclusion was allowed, she returned to her study of women's lives, preparing *Woman and Labour* for publication. Since her voluminous notes and chapter drafts had been destroyed during the pillaging of her home, the resulting study was a truncated version of her original design. Despite its brilliant argument for modern feminism, Schreiner regarded it as a disappointing fragment.

In 1913, believing herself near death and eager to see friends and relatives as well as doctors in Europe, Schreiner returned to England and remained there for the duration of World War I. For personal and economic reasons, her husband did not accompany her. Though in deteriorating health, she braved taunts and persecution for her vigorous support of conscientious objectors to the war as well as simply for her German name. Unable to complete *From Man to Man*, she commanded energy enough to compose "The Dawn of Civilization"—a piercing, original analysis of the interplay of irrational and self-interested impulses fomenting war.

When her husband joined her in London in July 1920, their reunion lasted one month. Rather than risk another damp English winter, Schreiner departed without him for South Africa. Though he planned to follow her back in a few months, she died on 11 December 1920, before his return. During the first year of her marriage, Schreiner had chosen her burial site, Buffels Kop, a stony summit overlooking an expanse of boundless space and diverse karoo vegetation. Her will, embodying her democratic ideals and healing vision, provided that sums be set aside for a medical scholarship for women at the South African College, Cape Town (the forerunner of the University of Cape Town). It was to be administered "without reference to race or colour or religion, poor women and girls to have preference."

Fortunately, though probably against his wife's wishes, Cronwright-Schreiner published the unfinished *From Man to Man*, Schreiner's most mature and intellectually penetrating fictional treatment of her lifelong devotion to social justice. *From Man to Man* traces the South African childhood and adult experiences of two sisters. The elder of the two, Rebekah, a voracious reader and horticulturist, finds her scientific and intellectual passions frustrated in her marriage to a callous, philandering husband. Though she loves him and cares deeply for preserving their marriage and family (they have three sons), she eventually asserts the legitimacy of her own needs: the priority of mutual trust and honesty for any meaningful intimacy. She separates from him and their Cape Town home and brings up her sons (as well as an adopted mulatto daughter of her husband's liaison with an African servant) in her country home on a vineyard she had bought years before. Late in the novel she meets the husband of a

Schreiner's coffin being carried to her burial site atop 5,000-foot-high Buffels Kop in South Africa

Cape Town neighbor with whom she shares an affinity of interests and an invigorating mutual respect. Given the unfinished state of the novel, it is not known whether this new relationship will result in any kind of deep or lasting bond.

Less heartening is the story of Rebekah's beloved younger sister, Baby Bertie, a victim of the Victorian sexual double standard. Seduced by her tutor on the family farm, Bertie is damned for life. When she confesses her "fallen" state to her fiancé, he discards her. Unable to escape the torment of social gossip and ostracism, she finally succumbs to the protection of a somewhat stereotyped, middle-aged, wealthy Jewish merchant and moneylender, who takes her with him to London. Pathetically in love with her, he suffocates her with material possessions as well as with his jealous behavior, finally ejecting her when he is led to believe (mistakenly) that she has seduced his young cousin. At the point where Schreiner breaks off the novel, Bertie is presumed to be a prostitute in a Soho brothel.

While the plot affords Schreiner opportunities to expose sexual injustice and female despondency, the intellectual meat of the novel emerges in Rebekah's searching social and philosophical reflections. In dreams, letters to her husband, introspective musings, and stories for her children, she ponders the nature and sources of social decadence and progress as well as the bias and malice of Social Darwinist support for social conflict, competition, and sexual, racial, and social-class inequality. She probes the dynamics between ideals and practical application, whether in politics, art, or human relationships, giving voice to Schreiner's socialist, pacifist, feminist, and antiracist convictions.

This novel, as indeed all Schreiner's fiction, has elicited a wide mixture of critical response. Schreiner's intellectual digressions are targets of considerable disapproval, both from opponents of her views and literary critics who deplore authorial didacticism and lengthy interruptions in plot action. More recently, in a period of renewed egalitarian fervor, these digressions, with their analytical detachment from reigning social norms and with their provocative insights into social relations, have been hailed as valid aesthetically and philosophically. While her character development is often regarded as uneven, Schreiner's poetic ability, especially in *The Story of an African Farm* and in her smaller works of fiction, to capture psychological and exterior landscapes through language rhythms and evocative and haunting images has been uniformly praised.

Letters:

The Letters of Olive Schreiner 1876-1920, edited by S. C. Cronwright-Schreiner (London: Unwin, 1924; Boston: Little, Brown, 1924).

Biographies:

S. C. Cronwright-Schreiner, *The Life of Olive Schreiner* (London: Unwin, 1924);

Ruth First and Ann Scott, *Olive Schreiner: A Biography* (London: Deutsch, 1980).

Reference:

Joyce Avrech Berkman, *Olive Schreiner: Feminism on the Frontier* (Montreal: Eden, 1979).

Joseph Henry Shorthouse

(9 September 1834–4 March 1903)

Frederick J. Wagner
University of Regina

BOOKS: *John Inglesant: A Romance* (Birmingham: Cornish, 1880; 2 volumes, London: Macmillan, 1881; 1 volume, New York: Munro, 1882; 2 volumes, Leipzig: Tauchnitz, 1882);

On the Platonism of Wordsworth (Birmingham: Cornish, 1882);

The Little Schoolmaster Mark: A Spiritual Romance (2 volumes, London: Macmillan, 1883-1884);

Sir Percival: A Story of the Past and of the Present (London & New York: Macmillan, 1886);

A Teacher of the Violin and Other Tales (London & New York: Macmillan, 1888);

The Countess Eve: A Novel (London & New York: Macmillan, 1888);

Blanche, Lady Falaise: A Tale (London & New York: Macmillan, 1891).

Though Joseph Henry Shorthouse wrote four other novels, some short stories, and a few essays, his reputation rests almost solely on his "philosophical romance," *John Inglesant* (1880). The novel was published and widely circulated in the supercharged atmosphere of the 1880s, an atmosphere of religious uncertainty and tension generated by the impact of the new science on philosophical thought and the erosive influence of the "Higher Criticism" on religious orthodoxy. This atmosphere was intensified by an awareness of the divisions resulting from the ritualist debate, and the rise of a vocal Evangelical party, in the Church of England. In addition, the loss of some prominent Anglicans (like Newman) to the church of Rome aroused, in Anglicans and Dissenters alike, a fear of possible Roman Catholic domination.

Thus, in a period of such widespread religious concern, *John Inglesant*, with its cultural and religious themes, found favor with a large, "earnest" public. Applauded by High Anglicans, warily viewed by many Evangelicals, condemned by some Roman Catholics (particularly the Jesuits), criticized by Lord Acton and Samuel Gardiner on grounds of historical inaccuracy, and denigrated by Ruskin, Andrew Lang, and Samuel Butler, the novel caused animated, often acrimonious, discussion. Begun in 1867, completed in 1876, and in manuscript twice

rejected by publishers, *John Inglesant* in its first, privately printed, Birmingham edition of 100 vellum-bound copies reached but few readers. Novelist James Payn acquired some dubious fame late in 1880 when, as reader for Smith, Elder, he turned down the novel as a poor publishing risk. But on Mrs. Humphry Ward's recommendation Alexander Macmillan in London ventured a cautious run of 750 copies in a two-volume edition (July 1881). Auspiciously attended by the unpremeditated publicity of Prime Minister W. E. Gladstone's untiring public praise of the novel, *John Inglesant* was hurried into rapid reprintings in several editions. Almost 10,000 copies were sold in the first year, and Shorthouse was lifted into unanticipated prominence as a lay spokesman for cultivated Anglicanism.

Born in Birmingham on 9 September 1834,

278

the oldest son of well-to-do, moderately conservative, third-generation Quakers, Shorthouse spent most of a comfortable, outwardly uneventful, sixty-eight year life in suburban Edgbaston. He was afflicted early with a painful stammer and delicate health; consequently, except for three very short and widely separated periods of attendance at private Quaker day schools, he had little formal education. For the most part he was taught at home by his parents, tutors, and his own wide reading. At sixteen, after a five-month residence at Grove House, Tottenham (a progressive Quaker school), he entered the family business, Joseph Shorthouse and Sons, manufacturers of vitriol and lacquer. In 1857 he married Sarah Scott, the elder daughter of a Birmingham accountant, whom he had known since childhood. Apart from a brief excursion with his cousins into southern Scotland and occasional family holidays in Llandudno, Wales, he was never out of England.

From early youth Shorthouse was impatient with the cultural and social restrictions (particularly on music, art, speech, and costume) of the Society of Friends. At the same time, though he was unsympathetic with the religious tenets and practices of the Society, he was not unaffected by them. Stimulated, however, by his study of the religious and political Anglican-Catholic-Puritan controversies of the seventeenth century, he was, like many of his Quaker contemporaries, drawn to the less restrictive, more socially acceptable, and more culturally satisfying Church of England. In August 1861 he and his wife joined the Church of England by baptism, and from 1864 to 1873 he served as people's warden in Anglican St. John's, Ladywood, near his home. Both his incurable stammer and the constant threat of epileptic attacks (the first of which occurred in 1862) barred him from public activity and confined him to a careful business routine and a quiet private life devoted to the study of seventeenth-century chroniclers and English divines.

In 1880 he was financially able to publish privately his first and best novel, *John Inglesant*, the fruit of over thirty years of scholarly reading and almost ten years of spare-time writing. Though the plot is simple, the encrustations which are the real substance of the book—religious and philosophical discussion, historical anecdote, aesthetic digressions—make summarization difficult, if not misleading. Historically based in seventeenth-century England and Italy, *John Inglesant* is a religious quest story of an "English saint," a half-mystic Cavalier with Roman Catholic leanings but with a restless,

inquiring mind. As courtier, soldier, diplomat, and traveler, he examines the various religious philosophies and institutions of his time—Anglicanism, Roman Catholicism, Puritanism, quietism, humanism. He meets and is influenced, positively or negatively, by such seventeenth-century figures as Thomas Hobbes, Nicholas Ferrar, Dr. Henry More, Hugh de Cressy, an Italian cardinal, and Miguel de Molinos, the quietist. Ever drawn to the church of Rome by the beauties of its services and edifices, he is repelled by what he considers in the Roman church a tyrannous repression of freedom of thought. Molinos comes into conflict with the Jesuits because of his advocacy of access to the sacrament without preliminary confession, and Inglesant is expelled from Italy for his politically injudicious defense at Molinos's heresy trial (1685). Finally, Inglesant finds spiritual equilibrium in the Church of England. For Inglesant the chief attraction of the Church of England lies in its uniqueness as an *English*, *national* church (established by law) with the *sovereign* as its head; for him it provides the "happy mean" between Roman Catholic authoritarianism and Puritan individualism. Like Shorthouse himself, Inglesant feels that in the Church of England he has independence of thought within a historically and legally authorized form. And what is perhaps even more important to him is an assurance that in the Church of England he has free access to the sacrament "barred by no confession, no human priest." In the Church of England he finds what satisfies the needs of his own nature, a proper balance of culture and restraint. In a sense, *John Inglesant* may be considered not only as a Cavalier's search for a satisfying faith but as an apologia, a fictional recreation of Shorthouse's own thinking as he groped his way from Quakerism to Anglicanism. Episodically loose in structure, uneven in style, covertly anti-Roman and anti-Evangelical, the novel, though flawed and now little read, still impresses with its evocation of seventeenth-century atmosphere, the vividness of its character portraits and scenes, and the religious sincerity of its author.

The four slighter novels and the book of short stories which followed mark a continual waning in his popularity as a writer. In these novels, Shorthouse, working on a smaller canvas, retouched the underlying themes and motifs of *John Inglesant* and further explored the interrelationships of religion, art, rank, and culture as these are manifested in the "noble living" of a "Christian gentleman" in an aristocratic setting. Hence, in *The Little Schoolmaster*

Mark (1883-1884), which is next to *John Inglesant* in importance and chronology, Shorthouse argues in an eighteenth-century German court setting that the "noble" life, the life of "culture," not only includes religion but must be dominated by it. His next novel, *Sir Percival* (1886), set in a nineteenth-century English manor, is a languorous, overpadded, unconvincing "Grail story" of a modern "knight" who demonstrates the efficacy of elevated, aristocratic cultural ideals by suffering martyrdom in Africa. In *The Countess Eve* (1888)—set in eighteenth-century Burgundy—Shorthouse rather nebulously undertakes an amplification of his "analysis of sin," which had been only oblique (though implicit) in *John Inglesant*: underlying the universe is an ever present evil, Sin; in turn, Sin causes particular sins and is vanquishable only by the "Divine Humanity," Christ. His last novel, and Shorthouse's favorite, *Blanche, Lady Falaise* (1891), repeats this theme—even less convincingly—in a Devonshire setting.

Invalided by muscular rheumatism, Shorthouse retired from business two years before his death at his home, Lansdowne, Edgbaston, on 4 March 1903. His wife survived him by six years; they had no children.

Lansdowne, Shorthouse's home in Edgbaston, where he lived from 1876 until his death in 1903

On a residue of inherited Quaker quietism Shorthouse imposed a Broad Church tolerance of dogma and a High Church feeling for "comely beauty" and liturgical form. The result was an amalgam, a distinctive Anglicanism—"Broad Church sacramentalism," he called it—as much aesthetic and cultural as religious, and especially congenial to an independent, if sometimes wayward, thinker seeking liberty of thought within the authority of a historically institutionalized church. Underlying most of his writing is the belief that all life is sacramental—symbolic of and permeated by the Divine—and reaches its highest, purest expression in the Eucharist as celebrated by an English national church.

In the novels, Shorthouse is less adept at detailed plot construction than at the swift sketching of capsule summaries and short dramatic scenes; the fictional characters of his own invention are less vivid and lifelike than those he recreated from historical and literary sources. But in all the novels one is impressed by Shorthouse's undisguised devoutness and his enthusiasm for the rarefied pleasure of high thought and the cultivated noble life.

Other:

George Herbert, *The Temple*, "Introductory Essay" by Shorthouse (London: Unwin, 1882);

Golden Thoughts from the Spiritual Guide of Molinos, the Quietist, preface by Shorthouse (Glasgow: Bryce, 1883);

Francis Morse, *Peace the Voice of the Church to Her Sick*, preface by Shorthouse (London: Christian Knowledge Society, 1888);

Arthur Galton, *The Message and Position of the Church of England*, "Preface on the Royal Supremacy" by Shorthouse (London: Kegan Paul, French, Trübner, 1899).

Periodical Publications:

"The Agnostic at Church," *Nineteenth Century*, 11 (April 1882): 650-652;

"The Humorous in Literature," *Macmillan's Magazine*, 47 (March 1883): 248-280;

"Frederick Denison Maurice," *Nineteenth Century*, 15 (May 1884): 849-866;

"Of Restraining Self-Denial in Art," *Century Guild Hobby Horse*, 3 (1888): 3-7.

Bibliography:

Frederick J. Wagner, "J. H. Shorthouse (1834-1903): A Bibliography," *Bulletin of Bibliography and Magazine Notes*, 28 (1971): 84-87, 108, 141-144.

Biographies:

Sarah Shorthouse, *Life, Letters, and Literary Remains of J. H. Shorthouse* (2 volumes, London: Macmillan, 1905);

Frederick J. Wagner, *J. H. Shorthouse* (Boston: Hall, 1979).

References:

Morchard Bishop, "*John Inglesant* and Its Author," in *Essays by Divers Hands*, 29 (1958): 73-86;

Raymond Chapman, "The Zeal of a Convert," in his *Faith and Revolt: Studies in the Literary Influence of the Oxford Movement* (London: Weidenfeld & Nicolson, 1970), pp. 252-279;

William Kaye Fleming, "Some Truths About 'John Inglesant,' " *Quarterly Review*, 245 (July 1925): 130-148;

Edmund Gosse, "The Author of *John Inglesant*," in his *Portraits and Sketches* (London: Heinemann, 1912), pp. 149-162;

Paul Elmer More, "J. Henry Shorthouse," in *Shelburne Essays, Third Series* (New York: Putnam's, 1905), pp. 213-243.

Robert Louis Stevenson

Robert Kiely
Harvard University

BIRTH: Edinburgh, Scotland, 13 November 1850, to Thomas and Margaret Isabella Balfour Stevenson.

EDUCATION: Edinburgh University, 1867-1872.

MARRIAGE: 19 May 1880 to Fanny Van de Grift Osbourne.

DEATH: Vailima, Samoa, 3 December 1894.

BOOKS: *An Appeal to the Clergy* (Edinburgh & London: Blackwood, 1875);

An Inland Voyage (London: Kegan Paul, 1878; Boston: Roberts, 1883);

Edinburgh: Picturesque Notes, with Etchings (London: Seeley, Jackson & Halliday, 1879; New York: Macmillan, 1889);

Travels with a Donkey in the Cévennes (London: Kegan Paul, 1879; Boston: Roberts, 1879);

Virginibus Puerisque and Other Papers (London: Kegan Paul, 1881; New York: Collier, 1881);

Familiar Studies of Men and Books (London: Chatto & Windus, 1882; New York: Dodd, Mead, 1887);

New Arabian Nights (2 volumes, London: Chatto & Windus, 1882; 1 volume, New York: Holt, 1882);

The Story of a Lie (London: Hayley & Jackson, 1882);

republished as *The Story of a Lie and Other Tales* (Boston: Turner, 1904);

The Silverado Squatters: Sketches from a Californian Mountain (London: Chatto & Windus, 1883; New York: Munro, 1884);

Treasure Island (London: Cassell, 1883; Boston: Roberts, 1884);

A Child's Garden of Verses (London: Longmans, Green, 1885; New York: Scribners, 1885);

More New Arabian Nights: The Dynamiter, by Stevenson and F. Van de G. Stevenson (London: Longmans, Green, 1885; New York: Holt, 1885);

Prince Otto: A Romance (London: Chatto & Windus, 1885; New York: Roberts, 1886);

Strange Case of Dr. Jekyll and Mr. Hyde (London: Longmans, Green, 1886; New York: Munro, 1886);

Kidnapped (London: Cassell, 1886; New York: Munro, 1886);

Some College Memories (Edinburgh: University Union Committee, 1886; New York: Mansfield & Wessels, 1899);

The Merry Men and Other Tales and Fables (London: Chatto & Windus, 1887; New York: Harper, 1887);

Underwoods (London: Chatto & Windus, 1887; New York: Scribners, 1887);

Memoirs and Portraits (London: Chatto & Windus, 1887; New York: Scribners, 1887);

The Misadventures of John Nicholson: A Christmas Story (New York: Lovell, 1887);

The Black Arrow: A Tale of the Two Roses (London: Cassell, 1888; New York: Scribners, 1888);

The Master of Ballantrae: A Winter's Tale (London: Cassell, 1889; New York: Collier, 1889);

The Wrong Box (London: Longmans, Green, 1889; New York: Scribners, 1889);

Ballads (London: Chatto & Windus, 1890; New York: Scribners, 1890);

Father Damien: An Open Letter to the Reverend Dr. Hyde of Honolulu (London: Chatto & Windus, 1890; Portland, Maine: Mosher, 1897);

Across the Plains, with Other Memories and Essays (London: Chatto & Windus, 1892; New York: Scribners, 1892);

A Footnote to History: Eight Years of Trouble in Samoa (London: Cassell, 1892; New York: Scribners, 1892);

Three Plays: Deacon Brodie, Beau Austin, Admiral Guinea, W. E. Henley (London: Nutt, 1892; New York: Scribners, 1892);

The Wrecker (London: Cassell, 1892; New York: Scribners, 1892);

Island Nights' Entertainments: Consisting of The Beach of Falesá, The Bottle Imp, The Isle of Voices (London: Cassell, 1893; New York: Scribners, 1893);

Catriona: A Sequel to "Kidnapped" (London: Cassell, 1893; New York: Scribners, 1893);

The Ebb-Tide: A Trio and a Quartette (Chicago: Stone & Kimball, 1894; London: Heinemann, 1894);

The Body-Snatcher (New York: Merriam, 1895);

The Amateur Emigrant from the Clyde to Sandy Hook (Chicago: Stone & Kimball, 1895, New York: Scribners, 1899);

The Strange Case of Dr. Jekyll and Mr. Hyde, with Other Fables (London: Longmans, Green, 1896);

Weir of Hermiston: An Unfinished Romance (London: Chatto & Windus, 1896; New York: Scribners, 1896);

A Mountain Town in France: A Fragment (New York & London: Lane, 1896);

Songs of Travel and Other Verses (London: Chatto & Windus, 1896);

In the South Seas (London: Chatto & Windus, 1896; New York: Scribners, 1896);

St. Ives: Being the Adventures of a French Prisoner in England (New York: Scribners, 1897; London: Heinemann, 1898);

The Morality of the Profession of Letters (Gouverneur, N.Y.: Brothers of the Book, 1899);

A Stevenson Medley, edited by S. Colvin (London: Chatto & Windus, 1899);

Essays and Criticisms (Boston: Turner, 1903);

Prayers Written at Vailima, with an Introduction by Mrs. Stevenson (New York: Scribners, 1904; London: Chatto & Windus, 1905);

Essays of Travel (London: Chatto & Windus, 1905);

Essays in the Art of Writing (London: Chatto & Windus, 1905);

Essays, edited by W. L. Phelps (New York: Scribners, 1906);

Lay Morals and Other Papers (London: Chatto & Windus, 1911; New York: Scribners, 1911);

Records of a Family of Engineers (London: Chatto & Windus, 1912);

The Waif Woman (London: Chatto & Windus, 1916);

On the Choice of a Profession (London: Chatto & Windus, 1916);

Poems Hitherto Unpublished, edited by G. S. Hellman (2 volumes, Boston: Bibliophile Society, 1916);

New Poems and Variant Readings (London: Chatto & Windus, 1918);

Poems Hitherto Unpublished, edited by Hellman and W. P. Trent (Boston: Bibliophile, 1921);

Robert Louis Stevenson: Hitherto Unpublished Prose Writings, edited by H. H. Harper (Boston: Bibliophile, 1921);

When the Devil Was Well, edited by Trent (Boston: Bibliophile, 1921);

Confessions of a Unionist: An Unpublished Talk on Things Current, Written in 1888, edited by F. V. Livingston (Cambridge, Mass.: Privately printed, 1921);

The Best Thing in Edinburgh: An Address to the Speculative Society of Edinburgh in March 1873, edited by K. D. Osbourne (San Francisco: Howell, 1923);

Selected Essays, edited by H. G. Rawlinson (London: Oxford University Press, 1923);

The Castaways of Soledad: A Manuscript by Stevenson Hitherto Unpublished, edited by Hellman (Buffalo: Privately printed, 1928);

Monmouth: A Tragedy, edited by C. Vale (New York: Rudge, 1928);

The Charity Bazaar (Westport, Conn.: Georgian Press, 1929);

The Essays of Robert Louis Stevenson edited by M. Elwin (London: Macdonald, 1950);

Salute to RLS, edited by F. Holland (Edinburgh: Cousland, 1950);

Tales and Essays, edited by G. B. Stern (London: Falcon, 1950);

Silverado Journal, edited by J. D. Hart (San Francisco: Book Club of California, 1954).

COLLECTIONS: *The Works of R. L. Stevenson*, Edinburgh Edition, edited by Sidney Colvin (28 volumes, London: Chatto & Windus, 1894-1898);

The Works of Robert Louis Stevenson, Vailima Edition, edited by L. Osbourne and F. Van de G. Stevenson, 26 volumes (London: Heinemann, 1922-1923; New York: Scribners, 1922-1923);

The Works of Robert Louis Stevenson, Tusitala Edition (35 volumes, London: Heinemann, 1924);

The Works of Robert Louis Stevenson, South Seas Edition (32 volumes, New York: Scribners, 1925).

One of the hallmarks of the Victorian literary achievement is genius wedded to industry and professionalism. One has only to think of Dickens and Trollope or George Eliot and Matthew Arnold to recall the persistence, self-discipline, and patiently sustained labor that resulted in the steady accumulation of a body of works as firm and fixed as the building blocks of a great edifice. It is one of the many paradoxes in the life of Robert Louis Stevenson that, though he was a worker and craftsman of extraordinary skill, his literary image is that of a whimsical amateur, an aesthetic drifter. Not only did he move from place to place, scribbling on trains, dictating in bed, but he seems to have written a bit of everything.

In fact, though Stevenson wrote poetry, essays, travel books, hundreds of wonderful letters, and a few plays, his reputation as an author writing for adults rests on his short stories and novels. Furthermore, despite the frequent travel, the velvet jacket and careless manner, the illness and relatively early death at the age of forty-four, his output betrays Victorian industry. Robert Louis Stevenson

Stevenson's birthplace: No. 8 Howard Place, Edinburgh

was, as Henry James said, a "figure," but he was also a writer of great determination, seriousness, and ever-increasing scope.

Stevenson was born in Edinburgh in 1850 of middle-class Church of Scotland parents who expected him to become an engineer like his father, uncles, and grandfather. Like so many gifted Victorian children, Stevenson wanted to please his parents but found that he could not do so and remain true to himself. His early schooling was limited, partly because of ill health caused by lung problems and partly because his father doubted the value of an orthodox education. His education at Mr. Henderson's school on India Street, near his Edinburgh home, was frequently interrupted by illness between 1855 and 1861. His later attendance at the Edinburgh Academy, beginning at age eleven, was similarly disrupted by poor health and trips to the Continent in search of better climates. He spent a brief time at boarding school in Isleworth, but, unhappy, he returned to Edinburgh and attended Mr. Thompson's school. At the university he studied first engineering, then law, a compromise with his father after the son confessed his religious skepticism and desire for a literary career. Stevenson was called to the bar in July 1875. In some ways, the early signs of frail health were a good omen for his career as a writer, for they enabled his parents to "make allowances" for him, to let him go abroad for his health, to rest, and write rather than pursue the rigors of a "manly" profession. Partly as a concession to their attitude, partly out of necessity and for the amusement of it, Stevenson approached the life of the writer as a long holiday.

Two of his earliest sustained pieces of writing are travel journals based on excursions in France. *An Inland Voyage* (1878) traces a somewhat damp, disappointing journey by canoe down the River Oise, and *Travels with a Donkey in the Cévennes* (1879) records a walking trip through the Cévennes mountains. Though these works are inevitably loose and discursive, they contain elements of local color and incidental vignettes that betray an early narrative gift. They also betray a tactic that Stevenson was to employ with particular effectiveness in his later suspense fiction: rococo dawdling. He never seems in a hurry, yet his delays are usually too rhetorically splendid, too entertaining in themselves to be irritating. After a while, one gives up worrying about the destination—which is precisely the state of mind Stevenson is trying to produce.

While still in his middle twenties Stevenson also began writing the occasional essays that eventu-

ally earned him a reputation as a popular philosopher. As Wordsworth and Thoreau had been among his favorite models as nature writers, so Hazlitt and Lamb inspired him to try his hand at the informal essay. In all of his writing, Stevenson liked moving from the personal, chatty, even frivolous to the elevated and moralistic. Though the pieces published in *Virginibus Puerisque and Other Papers* (1881), including "Aes Triplex," "Crabbed Age and Youth," "Ordered South," "An Apology for Idlers," and "Pan's Pipes," stand by themselves as complete and charming exercises, they, like his travel pieces, reveal the irrepressible traits of the future writer of fiction. Stevenson could not resist telling a story; and though in his essays he tries to fit his anecdotes to general observations, the tale is often superior to the moral tag to which it is applied. This does not necessarily mean, as some critics have asserted, that Stevenson was a hypocrite; rather it means that he came most naturally to terms with life through concrete and dramatic situations.

Readers of his own time were exhilarated by the freshness, the unexpected directness in the midst of luscious paragraphs in which he had seemed only to be marking time. Today the prose still sparkles in places, though the foot tapping seems less justifiable in exposition than in fiction and travel writing; the modern taste in essays demands that the writer get on with his point. But when, in fact, Stevenson does get on with his point, the twentieth-century reader is likely to feel let down: his observations about youth, age, marriage, work, suffering, play, and travel are rarely as original or stimulating as the fragmentary meditations, emotions, and incidents to which these themes are so loosely attached. In his essays, as in his life, Stevenson often challenges Victorian complacency, philistinism, and moral rigidity. Yet his antidotes are themselves deeply characteristic of the time: postromantic, personal, voluntaristic. His essays are sermons on self-help. He extols the imagination and the holiness of the heart's affections, but he also preaches duty, determination, self-reliance, and discipline.

If his essays reveal him to be a versatile and charming Victorian more than a truly rebellious or original thinker, they also show him developing and experimenting with a personal voice of considerable tonal range. Stevenson may not have created a new ethical system nor even cut very deeply into the faults of the existing one, but he learned in his essays to create a personality—or, more precisely, many personalities. Like other novelists who wrote

San Francisco and had set off with her three children for Europe to study art. Not long after arriving on the Continent, her youngest child, Hervey, had died of tuberculosis; and by the time she met Stevenson, she was in a state of extreme depression. Despite all the apparent obstacles, the two became friends and gradually over a two-year period developed an unusual bond. When Fanny returned to America, Stevenson's parents assumed the "danger" was over, but his close friends knew better and were not surprised when Stevenson responded to a telegram by dropping everything and setting off for the New World.

Never one to lose an opportunity to translate experience into words, Stevenson kept a travel journal of what for a person of his limited means and fragile health was an arduous, even hazardous, journey. *Across the Plains* (1892) and *The Amateur Emigrant from the Clyde to Sandy Hook* (1895) contain a good deal of the color and vivacity of the earlier travel books. Eccentric characters on shipboard, the

Stevenson shortly after being called to the bar in 1875

essays—Conrad, D. H. Lawrence, and Stevenson's friend, Henry James—Stevenson often sacrificed logical coherence to those sudden shifts in voice, argument, or atmosphere so essential to great narrative.

As his essays and travel pieces show, Stevenson's personal charm derives in large part from his unabashed interest in and affection for other people. It sometimes seems that the less his acquaintances were like him, the more fascinated in and sympathetic toward them he became. Men as different as James, Sidney Colvin, Edmund Gosse, and, for a time, William Ernest Henley (who collaborated with him on several plays) were devoted to him. His friendships with women were equally unpredictable. In the summer of 1876, Stevenson went with his cousin to an artist's colony near Fontainebleau and there met Fanny Van de Grift Osbourne, an American eleven years older than Stevenson. She had left an irresponsible husband in

Fanny Van de Grift Osbourne, Stevenson's American wife, whom he married in May 1880

mercantile bustle of the port of New York in 1879, the vast spaces of the American West, and the pioneer towns of California are presented with characteristic style. But no rhetorical polish is employed to conceal the fact that the trip was long, tedious, often painful, and, in the end, almost fatal to Stevenson. Though he had undertaken the voyage to save Fanny from ill health and a reckless husband, Stevenson literally collapsed on her doorstep in Monterey and was tenderly nursed by this woman who so often struck others as tough. During his eight months of illness and difficulty in California, he managed to write *The Amateur Emigrant from the Clyde to Sandy Hook* and to begin "A Vendetta in the West," an unfinished adventure novel. He was also working on such short stories as "The Pavillion on the Links" and contributing occasional pieces to the *Monterey Californian*, the local paper.

Once legally divorced from Osbourne, Fanny was free to marry Stevenson, and the wedding took place on 19 May 1880. Despite the fact that both had been ill, they were determined not to spend their honeymoon amid the comforts of San Francisco or Monterey but in the cabin of an abandoned mine at Silverado, over two thousand feet up the slope of Mount Saint Helena. During the weeks spent in this unlikely place, Stevenson not only gained in strength and equilibrium, but he returned to pieces he had begun during his travels and started on one of his most vivid and mature travel sketches, *The Silverado Squatters* (1883). Like his other American works, this one possesses a realism and confidence of tone missing in the earlier descriptions of his excursions in France. Stevenson was older, he had suffered and experienced more, and the American terrain, though challenging and often sublime, could not be trivialized or charmed into submission.

Though Stevenson's Scottish family and many of his friends adjusted to his unconventional marriage surprisingly well for the time, there is no doubt that some of his old associations, most particularly that with Henley, did not survive Fanny. From all accounts, she was a strong, protective, and opinionated woman, but it is difficult to deny that she and Stevenson loved one another or that from the time of their marriage his health and literary creativity took a marked turn for the better. In August 1880 they left the United States for a reunion with friends in Liverpool and London, a visit to Stevenson's family in Edinburgh, and a prolonged expedition to Switzerland. In the summer of 1881 Stevenson returned to Scotland, rented a cot-

tage in Braemar, and there, surrounded by his American family and the rough and rainy beauty of his own land, began to write *Treasure Island* (1883).

Originating in a water-color map Stevenson drew, *Treasure Island* describes the dangerous adventures of Jim Hawkins and his passage from adolescence to manhood. Set in the 1740s, the novel outlines Jim's discovery of a map to buried treasure in the possession of the pirate Billy Bones who, terrified by Blind Pew, dies in the inn run by Jim's mother and father. Under the leadership of Dr. Livesy and Squire Trelawney and with Jim as cabin boy, the *Hispaniola* sets sail in search of Treasure Island, somewhere off the Spanish Main (the coast of South America). The cook, however, is the one-legged Long John Silver, who, in league with the crew—mostly his cohorts—plans a mutiny. Jim learns of this, but before he can act, they sight the island. Smuggling himself on land, Jim meets Ben Gunn, once a pirate with Captain Flint, who buried the treasure. Suddenly, the mutiny breaks out, and Jim, with Dr. Livesy, the squire, and others, takes refuge in an abandoned stockade on the island. Courageously, Jim sneaks out to cut the *Hispaniola* adrift but is caught by the first mate, Israel Hands. They fight, and Jim proves his bravery; but upon returning to the island he is caught by the pirates and nearly killed. Long John Silver, however, protects him, and the pirates turn against them both. The pirates suspend their harmful actions while they search for the treasure, discovering only an empty chest. Returning to kill Silver and Jim, they are stopped by Ben Gunn and company, who free the two heroes. Escaping in the *Hispaniola* with the treasure Gunn had earlier dug up, the company travels to the West Indies; there, Silver leaves the ship, which finally returns safely to its home port, Bristol.

It is almost impossible to analyze the qualities of a classic of this kind without seeming to make an unnecessary academic fuss over an unpretentious adventure story. Yet to pass too quickly over *Treasure Island* would be to ignore a major turning point in Stevenson's career and an important key to his literary talent. Until the publication of this book, Stevenson's output had been promising but uneven: warm humor mixed with stiff sobriety and flashes of stylistic brilliance in the essays, increasing realism and irony in the travel sketches, interspersed with odd fantasies in the short stories of *New Arabian Nights* (1882). Aside from its other virtues, *Treasure Island* is a totally consistent, controlled, beautifully paced narrative; for the author,

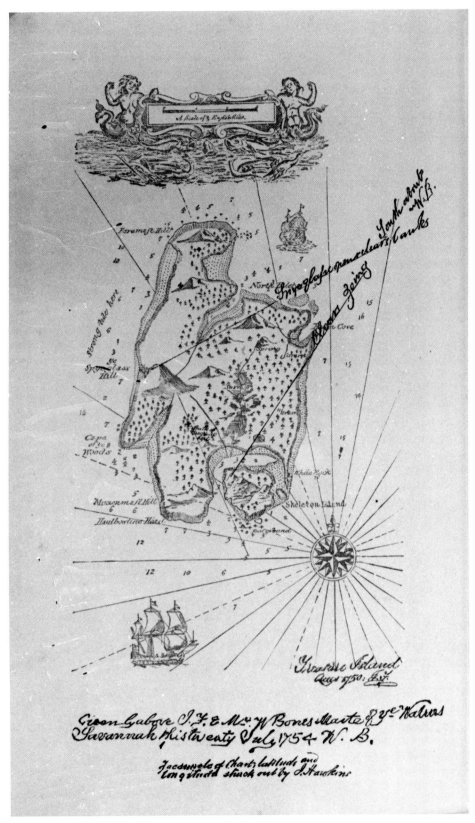

Map from first edition of Stevenson's classic 1883 novel about pirates, buried treasure, and the friendship of Jim Hawkins and Long John Silver (Thomas Cooper Library, University of South Carolina)

though obviously not for the characters, it is smooth sailing. Stevenson found a tone, a vocabulary, a convention and manipulated each with mastery. In one sense, it is the perfection of a familiar genre, but in another, it is a work of considerable originality. Most adventure books for young readers of the Victorian period are prosy, thick with schoolmaster's syntax, and heavy with the pieties of empire. To read *Treasure Island* today is still to find it fresh and exuberant, an absorbing imitation of a child's daydream, unhampered by adult guilt or moral justification. Jim Hawkins and Long John Silver do not smell musty even after a hundred years. Through them Stevenson succeeded in creating ac-

tions and emotions of a simple but timelessly comprehensible sort.

During the next two years (1882-1884), the Stevensons lived in France at the Chalet La Solitude in Hyères. Stevenson's health once again deteriorated; his early tendency to develop bronchial infections and correspondingly weak lungs led to hemorrhaging, and, suffering acute weakness, he was often required to remain in bed. Yet it was during this time that he solidified his reputation as a writer and completed some of his most successful and best-known works. He finished *A Child's Garden of Verses* (1885) and once more created a classic that the critic must be careful not to crush or ignore.

Pencil sketch by Stevenson of Alison Cunningham ("Cummy"), his nurse, to whom he dedicated A Child's Garden of Verses *(1885) (Anderson Galleries, #1171, 22 January 1929)*

These rhymes show a side of Stevenson that is musical, fey, unguarded, and very much of his own era. If *Treasure Island* survives as a timeless adventure, *A Child's Garden of Verses*, though still reprinted in innumerable children's editions, seems today to be a Victorian period piece. The adult world is solid, serious, busy, and detached. The child is often lonely or ill, secure in his bed, nursery, or enclosed garden, but with little to do but daydream. Lilting, gay, and earnest, the poems seem to reflect not entirely successful efforts to be cheerful in sad times.

Most of Stevenson's energy during this period went into the writing of fiction. He wrote *More New Arabian Nights: The Dynamiter* (1885), his only book written in collaboration with his wife. These stories, like the earlier *New Arabian Nights*, combine melodrama and a touch of the eerie with outcomes that are often wildly ludicrous. With some exceptions, Stevenson had still not made up his mind when he wished to write mystery and when comic satire. Sometimes he gives the impression that he cannot take his own grotesqueries seriously and ends up laughing at what he had first thought to be terrifying.

Following the success of *Treasure Island*, Stevenson set out to write another adventure novel. Perhaps fearing that the earlier book had been too unhistorical, he tried, without much success, to give *The Black Arrow* (1888; published serially in *Young Folks* in 1883) a recognizable setting. Yet Stevenson himself called the work "tushery" (his own term) and admitted that he wrote it quickly to earn money. His more serious and successful effort at combining history with adventure was his next novel, *Kidnapped* (1886). The year is 1751 (no exact time is ever given in *Treasure Island*), the place is the Highlands. Scotland is experiencing the aftermath of the Jacobites' return and their failed effort to reclaim the throne from the Hanoverians. Stevenson evokes the wild landscape as well as clan rivalries with great skill. But the most important difference from *Treasure Island* is in his rendering of the main characters. Whereas Jim Hawkins and Long John Silver are types, larger and simpler than life, David Balfour, the adolescent Lowlander, and Alan Breck, the daring Jacobite, are sharply realized personalities with habits, attitudes, and voices of their own. As in *Treasure Island*, the reader takes an interest in the sheer activity of the characters. David is orphaned, sold to slave traders by his uncle, engages in mutiny, is shipwrecked, and then flees across the Highlands

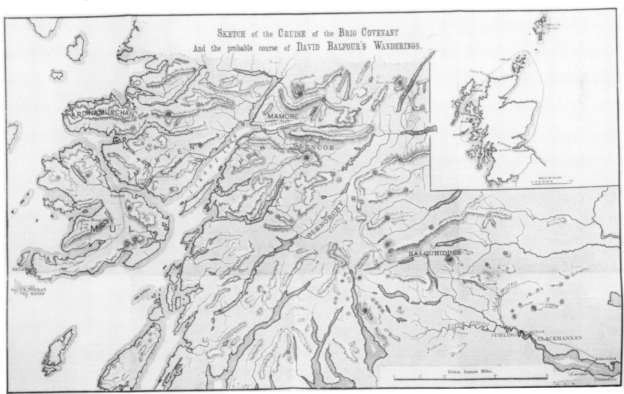

Map from first edition of Kidnapped, *Stevenson's 1886 historical novel set in the eighteenth-century Scottish Highlands (Thomas Cooper Library, University of South Carolina)*

with Alan Breck to escape political enemies and natural disaster.

All of this is exciting and entertaining, but throughout the central section of the novel, the relationship of David and Alan adds a moral and psychological dimension absent in *Treasure Island*. It is true that Jim Hawkins had found much in the nasty Silver to admire, but the ambiguity of villainy is left unresolved in that story. In *Kidnapped*, Stevenson explores in greater depth and with some subtlety a friendship between a loyal Protestant Whig Lowlander and a rebellious Catholic Jacobite Highlander. The innocent and prudent younger man is attracted by the courage and impetuosity of the older. During their flight together, they form a complex bond of trust, rivalry, and affection against which the political and religious conflicts of the times seem insanely simplistic and exaggerated. In some ways, the two characters seem to be in flight from the terrors of social reality, but, in the end, though the memory of their bond remains, they must return to the world of communal obligation. *Kidnapped* can be read as an adventure story; the historical detail is never so rich nor so deeply woven into the narrative as it is in Stendhal or Tolstoy or the best of Scott. Still, the daydream is no longer so free and pure as it had been in *Treasure Island*. The adult world encroaches both on the unsettled emotions of the young David and on the political ambitions of Alan Breck. In 1893, Stevenson wrote *Catriona*, a sequel to *Kidnapped*. Uneven, the work is transitional between the completeness of *Kidnapped* and the experimental fragments of fiction he left behind at his death.

In 1884 the Stevensons moved back to England and settled in Bournemouth in Skerryvore, a villa overlooking the sea, named after a famous lighthouse designed by his uncle Alan Stevenson. There it was possible for family and friends like Colvin, Henley, and William Archer to visit. From the literary point of view, the most important friendship that developed during this period was that with Henry James. During 1884, *Longman's Magazine* published "A Humble Remonstrance," Stevenson's reply to James's "The Art of Fiction" and probably his single most important critical statement. James had argued for moral and psychological "realism" in fiction and insisted that in order to be taken seriously literature had to "compete with life." With flare and apparent relish, Stevenson took the opposite view: "No art—to use the daring phrase of Mr. James—can successfully 'compete with life'; . . . To 'compete with life,'

Stevenson and some of the crew of the Casco, *the yacht in which he made his first Pacific cruise in 1888*

whose sun we cannot look upon, whose passions and diseases waste and slay us—to compete with the flavour of wine, the beauty of the dawn, the scorching of fire, the bitterness of death and separation—here is, indeed, a projected escalade of heaven . . . . Life is monstrous, infinite, illogical, abrupt, and poignant; a work of art, in comparison, is neat, finite, self-contained, rational, flowing, and emasculate." Anyone familiar with James's fiction and criticism will see how much, despite the apparent disagreement, he would have liked Stevenson's reply. Stevenson may seem to be reflecting an invalid's view of life and defending the literature of escape, but, more profoundly, he, like James, celebrates deliberate artistry, intelligent design, the craftsmanship of a work of art. Though many of their contemporaries might have spoken of poetry or painting and music in such terms, Stevenson and

James were almost alone in treating the novel with such respect. While vacationing in Bournemouth, James visited the Stevensons regularly and formed a friendship with Stevenson which developed into one of the most lively and thoughtful literary correspondences of the period.

If Braemar is associated with *Treasure Island* and Hyères with *Kidnapped*, Bournemouth is the notorious birthplace of the *Strange Case of Dr. Jekyll and Mr. Hyde* (1886). Stevenson had been intrigued by the ambiguities of evil since the beginning of his career. Long John Silver and Alan Breck are attrac-

The Stevensons' house at their estate, Vailima, in Samoa

Stevenson with his mother, his stepson Lloyd Osbourne, Fanny, his stepdaughter Isobel Strong, and servants on the porch at Vailima

A manuscript page from one of the letters Stevenson wrote for newspapers to finance his Pacific cruises. Some of this material was published as In the South Seas *(1896). (Anderson Galleries, #763, 9 April 1936)*

tive outlaws, and in two of his most important short stories, "Thrawn Janet," involving the Scottish fear of witchcraft and the Devil, and "Markheim," showing a murderer's confession and relief at turning to the Devil, he had probed the irrational specters of dream and the unconscious. Though he had abandoned literal adherence to the Calvinism of his parents, Stevenson's imagination and moral sensibility had obviously been influenced by a vision of good and evil forever locked in combat. Furthermore, he was continually irritated by hypocrisy and especially by the self-righteous moral superiority of those who claimed to be above the fray. In the novel (the idea for which came to Stevenson in a nightmare), Dr. Henry Jekyll, long interested in the problem of dual personality, has invented a chemical that can alter his character from that of a kind physician to that of the violent, criminally minded Edward Hyde. Gradually, Dr. Jekyll loses his ability to shift at will from one personality to another; at the same time, he loses control over Hyde's violent behavior, which leads to murder. In the end, lacking any chemical to transform him from Hyde back to Dr. Jekyll, the protagonist kills himself and reveals all by the means of a letter. This tale, narrated by a young lawyer, Utterson, achieves its impact through the vivid contrast between reason and the irrational.

In one sense, *Dr. Jekyll and Mr. Hyde* can be taken as a satire of the times in which a respectable and educated man is forced so to repress his animal nature as to turn it into an uncontrollably violent beast. Yet there is much in the tale that does not allow such an interpretation to go unqualified. There is a wildness in Hyde that does not really lend itself to possible accommodations to a moral world, even one more liberal and permissive than that of the 1880s. Furthermore, as it progresses the story seems preoccupied less with social and moral alternatives than with the inevitable progress into vice. Part of the appeal of the tale is, as the title suggests, its strangeness. It has its own obsessive logic and momentum that sweep the reader along. Thus, though various morals can be drawn from it (warnings against intellectual pride, hypocrisy, and indifference to the power of the evil within), the continuing attraction of the *Strange Case of Dr. Jekyll and Mr. Hyde* is perhaps the exact reverse of that of *Treasure Island*: one is an almost perfect literary rendition of a child's daydream of endless possibilities, the other of an adult's nightmare of disintegration.

Searching once again for an ideal climate, the Stevensons set out for America in 1887 with his stepson and recently widowed mother in tow and settled temporarily in Saranac Lake, New York. Encouraged by his popularity in the United States, Stevenson began work almost immediately on a new

Stevenson presiding over a feast for a group of Samoan chiefs who had built a road to his house

novel of history and adventure. *The Master of Ballantrae* (1889) departs even further than *Kidnapped* from the pure entertainment of *Treasure Island*. It is less well known than his earlier books and deserves more attention than it has received. Though, as in *Kidnapped*, the action turns on events connected with the Jacobite Rebellion of 1745, the political details and even the Scottish landscape are really secondary to a psychological and moral drama of rivalry and hatred between two brothers. At first glance, James and Henry Durrisdeer seem to be variants on Alan Breck and David Balfour. James, the older brother, is dark, handsome, reckless, a champion of the Stuart cause; Henry, the younger, is fair, mild, gentle, and cautious, a loyal Hanoverian. But whereas Alan and David brought out the best in one another and reflected the affinity and attraction of opposites, the Durrisdeer brothers drive one another to the worst extremes of their natural temperaments. As James becomes more and more flamboyant and brutal, Henry recedes into a near paralysis of blandness. It is as though Stevenson is deliberately weaving together caricatured versions of the conventional protagonists of domestic and romantic fiction. One brother almost defeats the reader with tedium, the other risks exhausting him with overactivity. However, at its best, the novel is neither a parody nor an incoherent double narrative but a powerful drama of blood hatred. The plot is convoluted but includes a dramatic duel between the brothers in which the wounded James is smuggled off to India, where he makes a fortune. He returns with the mysterious Secundra Dass, an East Indian who, in league with James, pursues Henry and his family to America. In a dramatic conclusion, Henry conspires to have James killed in the wilderness of New York State while searching for treasure. James appears to die, but as Henry watches, James returns momentarily to life under the care of Secundra Dass—and the shock kills Henry. But Dass cannot restore James completely to life because of the frigid temperatures in the wilderness. James dies, and the two brothers lie buried in the barren land.

As might have been predicted, New York did not answer Stevenson's needs. Indeed, it becomes clearer and clearer that although health was the immediate reason for his numerous moves, his restlessness ran very deep, and it is unlikely that he would have led a settled life even had he been robust. In addition to being solicitous of his health, Fanny seems to have shared his wanderlust. In 1888 she chartered the schooner *Casco*, and in June,

along with Fanny's son Lloyd, Stevenson's fifty-nine-year-old mother, and a family servant, they set sail for the Pacific islands, touching Nuku Hiva, the Paumotus, Tahiti, and Oahu in the Hawaiian Islands. During the next two years, on the *Equator* and then on the *Janet Nicoll*, they visited Australia and the Gilbert and Marshall islands and eventually bought 400 acres in Samoa, where they decided to build a house and establish themselves permanently. They named the estate Vailima, meaning "Five Rivers" in Samoan.

It is difficult to look at the photographs of the Stevenson clan in Samoa without reacting to the absurdity as well as the charm and spiritedness of their adventure. There they all are—Lloyd with his pince-nez, Fanny in a muumuu, Mrs. Stevenson wearing her widow's bonnet, Stevenson striking a pose in a funny hat. Like so much of Stevenson's life and writing, there is an impression of game playing, of flair and bravado, of an ultimate lack of seriousness. Yet, as in the case of the writing, if one looks carefully, the seriousness is there. In the first place, as his letters show, Stevenson never felt very far away from death. He continually suffered from the damp or cold climates of the various places he had tried to live. The warm sea air of Samoa did, for the first time in years, give him hope for a recovery or at least a partial easing of his pain.

Furthermore, once he came to know the islands and their history, Stevenson's interest in them and their inhabitants was sincere and far more understanding and sympathetic than that of many of his Victorian contemporaries. His famous *Father Damien: An Open Letter to the Reverend Dr. Hyde of Honolulu* (1890) in defense of the memory of Father Damien, the Catholic missionary to the lepers of Molokai, is as much a defense of the native islanders as it is of their priest. Father Damien's "sin," according to the appropriately named Dr. Hyde, was that he had "gone native," did not maintain a proper distance from his flock, was not always clean, and may have befriended a native woman. Stevenson's attack on the hypocrisy of these accusations is combined with a ringing defense of the true spirit of Christianity that preaches the common humanity of all men and women.

Stevenson's letters and journals reveal a growing concern for the health and well-being of the island population and an increasing irritation with the political and economic exploitation of the natives by European and American colonists. He and his family were rare among the white settlers in that they wanted nothing more than to live with the

The last photograph of Robert Louis Stevenson

Samoans. These attitudes are reflected in the fiction that deals with the Pacific: *The Wrecker* (1892), about murder and a treasure hunt to Midway Island; *Island Nights' Entertainments* (1893), a collection of short stories including "The Bottle Imp"; and *The Ebb-Tide* (1894), a story of three outcasts who descend on a small island where a miniature English society has been established. As in the earlier fiction, these narratives include strong elements of melodrama and high adventure, but they also contain searching studies of the behavior and motivation of the whites who are drawn to the islands and the destructive effects that their various searches for wealth and power have on the native populations. It is not too much to say that several of the narratives of this period, most particularly *The Ebb-Tide* and "The Beach of Falesa," anticipate Conrad. They are, in any case, far from the innocent dreams of *Treasure Island*, in which the search for gold is a

game played in a world without mixed motives or long-range consequences.

Finally, though he did remain playful and boyish and impulsive, Stevenson understood, as no modern reader or writer can, the vast distance he had placed between himself and home by coming to Samoa. Beneath the excitement of seeing new places and adjusting to a new life was the growing realization that he had cut himself off from the cultures and lands that had frustrated but also nourished him. Stevenson's homesickness for Scotland became, even as his physical health seemed to improve, the major psychological preoccupation of his last years. It was in Samoa that he wrote *Catriona*, the sequel to *Kidnapped*; and his last work—and one that promised to be his greatest if he had lived to finish it—was *Weir of Hermiston* (1896), a book that is Scottish to the core.

In presenting the Hermiston family—the father who is a brilliant but merciless judge, his pious wife, and their sensitive, rebellious son—Stevenson combines all his best talents. The richness of social and political history and local color are perfectly blended with characterizations of powerful psychological penetration. Archie, the judge's son, is sent to Hermiston, a moorland estate, for protesting a hanging ordered by his father. There he falls in love with Kirstie Elliott, but a visiting former schoolmate maligns Archie to Kirstie and her family. A stormy meeting between the two lovers breaks off because of Stevenson's sudden death, but Sidney Colvin, in a postscript, summarizes the notes Stevenson made concerning the remainder of the novel. Archie kills his former friend for betraying him; he is then condemned to die by his father, but he is rescued by Kirstie's brothers and escapes with her to America. However, the ordeal of the trial and sentencing of his son is too much for the judge, and he dies. In some ways it seems appropriate that Stevenson, who loved new starts and mysterious conclusions, left readers to speculate about some of his most intriguing characters.

His death came swiftly and unexpectedly on 3 December 1894. In the morning, he had been dictating the latest section of *Weir of Hermiston* to his stepdaughter Isobel Strong, who had arrived in Samoa in 1891. That evening he complained of a headache to Fanny. He appears to have suffered a stroke, and within a few hours he was dead at the age of forty-four. A burial procession of nearly sixty Samoans cut a path up a steep slope until they reached the summit of Mount Vaea, where he was laid to rest.

Stevenson's grave atop Mount Vaea, Samoa

The manner of his living and dying, in conjunction with the variety and popularity of much of his writing, has had a mixed effect on Stevenson's reputation as a writer. Immediately after his death, he was almost canonized as a literary and moral genius who lived courageously in the face of affliction. Inevitably there was a reaction to this sentimental portrait, but it too was excessive. In the 1920s and 1930s critics suddenly found his style imitative and pompous, and biographers discovered that he was mortal after all and for two or three decades took an almost lewd pleasure in detailing the ways in which he was not perfect. Though his books always had some faithful defenders and his younger readers were oblivious to the opinions of adults, it was not until the 1950s and 1960s that his work, especially his fiction, was reconsidered by scholars in a relatively unbiased way. Few would now disagree that he was an essayist of great charm and versatility or that his fiction belongs with that of Scott, Poe, Melville, and Conrad in that compelling tradition where mystery and psychology, adventure and moral choice converge.

Bibliography:

J. H. Slater, *Robert Louis Stevenson: A Bibliography of His Complete Works* (London: Bell, 1914).

Biographies:

Janet Adam Smith, *Robert Louis Stevenson* (London: Duckworth, 1937);

David Daiches, *Robert Louis Stevenson* (Norfolk, Conn.: New Directions, 1947);

J. C. Furnas, *Voyage to Windward: The Life of Robert Louis Stevenson* (New York: Sloane, 1951);

Jenni Calder, *RLS: A Life Study* (London: Hamish Hamilton, 1980).

References:

Jenni Calder, ed., *Stevenson and Victorian Scotland* (Edinburgh: University of Edinburgh Press, 1981);

G. K. Chesterton, *Robert Louis Stevenson* (London: Hodder & Stoughton, 1927);

Edwin M. Eigner, *Robert Louis Stevenson and Romantic Tradition* (Princeton, N.J.: Princeton University Press, 1966);

Lord Guthrie, *Robert Louis Stevenson: Some Personal Recollections* (Edinburgh: Green, 1924);

J. A. Hammerton, ed., *Stevensoniana* (Edinburgh: Grant, 1910);

Robert Kiely, *Robert Louis Stevenson and the Fiction of Adventure* (Cambridge, Mass.: Harvard University Press, 1965);

E. B. Simpson, *The Robert Louis Stevenson Originals* (New York: Scribners, 1913);

Janet Adam Smith, ed., *Henry James and Robert Louis*

Stevenson: A Record of Friendship and Criticism (London: Rupert Hart-Davis, 1948);

Isobel Strong and Lloyd Osbourne, *Memories of Vailima* (New York: Scribners, 1902);

Roger G. Swearingen, *The Prose Writings of Robert Louis Stevenson: A Guide* (Hamden, Conn.: Archon, 1980).

Papers:
There are collections of Stevenson's papers in the Beinecke Library at Yale University, the Pierpont Morgan Library in New York, the Huntington Library in San Marino, California, Widener Library at Harvard University, and the Edinburgh Public Library.

Mrs. Humphry Ward

(11 June 1851-24 March 1920)

Esther M. G. Smith

BOOKS: *Unbelief and Sin: A Protest Addressed to Those Who Attended the Bampton Lecture of Sunday, March 6*, anonymous (Oxford: Privately printed, 1881);

Milly and Olly; or, A Holiday among the Mountains (London: Macmillan, 1881; New York: Doubleday, Page, 1907);

Miss Bretherton (London: Macmillan, 1884; New York: Lowell, 1888);

Robert Elsmere (3 volumes, London: Smith, Elder, 1888; 1 volume, New York: Macmillan, 1888);

University Hall: Opening Address (London: Smith, Elder, 1891);

The Future of University Hall (London: Smith, Elder, 1892);

The History of David Grieve (3 volumes, London: Smith, Elder, 1892; 1 volume, New York: Macmillan, 1892);

Marcella (3 volumes, London: Smith, Elder, 1894; 2 volumes, New York: Macmillan, 1894);

Unitarians and the Future: The Essex Hall Lecture 1894 (London: Green, 1894);

The Story of Bessie Costrell (London: Smith, Elder, 1895; New York: Macmillan, 1895);

Sir George Tressady (London: Smith, Elder, 1896; New York: Macmillan, 1896);

Helbeck of Bannisdale (London: Smith, Elder, 1898; New York: Macmillan, 1898);

Eleanor (London: Smith, Elder, 1900; New York: Harper, 1900);

Agatha (play), by Ward and Louis N. Parker (London: Smith, Elder, 1903);

Lady Rose's Daughter (London: Smith, Elder, 1903; New York: Harper, 1903);

Eleanor (play), by Ward and Julian Sturgis (London: Smith, Elder, 1903);

The Marriage of William Ashe (London: Smith, Elder, 1905; New York: Harper, 1905);

Fenwick's Career (London: Smith, Elder, 1906; New York: Harper, 1906);

Mary A. Ward

Play-Time of the Poor (London: Smith, Elder, 1906);

William Thomas Arnold, Journalist and Historian, by Ward and C. E. Montague (Manchester: University Press, 1907);

Diana Mallory (London: Harper, 1908; New York: Harper, 1908);

Daphne; or, Marriage à la Mode (London: Cassell, 1909; New York: Harper, 1909);

Canadian Born (London: Smith, Elder, 1910); republished as *Lady Merton, Colonist* (Garden City: Doubleday, Page, 1910);

The Coming Election: Letters to My Neighbors (London: Smith, Elder, 1910);

Letters to My Neighbors on the Present Election (London: Smith, Elder, 1910);

The Case of Richard Meynell (London: Smith, Elder, 1911; New York: Hurst, 1911);

The Mating of Lydia (London: Smith, Elder, 1913; Garden City: Doubleday, Page, 1913);

The Coryston Family (London: Smith, Elder, 1913; New York: Harper, 1913);

Delia Blanchflower (New York: Hearst's International Library, 1914; London: Ward, Lock, 1915);

Eltham House (London: Cassell, 1915; New York: Hearst's International Library, 1915);

England's Effort: Six Letters to an American Friend, with a Preface by the Earl of Roseberry (London: Smith, Elder, 1916; New York: Scribners, 1916);

A Great Success (London: Smith, Elder, 1916; New York: Hearst's International Library, 1916);

Lady Connie (London: Smith, Elder, 1916; New York: Hearst's International Library, 1916);

"Missing" (London: Collins, 1917; New York: Dodd, Mead, 1917);

Towards the Goal, introduction by Theodore Roosevelt (London: Murray, 1917; New York: Scribners, 1917);

The War and Elizabeth (London: Collins, 1918); republished as *Elizabeth's Campaign* (New York: Dodd, Mead, 1918);

A Writer's Recollections (London: Collins, 1918; New York: Harper, 1918);

Cousin Philip (London: Collins, 1919); republished as *Helena* (New York: Dodd, Mead, 1919);

Fields of Victory: The Journey through the Battlefields of France (London: Hutchinson, 1919; New York: Scribners, 1919);

Harvest (London: Collins, 1920; New York: Dodd, Mead, 1920).

COLLECTION: *The Writings of Mrs. Humphry Ward, with Introductions by the Author*, Westmorland Edition (16 volumes, London: Smith, Elder, 1911-1912).

Mrs. Humphry Ward, born Mary Augusta Arnold, won worldwide recognition with the publication of *Robert Elsmere* (1888), which dramatized for countless readers the loss of faith in orthodox Christianity that resulted from the development of evolutionary science and historical criticism. Her total output—twenty-five novels, one children's book, three plays, three reports on World War I, an autobiography, a translation of a French mystic's journal, and numerous articles for reference books and leading periodicals—led many contemporaries to consider her the greatest living English author and supports the modern assessment that anyone wishing to understand England from 1880 to 1920 must have recourse to her work.

Mary Arnold was early introduced to the drama of men and women caught in the conflicts of religion, custom, and personality. In 1854, her father, Thomas Arnold, second son of Dr. Thomas Arnold of Rugby and brother of the poet and essayist Matthew Arnold, converted to Catholicism, largely under the influence of the *Tracts for the Times* (1833-1841). This series of papers was the vehicle of the Tractarian or Oxford Movement and was chiefly the work of John Henry Cardinal Newman, of whom Dr. Arnold had been the outstanding opponent. No longer acceptable as an educator in Tasmania (Australia), Thomas Arnold brought his family home to England, where, for financial reasons, Mary became the welcome charge of Dr. Arnold's widow and youngest daughter. While Thomas Arnold earned a precarious living teaching under Newman in Dublin and Birmingham, the family grew from three children to eight, but only the boys were trained in the Catholic faith, because Arnold's wife, Julia Sorrel Arnold, remained a staunch Protestant. In 1865, Thomas Arnold returned to Anglicanism and began tutoring at Oxford. In 1867 Mary left boarding school and came to Oxford to stay. There she fulfilled the duties of the oldest daughter in a large family but found time to develop musical, literary, and scholarly talents and to respond to the strong philosophical-religious currents of the academic community. On 6 April 1872, she became the wife of Thomas Humphry Ward, fellow and tutor of Brasenose College. The young couple soon began writing for a number of periodicals. Their first child, Dorothy, was born in 1872; a son, Arnold, arrived in 1876. In the same year, Thomas Arnold reconverted to Catholicism and went back to Dublin; this time Julia, slowly dying of cancer, did not go with him. Mary remained lovingly loyal to both parents, assisting in the care of her mother although she had added to her activities leadership in a movement to secure university education for women.

The Wards' last child, Janet, was born in 1879. In 1881 Humphry Ward began working as a political commentator, later art critic, for the *Times*. That winter, while the family remained in Oxford, Mary was so offended by a lecture of the Reverend Mr. John Wordsworth, which attacked her own religious convictions and the lives of such men as Thomas Hill Green, Benjamin Jowett, and her uncle, Matthew Arnold, that she wrote an anonymous pamphlet entitled *Unbelief and Sin: A Protest Addressed to Those Who Attended the Bampton Lecture of Sunday, March 6*. Ecclesiastical pressure forced the suppression of the unclaimed publication, but Mrs. Ward's long battle with religious prejudice had begun.

In London she continued her interest in education by establishing a cultural center for working young people, play centers for children forced onto the streets while their parents worked, and transportation and other assistance in educating physically handicapped children totally neglected by the regular schools. In 1885 Mary Ward's sister Julia married Leonard Huxley, further strengthening the Wards' ties with the nation's intellectual and influential people. In 1888 Ward's "best-selling" novel, *Robert Elsmere*, brought her worldwide but often hostile attention. Her defense of religious "heresy," with her later sympathy for the growing freedoms of women (although she was adamantly opposed to women's suffrage), upset clergymen and conservative critics, but her novels sold so well that the family was able to own both city and country homes and enjoy a life-style close to that of the aristocratic class she wrote about most of the time.

Robert Elsmere is the story of a young Anglican clergyman who studies himself out of orthodox convictions, resigns his "living," goes to London to establish a "new Christianity," but dies as success is imminent. The book struck a chord of popular response that made it a record-breaking best-seller, significant to all accounts of Victorian struggles of faith. However, the true value of the novel, as in all of Mrs. Ward's work, is the delineation of characters and the sympathetic dramatization of their interaction with each other and the circumstances that challenge them. While Elsmere represents the author's own religious convictions, his saintly or-

thodox wife, his artistic sister-in-law, his melancholy tutor, a gracious aristocrat, a cynical squire, and many minor characters are drawn from her family and friends.

Two more of her "religious" novels are outstanding: *The History of David Grieve* (1892) and *Helbeck of Bannisdale* (1898). In *The History of David Grieve* Mrs. Ward endeavored to "prove" that Elsmere's new faith would work for enlightened workingmen. Although the setting is the Westmorland countryside she knew and loved, all of the characters are more the work of artistic perception than personal acquaintance and achieve a Dickensian vividness without losing their naturalness. The hero, an intelligent orphan, experiences an evangelical conversion but quickly outgrows this "chapel" faith, tries Positivism, and ends an enlightened humanist. His devout High-Church cousin, his Catholic sister, his saintly friend, even the ignorant but persuasive chapel evangelist are integral parts of a long list of memorable characters.

Helbeck of Bannisdale is Mrs. Ward's best novel, though its tragic character recommends it to critics more than to the reading public. The plot involves the faith and love of a devout Catholic and the daughter of a "liberated" Cambridge professor. Laura Fountain comes to Bannisdale with her invalid widowed stepmother, Augustina, the older sister of Alan Helbeck. Alan and Laura discover their love for each other, but Alan's desire to glorify that love by converting Laura to his faith threatens her individuality and leads eventually to her suicide. The brooding sympathy with which each major, secondary, and minor character is drawn and placed in the haunting setting makes this a sane *Wuthering Heights*, a modern *Antigone*.

Levens Hall, near Kendal, where Mrs. Ward wrote the early chapters of Helbeck of Bannisdale *(1898). The hall served as one of the models for Bannisdale Park in the novel.*

Mrs. Ward shifted her major concern to social reform with *Marcella* (1894). As in a number of her works, a true incident inspired a fictional response; in this case it was the conviction and execution of poachers for the murder of a gamekeeper near their country home, Stocks. Beautiful, intelligent, idealistic, but immature Marcella Boyce comes to Mellor Park with her parents upon the death of her misanthropic uncle. Her engagement to a neighboring lord, Aldous Maxwell, is broken when he and his family refuse to sign a petition for the reprieve of a poacher convicted of killing their gamekeeper. Marcella becomes a public nurse in the London slums, matures, and is reunited with Aldous, Mrs. Ward's ideal British aristocrat—gracious, scholarly, and dedicated to the enlightened governing of England. Lord and Lady Maxwell continue their good work in *Sir George Tressady* (1896), in which Marcella persuades the young M.P. Tressady to switch parties and vote for the Factory Bill and to take an interest in improving the ugly conditions of his iron mines. Mrs. Ward made a careful study of all the political issues involved, but her significant achievement is the humanizing of history.

This concern with human drama so dominates the majority of her novels that they might safely be labeled "romances." One outstanding romance, *Eleanor* (1900), grew out of some months of 1899 that the Ward family spent at the old Villa Barberini at Castel Gandolfo, in the Alban Hills of Italy. During their stay, Henry James visited them, and together they visited the ruins of the temple of Diana Nemorensis, on the shores of Lake Nemi. This and other incidents of their Italian sojourn appear in the novel, but the story's initial concept was retelling with English characters—and morals—the eighteenth-century romance of the French statesman and author Chateaubriand and Madame de Beaumont. Eleanor Borgoyne, a widow of beauty and refinement, is helping her cousin, Edward Manisty, an arrogant aristocrat, write a treatise defending the cultural authority of the church in Italy, when a young evangelical American, Lucy Foster, becomes a guest of Manisty's Aunt Patti. Manisty falls in love with Lucy, but she realizes Eleanor's attachment to him and chooses to disappear with Eleanor. Before succumbing to a fatal illness, Eleanor is reconciled to her early Catholic rearing and finds peace in "ordering" Lucy to acknowledge her love and marry Manisty. This psychological drama of the emotions of super-refined individuals was Henry James's favorite and won such general

Stocks, the Wards' country home in the village of Aldbury, Hertfordshire

critical acclaim that it was made into a play (1903) with modest success. It also encouraged Mrs. Ward to use other historical romances as "seed" for other novels. The story of two famous French hostesses, Mlle Julie de Lespinasse and Mme de Deffand, stirred Mrs. Ward's imagination and produced *Lady Rose's Daughter* (1903), an excellent novel. Incidents in the life of the painter George Romney inspired *Fenwick's Career* (1906), one of her poorer novels. But the best-known recreated situation, that of William Lamb, Lord Melbourne, and his eccentric wife, Caroline, became *The Marriage of William Ashe* (1905).

A comparison of this novel with the life of Lord Melbourne as told by Lord David Cecil in *Melbourne* (1939) reveals that fiction and fact match at many points. William Lamb was first attracted to Caroline Ponsonby when she was fifteen; he fell in love with her when she was seventeen, he twenty-four. William Ashe falls in love with seventeen-year-old Kitty Bristol. However, it was not until Lamb's older brother died and William became heir to a peerage and a small fortune that he or Caroline were permitted to dream of marriage. The exalted position of Caroline, the only daughter of Lord Bessborough, seems in striking contrast to the unsavory brew from which Mrs. Ward's heroine springs until one discovers that Lady Bessborough's reputation was so tarnished that it was thought wise to have Caroline reared with her cousins at Devonshire House, then by her grandmother, Lady Spence, although neither household was willing to discipline this dynamic but erratic personality. Kitty is also charming but undisciplined. Caroline Lamb's notorious affair with the poet Byron is matched by

Kitty's tragic involvement with Geoffrey Cliffe. The Lambs' subnormal infant son is equated with the Ashes' delicate, crippled son. The factual episodes of the masked ball, the exposé novel, and the several attempts at separation are retold in the novel. And Ashe's betrayal of his love and obligations to his immature wife are a daring portrait of Lord Melbourne's failure to command Caroline's respect and save her from herself—because his self-image would not permit him to become passionately involved in anything. *The Marriage of William Ashe* was prepared for dramatization by Mrs. Ward and Margaret Mayo during 1905 and was performed by an American stock company with some success.

Dorothy Ward had become her mother's secretary at age sixteen and continued throughout her life as her mother's major assistant, managing the household and social duties, even traveling with her in 1916 and 1917 when Mrs. Ward went to war zones to write her influential *England's Effort: Six Letters to an American Friend* (1916) at the invitation of Theodore Roosevelt to win American sympathy for the Allied cause. Arnold Ward was an honor graduate of Oxford, became a *Times* correspondent in Egypt, Sudan, and India, and was elected to Parliament. However, he never married, and during the war he developed a serious gambling problem which the family sought to hide. Some of the driving force behind Mrs. Ward's last writing was financial strain from Arnold's debts. In 1904 Janet Ward married Macaulay Trevelyan, who became a distinguished historian; she wrote her mother's official biography (mentioning her brother's adult life only indirectly when telling of her mother's campaign for his election to Parliament).

Shortly before Mrs. Ward's death in 1920, she was chosen one of the first seven women magistrates of England. She also received an honorary doctorate from the University of Edinburgh. The Passmore Edwards Settlement House which she founded in 1897 is now known as the Mary Ward House.

Of considerable interest to modern critics are two novels that were "rewritten" by D. H. Lawrence. Mrs. Ward's *Lady Connie* (1916) became Lawrence's *Lady Chatterley's Lover* (1928), and Mrs. Ward's posthumous novel *Harvest* (1920) became *The Fox* (1923). In both novels, Lawrence turns her sympathetic interest in the expanding role of women into his cult of male dominance.

Lady Connie is the best of Mrs. Ward's late novels. Lady Constance Beldlow, orphaned daughter of the Earl of Risborough, comes to Oxford to

Mrs. Humphry Ward in 1903

live with her maternal uncle, Ewen Hooper, a professor. Among her many admirers are Douglas Falloden, a Greek scholar, "blood," athlete, and heir to a fortune and a title; and Otto Radowitz, a Polish musician, the handsome, orphaned protégé of Alexander Sorell, an ascetic professor of Greek and Latin who had been a youthful admirer of Connie's mother. Douglas and Connie are clearly destined for each other, but both are too proud to handle the "course of true love" smoothly. Her ill-advised favors to Otto lead to jealousy that spreads to group rivalry, and in a ragging incident Otto's right hand is permanently injured and his career as a pianist destroyed. Douglas's father dies, leaving little of the reputed fortune. Bitterness and tragedy turn to understanding and spiritual maturity that enable Connie and Douglas to achieve happiness.

U. C. Knoepflmacher makes a convincing case for Lawrence's use of plot, setting, and characters. The heroines have the same first names and similar backgrounds and personalities. They both must make a choice between men of strong physical attractiveness and men who are aesthetes. The metaphor of crippling is used in both novels. Crucial moments involve gamekeepers. Both heroes must seek success beyond their inherited position and classical scholarship. Of course it is in the differences that the crux of the comparison lies. Lady Connie's "surrender" to the musician, Radowitz, is the symbolic surrender of a dance; Lady Chatterley's surrender is to the writer Michaelis, but it is initiatory. Her second surrender, like that of the first heroine, is to the physically dynamic mate, but Mrs. Ward's heroine stays properly within the bonds of matrimony, while Lawrence's heroine breaks these bonds to secure fulfillment. Radowitz's crippling is limited to one hand, a disablement that destroys his career but neither his manhood nor his talent; Chatterley's crippling takes from him his power to be the mate Lady Chatterley needs. Falloden wins a chastened Connie, after both have been humbled and have matured; Sir Clifford loses his wife to Mellors, Lawrence's symbol of masculinity and fertility.

Harvest shows Mrs. Ward's usual contemporaneity with its beautiful but lower-middle-class heroine, Rachel Henderson, who does what many women learned to do during the war: she leases a farm that she plans to run with her friend Janet Leighton, whom she met while both were taking agricultural training at a college. She hopes to bury her past—marriage to an English cad, the death of her baby, three days spent with a sympathetic male neighbor—but love comes to renew guilt. Near the farm, timber has been commandeered by the government and is being cut by Canadian crews under the supervision of a New Englander, George Ellesborough. Janet helps Rachel find the courage to confess her secret, but just as George assures her of his forgiveness, her crazed former husband shoots her.

E. Smith's analysis of the novels *Harvest* and *The Fox* reveals similarities too numerous to be coincidental and changes that support Lawrence's philosophy that substituted the principle of human sexual union for what he considered the defunct dogma of Christianity. His statement of the necessary male dominance and female submission is the burden of the last six pages of *The Fox*. This point of view demands condemnation of the "new" independence of women of which Mrs. Ward approved, although her unorthodox religious beliefs assumed that all of Christianity's moral teachings would be maintained. Both stories have two young English women running a farm during the closing years of the war. Both heroes have spent the years immediately preceding the story in Canada; both respond promptly and forcefully to a letter from the heroine putting obstacles in the path of a desired marriage. Both heroines are moody; both have beautiful eyes and feminine softness that belie their frequent appearance in semimasculine garb. Both authors resolve their respective conflicts with the death of one of the young women—but Mrs. Ward kills her romantic heroine, while Lawrence kills the nonromantic companion. Lawrence's companion is spiritually parasitical; Mrs. Ward's companion is gracious and wise. Lawrence's hero combines Mrs. Ward's hero and her villain and adds the animal symbol of the fox to strengthen his contention that his philosophy is the natural one. Roger, the villain of *Harvest*, frequents the woods near Rachel and Janet's farm, sneaking in and out, chiefly at night; steals farm produce; frightens Rachel; finally he kills her and himself. George, the hero, takes two meetings to propose, plans marriage around the demands of his military commitment, cycles from his camp to the farm, and hopes to establish his new home in America. In *The Fox*, the fox sneaks in and out of the woods near March and Banford's (Lawrence uses the depersonalizing last names of the women) farm, chiefly at night; steals farm produce; casts a spell over March. Henry resembles the fox, takes over the fox's dominance of March, kills the fox, uses two occasions to secure March's consent to marriage, plans the marriage around his military schedule, cycles from his encampment to the farm, kills Banford, marries March, and counts on completing his dominance in Canada. There are many more altered similarities that support the conclusion that Lawrence was trying to refute Mrs. Ward's philosophy.

This philosophy was consistent throughout her work, both the fiction and the propaganda of the war years. She sincerely argued with artistic skill and humanistic idealism for her belief in the perfectibility of man and the superiority of English culture. She received respectable critical acclaim during her lifetime although she was occasionally moved to defend her techniques. The general turn against all things Victorian following the war increased the discordant evaluations. In 1973 Enid Huws Jones published an excellent biography, *Mrs. Humphry Ward*, enriched by Mrs. Ward's letters, diaries, and other material stored at the Mary Ward House, but Jones concentrates on Mrs. Ward's significant contributions to education and social reform. The only book-length recent criticism of her literary value is Esther M. G. Smith's *Mrs. Humphry Ward* (1980). The quantity of her work and her commitment to popularity may have cost her literary stature, but she succeeded more frequently than most writers in effectively blending setting, character, and plot, and her storytelling ability deserves to be rediscovered.

Other:

Amiel's Journal: The Journal Intime of Henri Frederic Amiel, translated with an introduction by Ward (London: Macmillan, 1885; New York: Brentano, 1928).

References:

Enid Huws Jones, *Mrs. Humphry Ward* (New York: St. Martin's Press, 1973);

U. C. Knoepflmacher, "The Rival Ladies: Mrs. Humphry Ward's *Lady Connie* and D. H. Lawrence's *Lady Chatterley's Lover*," *Victorian Studies*, 4 (December 1960): 141-158;

William S. Peterson, *Victorian Heretic: Mrs. Humphry Ward's "Robert Elsmere"* (Leicester, U.K.: Leicester University Press, 1976);

Esther M. G. Smith, *Mrs. Humphry Ward* (Boston: Twayne, 1980);

Janet Penrose Trevelyan, *The Life of Mrs. Humphry Ward* (New York: Dodd, Mead, 1923);

Robert Lee Wolff, *Gains and Losses: Novels of Faith and Doubt in Victorian England* (New York & London: Garland, 1977).

Mrs. Henry Wood

(17 January 1814-10 February 1887)

Lionel Adey
University of Victoria

BOOKS: *Danesbury House* (Glasgow: Scottish Temperance League, 1860; New York: Harper, 1860);

East Lynne (3 volumes, London: Bentley, 1861; 1 volume, New York: Dick & Fitzgerald, 1861);

Mrs. Halliburton's Troubles (3 volumes, London: Bentley, 1862; 1 volume, Richmond: West & Johnson, 1865);

The Channings (3 volumes, London: Bentley, 1862; 1 volume, Philadelphia: Peterson, 1862);

The Foggy Night at Offord: A Christmas Gift for the Lancashire Fund (Philadelphia: Peterson, 1862; London: Nisbet, 1863);

The Shadow of Ashlydyat (3 volumes, London: Bentley, 1863; 1 volume, Philadelphia: Peterson, 1863);

Verner's Pride (3 volumes, London: Bradbury & Evans, 1863; 1 volume, Philadelphia: Peterson, 1863);

William Allair; or, Running Away to Sea (Philadelphia: Peterson, 1863; London: Griffin & Farran, 1864);

Lord Oakburn's Daughters (3 volumes, London: Bradbury & Evans, 1864; 1 volume, Philadelphia: Peterson, 1865);

Oswald Cray (3 volumes, Edinburgh: Black, 1864; 1 volume: Philadelphia: Peterson, 1864);

Trevlyn Hold; or, Squire Trevlyn's Heir (3 volumes, London: Tinsley, 1864; 1 volume, London & New York: Macmillan, 1904);

Mildred Arkell: A Novel (3 volumes, London: Tinsley, 1865; 1 volume, Philadelphia: Peterson, 1865);

St. Martin's Eve: A Novel (3 volumes, London: Tinsley, 1866; 1 volume, Philadelphia: Peterson, 1866);

Elster's Folly: A Novel (3 volumes, London: Tinsley, 1866; 1 volume, Philadelphia: Peterson, 1866);

Lady Adelaide's Oath (3 volumes, London: Bentley, 1867; 1 volume, New York: Munro, 1877);

A Life's Secret, anonymous (2 volumes, London: Religious Tract Society, 1867; 1 volume, New York: Munro, 1877);

Orville College: A Story (2 volumes, London: Tinsley, 1867; 1 volume, New York: Munro, 1879);

Ellen Wood.

Castle Wafer; or, The Plain Gold Ring (New York: Dick & Fitzgerald, 1868);

The Red Court Farm: A Novel (3 volumes, London: Tinsley, 1868; 1 volume, Philadelphia: Peterson, 1869);

Anne Hereford: A Novel (3 volumes, London: Tinsley, 1868; 1 volume, London & New York: Macmillan, 1902);

Roland Yorke: A Novel (3 volumes, London: Bentley, 1869);

Bessy Rane: A Novel (3 volumes, London: Bentley, 1870; 1 volume, Philadelphia: Peterson, 1870);

George Canterbury's Will: A Novel (3 volumes, London: Tinsley, 1870; 1 volume, Philadelphia: Peterson, 1870);

Dene Hollow: A Novel (3 volumes, London: Bentley, 1871; 1 volume, Philadelphia: Peterson, 1871);

Within the Maze: A Novel (3 volumes, London: Bentley, 1872-1873; 1 volume, Philadelphia: Peterson, 1872);

The Master of Greylands (3 volumes, London: Bentley, 1873; 1 volume, Philadelphia: Peterson, 1873);

Johnny Ludlow (3 volumes, London: Bentley, 1874; 1 volume, New York: Carleton, 1875);

Told in the Twilight (3 volumes, London: Bentley, 1875);

Bessy Wells (London: Daldy, Isbister, 1875);

Adam Grainger: A Tale (London: Bentley, 1876);

Edina: A Novel (3 volumes, London: Bentley, 1876; 1 volume, Philadelphia: Peterson, 1876);

Parkwater, with Four Other Tales (London: Bentley, 1876; Philadelphia: Peterson, 1876);

Our Children (London: Daldy, 1876);

Pomeroy Abbey: A Romance (3 volumes, London: Bentley, 1878; 1 volume, New York: Munro, 1878);

Court Netherleigh: A Novel (3 volumes, London: Bentley, 1881; 1 volume, New York: Munro, 1881);

About Ourselves (London: Nisbet, 1883);

The Unholy Wish and Other Stories (New York: Munro, 1885; London: Bentley, 1890);

Lady Grace and Other Stories (3 volumes, London: Bentley, 1887; New York: Lovell, 1887);

The Story of Charles Strange: A Novel (3 volumes, London: Bentley, 1888; 1 volume, New York: Macmillan, 1901);

Featherston's Story (London: Bentley, 1889);

The House of Halliwell: A Novel (3 volumes, London: Bentley, 1890; 1 volume, New York: United States Book Company, 1890);

Ashley and Other Stories (London: Bentley, 1897; London & New York: Macmillan, 1901).

The novels of Mrs. Henry Wood were the quintessential Victorian best-sellers. *Danesbury House* (1860) penetrated an evangelical market normally closed to novels, and its Scottish sales exceeded those of any earlier novel. Within a year, metropolitan readers were besieging bookstores for *East Lynne* (1861), while printers worked day and night to produce four editions in six months. During an expedition to the Holy Land, the Prince of Wales played truant for a day to read this tale of desertion, adultery, and divorce, then handed it to Prof. (later Dean) A. P. Stanley, who read it in three hours, after which he and the prince crossexamined each other about it over dinner. For some years Mrs. Wood rivaled Dickens in being able to dictate her terms to her publishers. A born storyteller, Mrs. Wood incarnated the Victorian middle class's evangelical Christianity and its concern with domestic happiness and commercial probity.

Ellen Price was brought up by her maternal grandmother at Worcester, where her father was a glove manufacturer. The Midland cathedral city appears in *Mrs. Halliburton's Troubles* (1862) as Helstonleigh, a lesser analogue of Anthony Trollope's Barchester. A lifelong spinal curvature constrained her to write her forty novels and innumerable short stories from a reclining chair. In 1836 she married Henry Wood, who combined banking and shipping activities with consular service; from 1836 until 1856 the couple lived in France. In her latter years abroad, she contributed to *Bentley's Miscellany* and the *New Monthly Magazine* popular but ill-paid stories which, as the editor Harrison Ainsworth later admitted, kept these magazines afloat. After Henry Wood's early retirement, they resettled in London. Four years later, Ellen Wood won £ 100 from the Scottish Temperance Society for *Danesbury House*, her first novel, which she had written in just four weeks. This tale of a manufacturing family's fight against alcoholism bears the hallmarks of a Mrs. Henry Wood novel: a well-sustained plot, clearly drawn but stereotypical characters, conventional evangelical Christianity, and a melodramatic representation of life. Mr. and Mrs. Danesbury and their elder children eschew drink; their younger sons either die of delirium tremens, vividly depicted, or repent at the eleventh hour after a death-bed appeal by their father: " 'Arthur,' said the old man, with quivering lips and trembling hands, as he grasped those of his eldest son, 'there is no place for me much longer on earth. I question whether he or I shall go the quicker. My heart is broken. William,' reaching out to take his hand, and bring him side by side with Arthur, 'can you marvel at it? My son, can you marvel at it? Few and evil have the days of my old age been: my substance destroyed, my peace of mind wrecked. One of my children has gone before me; another—he, poor madman—is going with me, and I have no hope that I shall meet either of them hereafter. Do you act'—he wrung William's hand—'so as to come to me.' "

After two rejections, Mrs. Wood's most famous novel, *East Lynne*, became a best-seller and was accorded the rare privilege of a three-column review in the *Times*, which rarely reviewed novels. Within twenty years it had sold 130,000 copies, been translated into most European languages, and been several times adapted for the stage. A generation wept at this ingeniously contrived story—daring for its time—of Lady Isabel, who deserts her steadfast husband for an old flame and returns, broken-hearted and disguised by the ravages of smallpox, to nurse her children. The *Times* reviewer conceded the improbability of Lady Isabel's remaining unrec-

ognized and pointed to the errors regarding legal procedure, by which the "weak and commonplace" villain on trial for murder is testified against by another suspect and counsel for the defense assists in securing a conviction. Nevertheless, the reviewer found Mrs. Wood's portrayal of the deserted husband "masterly," her analysis of female characters "skillful," and the story "first-rate." Among several modern critics of this novel, Gail Cunningham points to the clichés that "batter the reader" and Mrs. Wood's inconsistency in heaping blame on Lady Isabel yet asserting that she cannot help loving Levison, while Peter Coveney claims that Lady Isabel treats her marital and social position as more important than morality as such.

Year by year Mrs. Wood poured out novels and short stories, outselling all major novelists save Dickens and perhaps George Eliot. *The Channings* (1862), on the trials of a model Christian family, sold 140,000 copies by 1895; *The Shadow of Ashlydyat* (1863), her own favorite, sold 150,000 by 1899. In the main plot of *The Channings*, a youth suspected of theft refuses to clear himself lest he incriminate the brother he believes responsible, while in the humorous underplot Mrs. Wood draws on her experience of cathedral choirboys and their antics. The Shadow of Ashlydyat appears before death or disaster in the Godolphin family, who have owned the house for generations. It fades after "graceless George" has ruined the family banking business and brought disgrace upon his upright brother and wife. Ashlydyat passes to his sister and her husband, who nobly forgives George for embezzlement and secures him a post abroad.

Ironically, as Mrs. Wood's popularity began to wane, she produced better work. In 1867, the year after her husband's death, she bought the magazine *Argosy*, editing it with her son's help. The magazine's immense success was due not to her serialized novels but her monthly short stories under the pseudonym "Johnny Ludlow." Few readers could have suspected the sexual identity of the youth who reports action set in the Worcestershire countryside. Recurrent names of the local squirearchy lend plausibility, and the narrator, Johnny Ludlow, supplies continuity to the tales, which tend toward the supernatural or melodramatic—the fallen girl abandoned with her baby, or the bridegroom arrested on his wedding day. Their popularity induced Mrs. Wood to bring out the Johnny Ludlow tales in book form (1874).

Mrs. Wood's extraordinary vogue over some thirty years, despite her careless, even ungrammati-

A manuscript page from The Red Court Farm *(1868) (Charles W. Wood,* Memorials of Mrs. Henry Wood)

cal writing, can in part be ascribed to her ingenious contrivance of suspense and the amazing variety of her plots. In large measure, however, it resulted from social circumstances: the dull, circumscribed lives and conventional religious values of her mainly female, lower-middle-class readers. The extreme conservatism of *A Life's Secret* (1867)—which pro-

voked angry workers to demonstrate outside the office of its publishers against its caricature of a strike, and to threaten the fortunately anonymous author's life—finds echoes in British middle-class society to this day.

Mrs. Wood suffered from bronchitis for many years and died of heart failure on 10 February 1887

Henry Wood–banker and diplomat who served as the model for boring husbands in novels by Mrs. Wood

at her home in the London suburb of South Hampstead. Her novels and stories are of interest today to the social historian bent on discovering what the mid-Victorian moral majority assumed about life, and what entertained it; they have often been disdained by critics. George Meredith, reader for Chapman and Hall, ignoring the advocacy of Ainsworth, pronounced *East Lynne* "foul." Mrs. Lynne Linton, critic for the *Saturday Review*, called Mrs. Wood a "shallow observer of society. . . puerile and vulgar." Her fellow novelist Adeline Sergeant, however, commended Mrs. Wood's skill in delineating "the bootmaker," "the grocer," and the boisterous schoolboy, as well as the central characters usually drawn from the professional or commercial classes. Ernest A. Baker dismissed her in a sentence as one of the "crude but far from unsuccessful" imitators of Charles Reade and Wilkie Collins, alluding to her "elaborate mystifications, solved by well-laid surprise." In 1935, Amy Cruse listed her among the "Philistines," all "lush sentimentalism" and "hectic melodrama." In recent years J. A. Sutherland has treated her as a shrewd

businesswoman who knew how to secure the best terms from publishers and retain a wide readership. Elaine Showalter comments perceptively on her success in "tapping female frustrations" and releasing her own. In *East Lynne*, Lady Isabel leaves an upright but passionless husband because (like Mr. Henry Wood, who never enjoyed novels) he bored her to desperation. Showalter considers the magnitude of Lady Isabel's punishment evidence of Mrs. Wood's self-repression. Certainly the similarities between Mrs. Wood's hero-figures and her own father, and the early deaths of blameless bankers and manufacturers as well as of saintly wives, suggest that her novels would repay study no less as psychological than as social documents.

Other:

Summer Stories from the "Argosy," by Mrs. Henry Wood and Other Authors (2 volumes, London: Bentley, 1890).

Biography:

Charles Wood, *Memorials of Mrs. Henry Wood* (London: Bentley, 1894).

References:

Ernest A. Baker, *History of the English Novel*, volume 9: *The Day before Yesterday* (New York: Barnes & Noble, 1950), p. 222;

Peter Coveney, *The Image of Childhood: The Individual and Society, A Study of the Theme in English Literature* (London: Penguin, 1967), pp. 179-184;

Amy Cruse, *Victorians and Their Reading* (Boston: Houghton Mifflin, 1935);

Gail Cunningham, *The New Woman and the Victorian Novel* (London: Macmillan, 1978);

M. Elwin, *Victorian Wallflowers* (London: Cape, 1934);

Michael Sadleir, "Bindings of Mrs. Henry Wood's Novels," *Times Literary Supplement*, 8 February 1936, p. 120;

Adeline Sergeant, *Women Novelists of Queen Victoria's Reign* (London: Hurst & Blackett, 1897), pp. 174-192;

Elaine Showalter, *A Literature of Their Own: British Women Novelists from Brontë to Lessing* (Princeton, N.J.: Princeton University Press, 1977), pp. 171-173;

J. A. Sutherland, *Victorian Novelists and Publishers* (Chicago: University of Chicago Press, 1978).

Charlotte Mary Yonge

Barbara J. Dunlap
City College, City University of New York

BIRTH: Otterbourne, Hampshire, 11 August 1823, to William Crawley and Frances Mary Bargus Yonge.

DEATH: Otterbourne, 24 March 1901.

SELECTED BOOKS: *Scenes and Characters; or, Eighteen Months at Beechcroft* (London: Mozley, 1847);

Abbey Church; or, Self-Control and Self-Conceit (London: Mozley, 1848);

Kings of England: A History for Young Children (London: Mozley, 1848);

Henrietta's Wish; or, Domineering: a Tale (London: Masters, 1850; New York: Munro, 1885);

Kenneth; or, The Rearguard of the Grand Army (London: Parker, 1850; New York: Appleton, 1855);

Langley School (London: Mozley, 1850);

Landmarks of History (3 volumes, London: Mozley & Smith, 1852-1857; New York: Leypoldt & Holt, 1867-1868);

The Two Guardians; or, Home in this World (London: Masters, 1852; New York: Appleton, 1855);

The Heir of Redclyffe (London: Parker, 1853; New York: Appleton, 1853);

The Herb of the Field (London: Mozley, 1853);

The Castle Builders; or, The Deferred Confirmation (London: Mozley, 1854; New York: Appleton, 1855);

Heartsease; or, The Brother's Wife (2 volumes, London: Parker, 1854; New York: Appleton, 1855);

The Little Duke; or, Richard the Fearless (London: Parker, 1854; New York: Macmillan, 1880);

The History of the Life and Death of the Good Knight Sir Thomas Thumb (London: Hamilton, Adams, 1855);

The Lances of Lynwood (London: Macmillan, 1855; New York: Appleton, 1856);

Ben Sylvester's Word (London: Mozley, 1856; New York: Appleton, 1859);

The Daisy Chain; or, Aspirations (2 volumes, London: Parker, 1856; 1 volume, New York: Appleton, 1856);

Harriet and Her Sister (London: Mozley, 1856);

Leonard the Lionheart (London: Mozley, 1856);

Dynevor Terrace; or, The Clue of Life (2 volumes, London: Parker, 1857; New York: Appleton, 1857);

The Instructive Picture Book: Lessons from the Vegetable World (London: Hamilton, 1857);

The Christmas Mummers (London: Mozley, Masters, 1858);

Conversations on the Catechism (London: Mozley, 1859);

Friarswood Post Office (London: Mozley, 1860; New York: Appleton, 1860);

Hopes and Fears; or, Scenes from the Life of a Spinster (2 volumes, London: Parker, 1860; New York: Appleton, 1861);

The Mice at Play (London: Groombridge, 1860);

The Strayed Falcon (London: Groombridge, 1860);

Pigeon Pie (London: Mozley, 1860; Boston: Roberts, 1864);

The Stokesley Secret; or, How the Pig Paid the Rent (London: Mozley, 1861; New York: Appleton, 1862);

The Young Stepmother; or, A Chronicle of Mistakes (2 volumes, London: Parker, 1861; New York: Appleton, 1862);

Biographies of Good Women (2 volumes, London: Mozley, 1862-1865);

The Chosen People: A Compendium of Sacred and Church History for School Children (London: Mozley, 1862; New York: Pott & Amery, 1868);

Countess Kate (London: Mozley, 1862; Boston: Loring, 1865);

Sea Spleenwort and Other Stories (London: Groombridge, 1862);

History of Christian Names (2 volumes, London: Parker, 1863);

The Apple of Discord: A Play (London: Groombridge, 1864);

A Book of Golden Deeds of All Times and All Lands (London: Macmillan, 1864; New York: Hurst, 1864);

Historical Dramas (London: Groombridge, 1864);

The Trial: More Links of the Daisy Chain (2 volumes, London: Macmillan, 1864; 1 volume, New York: Appleton, 1864);

The Wars of Wapsburgh (London: Groombridge, 1864);

The Clever Woman of the Family (2 volumes, London:

Charlotte Mary Yonge

Macmillan, 1865; 1 volume, New York: Appleton, 1865);

The Dove in the Eagle's Nest (2 volumes, London: Macmillan, 1866; 1 volume, New York: Appleton, 1866);

The Prince and the Page: A Story of the Last Crusade (London: Macmillan, 1866);

The Danvers Papers: An Invention (London: Macmillan, 1867);

A Shilling Book of Golden Deeds (London: Macmillan, 1867);

The Six Cushions (London: Mozley, 1867);

Cameos from English History (9 volumes, London: Macmillan, 1868-1899);

The Chaplet of Pearls; or, The White and Black Ribaumont: A Romance of French History, 1572 (London: Macmillan, 1868; New York: Burt, 1868);

Historical Selections: A Series of Readings in English and European History, by Yonge and E. Sewell (2 volumes, London: Macmillan, 1868-1870);

New Ground: Kaffirland (London: Mozley, 1868; New York: Pott & Amery, 1869);

The Pupils of St. John the Divine (London: Macmillan,

1868; Philadelphia: Lippincott, 1868);

A Book of Worthies, Gathered from the Old Histories and Written out Anew (London: Macmillan, 1869; London & New York: Macmillan, 1892);

Keynotes of the First Lessons for Every Day in the Year (London: Society for Promoting Christian Knowledge, 1869);

The Seal; or, The Inward Spiritual Grace of Confirmation (London: N.p., 1869);

The Caged Lion (London: Macmillan, 1870; New York: Appleton, 1870);

Little Lucy's Wonderful Globe (London & New York: Macmillan, 1871; Boston: Lothrop, 1872);

Musings over the "Christian Year" and "Lyra Innocentium," Together with a Few Gleanings of Recollections of the Rev. John Keble, Gathered by Several Friends (Oxford: Parker, 1871; New York: Pott & Amery, 1871);

A Parallel History of France and England, Consisting of Outlines and Dates (London: Macmillan, 1871);

Pioneers and Founders; or, Recent Works in the Mission Field (London: Macmillan, 1871; London & New York: Macmillan, 1890);

Scripture Readings for Schools, with Comments (5 volumes, London: Macmillan, 1871-1879);

P's and Q's: The Question of Putting Upon (London: Macmillan, 1872; London & New York: Macmillan, 1899);

Questions on the Prayer-Book (London: Mozley, 1872);

Aunt Charlotte's Stories of English History for the Little Ones (London: Ward, 1873);

Life of John Coleridge Patteson, Missionary Bishop of the Melanesian Islands (2 volumes, London: Macmillan, 1873; New York: Macmillan, 1894);

The Pillars of the House; or, Under Wode under Rode (4 volumes, London: Macmillan, 1873; 2 volumes, New York: Macmillan, 1874);

Aunt Charlotte's Stories of French History for the Little Ones (London: Ward, 1874);

Lady Hester; or, Ursula's Narrative (London: Macmillan, 1874);

Questions on the Collects (London: Mozley, 1874);

Questions on the Epistles (London: Mozley, 1874);

Questions on the Gospels (London: Mozley, 1874);

Aunt Charlotte's Stories of Bible History for the Little Ones (London: Ward, 1875; Philadelphia: Winston, 1951);

My Young Alcides: A Faded Photograph (London: Macmillan, 1875; New York: Macmillan, 1876);

Aunt Charlotte's Stories of Greek History for the Little Ones (London: Ward, 1876);

Eighteen Centuries of Beginnings of Church History

(London: Mozley, 1876);

The Three Brides (2 volumes, London: Macmillan, 1876; 1 volume, New York: Appleton, 1876);

Aunt Charlotte's Stories of German History for the Little Ones (London: Ward, 1877);

Aunt Charlotte's Stories of Roman History for the Little Ones (London: Ward, 1877);

Womankind (London: Mozley & Smith, 1877; New York: Macmillan, 1877);

The Disturbing Element; or, Chronicles of the Bluebell Society (London: Ward, 1878; New York: Appleton, 1879);

A History of France, in *History Primers*, edited by J. R. Green (London: Macmillan, 1878; New York: Appleton, 1882);

The Story of the Christians and Moors of Spain (London: Macmillan, 1878; New York: Macmillan, 1882);

Burnt Out: A Story for Mothers' Meetings (London: Smith, 1879);

A History of France, part 8 of *Historical Course for Schools*, edited by E. A. Freeman (London: Macmillan, 1879; New York: Holt, 1879);

Magnum Bonum; or, Mother Carey's Brood (3 volumes, London: Macmillan, 1879; 1 volume, New York: Munro, 1880);

Short English Grammar for Use of Schools (London: Longmans, 1879);

Bye-Words: A Collection of Tales New and Old (London: Macmillan, 1880);

Love and Life: An Old Story in Eighteenth-Century Costume (2 volumes, London: Macmillan, 1880; New York: Harper, 1880);

Verses on the Gospel for Sundays and Holy Days (London: Smith, 1880);

Aunt Charlotte's Evenings at Home with the Poets (London: Ward, 1880);

Cheap Jack (London: Smith, 1881);

Frank's Debt (London: Smith, 1881);

How to Teach the New Testament (London: National Society, 1881; New York: Pott, 1889);

Lads and Lasses of Langley (London: Smith, 1881; New York: Young, 1882);

Practical Work in Sunday Schools (London: National Society, 1881); republished as *Practical Work in Schools* (New York: Kellogg, 1888);

Questions on the Psalms (London: Smith, 1881);

Wolf (London: Smith, 1881);

Given to Hospitality (London: Smith, 1882);

Historical Ballads (London: National Society, 1882);

Langley Little Ones: Six Stories (London: Smith, 1882);

Pickle and His Page Boy; or, Unlooked for: A Story (London: Smith, 1882);

Sowing and Sewing: A Sexagesima Story (London: Smith, 1882);

Talks about the Laws We Live Under; or, At Langley Night School (London: Smith, 1882);

Unknown to History: A Story of the Captivity of Mary of Scotland (2 volumes, London: Macmillan, 1882; 1 volume, New York: Macmillan, 1882);

Aunt Charlotte's Stories of American History, by Yonge and J. H. Hastings Weld (London: National Society, 1883; New York: Appleton, 1883);

English Church History, Adapted for Use in Day and Sunday Schools (London: National Society, 1883);

Landmarks of Recent History, 1770-1883 (London: Smith, 1883);

Langley Adventures (London: Smith, 1883; New York: Dutton, 1884);

The Armourer's 'Prentices (London: Macmillan, 1884; New York: Munro, 1884);

The Daisy Chain Birthday Book (London: Smith, 1884);

Higher Reading-Book for Schools, Colleges, and General Use (London: National Society, 1885);

Nuttie's Father (2 volumes, London: Macmillan, 1885; 1 volume, New York: Munro, 1885);

The Two Sides of the Shield (London: Macmillan, 1885; New York: Munro, 1885);

Astray: A Tale of a Country Town, by Yonge and M. Bramston, C. Coleridge, and E. Stuart (London: Hatchards, 1886; New York: Dutton, 1887);

Chantry House (2 volumes, London: Macmillan, 1886; 1 volume, New York: Macmillan, 1886);

The Little Rick-Burners (London: Skeffington, 1886);

A Modern Telemachus (London: Macmillan, 1886; New York: Harper, 1886);

Teachings on the Catechism: For the Little Ones (London: Smith, 1886);

Victorian Half-Century: A Jubilee Book (London: Macmillan, 1886);

Under the Storm; or, Steadfast's Charge (London: National Society, 1887; New York: Munro, 1887);

What Books to Lend and What to Give (London: National Society, 1887);

Beechcroft at Rockstone (London: Macmillan, 1888; New York: Munro, 1889);

Preparation of Prayer-Book Lessons (London: Smith, 1888);

Deacon's Book of Dates: A Manual of the World's Chief Historical Landmarks, and an Outline of Universal History (London: Deacon, 1888);

Hannah More (London: Allen, 1888; Boston: Roberts, 1888);

Nurse's Memories (London: Eyre & Spottiswoode, 1888; New York: Young, 1888);

Our New Mistress; or, Changes at Brookfield Earl (London: National Society, 1888; New York: Munro, 1888);

The Cunning Woman's Grandson: A Tale of Cheddar a Hundred Years Ago (London: National Society, 1889; New York: Whittaker, 1889);

The Parent's Power: Address to the Conference of the Mother's Union (Winchester: Warren, 1889);

A Reputed Changeling; or, Three Seventh Years Two Centuries Ago (London: Macmillan, 1889);

Life of HRH the Prince Consort (London: Allen, 1890);

More Bywords (London: Macmillan, 1890);

The Slaves of Sabinus: Jew and Gentile (London: National Society, 1890; New York: Whittaker, 1890);

The Constable's Tower; or, The Times of Magna Carta (London: National Society, 1891; New York: Whittaker, 1891);

Old Times at Otterbourne (Winchester: Warren, 1891);

Seven Heroines of Christendom (London: Sonnenschein, 1891);

Twelve Stories from Early English History (London: National Society, 1891);

Two Penniless Princesses (London: Macmillan, 1891);

Westminster Historical Reading Books (2 volumes, London: National Society, 1891-1892);

The Cross Roads; or, A Choice in Life (London: National Society, 1892; New York: Whittaker, 1892);

That Stick (London: Macmillan, 1892);

The Tudor Period, with Biographies of Leading Persons (London: National Society, 1892);

An Old Woman's Outlook in a Hampshire Village (London: Macmillan, 1892; New York: Macmillan, 1892);

Chimes for the Mothers: A Reading for Each Week in the Year (London: Gardner, 1893);

The Girl's Little Book (London: Skeffington, 1893; New York: Pott, N.d.);

Grisly Grisell; or, The Laidly Lady of Whitburn: A Tale of the Wars of the Roses (London: Macmillan, 1893);

The Strolling Players: A Harmony of Contrasts, with C. Coleridge (London: Macmillan, 1893; New York: Macmillan, 1893);

The Treasures in the Marshes (London: National Society, 1893);

The Cook and the Captive; or, Attalus the Hostage (New York: Whittaker, 1893; London: National Society, 1894);

The Rubies of St. Lo (London: Macmillan, 1894);

The Story of Easter (London: Ward, 1894);

The Carbonels (London: National Society, 1895; New York: Whittaker, 1895);

The Long Vacation (London: Macmillan, 1895; New York: Macmillan, 1895);

The Release; or, Caroline's French Kindred (London: Macmillan, 1896);

The Wardship of Steepcombe (London: National Society, 1896; New York: Whittaker, 1896);

The Pilgrimage of the Ben Beriah (London: Macmillan, 1897);

Founded on Paper; or, Uphill and Downhill between the Two Jubilees (New York: Whittaker, 1897; London: National Society, 1898);

John Keble's Parishes: A History of Hursley and Otterbourne (London: Macmillan, 1898; New York: Macmillan, 1898);

The Patriots of Palestine: A Story of the Maccabees (London: National Society, 1898; New York: Whittaker, 1898);

Scenes from "Kenneth," etc. (London: Arnold, 1899);

The Herd Boy and His Hermit (New York: Whittaker, 1899; London: National Society, 1900);

The Making of a Missionary; or, Day Dreams in Earnest (London: National Society, 1900; New York: Whittaker, 1900);

Modern Broods; or, Developments Unlooked For (London: Macmillan, 1900; New York: Macmillan, 1900);

Reasons Why I Am a Catholic, and not a Roman Catholic (London: Wells Gardner, Darton, 1901);

COLLECTION: *Novels and Tales of Charlotte Mary Yonge*, New Edition (40 volumes, London: Macmillan, 1879-1899).

Charlotte Mary Yonge may be "placed" in literary history as the leading novelist of that Anglo-Catholic revival known as Tractarianism, or the Oxford Movement; but this classification cannot explain why her domestic novels have always been enjoyed by many readers to whom her religious views are a matter of indifference or even hostility. Firmly opposed to crudely didactic fiction—especially for children—she had the ability to extract dramatic tension from almost any family situation and relationship and to develop it with delicate moral and psychological notation. In her own day her domestic novels were admired by

Henry James, Tennyson, and a wide public of discriminating reviewers and readers. In the twentieth century her enormous output of over 200 books—historical novels; histories; biographies; children's stories; tales of village life; and volumes on religion, geography, and names—has tended to be held against her. While there is much of interest throughout her writings, her claim to importance rests on her domestic fictions; in those long chronicles of large, middle-class Victorian broods, family life is presented, in the phrase of her admirer C. S. Lewis, as an "arduous vocation."

Charlotte Yonge lived all her life in the village of her birth. Strongly attached by bonds of love and admiration to her parents, she remained in some respects a devoted and submissive daughter until her death at seventy-seven. Her father, William Yonge, had sacrificed his military career, his beloved Devonshire home, and many of his artistic tastes in order to gain the consent of his mother-in-law, a woman considered narrow by her own contemporaries, to his marriage to Frances Mary Bargus. He and his wife settled down on Mrs. Bargus's small estate in Otterbourne, near Winchester. Here he made a new life for himself out of village interests, church building, and the education of his daughter. He and his wife taught her Latin, French, German, history, and mathematics, in addition to giving her religious instruction. At the age of seven she began to hear lessons in the Otterbourne Sunday School; she went on to teach in the school, seldom missing more than a few weeks each year, until her death.

In 1836 John Keble became rector of the neighboring parish of Hursley and would be, after her father, the greatest influence on the entire cast of her mind and thought. Keble's life paralleled William Yonge's: he had given up a brilliant career at Oxford, where his sermon on "National Apostasy" launched the Oxford Movement in 1833, first to fulfill family duties and then to take up the work of a parish priest. In preparing Charlotte Yonge for confirmation he recognized her brilliant mind and passionate love of history. She absorbed all he had to teach her about the doctrine of the Church of England; and in her later life, neither the claims of the Roman Catholic church on the one hand nor the prevalence of religious doubt on the other seem ever to have troubled her faith. Indeed, religious doubt is the only "sin" for which she, as a novelist, could find little sympathy. Her circle also included the family—which eventually numbered fifteen children—of George Moberly, headmaster of Win-

John Keble, Yonge's friend and mentor for thirty years
(National Portrait Gallery)

chester College. The Kebles, Moberlys, Yonges, and the Yonges' Coleridge relations formed a close circle of mutual interests and stimulation. When this group broke up in the 1860s from the inevitable causes of change and decay, Charlotte Yonge, who was excessively shy, never developed another group to replace it. From 1859 to 1874 Miss Yonge met periodically in London with a group of teenage girls who corresponded under her direction on literary and historical questions for the purpose of self-cultivation. For a short time Mary Augusta Arnold, later Mrs. Humphry Ward, was one of these "goslings" to Miss Yonge's Mother Goose. The group briefly published a magazine, the *Barnacle*. While this coterie gave Miss Yonge much enjoyment, it was no substitute for the company of those distinguished adult contemporaries who were eager to have her friendship. Her shyness outside of small circles of like-minded old friends prevented her from making new ones. Her direct experience was thus limited; how limited seems best indicated by a remark in an autobiographical sketch she wrote in middle age: "on the thirty-first of January 1830 came the greatest event of my life: my only brother, Julian, was born."

As she grew older, Charlotte Yonge made a practice of writing down the dinner table conversations of her friends and Devonshire cousins. From these exercises she learned how dialogue could reveal and distinguish characters. The enormous skill she developed with dialogue is most evident in her novels about large families whose members share a common physical resemblance and family traits, yet reveal their personalities through conversation so clearly that characters seldom need to be identified once a dialogue has been established. After some apprentice work, she published in 1847 *Scenes and Characters; or, Eighteen Months at Beechcroft*, whose early pages reveal the strong influence of another Hampshire novelist, Jane Austen. The Mohuns of Beechcroft Court, the first of the four families who intermarry and interact throughout many of her novels, grew out of a family of boys and girls Charlotte Yonge had created to alleviate the loneliness of her essentially solitary childhood at Otterbourne.

Eleanor Mohun, the eldest of twelve children, has postponed her marriage in order to provide companionship for her widowed father and educate her younger sisters. Her cold, repressed manner has been greatly resented by the others and when, at Eleanor's marriage, her duties descend to Emily and Lilias, they vow to be guided in their running of the household by the "rule of love"—that all action must spring from spontaneous emotion—rather than that of duty. The indolent Emily soon gives up her work, and the increased responsibilities descend to Lilias, an imaginative girl of sixteen. After making several serious mistakes, she learns—and it is a Tractarian teaching—that where the "daily round, the common task" are concerned, the rule of duty is a surer guide than the rule of love, but that love must inform duty to make it a blessing. Here, as in other of Miss Yonge's novels, the helpful influence of a perceptive and sympathizing brother of high ideals is essential to the heroine's development. Many years later Charlotte Yonge referred to this "crude and inexperienced tale" as devoid of plot and incident; yet a student of her work should not ignore it. *Scenes and Characters* contains the germs of many of her later novels and shows that she had developed her skills at dialogue by the time she was twenty-three. Forty years later she took up the Mohuns again and downright, honest Phyllis, vain little Ada, and pertinacious Jane reappear as the adults they would inevitably have become.

In 1850 Marianne Dyson, an invalid friend of Miss Yonge's, suggested that she develop a story which would contrast two characters, the essentially contrite and the essentially self-satisfied. The result, finished late in 1851, was *The Heir of Redclyffe* (1853). Miss Yonge read the manuscript while it was in progress to her parents and the Kebles, as she generally did, and wrote to "Guy's mother," Miss Dyson, about his progress. Guy Morville shares many of the traits of Hurrell Froude, the intimate of Keble and John Henry Newman. The title is more subtle than first appears. When the story opens, Guy is the reigning baronet of Redclyffe; the heir of Redclyffe will be Philip, and the novel is as much about Philip's awakening from his self-deceptions as it is about Guy's trials at Philip's hands, Guy's marriage to Amy Edmonstone, and his early death as a result of Philip's having acted on his habitual assumption of always being right.

Like Flora May's in *The Daisy Chain* (1856), Philip's punishment for his worldliness is the attainment of his wishes: a seat in Parliament, the Redclyffe estate, and marriage to his cousin Laura. Like Flora, Philip has a harsh measure of mental and spiritual suffering meted out to him because the author feels he is worth it and has the ability to profit from it. "Silly little Amy Edmonstone" is the kind of heroine her author most admired: unpretending and meek but capable of rising to heights of heroism and firmness at a crisis. The warm domestic circle of Amy's home in placid Hampshire is effectively contrasted with the rough scenery of Redclyffe, Guy's estate on the Cumberland coast. In Guy Morville Miss Yonge domesticated the Byronic hero and allowed him to surmount through inner discipline a wretched family history, a violent temper, and the crossing of his purposes. To a modern reader the more interesting character is Philip, with his self-deception, his thwarted career, and his despair at the self-inflicted poverty which makes him an ineligible suitor for his cousin. The last quarter of the book, which deals with the first two years of Amy's widowhood and Philip's awakening, are typical of Charlotte Yonge's need to follow the destiny of her characters. She drew here characters she would use in varied forms throughout her works: the ineffective father who must nonetheless be obeyed, the invalid, and the pert younger sister.

Shortly after the publication of *The Heir of Redclyffe* in January 1853, Charlotte Yonge found herself famous. Keble, doubtless thinking of his own book of hymns, *The Christian Year* (1827), counseled her that a successful book could be the trial of one's life, but Miss Yonge seems to have been almost

Yonge and her mother

completely free of authorial vanity. Among the best-known admirers of *The Heir of Redclyffe* were William Morris and his friends, the artists Edward Burne-Jones and Dante Gabriel Rossetti. Very likely they were fired by Guy's love of the Middle Ages and Malory, of English cathedrals, and of de La Motte-Fouqué's romance *Sintram* with its hero's appreciation of the value of symbols. The reviewer for the *Times* remarked of Guy that "never before did the beauty of holiness appear more beautiful or more winning." Henry James liked it; Wilkie Collins abhorred it. It was *the* novel of the Crimean War period and helped inspire the ideals of a generation.

While working on *The Heir of Redclyffe*, Charlotte Yonge was also writing her best children's book, *The Little Duke* (1854), about the tenth-century Richard of Normandy, and beginning two series, *Cameos from English History* (1868-1899) and *Conversations on the Catechism* (1859). All three were serialized in the magazine she founded in 1851 and edited until 1894, the *Monthly Packet of Evening Readings for Members of the Church of England*. The

magazine, which probably never had more than 1,500 subscribers, was thoroughly an expression of her personality and interests: fiction, history, literary history, theology, and botany were the leading subjects. Later, more scientific material was added, and Lewis Carroll contributed some mathematical recreations. For a periodical with such a restricted purpose, the literary and historical interests of the *Monthly Packet* were wide-ranging and included articles on such topics as Hungarian and Polish history and literature. At a time when Matthew Arnold was lamenting the insularity of British culture, articles in the *Monthly Packet* dealt soundly with all periods of European culture and history. In the 1870s and 1880s as the question of occupations for women grew more pressing, Miss Yonge invited many contributions on this subject, and her novels, serialized in the *Monthly Packet*, showed her increasing concern with it.

Charlotte Yonge published two novels in 1854. *The Castle Builders* provides a link in the person of Lady Herbert Somerville with the personnel of *The Pillars of the House* (1873) and dwells on a religious theme of great meaning to the Tractarians: the importance of confirmation. *Heartsease* is the more considerable novel and won Charles Kingsley's unstinted praise, despite Miss Yonge's disapproval of his own writings. The reviewer for the *Athenaeum* commented that "the authoress throughout thinks more of her book than of herself and keeps out everything that does not immediately concern it," and a similar comment could be made about the selfless narrator of *The Pillars of the House*. *Heartsease* is a good example of how Charlotte Yonge's total lack of self-consciousness and her imaginative sympathies allowed her to transcend the limits of her own direct experience. "Heartsease" is a plant of the genus *Viola*, or violet, and the title both plays on the name of the heroine and describes her function of reconciler and healer.

Arthur Martindale, a handsome, careless young officer in the Queen's Life Guards, marries Violet Moss, a timid girl of sixteen, and, without any warning, launches her on his cold, reserved family. Arthur's father, Lord Martindale, is a well-meaning, upright man who is devoted to his children but has left their moral training in the hands of governesses. His wife has been dominated all her life by an aunt, who has systematically separated her from each of her children at birth lest she should become too attached to them and fail to keep up her "accomplishments." Violet's best friend in the family is Arthur's older brother, John, whose guidance of her readings and devotions helps her develop the inner strength to undergo the severe trials Arthur's thoughtlessness inflicts upon her. Eventually Violet knits the family together. *Heartsease* takes up where most Victorian novels would have left off—after an almost fairy-tale marriage—and presents both the elder Martindales and Arthur and Violet as parents who have to learn their jobs. Violet's anemia during pregnancy, her terror of childbirth when Arthur forbids her mother to come and help her, her quiet struggle to remain with (and by implication nurse) her fragile child when Arthur wishes her to go out with him, and, most of all, the couple's sexual attraction are no less clear for being implied rather than declared.

Lack of affection in early life from remote parents who stuff their children with "accomplishments" while ignoring their emotional needs is very clearly made the cause of personality and relational difficulties in young adulthood. Indeed, a pioneering vein in many of Charlotte Yonge's novels is the implication that the nurture of young children is a worthy occupation for *men*. Arthur Martindale's maturation is indicated, in part, by the interest he begins to take in his children.

Heartsease appears to have been the most extensively reviewed of Miss Yonge's works. There were some critics who found her religious views antipathetic and thus dismissed the book out of hand, but the general opinion on *Heartsease*, as well as on *The Heir of Redclyffe*, was that she suffered from the faults of prolixity and plotlessness but more than compensated for them by fine character drawing and truthfulness. The anonymous reviewer for *Fraser's Magazine* in 1854 anticipated many later commentators: "When we bid her characters farewell, it is ever hereafter to recall them to our affectionate remembrance as friends whom we have known and loved on earth, and whom we may hope to one day meet in heaven."

Heartsease was the last manuscript that her father read and approved. He died of apoplexy quite suddenly in February 1854 after having seen his son, Julian, take ship with his regiment for the Crimea. Shortly before his death, Charlotte Yonge had written to a friend about the value of his steadying influence but added, "I don't think he is my pope." Despite, or because of, his primary role in his daughter's life, none of the fathers in Charlotte Yonge's best novels are at all like William Yonge; rather they are usually ineffectual, indecisive, or even corrupt. Julian Yonge is a shadowy figure, but it is fairly clear that from the time he was

ingloriously invalided home from the Crimea with sunstroke before his regiment could join the fighting until his death in 1892, he had something unsatisfactory about him. His financial miscalculations eventually resulted in the sale of his and Charlotte's childhood home, Otterbourne House, and she used monies she had earned and wished to give for church work to support his family. That the figure of the beautiful, brilliant, spiritual boy who never fulfills his early promise recurs in Charlotte Yonge's books, and is often contrasted with a less-gifted brother who succeeds because he perseveres, may not be mere happenstance.

In 1853 Charlotte Yonge began the serialization of the first part of *The Daisy Chain; or, Aspirations* in the *Monthly Packet*; the entire book appeared in 1856. This "family chronicle" begins with the death of Dr. Richard May's wife in a driving accident for which he is largely to blame, and covers seven years in the development of him and his eleven children. Intellectual Ethel's pain upon realizing that increased family responsibilities must compel her to give up her study of Greek and "fall behind" her brilliant brother Norman is not without relevance today. Subtly conveyed is the increasing trial the invalidism of the eldest sister, Margaret, becomes to the family which loves her. In the character of Flora May, "so quiet, reasonable and determined," Charlotte Yonge chastises worldliness. Flora marries a dull but rich man and manages his parliamentary career, writing his speeches and explaining reports to him "so George will know what he has heard in the House." When their baby is drugged to death by an inexperienced nurse after Flora's social and political activities have forced her to wean prematurely, she realizes her errors but also that she must keep on in the "dreary" way she has chosen. Norman May's religious doubts are overcome, and he rejects a public career to go to New Zealand as a missionary. This and Ethel's success in bringing the church, which is the bearer of food, sanitation, and self-respect—as well as salvation—to the wild hamlet of Cocksmoor popularized the cause of missions with young people.

While the word *God* never appears in the book, Charlotte Yonge's motto, *Pro Ecclesia Dei* ("for the Glory of God"), informs the entire story. Her gift for dialogue and for portraying the development of character and the tensions, rivalries, and intense affections which bind together a large family are nowhere better displayed. Dr. May has much to learn as he becomes the sole parent to his children and makes several mistakes. A clever, highly trained physician, he has chosen voluntarily to take up his own father's practice in a little country town. He is favorably contrasted with his former fellow student, Sir Matthew Fleet, who has become a wealthy Harley Street practitioner but is May's inferior in humane qualities and actually less acute in his diagnosis of the course of Margaret May's paralysis than is her father.

The May saga is continued in *The Trial* (1864), which is the story of Leonard Ward's unjust imprisonment for murder and his vindication through the efforts of Tom May. This was the last of Charlotte Yonge's books which Keble read in manuscript, and he persuaded her to soften her account of the degrading effects of prison life on a sensitive and intellectual young man. The real theme of *The Trial* is Tom May's reconciliation with his father's values and way of life. From the dirty, untruthful little boy of *The Daisy Chain* he has grown up into something of a dandy, a Cambridge scholar, and a doctor who has studied in Edinburgh and Paris as his father did before him. Unlike the older Dr. May, Tom is more interested in research than in patients, and his aversions are his hometown, sick people, and Leonard Ward's family. Yet at the end of the book, through a process so gradual that the actions seem inevitable, he embraces all three. His marriage to Leonard Ward's invalid sister brings her into the orbit of the May family. This is a pattern in Charlotte Yonge: desirable marriage partners become truly absorbed into the family they marry into while undesirable marriage partners generally try to separate husbands or wives from their families. After reading *The Trial*, Henry Sidgwick, professor of philosophy and ethics at Cambridge, wrote to a friend: "Did you ever read *Madame Bovary* by Flaubert? It is very powerful, and Miss Yonge reminds me of it by force of contrast. It describes how the terrible *ennui* of mean French rural domestic life drags down the soul of an ambitious woman, whereas Miss Yonge makes one feel how full of interest the narrowest sphere of life is."

Julian Yonge married in 1858 and brought his bride to Otterbourne House. By 1862 their growing family, and possibly also unspecified frictions, led Charlotte Yonge and her mother to move to the nearby Elderfield Cottage, which remained Miss Yonge's home until her death. During the early 1860s she published three novels which examine the question of the gentlewoman's place in society. *The Young Stepmother* was serialized in the *Monthly Packet* in the late 1850s but did not appear in book form, somewhat shortened, until 1861. It is the history of the robust and charming Albinia Kendal, who brings vitality, energy, and social responsibility to the depressing home of her husband. Edmund Kendal, a wealthy scholar in Persian and other Eastern languages, lives in his books and shuts himself out from the knowledge of his daughters' characters as well as the fact that his son's inherited property consists of slum dwellings from which his agent exacts exorbitant rents. Albinia rouses him to interest himself in these matters, but her influence on her weak-willed stepson, Gilbert, is less happy. His death in the Crimea is directly attributable to her belief that the church and the army are the only two careers truly worthy of a gentleman. Charlotte Yonge's satire of the narrow minds and tasteless manners of the leading citizens of the little provincial town of Bayford is a success of a kind she did not repeat until *The Three Brides* (1876).

Implicit in Albinia's mixed achievements as a stepmother is Miss Yonge's conviction that no person, no matter how loving or well-intentioned, can be a wholly successful parent to children not his or her own, because stepparents lack that natural authority which she seems to have regarded as an earthly manifestation of the divine authority of the church. This theme is also met in *Hopes and Fears; or, Scenes from the Life of a Spinster*. The idea for this novel was developed as early as 1853, but other work intervened, and the book was not finished and published until 1860. It is unusual for a Victorian novel in that the heroine, the unmarried Honor Charlecote, is treated most fully in the years between thirty and fifty. Honor's infatuation with Owen Sandbrook persists, if unacknowledged to herself, even after he "jilts" her; and she refuses the steady love of her cousin, Squire Humpfrey, until he is dying. Humpfrey, with his unselfish devotion and oneness with nature, presages Hardy's Giles Winterborne in *The Woodlanders* (1887). Honor devotes herself to Owen's orphaned children, and her blindness to their characters and worship of the younger Owen cause a series of mistakes in judgment which result in Owen's foolish marriage and Lucilla's alienation. With these children, Honor knows all the pains of parenthood but few of its joys. By the end of the novel she has surrendered her estate and her judgment to other members of the younger generation who share her idealism and Christian chivalry but not her wooliness and fatal capacity for self-deception. Honor's development from an eager and lovable young girl to a still admirable but rather tiresome middle-aged woman is well done. In Squire Humpfrey, Charlotte Yonge

Yonge's writing table in Elderfield Cottage, where she lived from 1862 until her death

located qualities she most admired. He is a good churchman, a conscientious landowner, and totally unselfish. His role in the novel is over very early, as is the role of such other paragons as Mrs. May and Mr. Underwood in *The Pillars of the House*; but, like them, his influence remains to inspire others. He is the one to tell Honor, "There are ways of loving without setting one's heart," a truth it takes her twenty years to learn.

The 1860s were a difficult time in Charlotte Yonge's life. Both of the Kebles died in 1866, and the Moberlys left Winchester the next year. Her mother began a decline into senility, possibly through a series of small strokes, which Miss Yonge found all the more difficult to bear because they had been such inseparable companions. Her novels of this period share a depressed tone, but her output remained as high as ever. *Countess Kate* (1862) is one of her best stories for younger readers. Ten-year-old Kate Caergwent actually lives out a common childhood fantasy of discovering that she really is, if not a princess, at least a countess. In her passion for poetry, play acting, and history, her harum-scarum manners, and her total unmusicality, she is a portrait of the young Charlotte.

The following year saw the publication of her *History of Christian Names*. Taken with all the other work Charlotte Yonge had on hand, *History of Chris-*

tian Names is an awesome achievement. The book tries to record the derivation and meaning of all European given names, trace their variations in popularity, and note the most important persons in history, poetry, or fiction who bore them. The book leads to all sorts of byways of history, particularly of the medieval period. Charlotte Yonge begins with an apology for her lack of qualifications in undertaking such a work, as it requires "a perfect acquaintance with language, philology, ethnology, hagiology, universal history, and provincial antiquities," but the ground is "almost untrodden," and that must be her excuse. The list of sources she consulted is formidable, and she placed particular emphasis on Teutonic and Celtic names as they were at that time less familiar than scriptural and classical ones. The study of names has become a sophisticated, specialized study in this century, but her pioneering work still merits respect.

An outstanding trait of Charlotte Yonge as a domestic novelist is her ability to present in the round and with considerable sympathy characters whom she does not like or cannot approve. The glaring exception to this rule is Rachel Curtis in *The Clever Woman of the Family* (1865). The initial situation is promising as Rachel chafes against her role as a useless "young lady" in a seaside resort. In this she anticipates George Eliot's Dorothea Brooke, in

Middlemarch (1871-1872), but Rachel is deprived of the author's sympathy because her reading has unsettled her religious views. She burns with the desire to help others and share in the intellectual and social ferment of which she reads in the leading quarterlies; but since her efforts to help the exploited child lacemakers are undertaken without the benefit of church guidance, they are doomed. Rachel is strident and unpleasant in cruel contrast to the charming invalid, Ermine Williams, who edits a magazine from her wheelchair, and the seemingly weak Lady Temple who uncovers the fact that Rachel has been taken in by a scoundrel. After Rachel's amateur medical treatment has allowed a child to die of scarlet fever and she has barely escaped prosecution, she is rescued from her errors by a handsome cavalry officer who appreciates her for her good qualities. He effects her spiritual healing and intellectual humbling at the home of his clergyman uncle, Mr. Clare. Keble was surely the model for Clare, whose home suggests the refined, serious atmosphere in which Charlotte Yonge grew up. Implicit obedience to one's parents and to the church are the laws of Yonge's moral universe, and Rachel transgresses both of them. While many

characters fail in duty to their families but are treated with entire sympathy, failure of faith is like a disease which can infect all around it if it is not rooted out, and must be severely dealt with. Doubt is the one subject she cannot treat with detachment, and it is well for her art as a novelist that she dealt with it so little.

Miss Yonge's only trip abroad took place in 1869, the year following her mother's death. She visited Paris and the French countryside at the invitation of a distinguished French family, the Guizots, who wished to translate some of her books. History and geography were thrilling and living subjects to her, and she had the skill to develop backgrounds distant in time and space for her books, which are fairly free of the taint of having been "gotten up" for the occasion. Her work is quintessentially English, and no amount of travel would have made it less so; yet her closest friends regretted that she almost completely shut herself off from new impressions. Charlotte Yonge insured that she could not easily leave Otterbourne, when, in 1873, she took her invalid sister-in-law, Gertrude Walter, to live with her. Miss Walter, who called herself "Char's wife," seems to have been a sym-

Yonge with one of her Sunday school classes in the early 1870s. She taught in the Otterbourne Sunday school most of her life.

pathetic and helpful companion within her limits. Nonetheless, the arrangement circumscribed Charlotte Yonge's ability to visit or to receive friends for over twenty years.

The early 1870s saw Miss Yonge at the height of her powers. In addition to beginning the series of "nursery histories" known as "Aunt Charlotte's Stories" and a series of religious pamphlets to be used in preparing young people for confirmation, she serialized in the *Monthly Packet* her tribute to John Keble, *Musings over the "Christian Year" and "Lyra Innocentium"* (1871), a series of meditations on the poems which had directed the spiritual development of two generations of Anglo-Catholics. In 1870 she began to serialize in the *Monthly Packet* a novel which, along with *The Daisy Chain*, represents the summit of her achievement as a domestic novelist: *The Pillars of the House*.

Charlotte Yonge's facility as a writer—remarkable even in an age of fecund writers—is best illustrated by an anecdote told by Annie Moberly about a visit to Miss Yonge in 1873. The author appeared one day at lunch and exclaimed, "I have had a dreadful day; I have killed the Bishop and Felix." She had obviously been working on two books in the forenoon. The Bishop's death brought to a conclusion her widely praised *Life of John Coleridge Patteson* (1873). The Coleridges and Yonges had been united through a series of marriages around 1780 which also gave them both Duke and Taylor relations. All these connections were, as Charlotte Yonge wrote in a footnote to her biography of Patteson, "happily strengthened by ties of friendship in each generation." Patteson's life followed the paradigm Charlotte Yonge most valued. He had abandoned the possibility of a truly distinguished career as a linguistics scholar to serve as a parish priest and then to go as a missionary to Melanesia. His work there was remarkable for his total lack of condescension to the islanders and his determination to preserve their culture. He was killed by Melanesians who mistook him for one of the illegal slave traders who used to come among them disguised as clergymen, and thus was for Charlotte Yonge the truest type of hero: in addition to incarnating all of Charlotte Yonge's ideals of Christian chivalry, Patteson's sacrifice of his most congenial tastes and ambitions to a higher service linked him in her eyes to John Keble and her own Norman May; but Patteson had the added glory of martyrdom. The early portions of the biography, which deal with Patteson's remarkable family, their Coleridge relations, and his years at Eton and Ox-

ford, have all the freshness which mark her domestic novels. For his later life she relied on letters, diaries, and testimony, allowing Patteson to tell his own story as much as possible. The bishop's sisters had asked her to undertake the work shortly after his death in 1871, and she did so despite murmurs among the bishop's fellow clergy that this was an unsuitable job for a woman. Her delicacy of perception and sureness of method resulted in a book greatly admired by Henry James and other critics to whom the prospect of two thick volumes about a missionary bishop were not immediately appealing. Patteson himself is revealed as a delightful person, yet another illustration of Charlotte Yonge's ability to make goodness blindingly attractive—a talent as great as the ability to create sympathetic villains.

In 1872 and 1873 Miss Yonge was visited by Elizabeth Wordsworth, principal of Lady Margaret Hall at Elderfield. These two scholarly women stimulated each other greatly. Miss Wordsworth's memoirs present many attractive glimpses of Miss Yonge, such as the picture of her lying on the sofa "and showing a very pretty pair of feet in white open-work stockings" while they "capped [quotations from] Miss Austen con amore." She told her visitor, "I have had a great deal of affection in my life, but not from the people I cared for most." The year 1873 was also notable for the publication in book form of her longest and perhaps greatest novel: *The Pillars of the House*. In narrating the histories of the thirteen Underwood children over a period of eighteen years, Charlotte Yonge dramatized two of her strongest beliefs: the development of strong characters through continuous testing in the domestic circle and the ability of the most unpromising circumstances to bring about spiritual good. Her distrust of ritualism and her belief in the strength to be drawn from attending daily church services are worked into the texture of the book. Yet the reader caught up in this story for the first time will be primarily conscious of experiencing the dense texture of life in a Victorian family.

Upon the death of his father, Felix Underwood holds the family together by working for a bookseller. Their descent into "trade," a drastic step for a "gentleman's family," cuts the Underwoods off from their natural social sphere; yet buoyed up by his "gentle birth," family solidarity, and unostentatious faith, Felix turns this trial into an exercise in Christian chivalry. Edgar Underwood is Charlotte Yonge's portrait of the bohemian artist who rejects his family's values but has nothing to put in their place and whose lack of self-discipline proves as fatal to his art as it does to his morals. His crippled sister, Geraldine, works quietly but steadily and eventually wins success with her own painting. The suffering of the beauty-starved Geraldine in the smoky, nasty industrial town of Bexley is sensitively portrayed. Over the struggles of the Underwoods Miss Yonge manages to cast the same halo of romance she cast over the prosperous drawing room of the Edmonstones in *The Heir of Redclyffe*. The family's desire to remain together despite dissensions and conflicting ambitions, and their attempts to live up to the high moral and intellectual values of their father, create tensions which hold the disparate threads of the narrative together. By the novel's end the family has been restored to its unjustly lost inheritance but uses it for social and religious good. With Felix dead and his sister Wilmet absorbed in her own home cares, the new pillars of the house are Geraldine and her clergyman brother, Clement. Clement has overcome a youth steeped in incense and ritual to develop into an effective priest. Most of the Underwoods are gifted in art or music, and the question of the proper way to use these gifts is another theme of the book.

Had Charlotte Yonge written only *The Three Brides* instead of scores of books for readers of all ages, she would never have been mislabeled as a children's writer. Here the atmosphere is redolent with bad drains, sexuality, and familial tension. Three young women are forced by circumstances to live in the great English house of their mother-in-law, Julia Charnock Poynsett. Mrs. Charnock Poynsett holds her five sons in willing subjection through her highly cultivated charm and the pity they feel for her spinal paralysis—the result of a riding accident. Raymond, the eldest and most deeply attached, marries "for his mother's sake" and chooses his cousin, Cecil, a prig who resents living in her mother-in-law's house. Raymond treats his wife with a merely "elder brother tone of kindness," and the reason for this becomes apparent: despite his refusal to acknowledge his feelings, he is still drawn to the siren Camilla Vivien, to whom he was once engaged, and who has returned to her old neighborhood reeking of adulterous passion. When the typhoid strikes, Raymond and Camilla die within an hour of each other, each obsessed on the deathbed with the notion that the other is in the room.

The fruitful physical union and deepening love—despite a number of quarrels—between Raymond's clergyman brother, Julius, and his spir-

ited Irish wife, Lady Rosamond, further point up the sterility of Raymond's marriage. The third bride, Anne, a South African colonist raised in a rigidly "Puritanical" atmosphere, finds her card-playing, dancing in-laws almost immoral. In Mrs. Duncombe, whose husband lives "on the turf," Charlotte Yonge presents a surprisingly sympathetic portrait of an agnostic who neglects her own children while she pursues women's rights and schemes of social betterment. Far from being a monster like Dickens's Mrs. Jellyby in *Bleak House* (1852-1853), she is a clearheaded, complex woman who wins respect by her excellent plans after a fire has gutted the factory which is a major source of income for the poor women of the town, and by her heroic nursing during the typhoid epidemic after many of the conventionally pious have fled in fear.

The Three Brides contains several lively discussions about the equality of men and women; from the point of view of a modern reader, the supporters of equality are given the best arguments. The opponents, who include most of the admirable and likable persons in the book, take refuge in platitudes and scriptural authority to refute these arguments. It is a measure of Miss Yonge's ability that the contemporary reader will probably disagree totally with the views of Raymond, Julius, and Rosamond while liking them enormously.

With *The Three Brides* Charlotte Yonge's important work as a domestic novelist came to an end. She elaborated on the relationships of her four families—the Mohuns, Mays, Underwoods, and Merrifields—in such later books as *The Two Sides of the Shield* (1885), *Beechcroft at Rockstone* (1888), *The Long Vacation* (1895) and *Modern Broods* (1900). While these novels have much of interest—especially in the development of the difficult character of Dolores Mohun, who is last seen in *Modern Broods* taking ship for Australia to work as a scientific lecturer—they are written to a lower standard. The true lover of Miss Yonge's novels will relish each detail, but the latter two are essentially shapeless and poorly written.

Beechcroft at Rockstone and *Magnum Bonum* (1879) exhibit Miss Yonge's growing concern with the matter of education and careers for women. She has been portrayed as opposed to higher education for women; nothing could be further from the truth. Her own upbringing and wholehearted devotion to her parents' standards caused her to believe that the education of upper-middle-class girls could best be given in the family circle. The regime she proposed, with governesses and tutors, was

Yonge in the garden at Elderfield Cottage

quite stringent and reminiscent of her own curriculum. She was most emphatically opposed to the trivial, superficial curricula of boarding schools for "young ladies" of the type which formed Rosamond Vincy in George Eliot's *Middlemarch*. The accession of two of her closest friends, Annie Moberly and Elizabeth Wordsworth, to the principalships of Oxford women's colleges did much to reconcile her to such institutions; and in her last years a scholarship in her name was established at the Winchester High School to help young women pay their way at Oxford or Cambridge.

Between 1874 and 1877 Charlotte Yonge published in the *Monthly Packet* a series of essays designed to guide the Church of England gentlewoman from the cradle to the grave. Collected under the title *Womankind* (1877), these essays are rich in shrewd observations, but they do show Miss Yonge at her most limited. She describes a class-bound world in which the greatest danger to

a young girl is that she might lose the "delicate home bloom of maidenliness." She comes out squarely for the inferiority of women, basing her view on Eve's betrayal of her role of helpmate when she enticed Adam to share the forbidden fruit. For this transgression she was punished with physical weakness and inferior mental capacity. Charlotte Yonge softens this view a bit by noting how, throughout history, living conditions in various parts of the world have varied the proportions of this inequality while never wholly eradicating it. The religious, moral, educational, and social standards she actually sets for her gentlewomen are so high that only superior men could surpass them. She inveighs against the double standard because she believes that men and women should be equally chaste. Women should work outside the home only when they must and be always "strong-minded" to speak out against improprieties at home and evils abroad. That the married woman's noblest role lies in making her home a center of refuge, repose, and stimulation for her family is a conventional view of the time; but Miss Yonge also insists that the unmarried woman has a vital role to play in society, provided she do so as a "daughter of the Church." In either role Miss Yonge praises "self-denial, patience, meekness, pity and modesty," but reminds her readers that "meekness does not mean looking like a reproachful victim." Her beautiful chapters on aging and on the necessity of yielding authority to the young are the best things in *Womankind*, but basically these essays are a measure of Charlotte Yonge's ability as a creative artist. In her best novels she transcends her own limits, not by being false to her ideals but by dramatizing possibilities and ramifications her "theoretical" writings could not comprehend.

Charlotte Yonge wrote many of her historical novels in the 1880s and 1890s as a means of painlessly educating younger readers in history. Her Cameos and Landmarks series were based on extensive reading in source materials and, while emphasizing her love of heroes, kept to events as they were known to have happened. In the novels she used historical events as background for personal drama, much as did her beloved Sir Walter Scott. But most of her heroes and heroines resemble Tractarians born before their time in their ideals and religious observances, and these novels have tended to drag her reputation down. The best of them is clearly *The Little Duke*, written early in her life, but another of great interest is *Unknown to History* (1882), based on the legend that Mary of Scotland and Bothwell had a daughter. The daughter is separated from the queen soon after birth and not reunited with her until shortly before the uncovering of the Babington plot which results in Mary's execution. Mary's charm and deviousness, the tedium of her life, and the perplexities of her jailers are skillfully woven into a well-paced narrative. Anthony Babington is first introduced as a beautiful and delightful child. With the respect and concern typical of her handling of children in fiction, Miss Yonge traces the development of Babington's romantic illusions concerning Mary and his inextricable involvement in the plot against Elizabeth which leads to his conviction as a traitor and his horrible death. It is typical of Charlotte Yonge's care that she inspected original records of the Queen of Scots at Hatfield House.

Miss Yonge was an enthusiastic botanist. While she seldom wrote lyrical descriptions of natural scenery—her upbringing had been neoclassical rather than romantic—she was a close observer and could use nature to dramatic effect, as she showed in such novels as *The Heir of Redclyffe* and *Hopes and Fears*. In 1892 she published *An Old Woman's Outlook in a Hampshire Village*, a very quiet book in the tradition of Gilbert White's *Natural History of Selborne* (1789) and Mary Russell Mitford's *Our Village* (1824-1832). Details of life in Otterbourne as they had changed in her lifetime are mingled with meticulous descriptions, which clearly show the influence of Ruskin, of the flora and fauna of the vicinity during the four seasons. She calls the book "an old woman's outlook through a keyhole, for all my life has been spent in one place, and one which can boast of nothing extraordinary; but then it has always been looked at with loving eyes. . . . Otterbourne's absence of peculiarities may make it serve to assist others to make the most of their surroundings, so as to find no country walk devoid of the homely delights that sustain and lift up the spirit. . . ." This book and *The Carbonels* (1895) recreate the background of her own girlhood and should be read in conjunction with the hundred pages or so of autobiography available in the biography by Christabel Coleridge.

Charlotte Yonge was occupied with her writing and her village pursuits until March 1901, when she was overtaken by bronchitis and pneumonia; she died on 24 March. The suggestion was made that she be interred next to Jane Austen in Winchester Cathedral, but she was buried in the Otterbourne churchyard at the foot of Keble's memorial cross. For several months after her death there was an outpouring of published tributes, most of which lamented the passing of an old if unseen friend. The great appeal of her novels even to those with absolutely no religious convictions was frequently stressed. In a brief obituary, her future biographer, Samuel Taylor Coleridge's granddaughter, Christabel, indicated that Miss Yonge's ability to differentiate numerous characters from a similar class and milieu was an achievement in its own way as remarkable as the depiction of a broad spectrum of classes and beliefs. If earlier critics had compared facets of her work to that of Balzac and Rousseau, Edith Sichel—a well-known critic of French literature—went further: in the size of her canvas, in the multiplicity of characters and their recurrences with numerous descendants, in "courage in the face of tediousness," and in "prolixity," Miss Yonge may best be compared with Émile Zola. Their themes, Miss Sichel allowed, were very different. She stressed the author's ability to put her readers in touch with the deepest aspects of family

Charlotte Yonge in 1898

life. Other obituary tributes compared and contrasted her with Anthony Trollope. The *Edinburgh Review* noted that both are to be "sought in the whole rather than the part of any given book" and share the gift of "shaping in their minds a large group of individuals for the most part neither witty nor exceptional, yet interesting as a group just because their creators are so profoundly alive to their idiosyncracies and realize so thoroughly their impact on each other." There was general agreement that her domestic novels strike into the currents of a reader's deepest feelings and that the "obsolete orthodoxies" she often championed are merely the accidentals of her works. This latter comment would not have pleased her, but she would have agreed that her "governing idea is the duty of self-discipline." Charlotte Yonge's power as a novelist was limited only by her sympathies.

The increased attention afforded Victorian women writers during the past decade has led to some revival of interest in Charlotte Yonge's work. Frequently, however, these reexaminations contain errors of fact about details of her life or incidents in

her books. A more serious difficulty arises from the fact that her ethics of chastity, humility, resignation, and filial piety so antagonize most feminist writers that they fail to apply the tools of literary analysis to her texts. Queenie Leavis expressed some of their feeling in a *Scrutiny* essay of 1944 in which her dislike of Miss Yonge's ideals appears to be the primary reason she denies any literary value to her work. Mrs. Leavis accuses Miss Yonge of "selecting the anti-Life elements in Christianity for stress and idealization" and writes as if the novels are peopled only, or principally, by "saintly" invalids, "physically incapable marriage partners," and the like. Mrs. Leavis definitely does not admire a man who gives up "the natural field for his abilities in order to become a South Seas missionary. . . ." Actually her quarrel is as much with her critical adversaries—disciples of T. S. Eliot who were in the 1940s making high literary claims for literature written by orthodox Anglicans—as it is with Miss Yonge. The *Scrutiny* attack on Miss Yonge and on Dorothy L. Sayers is based on the contention that their theological orthodoxy represses a "full and real understanding of the world we are part of." "Life" and "real understanding" are key words in the Leavis critical canon but they are never explained in this article. Into this crossfire of attacks Mrs. Leavis drags C. S. Lewis as a supporter of the orthodox Anglican position. In 1945, a year after Mrs. Leavis wrote her diatribe, Lewis himself wrote an essay on the importance of courtesy in family life. Here, in a passing reference, he strikes a vital nerve of her work, the aspect which makes it so attractive to readers with a wide variety of backgrounds and values: "In the Middle Ages some people thought that if only they entered a religious order they would find themselves automatically becoming holy and happy: the whole native literature of the period echoes with the exposure of that fatal error. In the nineteenth century some people thought that monogamous family life would automatically make them holy and happy: the savage anti-domestic literature of modern times—the Samuel Butlers, the Gosses, the Shaws—delivered the answer. In both cases the 'debunkers' may have been wrong about principles . . . but in both cases they were pretty right about matter of fact. Both family life and monastic life were often detestable, and it should be noticed that the serious defenders of both are well aware of the dangers and free of the sentimental illusion. The author of the *Imitation of Christ* knows (no one better) how easily monastic life goes wrong. Charlotte M. Yonge makes it abundantly clear that domesticity is no passport to heaven on earth but an arduous vocation—a sea full of hidden rocks and perilous ice shores only to be navigated by one who uses a celestial chart."

An oblique retort to Mrs. Leavis's charges that doctrinal rigidity and provincialism are the dominant qualities in Charlotte Yonge's domestic novels comes from Kathleen Tillotson, an outstanding scholar of Victorian fiction and Dickens editor. Writing in 1953 for a centenary broadcast on the BBC on *The Heir of Redclyffe*, she claims that "the moral content of *The Heir of Redclyffe* is easily disengaged from the social content and is not seriously out of date." After praising Yonge's use of symbols in this novel, Mrs. Tillotson notes that the final chapters trace the progress of the heroine after Guy Morville's death; "It was, I think, Charlotte Yonge's keen sense of [domestic] life that kept her from vapid sentimentality. . . ." To provoke such strong reactions in two such distinguished critics is itself an accomplishment. No doubt Barbara Dennis is correct in asserting that Miss Yonge's work is weakened by "her inability to come to terms with the movement of mind in the nineteenth century" and the lack of sympathy she displays toward manifestations of religious doubt. She was not George Eliot, nor even Mrs. Humphry Ward. Her best novels—*The Daisy Chain*, *The Pillars of the House*—draw the reader into her world and recreate the texture of Victorian family life as she knew it; these novels triumphantly demonstrate her feeling for the value of symbols, her faculty for minute observation, and her delicate moral and psychological discrimination.

Biographies:

Christabel Rose Coleridge, *Charlotte Mary Yonge: Her Life and Letters* (London: Macmillan, 1903);

Ethel Romanes, *Charlotte Mary Yonge: An Appreciation* (London: Mowbray, 1908);

Georgina Battiscombe, *Charlotte Mary Yonge: The Story of an Uneventful Life* (London: Constable, 1943);

Margaret Mare and Alicia Percival, *Victorian Best Seller: The World of Charlotte M. Yonge* (London: Murray, 1948).

References:

Georgina Battiscombe and Marghanita Laski, eds., *A Chaplet for Charlotte Yonge* (London: Cresset Press, 1965);

Yonge's grave in the Otterbourne churchyard, at the foot of the memorial to Keble which she had erected

David B. Brownell, "The Two Worlds of Charlotte Yonge," in *The World of Victorian Fiction* (Cambridge, Mass.: Harvard University Press, 1975), pp. 165-178;

Barbara Dennis, "The Two Voices of Charlotte Yonge," *Durham University Journal*, 65 (1973): 181-188;

Alethea Hayter, "The Sanitary Idea and a Victorian Novelist," *History Today*, 19 (December 1969): 840-847;

Queenie Dorothy Leavis, "Charlotte Yonge and 'Christian Discrimination,' " *Scrutiny*, 12 (Spring 1944): 152-160;

C. S. Lewis, *God in the Dock: Essays on Theology and Ethics*, edited by Walter Hooper (Grand Rapids: Eerdmans, 1970);

Sally Mitchell, "Sentiment and Suffering: Women's Recreational Reading in the 1860s," *Victorian Studies*, 21 (Spring 1977): 29-45;

Charlotte Anne Elizabeth Moberly, *Dulce Domum:*

George Moberly (D.C.L. . .): His Family and Friends (London: Murray, 1916);

Elaine Showalter, *A Literature of Their Own: British Women Novelists from Brontë to Lessing* (Princeton: Princeton University Press, 1977);

June Sturrock, "A Personal View of Women's Education 1838-1900: Charlotte Yonge's Novels," *Victorians' Institute Journal*, 7 (1979): 7-18;

Kathleen Tillotson, *Mid-Victorian Studies* (London: Athlone Press, 1965), pp. 49-55.

Papers:

Christabel Coleridge destroyed most of C. M. Yonge's personal papers after finishing her memoir. Such letters as do turn up from time to time bear primarily on her activities as an editor. The following collections contain the most sizable numbers of letters: British Library (Letterbooks of Alexander Macmillan); Harvard University (Houghton Library); Princeton University (Firestone Library).

Appendix

Literature at Nurse, or Circulating Morals

From "The Decay of Lying"

Candour in English Fiction

The Present State of the English Novel, 1892

The Place of Realism in Fiction

The Future of the Novel

Editors' Note

This appendix makes available several important documents relevant to the late Victorian novel. The six essays reprinted here have been selected for their broad discussions of concepts, their attention to the nature of the novel, and their general inaccessibility. Unlike essays on individual Victorian authors reprinted in such series as *Critical Heritage*, late-nineteenth-century discussions of the state of the novel and the status of fiction have only occasionally been republished. (George Moore's *Literature at Nurse* has recently been edited by Pierre Coustillas [Sussex, U.K.: Harvester Press, 1976], but since it is pivotal in marking the division between the periods covered by the two *Dictionary of Literary Biography* volumes on Victorian novelists, the editors felt it had to be included.)

These six works range widely over a variety of topics: from George Moore's rare pamphlet on the circulating libraries, *Literature at Nurse*, to a passage from Oscar Wilde's "The Decay of Lying" which displays the reaction of the aesthetes to the novel; from Thomas Hardy's important essay on frankness in fiction to George Saintsbury's survey of English fiction to 1892; from George Gissing's little-known discussion of realism in the English novel to Henry James's essay on the possibilities of English fiction. Collectively the works register the changes in attitude, practices, and reading habits of the late Victorians while at the same time pointing to some of the new directions that later novelists were to follow.

Literature at Nurse,
or Circulating Morals

George Moore

First published in pamphlet form (London: Vizetelly, 1885).

This paper should have been offered to *The Nineteenth Century*, but as, for purely commercial reasons, it would be impossible for any English magazine to print it, I give it to the public in pamphlet form.

In an article contributed to the *Pall Mall Gazette* last December, I called attention to the fact that English writers were subject to the censorship of a tradesman who, although doubtless an excellent citizen and a worthy father, was scarcely competent to decide the delicate and difficult artistic questions that authors in their struggles for new ideals might raise: questions that could and should be judged by time alone. I then proceeded to show how, to retain their power, the proprietors of the large circulating libraries exact that books shall be issued at extravagant prices, and be supplied to them at half the published rate, or even less, thus putting it out of the power of the general public to become purchasers, and effectually frustrating the right of the latter to choose for themselves.

The case, so far as I am individually concerned, stands thus: In 1883, I published a novel called "A Modern Lover." It met with the approval of the entire press; *The Athenaeum* and *The Spectator* declared emphatically that it was not immoral; but Mr. Mudie told me that two ladies in the country had written to him to say that they disapproved of the book, and on that account he could not circulate it. I answered, "You are acting in defiance of the opinion of the press—you are taking a high position indeed, and one from which you will probably be overthrown. I, at least, will have done with you; for I shall find a publisher willing to issue my next book at a purchasable price, and so enable me to appeal direct to the public." Mr. Mudie tried to wheedle, attempted to dissuade me from my rash resolution; he advised me to try another novel in three volumes. Fortunately I disregarded his suggestion, and my next book, "A Mummer's Wife," was published at the price of six shillings. The result exceeded my expectations, for the book is now in its fourth edition. The press saw no immoral tendency in it, in-

deed *The Athenaeum* said that it was "remarkably free from the elements of uncleanness." Therefore it is not with a failing but with a firm heart that I return to the fight—a fight which it is my incurable belief must be won if we are again to possess a literature worthy of the name. This view of the question may be regarded by some as quixotic, but I cannot forget that my first article on the subject awakened a polemic that lasted several weeks, giving rise to scores of articles and some hundreds of paragraphs. The *Saturday Review* wrote, "Michel Lévy saved France with cheap publications, who will save England?" Thus encouraged, I yield again to the temptation to speak upon a subject which on such high authority is admitted to be one of national importance. Nor do I write influenced by fear of loss or greed of gain. The "select" circulating libraries can no longer injure me; I am now free to write as I please, and whether they take or refuse my next novel is to me a matter of indifference. But there are others who are not in this position, who are still debutants, and whose artistic aspirations are being crushed beneath the wheels of these implacable Juggernauts. My interest in the question is centred herein, and I should have confined myself to merely denouncing the irresponsible censorship exercised over literature if I did not hear almost daily that when "A Mummer's Wife" is asked for at Mudie's, and the assistants are pressed to say why the book cannot be obtained, they describe it as an immoral publication which the library would not be justified in circulating.

Being thus grossly attacked, it has occurred to me to examine the clothing of some of the dolls passed by our virtuous librarian as being decently attired, and to see for myself if there be not an exciting bit of bosom exhibited here and a naughty view of an ankle shown there; to assure myself, in fact, if all the frocks are modestly set as straight as the title Select Library would lead us to expect.

Perhaps of all moral theories, to do unto others as you would be done unto meets with the most unhesitating approval. Therefore my *confrères*, of whose works I am going to speak, will have nothing to complain of. I shall commence by indicating the main outlines of my story of "A Mummer's Wife," appending the passage that gained it refusal at Mudie's; then I shall tell the stories of three fashionable novels (all of which were, and no doubt still are, in circulation at Mudie's Select Library), appending extracts that will fairly set before the reader the kind of treatment adopted in each case. The public will thus be able to judge between Mr. Mudie and me.

Now as to "A Mummer's Wife." Kate Ede is the wife of an asthmatic draper in Hanley. Attending her husband's sick-bed and selling reels of cotton over the little counter, her monotonous life flows unrelieved by hope, love, or despair. To make a few extra shillings a week the Edes let their front rooms, which are taken by Mr. Dick Lennox, the manager of an opera bouffe company on tour. He makes love to the draper's wife, seduces her, and she elopes with him. She travels about with the actors, and gradually becomes one of them; she walks among the chorus, speaks a few words, says a few verses, and is eventually developed into a heroine of comic opera. The life, therefore, that up to seven-and-twenty knew no excitement, no change of thought or place, now knows neither rest nor peace. Even marriage—for Dick Lennox marries her when Ralph Ede obtains his divorce—is unable to calm the alienation of the brain that so radical a change of life has produced, and after the birth of her baby she takes to drink, sinks lower and lower until death from dropsy and liver complaint in a cheap lodging saves her from becoming one of the street-walkers with whom she is in the habit of associating. That is my story; here is the passage objected to:—

> At last she felt him moving like one about to awake, and a moment after she heard him say, "There's Mr. Lennox at the door; he can't get in; he's kicking up an awful row. Do go down and open for him."
>
> "Why don't you go yourself," she answered, starting into a sitting position.
>
> "How am I to go? you don't want me to catch my death at that door?" Ralph replied angrily.
>
> Kate did not answer, but quickly tying a petticoat about her, and wrapping herself in her dressing gown, she went downstairs. It was quite dark and she had to feel her way along. At last, however, she found and pulled back the latch, but when the white gleam of moonlight entered she retreated timidly behind the door.
>
> "I am sorry," said Dick, trying to see who was the concealed figure, "but I forgot my

> latch-key."
>
> "It does not matter," said Kate.
>
> "Oh, it is you, dear! I have been trying to get home all day, but couldn't. Why didn't you come down to the theatre?"
>
> "You know that I can't do as I like."
>
> "Well, never mind; don't be cross; give me a kiss."
>
> Kate shrunk back, but Dick took her in his arms. "You were in bed then?" he said, chuckling.
>
> "Yes, but you must let me go."
>
> "I should like never to let you go again."
>
> "But you are leaving to-morrow."
>
> "Not unless you wish me to, dear."
>
> Kate did not stop to consider the impossibility of his fulfilling his promise, and, her heart beating, she went upstairs. On the first landing he stopped her, and laying his hand on her arm, said, "And would you be really be very glad if I were to stay with you?"
>
> "Oh, you know I would, Dick!"
>
> They could not see each other. After a long silence she said, "We must not stop talking here. Mrs. Ede sleeps, you know, in the room at the back of the work-room, and she might hear us."
>
> "Then come into the sitting-room," said Dick, taking her hands and drawing her towards him.
>
> "Oh, I cannot!"
>
> "I love you better than anyone in the world."
>
> "No, no; why should you love me?"
>
> Although she could not see his face she felt his breath on her neck. Strong arms were wound about her, she was carried forward, and the door was shut behind her.
>
> Only the faintest gleam of starlight touched the wall next to the window; the darkness slept profoundly on the landing and staircase; and when the silence was again broken, a voice was heard saying, "Oh, you shouldn't have done this! What shall I tell my husband if he asks me where I've been?"
>
> "Say you have been talking to me about my bill, dear. I'll see you in the morning."

The story of "Nadine," by Mrs. Campbell Praed, runs as follows:—Nadine, a young girl of twenty, is staying in a fashionable country house. There she meets Dr. Bramwell and Colonel Halkett, a married man; the latter she admits into her bedroom in the dead of night; he dies there of heart disease, and, in her nightdress, she is seen dragging the corpse down the passage by Dr. Bramwell. Next morning the servant informs the house that he has found Colonel Halkett dead in his bed. Dr. Bramwell examines the body, says nothing of what he has seen overnight, and there the matter for the present ends. But Dr. Bramwell is hopelessly in love with Nadine, and he meets her a few weeks after at a great ball in London. She begs of him to take her out into the garden. There they talk of Colonel Halkett's death, and Dr. Bramwell begs of Nadine to say that she tried to repulse the colonel; she declines to do so.

Six months after they meet again in the same country house where Colonel Halkett died. Dr. Bramwell is brooding over his love in the dead of night, when he is startled by a knock at the door. It is Nadine. At a glance he sees that she is in labour; she begs of him to come to her room and deliver her of the child. Next morning a nurse is called in. Dr. Bramwell, for the sake of Nadine, tells a tissue of falsehoods; he declares that she is suffering from a severe shock to her nervous system, and that her safety depends on nobody being admitted to her room. As soon as she possibly can Nadine gets away, leaving the child with Dr. Bramwell, who adopts it.

Years pass. Nadine meets a Russian prince at Nice, marries him, and comes to live in England. Dr. Bramwell falls in love with Miss Blundell, a friend of Nadine's, whose mother will not accept him as a suitor for her daugher's hand on account of the mystery that hangs about the parentage of his ward—Nadine's child. Dr. Bramwell goes to Nadine, begs of her to use her influence with Mrs. Blundell (Mrs. Blundell owes Nadine money) to make her consent to his marriage with her daughter. But instead Nadine talks to Dr. Bramwell of their past, and ends by proposing to become his mistress. After some hesitation he declines: Nadine turns upon him fiercely, and refuses to assist him in his endeavours to marry Miss Blundell; she denies ever having borne a child, and challenges him to do his worst. Dr. Bramwell returns home dumbfounded; but that night Nadine comes to his house repentant, holding a written confession in her hand. This is sent to Mrs. Blundell. The doctor marries the girl, and Nadine goes off to Russia with her husband.

The first extract I give is from the chapter entitled "In the Pavilion." Bramwell has led Nadine away from the dancers; he shows her a ring in proof of what he saw in the house at Croxham. Nadine

faints. He tries to reanimate the motionless form:—

> "Oh, Nadine," he murmured, "my love, my darling! you bade me be kind, and idiot-like, I have smitten you as though you were my enemy." He pressed his lips to hers in a transport of passion. Never before had he so forgotten himself. She opened her eyes, and he saw in them something of the same blank horror as had transfixed her features during that momentary flash of moonlight in the corridor at Croxham.

Then when Nadine recovers consciousness,

> "There is one solution," he said hoarsely. "I have repeated it to myself so often, that it has become borne in upon me as truth, and has comforted me in my despair. Nadine, let me speak as though I were your brother. Trust in my loyalty, my reverence. That night—listen—is not this how it was? He forced his way into your room. You repulsed him. In the excitement and agitation death struck him."
>
> Bramwell paused and waited breathlessly for her reply. None came. She sat motionless, her eyes bent downwards. In his agony he quitted her side and walked towards the door of the tent. Here he stood for several moments looking earnestly upon her, while there was still silence. At length the strain became unbearable, and he turned his face resolutely away from her. Aware of the movement, she seemed to interpret it as a sign of desertion. For a second the old defiance revived. She uplifted her head, her lips framed the words, "Go! think the worst of me that you choose; I can live without you."

Then when Nadine comes to Bramwell's room to ask him to deliver her of her child:—

> Bramwell gave her admission; and she stood in his presence white and almost as terror-stricken as upon the night to which his thoughts now involuntarily reverted. She was dressed in a loose cashmere robe that, clinging to her form, displayed its outlines clearly. In an instant his practised intelligence had grasped her imminent need. His worst horror confronted him. She had come to him for aid in the direst extremity which can befall a woman. He stood, almost as pale as she was, waiting for her to speak. Suddenly she divined that he knew her secret. A wave of crimson swept over her face. She advanced

with drooped eyes, and said in an imperative whisper, "I want you to come at once to my room." He bowed his head, and still without speaking followed her down the long dim corridor till they turned into the west wing. Here she paused, and motioned him to enter a room, the door of which stood partially open; then closed it behind them both and turned the key.

It being well known that I am no judge of such things, tell me, Mr. Mudie, if there be not in this doll just a little too much bosom showing, if there be not too much ankle appearing from under this skirt? Tell me, I beseech you.

The story of "A Romance of the Nineteenth Century," by W. H. Mallock, runs as follows:—

Ralph Vernon, a young man half philosopher, half poet, is living at Nice. There he meets Miss Walters, who had been seduced a year or two before by Colonel Stapleton. The colonel has been away in Palestine, but he has returned to Europe, and when the story opens he also is staying at Nice. The grossness of the lines on which their sensual intercourse has been conducted is easily imagined when we are told that the colonel has generally in his pocket a collection of obscene photographs, which he shows to his acquaintances, and which he sends to Miss Walters, who in turn shows them to the religious sensualist, Mr. Vernon. The latter falls hopelessly in love with Miss Walters. He wastes his time in talking religion, and she reflects, "Were you all a man ought to be you would be able to love in a more human way than you do." Vernon, however, is unable to do this, and Miss Walters goes to see the colonel in a very pretty room which he has taken for the purpose in the Hotel Victoria. Meanwhile Vernon strives to console himself with a depraved married woman called Mrs. Crane. But the memory of Miss Walters haunts him, and, after indulging in much kissing, he resists temptation. Then, in the last chapter, all meet at a masquerade ball. Miss Walters takes Vernon away into the garden; she tells him that the colonel "has recovered all," and dies of heart disease in his arms. He, not knowing that she is dead, runs to dip his handkerchief in a fountain, but at that moment the colonel, singing a comic song, passes down the pathway, and Vernon (who is in the costume of a Spanish pedlar) seizes him by the throat; the colonel, fancying he is attacked by some vagrant, pulls out a revolver and shoots his assailant dead. Here are a few extracts from one of the differ-

ent love scenes between Vernon and Miss Walters:—

The temptation was too much for Vernon. He put his hand on her shoulder, and let it slip down to her waist. She made no struggle; he felt her yield to his touch; and, still holding her, he led her back to her seat.

"You are looking beautiful to-day," he murmured.

"I'm glad of that," she said. "I should like your last impressions to be nice of me. Don't you admire my rose too?"

It was in her button-hole, and Vernon stooped forward to smell it. As he was slowly drawing back, her breath stirred his hair. He raised his eyes, and his lips were close to hers. Neither of them spoke: they each drew a breath sharply: in another instant the outer world was dark to them, and their whole universe was nothing but a single kiss. . . . Her lips parted a little, a flush stole over her cheek, she opened her arms as if to call him to herself, and at last, in a breathless whisper, she said "Come!" She saw that he did not stir, and she moved her head imperiously: "Come!" she repeated, "come closer. I want you here. There is something I wish to tell you."

He did as she commanded; he moved quite close to her, and in another instant her fair arms were round him, pressing him to her breathing bosom. Her lips were close to his ear. "My own one," she said, "I love you"; and still holding him, and almost in the same breath, "you must pay me," she said, "for having told you that. Kiss me—kiss me on the mouth, and say that you love me too.". . . At last her arms released him, and the two exchanged glances. "Tell me," she murmured, "are you happy now?"

"Yes, and no," he said; and there was then a long silence. "Cynthia, even yet you have not answered my question."

"What question?" she said. "Do you mean if I love goodness? Oh, if I do not yet (and she pressed his hand to her lips), you shall teach me to. You shall teach me everything. You shall do exactly what you will with me."

Notwithstanding, Vernon's love could not be sufficiently humanized, and at the end of the scene Colonel Stapleton is announced. This is how his arrival is led up to:—

"My memory is still full of the past; no

magic can alter that; and if you went from me, and made a vacuum in my present, the past would probably rush in and fill it up."

"Listen to me," said Vernon, with a sudden coldness in his voice. "Let us suppose I am very fond of the smell of eau-de cologne. Do you think that if I had none left in my bottle, I should dip my pocket-handkerchief in the next drain as a substitute?"

"I think you would be very silly if you did," she said, her voice growing cold also.

"Then would you not be equally or even more silly, if, on losing a comrade in the search of the thing you loved, you were to try to console yourself by seeking the thing you hated?"

"Only, the worst of it is, you see," she said with a slight laugh, "that the things that would console me are not things I hate. If it were so, I should not be what I am. When drunkards have not got wine they will drink stuff out of the next spirit lamp." . . .

"What then is it? you are a complete mystery to me. If I only knew the truth, I could be of so much more help to you."

"Don't ask me," she said; "why harp upon this one subject? Is there any use in trying to stir up all the dregs of my nature? In all conscience I have told you enough already. Do you know," she went on with a smile of expiring tenderness, "you must be, I think, a very innocent-minded person, or you would have understood it pretty well by this time."

Soon after the servant announces that the colonel is in the drawing-room:—

"Tell him," she said, "that I am coming up immediately. I will be with him in a few minutes." She waited till the man (the servant) was out of sight, and then she rose to go. "Good morning, Mr. Vernon," she said coldly as she swept past him [her still unhumanized lover]. "I suppose I shall hardly see you again to-day—or, indeed, for some time to come—as we may possibly go to-morrow."

Then Vernon returns home in a state verging on stupor. He, however, writes to her, and begs of her to meet him again at the same place. She consents, and this time, it must be admitted, lost not a moment, and made every possible effort to humanize him to her satisfaction. He was about to speak, but she did not give him time:—

"Come," she said, "am I not looking well to-night? Why don't you kiss me and tell me how soft and pretty I am? Isn't that what you say generally when you talk to girls like me? By the way, I have found a word that will at least describe what I might have been, had circumstances only favoured me, an *hetaira*. If I had lived in Athens I should have performed that part capitally. I was made for a life of pleasure, I think, if—, if—." She stopped abruptly for a moment, and then broke out once more, "If only there were not something in me that had made all my pleasure a hell."

But notwithstanding all this encouragement, Vernon lapses into religious talk—sermonings of all kind—and in despair at not being able to make him understand her, she takes him up to the house, and shows him the obscene photographs. He is terribly shocked, and confesses his folly in "wishing her to become an innocent girl again."

"Amongst the highest saints in heaven," he says, "there will be faces deeply scarred by the battle. You are right, very likely, that there is no way back to Eden; but—I am not a great quoter of texts, yet I still remember this one—'We all die in Adam, but we may all live in Christ.' "

She asks him if he really believes what he says, and being assured that he does, in front of the obscene photographs that have fallen on the floor she kneels down and murmurs "Our Father"; he, staring at the stars and palm-trees, "wondered if prayer meant anything?"

After this scene the lovers are separated for some time, but Miss Walters sends her picture to Vernon; on looking at it he declares: "If she will not be God's she must and shall be mine!" She, while contemplating herself in the glass, said to herself, with her heart full of Vernon, "My body at least is worthy of your acceptance." But at that moment the servant brought her a telegram from the colonel, announcing his arrival by the next train:—

"Come," said he, "what on earth is the matter with you? You shouldn't treat me in this way, for I can only stay ten minutes. I have come over with some lawyer's papers for Molly Crane to sign, and in another half-hour I shall have to start for Nice again. I heard you were in the garden, so I couldn't help having one try at finding you."

The news that the Colonel was going

gave Miss Walters great relief, and brought a smile to her face that was perhaps more cordial than she meant it to be, for the Colonel took her by the chin and turned her face towards him. At his touch, however, she started back abruptly, though the smile did not desert her.

"Remember, Jack," she said, "I'm going to have no more of your nonsense. We are too old, both of us, for that kind of thing."

"I'm not," said the Colonel, "though I believe at this moment, I'm in too great a hurry for it. However, I shall be back here to have another look at our Molly in a couple of days. I've engaged a room, a first-rate one, at the Hotel Victoria. Such a view from it, I can tell you! You must come," he went on fixing his gleaming eyes on her, "and see it yourself one of these days, little cross vindictive minx that you are!"

It being well known that I am no judge of such things, tell me, Mr. Mudie, if there be not in this doll just a little too much bosom showing, if there be not just a little too much ankle appearing from under this skirt? Tell me, I beseech you.

The story of "Foxglove Manor," by Robert Buchanan, reeks of the pulpit and the alcove. The hero is a young parson who uses religion for the purpose of seducing his congregation—he, in fact, uses it very much in the same way as Colonel Stapleton did the obscene photographs. When he has ruined Miss Edith Dove he deserts her for Mrs. Haldane, who, after much kissing and tying of pocket-handkerchiefs round swollen ankles, is saved from him by the machinations of her husband, a great scientist. On leaving Mrs. Haldane, the Rev. Mr. Santley muses to the following effect:—

"I love this woman. In her heart she loves me. Her superior spiritual endowments are mystically alive to those I myself possess. Her husband is a clod, an unbeliever, with no spiritual promptings. In his sardonic presence, her aspirations are chilled, frozen at the fountain-head, whereas in mine, all the sweetness and the power of her nature are aroused, though with a certain irritation. If I persist, she must yield to the slow moral mesmerism of my passion, and eventually fall. Is this necessarily evil? Am I of set purpose sinning? Is it not possible that even a breach of the moral law might under certain conditions lead us both to a higher religious place—yes,

even to a deeper and intenser consciousness of God?"

And again—

"What is sin? Surely it is better than moral stagnation, which is death. There are certain deflections from duty which, like the side stroke of a bird's wing, may waft us higher. In the arms of this woman I should surely be nearer God than crawling alone on the bare path of duty, loving nothing, hoping nothing, becoming nothing. What is it that Goethe says of the Eternal Feminine which leads us ever upwards and onwards? Which was the highest, Faust before he loved Marguerite, or Faust after he passed out of the shadow of his sin into the sphere of empirical and daring passion? I believe in God, I love this woman. Out of that belief, and that love, shall I not become a living soul?"

Later on in the book we find a meeting between our libidinous clergyman and his victim Miss Edith Dove, described as follows—

"She wore a light dress of some soft material, a straw hat, a country cloak, and gloves of Paris kid—a civilized nymph, as you perceive! To complete her modern appearance she carried a closed parasol and a roll which looked like music . . . And the satyr? Ah! I knew him at a glance, despite the elegant modern boots used to disguise the cloven foot. He wore black broadcloth and snowy linen, too, and a broad-brimmed clerical hat. His face was seraphically pale, but I saw (or fancied I saw), the twinkle of the hairy ears of the ignoble, sensual, nymph-compelling, naiad-pursuing breed."

In the third volume, in a chapter entitled "And lo! within her something leapt," the result of the love encounter is made known to the reader.

She arose shivering; and at that very instant there came to her a warning, an omen full of nameless terror. It seemed to her as if faces were flashing before her eyes, voices shrieking in her ears; her heart leapt, her head went round, and at the same moment she felt her whole being miraculously thrilled by the quickening of a new life within her own. With a loud moan, she fainted away upon the floor. When she returned to consciousness, she was lying nearly naked by the bedside and the moonlight was flooding the little room.

Now a writer like myself, whom you had proved to be no better than he should be, might be said to be capable of comparing a clergyman of the Church of England to a satyr, of even calling him "the snake of the parish," but you, Mr. Mudie, Methodist or Baptist, I forget which you are, how can you allow such a book in your Select Library? Two old ladies in the country wrote to you about my "Modern Lover," and you suppressed it; but did not one of the thousands of young ladies in the many thousand parsonages you supply with light literature write to tell you that papa was not "the snake of the parish," and your great friend the British Matron, did she never drop you a line on the subject? Tell me, I beseech you.

I say your great friend, my dear Mr. Mudie, because I wish to distinguish between you, for latterly your identities have got so curiously interwoven that it would need a critical insight that few—I may say none—possess, to separate you. Indeed on this subject many different opinions are afloat. Some hold that being the custodian of the national virtue you have by right adopted the now well-known signature as your *nom de plume*, others insist that the lady in question is your better half (by that is it meant the better half of your nature or the worthy lady who bears your name?), others insist that you yourself are the veritable British Matron. How so strange a belief could have obtained credence I cannot think, nor will I undertake to say if it be your personal appearance, or the constant communication you seem to be in with this mysterious female, or the singularly obtrusive way you both have of forcing your moral and religious beliefs upon the public that has led to this vexatious confusion of sex. It is, however, certain that you are popularly believed to be an old woman; and assuming you to be the British Matron I would suggest, should this pamphlet cause you any annoyance, that you write to *The Times* proving that the books I have quoted from are harmless, and differ nowise from your ordinary circulating corals whereon young ladies are supposed to cut their flirtation teeth. The British Matron has the public by the ear, and her evidence on the subject of impure literature will be as greedily listened to as were her views on painting from the nude. But although I am willing to laugh at you, Mr. Mudie, to speak candidly, I hate you; and I love and am proud of my hate of you. It is the best thing about me. I hate you because you dare question the sacred right of the artist to obey the impulses of his temperament; I hate you because you are the great purveyor of the worthless, the false and the commonplace; I hate you because you are a fetter about the ankles of those who would press forward towards the light of truth; I hate you because you feel not the spirit of scientific inquiry that is bearing our age along; I hate you because you pander to the intellectual sloth of to-day; I hate you because you would mould all ideas to fit the narrow limits in which your own turn; I hate you because you impede the free development of our literature. And now that I have told you what I think of you, I will resume my examination of the ware you have in stock.

Without in the least degree attempting to make an exhaustive list of the books which to my surprise this most virtuous literary tradesman consents to circulate, I may venture to call attention to "Puck," by Ouida. This is the history of a courtezan through whose arms, in the course of the narrative, innumerable lovers pass. "Moths," by the same author, tells how a dissolute adventuress sells to her lover the pure white body and soul of her daughter, and how in the end Vera, disgraced and degraded by her ignoble husband, goes off to live with the tenor with whom she fell in love at the beginning of the story. In a book I opened the other day at haphazard, "Phillida," by Florence Marryat, I find a young lady proposing to a young parson to be his mistress. It is true that the feelings that prompt her are not analyzed, but does the cause of morals gain I wonder by this slightness of treatment?

It is not for me to put forward any opinion of my own. I have spoken of and quoted only from the works of writers longer and better known to the public than I am. They do not need defence against the Philistine charge of immorality, and it would be ridiculous for me—ostracised as I am by the founder and president of our English Academy, the Select Circulating Library—to accuse them, or even to hint that they have offended against the Mudie code more deeply than myself. I therefore say nothing. I cast no stone. All I seek is to prove how absurd and how futile is the censorship which a mere tradesman assumes to exercise over the literature of the nineteenth century, and how he overrules the decisions of the entire English press.

Were I indeed the only writer who has suffered from this odious tyranny the subject might well be permitted to drop. Many cases might be brought forward, but I will not look further than last month. I am informed on good authority that on being written to repeatedly for a book called

"Leicester," Mr. Mudie sent back word to the Athenaeum Club that he did not keep naturalistic literature—that he did not consider it "proper." And thus an interesting, if not a very successful, literary experiment is stamped out of sight, and the strange paradox of a tradesman dictating to the bishops of England what is proper and improper for them to read is insolently thrust upon us. However the matter has been brought before the committee of the club, and the advisability of withdrawing the subscription from this too virtuous library is under consideration.

It has been and will be again advanced that it is impossible to force a man to buy goods if he does not choose to do so: but with every privilege comes a duty. Mr. Mudie possesses a monopoly, and he cannot be allowed to use that monopoly to the detriment of all interests but his own. But even if this were not so, it is no less my right to point out to the public, that the character for strength, virility, and purpose, which our literature has always held, the old literary tradition coming down to us through a long line of glorious ancestors, is being gradually obliterated to suit the commercial views of a narrow-minded tradesman. Instead of being allowed to fight, with and amid, the thoughts and aspirations of men, literature is now rocked to an ignoble rest in the motherly arms of the librarian. That of which he approves is fed with gold; that from which he turns the breast dies like a vagrant's child; while in and out of his voluminous skirts run a motley and monstrous progeny, a callow, a whining, a puking brood of bastard bantlings, a race of Aztecs that disgrace the intelligence of the English nation. Into this nursery none can enter except in baby clothes; and the task of discriminating between a divided skirt and a pair of trousers is performed by the librarian. Deftly his fingers lift skirt and underskirt, and if the examination prove satisfactory the sometimes decently attired dolls are packed in tin-cornered boxes, and scattered through every drawing-room in the kingdom, to be in rocking-chairs fingered and fondled by the "young person" until she longs for some newer fashion in literary frills and furbelows. Mudie is the law we labour after; the suffrage of young women we are supposed to gain: the paradise of the English novelist is in the school-room: he is read there or nowhere. And yet it is certain that never in any age or country have writers been asked to write under such restricted conditions; if the same test by which modern writers are judged were applied to their forefathers, three-fourths of the contents of our

libraries would have to be condemned as immoral publications. Now of the value of conventional innocence I don't pretend to judge, but I cannot help thinking that the cultivation of this curiosity is likely to run the nation into literary losses of some magnitude.

It will be said that genius triumphs over circumstances, but I am not sure that this is absolutely the case; and turning to Mr. Mathew Arnold, I find that he is of the same opinion. He says, . . . "but it must have the atmosphere, it must find itself in the order of ideas, to work freely, and this is not so easy to command. This is why the great creative epochs in literature are so rare . . . because for the creation of a master work of literature two powers must concur, the power of the man and the power of the moment; the creative has for its happy exercise appointed elements, and those elements are not in its own control." I agree with Mr. Mathew Arnold. Genius is a natural production, just as are chickweed and roses; under certain conditions it matures; under others it dies; and the deplorable dearth of talent among the novelists of to-day is owing to the action of the circulating library, which for the last thirty years has been staying the current of ideas, and quietly opposing the development of fresh thought. The poetry, the history, the biographies written in our time will live because they represent the best ideas of our time; but no novel written within the last ten years will live through a generation, because no writer pretends to deal with the moral and religious feeling of his day; and without that no writer will, no writer ever has been able to, invest his work with sufficient vitality to resist twenty years of criticism. When a book is bought it is read because the reader hopes to find an expression of ideas of the existence of which he is already dimly conscious. A literature produced to meet such hopes must of necessity be at once national and pregnant with the thought of the epoch in which it is written. Books, on the contrary, that are sent by the librarian to be returned in a few days, are glanced at with indifference, at most with the vapid curiosity with which we examine the landscape of a strange country seen through a railway-carriage window. The bond of sympathy that should exist between reader and writer is broken—a bond as sacred and as intimate as that which unites the tree to the earth—and those who do not live in communion with the thought of their age are enabled to sell their characterless trash; and a writer who is well known can command as large a sale for a bad book as a good one. The struggle for existence, therefore, no longer exists; the librarian rules the roost; he crows, and every chanticleer pitches his note in the same key. He, not the ladies and gentlemen who place their names on the title-pages, is the author of modern English fiction. He models it, fashions it to suit his purpose, and the artistic individualities of his employes count for as little as that of the makers of the pill-boxes in which are sold certain well-known and mildly purgative medicines. And in accordance with his wishes English fiction now consists of either a sentimental misunderstanding, which is happily cleared up in the end, or of singular escapes over the edges of precipices, and miraculous recoveries of one or more of the senses of which the hero was deprived, until the time has come for the author to bring his tale to a close. The novel of observation, of analysis, exists no longer among us. Why? Because the librarian does not feel as safe in circulating a study of life and manners as a tale concerning a lost will.

To analyze, you must have a subject; a religious or sensual passion is as necessary to the realistic novelist as a disease to the physician. The dissection of a healthy subject would not, as a rule, prove interesting, and if the right to probe and comment on humanity's frailties be granted, what becomes of the pretty schoolroom, with its piano tinkling away at the "Maiden's Prayer," and the water-colour drawings representing mill-wheels and Welsh castles? The British mamma is determined that her daughter shall know nothing of life until she is married; at all events, that if she should learn anything, there should be no proof of her knowledge lying about the place—a book would be a proof; consequently the English novel is made so that it will fit in with the "Maiden's Prayer" and the water-mill. And as we are a thoroughly practical nation, the work is done thoroughly; root and branch are swept away, and we begin on a fresh basis, just as if Shakespeare and Ben Jonson had never existed. A novelist may say, "I do not wish to enter into those pretty schoolrooms. I agree with you, my book is not fit reading for young girls; but does this prove that I have written an immoral book?" The librarian answers, "I cater for the masses, and the masses are young unmarried women who are supposed to know but one side of life. I cannot therefore take your book." And so it comes to pass that English literature is sacrificed on the altar of Hymen.

But let me not be misunderstood. I would not have it supposed that I am of opinion that literature can be glorified in the Temples of Venus. Were the freedom of speech I ask for to lead to this, we should have done no more than to have substituted one evil for another. There is a middle course, and I think it is this—to write as grown-up men and women talk of life's passions and duties. On one hand there must be no giggling over stories whispered in the corners of rooms; on the other, there must be no mock moral squeamishness about speaking of vice. We must write as our poems, our histories, our biographies are written, and give up once and for ever asking that most silly of all silly questions, "Can my daughter of eighteen read this book?" Let us renounce the effort to reconcile those two irreconcilable things—art and young girls. That these young people should be provided with a literature suited to their age and taste, no artist will deny; all I ask is that some means may be devised by which the novelist will be allowed to describe the moral and religious feeling of his day as he perceives it to exist, and to be forced no longer to write with a view of helping parents and guardians to bring up their charges in all the traditional beliefs.

It is doubtless a terrible thing to advocate the breaking down of the thirty-one and sixpenny safeguards, and to place it in the power of a young girl to buy an immoral book if she chooses to do so; but I am afraid it cannot be helped. Important an element as she undoubtedly is in our sociological system, still we must not lose sight of everything but her; and that the nineteenth century should possess a literature characteristic of its nervous, passionate life, I hold is as desirable, and would be as far-reaching in its effects, as the biggest franchise bill ever planned. But even for the alarmed mother I have a word of consolation. For should her daughter, when our novels are sold for half-a-crown in a paper cover, become possessed of one written by a member of the school to which I have the honour to belong, I will vouch that no unfortunate results are the consequence of the reading. The close analysis of a passion has no attraction for the young girl. When she is seduced through the influence of a novel, it is by a romantic story, the action of which is laid outside the limits of her experience. A pair of lovers—such as Paul and Virginia—separated by cruel fate, whose lives are apparently nothing but a long cry of yearning and fidelity, who seem to live, as it were, independent of the struggle for life, is the book that more often than any other leads to sin; it teaches the reader to look to a false ideal, and gives her—for men have ceased to read novels in England—erroneous and superficial notions of the value of life and love.

All these evils are inherent in the "select" circulating library, but when in addition it sets up a censorship and suppresses works of which it does not approve, it is time to appeal to the public to put an end to such dictatorship, in a very practical way, by withdrawing its support from any library that refuses to supply the books it desires to read.

From "The Decay of Lying"

Oscar Wilde

First published in Nineteenth Century, 25 (*January 1889*): 35-56.

VIVIAN

Shall I read you what I have written? It might do you a great deal of good.

CYRIL

Certainly, if you give me a cigarette. Thanks. By the way, what magazine do you intend it for?

VIVIAN

For the *Retrospective Review*. I think I told you that the elect had revived it.

CYRIL

Whom do you mean by "the elect"?

VIVIAN

Oh, The Tired Hedonists of course. It is a club to which I belong. We are supposed to wear faded roses in our buttonholes when we meet, and to have a sort of cult for Domitian. I am afraid you are not eligible. You are too fond of simple pleasures.

CYRIL

I should be black-balled on the ground of animal spirits, I suppose?

VIVIAN

Probably. Besides, you are a little too old. We don't admit anybody who is of the usual age.

CYRIL

Well, I should fancy you are all a good deal bored with each other.

VIVIAN

We are. That is one of the objects of the club.

Now, if you promise not to interrupt too often, I will read you my article.

CYRIL

You will find me all attention.

VIVIAN

(*reading in a very clear, musical voice*)

"THE DECAY OF LYING: A PROTEST.—One of the chief causes that can be assigned for the curiously commonplace character of most of the literature of our age is undoubtedly the decay of Lying as an art, a science, and a social pleasure. The ancient historians gave us delightful fiction in the form of fact; the modern novelist presents us with dull facts under the guise of fiction. The Blue-Book is rapidly becoming his ideal both for method and manner. He has his tedious *document humain*, his miserable little *coin de la création*, into which he peers with his microscope. He is to be found at the Librairie Nationale, or at the British Museum, shamelessly reading up his subject. He has not even the courage of other people's ideas, but insists on going directly to life for everything, and ultimately, between encyclopaedias and personal experience, he comes to the ground, having drawn his types from the family circle or from the weekly washerwoman, and having acquired an amount of useful information from which never, even in his most meditative moments, can he thoroughly free himself.

"The loss that results to literature in general from this false idea of our time can hardly be overestimated. People have a careless way of talking about a 'born liar,' just as they talk about a 'born poet.' But in both cases they are wrong. Lying and poetry are arts—arts, as Plato saw, not unconnected with each other—and they require the most careful study, the most disinterested devotion. Indeed, they have their technique, just as the more material arts of painting and sculpture have, their subtle secrets of form and colour, their craft-mysteries, their deliberate artistic methods. As one knows the poet by his fine music, so one can recognize the liar by his rich rhythmic utterance, and in neither case will the casual inspiration of the moment suffice. Here, as elsewhere, practice must precede perfection. But in modern days while the fashion of writing poetry has become far too common, and should, if possible, be discouraged, the fashion of lying has almost fallen into disrepute. Many a young man starts in life with a natural gift for exaggeration which, if nurtured in congenial and sympathetic surroundings, or by the imitation of the best models, might grow into something really great and wonderful. But, as a rule, he comes to nothing. He either falls into careless habits of accuracy————"

CYRIL

My dear fellow!

VIVIAN

Please don't interrupt in the middle of a sentence. "He either falls into careless habits of accuracy, or takes to frequenting the society of the aged and the well-informed. Both things are equally fatal to his imagination, as indeed they would be fatal to the imagination of anybody, and in a short time he develops a morbid and unhealthy faculty of truth-telling, begins to verify all statements made in his presence, has no hesitation in contradicting people who are much younger than himself, and often ends by writing novels which are so like life that no one can possibly believe in their probability. This is no isolated instance that we are giving. It is simply one example out of many; and if something cannot be done to check, or at least to modify, our monstrous worship of facts, Art will become sterile, and Beauty will pass away from the land.

"Even Mr. Robert Louis Stevenson, that delightful master of delicate and fanciful prose, is tainted with this modern vice, for we know positively no other name for it. There is such a thing as robbing a story of its reality by trying to make it too true, and *The Black Arrow* is so inartistic as not to contain a single anachronism to boast of, while the transformation of Dr. Jekyll reads dangerously like an experiment out of the *Lancet*. As for Mr. Rider Haggard, who really has, or had once, the makings of a perfectly magnificent liar, he is now so afraid of being suspected of genius that when he does tell us anything marvellous, he feels bound to invent a personal reminiscence, and to put it into a footnote

as a kind of cowardly corroboration. Nor are our other novelists much better. Mr. Henry James writes fiction as if it were a painful duty, and wastes upon mean motives and imperceptible 'points of view' his neat literary style, his felicitous phrases, his swift and caustic satire. Mr. Hall Caine, it is true, aims at the grandiose, but then he writes at the top of his voice. He is so loud that one cannot hear what he says. Mr. James Payn is an adept in the art of concealing what is not worth finding. He hunts down the obvious with the enthusiasm of a short-sighted detective. As one turns over the pages, the suspense of the author becomes almost unbearable. The horses of Mr. William Black's phaeton do not soar towards the sun. They merely frighten the sky at evening into violent chromolithographic effects. On seeing them approach, the peasants take refuge in dialect. Mrs. Oliphant prattles pleasantly about curates, lawn-tennis parties, domesticity, and other wearisome things. Mr. Marion Crawford has immolated himself upon the altar of local colour. He is like the lady in the French comedy who keeps talking about 'le beau ciel d'Italie.' Besides, he has fallen into a bad habit of uttering moral platitudes. He is always telling us that to be good is to be good, and that to be bad is to be wicked. At times he is almost edifying. *Robert Elsmere* is of course a masterpiece—a masterpiece of the 'genre ennuyeux,' the one form of literature that the English people seem thoroughly to enjoy. A thoughtful young friend of ours once told us that it reminded him of the sort of conversation that goes on at a meat tea in the house of a serious Nonconformist family, and we can quite believe it. Indeed it is only in England that such a book could be produced. England is the home of lost ideas. As for that great and daily increasing school of novelists for whom the sun always rises in the East End, the only thing that can be said about them is that they find life crude, and leave it raw.

"In France, though nothing so deliberately tedious as *Robert Elsmere* has been produced, things are not much better. M. Guy de Maupassant, with his keen mordant irony and his hard vivid style, strips life of the few poor rags that still cover her, and shows us foul sore and festering wound. He writes lurid little tragedies in which everybody is ridiculous; bitter comedies at which one cannot laugh for very tears. M. Zola, true to the lofty principle that he lays down in one of his pronunciamentos on literature, 'L'homme de génie n'a jamais d'esprit,' is determined to show that, if he has not got genius, he can at least be dull. And how well he succeeds! He is not without power. Indeed at times, as in *Germinal* there is something almost epic in his work. But his work is entirely wrong from beginning to end, and wrong not on the ground of morals, but on the ground of art. From any ethical standpoint it is just what it should be. The author is perfectly truthful, and describes things exactly as they happen. What more can any moralist desire? We have no sympathy at all with the moral indignation of our time against M. Zola. It is simply the indignation of Tartuffe on being exposed. But from the standpoint of art, what can be said in favour of the author of *L'Assommoir*, *Nana*, and *Pot-Bouille*? Nothing. Mr. Ruskin once described the characters in George Eliot's novels as being like the sweepings of a Pentonville omnibus, but M. Zola's characters are much worse. They have their dreary vices, and their drearier virtues. The record of their lives is absolutely without interest. Who cares what happens to them? In literature we require distinction, charm, beauty, and imaginative power. We don't want to be harrowed and disgusted with an account of the doings of the lower orders. M. Daudet is better. He has wit, a light touch, and an amusing style. But he has lately committed literary suicide. Nobody can possibly care for Delobelle with his 'Il faut lutter pour l'art,' or for Valmajour with his eternal refrain about the nightingale, or for the poet in *Jack* with his 'mots cruels,' now that we have learned from *Vingt Ans de ma Vie littéraire* that these characters were taken directly from life. To us they seem to have suddenly lost all their vitality, all the few qualities they ever possessed. The only real people are the people who never existed, and if a novelist is base enough to go to life for his personages he should at least pretend that they are creations, and not boast of them as copies. The justification of a character in a novel is not that other persons are what they are, but that the author is what he is. Otherwise the novel is not a work of art. As for M. Paul Bourget, the master of the *roman psychologique*, he commits the error of imagining that the men and women of modern life are capable of being infinitely analysed for an innumerable series of chapters. In point of fact what is interesting about people in good society—and M. Bourget rarely moves out of the Faubourg St. Germain, except to come to London—is the mask that each one of them wears, not the reality that lies behind the mask. It is a humiliating confession, but we are all of us made out of the same stuff. In Falstaff there is something of Hamlet, in Hamlet there is not a little of Falstaff. The fat knight has his moods of melancholy, and the young prince his moments of coarse humour.

Where we differ from each other is purely in accidentals: in dress, manner, tone of voice, religious opinions, personal appearance, tricks of habit, and the like. The more one analyses people, the more all reasons for analysis disappear. Sooner or later one comes to that dreadful universal thing called human nature. Indeed, as any one who has ever worked among the poor knows only too well, the brotherhood of man is no mere poet's dream, it is a most depressing and humiliating reality; and if a writer insists upon analysing the upper classes, he might just as well write of match-girls and coster-mongers at once." However, my dear Cyril, I will not detain you any further just here. I quite admit that modern novels have many good points. All I insist on is that, as a class, they are quite unreadable.

CYRIL

That is certainly a very grave qualification, but I must say that I think you are rather unfair in some of your strictures. I like *The Deemster*, and *The Daughter of Heth*, and *Le Disciple*, and *Mr. Isaacs*, and as for *Robert Elsmere* I am quite devoted to it. Not that I can look upon it as a serious work. As a statement of the problems that confront the earnest Christian it is ridiculous and antiquated. It is simply Arnold's *Literature and Dogma* with the literature left out. It is as much behind the age as Paley's *Evidences*, or Colenso's method of Biblical exegesis. Nor could anything be less impressive than the unfortunate hero gravely heralding a dawn that rose long ago, and so completely missing its true significance that he proposes to carry on the business of the old firm under the new name. On the other hand, it contains several clever caricatures, and a heap of delightful quotations, and Green's philosophy very pleasantly sugars the somewhat bitter pill of the author's fiction. I also cannot help expressing my surprise that you have said nothing about the two novelists whom you are always reading, Balzac and George Meredith. Surely they are realists, both of them?

VIVIAN

Ah! Meredith! Who can define him? His style is chaos illumined by flashes of lightning. As a writer he has mastered everything except language: as a novelist he can do everything, except tell a story: as an artist he is everything, except articulate. Somebody in Shakespeare—Touchstone, I think—talks about a man who is always breaking his shins over his own wit, and it seems to me that this might serve as the basis for a criticism of Meredith's method. But whatever he is, he is not a realist. Or rather I would say that he is a child of realism who is not on speaking terms with his father. By deliberate choice he has made himself a romanticist. He has refused to bow the knee to Baal, and after all, even if the man's fine spirit did not revolt against the noisy assertions of realism, his style would be quite sufficient of itself to keep life at a respectful distance. By its means he has planted round his garden a hedge full of thorns, and red with wonderful roses. As for Balzac, he was a most remarkable combination of the artistic temperament with the scientific spirit. The latter he bequeathed to his disciples: the former was entirely his own. The difference between such a book as M. Zola's *L'Assommoir* and Balzac's *Illusions Perdues* is the difference between unimaginative realism and imaginative reality. "All Balzac's characters," said Baudelaire, "are gifted with the same ardour of life that animated himself. All his fictions are as deeply coloured as dreams. Each mind is a weapon loaded to the muzzle with will. The very scullions have genius." A steady course of Balzac reduces our living friends to shadows, and our acquaintances to the shadows of shades. His characters have a kind of fervent fiery-coloured existence. They dominate us, and defy scepticism. One of the greatest tragedies of my life is the death of Lucien de Rubempré. It is a grief from which I have never been able completely to rid myself. It haunts me in my moments of pleasure. I remember it when I laugh. But Balzac is no more a realist than Holbein was. He created life, he did not copy it. I admit, however, that he set far too high a value on modernity of form, and that, consequently, there is no book of his that, as an artistic masterpiece, can rank with *Salammbô* or *Esmond*, or *The Cloister and the Hearth*, or *The Vicomte de Bragelonne*.

CYRIL

Do you object to modernity of form, then?

VIVIAN

Yes. It is a huge price to pay for a very poor result. Pure modernity of form is always somewhat vulgarizing. It cannot help being so. The public imagine that, because they are interested in their immediate surroundings, Art should be interested in them also, and should take them as her subject-matter. But the mere fact that they are interested in these things makes them unsuitable subjects for Art. The only beautiful things, as somebody once said, are the things that do not concern us. As long as a thing is useful or necessary to us, or affects us in any

way, either for pain or for pleasure, or appeals strongly to our sympathies, or is a vital part of the environment in which we live, it is outside the proper sphere of art. To art's subject-matter we should be more or less indifferent. We should, at any rate, have no preferences, no prejudices, no partisan feeling of any kind. It is exactly because Hecuba is nothing to us that her sorrows are such an admirable motive for a tragedy. I do not know anything in the whole history of literature sadder than the artistic career of Charles Reade. He wrote one beautiful book, *The Cloister and the Hearth*, a book as much above *Romola* as *Romola* is above *Daniel Deronda*, and wasted the rest of his life in a foolish attempt to be modern, to draw public attention to the state of our convict prisons, and the management of our private lunatic asylums. Charles Dickens was depressing enough in all conscience when he tried to arouse our sympathy for the victims of the poor-law administration; but Charles Reade, an artist, a scholar, a man with a true sense of beauty, raging and roaring over the abuses of contemporary life like a common pamphleteer or a sensational journalist, is really a sight for the angels to weep over. Believe me, my dear Cyril, modernity of form and modernity of subject-matter are entirely and absolutely wrong. We have mistaken the common livery of the age for the vesture of the Muses, and spend our days in the sordid streets and hideous suburbs of our vile cities when we should be out on the hillside with Apollo. Certainly we are a degraded race, and have sold our birthright for a mess of facts.

CYRIL

There is something in what you say, and there is no doubt that whatever amusement we may find in reading a purely modern novel, we have rarely any artistic pleasure in re-reading it. And this is perhaps the best rough test of what is literature and what is not. If one cannot enjoy reading a book over and over again, there is no use reading it at all. But what do you say about the return to Life and Nature. This is the panacea that is always being recommended to us.

VIVIAN

I will read you what I say on that subject. The passage comes later on in the article, but I may as well give it to you now:

"The popular cry of our time is 'Let us return to Life and Nature; they will recreate Art for us, and send the red blood coursing through her veins; they will shoe her feet with swiftness and make her hand strong.' But, alas! we are mistaken in our amiable and well-meaning efforts. Nature is always behind the age. And as for Life, she is the solvent that breaks up Art, the enemy that lays waste her house."

CYRIL

What do you mean by saying that Nature is always behind the age?

VIVIAN

Well, perhaps that is rather cryptic. What I mean is this. If we take Nature to mean natural simple instinct as opposed to self-conscious culture, the work produced under this influence is always old-fashioned, antiquated, and out of date. One touch of Nature may make the whole world kin, but two touches of Nature will destroy any work of Art. If, on the other hand, we regard Nature as the collection of phenomena external to man, people only discover in her what they bring to her. She has no suggestions of her own. Wordsworth went to the lakes, but he was never a lake poet. He found in stones the sermons he had already hidden there. He went moralizing about the district, but his good work was produced when he returned, not to Nature, but to poetry. Poetry gave him *Laodamia*, and the fine sonnets, and the great Ode, such as it is. Nature gave him *Martha Ray* and *Peter Bell*, and the

address to Mr. Wilkinson's spade.

CYRIL

I think that view might be questioned. I am rather inclined to believe in the "impulse from a vernal wood," though of course the artistic value of such an impulse depends entirely on the kind of temperament that receives it, so that the return to Nature would come to mean simply the advance to a great personality. You would agree with that, I fancy. However, proceed with your article.

VIVIAN
(*reading*)

"Art begins with abstract decoration, with purely imaginative and pleasurable work dealing with what is unreal and non-existent. This is the first stage. Then Life becomes fascinated with this new wonder, and asks to be admitted into the charmed circle. Art takes life as part of her rough material, recreates it, and refashions it in fresh forms, is absolutely indifferent to fact, invents, imagines, dreams, and keeps between herself and reality the impenetrable barrier of beautiful style, of decorative or ideal treatment. The third stage is when Life gets the upper hand, and drives Art out into the wilderness. This is the true decadence, and it is from this that we are now suffering."

Candour in English Fiction

Thomas Hardy

First published in the New Review, 2 *(January 1890): 15-21.*

Even imagination is the slave of stolid circumstance; and the unending flow of inventiveness which finds expression in the literature of Fiction is no exception to the general law. It is conditioned by its surroundings like a river-stream. The varying character and strength of literary creation at different times may, indeed, at first sight seem to be the symptoms of some inherent, arbitrary, and mysterious variation; but if it were possible to compute, as in mechanics, the units of power or faculty, revealed and unrevealed, that exist in the world at

stated intervals, an approximately even supply would probably be disclosed. At least there is no valid reason for a contrary supposition. Yet of the inequality in its realisations there can be no question; and the discrepancy would seem to lie in contingencies which, at one period, doom high expression to dumbness and encourage the lower forms, and at another call forth the best in expression and silence triviality.

That something of this is true has indeed been pretty generally admitted in relation to art-products of various other kinds. But when observers and critics remark, as they often do remark, that the great bulk of English fiction of the present day is characterised by its lack of sincerity, they usually omit to trace this serious defect to external, or even eccentric causes. They connect it with an assumption that the attributes of insight, conceptive power, imaginative emotion, are distinctly weaker nowadays than at particular epochs of earlier date. This may or may not be the case to some degree; but, on considering the conditions under which our popular fiction is produced, imaginative deterioration can hardly be deemed the sole or even chief explanation why such an undue proportion of this sort of literature is in England a literature of quackery.

By a sincere school of Fiction we may understand a Fiction that expresses truly the views of life prevalent in its time, by means of a selected chain of action best suited for their exhibition. What are the prevalent views of life just now is a question upon which it is not necessary to enter further than to suggest that the most natural method of presenting them, the method most in accordance with the views themselves, seems to be by a procedure mainly impassive in its tone and tragic in its developments.

Things move in cycles; dormant principles renew themselves, and exhausted principles are thrust by. There is a revival of the artistic instincts towards great dramatic motives—setting forth that "collision between the individual and the general"—formerly worked out with such force by the Periclean and Elizabethan dramatists, to name no other. More than this, the periodicity which marks the course of taste in civilised countries does not take the form of a true cycle of repetition, but what Comte, in speaking of general progress, happily characterises as "a looped orbit": not a movement of revolution but—to use the current word—evolution. Hence, in perceiving that taste is arriving anew at the point of high tragedy, writers are conscious that its revived presentation demands enrichment by further truths—in other words, original treatment: treatment which seeks to show Nature's unconsciousness not of essential laws, but of those laws framed merely as social expedients by humanity, without a basis in the heart of things; treatment which expresses the triumph of the crowd over the hero, of the commonplace majority over the exceptional few.

But originality makes scores of failures for one final success, precisely because its essence is to acknowledge no immediate precursor or guide. It is probably to these inevitable conditions of further acquisition that may be attributed some developments of naturalism in French novelists of the present day and certain crude results from meritorious attempts in the same direction by intellectual adventurers here and there among our own authors.

Anyhow, conscientious fiction alone it is which can excite a reflective and abiding interest in the minds of thoughtful readers of mature age, who are weary of puerile inventions and famishing for accuracy; who consider that, in representations of the world, the passions ought to be proportioned as in the world itself. This is the interest which was excited in the minds of the Athenians by their immortal tragedies, and in the minds of Londoners at the first performance of the finer plays of three hundred years ago. They reflected life, revealed life, criticised life. Life being a physiological fact, its honest portrayal must be largely concerned with, for one thing, the relations of the sexes, and the substitution for such catastrophes as favour the false colouring best expressed by the regulation finish that "they married and were happy ever after," of catastrophes based upon sexual relationship as it is. To this expansion English society opposes a well-nigh insuperable bar.

The popular vehicles for the introduction of a novel to the public have grown to be, from one cause and another, the magazine and the circulating library; and the object of the magazine and circulating library is not upward advance but lateral advance; to suit themselves to what is called household reading, which means, or is made to mean, the reading of the majority in a household or of the household collectively. The number of adults, even in a large household, being normally two, and these being the members which, as a rule, have least time on their hands to bestow on current literature, the taste of the majority can hardly be, and seldom is, tempered by the ripe judgment which desires fidelity. However, the immature members of a household often keep an open mind, and they might, and no doubt would, take sincere fiction with the rest but for another condition, almost generally co-existent: which is that adults who would desire true views for their own reading insist, for a plausible but questionable reason, upon false views for the reading of their young people.

As a consequence, the magazine in particular and the circulating library in general do not foster the growth of the novel which reflects and reveals life. They directly tend to exterminate it by monopolising all literary space. Cause and effect were never more clearly conjoined, though commentators upon the result, both French and English, seem seldom if ever to trace their connection. A sincere and comprehensive sequence of the ruling passions, however moral in its ultimate bearings, must not be put on paper as the foundation of imaginative works, which have to claim notice through the above-named channels, though it is extensively welcomed in the form of newspaper reports. That the magazine and library have arrogated to themselves the dispensation of fiction is not the fault of the authors, but of circumstances over which they, as representatives of Grub Street, have no control.

What this practically amounts to is that the patrons of literature—no longer Peers with a taste—acting under the censorship of prudery, rigorously exclude from the pages they regulate subjects that have been made, by general approval of the best judges, the bases of the finest imaginative compositions since literature rose to the dignity of an art. The crash of broken commandments is as necessary an accompaniment to the catastrophe of a tragedy as the noise of drum and cymbals to a triumphal march. But the crash of broken commandments shall not be heard; or, if at all, but gently, like the roaring of Bottom—gently as any sucking dove, or as 'twere any nightingale, lest we should fright the ladies out of their wits. More precisely, an arbitrary proclamation has gone forth that certain picked commandments of the ten shall be preserved intact—to wit, the first, third, and seventh; that the ninth shall be infringed but gingerly; the sixth only as much as necessary; and the remainder alone as much as you please, in a genteel manner.

It is in the self-consciousness engendered by interference with spontaneity, and in aims at a compromise to square with circumstances, that the real secret lies of the charlatanry pervading so much of English fiction. It may be urged that abundance of great and profound novels might be written which should require no compromising, contain not an episode deemed questionable by prudes. This I venture to doubt. In a ramification of the profounder passions the treatment of which makes the great style, something "unsuitable" is sure to arise; and then comes the struggle with the literary conscience. The opening scenes of the would-be great story may, in a rash moment, have been printed in some popular magazine before the remainder is written; as it advances month by month the situations develop, and the writer asks himself, what will his characters do next? What would probably happen to them, given such beginnings? On his life and conscience, though he had not foreseen the thing, only one event could possibly happen, and that

therefore he should narrate, as he calls himself a faithful artist. But, though pointing a fine moral, it is just one of those issues which are not to be mentioned in respectable magazines and select libraries. The dilemma then confronts him, he must either whip and scourge those characters into doing something contrary to their natures, to produce the spurious effect of their being in harmony with social forms and ordinances, or, by leaving them alone to act as they will, he must bring down the thunders of respectability upon his head, not to say ruin his editor, his publisher, and himself.

What he often does, indeed can scarcely help doing in such a strait, is, belie his literary conscience, do despite to his best imaginative instincts by arranging a *denouement* which he knows to be indescribably unreal and meretricious, but dear to the Grundyist and subscriber. If the true artist ever weeps it probably is then, when he first discovers the fearful price that he has to pay for the privilege of writing in the English language—no less a price than the complete extinction, in the mind of every mature and penetrating reader, of sympathetic belief in his personages.

To say that few of the old dramatic masterpieces, if newly published as a novel (the form which, experts tell us, they would have taken in modern conditions), would be tolerated in English magazines and libraries is a ludicrous understatement. Fancy a brazen young Shakespeare of our time—"Othello," "Hamlet," or "Antony and Cleopatra" never having yet appeared—sending up one of those creations in narrative form to the editor of a London magazine, with the author's compliments, and his hope that the story will be found acceptable to the editor's pages; suppose him, further, to have the temerity to ask for the candid remarks of the accomplished editor upon his manuscript. One can imagine the answer that young William would get for his mad supposition of such fitness from any one of the gentlemen who so correctly conduct that branch of the periodical Press.[1]

Were the objections of the scrupulous limited to a prurient treatment of the relations of the sexes, or to any view of vice calculated to undermine the essential principles of social order, all honest lovers of literature would be in accord with them. All really true literature directly or indirectly sounds as its refrain the words in the "Agamemnon": 'Chant Aelinon, Aelinon! but may the good prevail.' But the writer may print the *not* of his broken commandment in capitals of flame; it makes no difference. A question which should be wholly a question of treatment is confusedly regarded as a question of subject.

Why the ancient classic and old English tragedy can be regarded thus deeply, both by young people in their teens and by old people in their moralities, and the modern novel cannot be so regarded; why the honest and uncompromising delineation which makes the old stories and dramas lessons in life must make of the modern novel, following humbly on the same lines, a lesson in iniquity, is to some thinkers a mystery inadequately accounted for by the difference between old and new.

Whether minors should read unvarnished fiction based on the deeper passions, should listen to the eternal verities in the form of narrative, is somewhat a different question from whether the novel ought to be exclusively addressed to those minors. The first consideration is one which must be passed over here; but it will be conceded by most friends of literature that all fiction should not be shackled by conventions concerning budding womanhood, which may be altogether false. It behoves us then to inquire how best to circumvent the present lording of nonage over maturity, and permit the explicit novel to be more generally written.

That the existing magazine and book-lending system will admit of any great modification is scarcely likely. As far as the magazine is concerned it has long been obvious that as a vehicle for fiction dealing with human feeling on a comprehensive scale it is tottering to its fall; and it will probably in the course of time take up openly the position that it already covertly occupies, that of a purveyor of tales for the youth of both sexes, as it assumes that tales for those rather numerous members of society ought to be written.

There remain three courses by which the adult may find deliverance. The first would be a system of publication under which books could be bought and not borrowed, when they would naturally resolve themselves into classes instead of being, as now, made to wear a common livery in style and subject, enforced by their supposed necessities in addressing indiscriminately a general audience.

But it is scarcely likely to be convenient to either authors or publishers that the periodical

form of publication for the candid story should be entirely forbidden, and in retaining the old system thus far, yet ensuring that the emancipated serial novel should meet the eyes of those for whom it is intended, the plan of publication as a *feuilleton* in newspapers read mainly by adults might be more generally followed, as in France. In default of this, or co-existent with it, there might be adopted what, upon the whole, would perhaps find more favour than any with those who have artistic interests at heart, and that is, magazines for adults; exclusively for adults, if necessary. As an offshot there might be at least one magazine for the middle-aged and old.

There is no foretelling; but this (since the magazine form of publication is so firmly rooted) is at least a promising remedy, if English prudery be really, as we hope, only a parental anxiety. There should be no mistaking the matter, no half measures. *La dignite de la pensee*, in the words of Pascal, might then grow to be recognised in the treatment of fiction as in other things, and untrammelled adult opinion on conduct and theology might be axiomatically assumed and dramatically appealed to. Nothing in such literature should for a moment exhibit lax views of that purity of life upon which the well-being of society depends; but the position of man and woman in nature, and the position of belief in the minds of man and woman—things which everybody is thinking but nobody is saying—might be taken up and treated frankly.

---

[1] It is, indeed, curious to consider what great works of the past the notions of the present day would aim to exclude from circulation, if not from publication, if they were issued as new fiction. In addition to those mentioned, think of the "King Oedipus" of Sophocles, the "Agamemnon" of Aeschylus, Goethe's "Faust" and "Wilhelm Meister," the "Prometheus" of Aeschylus, Milton's "Paradise Lost." The "unpleasant subjects" of the two first-named compositions, the "unsuitableness" of the next two, would be deemed equalled only by the profanity of the two last; for Milton, as it is hardly necessary to remind the reader, handles as his puppets the Christian divinities and fiends quite as freely as the Pagan divinities were handled by the Greek and Latin imaginative authors.

The Present State of the English Novel, 1892

George Saintsbury

First published in Miscellaneous Essays *(London: Percival, 1892).*

In discussing the state of the English novel at a time which seems likely to be a rather exceptionally interesting one in the history of a great department of literature in England, it will probably be as well to make the treatment as little of a personal one as possible. Reviews of the *personnel* are in some cases allowable, and are at times not uninteresting: but they are rarely desirable, except when something like ignorance of it is presumable in the reader. When the survey is presented in a form which aims at a certain permanence they are better omitted, and so far as I have availed myself of anything formerly written on the present subject, or subjects akin to it, I have weeded out almost entirely anything like personal and individual reference. An exception or two to this may be found, but they shall be exceptions which certainly do not infringe the rule. In regard, I think, to most living practitioners of the craft, it will be more than possible—it will be a very great advantage—altogether to avoid either naming examples or expressing like and dislike for them.

For the question happens not to be one of liking at all, still less one of ranking novelists, old and new, in order of merit. It is one of setting in order, as well as may be, the chief characteristics of the English novels of the day, and of indicating, with as little rashness as possible, which of them are on the mounting hand and which are on the sinking. And for my part, and in the first place, I do not see any reason to think the reappearance of the romance of adventure at all likely to be a mere passing phenomenon. For the other kind has gone hopelessly sterile in all countries, and is very unlikely to be good for anything unless it is raised anew from seed, and allowed a pretty long course of time. In more than one sense its state was and is (for it still flourishes after a sort) less perilous with us than elsewhere. The habits and public opinion of the nation have kept us from that curious scholasticism of dull uncleanness on which too many French novelists spend their time. There is still too much healthy beefiness and beeriness (much of both as it

has lost) in the English temperament to permit it to indulge in the sterile pessimism which seems to dominate Russian fiction. When we come to the comparison with America, we are getting on very delicate ground. Perhaps the best way of putting the difference is to recall a pleasant observation of Thackeray's, in his remarks on Maginn's *Maxims of O'Doherty*. O'Doherty laid it down (though for himself he thought it "nonsense") as a maxim of fashionable life, that you were to drink champagne after white cheeses, water after red; and Thackeray rejoined very truly that fashionable society did not trouble itself whether you did both, or neither, or either. Now America, a little young at "culture," is taking her literary etiquette books very seriously and trying to obey their minutest directions; while Englishmen, whose literary breeding is of an older stamp and tolerably well established, do not trouble themselves about it at all. For my part, I have said before that I think some of my friends are very hard on Mr. Howells when he makes those comic little critical excursions of his, of which, my prayers having been heard, he has since made a most valuable and instructive collection. Your virtuous beginner always plays the game with surpassing strictness, and is shocked at the lax conduct of oldsters.

In England we have escaped the worst of all these things even yet: though we have been drawing nearer and nearer to them. Half a score at least of writers possessing gifts which range from very considerable talent to decided genius, and perhaps not less than half a thousand possessing gifts ranging from very considerable talent to none at all, have elaborated, partly by their own efforts and partly by following the great models of the last generation, a kind of mixed mode of half-incident, half-character novel, which at its best is sometimes admirable, and at its average is often quite tolerable pastime. We are still curiously behindhand in the short story, the *nouvelle* properly so called, which is not a *märchen*, or a burlesque, or a tale of terror (these three we can sometimes do very well). If there is any falling off, the determined optimist may remember the mercies which tempered the domination of the Campaigner to poor Mr. Binney. If we have cut off the cigars we have considerably improved the claret; or

346

in other words, if we have lost some graces, some charms of the finest and rarest kind, we have greatly bettered the *average*—(I must be pardoned italics here)—the average structure and arrangement of the average novel. How weak a point this has always been with our great novelists, at any rate since the beginning of this century, everybody who has studied literary history knows. Scott never seems to have had the slightest idea of what was going to happen, or how it was going to happen, though as a matter of fact it generally did happen delightfully if irregularly enough. Dickens is supposed to have been very careful about his schemes, though if any man can explain to me what the plot of *Little Dorrit* is; why Mr. Tulkinghorn chose in that entirely irrational and unprofitable manner to persecute Lady Dedlock; why anything, no matter what, happens as it actually does happen in *Hard Times*; and what the sense or meaning of Estella's general conduct is in *Great Expectations*, he will do more than I have ever been able to do for me. Thackeray's sins (if in novel-writing it be not blasphemy to say that Thackeray sinned at all) are gross, palpable, and, for the matter of that, confessed by the sinner. In particular, if any one will try to arrange the chronology of the various Pendennis books, and if his hair does not turn white in the process, he may be guaranteed against any necessity for a peruke arising from similarly hopeless intellectual labour. Of course these things are usually very small faults. But they are faults, and I think that, on the whole, the tendency in average novel-writing during the last twenty years has been to correct them. Again, the average writing of the said novel is decidedly better, and, generally speaking, a distinct advance has been made in the minor details of craftsmanship. There are one or two popular writers, and many not yet popular, who still sin flagrantly in the old direction of taking fair pains over the first and the third volumes and flinging to the public the slovenliest botch of a second that it is likely to tolerate. But this want of literary conscience and literary self-respect is much rarer than it used to be, and appears to be regarded, by younger hands especially, with proper disgust.

Nevertheless I do not think, much as I respect many of its individual practitioners, that the English novel of the day in its average form is a work of art which ranks very high. In the first place, though it has for many years almost wholly devoted itself to character, how many characters has it produced that will live, that will accompany in the memories of posterity the characters of the masters of the past? Very few, I think. We read its books often with pleasure, and sometimes with admiration, at the moment, but they add little to the abiding furniture of our minds and memories. And here let me guard against an objection which is obvious enough, that a man furnishes his mind pretty early, and by the time he comes to forty has no room left. I do not find it so. I have within the last few years, within the last few months, read books for the first time whose characters I am quite certain I shall not forget till I forget everything. Nor am I short of memory, for, as far as mere facts go, I could give plenty of details of many novels published in the last twenty years and more. But very few indeed of their characters and their incidents and stories have taken rank with Partridge at the theatre, with Habakkuk Mucklewrath's dying denunciation of Claverhouse, with Elizabeth Bennet's rejection of Darcy, with Esmond breaking his weapon before Beatrix's princely lover, with Lavengro teaching Armenian to Isopel Berners, with Amyas flinging his sword into the sea. I must confess also that I hold a creed which may seem to some people, perhaps to most, irrational and even childish. I do not think that there is exactly the same amount of genius and of talent always present on the earth, but I do think that in the blossoming times of the intellect the genius and the talent are pretty constant in their total amount. If you get the sum spread widely about you get the kind of work which is now abundant, and nowhere so abundant as in the novel. Of the immense numbers of novels which are now written, a very large proportion cannot be called in any true sense bad, and of the still considerable number which are written by our best men there are few which may not be called in a very real sense good. The great models which they have before them, the large rewards of successful writing, and (for why should not a man magnify his own office?) the constant exposure and reprobation of the grosser faults of novel-writing on the part of critics,[1] have brought about a much higher general level of excellence, a better turn-out of average work, than was ever known before. But, either from the very fact of this imitating and schoolmastering, or from sheer haste, or what not, we do not seem to get the very best things.

Undoubtedly, therefore, the return to the earliest form of writing, to the pure romance of adventure, is a very interesting thing indeed. We do not want here a detailed criticism of the books which have shown it. The point is, that in all the writers have deliberately reverted to the simpler instead of the more complicated kind of novel, trusting more to incident, less to the details of manners and character. I hold that they have done rightly and wisely. For the fictitious (as distinguished from the poetic) portraiture of manners and the fictitious dissection of character deal for the most part with minute and superficial points, and when those points have been attacked over and over again, or when the manners and characters of a time have become very much levelled and mannerised, an inevitable monotony and want of freshness in the treatment comes about. This seems to have been the case more or less in all European languages for a long time past. Except in the most insignificant details, manners have altered very little for the last half-century—a stability which has not been a little increased by the very popularity of novels themselves. A boy or girl now learns manners less from life than from books, and reproduces those manners in his or her own fresh generation. The novel has thus "bred in and in," until the inevitable result of feebleness of strain has been reached. But the incidents, and the broad and poetic features of character on which the romance relies, are not matters which change at all. They are always the same, with a sameness of nature, not of convention. The zest with which we read novels of character and manners is derived, at least in the main, from the unlikeness of the characters and manners depicted. The relish with which we read the great romances in prose, drama, and verse is derived from the likeness of the passions and actions, which are always at bottom the same. There is no danger of repetition here; on the contrary, the more faithful the repetition the surer the success, because the artist is only drawing deeper on a perennial source. In the other case he is working over and over again in shallow ground, which yields a thinner and weedier return at every cropping.

But it will be said, Are we to have nothing new? Are we simply to hunt old trails? Whereto I reply with a *distinguo*. A time may possibly come, may be near at hand, when some considerable change of political or social life may bring about so new a state of manners, and raise into prominence as an ordinary phase so different a side of human character, that the analytic novelist may once more find ready to his hand new material. This in its turn will grow stale, just as the ordinary middle-class person, fairly educated and acquainted with the novelists from Scott downwards, is now getting stale in all European countries, even in those which, like Russia and America, seem as if they ought to have plenty of virgin soil to cultivate. And then that generation, whether it is the next or the next after, will have to return as we are doing to the romance for some-

thing fresh. For the romance is of its nature eternal and preliminary to the novel. The novel is of its nature transitory and is parasitic on the romance. If some of the examples of novels themselves partake of eternity, it is only because the practitioners have been cunning enough to borrow much from the romance. Miss Austen is the only English novelist I know who attains the first rank with something like a defiance of interest of story, and we shall see another Homer before we see another Jane. As for what we often hear about the novel of science, the novel of new forms of religion, the novel of altruism, and Heaven knows what else, it is all stark naught. The novel has nothing to do with any beliefs, with any convictions, with any thoughts in the strict sense, except as mere garnishings. Its substance must always be life not thought, conduct not belief, the passions not the intellect, manners and morals not creeds and theories. Its material, its bottom, must always be either the abiding qualities or the fleeting appearances of social existence, *quicquid agunt homines* not *quicquid cogitant*. In the first and most important division there has been no change within recorded history, and if esoteric Buddhism were to become the Church of England established by law, and a Great British Republic were to take the place of the monarchy, there would be no change in these. There would probably be none if the whole human race were evicted from this earth and re-established in Mars. In the other class of materials there *is* a change, and the very fact of this change necessitates a certain intermission of dead seasons to let the new form germinate and ripen. There is perhaps no reason why a really great romance should not be written at any time. But it is almost impossible that a continuous supply of great character-novels or novels of manners should be kept up and no one will deny that the novel of character and manners has been the favourite until quite recently. And so in a manner *consummatum est*. The average man and woman in England of the middle and late nineteenth century, has been drawn and quartered, analysed and "introspected," till there is nothing new to be done with him or her either as an *écorché*, or with the skin on, or with clothes on the skin. Merely as a man or woman, he or she can still be dealt with profitably, but then you have a romance and not a novel. Unfortunately, many of our best proved writers continue to write the novel and not the romance, or to treat the romance as if it were the novel. Thus we do not, and for this and the other reasons given and to be given, we cannot, get the best things.

We get indeed many things that are good: good in ways which not so many years ago were unexpected if not undesired. The present year is the twentieth from that in which I first began to review novels, and during the earlier part of the intervening period it was possible, without being unduly given to pessimism, to take a very gloomy view of the future of English fiction, not merely on the considerations just advanced but for other reasons. The novelists of the elder generation were dropping off one by one, and were not in their later years giving anything that could on just critical estimate rank with even their own best work. No actual "youngsters" of decided genius or even very remarkable talent had appeared in the early seventies. Between the old and the new there were practitioners of various, sometimes of great, ability, but hardly any who fulfilled the two conditions of absolutely great literature. The first of these is that something—phrase, personality, situation, what not—shall survive the reading of the book, the second that it shall be impossible to read it once only—that it shall of necessity and imperatively take its place on the shelves of that smaller library of predilection which the greater library even of the most limited book-collector contains. One exception there has been indeed to this throughout the whole period, and he to whom I refer remains an exception still. I remember when as a boy I read *The Ordeal of Richard Feverel*, thinking more or less dimly that here was a man from whom at any time an *Esmond* or an *Antiquary*, a *Manon Lescaut* (though I do not think I had read *Manon* then) or a *Trois Mousquetaires* might be expected. Thirty years later I read *One of Our Conquerors* with feelings almost exactly the same. I do not know whether Mr. Meredith will write that book yet—I know no reason why he should not. Defoe was on the eve of sixty when he wrote *Robinson Crusoe*, and Dryden was on the eve of seventy when he wrote the *Fables*.

During the last ten or fifteen years, but especially during the last five or ten, things have been different. There has been a great stir among the dry bones. Some new comers, of power which would have been remarkable at any time, have arisen: not a few oldsters have aroused themselves to take their craft very seriously, and perhaps to magnify their office even a little overmuch: journeyings have been made by well-willing neophytes and others to the ends of the earth for models and motives: an immense enthusiasm has been shown for that one representative of the giant race before the flood who has just been referred to. There have been

schools, methods, a propaganda, and indeed more than one—

> Principle! principle! principle! that's what I
>   hears 'em say,

if the Laureate will pardon me. Our novelists have been, whether by self-examination or by stress of critics, convinced of sin in the matter of not taking enough trouble with the style of their books, with the plot, with the general stage management and stage carpentry. One has said to himself, "Go to, let us treat life with candour"; another, "Shall I live and die in respect of the young person?"; a third, "Is there not something to be made of the undogmatically Christian romance?"; a fourth, "Let us cease to be insular"; a fifth, "A bas l'incident!"; a sixth (this is a rather favourite cry just now), "Let us raise language to a higher power and never say anything simply." Even that other symptom of the uprising of novelists against critics, and their demand that every newspaper shall give at least a column to the sober and serious laudation (for nothing else is to be thought of) of every serious work of fiction that issues from the press, is, though rather a grotesque, a cheering and healthy sign. The novelist, like the actor and the poet, is taking his *sacerdoce* sacerdotally, and is indignant at being treated lightly by the profane. This is, I say, a healthy sign: and should be reverently treated by those who have only too much difficulty in taking themselves or anything else with due seriousness.

But when we come to look a little narrowly into the results of this activity it may be that they will not strike us as altogether in correspondence. I saw not long ago a half-shamefaced apology for the singular succession of roars which has of late years hailed the advent of divers new novelists and novels. This vociferation, it was urged, was at any rate better than a nasty cold system of ignoring or sneering at the lambs of the flock. I am not quite so sure of that. As a critic I begin to feel myself like Mr. Browning's legate, and am constantly murmuring, "I have known *four*-and-twenty new stars in the firmament of the English novel." This state of things, looked at from a personal point of view, is no doubt pleasant—for the four-and-twentieth, and until the five-and-twentieth appears. But I doubt whether the three-and-twenty like it, and what is of much more importance, I doubt whether it is a good state of things either for the stars or the star-gazers, the latter especially. It must sometimes have seemed to cool-headed onlookers during the last few years that the British public, critics and all, had simply lost all faculty of distinguishing good from bad. Among the new reputations of the last decade we all know some cases not merely of undoubted and quite remarkable talent—of talent that must have made its way at any time, though it might have made it more healthily under a less forcing system—but of something that may be called genius by those who are least prodigal of the word. And we all—all of us who are in the least critical—know some cases either of utter worthlessness or of worth so excessively small that one wonders how on earth it has come to be recognised. This can hardly be a healthy state of things—states of "boom" seldom or never are signs of real health in the business in which they from time to time occur. Indeed, if nothing else were considered save the encouragement to over-production, the case would be perilous enough. It is sometimes the fashion to throw Scott in the face of those who demur to it, and who are very often admirers of Scott. But it seems to be forgotten that when Scott began novel-writing seriously he was a man far advanced in life, with an immense accumulated experience of reading, of society, of business, even of the practice of literature in other kinds. This is not usually the case with those new novelists of whom we have recently had about one a year, and of whom we may, it seems, shortly expect one a month. Once more let it be said that some at least of these new novelists would have made their way at any time and against any odds. But the others—would not.

However, let us count the positive gains of this recent bustle. These are at least three—variety of method and subject, increased carefulness of treatment, and increased carefulness of style. Perhaps all three are chequered advantages, but they are advantages. Some fifteen years ago the novel, the unconquerable unconventionality of Mr. Meredith once more excepted, had certainly got rather into a rut. The difference between George Eliot and Miss Yonge, between Mr. Trollope and Mr. Black—to take examples as widely different in appearance as possible, but all of the upper class of novelists—might at first seem huge, but when it was subjected to true critical analysis it became very much smaller. Hardly anything—I do not say nothing—was cultivated but the novel as opposed to the romance; and the novel was for the most part further narrowed to ordinary upper middle-class English life. Now we have at least altered all that. The differences may still be a little more apparent than real, but the reality has advanced in proportion

far more than the appearance. We have revived the romance, if not on the greatest scale, on a scale which, with almost the solitary exceptions in the first class of *Lorna Doone* and *Westward Ho!* a whole generation had not seen. We have wound ourselves up to something like the pitch of the Romantics of sixty or seventy years ago in our demand for local colour, and that not merely external, as theirs too often was, but the local colour which derives from local peculiarities of thought and feeling, of manners and life. We have to a great extent shaken off the "diffusion-of-knowledge" Philistinism and the "sword-and-pen" cant of the middle of the century. If we are not more gay in some sense (for 'tis a generation which jocks wi' extreme deeficulty), we are much more what I believe the very newest school of critics calls *bunt*. In short, we are "boxing it about" merrily, with the old Jacobite confidence that "it will come to our father." Let us hope it will.

At the same time there is no doubt that the English novelist of the present day, incited partly by his study of foreign models and partly by the exhortations of the wicked critics, whose crimes he is never tired of denouncing (especially when, as frequently happens, he is holding the pen of the critic himself), has bestirred himself mightily in the matter of construction. Something has been said already on this point, and there is no doubt that, from having been the most scholarly of all novelists in the last century, Englishmen had become the most haphazard and lawless in this. We have altered that too to some extent—nay, to a great one. From the teller of short tales who bestirs himself to take away the well-known reproach from England, to the constructor of three-deckers who labours to avoid the razeeing of that time-honoured form, by constructing it more conscientiously and scientifically, all our "fictionists" (as, I regret to observe, they allow some of their admirers to call them without instantly taking the offenders' lives) are as busy as bees. And they are as busy once more in the direction of style, where also their predecessors, good easy men, used to be a little, nay, more than a little, remiss. Here Mr. Meredith's epigrams and his quaint remotely worded pictures in phrase are religiously copied as far as the copier can. There the dissection and mounting on microscopic slides of action and thought which have become fashionable in America occupy the reformers. A third set shall be found vying with one another in the endeavour to select and stick together the most gorgeous adjectives, to use words in the most unfamiliar, not to say impossible senses. In short, there is, as Mr. Carlyle observed in one of the best because one of the quietest of his sardonic passages, a cheerful appearance of work going forward. And to do the workers justice, their intention is not, as in that case, destruction at all, but on the contrary construction.

How far has that intention been attained, and what are the drawbacks attending these efforts? This is the less cheerful, but perhaps also the more important, side of the subject. It would be uncritical to attack it by asking whether any, and if so what, remarkable books have been produced. Remarkable books may be and are produced at any time when there happen to be remarkable book-producers. The last decade in England has seen at least three, perhaps more, new writers of fiction who would have been remarkable at any time. But the things to put the finger on if possible are not these prize specimens, but the general results of the efforts just described. And perhaps here we shall have occasion to remember once more that exceedingly uncomfortable proverb "Seldom comes a better."

For the advantages above chronicled, with, I trust, impartiality and the absence of prejudice, have brought divers disadvantages in their train. To begin with, there is that extraordinary oppression which weighs upon so many of our novelists in regard to what is called the Young Person. For some time past divers of our most eminent hands have been lifting themselves up against the Young Person, deploring the terrible restraints that she imposes on their growing reputation, occasionally even emancipating themselves from her in a timid British way, and committing excesses in another variety of that shivering consciousness of sin which made Leigh Hunt, when he was a little boy of seven, and had said a naughty word, for a long time afterwards, when anybody took kind notice of him, say to himself, "Ah, they little think I'm the boy who said d—n!" Ambition to be the boy who says d—n causes these fiery souls to languish. But why do they not say d—n, and have done with it? The creeping and gingerly approaches to continental licenses of speech and subject which we have seen lately seem to me, I confess, inexpressibly puerile.

Nor can I doubt that on the whole the general convention of English novelists during this century has been a sound one. There is, so far as I know, only one instance—Scott's alteration of the plot of *St. Ronan's Well*—where it did distinct, unremedied, irremediable harm. I very much doubt whether *Pendennis* would have been improved by the different cast of one of its episodes which some of my friends desiderate, and I am sure *Vanity Fair* positively gains by the ambiguity in which Becky's technical "guilt" is left. The fact is that the spring of what is very liberally called passion is one which, in appearance facile and powerful, is really a very difficult one to bring into play, and is lamentably monotonous and ineffective when abused, as it is apt to be. For my part, I would excuse either novelist or poet for violating any convention of the kind, but only on the admirable old condition that he comes in with a rope about his neck and is strung up ruthlessly if he fails to produce a masterpiece.

This, however, is of course only part of the great Realist mistake, and that has been spoken of already, and elsewhere. The rules as I take it, if rules can be spoken of in such a matter, are two only. The first is "Disrealise everything, and never forget that whatever art is, it is not nature." The second is the same as that just given, "Try all things if you like: but if you try the exceptional, the abnormal, the unconventional, remember that you try it at your own peril, and that you must either make a great success or an intolerable and inexcusable failure."

So far, however, we are concerned simply with the subject; and as a rule very little depends in any art on the subject. The most that the subject can do is to give the measure of the artist in point of strength. If he is a good artist it does not matter how bad the subject is: if he is a bad artist it does not matter how good the subject is. All really depends on the treatment; and here we get into quite a different region—a region, however, which happens to be that which chiefly invites our attention. The two chief innovations in treatment which have been seen in the period under discussion, and the signs of which are most particularly evident at the present moment, are innovations, the one in handling incident, situation, motive, and so forth, the other in style.

The first may be said to consist in a great extension, as compared with the practice ever since the revival of the novel some eighty years ago, of the representation of the component parts, the intermediate processes, of thought and action. This is not in itself new: nothing is. Another form was, or, rather, other forms of this extension were conspicuous in the novel of Richardson in England and Marivaux in France. The last great practitioner of it was Miss Austen, who indeed raised it to something like absolute perfection; but it died with her among ourselves, at the same time, within a few years, as that at which Benjamin Constant in *Adolphe* was producing the last masterpiece of its older manner in France. With us it had no immediate resurrection: it was hardly dead in France before it was revived with a considerable difference by Beyle and Balzac on the other side of the Channel: and this later form, with many alterations and variants, is that which has survived in other countries to this day, is more popular in some of them than ever, and has from their practice been regrafted upon the English novel. The completest exaggerations of it are to be found in America and Russia. Now of this kind of novel (to use the singular for convenience sake) it is sometimes said that "the story is abolished," that "nothing happens," and so forth. This is, of course, not strictly true. A good deal often happens in Russian novels, and I have read American stories of the straitest sect in which incident was not entirely tabooed. But in both the poor creature is taught to know its place. The story, even if there is one, is of the last importance: the solemn and painstaking indication, as was said of Marivaux, of "everything you have said, and everything you have thought, and everything you would have liked to think but did not," is of the first. Instead of the presentation of the result you have an endless description of the process; instead of a succinctly presented quotient, an endless array of dividends and divisors. To say that this is never satisfactory would be too much: I know at least one instance, Count Tolstoi's *Ivan Ilyitch*, which may defy criticism. But this very instance shows that the success is a *tour de force*, and it has never, that I know of, been reached in a long story by any one. As a contrast to the average Russian and American novel, take that admirable masterpiece *Pepita Jimenez*. Señor Valera is, I believe, sometimes pointed at for theirs by the ghostly Banquos of the analytic school. O creatures as unfortunate as doleful! It would be impossible to find a more complete or convincing *instantia contradictoria* of their principles. The only weak points in the book are those which draw to their side. Its interest depends on the manners-painting, the characters, and the story, the three things that they never reach, or reach in spite of their tendency to potter and trifle. Fortunately it cannot be said that this particular form has laid much hold on us, but it has laid some, and I expect it to lay more. For it is naturally attractive to the half-educated: and half-education is advancing with us by leaps and bounds.

It is also to this kind of imperfect culture that the other innovation of treatment, which has been widely described as one of style, appeals. This is more rampant with us, but it has also a more plausible pretext for ramping, for it has excuses of precedent contrast, and excuses of precedent pattern. Scott was notoriously and confessedly a rather careless writer, and the fashion of writing, either in parts separately published or in chapters of magazines, which set in after his death was the very likeliest fashion in the world to encourage careless writing. On the other hand, some of the most popular, and some of the greatest novelists of the second and third quarters of the century—Dickens, George Eliot, Mr. Meredith—wide apart as they were in other ways, agreed in having styles the reverse of careless, styles mannered and mannerised to the very *n*-th. We know from their own descriptions how some much younger writers of fiction have set themselves to acquire manners of their own: we know from their books how they and others have succeeded.

It would be superfluous to repeat here the various remarks bearing on the exact amount and character of that success which will be found in certain earlier essays of this volume. But, as I was writing this paper, a passage remarkably to the point came before me in the latest published volume of the *Journal des Goncourt*, the last, as M. Edmond de Goncourt assures us, that we shall have in his lifetime. He was a little annoyed, it seems, at finding that his old friend Flaubert had, in his correspondence with George Sand, spoken disrespectfully of the Goncourtian epithet. "No, my dear Flaubert," retorts M. de Goncourt, "*you* had not the epithets *osées, téméraires et personnelles* which authors who shall be nameless have. You had only *les épithètes, excellemment bonnes, de tout le monde.*" Now there is no doubt that "les deux Goncourt," whatever may be thought of the positive value of their work, did anticipate, and have for many years (less excellently, perhaps, since the death of M. Jules, but that is neither here nor there) exhibited the tendencies and preoccupations as to style which have prevailed among the more careful men of letters in all European countries during the last quarter of the nineteenth century. Unfortunately, it seems to me that the distinction which M. de Goncourt here puts sharply and well tells in a direction exactly opposite to that in which he intended it to tell. The epithets of genius are exactly the epithets *de tout le monde*, but "good to an excellent degree." These are the epithets of Shakespeare, of Dante, of Homer, of all who have the Shakespearian, the Homeric, the Dantesque qualities. It is the attainment of this "excellent" degree that is the test-rub of genius. Whereas the "daring," the "rash," the "personal" epithet, which is the special game and object of talent, and especially of the talent of our day, stands in an entirely different category. When the talent is great the epithet is sometimes very happy, and you give it a hearty hand of approbation, as to the successful trick of a master in conjuring. It is sometimes anything but happy, and if you are well-bred you do not hiss it, but let it pass with as much indulgence as may be, like the *couac* of a generally well-graced singer. In the lower order of attempts, it is at its best a little fatiguing, at its worst utterly unendurable. Never does it excite the immediate assent, the almost silent rapture, the intense unceasing ever-novel admiration which are aroused by the great efforts of genius in making the common as though it were not common, in sublimating the ordinary language terrestrial to the seventh heaven.

Now it stands, I think, to reason that the deliberate seeker after style will too often stray in the direction of the *osé*, the *téméraire*, the *personnel*, not merely in epithets but in other things. Whether it stands to reason or not he certainly does it; and though there may not be many at the moment who perceive his error, the meet consequences of that error never have failed, and are never likely to fail. They are also, as it happens, illustrated unusually well in the history of novels. I have myself gone about for many years—a very different and inferior La Fontaine—asking "Avez vous lu?" *Hysminias and Hysmine*, which the books of reference sometimes call *Ismenias and Ismene*. There must be people who have read it, though I never personally met one. Here, in a very wonderful kind of Greek (it is perfectly useless to attempt to read the book in a translation, for all its charms are necessarily lost), did a certain person of the twelfth century, by genius of anticipation or following of originals mostly lost to us, concentrate in one book Euphuism, Marivauage, aestheticism, divers isms of the present day—which I could only indicate by taking divers respected proper names in vain—even Naturalism in a way, except that the author was a gentleman after his Lower Empire fashion. If the task of reading him is too great—and I must own that his lingo is extraordinary and his matter of a marvellous tediousness—there is Lyly, there is Madeleine de Scudery, there is Marivaux, there is the Mr. Cumberland whom gods call Sir Fretful, there are the followers of Mrs. Radcliffe, there are many others, great and small, persons of genius, persons of talent, and persons equally destitute of either. They do not always aim especially or principally at style, but they often do so, and they always expend an immense determination, an almost piteous en-

deavour, on the attempt to do something great by taking thought, by exaggerating popular fashions, by running directly counter to them, by being eccentric, by being scrupulously correct, by anything, in short, but waiting for the shepherd's hour and profiting thereby in the best and most straightforward way they can.

The point to which we are coming will no doubt have been foreseen for a long time. It is that in this busy, this conscientious, this serious period of novel-writing, our novelists are, as a rule, far too much of Marthas and far too little of Maries. They cumber themselves tremendously about the fashion of serving us, and it seems horribly ungracious to criticise the viands served; yet it may be permissible to suggest that they are in the wrong way. They seem to be beguiled by the dictum—true and important enough in itself—that novel-writing is an art. It is—and a fine art. No doubt also all art has its responsibilities. But the responsibilities of different arts are different, and the methods of discharging them are different too. What makes the art of literature in general the most difficult of all is the fact that nowhere is it more necessary to take pains, and yet that nowhere is mere painstaking not merely so insufficient but so likely to lead the artist wrong. And in this particular division of the literary art there is the still further difficulty that it is easiest, most obvious, and in the special circumstances of recent English literature apparently most praiseworthy, to take pains about those things which are not the root of the matter. In poetry the so-called "formal" part is of the essence. A halting verse, a cacophonous rhyme, a lack of musical accompaniment and atmosphere, will render unpoetical the very finest, and in happier circumstances the most really poetical, thoughts. Yet even in poetry attention to these formal matters will but rarely—it will sometimes when it is extraordinary—do of itself. In prose fiction, the nearest to poetry of the kinds of literature when it is at its best, the case is quite different. It is a pity that a novel should not be well written: yet some of the greatest novels of the world are, as no one of the greatest poems of the world is, or could possibly be, written anything but well. It is, at any rate, rather annoying that the plot of a novel should hang loosely together, that the chronology should be obviously impossible, that the author should forget on page 200 what page 100 has told his readers, that there should be little beginning, less middle, and no end. Yet some of the great, some of the greatest novels of the world, are open to objections of this kind. The truth is, that the novel is, while the poem is not, mainly and firstly a criticism of life. Great truths always lurk in great errors, and Naturalism, with its kindred faults, reveals this truth at once. The life may be life as it is, and we have the novel proper—life as we would have it to be, and we have the romance; but one or the other, not photographed, not grovellingly dissected, but rendered in the mediums and by the methods proper to art, it must be. All the requirements of the novelist are subsidiary and secondary to this, that he shall in his pages show us the result of the workings of the heart and brain, of the body, soul, and spirit of actual or possible human beings. Poetry is not limited—novel writing is.

Now the mistake of many of our careful and clever ones at the present day seems to me sometimes that, forgetting this chief and principal thing, they concentrate themselves on the secondary and subsidiary matters; sometimes that, accepting the requirement of rendering life, they prove unequal to it. I have already said that I would not have any subject ruled out as such. Remembering what a certain dramatist did with a certain Bellafront centuries ago, I should not be disposed to refuse permission to a certain novelist to experiment with a certain Tess, though I greatly prefer the straightforwardness of the earlier artist's title. I think that many attempts, and an exactly equal number of failures, have shown the impossibility of making a great historical character of whom much is directly known the central and ostensible hero or heroine of a novel: but if any will try it, he or she may try it at their own peril, and I will applaud if they succeed. I can even conceive (though I have never read one) a novel in which undogmatic Christianity might play a considerable part, and which yet might be readable, and a novel. We have not, as it seems to me, a right to complain of any experiments: we have only a right to complain when experiments are made in the teeth of the teaching of experience, and do not succeed. Paradox, crotchet, new moralities, new theories of religion—all may be susceptible of being made into novels that ought to live and will live. It only seems to me that at the present day our clever novelists are a great deal too fond of deliberately selecting the most unsuitable materials and then endeavouring to varnish over the rickety construction with fine writing, with fashionable tricks of expression or treatment, with epithets *osées*, *téméraires et personnelles*, with doses of popular talk.

One special difficulty which besets the novelist, and of which he not infrequently complains when he aims at excellence, remains to be noticed. He is at the present moment, perhaps, the only artist whose art is liable to be confounded with the simple business of the ordinary tradesman. There is, and has been for at least two generations—perhaps indeed for three or four—a certain steady and increasing demand for "something to read" in the way of fiction. There are no parallels, so far as I know, to his difficulty in this respect. The only persons who stand in the same position are the purveyor of sermons and the purveyor of newspaper articles. But neither of these is expected, and it is entirely at his own risk if either undertakes, to present himself as a maker of books, that is to say, as a producer of something which is intended to last. The novel-producer, as distinguished from the novelist, is in really evil case in this matter: and the novelist, as distinguished from the novel-producer, is perhaps in worse. Nobody insists (thank Heaven!) that the usual journalist shall produce all his articles, or the usual preacher all his sermons, for the year in book form:—I can answer for one class that some representatives of it, at any rate, though they may try to do their work as well as possible, would be horrified at the idea. The requirements of the circulating library insist upon the novel-producer doing this very thing: and as we know, the novelist, or he who hopes that he is a novelist, is very angry at the confusion which thus arises from their both addressing the same lady. It is natural, it is inevitable, that the results of this confusion should be almost always bad. When a man, as has just been said, caters for the general in sermon or article or platform speech, it is perfectly understood that he does not, except as a secondary thing and at his own peril and distinct volition, enter for any other stakes or seek to gain the Land of Matters Unforgot. When a man writes verse and publishes it, he does in form enter for the stakes, but the race is not run in public. The minor bard competes, except in the rarest instances, for his own pleasure before an extremely select audience composed of a few critics and a number, which it rests with him to limit in one direction and with themselves to limit in another, of holders of presentation copies. For myself I own that I am rather fond of reading minor poetry—much fonder of it than of reading minor novels. But that is a purely personal detail. It is an understood thing that the minor poet is not—I do not say that he does not wish to be—read. He publishes either because he cannot help it or because he likes it. The ambition of the curate, of the leader-writer, of the platform speaker, is sufficed by the day or the day after. But the unhappy novelist is obliged by the state of the demand to divulge himself widely, and put himself on more or less perpetual record. There are those of his kind who are very angry with the managers of literary newspapers for taking account of this fact. They would have literary notice restricted to novels which aim at something higher than the circulating library demand. I have never indeed, being a person with some experience of newspapers, understood quite how their demand is to be complied with. Is the editor to read every novel and decide whether it is novel-journalism or novel-literature? I think this is barely feasible, for even an editor's day has but twenty-four hours, and even an editor's brain requires occasional rest and refreshment. Is he to have a special novel-referee, one, in fact, to whom all novels are to be handed over, and according to whose dictum they are to be reviewed or not? The selection of such referees would be difficult, and would, to take an abominably prosaic view, cost the proprietors of newspapers a vast sum of money, for which, except in prayers and curses, they would certainly not receive any appreciable return. Or are the deciding persons to be guided by name, vogue, previous work? In this I am bound again, from no small experience, to express my fear that a great deal of injustice would be done by inclusion in the selected circle, and a little (but the most serious in the long-run) by exclusion from it.

This may seem something of a digression: but it has a real connection with our subject. It is easily conceivable that when journalism and literature are in this way inextricably mixed and blended, almost any means will seem justifiable, nay, praiseworthy, to the aspirant to literature who wishes to declare himself, at once and unmistakably, to be other than those who are content with journalism. And this being so, we can hardly wonder at that strain and stress which I have noticed as marking our present more ambitious novels, without on the whole any corresponding excellence of result. Except at very rare intervals, it is acknowledged that a nation is a lucky nation if it possesses half a dozen persons who really deserve the name of poet: and if the poets in the course of an ordinary human life fill half a dozen volumes of the ordinary content of the volume of a circulating library novel, it is acknowledged that they have done very handsomely. We expect to have our novelists by dozens, by scores, by hundreds, and we expect them to produce their volumes, if not by hundreds, yet almost by scores,

and certainly by dozens. Is this reasonable? Is this treating the artist as he deserves to be treated?[2] I do not take the other side and say, Is the acceptance of such an expectation and the attempt to fulfil it worthy of the novelist? For then we get into that hopeless and endless question of what Mr. Anthony Trollope used delicately to call "details"—meaning thereby pounds, shillings, and pence—of the arguing of which there is no end, and which, after all, does not concern novel-writing more than any other kind of literature except in one point which is a little important. It *is* much more difficult for the novelist pure and simple to write, as it has been phrased, "articles for money and books for love," than for almost any other variety of man of letters. His novel-journalism without his name would be a drug: and with his name it at once enters into competition with his novel-literature.

It may seem as if I were shaping a course towards the somewhat paradoxical proposition that it will never be merry with novelists till the public gives over reading novels. And indeed there might be something to be said for this, for as long as the public insists on novels by the hundred and five hundred every year to read, certain things will follow. There will be a vast amount of unworthy stuff produced: there will be now and then for popular (not necessarily or probably for good) novels those huge prizes which entice more and more competitors into the race. There will be more and more the inducement, subtly extending, at once for the tradesman who aspires to be popular and for the artist who aspires to be good, to strive for distinction of whatever kind by illegitimate or scarcely legitimate means—by oddity, by license, by quaintness, by strangeness, by spreading the sail, no matter at what angle, to the *popularis aura*. Demand no doubt creates supply, and supply stimulates demand: but what sort of each does the reflex action produce? I fear that churlish thing, the study of history, would reply, A supply that is by turns cheap and nasty, or distinguished from the cheap and nasty by fantastic preciousness; a demand that is by turns coarse and uncritical or squeamish and morbid.

And all this while there may be some who remember that the novel has never yet shown itself an enduring form in literature; that it rose very late, and so may be expected not to die—nothing dies—but to dwindle or change very early; that it has already had an almost unexampled flourishing time in slightly different varieties of one particular form; and that as for many centuries of ascertained progress, or rather continuance, in literature the unchanging human mind was content with brief and occasional indulgences in it, it is by no means impossible that the period of this particular indulgence is drawing to a close. To such reminders I neither assent wholly nor do I wholly rule them out. The printing-press and the common half-educated reader must be taken into consideration. No former age possessed this combination of means to produce supply and circumstances to create demand. The newspaper and the novel, though each has produced in its time literature of the highest value, are both in themselves rather low forms of literature, and it is, I believe, an axiom of physical science, which has given itself to observing such things, that the low form is the most tenacious of life. As long as the Board School lasts, the ordinary manufacture of newspapers and novels must go on—a reflection which may have its consolations to those who are obliged to get their living by working at either mill. But whether either art or craft is likely to develop improvements such as will render it more prolific of real literature, that is one of the too numerous things which are "obscure to all except to God." The novel has at least produced some of nearly the greatest things in literature; this is its great, its exceeding great merit. That it has produced vast volumes of things that to-day are and tomorrow are cast into the oven, is not perhaps, rightly considered, a fact for regret.

And so we end with *Quien sabe?* Enormous fatalism, I take it, impresses itself on careful students of the history of literature—so obstinate is the wind in blowing where it listeth without the slightest reference either to the literary clerk of the weather, or to ingenious and diligent persons who, like our young officers in Burmah, get up on high places and explode large quantities of blasting powder in the hope of coaxing or forcing the wind and the rain with it. All things are possible in a time when a novelist of real talent like M. Zola dismisses Sir Walter Scott as a "boarding-school novelist," and when a critic of real intelligence like my friend Mr. Brander Matthews takes Mr. Howells for an excellent critic. The safer plan is to stand still and see the wondrous works of the Lord. After all, the critic and the prophet are two extremely different persons: and criticism has not been usually most happy when it meddled with prophecy.

---

[1] At the same time I must admit that I could not undertake to teach the complete art of novel-writing in so many lessons. I was obliged once to confess as much, to a very amiable person who, in consequence of a critique of mine, sent me a cheque with an agreeable apology for its not being larger, and a request for more of that excellent advice. It was not possible to keep his cheque; but I have always thought that he must have been a very nice man. As a general rule authors do not send such documents to their critics; you may go a long way "without a cheque" on that road.

[2] Since this was written I have found a counterpart of this argument in M. Ferdinand Brunetière's just published *Essais sur la Littérature Contemporaine*, art. "Critique et Roman," an excellent example of the author's robust polemic, which, however, takes more of a side than I think it necessary to take in a quarrel which would be much better unfought.

The Place of Realism in Fiction

George Gissing

First published in the Humanitarian *(July 1895).*

One could wish, to begin with, that the words *realism* and *realist* might never again be used, save in their proper sense by writers on scholastic philosophy. In relation to the work of novelists they never had a satisfactory meaning, and are now become mere slang. Not long ago I read in a London newspaper, concerning some report of a miserable state of things among a certain class of work-folk, that "this realistic description is absolutely truthful," where by *realistic* the writer simply meant painful or revolting, with never a thought of tautology. When a word has been so grievously mauled, it should be allowed to drop from the ranks.

Combative it was, of course, from the first. Realism, naturalism, and so on signified an attitude of revolt against insincerity in the art of fiction. Go to, let us picture things as they are. Let us have done with the conventional, that is to say, with mere tricks for pleasing the ignorant and the prejudiced. Let the novelist take himself as seriously as the man of science; be his work to depict with rigid faithfulness the course of life, to expose the secrets of the mind, to show humanity in its eternal combat with fate. No matter how hideous or heartrending the results; the artist has no responsibility save to his artistic conscience. The only question is, has he wrought truly, in matter and form? The leaders of this revolt emphasized their position by a choice of vulgar, base, or disgusting subjects; whence the popular understanding of the term *realist*. Others devoted themselves to a laborious picturing of the dullest phases of life; inoffensive, but depressing, they invested *realism* with another quite accidental significance. Yet further to complicate and darken the discussion, it is commonly supposed that novelists of this school propound a theory of life, by preference that known as "pessimism." There is but one way out of this imbroglio: to discard altogether the debated terms, and to inquire with regard to any work of fiction, first, whether it is sincere, secondly, whether it is craftsmanlike.

Sincerity I regard as of chief importance. I am speaking of an art, and, therefore, take for granted that the worker has art at his command; but art, in the sense of craftsman's skill, without sincerity of vision will not suffice. This is applicable to both branches of fiction, to romance and to the novel; but with romance we are not here concerned. It seems to me that no novel can possess the slightest value which has not been conceived, fashioned, elaborated, with a view to depicting some portion of human life as candidly and vividly as is in the author's power. Other qualities may abound in the work; some others must needs be present. Tragic power, pathos, humour, sportiveness, tenderness: the novelist may have them one or all; constructive ability and the craft of words he cannot dispense with. But these gifts will not avail him as a novelist if he lack the spirit of truthfulness, which, be it added, is quite a different thing from saying that no novel can be of worth if it contain errors of observation, or fall short of the entire presentment of facts.

What do we mean by "reality"? Science concerns itself with facts demonstrable to every formal understanding; the world of science we call "real," having no choice but to accept it as such. In terms of art, reality has another signification. What the artist sees is to him only a part of the actual; its complement is an emotional effect. Thus it comes about that every novelist beholds a world of his own, and the supreme endeavour of his art must be to body forth that world as it exists for him. The novelist works, and must work, subjectively. A demand for objectivity in fiction is worse than meaningless, for apart from the personality of the workman no literary art can exist. The cry arose, of course, in protest against the imperfect method of certain novelists, who came forward in their own pages, and spoke as showmen; but what can be more absurd than to talk about the "objectivity" of such an author as Flaubert, who triumphs by his extraordinary power of presenting life as he, and no other man, beheld it? There is no science of fiction. However energetic and precise the novelist's preparation for his book, all is but dead material until breathed upon by "the shaping spirit of imagination," which is the soul of the individual artist. Process belongs to the workshop; the critic of the completed work has only to decide as to its truth—that is to say, to judge the spirit in which it was conceived, and the technical merit of its execution.

Realism, then, signifies nothing more than artistic sincerity in the portrayal of contemporary life; it merely contrasts with the habit of mind which assumes that a novel is written "to please people," that disagreeable facts must always be kept out of sight, that human nature must be systematically flattered, that the book must have a "plot," that the story should end on a cheerful note, and all the rest of it. Naturally the question arises: What limits does the independent novelist impose upon himself? Does he feel free to select *any* theme, from the sweetest to the most nauseating? Is it enough to declare that he has looked upon this or that aspect of life, has mirrored it in his imagination, and shows it forth candidly, vividly? For my own part, I believe that he must recognise limits in every direction; that he will constantly reject material as unsuitable to the purposes of art; and that many features of life are so completely beyond his province that he cannot dream of representing them. At the same time I joyfully compare the novelist's freedom in England of to-day with his bondage of only ten or twelve years ago. No doubt the new wine of liberty tempts to excess. Moreover, novels nowadays are not always written for the novel's sake, and fiction cries aloud as the mouthpiece of social reform. The great thing is, that public opinion no longer constrains a novelist to be false to himself. The world lies open before him, and it is purely a matter for his private decision whether he will write as the old law dictates or show to life its image as he beholds it.

The Future of the Novel

Henry James

First published in International Library of Famous Literature, *Richard Garnett, et al., eds. (London: The Standard, 1899), pp. xi-xxii.*

Beginnings, as we all know, are usually small things, but continuations are not always strikingly great ones, and the place occupied in the world by the prolonged prose fable has become, in our time, among the incidents of literature, the most surprising example to be named of swift and extravagant growth, a development beyond the measure of every early appearance. It is a form that has had a fortune so little to have been foretold at its cradle. The germ of the comprehensive epic was more recognizable in the first barbaric chant than that of the novel as we know it today in the first anecdote retailed to amuse. It arrived, in truth, the novel, late at self-consciousness; but it has done its utmost ever since to make up for lost opportunities. The flood at present swells and swells, threatening the whole field of letters, as would often seem, with submersion. It plays, in what may be called the passive consciousness of many persons, a part that directly marches with the rapid increase of the multitude able to possess itself in one way and another of the *book*. The book, in the Anglo-Saxon world, is almost everywhere, and it is in the form of the voluminous prose fable that we see it penetrate easiest and farthest. Penetration appears really to be directly aided by mere mass and bulk. There is an immense public, if public be the name, inarticulate, but abysmally absorbent, for which, at its hours of ease, the printed volume has no other association. This public—the public that subscribes, borrows, lends, that picks up in one way and another, sometimes even by purchase—grows and grows each year, and nothing is thus more apparent than that of all the recruits it brings to the book the most numerous by far are those that it brings to the "story."

This number has gained, in our time, an augmentation from three sources in particular, the first of which, indeed, is perhaps but a comprehensive name for the two others. The diffusion of the rudiments, the multiplication of common schools, has had more and more the effect of making readers of women and of the very young. Nothing is so striking in a survey of this field, and nothing to be so much borne in mind, as that the larger part of the great multitude that sustains the teller and the publisher of tales is constituted by boys and girls; by girls in especial, if we apply the term to the later stages of the life of the innumerable women who, under modern arrangements, increasingly fail to marry—fail, apparently, even, largely, to desire to. It is not too much to say of many of these that they live in a great measure by the immediate aid of the novel—confining the question, for the moment, to the fact of consumption alone. The literature, as it may be called for convenience, of children is an industry that occupies by itself a very considerable quarter of the scene. Great fortunes, if not great reputations, are made, we learn, by writing for schoolboys, and the period during which they consume the compound artfully prepared for them appears—as they begin earlier and continue later—to add to itself at both ends. This helps to account for the fact that public libraries, especially those that are private and money-making enterprises, put into circulation more volumes of "stories" than of all other things together of which volumes can be made. The published statistics are extraordinary, and of a sort to engender many kinds of uneasiness. The sort of taste that used to be called "good" has nothing to do with the matter: we are so demonstrably in presence of millions for whom taste is but an obscure, confused, immediate instinct. In the flare of railway bookstalls, in the shop-fronts of most booksellers, especially the provincial, in the advertisements of the weekly newspapers, and in fifty places besides, this testimony to the general preference triumphs, yielding a good-natured corner at most to a bunch of treatises on athletics or sport, or a patch of theology old and new.

The case is so marked, however, that illustrations easily overflow, and there is no need of forcing doors that stand wide open. What remains is the interesting oddity or mystery—the anomaly that fairly dignifies the whole circumstances with its strangeness: the wonder, in short, that men, women, and children *should* have so much attention to spare for improvisations mainly so arbitrary and frequently so loose. That, at the first blush, fairly leaves us gaping. This great fortune then, since fortune it seems, has been reserved for mere unsupported and unguaranteed history, the *inexpensive* thing, written in the air, the record of what, in any particular case, has *not* been, the account that remains responsible, at best, to "documents" with which we are practically unable to collate it. This is the side of the whole business of fiction on which it can always be challenged, and to that degree that if the general venture had not become in such a manner the admiration of the world it might but too easily have become the derision. It has in truth, I think, never philosophically met the challenge, never found a formula to inscribe on its shield, never defended its position by any better argument than the frank, straight blow: "Why am I not so

unprofitable as to be preposterous? Because I can do *that*. There!" And it throws up from time to time some purely practical masterpiece. There is nevertheless an admirable minority of intelligent persons who care not even for the masterpieces, nor see any pressing point in them, for whom the very form itself has, equally at its best and at its worst, been ever a vanity and a mockery. This class, it should be added, is beginning to be visibly augmented by a different circle altogether, the group of the formerly subject, but now estranged, the deceived and bored, those for whom the whole movement too decidedly fails to live up to its possibilities. There are people who have loved the novel, but who actually find themselves drowned in its verbiage, and for whom, even in some of its approved manifestations, it has become a terror they exert every ingenuity, every hypocrisy, to evade. The indifferent and the alienated testify, at any rate, almost as much as the omnivorous, to the reign of the great ambiguity, the enjoyment of which rests, evidently, on a primary need of the mind. The novelist can only fall back on that—on his recognition that man's constant demand for what he has to offer is simply man's general appetite for a *picture*. The novel is of all pictures the most comprehensive and the most elastic. It will stretch anywhere—it will take in absolutely anything. All it needs is a subject and a painter. But for its subject, magnificently, it has the whole human consciousness. And if we are pushed a step farther backward, and asked why the representation should be required when the object represented is itself mostly so accessible, the answer to that appears to be that man combines with his eternal desire for more experience an infinite cunning as to getting his experience as cheaply as possible. He will steal it whenever he can. He likes to live the life of others, yet is well aware of the points at which it may too intolerably resemble his own. The vivid fable, more than anything else, gives him this satisfaction on easy terms, gives him knowledge abundant yet vicarious. It enables him to select, to take and to leave; so that to feel he can afford to neglect it he must have a rare faculty, or great opportunities, for the extension of experience—by thought, by emotion, by energy—at first hand.

Yet it is doubtless not this cause alone that contributes to the contemporary deluge; other circumstances operate, and one of them is probably, in truth, if looked into, something of an abatement of the great fortune we have been called upon to admire. The high prosperity of fiction has marched, very directly, with another "sign of the times," the demoralization, the vulgarization of literature in general, the increasing familiarity of all such methods of communication, the making itself supremely felt, as it were, of the presence of the ladies and children—by whom I mean, in other words, the reader irreflective and uncritical. If the novel, in fine, has found itself, socially speaking, at such a rate, the book *par excellence*, so on the other hand the book has in the same degree found itself a thing of small ceremony. So many ways of producing it easily have been discovered that it is by no means the occasional prodigy, for good or for evil, that it was taken for in simpler days, and has therefore suffered a proportionate discredit. Almost any variety is thrown off and taken up, handled, admired, ignored by too many people, and this, precisely, is the point at which the question of its future becomes one with that of the future of the total swarm. How are the generations to face, at all, the monstrous multiplications? Any speculation on the further development of a particular variety is subject to the reserve that the generations may at no distant day be obliged formally to decree, and to execute, great clearings of the deck, great periodical effacements and destructions. It fills, in fact, at moments the expectant ear, as we watch the progress of the ship of civilization—the huge splash that must mark the response to many an imperative, unanimous "Overboard!" What at least is already very plain is that practically the great majority of volumes printed within a year cease to exist as the hour passes, and give up by that circumstance all claim to a career, to being accounted or provided for. In speaking of the future of the novel we must of course, therefore, be taken as limiting the inquiry to those types that have, for criticism, a present and a past. And it is only superficially that confusion seems here to reign. The fact that in England and in the United States every specimen that sees the light may look for a "review" testifies merely to the point to which, in these countries, literary criticism has sunk. The review is in nine cases out of ten an effort of intelligence as undeveloped as the ineptitude over which it fumbles, and the critical spirit, which knows where it is concerned and where not, is not touched, is still less compromised, by the incident. There are too many reasons why newspapers must live.

So, as regards the tangible type, the end is that in its undefended, its positively exposed state, we continue to accept it, conscious even of a peculiar beauty in an appeal made from a footing so precarious. It throws itself wholly on our generosity, and

very often indeed gives us, by the reception it meets, a useful measure of the quality, of the delicacy, of many minds. There is to my sense no work of literary, or of any other, art, that any human being is under the smallest positive obligation to "like." There is no woman—no matter of what loveliness—in the presence of whom it is anything but a man's unchallengeably *own* affair that he is "in love" or out of it. It is not a question of manners; vast is the margin left to individual freedom; and the trap set by the artist occupies no different ground—Robert Louis Stevenson has admirably expressed the analogy—from the offer of her charms by the lady. There only remain infatuations that we envy and emulate. When we do respond to the appeal, when we *are* caught in the trap, we are held and played upon; so that how in the world can there *not* still be a future, however late in the day, for a contrivance possessed of this precious secret? The more we consider it the more we feel that the prose picture can never be at the end of its tether until it loses the sense of what it can do. It can do simply everything, and that is its strength and its life. Its plasticity, its elasticity are infinite; there is no color, no extension it may not take from the nature of its subject or the temper of its craftsman. It has the extraordinary advantage—a piece of luck scarcely credible—that, while capable of giving an impression of the highest perfection and the rarest finish, it moves in a luxurious independence of rules and restrictions. Think as we may, there is nothing we can mention as a consideration outside itself with which it must square, nothing we can name as one of its peculiar obligations or interdictions. It must, of course, hold our attention and reward it, it must not appeal on false pretenses; but these necessities, with which, obviously, disgust and displeasure interfere, are not peculiar to it—all works of art have them in common. For the rest it has so clear a field that if it perishes this will surely be by its fault—by its superficiality, in other words, or its timidity. One almost, for the very love of it, likes to think of its appearing threatened with some such fate, in order to figure the dramatic stroke of its revival under the touch of a life-giving master. The temperament of the artist can do so much for it that our desire for some exemplary felicity fairly demands even the vision of that supreme proof. If we were to linger on this vision long enough, we should doubtless, in fact, be brought to wondering—and still for very loyalty to the form itself—whether our own prospective conditions may not before too long appear to many critics to call for some such happy *coup* on the part of a great artist yet to come.

There would at least be this excuse for such a reverie: that speculation is vain unless we confine it, and that for ourselves the most convenient branch of the question is the state of the industry that makes its appeal to readers of English. From any attempt to measure the career still open to the novel in France I may be excused, in so narrow a compass, for shrinking. The French, as a result of having ridden their horse much harder than we, are at a different stage of the journey, and we have doubtless many of their stretches and baiting-places yet to traverse. But if the range grows shorter from the moment we drop to inductions drawn only from English and American material, I am not sure that the answer comes sooner. I should have at all events—a formidably large order—to plunge into the particulars of the question of the present. If the day *is* approaching when the respite of execution for almost any book is but a matter of mercy, does the English novel of commerce tend to strike us as a production more and more equipped by its high qualities for braving the danger? It would be impossible, I think, to make one's attempt at an answer to that riddle really interesting without bringing into the field many illustrations drawn from individuals—without pointing the moral with names both conspicuous and obscure. Such a freedom would carry us, here, quite too far, and would moreover only encumber the path. There is nothing to prevent our taking for granted all sorts of happy symptoms and splendid promises—so long, of course, I mean, as we keep before us the general truth that the future of fiction is intimately bound up with the future of the society that produces and consumes it. In a society with a great and diffused literary sense the talent at play can only be a less neglible thing than in a society with a literary sense barely discernible. In a world in which criticism is acute and mature such talent will find itself trained, in order successfully to assert itself, to many more kinds of precautionary expertness than in a society in which the art I have named holds an inferior place or makes a sorry figure. A community addicted to reflection and fond of ideas will try experiments with the "story" that will be left untried in a community mainly devoted to traveling and shooting, to pushing trade and playing football. There are many judges, doubtless, who hold that experiments—queer and uncanny things at best—are not necessary to it, that its face has been, once for all, turned in one way, and that it has only to go straight before it. If that is what it is actually doing in

England and America the main thing to say about its future would appear to be that this future will in very truth more and more define itself as negligible. For all the while the immense variety of life will stretch away to right and to left, and all the while there may be, on such lines, perpetuation of its great mistake of failing of intelligence. That mistake will be, ever, for the admirable art, the only one really inexcusable, because of being a mistake about, as we may say, its own soul. The form of novel that is stupid on the general question of its freedom is the single form that may, *a priori*, be unhesitatingly pronounced wrong.

The most interesting thing today, therefore, among ourselves is the degree in which we may count on seeing a sense of that freedom cultivated and bearing fruit. What else is this, indeed, but one of the most attaching elements in the great drama of our wide English-speaking life! As the novel is at any moment the most immediate and, as it were, admirably *treacherous* picture of actual manners—indirectly as well as directly, and by what it does not touch as well as by what it does—so its present situation, where we are most concerned with it, is exactly a reflection of our social changes and chances, of the signs and portents that lay most traps for most observers, and make up in general what is most "amusing" in the spectacle we offer. Nothing, I may say, for instance, strikes me more as meeting this description than the predicament finally arrived at, for the fictive energy, in consequence of our long and most respectable tradition of making it defer supremely, in the treatment, say, of a delicate case, to the inexperience of the young. The particular knot the coming novelist who shall prefer not simply to beg the question, will have here to untie may represent assuredly the essence of his outlook. By what it shall decide to do in respect to the "young" the great prose fable will, from any serious point of view, practically see itself stand or fall. What is clear is that it has, among us, veritably never chosen—it has, mainly, always obeyed an unreasoning instinct of avoidance in which there has often been much that was felicitous. While society was frank, was free about the incidents and accidents of the human constitution, the novel took the same robust ease as society. The young then were so very young that they were not table-high. But they began to grow, and from the moment their little chins rested on the mahogany, Richardson and Fielding began to go under it. There came into being a mistrust of any but the most guarded treatment of the great relation between men and women, the constant world-renewal, which was the conspicuous sign that whatever the prose picture of life was prepared to take upon itself, it was not prepared to take upon itself not to be superficial. Its position became very much: "There are other things, don't you know? For heaven's sake let *that* one pass!" And to this wonderful propriety of letting it pass the business has been for these so many years—with the consequences we see today—largely devoted. These consequences are of many sorts, not a few altogether charming. One of them has been that there is an immense omission in our fiction—which, though many critics will always judge that is has vitiated the whole, others will continue to speak of as signifying but a trifle. One can only talk for one's self, and of the English and American novelists of whom I am fond, I am so superlatively fond that I positively prefer to take them as they are. I cannot so much as imagine Dickens and Scott *without* the "*love-making*" left, as the phrase is, out. They were, to my perception, absolutely right—from the moment their attention to it could only be perfunctory—practically not to deal with it. In all their work it is, in spite of the number of pleasant sketches of affection gratified or crossed, the element that matters least. Why not therefore assume, it may accordingly be asked, that discriminations which have served their purpose so well in the past will continue not less successfully to meet the case? What will you have better than Scott and Dickens?

Nothing certainly *can* be, it may at least as promptly be replied, and I can imagine no more comfortable prospect than jogging along perpetually with a renewal of such blessings. The difficulty lies in the fact that two of the great conditions have changed. The novel is older, and so are the young. It would seem that everything the young can possibly do for us in the matter has been successfully done. They have kept out one thing after the other, yet there is still a certain completeness we lack, and the curious thing is that it appears to be they themselves who are making the grave discovery. "You have kindly taken," they seem to say to the fiction-mongers, "our education off the hands of our parents and pastors, and that, doubtless, has been very convenient for *them*, and left them free to amuse themselves. But what, all the while, pray, if it is a question of education, have you done with your own? These are directions in which you seem dreadfully untrained, and in which *can* it be as vain as it appears to apply to you for information?" The point is whether, from the moment it is a question of averting discredit, the novel can afford to take things quite so easily as it has, for a good while now, settled down into the way of doing. There are too many sources of interest neglected—whole categories of manners, whole corpuscular classes and provinces, museums of character and condition, unvisited; while it is on the other hand mistakenly taken for granted that safety lies in all the loose and thin material that keeps reappearing in forms at once ready-made and sadly the worse for wear. The simple themselves may finally turn against our simplifications; so that we need not, after all, be more royalist than the king or more childish than the children. It is certain that there is no real health for any art—I am not speaking, of course, of any mere industry—that does not move a step in advance of its farthest follower. It would be curious—really a great comedy—if the renewal were to spring just from the satiety of the very readers for whom the sacrifices have hitherto been supposed to be made. It bears on this that as nothing is more salient in English life today, to fresh eyes, than the revolution taking place in the position and outlook of women—and taking place much more deeply in the quiet than even the noise on the surface demonstrates—so we may very well yet see the female elbow itself, kept in increasing activity by the play of the pen, smash with final resonance the window all this time most superstitiously closed. The particular draught that has been most deprecated will in that case take care of the question of freshness. It is the opinion of some observers that when women do obtain a free hand they will not repay their long debt to the precautionary attitude of men by unlimited consideration for the natural delicacy of the latter.

To admit, then, that the great anodyne can ever totally fail to work, is to imply, in short, that this will only be by some grave fault in some high quarter. Man rejoices in an incomparable faculty for presently mutilating and disfiguring any plaything that has helped create for him the illusion of leisure; nevertheless, so long as life retains its power of projecting itself upon his imagination, he will find the novel work off the impression better than anything he knows. Anything better for the purpose has assuredly yet to be discovered. He will give it up only when life itself too thoroughly disagrees with him. Even then, indeed, may fiction not find a second wind, or a fiftieth, in the very portrayal of that collapse? Till the world is an unpeopled void there will be an image in the mirror. What need more immediately concern us, therefore, is the care of seeing that the image shall continue various and vivid. There is much, frankly, to be said for those who, in spite of all brave pleas, feel it to be considerably menaced, for very little reflection will help to show us how the prospect strikes them. They see the whole business too divorced on the one side from observation and perception, and on the other from the art and taste. They get too little of the first-hand impression, the effort to penetrate—that effort for which the French have the admirable expression to *fouiller*—and still less, if possible, of any science of composition, any architecture, distribution, proportion. It is not a trifle, though indeed it is the concomitant of an edged force, that "mystery" should, to so many of the sharper eyes, have disappeared from the craft, and a facile flatness be, in place of it, in acclaimed possession. But these are, at the worst, even for such of the disconcerted, signs that the novelist, not that the novel, has dropped. So long as there is a subject to be treated, so long will it depend wholly on the treatment to rekindle the fire. Only the ministrant must really approach the altar; for if the novel *is* the treatment, it is the treatment that is essentially what I have called the anodyne.

Contributors

Lionel Adey ....*University of Victoria*
Joyce Avrech Berkman ....*University of Massachusetts-Amherst*
Kathleen Blake ....*University of Washington*
Michael Collie...*York University*
Philip B. Dematteis ....*Columbia, South Carolina*
Susan Dick ....*Queen's University*
Patrick A. Dunae...*University of Victoria*
Barbara J. Dunlap.......................*City College, City University of New York*
Joseph R. Dunlap ....*New York, New York*
George Grella..*University of Rochester*
Catherine Harland ....*Queen's University*
Lee E. Holt ....*Amherst, Massachusetts*
Winifred Hughes...*Princeton University*
Anne Humpherys ....*Herbert H. Lehman College, City University of New York*
Robert Kiely ....*Harvard University*
Jacob Korg..*University of Washington*
Marjory Lang ....*University of British Columbia*
Christopher D. Murray..*University of Regina*
Ira B. Nadel ....*University of British Columbia*
Norman Page ....*University of Alberta*
Barry V. Qualls ....*Rutgers University*
Esther M. G. Smith ....*Lutz, Florida*
Roy B. Stokes..*University of British Columbia*
Max Keith Sutton...*University of Kansas*
R. C. Terry...*University of Victoria*
Dorothea M. Thompson..*Carnegie-Mellon University*
Craig Turner..*Texas A&M University*
Frederick J. Wagner ....*University of Regina*
Tom Winnifrith ....*University of Warwick*
George J. Worth..*University of Kansas*

Cumulative Index

Dictionary of Literary Biography, Volumes 1-18
Dictionary of Literary Biography Yearbook, 1980, 1981, 1982
Dictionary of Literary Biography Documentary Series, Volumes 1-3

Cumulative Index

DLB before number: *Dictionary of Literary Biography*, Volumes 1-18
Y before number: *Dictionary of Literary Biography Yearbook*, 1980, 1981, 1982
DS before number: *Dictionary of Literary Biography Documentary Series*, Volumes 1-3

A

Abbott, Jacob 1803-1879 ....DLB1

Adamic, Louis 1898-1951 ....DLB9

Adams, Henry 1838-1918 ....DLB12

Adams, James Truslow 1878-1949 ....DLB17

Ade, George 1866-1944...............................DLB11

Adeler, Max (see Clark, Charles Heber)

Agassiz, Jean Louis Rodolphe 1807-1873
....DLB1

Agee, James 1909-1955 ....DLB2

Aiken, Conrad 1889-1973 ....DLB9

Albee, Edward 1928- DLB7

Alcott, Amos Bronson 1799-1888.................DLB1

Alcott, Louisa May 1832-1888.......................DLB1

Alcott, William Andrus 1798-1859 ....DLB1

Aldiss, Brian W. 1925- DLB14

Algren, Nelson 1909-1981...............DLB9; Y81,82

Alldritt, Keith 1935- DLB14

Allen, Hervey 1889-1949...............................DLB9

Josiah Allen's Wife (see Holly, Marietta)

Allston, Washington 1779-1843 ....DLB1

Alvarez, A. 1929- DLB14

Amis, Kingsley 1922- DLB15

Amis, Martin 1949- DLB14

Ammons, A. R. 1926- DLB5

Anderson, Margaret 1886-1973 ....DLB4

Anderson, Maxwell 1888-1959.....................DLB7

Anderson, Poul 1926- DLB8

Anderson, Robert 1917- DLB7

Anderson, Sherwood 1876-1941
....DLB4, 9; DS1

Andrews, Charles M. 1863-1943.................DLB17

Anthony, Piers 1934- DLB8

Archer, William 1856-1924 ....DLB10

Arden, John 1930- DLB13

Arensberg, Ann 1937- Y82

Arnow, Harriette Simpson 1908- DLB6

Arp, Bill (see Smith, Charles Henry)

Arthur, Timothy Shay 1809-1885................DLB3

Asch, Nathan 1902-1964 ....DLB4

Ashbery, John 1927- DLB5; Y81

Ashton, Winifred (see Dane, Clemence)

Asimov, Isaac 1920- DLB8

Atherton, Gertrude 1857-1948 ....DLB9

Auchincloss, Louis 1917- DLB2; Y80

Auden, W. H. 1907-1973 ....DLB10

Austin, Mary 1868-1934...............................DLB9

Ayckbourn, Alan 1939- DLB13

B

Bacon, Delia 1811-1859.................................DLB1

Bagnold, Enid 1889-1981............................DLB13

Bailey, Paul 1937- DLB14

Bailyn, Bernard 1922- DLB17

Bainbridge, Beryl 1933- DLB14

Bald, Wambly 1902- DLB4

Baldwin, James 1924- DLB2, 7

Baldwin, Joseph Glover 1815-1864
....DLB3, 11

Ballard, J. G. 1930- DLB14

Bancroft, George 1800-1891 ....DLB1

Bangs, John Kendrick 1862-1922 ....DLB11

Banville, John 1945- DLB14

Baraka, Amiri 1934- DLB5, 7, 16

Barker, A. L. 1918- DLB14

Barker, Harley Granville 1877-1946
     ....DLB10

Barker, Howard 1946- DLB13

Barks, Coleman 1937- DLB5

Barnes, Djuna 1892-1982.................DLB4, 9

Barnes, Margaret Ayer 1886-1967.................DLB9

Barnes, Peter 1931- DLB13

Barney, Natalie 1876-1972.................DLB4

Barrie, James M. 1860-1937.................DLB10

Barry, Philip 1896-1949 ....DLB7

Barstow, Stan 1928- DLB14

Barth, John 1930- DLB2

Barthelme, Donald 1931- DLB2; Y80

Bartlett, John 1820-1905.................DLB1

Bartol, Cyrus Augustus 1813-1900.................DLB1

Bass, T. J. 1932- Y81

Bassett, John Spencer 1867-1928.................DLB17

Bassler, Thomas Joseph (see T. J. Bass)

Baumbach, Jonathan 1933- Y80

Bawden, Nina 1925- DLB14

Bax, Clifford 1886-1962.................DLB10

Beach, Sylvia 1887-1962.................DLB4

Beagle, Peter S. 1939- Y80

Beal, M. F. 1937- Y81

Beale, Howard K. 1899-1959.................DLB17

Beard, Charles A. 1874-1948.................DLB17

Beattie, Ann 1947- Y82

Becker, Carl 1873-1945.................DLB17

Beckett, Samuel 1906- DLB13, 15

Beecher, Catharine Esther 1800-1878
     ....DLB1

Beecher, Henry Ward 1813-1887.................DLB3

Behan, Brendan 1923-1964 ....DLB13

Behrman, S. N. 1893-1973.................DLB7

Belasco, David 1853-1931.................DLB7

Belitt, Ben 1911- DLB5

Bell, Marvin 1937- DLB5

Bellamy, Edward 1850-1898 ....DLB12

Bellow, Saul 1915- DLB2; DS3; Y82

Bemis, Samuel Flagg 1891-1973 ....DLB17

Benchley, Robert 1889-1945 ....DLB11

Benedictus, David 1938- DLB14

Benedikt, Michael 1935- DLB5

Benét, Stephen Vincent 1898-1943
     ....DLB4

Benford, Gregory 1941- Y82

Benjamin, Park 1809-1864.................DLB3

Bennett, Arnold 1867-1931.................DLB10

Berg, Stephen 1934- DLB5

Berger, John 1926- DLB14

Berger, Thomas 1924- DLB2; Y80

Berrigan, Daniel 1921- DLB5

Berrigan, Ted 1934- DLB5

Berry, Wendell 1934- DLB5, 6

Bester, Alfred 1913- DLB8

Betts, Doris 1932- Y82

Beveridge, Albert J. 1862-1927.................DLB17

Bierce, Ambrose 1842-1914? DLB11, 12

Biggle, Lloyd, Jr. 1923- DLB8

Biglow, Hosea (see Lowell, James Russell)

Billings, Josh (see Shaw, Henry Wheeler)

Bird, William 1888-1963 ....DLB4

Bishop, Elizabeth 1911-1979.................DLB5

Bishop, John Peale 1892-1944.................DLB4, 9

Blackburn, Paul 1926-1971.................Y81; DLB 16

Blackmore, R. D. 1825-1900.................DLB 18

Blackwood, Caroline 1931- DLB14

Bledsoe, Albert Taylor 1809-1877.................DLB3

Blish, James 1921-1975 ....DLB8

Bly, Robert 1926- DLB5

Bodenheim, Maxwell 1892-1954..................DLB9

Boer, Charles 1939- DLB5

Bogarde, Dirk 1921- DLB14

Bolt, Robert 1924- DLB13

Bolton, Herbert E. 1870-1953....................DLB17

Bond, Edward 1934- DLB13

Boorstin, Daniel J. 1914- DLB17

Booth, Philip 1925- Y82

Botta, Anne C. Lynch 1815-1891 ....DLB3

Bottomley, Gordon 1874-1948...................DLB10

Boucher, Anthony 1911-1968.....................DLB8

Bourjaily, Vance 1922- DLB2

Bova, Ben 1932- Y81

Bowen, Elizabeth 1899-1973 ....DLB15

Bowen, Francis 1811-1890 ....DLB1

Bowen, John 1924- DLB13

Bowers, Claude G. 1878-1958....................DLB17

Bowers, Edgar 1924- DLB5

Bowles, Paul 1910- DLB5, 6

Boyd, James 1888-1944............................DLB9

Boyd, John 1919- DLB8

Boyd, Thomas 1898-1935 ....DLB9

Boyesen, Hjalmar Hjorth 1848-1895..........DLB12

Boyle, Kay 1902- DLB4, 9

Brackett, Leigh 1915-1978 ....DLB8

Brackenridge, Hugh Henry 1748-1816
....DLB11

Bradbury, Malcolm 1932- DLB14

Bradbury, Ray 1920- DLB2, 8

Braddon, Mary Elizabeth 1835-1915
....DLB18

Bradford, Gamaliel 1863-1932...................DLB17

Bradley, Marion Zimmer 1930- DLB8

Bradley, William Aspenwall 1878-1939
....DLB4

Bragg, Melvyn 1939- DLB14

Braine, John 1922- DLB15

Brautigan, Richard 1935- DLB2, 5; Y80

Bremser, Bonnie 1939- DLB16

Bremser, Ray 1934- DLB16

Brenton, Howard 1942- DLB13

Bridie, James 1888-1951 ....DLB10

Briggs, Charles Frederick 1804-1877
....DLB3

Brighouse, Harold 1882-1958....................DLB10

Brisbane, Albert 1809-1890.......................DLB3

Bromfield, Louis 1896-1956 ....DLB4, 9

Brooke-Rose, Christine 1926- DLB14

Brooks, Charles Timothy 1813-1883 ....DLB1

Brooks, Gwendolyn 1917- DLB5

Brooks, Jeremy 1926- DLB14

Brophy, Brigid 1929- DLB14

Brossard, Chandler 1922- DLB16

Brother Antoninus (see Everson, William)

Brougham, John 1810-1880.......................DLB11

Broughton, James 1913- DLB5

Broughton, Rhoda 1840-1920....................DLB18

Brown, Bob 1886-1959.............................DLB4

Brown, Christy 1932-1981.........................DLB14

Brown, Dee 1908- Y80

Brown, Fredric 1906-1972 ....DLB8

Brown, George Mackay 1921- DLB14

Brown, William Wells 1813-1884..................DLB3

Browne, Charles Farrar 1834-1867 ....DLB11

Browne, Wynyard 1911-1964.....................DLB13

Brownson, Orestes Augustus 1803-1876......DLB1

Bryant, William Cullen 1794-1878................DLB3

Buchanan, Robert 1841-1901.....................DLB18

Buck, Pearl S. 1892-1973 ....DLB9

Buckley, William F., Jr. 1925- Y80

Budrys, A. J. 1931- DLB8

Buechner, Frederick 1926- Y80

Bukowski, Charles 1920- DLB5

Bullins, Ed 1935- DLB7

Bumpus, Jerry 1937- Y81

Burgess, Anthony 1917- DLB14

Burgess, Gelett 1866-1951.........................DLB11

Burnett, W. R. 1899- DLB9

Burns, Alan 1929- DLB14

Burroughs, Edgar Rice 1875-1950 ....DLB8

Burroughs, William S., Jr. 1947-1981 ....DLB16

Burroughs, William Seward 1914-
................................DLB2, 8, 16; Y81

Burroway, Janet 1936- DLB6

Busch, Frederick 1941- DLB6

Butler, Samuel 1835-1902.........................DLB18

Byatt, A. S. 1936- DLB14

Byrne, John Keyes (see Leonard, Hugh)

C

Cabell, James Branch 1879-1958 ....DLB9

Cable, George Washington 1844-1925
....DLB12

Cahan, Abraham 1860-1951 ....DLB9

Caldwell, Erskine 1903- DLB9

Calhoun, John C. 1782-1850.......................DLB3

Calisher, Hortense 1911- DLB2

Calmer, Edgar 1907- DLB4

Calvert, George Henry 1803-1889...............DLB1

Campbell, John W., Jr. 1910-1971..............DLB8

Cannan, Gilbert 1884-1955 ....DLB10

Cannell, Kathleen 1891-1974.....................DLB4

Cantwell, Robert 1908-1978......................DLB9

Capote, Truman 1924- DLB2; Y80

Carroll, Gladys Hasty 1904- DLB9

Carroll, Lewis 1832-1898..........................DLB18

Carroll, Paul 1927- DLB16

Carroll, Paul Vincent 1900-1968................DLB10

Carruth, Hayden 1921- DLB5

Carter, Angela 1940- DLB14

Carter, Lin 1930- Y81

Caruthers, William Alexander 1802-1846
....DLB3

Cary, Joyce 1888-1957..............................DLB15

Casey, Juanita 1925- DLB14

Casey, Michael 1947- DLB5

Cassady, Carolyn 1923- DLB16

Cassady, Neal 1926-1968..........................DLB16

Cassill, R. V. 1919- DLB6

Cather, Willa 1873-1947......................DLB9; DS1

Catton, Bruce 1899-1978..........................DLB17

Caute, David 1936- DLB14

Chambers, Charles Haddon 1860-1921
....DLB10

Channing, Edward 1856-1931 ....DLB17

Channing, Edward Tyrrell 1790-1856
....DLB1

Channing, William Ellery 1780-1842
....DLB1

Channing, William Ellery, II 1817-1901
....DLB1

Channing, William Henry 1810-1884
....DLB1

Chappell, Fred 1936- DLB6

Charles, Gerda 1914- DLB14

Chayefsky, Paddy 1923-1981 ....DLB7; Y81

Cheever, John 1912-1982..............DLB2; Y80, 82

Cheever, Susan 1943- Y82

Cheney, Ednah Dow (Littlehale) 1824-1904
....DLB1

Cherryh, C. J. 1942- Y80

Chesnutt, Charles Waddell 1858-1932
....DLB12

Chesterton, G. K. 1874-1936......................DLB10

Child, Francis James 1825-1896...................DLB1

Child, Lydia Maria 1802-1880 ....DLB1

Childress, Alice 1920- DLB7

Chivers, Thomas Holley 1809-1858
....DLB3

Chopin, Kate 1851-1904.............................DLB12

Christie, Agatha 1890-1976.........................DLB13

Churchill, Caryl 1938- DLB13

Ciardi, John 1916- DLB5

Clark, Charles Heber 1841-1915 ....DLB11

Clark, Eleanor 1913- DLB6

Clark, Lewis Gaylord 1808-1873....................DLB3

Clark, Walter Van Tilburg 1909-1971.........DLB9

Clarke, Austin 1896-1974...........................DLB10

Clarke, James Freeman 1810-1888
....DLB1

Clausen, Andy 1943- DLB16

Clemens, Samuel Langhorne 1835-1910
....DLB11, 12

Clement, Hal 1922- DLB8

Clifton, Lucille 1936- DLB5

Coates, Robert M. 1897-1973
....DLB4, 9

Cobb, Irvin S. 1876-1944 ....DLB11

Cochran, Thomas C. 1902- DLB17

Cole, Barry 1936- DLB14

Colegate, Isabel 1931- DLB14

Coleman, Emily Holmes 1899-1974
....DLB4

Collins, Wilkie 1824-1889...........................DLB18

Colwin, Laurie 1944- Y80

Commager, Henry Steele 1902- DLB17

Connell, Evan S., Jr. 1924- DLB2; Y81

Connelly, Marc 1890- DLB7; Y80

Conrad, Joseph 1857-1924.........................DLB10

Conroy, Jack 1899- Y81

Conroy, Pat 1945- DLB6

Conway, Moncure Daniel 1832-1907
....DLB1

Cooke, John Esten 1830-1886......................DLB3

Cooke, Philip Pendleton 1816-1850
....DLB3

Cooke, Rose Terry 1827-1892 ....DLB12

Cooper, Giles 1918-1966 ....DLB13

Cooper, James Fenimore 1789-1851
....DLB3

Coover, Robert 1932- DLB2; Y81

Corman, Cid 1924- DLB5

Corn, Alfred 1943- Y80

Corrington, John William 1932- DLB6

Corso, Gregory 1930- DLB5, 16

Costain, Thomas B. 1885-1965....................DLB9

Coward, Noel 1899-1973...........................DLB10

Cowley, Malcolm 1898- DLB4; Y81

Coxe, Louis 1918- DLB5

Cozzens, James Gould 1903-1978
....DLB9; DS2

Craddock, Charles Egbert (see Murfree, Mary N.)

Cranch, Christopher Pearse 1813-1892
....DLB1

Crane, Hart 1899-1932...............................DLB4

Crane, Stephen 1871-1900.........................DLB12

Craven, Avery 1885-1980...........................DLB17

Crayon, Geoffrey (see Irving, Washington)

Creeley, Robert 1926- DLB5, 16

Cregan, David 1931- DLB13

Crews, Harry 1935- DLB6

Crichton, Michael 1942- Y81

Cristofer, Michael 1946- DLB7

Crockett, David 1786-1836.......................DLB3, 11

Crosby, Caresse 1892-1970 and Crosby,
     Harry 1898-1929...............................DLB4

Crothers, Rachel 1878-1958......................DLB7

Crowley, John 1942- Y82

Crowley, Mart 1935- DLB7

Croy, Homer 1883-1965.............................DLB4

Cullen, Countee 1903-1946........................DLB4

Cummings, E. E. 1894-1962.....................DLB4

Cummings, Ray 1887-1957 ....DLB8

Cunningham, J. V. 1911- DLB5

Cuomo, George 1929- Y80

Cuppy, Will 1884-1949.............................DLB11

Curti, Merle E. 1897- DLB17

Curtis, George William 1824-1892
....DLB1

D

Dall, Caroline Wells (Healey) 1822-1912
....DLB1

Daly, T. A. 1871-1948 ....DLB11

D'Alton, Louis 1900-1951........................DLB10

Dana, Charles A. 1819-1897 ....DLB3

Dana, Richard Henry, Jr. 1815-1882
....DLB1

Dane, Clemence 1887-1965......................DLB10

Davidson, Avram 1923- DLB8

Davidson, Lionel 1922- DLB14

Daviot, Gordon 1896-1952.......................DLB10

Davis, Charles A. 1795-1867 ....DLB11

Davis, Clyde Brion 1894-1962...................DLB9

Davis, H. L. 1894-1960 ....DLB9

Davis, Margaret Thomson 1926- DLB14

Davis, Ossie 1917- DLB7

Davis, Richard Harding 1864-1916
....DLB12

Davison, Peter 1928- DLB5

Day, Clarence 1874-1935.........................DLB11

Day Lewis, C. 1904-1972.........................DLB15

Deal, Borden 1922- DLB6

De Bow, James D. B. 1820-1867.................DLB3

de Camp, L. Sprague 1907- DLB8

De Forest, John William 1826-1906
....DLB12

de Graff, Robert 1895-1981 ....Y81

Delaney, Shelagh 1939- DLB13

Delany, Samuel R. 1942- DLB8

Delbanco, Nicholas 1942- DLB6

DeLillo, Don 1936- DLB6

Dell, Floyd 1887-1969.............................DLB9

del Rey, Lester 1915- DLB8

Dennis, Nigel 1912- DLB13, 15

Derby, George Horatio 1823-1861 ....DLB11

Derleth, August 1909-1971 ....DLB9

DeVoto, Bernard 1897-1955.....................DLB9

De Vries, Peter 1910- DLB6; Y82

Dick, Philip K. 1928- DLB8

Dickey, James 1923- DLB5; Y82

Dickey, William 1928- DLB5

Dickinson, Emily 1830-1886......................DLB1

Dickson, Gordon R. 1923- DLB8

Didion, Joan 1934- DLB2; Y81

Di Donato, Pietro 1911- DLB9

Dillard, Annie 1945- Y80

Dillard, R. H. W. 1937- DLB5

Diogenes, Jr. (see Brougham, John)

DiPrima, Diane 1934- DLB5

Disch, Thomas M. 1940- DLB8

Dix, Dorothea Lynde 1802-1887..................DLB1

Doctorow, E. L. 1931- DLB2; Y80

Dodd, William E. 1869-1940 ....DLB17

Dodgson, Charles Lutwidge (see Carroll, Lewis)

Doesticks, Q. K. Philander, P. B. (see Thomson, Mortimer)

Donald, David H. 1920- DLB17

Donnelly, Ignatius 1831-1901 ....DLB12

Donleavy, J. P. 1926- DLB6

Doolittle, Hilda 1886-1961 ....DLB4

Dorn, Edward 1929- DLB5

Dos Passos, John 1896-1970
....DLB4, 9; DS1

Douglass, Frederick 1817?-1895 ....DLB1

Downing, J., Major (see Davis, Charles A.)

Downing, Major Jack (see Smith, Seba)

Doyle, Arthur Conan 1859-1930
....DLB18

Doyle, Kirby 1932- DLB16

Drabble, Margaret 1939- DLB14

Dreiser, Theodore 1871-1945
....DLB9, 12; DS1

Drinkwater, John 1882-1937...................DLB10

Duffy, Maureen 1933- DLB14

Dugan, Alan 1923- DLB5

Dukes, Ashley 1885-1959 ....DLB10

Duncan, Robert 1919- DLB5, 16

Duncan, Ronald 1914-1982......................DLB13

Dunne, Finley Peter 1867-1936 ....DLB11

Dunne, John Gregory 1932- Y80

Dunning, Ralph Cheever 1878-1930
....DLB4

Dunning, William A. 1857-1922 ....DLB17

Plunkett, Edward John Moreton Drax,
   Lord Dunsany 1878-1957 ....DLB10

Durrell, Lawrence 1912- DLB15

Duyckinck, Evert A. 1816-1878 ....DLB3

Duyckinck, George L. 1823-1863................DLB3

Dwight, John Sullivan 1813-1893 ....DLB1

Dyer, Charles 1928- DLB13

Dylan, Bob 1941- DLB16

E

Eastlake, William 1917- DLB6

Edgar, David 1948- DLB13

Edmonds, Walter D. 1903- DLB9

Effinger, George Alec 1947- DLB8

Eggleston, Edward 1837-1902....................DLB12

Eigner, Larry 1927- DLB5

Elder, Lonne, III 1931- DLB7

Eliot, T. S. 1888-1965........................DLB7, 10

Elkin, Stanley 1930- DLB2; Y80

Elliott, Janice 1931- DLB14

Elliott, William 1788-1863 ....DLB3

Ellison, Harlan 1934- DLB8

Ellison, Ralph 1914- DLB2

Emerson, Ralph Waldo 1803-1882
....DLB1

Erskine, John 1879-1951 ....DLB9

Ervine, St. John Greer 1883-1971
....DLB10

Eshleman, Clayton 1935- DLB5

Everett, Edward 1794-1865......................DLB1

Everson, William 1912- DLB5, 16

Exley, Frederick 1929- Y81

F

Farmer, Philip José 1918- DLB8

Farrell, J. G. 1935-1979........................DLB14

Farrell, James T. 1904-1979
....DLB4, 9; DS2

Fast, Howard 1914- DLB9

Faulkner, William 1897-1962
....DLB9, 11; DS2

Faust, Irvin 1924- DLB2; Y80

Fearing, Kenneth 1902-1961......................DLB9

Federman, Raymond 1928- Y80

Feiffer, Jules 1929- DLB7

Feinstein, Elaine 1930- DLB14

Felton, Cornelius Conway 1807-1862
....DLB1

Ferber, Edna 1885-1968............................DLB9

Ferlinghetti, Lawrence 1919- DLB5, 16

Field, Rachel 1894-1942 ....DLB9

Fields, James Thomas 1817-1881 ....DLB1

Figes, Eva 1932- DLB14

Finney, Jack 1911- DLB8

Finney, Walter Braden (see Finney, Jack)

Fisher, Dorothy Canfield 1879-1958
....DLB9

Fisher, Vardis 1895-1968 ....DLB9

Fitch, William Clyde 1865-1909
....DLB7

Fitzgerald, F. Scott 1896-1940
....DLB4, 9; Y81; DS1

Fitzgerald, Penelope 1916- DLB14

Fitzgerald, Robert 1910- Y80

Flanagan, Thomas 1923- Y80

Flanner, Janet 1892-1978 ....DLB4

Flavin, Martin 1883-1967 ....DLB9

Flecker, James Elroy 1884-1915
....DLB10

Fletcher, John Gould 1886-1950
....DLB4

Follen, Eliza Lee (Cabot) 1787-1860
....DLB1

Follett, Ken 1949- Y81

Foote, Shelby 1916- DLB2, 17

Forché, Carolyn 1950- DLB5

Ford, Charles Henri 1913- DLB4

Ford, Corey 1902-1969................................DLB11

Ford, Jesse Hill 1928- DLB6

Fornés, María Irene 1930- DLB7

Foster, Michael 1904-1956 ....DLB9

Fowles, John 1926- DLB14

Fox, John, Jr. 1862 or 1863-1919
....DLB9

Fox, William Price 1926- DLB2; Y81

Fraenkel, Michael 1896-1957 ....DLB4

France, Richard 1938- DLB7

Francis, Convers 1795-1863 ....DLB1

Frank, Waldo 1889-1967 ....DLB9

Frantz, Ralph Jules 1902- DLB4

Frayn, Michael 1933- DLB13, 14

Frederic, Harold 1856-1898........................DLB12

Freeman, Douglas Southall 1886-1953.......DLB17

Freeman, Mary Wilkins 1852-1930
....DLB12

Friedman, Bruce Jay 1930- DLB2

Friel, Brian 1929- DLB13

Friend, Krebs 1895?-1967?..........................DLB4

Frothingham, Octavius Brooks 1822-1895
....DLB1

Froude, James Anthony 1818-1894
....DLB18

Fry, Christopher 1907- DLB13

Fuchs, Daniel 1909- DLB9

Fuller, Henry Blake 1857-1929...................DLB12

Fuller, Roy 1912- DLB15

Fuller, Sarah Margaret, Marchesa
D'Ossoli 1810-1850..............................DLB1

Furness, William Henry 1802-1896
....DLB1

G

Gaddis, William 1922- DLB2

Gaines, Ernest J. 1933- DLB2; Y80

Gale, Zona 1874-1938.................................DLB9

Gallico, Paul 1897-1976 ....DLB9

Galsworthy, John 1867-1933 ....DLB10

Galvin, Brendan 1938- DLB5

Gardam, Jane 1928- DLB14

Gardner, John 1933-1982 ....DLB2; Y82

Garland, Hamlin 1860-1940........................DLB12

Garraty, John A. 1920- DLB17

Garrett, George 1929- DLB2, 5

Garrison, William Lloyd 1805-1879
....DLB1

Gass, William 1924- DLB2

Geddes, Virgil 1897- DLB4

Gelber, Jack 1932- DLB7

Gellhorn, Martha 1908- Y82

Gems, Pam 1925- DLB13

Genovese, Eugene D. 1930- DLB17

Gent, Peter 1942- Y82

Gernsback, Hugo 1884-1967.....................DLB8

Gerrold, David 1944- DLB8

Geston, Mark S. 1946- DLB8

Gibson, William 1914- DLB7

Gillespie, A. Lincoln, Jr. 1895-1950
....DLB4

Gilliam, Florence DLB4

Gilliatt, Penelope 1932- DLB14

Gillott, Jacky 1939-1980 ....DLB14

Gilman, Caroline H. 1794-1888
....DLB3

Gilroy, Frank D. 1925- DLB7

Ginsberg, Allen 1926- DLB5, 16

Giovanni, Nikki 1943- DLB5

Gipson, Lawrence Henry 1880-1971 ....DLB17

Gissing, George 1857-1903........................DLB18

Glanville, Brian 1931-...............................DLB15

Glasgow, Ellen 1873-1945 ....DLB9, 12

Glaspell, Susan 1882-1948.......................DLB7, 9

Glass, Montague 1877-1934 ....DLB11

Gluck, Louise 1943- DLB5

Godwin, Gail 1937- DLB6

Godwin, Parke 1816-1904 ....DLB3

Gogarty, Oliver St. John 1878-1957 ....DLB15

Gold, Herbert 1924- DLB2; Y81

Gold, Michael 1893-1967...........................DLB9

Goldberg, Dick 1947- DLB7

Golding, William 1911-..............................DLB15

Goodrich, Samuel Griswold 1793-1860
....DLB1

Goodwin, Stephen 1943- Y82

Gordon, Caroline 1895-1981
....DLB4, 9; Y81

Gordon, Giles 1940- DLB14

Gordon, Mary 1949- DLB6; Y81

Gordone, Charles 1925- DLB7

Goyen, William 1915- DLB2

Grau, Shirley Ann 1929- DLB2

Gray, Asa 1810-1888 ....DLB1

Gray, Simon 1936- DLB13

Grayson, William J. 1788-1863
....DLB3

Greeley, Horace 1811-1872.........................DLB3

Green, Henry 1905-1973............................DLB15

Green, Julien 1900- DLB4

Green, Paul 1894-1981....................DLB7, 9; Y81

Greene, Asa 1789-1838 ....DLB11

Greene, Graham 1904- DLB13, 15

Greenough, Horatio 1805-1852
....DLB1

Greenwood, Walter 1903-1974
....DLB10

Greer, Ben 1948- DLB6

Persse, Isabella Augusta,
    Lady Gregory 1852-1932...................DLB10

Grey, Zane 1872-1939 ....DLB9

Griffiths, Trevor 1935- DLB13

Griswold, Rufus 1815-1857.........................DLB3

Gross, Milt 1895-1953................................DLB11

Grubb, Davis 1919-1980.............................DLB6

Guare, John 1938- DLB7

Guest, Barbara 1920- DLB5

Guiterman, Arthur 1871-1943....................DLB11

Gunn, James E. 1923- DLB8

Gunn, Neil M. 1891-1973........................DLB15

Guthrie, A. B., Jr. 1901- DLB6

Guthrie, Ramon 1896-1973........................DLB4

Gwynne, Erskine 1898-1948........................DLB4

Gysin, Brion 1916- DLB16

H

H. D. (see Doolittle, Hilda)

Hailey, Arthur 1920- Y82

Haines, John 1924- DLB5

Haldeman, Joe 1943- DLB8

Hale, Edward Everett 1822-1909
........................DLB1

Hale, Nancy 1908- Y80

Hale, Sara Josepha (Buell) 1788-1879
........................DLB1

Haliburton, Thomas Chandler 1796-1865
........................DLB11

Hall, Donald 1928- DLB5

Halleck, Fitz-Greene 1790-1867
........................DLB3

Halper, Albert 1904- DLB9

Hamilton, Cicely 1872-1952........................DLB10

Hamilton, Edmond 1904-1977
........................DLB8

Hamilton, Patrick 1904-1962........................DLB10

Hamner, Earl 1923- DLB6

Hampton, Christopher 1946- DLB13

Handlin, Oscar 1915- DLB17

Hankin, St. John 1869-1909
........................DLB10

Hanley, Clifford 1922- DLB14

Hannah, Barry 1942- DLB6

Hansberry, Lorraine 1930-1965
........................DLB7

Hardwick, Elizabeth 1916- DLB6

Hardy, Thomas 1840-1928........................DLB18

Hare, David 1947-........................DLB13

Hargrove, Marion 1919- DLB11

Harness, Charles L. 1915- DLB8

Harris, George Washington 1814-1869
........................DLB3, 11

Harris, Joel Chandler 1848-1908
........................DLB11

Harris, Mark 1922- DLB2; Y80

Harrison, Harry 1925- DLB8

Harrison, Jim 1937- Y82

Hart, Albert Bushnell 1854-1943........................DLB17

Hart, Moss 1904-1961........................DLB7

Harte, Bret 1836-1902........................DLB12

Hartley, L. P. 1895-1972........................DLB15

Harwood, Ronald 1934- DLB13

Hawkes, John 1925- DLB2; Y80

Hawthorne, Nathaniel 1804-1864
........................DLB1

Hay, John 1838-1905........................DLB12

Hayden, Robert 1913-1980........................DLB5

Hayne, Paul Hamilton 1830-1886
........................DLB3

Hazzard, Shirley 1931- Y82

Hearn, Lafcadio 1850-1904........................DLB12

Heath, Catherine 1924- DLB14

Hecht, Anthony 1923- DLB5

Hecht, Ben 1894-1964........................DLB7, 9

Hecker, Isaac Thomas 1819-1888
........................DLB1

Hedge, Frederic Henry 1805-1890
........................DLB1

Heidish, Marcy 1947- Y82

Heinlein, Robert A. 1907- DLB8

Heller, Joseph 1923- DLB2; Y80

Hellman, Lillian 1906- DLB7

Hemingway, Ernest 1899-1961
........................DLB4, 9; Y81; DS1

Henderson, Zenna 1917- DLB8

Henry, Robert Selph 1889-1970........................DLB17

Henty, G. A. 1832-1902 ....DLB18

Hentz, Caroline Lee 1800-1856
....DLB3

Herbert, Alan Patrick 1890-1971
....DLB10

Herbert, Frank 1920- DLB8

Herbert, Henry William 1807-1858
....DLB3

Herbst, Josephine 1892-1969
....DLB9

Hergesheimer, Joseph 1880-1954
....DLB9

Herrick, Robert 1868-1938
....DLB9, 12

Herrmann, John 1900-1959
....DLB4

Hersey, John 1914- DLB6

Heyen, William 1940- DLB5

Heyward, Dorothy 1890-1961 and
    Heyward, DuBose 1885-1940 ....DLB7

Heyward, DuBose 1885-1940
....DLB9

Higgins, Aidan 1927- DLB14

Higgins, George V. 1939- DLB2; Y81

Higginson, Thomas Wentworth 1822-1911
....DLB1

Hildreth, Richard 1807-1865 ....DLB1

Hill, Susan 1942- DLB14

Himes, Chester 1909- DLB2

Hoagland, Edward 1932- DLB6

Hochman, Sandra 1936- DLB5

Hodgman, Helen 1945- DLB14

Hoffenstein, Samuel 1890-1947
....DLB11

Hoffman, Charles Fenno 1806-1884
....DLB3

Hoffman, Daniel 1923- DLB5

Hofstadter, Richard 1916-1970.................DLB17

Hogan, Desmond 1950- DLB14

Holbrook, David 1923- DLB14

Hollander, John 1929- DLB5

Holley, Marietta 1836-1926.......................DLB11

Holmes, John Clellon 1926 ....DLB16

Holmes, Oliver Wendell 1809-1894
....DLB1

Home, William Douglas 1912- DLB13

Honig, Edwin 1919- DLB5

Hooper, Johnson Jones 1815-1862
....DLB3, 11

Horovitz, Israel 1939- DLB7

Hough, Emerson 1857-1923 ....DLB9

Houghton, Stanley 1881-1913....................DLB10

Housman, Laurence 1865-1959..................DLB10

Howard, Richard 1929- DLB5

Howard, Sidney 1891-1939........................DLB7

Howe, E. W. 1853-1937............................DLB12

Howe, Julia Ward 1819-1910......................DLB1

Howells, William Dean 1837-1920
....DLB12

Hoyem, Andrew 1935- DLB5

Hubbard, Kin 1868-1930 ....DLB11

Hughes, David 1930- DLB14

Hughes, Langston 1902-1967
....DLB4, 7

Hughes, Richard 1900-1976.......................DLB15

Hughes, Thomas 1822-1896.......................DLB18

Hugo, Richard 1923-1982.........................DLB5

Humphrey, William 1924- DLB6

Humphreys, Emyr 1919- DLB15

Huncke, Herbert 1915- DLB16

Hunter, Evan 1926- Y82

Hunter, Jim 1939- DLB14

Hunter, N. C. 1908-1971...........................DLB10

I

Ignatow, David 1914- DLB5

Imbs, Bravig 1904-1946 ....DLB4

Inge, William 1913-1973 ....DLB7

Ingraham, Joseph Holt 1809-1860 ....DLB3

Irving, John 1942- DLB6; Y82

Irving, Washington 1783-1859 ....DLB3, 11

Isherwood, Christopher 1904- DLB15

J

Jackson, Shirley 1919-1965 ....DLB6

Jacob, Piers Anthony Dillingham (see Anthony, Piers)

Jacobson, Dan 1929- DLB14

James, Henry 1843-1916 ....DLB12

Jameson, J. Franklin 1859-1937 ....DLB17

Jellicoe, Ann 1927- DLB13

Jenkins, Robin 1912- DLB14

Jenkins, William Fitzgerald (see Leinster, Murray)

Jensen, Merrill 1905-1980 ....DLB17

Jerome, Jerome K. 1859-1927 ....DLB10

Jewett, Sarah Orne 1849-1909 ....DLB12

Joans, Ted 1928- DLB16

Johnson, B. S. 1933-1973 ....DLB14

Johnson, Diane 1934- Y80

Johnson, Pamela Hansford 1912- DLB15

Johnson, Samuel 1822-1882 ....DLB1

Johnston, Denis 1901- DLB10

Johnston, Jennifer 1930- DLB14

Johnston, Mary 1870-1936 ....DLB9

Jolas, Eugene 1894-1952 ....DLB4

Jones, Glyn 1905- DLB15

Jones, Gwyn 1907- DLB15

Jones, Henry Arthur 1851-1929 ....DLB10

Jones, James 1921-1977 ....DLB2

Jones, LeRoi (see Baraka, Amiri)

Jones, Lewis 1897-1939 ....DLB15

Jones, Major Joseph (see Thompson, William Tappan)

Jones, Preston 1936-1979 ....DLB7

Jong, Erica 1942- DLB2, 5

Josephson, Matthew 1899-1978 ....DLB4

Josipovici, Gabriel 1940- DLB14

Joyce, James 1882-1941 ....DLB10

Judd, Sylvester 1813-1853 ....DLB1

K

Kandel, Lenore 1932- DLB16

Kanin, Garson 1912- DLB7

Kantor, Mackinlay 1904-1977 ....DLB9

Kaufman, Bob 1925- DLB16

Kaufman, George S. 1889-1961 ....DLB7

Kavanagh, Patrick 1904-1967 ....DLB15

Keane, John B. 1928- DLB13

Keeffe, Barrie 1945- DLB13

Kelley, Edith Summers 1884-1956 ....DLB9

Kelly, George 1887-1974 ....DLB7

Kelly, Robert 1935- DLB5

Kennedy, John Pendleton 1795-1870 ....DLB3

Kennedy, X. J. 1929- DLB5

Kerouac, Jack 1922-1969 ....DLB2, 16; DS3

Kerouac, Jan 1952- DLB16

Kerr, Orpheus C. (see Newell, Robert Henry)

Kesey, Ken 1935- DLB2, 16

Kiely, Benedict 1919- DLB15

Kiley, Jed 1889-1962 ....DLB4

King, Clarence 1842-1901 ....DLB12

King, Grace 1852-1932 ....DLB12

Nye, Bill 1850-1896 ....DLB11

Nye, Robert 1939- DLB14

O

Oates, Joyce Carol 1938- DLB2, 5; Y81

O'Brien, Edna 1932- DLB14

O'Brien, Kate 1897-1974.............................DLB15

O'Brien, Tim 1946- Y80

O'Casey, Sean 1880-1964 ....DLB10

O'Connor, Flannery 1925-1964
....DLB2; Y80

Odets, Clifford 1906-1963...........................DLB7

O'Faolain, Julia 1932- DLB14

O'Faolain, Sean 1900- DLB15

O'Hara, Frank 1926-1966 ....DLB5, 16

O'Hara, John 1905-1970.....................DLB9; DS2

O. Henry (see Porter, William S.)

Oliphant, Laurence 1829-1888 ....DLB18

Oliphant, Margaret 1828-1897...................DLB18

Oliver, Chad 1928- DLB8

Oliver, Mary 1935- DLB5

Olsen, Tillie 1912 or 1913- Y80

Olson, Charles 1910-1970 ....DLB5, 16

O'Neill, Eugene 1888-1953 ....DLB7

Oppen, George 1908- DLB5

Oppenheimer, Joel 1930- DLB5

Orlovitz, Gil 1918-1973 ....DLB2, 5

Orlovsky, Peter 1933- DLB16

Orton, Joe 1933-1967 ....DLB13

Orwell, George 1903-1950 ....DLB15

Osborne, John 1929- DLB13

Ouida 1839-1908 ....DLB18

Owen, Guy 1925- DLB5

Owsley, Frank L. 1890-1956 ....DLB17

Ozick, Cynthia 1928- Y82

P

Pack, Robert 1929- DLB5

Padgett, Ron 1942- DLB5

Page, Thomas Nelson 1853-1922
....DLB12

Palfrey, John Gorham 1796-1881
....DLB1

Pangborn, Edgar 1909-1976 ....DLB8

Panshin, Alexei 1940- DLB8

Parker, Dorothy 1893-1967........................DLB11

Parker, Theodore 1810-1860 ....DLB1

Parkman, Francis, Jr. 1823-1893
....DLB1

Parrington, Vernon L. 1871-1929 ....DLB17

Pastan, Linda 1932- DLB5

Patchen, Kenneth 1911-1972 ....DLB16

Patrick, John 1906- DLB7

Paul, Elliot 1891-1958................................DLB4

Paulding, James Kirke 1778-1860
....DLB3

Payn, James 1830-1898...............................DLB18

Peabody, Elizabeth Palmer 1804-1894
....DLB1

Peake, Mervyn...DLB15

Pennington, Lee 1939- Y82

Percy, Walker 1916- DLB2; Y80

Perelman, S. J. 1904-1979...........................DLB11

Perkoff, Stuart Z. 1930-1974......................DLB16

Peterkin, Julia 1880-1961 ....DLB9

Phillips, David Graham 1867-1911
....DLB9, 12

Phillips, Jayne Anne 1952- Y80

Phillips, Stephen 1864-1915 ....DLB10

Phillips, Ulrich B. 1877-1934 ....DLB17

Phillpotts, Eden 1862-1960 ....DLB10

Phoenix, John (see Derby, George Horatio)

Pinckney, Josephine 1895-1957
....DLB6

Pinero, Arthur Wing 1855-1934
....DLB10

Pinsky, Robert 1940- Y82

Pinter, Harold 1930- DLB13

Piper, H. Beam 1904-1964 ....DLB8

Plath, Sylvia 1932-1963 ....DLB5, 6

Plumly, Stanley 1939- DLB5

Plunkett, James 1920- DLB14

Plymell, Charles 1935- DLB16

Poe, Edgar Allan 1809-1849 ....DLB3

Pohl, Frederik 1919- DLB8

Poliakoff, Stephen 1952- DLB13

Poole, Ernest 1880-1950 ....DLB9

Porter, Eleanor H. 1868-1920
....DLB9

Porter, Katherine Anne 1890-1980
....DLB4, 9; Y80

Porter, William S. 1862-1910 ....DLB12

Porter, William T. 1809-1858 ....DLB3

Portis, Charles 1933- DLB6

Potter, David M. 1910-1971 ....DLB17

Pound, Ezra 1885-1972 ....DLB4

Powell, Anthony 1905- DLB15

Pownall, David 1938- DLB14

Powys, John Cowper 1872-1963 ....DLB15

Prescott, William Hickling 1796-1859
....DLB1

Price, Reynolds 1933- DLB2

Price, Richard 1949- Y81

Priest, Christopher 1943- DLB14

Priestley, J. B. 1894- DLB10

Pritchett, V. S. 1900- DLB15

Propper, Dan 1937- DLB16

Purdy, James 1923- DLB2

Putnam, George Palmer 1814-1872
....DLB3

Putnam, Samuel 1892-1950..........................DLB4

Puzo, Mario 1920- DLB6

Pym, Barbara 1913-1980 ....DLB14

Pynchon, Thomas 1937- DLB2

Q

Quad, M. (see Lewis, Charles B.)

Quin, Ann 1936-1973...............................DLB14

R

Rabe, David 1940- DLB7

Rameé, Marie Louise de la (see Ouida)

Randall, James G. 1881-1953 ....DLB17

Raphael, Frederic 1931- DLB14

Rattigan, Terence 1911-1977 ....DLB13

Rawlings, Marjorie Kinnan 1896-1953
....DLB9

Ray, David 1932- DLB5

Read, Piers Paul 1941- DLB14

Rechy, John 1934- Y82

Reed, Ishmael 1938- DLB2, 5

Reed, Sampson 1800-1880 ....DLB1

Remington, Frederic 1861-1909 ....DLB12

Rexroth, Kenneth 1905-1982.............DLB16; Y82

Reynolds, Mack 1917- DLB8

Rice, Elmer 1892-1967 ....DLB4, 7

Rich, Adrienne 1929- DLB5

Richardson, Jack 1935- DLB7

Richter, Conrad 1890-1968 ....DLB9

Riddell, John (see Ford, Corey)

Ripley, George 1802-1880 ....DLB1

Ritchie, Anna Mowatt 1819-1870
....DLB3

Ritchie, Anne Thackeray 1837-1919
....DLB18

Robbins, Tom 1936- Y80

Roberts, Elizabeth Madox 1881-1941
....DLB9

Roberts, Kenneth 1885-1957.......................DLB9

Robinson, Lennox 1886-1958 ....DLB10

Roethke, Theodore 1908-1963 ....DLB5

Rogers, Will 1879-1935 ....DLB11

Roiphe, Anne 1935- Y80

Rölvaag, O. E. 1876-1931 ....DLB9

Root, Waverley 1903-1982 ....DLB4

Rosenthal, M. L. 1917- DLB5

Ross, Leonard Q. (see Rosten, Leo)

Rossner, Judith 1935- DLB6

Rosten, Leo 1908- DLB11

Roth, Philip 1933- DLB2; Y82

Rothenberg, Jerome 1931- DLB5

Rubens, Bernice 1928- DLB14

Rudkin, David 1956- DLB13

Rumaker, Michael 1932- DLB16

Runyon, Damon 1880-1946 ....DLB11

Russ, Joanna 1937- DLB8

Rutherford, Mark 1831-1913......................DLB18

Ryan, Michael 1946- Y82

S

Saberhagen, Fred 1930- DLB8

Sackler, Howard 1929-1982 ....DLB7

Sage, Robert 1899-1962...............................DLB4

Salemson, Harold J. 1910- DLB4

Salinger, J. D. 1919- DLB2

Sanborn, Franklin Benjamin 1831-1917
....DLB1

Sandburg, Carl 1878-1967 ....DLB17

Sanders, Ed 1939- DLB16

Sandoz, Mari 1896-1966 ....DLB9

Sargent, Pamela 1948- DLB8

Saroyan, William 1908-1981
....DLB7, 9; Y81

Sarton, May 1912- Y81

Saunders, James 1925- DLB13

Sayers, Dorothy L. 1893-1957....................DLB10

Schlesinger, Arthur M., Jr. 1917- DLB17

Schmitz, James H. 1911- DLB8

Schreiner, Olive 1855-1920 ....DLB18

Schulberg, Budd 1914- DLB6; Y81

Schuyler, James 1923- DLB5

Schwartz, Jonathan 1938- Y82

Scott, Evelyn 1893-1963 ....DLB9

Scott, Paul 1920-1978 ....DLB14

Seabrook, William 1886-1945......................DLB4

Sedgwick, Catharine Maria 1789-1867
....DLB1

Selby, Hubert, Jr. 1928- DLB2

Settle, Mary Lee 1918- DLB6

Sexton, Anne 1928-1974 ....DLB5

Shaffer, Anthony 1926- DLB13

Shaffer, Peter 1926- DLB13

Shairp, Mordaunt 1887-1939.....................DLB10

Sharpe, Tom 1928- DLB14

Shaw, Bernard 1856-1950 ....DLB10

Shaw, Henry Wheeler 1818-1885
....DLB11

Shaw, Irwin 1913- DLB6

Shaw, Robert 1927-1978 ....DLB13, 14

Sheckley, Robert 1928- DLB8

Sheed, Wilfred 1930- DLB6

Sheldon, Alice B. (see Tiptree, James, Jr.)

Sheldon, Edward 1886-1946 ....DLB7

Shepard, Sam 1943- DLB7

Sherriff, R. C. 1896-1975 ....DLB10

Sherwood, Robert 1896-1955.......................DLB7

Shiels, George 1886-1949............................DLB10

Shillaber, Benjamin Penhallow 1814-1890
....DLB1, 11

Shirer, William L. 1904- DLB4

Shorthouse, Joseph Henry 1834-1903
....DLB18

Shulman, Max 1919- DLB11

Shute, Henry A. 1856-1943 ....DLB9

Shuttle, Penelope 1947- DLB14

Sigourney, Lydia Howard (Huntley) 1791-1865
....DLB1

Sillitoe, Alan 1928- DLB14

Silverberg, Robert 1935- DLB8

Simak, Clifford D. 1904- DLB8

Simms, William Gilmore 1806-1870
....DLB3

Simon, Neil 1927- DLB7

Simpson, Louis 1923- DLB5

Simpson, N. F. 1919- DLB13

Sinclair, Andrew 1935- DLB14

Sinclair, Upton 1878-1968.........................DLB9

Singer, Isaac Bashevis 1904- DLB6

Singmaster, Elsie 1879-1958.........................DLB9

Sissman, L. E. 1928-1976.........................DLB5

Slavitt, David 1935- DLB5, 6

Slick, Sam (see Haliburton, Thomas Chandler)

Smith, Betty 1896-1972 ....Y82

Smith, Carol Sturm 1938- Y81

Smith, Charles Henry 1826-1903
....DLB11

Smith, Cordwainer 1913-1966 ....DLB8

Smith, Dave 1942- DLB5

Smith, Dodie 1896- DLB10

Smith, E. E. 1890-1965.........................DLB8

Smith, Elizabeth Oakes (Prince) 1806-1893
....DLB1

Smith, George O. 1911- DLB8

Smith, H. Allen 1907-1976.........................DLB11

Smith, Mark 1935- Y82

Smith, Seba 1792-1868.........................DLB1, 11

Smith, William Jay 1918- DLB5

Snodgrass, W. D. 1926- DLB5

Snow, C. P. 1905-1980.........................DLB15

Snyder, Gary 1930- DLB5, 16

Solano, Solita 1888-1975 ....DLB4

Solomon, Carl 1928- DLB16

Sontag, Susan 1933- DLB2

Sorrentino, Gilbert 1929- DLB5; Y80

Southern, Terry 1924- DLB2

Spark, Muriel 1918- DLB15

Sparks, Jared 1789-1866 ....DLB1

Spencer, Elizabeth 1921- DLB6

Spicer, Jack 1925-1965 ....DLB5, 16

Spielberg, Peter 1929- Y81

Spinrad, Norman 1940- DLB8

Squibob (see Derby, George Horatio)

Stafford, Jean 1915-1979 ....DLB2

Stafford, William 1914- DLB5

Stallings, Laurence 1894-1968
....DLB7, 9

Stampp, Kenneth M. 1912- DLB17

Stanford, Ann 1916- DLB5

Stapledon, Olaf 1886-1950.........................DLB15

Starkweather, David 1935- DLB7

Steadman, Mark 1930- DLB6

Stearns, Harold E. 1891-1943 ....DLB4

Steele, Max 1922- Y80

Stegner, Wallace 1909- DLB9

Stein, Gertrude 1874-1946.........................DLB4

Stein, Leo 1872-1947.........................DLB4

Steinbeck, John 1902-1968
....DLB7, 9; DS2

Stephens, Ann 1813-1886 ....DLB3

Stevenson, Robert Louis 1850-1894
....DLB18

Stewart, Donald Ogden 1894-1980
....DLB4, 11

Stewart, George R. 1895-1980 ....DLB8

Still, James 1906- DLB9

Stoddard, Richard Henry 1825-1903
....DLB3

Stoppard, Tom 1937- DLB13

Storey, Anthony 1928- DLB14

Storey, David 1933- DLB13, 14

Story, William Wetmore 1819-1895
....DLB1

Stowe, Harriet Beecher 1811-1896
....DLB1, 12

Strand, Mark 1934- DLB5

Streeter, Edward 1891-1976.......................DLB11

Stribling, T. S. 1881-1965............................DLB9

Strother, David Hunter 1816-1888
....DLB3

Stuart, Jesse 1907- DLB9

Stubbs, Harry Clement (see Hal Clement)

Sturgeon, Theodore 1918- DLB8

Styron, William 1925- DLB2; Y80

Suckow, Ruth 1892-1960............................DLB9

Suggs, Simon (see Hooper, Johnson Jones)

Sukenick, Ronald 1932- Y81

Sullivan, Frank 1892-1976.........................DLB11

Summers, Hollis 1916- DLB6

Sutro, Alfred 1863-1933............................DLB10

Swados, Harvey 1920-1972 ....DLB2

Swenson, May 1919- DLB5

Synge, John Millington 1871-1909
....DLB10

T

Tarkington, Booth 1869-1946......................DLB9

Tate, Allen 1896-1979..............................DLB4

Tate, James 1943- DLB5

Taylor, Bayard 1825-1878...........................DLB3

Taylor, Henry 1942- DLB5

Taylor, Peter 1917- Y81

Tenn, William 1919- DLB8

Tennant, Emma 1937- DLB14

Terhune, Albert Payson 1872-1942
....DLB9

Terry, Megan 1932- DLB7

Terson, Peter 1932- DLB13

Theroux, Paul 1941- DLB2

Thoma, Richard 1902- DLB4

Thomas, Dylan 1914-1953 ....DLB13

Thomas, Gwyn 1913-1981.........................DLB15

Thomas, John 1900-1932.........................DLB4

Thompson, John R. 1823-1873
....DLB3

Thompson, William Tappan 1812-1882
....DLB3, 11

Thomson, Mortimer 1831-1875
....DLB11

Thoreau, Henry David 1817-1862
....DLB1

Thorpe, Thomas Bangs 1815-1878
....DLB3, 11

Thurber, James 1894-1961 ....DLB4, 11

Ticknor, George 1791-1871 ....DLB1

Timrod, Henry 1828-1867........................DLB3

Tiptree, James, Jr. 1915- DLB8

Titus, Edward William 1870-1952
....DLB4

Toklas, Alice B. 1877-1967 ....DLB4

Tolkien, J. R. R. 1892-1973......................DLB15

Tonks, Rosemary 1932- DLB14

Toole, John Kennedy 1937-1969
....Y81

Tracy, Honor 1913- DLB15

Traven, B. 1882? or 1890?-1969..................DLB9

Travers, Ben 1886-1980...........................DLB10

Tremain, Rose 1943- DLB14

Trevor, William 1928- DLB14

Trocchi, Alexander 1925- DLB15

Troop, Elizabeth 1931- DLB14

Tucker, George 1775-1861 ....DLB3

Tucker, Nathaniel Beverley 1784-1851
.................................DLB3

Tuohy, Frank 1925- DLB14

Turner, Frederick Jackson 1861-1932........DLB17

Twain, Mark (see Clemens, Samuel Langhorne)

Tyler, Anne 1941- DLB6; Y82

U

Upchurch, Boyd B. (see Boyd, John)

Updike, John 1932- DLB2, 5; Y80, 82; DS3

Upton, Charles 1948- DLB16

Ustinov, Peter 1921- DLB13

V

Vail, Laurence 1891-1968 ....DLB4

Vance, Jack 1916?- DLB8

van Druten, John 1901-1957.............DLB10

Van Duyn, Mona 1921- DLB5

van Itallie, Jean-Claude 1936- DLB7

Vane, Sutton 1888-1963 ....DLB10

Van Vechten, Carl 1880-1964
.............................DLB4, 9

van Vogt, A. E. 1912- DLB8

Varley, John 1947- Y81

Vega, Janine Pommy 1942- DLB16

Very, Jones 1813-1880 ....DLB1

Vidal, Gore 1925- DLB6

Viereck, Peter 1916- DLB5

Vonnegut, Kurt 1922-
......................DLB2, 8; Y80; DS3

W

Wagoner, David 1926- DLB5

Wain, John 1925- DLB15

Wakoski, Diane 1937- DLB5

Walcott, Derek 1930- Y81

Waldman, Anne 1945- DLB16

Walker, Alice 1944- DLB6

Wallant, Edward Lewis 1926-1962
.............................DLB2

Walsh, Ernest 1895-1926.............DLB4

Wambaugh, Joseph 1937- DLB6

Ward, Artemus (see Browne, Charles Farrar)

Ward, Douglas Turner 1930- DLB7

Ward, Mrs. Humphry 1851-1920 ....DLB18

Ware, William 1797-1852 ....DLB1

Warner, Rex 1905- DLB15

Warner, Susan B. 1819-1885 ....DLB3

Warren, Robert Penn 1905-
.............................DLB2; Y80

Wasson, David Atwood 1823-1887
.............................DLB1

Waterhouse, Keith 1929- DLB13

Watts, Alan 1915-1973 ....DLB16

Waugh, Auberon 1939- DLB14

Waugh, Evelyn 1903-1966.............DLB15

Webb, Walter Prescott 1888-1963.............DLB17

Webster, Noah 1758-1843 ....DLB1

Weinbaum, Stanley Grauman 1902-1935
.............................DLB8

Weiss, John 1818-1879 ....DLB1

Weiss, Theodore 1916- DLB5

Welch, Lew 1926-1971?.............DLB16

Weldon, Fay 1931- DLB14

Wells, Carolyn 1862-1942............DLB11

Welty, Eudora 1909- DLB2

Wescott, Glenway 1901- DLB4, 9

Wesker, Arnold 1932- DLB13

West, Anthony 1914- DLB15

West, Jessamyn 1902- DLB6

West, Nathanael 1903-1940
.................DLB4, 9

West, Paul 1930- DLB14

Whalen, Philip 1923- DLB16

Wharton, Edith 1862-1937 ....DLB4, 9, 12

Wharton, William 1920s?- Y80

Wheeler, Charles Stearns 1816-1843
.................DLB1

Wheeler, Monroe 1900- DLB4

Whetstone, Colonel Pete (see Noland, C. F. M.)

Whipple, Edwin Percy 1819-1886
.................DLB1

Whitcher, Frances Miriam 1814-1852 ....DLB11

White, E. B. 1899- DLB11

White, William Allen 1868-1944
.................DLB9

White, William Anthony Parker (see Boucher, Anthony)

White, William Hale (see Rutherford, Mark)

Whitehead, James 1936- Y81

Whiting, John 1917-1963 ....DLB13

Whitlock, Brand 1869-1934 ....DLB12

Whitman, Sarah Helen (Power) 1803-1878
.................DLB1

Whitman, Walt 1819-1892.................DLB3

Whittemore, Reed 1919- DLB5

Whittier, John Greenleaf 1807-1892
.................DLB1

Wieners, John 1934- DLB16

Wilbur, Richard 1921- DLB5

Wild, Peter 1940- DLB5

Wilde, Oscar 1854-1900 ....DLB10

Wilde, Richard Henry 1789-1847
.................DLB3

Wilder, Thornton 1897-1975
.................DLB4, 7, 9

Wiley, Bell Irvin 1906-1980 ....DLB17

Wilhelm, Kate 1928- DLB8

Willard, Nancy 1936- DLB5

Williams, C. K. 1936- DLB5

Williams, Emlyn 1905- DLB10

Williams, Heathcote 1941- DLB13

Williams, Joan 1928- DLB6

Williams, John A. 1925- DLB2

Williams, John E. 1922- DLB6

Williams, Jonathan 1929- DLB5

Williams, Raymond 1921- DLB14

Williams, T. Harry 1909-1979 ....DLB17

Williams, Tennessee 1911- DLB7

Williams, William Appleman 1921- DLB17

Williams, William Carlos 1883-1963
.................DLB4, 16

Williams, Wirt 1921- DLB6

Williamson, Jack 1908- DLB8

Willingham, Calder, Jr. 1922- DLB2

Willis, Nathaniel Parker 1806-1867
.................DLB3

Wilson, A. N. 1950- DLB14

Wilson, Angus 1913- DLB15

Wilson, Colin 1931- DLB14

Wilson, Harry Leon 1867-1939
.................DLB9

Wilson, Lanford 1937- DLB7

Wilson, Margaret 1882-1973 ....DLB9

Windham, Donald 1920- DLB6

Wister, Owen 1860-1938 ....DLB9

Woiwode, Larry 1941- DLB6

Wolfe, Gene 1931- DLB8

Wolfe, Thomas 1900-1938
.................DLB9; DS2

Wood, Charles 1932-1980 ....DLB13

Wood, Mrs. Henry 1814-1887 ....DLB18

Woodson, Carter G. 1875-1950 ....DLB17

Woodward, C. Vann 1908- DLB17

Woolson, Constance Fenimore 1840-1894
....DLB12

Worcester, Joseph Emerson 1784-1865
....DLB1

Wouk, Herman 1915- Y82

Wright, Charles 1935- Y82

Wright, Harold Bell 1872-1944 ....DLB9

Wright, James 1927-1980 ....DLB5

Wright, Louis B. 1899- DLB17

Wright, Richard 1908-1960 ....DS2

Wylie, Elinor 1885-1928 ....DLB9

Wylie, Philip 1902-1971 ....DLB9

Y

Yates, Richard 1926- DLB2; Y81

Yeats, William Butler 1865-1939 ....DLB10

Yonge, Charlotte Mary 1823-1901
....DLB18

Young, Stark 1881-1963 ....DLB9

Z

Zangwill, Israel 1864-1926 ....DLB10

Zebrowski, George 1945- DLB8

Zelazny, Roger 1937- DLB8

Zimmer, Paul 1934- DLB5

Zindel, Paul 1936- DLB7

Zukofsky, Louis 1904-1978
....DLB5